T0309186

SAP PRESS e-books

Print or e-book, Kindle or iPad, workplace or airplane: Choose
where and how to read your SAP PRESS books! You can now
get all our titles as e-books, too:

- By download and online access
- For all popular devices
- And, of course, DRM-free

Convinced? Then go to www.sap-press.com and get your
e-book today.

SAP° Activate

SAP PRESS is a joint initiative of SAP and Rheinwerk Publishing. The know-how offered by SAP specialists combined with the expertise of Rheinwerk Publishing offers the reader expert books in the field. SAP PRESS features first-hand information and expert advice, and provides useful skills for professional decision-making.

SAP PRESS offers a variety of books on technical and business-related topics for the SAP user. For further information, please visit our website: *www.sap-press.com.*

Aditya Lal, Jeyaganesh Viswanathan
SAP Activate Project Management Certification Guide:
Certified Associate Exam (2nd Edition)
2025, approx. 400 pp., paperback and e-book
www.sap-press.com/6032

Saueressig, Gilg, Grigoleit, Shah, Podbicanin, Homann
SAP S/4HANA Cloud: An Introduction (2nd Edition)
2022, 538 pages, hardcover and e-book
www.sap-press.com/5457

Bardhan, Baumgartl, Dudgeon, Górecki, Lahiri, Meijerink,
Worsley-Tonks, Maund, Dascalescu
SAP S/4HANA: An Introduction (5th Edition)
2025, approx. 640 pp., hardcover and e-book
www.sap-press.com/5973

Banda, Chandra, Gooi
SAP Business Technology Platform (2nd Edition)
2024, 729 pages, hardcover and e-book
www.sap-press.com/5919

Strasser, Sokollek, Sänger, Spierling, Schönwälder
SAP Signavio: Business Process Transformation
2024, 424 pages, hardcover and e-book
www.sap-press.com/5855

Sven Denecken, Jan Musil, Srivatsan Santhanam

SAP® Activate

Project Management for SAP S/4HANA® Cloud and SAP S/4HANA®

Rheinwerk
Publishing

Editor Megan Fuerst
Acquisitions Editor Emily Nicholls
Copyeditor Julie McNamee
Cover Design Graham Geary
Photo Credit iStockphoto: 1307940242/© petesphotography
Layout Design Vera Brauner
Production Hannah Lane
Typesetting III-satz, Germany
Printed and bound in the United States of America, on paper from sustainable sources

ISBN 978-1-4932-2650-4
3rd edition 2025

© 2025 by:
Rheinwerk Publishing, Inc.
2 Heritage Drive, Suite 305
Quincy, MA 02171
USA
info@rheinwerk-publishing.com

Represented in the E.U. by:
Rheinwerk Verlag GmbH
Rheinwerkallee 4
53227 Bonn
Germany
service@rheinwerk-verlag.de

Library of Congress Cataloging-in-Publication Control Number: 2024046345

Contents at a Glance

Contents

4   Starting with a Working System   153

5   Implementation Activities   175

6   Agile Project Delivery

7   New Implementation of SAP S/4HANA

8 System Conversion and Selective Data Transition to SAP S/4HANA

Appendices

Foreword by Jan Gilg

In recent years, we've faced significant disruptions in the business environment and rapid changes in our world. Regional conflicts, the global pandemic, and supply chain challenges, alongside new opportunities such as business AI, have underscored the need for businesses to adapt quickly to continue thriving.

To manage change effectively, businesses need to modernize and adapt their processes using agile, intelligent, and sustainable ERP platforms. With SAP S/4HANA Cloud, businesses are well-positioned to make the right decisions at the right time and drive positive business outcomes. Business AI-powered technologies can transform how business is done and improve user experience by simplifying and automating business processes.

Organizations can achieve and maintain business agility by embracing cloud or hybrid deployment approaches for their ERP systems. A cloud approach offers businesses a much quicker time to value by providing best practices that can be adopted via a fit-to-standard approach to rapidly deploy a new solution. It provides the business with a lean and effective strategy to support the changing business environment that the digital marketplace demands.

It has become clear that prescriptive guidance coupled with preconfigured business content is the key to ensuring the aspirational benefits of a cloud approach, enabling rapid solution deployment at a lower total cost of ownership (TCO) or total cost of implementation (TCI) for the business. I am proud to say that SAP Activate delivers on this promise. The combination of SAP S/4HANA Cloud and SAP Activate is unique in the marketplace, showcasing the thought leadership that SAP brings to the table based on its decades of experience delivering ERP solutions for customers across the world and in all industries. It equips system integrators and ecosystem partners with the knowledge needed to guide their customers on this journey.

As you'll discover throughout this book, the broad span of SAP Activate not only covers initial deployment—focusing on enabling and supporting a fit-to-standard approach—but also supports the customer running the solution to continuously adopt the innovations that SAP S/4HANA Cloud delivers through regular updates. The past few years have also transformed how we get work done. SAP Activate fully supports teams working in hybrid or fully remote setups with dedicated playbooks and tools that help project teams deliver business value seamlessly. While this book focuses on the efficient deployment of SAP S/4HANA Cloud solutions, the authors also address important considerations when adopting new AI-powered business processes in your organization.

Finally, I would like to thank the authors of this book for their efforts in constructively and concisely laying out all aspects of SAP Activate and its strategic importance for SAP

S/4HANA Cloud customers and partners. Their expertise is market leading with hands-on experience in numerous projects worldwide, and you can be confident that what follows in this book is the most up-to-date and relevant information about SAP Activate from the most trusted sources.

Jan Gilg
President and Chief Product Officer, Cloud ERP, SAP SE

Foreword by Sven Denecken

Your organization needs agility to transform, grow new business, and run cost-efficient operations. We're proud to support you on that journey by enabling business transformation and continuous innovation. Our solutions are designed to digitize and automate your business processes, provide real-time insights, and offer innovations that help you quickly adapt and scale in response to market opportunities and disruptions. We're more than just a technology provider; we like to see ourselves as engineers of progress co-innovating with clients and the ecosystem. We're in the unique position to help companies maximize performance and have a positive impact in a fast-changing world where technology and business have become inseparable. The need for speed calls for best-practice business solutions that use the latest digital technologies, are instantly delivered in the cloud, can be rapidly adopted to your specific business needs, and can be quickly deployed to business departments with their end users—enabling the best constant digital transformation.

Every industry is unique in the opportunities and challenges they deal with and the business capabilities they need. At SAP, we're proud to serve more than 25 industries and a dozen lines of business (LoBs); interestingly, we also see industry convergence and capabilities that will be leveraged by many clients, irrespective of which industry defines their core business. We deliver a rich set of industry-specific capabilities that support core business processes that directly determine business outcomes: from providing natural resources and energy to engineering and manufacturing goods, to trading and retailing, to transportation and logistics, to operating infrastructure, and to providing financial and public services. The industry-specific business capabilities are deeply embedded in our cloud ERP and LoB solutions or delivered by industry-specific solutions and configuration content developed by SAP and by our rich ecosystem of partners.

Cloud solutions by SAP and our partners are the building blocks for your business solutions architecture and your specific digital and business transformation. Now you need a way to rapidly adapt and deploy them to create business impact. SAP Activate offers exactly this smooth transition toward a solid cloud ERP and the supporting business technology platform, and continues to realize value for your organization by delivering agility at scale. "Activate" sounds like flipping a switch to magically transform your organization, but we all know that technology alone doesn't really get you there. That's why SAP Activate comes with the technology, tools, and best practices to make our SAP solutions work in your business and organizational context, fueled by a large and engaged community that collaborates at its best and serves you best. Providing our solutions is only the first step for us: we only call it "success" when we see you run and perform at your best!

Sven Denecken
Chief Marketing Officer, SAP Industries

Preface

Welcome to the third edition of the most comprehensive book about SAP Activate for deployment of all versions of SAP S/4HANA software, including SAP S/4HANA Cloud Public Edition, SAP S/4HANA Cloud Private Edition, and SAP S/4HANA (on-premise). In this book, we'll take you on a journey of deploying and innovating your software environment in your organization, including the new topics of leveraging business artificial intelligence (AI).

In today's rapidly evolving business world, companies encounter disruptions constantly and must adapt their practices accordingly to keep up with these changes. But the challenges we're all facing are bigger than that, whether our organizations are faced by new entrants or existing competitors who are faster and more agile in the adoption of new business models or the use of intelligent technologies. Businesses need to constantly innovate in how they create value through new ways to interact with customers and business partners, as well as how they compete with other companies to continue to grow.

As we write this book, the world continues recovering from the enormous impact of the global pandemic and the regional conflicts in Ukraine and the Middle East. At the same time, businesses are working hard to figure out how to benefit from the use of new technologies such as AI. The ever-changing world constantly demands that organizations adapt and transform to stay aligned with the shifting business landscape. Adopting modern cloud enterprise resource planning (ERP) software in the organization is critical for their success while transforming their business processes and practices.

This book provides a blueprint for how your organization can prepare for, plan, and adopt an SAP S/4HANA Cloud (or on-premise) solution that provides a flexible digital core for rapidly and continuously innovating business processes. SAP has designed the SAP Activate approach to help organizations not only deploy their SAP S/4HANA Cloud (or on-premise) solution fast but also apply principles that enable them to adopt the new capabilities and innovate their business processes as SAP delivers new functionality and as businesses and organizations evolve.

With the rapid innovation cycles of SAP S/4HANA Cloud Public Edition, your business can take advantage of key innovations such as robotic process automation (RPA), AI, embedded analytics capabilities, machine learning scenarios, and key usability innovations in SAP Fiori to unlock the potential of this next-generation intelligent ERP system for your organization.

No matter which deployment strategy you choose, each is covered in its own chapter or unit in this book. This book takes you on a journey through SAP Activate, from introducing the key concepts and components to discussing the tools and applications you'll use during your deployment. We then provide comprehensive coverage of the deployment approaches: new implementation, system conversion, and selective data transition. We truly hope you enjoy this book and wish you luck on your journey of transition to SAP S/4HANA Cloud or SAP S/4HANA.

The Objective of This Book

Our goal in writing this book is to provide one comprehensive guide to SAP Activate for IT professionals, business users, and consultants who are planning or implementing SAP S/4HANA Cloud (or on-premise) in their organizations. This book aims to provide details about the implementation and operation of SAP S/4HANA Cloud, SAP S/4HANA (on-premise), and a hybrid environment combining both the cloud and on-premise solutions in a federated deployment model. You'll not only learn the fundamentals and principles of SAP Activate but also discover how to access SAP Activate content and methodology and use the expertise and knowledge of the SAP Activate community of experts. In addition, you'll learn about the subtle differences between using SAP Activate for the implementation of cloud solutions and on-premise solutions. Finally, this book provides a set of practice questions that you can review as preparation for your SAP Activate certification exam.

Who This Book Is For

This book is targeted at a wide range of people in roles that plan, execute, contribute to, or influence the deployment of SAP software solutions in their organizations or their client organizations. Specifically, the following roles will benefit from reading this book and following the SAP Activate approach during the deployment of SAP S/4HANA Cloud and SAP S/4HANA in their organizations:

- Sponsors of transformation programs
- IT executives and managers
- Leaders of line of business (LoB) organizations, such as finance and logistics
- Program managers and project managers
- Agile coaches and agile practitioners
- Solution, application, and technology architects
- Application experts and consultants
- Technology experts and consultants
- Developers
- Students interested in a career in IT or consulting services

How This Book Is Organized

This book is structured into 11 chapters and an appendix:

- **Chapter 1: SAP S/4HANA Fundamentals**
  We begin by introducing SAP S/4HANA Cloud and SAP S/4HANA, including the discussion of these key technologies: SAP Business Technology Platform (SAP BTP), SAP Business AI, and SAP Fiori. Then, we dive into the discussion of the deployment strategies customers can apply to bring their organization to SAP S/4HANA in the cloud, on-premise, or in a hybrid two-tier setup.

- **Chapter 2: Introduction to SAP Activate**
  This chapter takes you on a journey through SAP Activate, explaining the fundamentals of the approach, discussing the structure of the methodology, and introducing the clean core strategy and golden rules for deployment of SAP S/4HANA Cloud, including the recommended governance to follow the rules in your project to deploy a solution that enables your organization to innovate continually. We close with the introduction of the SAP Activate community on *www.sap.com* and the learning offerings for SAP Activate practitioners.

- **Chapter 3: Accessing SAP Activate**
  In this chapter, we'll dive into the details of the key tools to support users of SAP Activate in their journey, including SAP Cloud ALM, the SAP Activate Roadmap Viewer, and SAP Signavio Process Navigator. You'll learn what each of these tools does and how you can leverage them in your project.

- **Chapter 4: Starting with a Working System**
  In Chapter 4, we'll focus on the ready-to-run business processes preconfiguration that customers will use in their deployment of SAP S/4HANA Cloud: SAP Best Practices and the enterprise management layer for SAP S/4HANA. We provide comprehensive descriptions of the business process content structure and consumption of these assets in your project. We also discuss the importance of the business content for successfully running fit-to-standard workshops.

- **Chapter 5: Implementation Activities**
  In Chapter 5, we'll focus on the fundamentals of how the solution is configured, extended, integrated with other solutions, and tested. We'll also introduce the key considerations for organizations adopting business AI in their business processes. This chapter provides an overview of the concepts for these topics and sets the foundation for Chapter 7 and Chapter 8, in which we'll focus on the deployment of SAP S/4HANA Cloud and SAP S/4HANA.

- **Chapter 6: Agile Project Delivery**
  Before you get to the deployment processes, Chapter 6 offers a detailed explanation of how SAP Activate incorporates agile concepts in the approach and how agile can be scaled in large organizations and projects. We discuss the roles, organization, governance, and processes agile teams apply in their implementation process.

- **Chapter 7: New Implementation of SAP S/4HANA**
  In Chapter 7, you'll learn how to perform a new implementation of all versions of the SAP S/4HANA solutions. We start the chapter with the new implementation of SAP S/4HANA Cloud Public Edition in a three-system landscape; continue with the new implementation of SAP S/4HANA Cloud Private Edition; and close the chapter with the review of the new implementation of the SAP S/4HANA (on-premise) solution. For each of the solutions, we'll take you through all the phases of SAP Activate to help you understand the key steps for deployment of the solution and learn how to prepare for regular upgrades and innovation shipments from SAP.

- **Chapter 8: System Conversion and Selective Data Transition to SAP S/4HANA**
  Chapter 8 will then discuss the strategies and steps for system conversion and selective data transition to SAP S/4HANA Cloud Private Edition and SAP S/4HANA. For each of these deployment approaches, we'll take you through the key steps your project team will follow from the discover phase to the run phase of SAP Activate.

- **Chapter 9: Deploying Hybrid System Landscapes**
  Chapter 9 will explore the deployment of SAP S/4HANA in hybrid landscapes and will explain the hybrid scenarios across finance, sales, procurement, manufacturing, and supply chain. We also cover recommendations for organizations deploying SAP S/4HANA Cloud in their existing environments while maximizing the use of their existing investment in their IT infrastructure.

- **Chapter 10: Organizational Change Management**
  Everybody deploying SAP S/4HANA Cloud and SAP S/4HANA in their organizations needs to be familiar with critical concepts and approaches for organizational change management (OCM). These are fundamental for successful solution adoption and customer lifetime value realization. Change management topics are often underestimated, negatively impacting the adoption of the solution in the business. Additionally, we'll discuss the importance of the Customer Center of Expertise (Customer COE) for establishing operational excellence for your ERP solution. This chapter is a must-read for all transformation managers.

- **Chapter 11: SAP Activate for Other SAP Products**
  Finally, Chapter 11 provides several examples of SAP Activate assets for other SAP products, such as SAP SuccessFactors, and detailed guidance for the implementation of multiple products in SAP Activate for the intelligent enterprise. We also discuss SAP Activate for SAP BTP, which provides guidance for customers leveraging SAP BTP services in their organization, and we introduce the methodology for converting your SAP S/4HANA Cloud Public Edition solution from a two-system landscape to a three-system landscape. We then discuss the methodology for upgrading your SAP S/4HANA solution and for additional product integration. Finally, this chapter closes with a complete list of SAP Activate roadmaps that are available at the time of writing this book (fall 2024).

- **Appendix A: SAP Activate Certification Preparation**
  In Appendix A, you'll find practice questions for your preparation for the SAP Activate certification exam. These questions are different from the actual certification exam questions but follow the same structure that you'll encounter while taking the SAP Activate certification exam. They cover the scope of topics this book addresses, with a focus on topics and categories listed in the certification exam.

Acknowledgments

We thank our families for their patience and support while we were working on this book. Your support and encouragement helped us get through long nights of writing and revising the text to make this book something we're all proud of.

We also thank all the contributors and reviewers who helped make this book a comprehensive compendium of SAP Activate approaches, content, tools, and methods. You'll find short biographies for all the contributors in Appendix B.

Chapter 1

SAP S/4HANA Fundamentals

In the current era of relentless market shifts, evolving business expectations, altering customer demands, and competitive dynamics, orchestrating and implementing digital business transformation is critical for the success of any enterprise. SAP S/4HANA Cloud enables businesses to rapidly transform their operations, innovate, and empower their business users to deliver lasting value to their customers across a wide range of industries.

For today's enterprises, success comes when business users can work together across all domains and jointly focus on business outcomes. However, visibility of information across business domains and the ability to perform periodic course corrections based on forecasting and reporting aren't enough. This doesn't guarantee survival unless companies are able to innovate at a rapid pace.

The ability to evolve a business model swiftly hinges on having systems and operations ready for fast adoption of business innovations, which is the advantage offered by cloud technology. Today's businesses are rapidly transitioning their business systems from traditional on-premise operations to cloud-first infrastructure augmented with artificial intelligence (AI) technology that empowers them to adjust more rapidly to changing business and competitive environments as well as to grow.

SAP provides organizations with the foundation to become intelligent enterprises, enabling them to run business operations better, become more resilient to changes in the marketplace, increase profitability, and become more sustainable. To achieve this objective, SAP brings together a comprehensive portfolio of business solutions and technology to serve customers' business process needs, which we'll discuss in this chapter.

The challenge for enterprise resource planning (ERP) systems is to overcome today's fragmentation of business decision-making and execution to bring about truly integrated business management without the limitations and complexity of legacy environments. Informed decisions powered by AI and agile simulations of alternative business scenarios will allow enterprises to adapt and continuously evolve. Modern cloud ERP systems need to help businesses transform from reactive decision-making and partially informed execution to continuous and proactive simulation of possible business outcomes. Such outcomes will be executed by a fully informed workforce augmented by capable AI functions that can together wholly focus on value-adding activities and offloading low-value tasks to system-automated processes—all to the delight of customers at every touchpoint with the company.

Enterprises will also be able to supplement these capabilities with automatically identified patterns and predicted data points, providing them as insights to effectively engage them in collaborative value creation and customer focus.

While this book isn't centering on the SAP solutions portfolio, we will introduce the technologies that play a critical role in the deployment of SAP S/4HANA Cloud (or on-premise) solutions.

In this chapter, we'll establish the SAP S/4HANA Cloud basics, including technologies such as SAP Business Technology Platform (SAP BTP), SAP Business AI, SAP HANA, and SAP Fiori. We'll also discuss the available offerings, deployment models, and transition options. To begin, we'll explore the context in which SAP S/4HANA Cloud is positioned: the intelligent, sustainable enterprise.

1.1   Transition into an Intelligent, Sustainable Enterprise

Today's businesses are constantly tested with changing business environments, evolving customer needs, and emerging competitive market situations. Over the past years, the entire world experienced massive changes to the way consumers behave, employees work, supply chains react, and governments respond to crises and disruptions. If anything, the pace of change each business needs to respond to has only accelerated.

In the following sections, we'll explain how today's market leaders are making this transition, including overall market trends that set the bar for differentiation.

1.1.1   What Makes an Enterprise Intelligent and Sustainable?

Many businesses are in the thick of the transition to an intelligent, sustainable enterprise and need to develop business models that are resilient to disruption. Table 1.1 notes the key differences between traditional enterprise management and enterprise management suited for the intelligent, sustainable enterprise.

Traditional Enterprise	Intelligent, Sustainable Enterprise
Focus on supply/demand matching and profitability	Focus on customer experience along the entire value chain
Bottom-up versus top-down (strategy, business plan, and directives)	Strategy execution at all levels of the corporate structure
Periodic planning of resources to meet time-bound profitability goals	Ongoing business optimization via simulation of scenarios powered by AI
Management process focused on forward projections and results review	Management exploiting strategic opportunities through organizational agility

Table 1.1 Differences between Enterprise Management Today and in the Future

Traditional Enterprise	Intelligent, Sustainable Enterprise
Automation of simple recurring tasks only	Automation of comprehensive processes that used to require human intervention
Enterprise focuses on top line and bottom line	Social, sustainable enterprise focusing on top line, bottom line, and green line

Table 1.1 Differences between Enterprise Management Today and in the Future (Cont.)

The effectiveness of this new style of management hinges on the extent to which meaningful insights for game-changing outcomes can be generated fast enough to be ahead of competitive pressures. Therefore, we need to ensure that all relevant streams of information are brought together with the business information traditionally seen in the scope of ERP (operational data), such as relevant patterns emerging from big data pools (market and resource signals, device information) and customer experience feedback (experience data). Today's enterprise needs to drive business innovation to grow the top line, drive operational excellence to improve the bottom line and do all this in a sustainable and socially responsible way to sustain the green line.

Figure 1.1 shows the components of the intelligent enterprise. It starts with SAP BTP, which provides the foundation of application integration and extension to a robust ecosystem of solutions, data, and AI. Building on this solid foundation is SAP cloud ERP and business applications that empower organizations with a wide range of business process capabilities augmented with AI technology supporting business users across front-office and back-office functions. These core applications are further strengthened by a rich portfolio of solutions from the ecosystem partners. With such a range of capabilities at play, enterprises can transform their business operations at rapid speed.

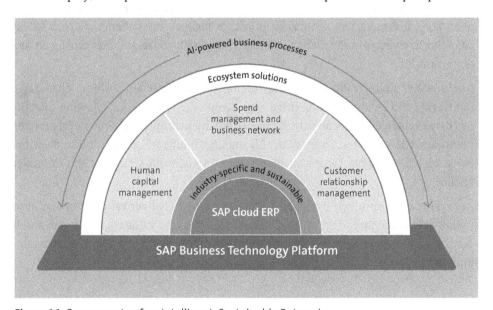

Figure 1.1 Components of an Intelligent, Sustainable Enterprise

1.1.2   Preparing Businesses for a Fast-Changing Future

Uncertainty is among the biggest challenges businesses face today as the pace of change continues to accelerate. In this climate, most organizations must make the right decisions to ensure survival and growth. However, they don't necessarily know how, when, and where change will happen; as we all experienced in the past years, change can come rapidly and accelerate business trends, impact the business environment, and change consumer behaviors. For example, a significant shift in buying patterns to online shopping, increased use of delivery services, and much more strained supply chains. In other words, organizations must have the structural and financial flexibility to make swift decisions and grab opportunities as soon as they appear. In the same way, they need to reinvent the enterprise. However, businesses focused on the existing digital landscape for predicting the future will find this landscape inappropriate for modernizing their business into an intelligent, sustainable enterprise.

One of the first steps is to refresh your digital landscape to support your organization in evolving its business processes. This requires a sequential path of technology adoption that allows you to transform the business, connect the dots between current and future digital capabilities, and enable new opportunities. You need agile IT solutions to be well-prepared for an unpredictable future.

1.1.3   Achieving More across the Value Chain

Companies that integrate insights from their own systems with those obtained from external partnerships can enhance efficiency, reduce costs, and improve performance. By adopting this integrated approach, businesses can use information from both their operations and interactions with partners, leading to more dynamic relations with suppliers and consumers. This results in a more agile business ecosystem capable of swiftly adjusting to changes in the market, effectively managing risks, and capitalizing on new opportunities.

Additionally, strategically combining intelligence in these ecosystems encourages innovation and creates a competitive edge. Removing barriers and allowing continuous data exchange among all parties gives companies complete visibility of their operations and the market at large. With this understanding, leaders can make decisions based on solid insights, which results in more thought-out strategies and improved results.

As organizations continue to face increasing pressure to deliver value faster and more sustainably, the ability to optimize performance across the value chain through a well-connected and intelligent ecosystem becomes a critical differentiator in achieving long-term success.

1.1.4   Sustainability at the Core of Your Organization

All enterprises are under growing pressure from stakeholders, including consumers, investors, and regulators, to adopt sustainable practices that reduce environmental impact and promote social responsibility. By leveraging advanced technologies and data-driven tools, companies can drive more accurate and actionable sustainability management across their entire enterprise.

These solutions enable organizations to monitor, measure, and manage their environmental footprint with greater precision, ensuring that sustainability efforts are not only compliant with global standards but also contribute to a more sustainable future.

The importance of sustainability for modern businesses can't be overstated. It's no longer just a matter of corporate social responsibility but a strategic imperative that directly impacts profitability, brand reputation, and competitiveness. Organizations that prioritize sustainability are better positioned to adapt to regulatory changes, meet consumer expectations, and mitigate risks associated with environmental degradation and resource scarcity.

1.1.5   RISE with SAP and GROW with SAP

SAP introduced RISE with SAP in 2021 and added GROW with SAP in 2023 as new offerings for SAP customers looking to transition their business operations to the cloud. These offerings are designed to provide the right-sized cloud ERP solution for any organization or business. We won't cover the details of these offerings in this book but instead continue to focus on the deployment of specific SAP S/4HANA Cloud solutions that customers gain entitlements to use through these offerings.

We may make brief references to RISE with SAP or GROW with SAP later in the book. For readers aiming to understand the details, entitlements, and options, we'll briefly outline these offerings here:

- **GROW with SAP**

  Midsize enterprises are the drivers of future growth. They drive groundbreaking innovations and fresh concepts destined to transform our world. Concurrently, they face similar challenges in running their businesses as larger corporations. These companies need adaptable and nimble business solutions that enable efficient business management, propelling them to new heights in the dynamic, competitive, and often volatile marketplace.

  GROW with SAP is designed to help midsize companies deploy the solution rapidly to fully take advantage of cloud ERP and all of its benefits. It gives customers the confidence that they will be up and running quickly with technology that allows them to keep growing and continuously innovate. Customers leveraging GROW with SAP are deploying SAP S/4HANA Cloud Public Edition, the ready-to-run business solution, along with other capabilities such as SAP BTP, adoption acceleration services, and community and learning. For more details about what is included in GROW with SAP, go to *www.sap.com/products/erp/grow.html*.

- **RISE with SAP**

  This offering is designed for customers migrating their ERP solution to the cloud to achieve the next level of innovation. Customers who leverage RISE with SAP are on the path of continuous digital transformation that empowers their business users to innovate. They leverage intelligence and automation in their business processes. Organizations using RISE with SAP establish an agile operating model to free up their IT resources from the burden of maintenance and tactical execution to shift toward evolving the business processes and serving their business users as business needs evolve. This often includes the adoption of technology and business process innovation such as business AI or automation.

  Customers adopting RISE with SAP are deploying SAP S/4HANA Cloud Private Edition coupled with additional capabilities and services. This includes migration and adoption services, cloud infrastructure managed by SAP, hosting on a hyperscaler of the customer's choice, and platform extensibility through SAP BTP.

  You can find more details about RISE with SAP on the SAP website at *www.sap.com/products/erp/rise.html*.

Note that both offerings include access to SAP Business AI, which we'll introduce as a capability in Section 1.2.3.

1.2   Key Technologies

In this section, we'll examine the foundational technologies for delivering intelligent ERP in SAP S/4HANA Cloud. We'll detail the technologies of SAP S/4HANA Cloud, SAP Business AI, SAP BTP, and SAP HANA, the modern in-memory database that powers intelligent ERP. We'll also discuss the benefits of one user experience (UX) across the entire application suite, powered by SAP Fiori. Let's start with the introduction to the SAP cloud ERP applications in SAP S/4HANA Cloud.

1.2.1   SAP S/4HANA Cloud

SAP S/4HANA Cloud is an intelligent and integrated ERP solution that runs on SAP's in-memory database, SAP HANA (discussed in Section 1.2.4). It provides organizations with software that addresses their business requirements across business verticals and enables organizations to evolve their business models as their industry changes over time. Organizations that adopt SAP S/4HANA Cloud gain the following advantages:

- **Create innovative business models at a global scale**
  Accelerate revenue growth, discover new opportunities for expansion by seamlessly shifting from a product-centric to a service-oriented model, and modify strategies flexibly in response to real-time data on usage and customer feedback.

- **Benefit from proven business processes for your industry**
  Achieve bottom-line growth; collaborate more efficiently with instant, tailored business insights accessible from any location; and improve profit margins consistently through smart automation of operational procedures.

- **Build sustainability directly into your business**
  Deliver green-line growth, and adjust business practices and procedures to continuously minimize emissions, reduce waste, lessen ecological effects, and handle legal compliance ahead of time through comprehensive organizational controls and detailed reporting.

- **Bring your business wherever it needs to go**
  Grow without limits, maintain compliance and security through adherence to updated global standards, and drive innovation with a scalable platform and extensive partner network that consistently delivers new value.

With SAP S/4HANA Cloud, business users and organizations are equipped for better and faster decision-making with embedded analytics. They get faster answers with conversational interfaces powered by business AI capabilities built into the solution. SAP S/4HANA Cloud provides organizations with a choice of deployment in hybrid, cloud, and on-premise scenarios to optimize their IT landscapes. We'll discuss the options later in this chapter.

SAP S/4HANA Cloud provides organizations with a broad range of capabilities in the following areas (see Figure 1.2):

- **Finance**
  These capabilities help organizations simplify accounting processes and the financial close, enable improvements to the treasury and financial risk processes, provide support for collaborative financial operations, help simplify real estate management, and more.

- **Procurement**
  The sourcing and procurement capability helps organizations gain in-depth insight into their purchasing operations, streamlines their operational purchasing, automates contract management and sourcing, centralizes procurement processes, reduces supply chain risk, manages commodity procurement, and more.

- **Sales**
  The sales capability enables organizations to drive and manage sales force performance, supports sales professionals and sales managers, maximizes revenue with optimized sales processes for contract and order management, and more.

- **Service**
  The service capability provides organizations with processes to optimize engagement profitability, achieve better staffing levels, help capture time sheets faster with simplified time entry, streamline quote-to-cash processes, reimagine bid management processes, and more.

- **Cross functions**
  The cross-functional capabilities cover topics like integration with other systems, data loads into the system, data protection and data privacy, and information lifecycle management.

- **Asset management**
  Asset management capabilities help organizations achieve operational excellence through planning, scheduling, and executing asset maintenance activities.

- **Supply chain**
  The supply chain capability enables excellence in your supply processes to provide more accurate commitment dates, achieve more streamlined warehouse management, optimize inventory processes for optimal inventory levels, integrate transportation management, and more.

- **Manufacturing**
  The manufacturing capability helps organizations implement processes to support complex assembly execution, improve production planning, support seamless manufacturing engineering, and accelerate manufacturing operations, including enhanced quality management.

- **R&D**
  The R&D and engineering capabilities provide organizations with processes to improve product development and project control, as well as help achieve effective management of enterprise-wide projects, better product lifecycle management, and improved efficiency through requirement-driven processes.

- **Industry capabilities**
  Industry capabilities are used across 31 industries, such as automotive, consumer, chemicals, mill, mining, media, public services, retail, sports and entertainment, and wholesale distribution.

Feature Scope Description Document

As the list of capabilities in SAP S/4HANA Cloud continues to evolve, we recommend you refer to the full list of capabilities in the following resources:

- SAP S/4HANA Cloud Public Edition: *https://help.sap.com/docs/SAP_S4HANA_CLOUD*
- SAP S/4HANA Cloud Private Edition: *https://help.sap.com/docs/SAP_S4HANA_CLOUD_PE*

Then, open the feature scope description document that you'll find on these SAP Help pages.

Finance	Procurement	Sales	Service	Cross Functions
• Accounting and financial close • Financial operations • Cost management • Treasury • Enterprise risk and compliance	• Procurement of direct materials and services • Supplier management • Central procurement	• Sell from stock • Sell services • Rebates and commissions • Convergent and external billing	• Sell, deliver, bill, and monitor a combination of physical goods and services as one solution offering	• Master data, data migration, data protection and privacy, information lifecycle management • Integration capabilities • Legal content management

SAP S/4HANA Cloud

Asset Management	Supply Chain	Manufacturing	R&D	Industry Capabilities
• Resource scheduling for maintenance planner • Enhanced collaboration and review	• Warehouse outbound and inbound processing • Core inventory management • Advanced ATP processing	• Material requirements planning (MRP) with demand-driven and/or predictive MRP • Make-to-stock and make-to-order • Quality management	• Product compliance • Enterprise portfolio and project management • Variant configuration	• Professional services • Public sector • Higher education • Manufacturing • Mining services

Figure 1.2 SAP S/4HANA Cloud Scope Highlights

As outlined earlier, these capabilities enable organizations to achieve higher efficiency and better performance across a wide range of processes in their enterprise, such as the following:

- Engineer-to-order
- Invoice-to-pay
- Invoice-to-cash
- Produce-to-invoice
- Make-to-order
- Treasury management
- Sell-from-stock
- Financial planning and analysis
- Idea-to-product
- Engagement-to-cash
- Asset maintenance and operations
- Quote-to-order
- Managing real estate and facilities
- Record-to-report
- Return-to-restock

Further SAP S/4HANA Resources

For more in-depth information about the SAP S/4HANA and SAP S/4HANA Cloud solutions, refer to the following SAP PRESS books:

- *SAP S/4HANA: An Introduction* (SAP PRESS, 2021, *www.sap-press.com/5232*)
- *SAP S/4HANA Cloud: An Introduction* (SAP PRESS, 2022, *www.sap-press.com/5457*)

You can also find additional information about SAP S/4HANA Cloud functions and capabilities on SAP's website at *https://www.sap.com/products/erp/s4hana.html* for SAP S/4HANA Cloud Public Edition and *www.sap.com/products/erp/s4hana-private-edition.html* for SAP S/4HANA Cloud Private Edition.

1.2.2   SAP Business Technology Platform

SAP Business Technology Platform (SAP BTP) provides customers with one platform that brings together intelligent enterprise applications, database and data management, analytics, and integration and extension capabilities. As we discussed earlier in the chapter, SAP BTP is the foundation of the intelligent, sustainable enterprise (refer to Figure 1.1).

SAP BTP provides a wide range of services for building powerful business solutions, including the following:

- **Application development and automation**
  SAP BTP provides users with a set of low-code and no-code capabilities such as SAP Build to create business applications, create automation, and visually design the business applications. It also offers full-fledged development tools for developers with SAP Build Code and the ABAP cloud environment for building powerful applications. We'll touch on these topics in Chapter 5 when we talk about the extensibility of standard applications.

- **AI**
  These capabilities allow organizations to transform business applications with ready-to-use business-specific pretrained AI models. You can leverage conversational AI to build user-friendly chatbots and run AI responsibly with compliance and transparency. We'll cover the SAP Business AI capabilities that leverage the AI capabilities of SAP BTP in more detail in the next section.

- **Data and analytics**
  These services and capabilities enable organizations to access data anywhere, analyze the data, and leverage the insight to run the organization more efficiently and grow. The capabilities in this category include SAP HANA, which we'll cover in Section 1.2.4, as one of the key technologies powering SAP S/4HANA Cloud applications.

- **Extended planning and analysis (xP&A)**
  The capabilities in this category empower organizations to interconnect and integrate data across their SAP and other enterprise applications. This facilitates collaborative planning by integrating financial, supply chain, and operational planning into one AI-powered solution.

- **Integration**
  This set of capabilities enables organizations to integrate the various SAP and non-SAP applications in their landscape with powerful integration technology delivered in SAP Integration Suite. We'll discuss the topic of integration in the context of implementation with SAP Activate in Chapter 5.

Other SAP BTP Resources

Our intent is to only introduce SAP BTP, not to cover it comprehensively. If you're interested in SAP BTP topics and integration, you can explore these areas in the following SAP PRESS books:

- *SAP Business Technology Platform* (SAP PRESS, 2024, *www.sap-press.com/5919*)
- *Cloud Integration with SAP Integration Suite* (SAP PRESS, 2024, *www.sap-press.com/5760*)

Additionally, you can learn more about SAP BTP and individual capabilities at *www.sap.com/products/business-technology-platform.html.*

1.2.3   SAP Business AI

SAP Business AI provides customers of SAP solutions with the power of AI capabilities across the entire range of SAP applications and solutions. It's deeply embedded directly into the applications and business processes encoded in these applications, as you can see in Figure 1.3.

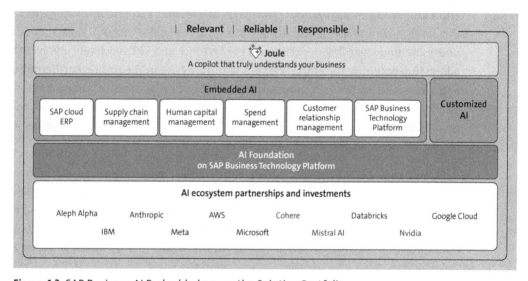

Figure 1.3 SAP Business AI Embedded across the Solution Portfolio

As Figure 1.3 shows, SAP Business AI is designed to be relevant, reliable, and responsible. Let's briefly explore what that means:

- **Relevant**

  SAP Business AI enhances user interaction with SAP software by leveraging Joule—the digital assistive copilot available across various SAP applications. This innovation is ready to boost efficiency and productivity for hundreds of millions of users, who can now simply express their ideas, inquire about analytics, or command the system through speech instead of navigating through transaction menus or writing application code. Consequently, SAP systems will grasp user intentions, going beyond mere voice commands. SAP Business AI enhances the capabilities of SAP applications and enables them to learn and improve business outcomes. This leads to significant improvements in key business processes such as recruit-to-retire, source-to-pay, design-to-operate, and lead-to-cash, giving customers access to more intelligent and automated solutions.

- **Reliable**
  The quality of your AI directly depends on the quality of your data, and SAP leads in this respect, maintaining intact business data context like no other organization. Combining immense business process data, industry best practices from both SAP and third-party applications, and state-of-the-art large language models, SAP Business AI is grounded in real customer business insights. It uses generative AI informed by current data to help guarantee reliable results.

- **Responsible**
  SAP upholds a deep commitment to the ethical use of AI, aligning with its fundamental values. The approach with SAP Business AI focuses on enhancing human effort and decision-making. SAP proactively tackles bias and discrimination during the development phase of AI in its applications. The goal is to maintain clarity and understanding regarding the actions of the systems, and SAP is actively involved in addressing potential societal challenges that may arise in the future. Furthermore, SAP's excellent business authorization concepts can be used to safeguard both employees and business partners against unintended results. Responsible and secure integration of business information in SAP systems with cutting-edge AI technologies is at the center of SAP Business AI design.

SAP introduced Joule, the copilot, in 2024 as an interface for business users to interact with SAP business applications conversationally to accomplish their business objectives. It facilitates faster work by providing a simple interface to perform tasks and to get insight. The AI responses are grounded in your business application data and follow the authorizations that the business user has in the application. The Joule interface is seamlessly integrated into the user interaction in the SAP Fiori UX (we'll discuss this UX technology in Section 1.2.5) on the business screen, as you can see in Figure 1.4. This also means Joule has one consistent UX, which makes its usage as seamless as possible for all business users.

Now, let's look at some examples of how SAP has embedded business AI capabilities into various applications across the SAP product portfolio today:

- **Cloud ERP**
  The SAP Business AI capabilities span a wide range of applications in the enterprise resource management solution from accounting and financial close areas where AI is used to reduce the processing time of financial close through enhancing the goods receipt/invoice receipt account reconciliation process and to improve the resolution of common errors during the financial close. In the compliance optimization area, AI can be used to streamline and automate tax compliance checks to reduce

risk exposure where AI learns from manual decisions made by the tax experts and increases automation of these actions over time. These are just a few examples of AI improving the business process efficiency, quality, and responsiveness.

Figure 1.4 Joule Interface in an SAP S/4HANA Cloud System

- **Human capital management**
  Leverage SAP Business AI to streamline HR processes and improve efficiency anywhere from requesting time off work to requesting or providing feedback to getting answers about HR policies. In recruiting processes, AI can be used to enhance job descriptions to make them more inclusive and personalized to your business. It can be used to prepare for candidate interviews with tailored question lists for the specific role. Additionally, AI can recommend specific learning to employees for advancing their career and developing new skills needed in the role they are aiming to achieve.

- **Supply chain**
  Organizations can continue transforming their supply chain processes with SAP Business AI across product lifecycle management, where generative AI can be used to connect the 2D and 3D product models with the corresponding business information from the ERP system to ensure the accuracy of product data. In supply chain planning, AI capabilities facilitate forecasting based on near real-time information that reflects market variability and evolving sales trends; predictive material and resource planning helps to reduce inventory carrying cost and improve utilization. In manufacturing, AI can provide improved visibility and insights where machine learning for visual inspections improves operator productivity.

- **Procurement**

  There are wide applications of AI in procurement where it can be used to streamline processes to make better decisions with onscreen recommendations. Joule can be used to streamline and automate the sourcing event processes with recommendations of relevant suppliers and specific items to source. In the procurement process, AI helps improve delivery date predictions, and during invoice processing, it helps with automating invoice classification and data enrichment.

- **SAP BTP**

  Joule empowers the developers with code generation capabilities, prebuilt integration content, data insight, and administration support. The generative AI hub provides access to AI development tools, enterprise-grade access to AI models, and data control for building AI-powered applications in SAP BTP. The SAP HANA Cloud vector engine supports the management and examination of intricate, nonstructured vector data (embeddings). This allows for the smooth handling, assessment, and use of embeddings in the creation of business applications and provides additional business relevance for generative AI use cases.

> **Note**
>
> These are only select applications of SAP Business AI, so we recommend you review the complete list of capabilities on SAP's website at *www.sap.com/products/artificial-intelligence.html*.

Now that we've introduced SAP Business AI, we'll examine other key technologies powering SAP cloud ERP. Additionally, in Chapter 5, we'll expand on considerations for implementing SAP Business AI in your organization, including the capabilities of Joule, the digital business assistant in SAP S/4HANA Cloud Public Edition.

1.2.4   SAP HANA

The SAP HANA Master Guide, used by IT professionals when planning the installation of SAP HANA system landscapes, defines SAP HANA as "a modern, in-memory database and platform that is deployable on-premise or in the cloud." Let's delve a little deeper to evaluate why SAP HANA provides the next-generation data management foundation for all the industry-leading SAP solutions necessary to build an intelligent enterprise.

In-Memory Database

SAP HANA revolutionized the data management industry by delivering the first in-memory data platform to the market in 2010 with its in-memory-first architecture. With SAP HANA, data is maintained in memory by default. Other storage media, such as SSDs or HDs, can also be used to manage larger data sets that don't fit in memory and data that is rarely accessed to lower storage costs.

This is fundamentally different from how traditional databases operate. They are designed to store data on disk and move data to memory only for processing. Even with the most recent introduction of in-memory extensions, these legacy databases carry the intrinsic complexity of having to manage all the data on disk and having to be told what data needs to be copied into memory and when. This translates into higher data latency, unnecessary data duplication, and higher administration costs. Instead, SAP HANA's architecture supports true real-time performance without latency or data duplication, allowing you to support more diverse and complex workloads and applications.

Database and Platform

SAP HANA allows online transactional processing (OLTP) and online analytical processing (OLAP) on one system, without the need for redundant data storage or aggregates. The "online" in OLTP and OLAP once expressed the novelty that transactions occurred in real time and not with punch cards updating the system overnight. But analytics still requires special processing to get the data out of the system of record and into multidimensional cubes. With SAP HANA, this special processing isn't required because it's a single database system with a single data copy.

SAP HANA is called a *platform* because different technologies are integrated with the database server. When you start up an SAP HANA system, you're also starting up an application server. This built-in functionality promotes the concept of in-database processing and keeping a single data copy.

Besides database and application services, the platform also includes a graph engine and a spatial engine; both are built into one system in real time without tuning and are accessible through the same SQL interface used for transactions and analytics. Other advanced analytics "capabilities" (features and functions) concern the execution of predictive analytics and business functions, as well as the manipulation of unstructured data (as opposed to structured relational data).

SAP HANA in the Cloud or On-Premise

The term *on-premise* refers to running the system in your own corporate data center. In this case, you'll rely on certified hardware and certified engineers to install and operate the platform. Deploying *in the cloud* refers to running SAP HANA as a data platform as a service (DPaaS) that can run on a hyperscaler infrastructure or as a service in SAP BTP.

With SAP HANA, you gain access to a modern data platform that can support all of your data management needs and that works synergistically with your technology landscape, including Hadoop, Spark, and other data sources, to accelerate your ability to get value from your data by simplifying your application architectures and IT landscapes. The SAP HANA platform encompasses the following capabilities:

- **Application development**
  These tools simplify the application architecture, achieve optimal application performance, and reduce complexity in the IT environment. In this area, SAP HANA offers capabilities geared for application development—for example, SAP HANA extended application services (SAP HANA XS) with a built-in application server that allows development of services, such as REST or OData, and web applications. Client access provides access to other client libraries such as Python, JavaScript, R, and so on. Additionally, SAP HANA provides capabilities for application lifecycle management (ALM) and more.

- **Advanced analytics**
  Advanced analytics are processed natively on relational and nonrelational data by effectively managing multi-model data—for example, relational, JavaScript Object Notation (JSON), graph, and spatial data—and by applying specialized analytical processing, such as predictive analysis/machine learning, text mining, time series analysis, and more.

- **Data virtualization**
  The platform provides comprehensive features to handle various data integration scenarios. These include extract, transform, load (ETL); extract, load, transform (ELT); real-time data replication; bulk-load processing; data transformation; and built-in data quality and enrichment services. Additionally, you can perform queries on remote data sources, such as external cloud-native sources, Apache Hadoop, and other databases. It also supports data caching to optimize federated queries against remote sources of data.

- **Database management**
  Data of any size is managed efficiently, allowing rarely accessed data to be moved from memory to more economical storage media with its policy-driven dynamic storage tiering capability. Additionally, this area offers tools for database administration, security, and high availability disaster recovery.

1.2.5   SAP Fiori

As part of a digital transformation, the way users access ERP solutions is different than in the past. In recent years, there has been a massive change in the behavior of specific target groups, such as Generation Y or millennials—they're looking for a customized, personalized, responsive, and focused UX that's intuitive and easy to handle across all devices (e.g., mobile, desktop, and tablet). Based on changing requirements and the future of digitally enabled enterprises, SAP provided a new UX called SAP Fiori. SAP Fiori applies the following new design principles to reimagine the UX:

- **Role-based**

  SAP Fiori is designed to meet users' business needs and support their work in the application. It draws from deep insight into today's workforce to provide users with the right information at the right time and reflect their work in their business roles.

- **Adaptive**

  SAP Fiori enables users to work from anywhere and access their applications using any device they prefer. This allows users to gain instant insight by having relevant information at their fingertips.

- **Simple**

  Users can perform their jobs in an intuitive and simple environment that is responsive to their needs. SAP Fiori helps users focus on important functions via an easy-to-use environment that users can personalize to fit their needs.

- **Coherent**

  No matter your role and function in the organization, SAP Fiori will provide a consistent experience and unified visual design language. Users across the organization will enjoy the same consistent and intuitive experience whether they manage leave requests, analyze the latest sales performance metrics, or fulfill a sales order.

- **Delightful**

  SAP Fiori helps users work smarter by providing a rich UX that allows them to focus on their jobs and perform them more efficiently.

With the usage of SAP Fiori, there is a significant shift from the purely functional view that was available in the old SAP ERP to a role-based UX with a single entry point and a common design in SAP S/4HANA across business applications, whether cloud or on-premise.

SAP Start and SAP Mobile Start

SAP Start is an application that provides a central entry point for users of the SAP cloud business solutions integrated through it. SAP Start displays user-specific business content from these solutions respecting the user access and authorizations in all the applications accessible through SAP Start. The access is role-based across solutions such as SAP S/4HANA Cloud Public Edition, SAP S/4HANA Cloud Private Edition, and SAP SuccessFactors. You can find more information about SAP Start on SAP Help here: *http://s-prs.co/v596600*.

SAP Mobile Start is a native mobile application that provides the same capability as SAP Start, but on mobile devices. It acts as the gateway to SAP's suite of business applications and content, delivering a user-friendly experience. Its carefully preconfigured content caters to common industry roles and persona-based duties, enabling the execution of business processes on mobile devices.

SAP Mobile Start is a perfect companion for business users, enriching their experience of accessing various applications using SAP Fiori design elements. You can easily access content, apps, and tasks in one place so that you can stay informed and carry out all of your tasks no matter where you are. You'll find more information about SAP Mobile Start on SAP Help Portal here: *https://help.sap.com/docs/mobile-start*.

The changing UX strategy aims to support the simplification of the SAP S/4HANA Cloud solution, which is why SAP S/4HANA Cloud and SAP Fiori are tightly integrated. At present, not all SAP solutions are enabled fully with SAP Fiori, but solution development will continue. More SAP Fiori apps will be available in later releases that will simplify the overall solution. In addition, not all transactions are being replaced with SAP Fiori apps because there will be a move to a more role-based UX, and the processes will be streamlined and condensed to the necessary core functionality.

To identify currently available SAP Fiori apps, you can browse the SAP Fiori apps reference library (see Figure 1.5) at *http://s-prs.co/v502701*.

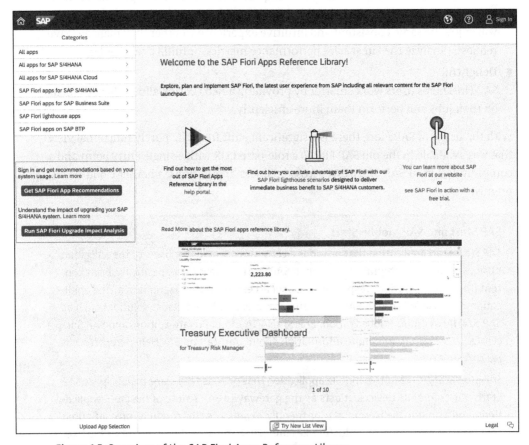

Figure 1.5 Overview of the SAP Fiori Apps Reference Library

1

SAP Fiori 3

The later version of SAP Fiori is SAP Fiori 3 UX, which is adopted by SAP products, resulting in consistency and integration across the portfolio. SAP Fiori 3 provides a coherent UX across the various SAP products to facilitate seamless integration and promote the intelligent suite.

If you're interested in SAP Fiori, be sure to explore the SAP Fiori design guidelines at *https://experience.sap.com/fiori-design-web/.*

1.3   Deployment and Operating Models

SAP S/4HANA can be deployed in multiple deployment models to support your organization's specific needs and to fit your IT architecture and strategy. We'll discuss the various deployment models in this section, and we'll outline how to deploy the SAP S/4HANA solution based on your needs and preferences later in the book.

The three key deployment models and respective operating models are as follows:

- Cloud
- On-premise
- Hybrid

Let's discuss each in more detail.

1.3.1   Cloud

In cloud operating models, instead of you operating or managing the software, a service provider is engaged for this purpose. The software and the corresponding services are leased for a defined period in the cloud operating model. Hardware and operating system software aren't required on-premises. The enterprise's IT staff can thus focus on other value-added tasks. Internet access is necessary to make use of the solution, and users can access the cloud software from anywhere and via mobile devices. One of the major benefits of the cloud operating model is the associated cost transparency and the ability to stay current with future innovations.

SAP offers companies full flexibility in their choice of how SAP S/4HANA Cloud is deployed. This choice is typically made by an organization after considering the available capabilities, localization needs, deployment model needed for the business, and so on. Companies can choose from two primary landscape options in the cloud:

- **Public cloud**
  In a public cloud scenario, the SAP S/4HANA Cloud Public Edition application runs as a service provided to business users. In the public cloud, the infrastructure and software are shared by multiple businesses. The software is on the same release level for

all customers at all times. The operational model ensures that in this shared model, no changes made for one client impact another client, and the data is strictly separated. To ensure efficient operation, SAP sets the maintenance cycles and upgrade schedules of the cloud software. This ensures faster delivery of innovation, and customers running in the public cloud can activate new capabilities much faster than in any other landscape option or deployment model (e.g., faster than on-premise or private cloud offerings).

- **Private cloud**
  In a private cloud scenario with SAP S/4HANA Cloud Private Edition, the software and infrastructure are operated by SAP or a hyperscaler and provided to the company as a service. This landscape option provides companies with the full scope of SAP S/4HANA Cloud, coverage of a wide range of industries, and availability of a range of SAP partner add-ons across multiple country and regional versions in more than 40 languages. One of the key differences of this landscape option as compared to the public cloud is that a company has more granular control over upgrades and software updates. As a result, the adoption of new capabilities can be somewhat slower than in the public cloud, depending on the upgrade strategy that the customer chooses.

Clean Core Strategy

Be sure to pay attention to the detailed discussion of the clean core strategy in Chapter 2 as a critical component for the successful adoption of the SAP S/4HANA Cloud Private Edition solution.

For deployment of SAP S/4HANA Cloud in both landscape options, data security and cloud security are critical topics for every customer. SAP sets up the data center operations, security standards, and processes to provide the highest level of security and protection. These standards are detailed in the SAP Trust Center, and you can access them here: *www.sap.com/about/trust-center.html*. In general, the security provided by trustworthy cloud providers is higher than that of typical enterprise IT organizations. Cloud providers document their security and operational capabilities via Service Organization Control (SOC) reports. You can access SAP's SOC reports in the SAP Trust Center.

Deploying SAP S/4HANA Cloud involves several characteristics, and many are related to the nature of the deploying software as a service (SaaS) solution. The key characteristics are as follows:

- **Ability to innovate rapidly by using standard functionality**
  Cloud solutions such as SAP S/4HANA Cloud allow you to adopt the solution quickly and continuously add new capabilities as SAP adds new capabilities to the solution. During the initial deployment, the objective is to implement the solution fast by staying close to the standard functionality, which enables you to adopt the new

capabilities SAP delivers in future releases much faster. We'll dedicate a significant part of this book to this topic and explore it in more detail in later chapters. The speed of innovation will be generally the fastest in the public cloud landscape option.

- **Stronger focus on organizational change management (OCM)**
Adopting a cloud solution often requires companies to adjust their existing business processes, which increases the effort and focus that project teams need to spend on assisting business users with the changing environment. This also increases the need to plan, execute, and monitor the implementation of the OCM activities in the project. We'll discuss this topic in more detail in Chapter 10.

- **Rapid deployment and innovation cycles**
In general, SAP S/4HANA Cloud has much shorter deployment and innovation cycles than on-premise solutions. This is especially true when you apply the cloud mindset of minimizing the number of extensions and focusing on deploying the minimally viable solution in the first implementation cycle and then adding to it in short innovation cycles. We've seen this approach applied more often with project teams deploying cloud solutions than with project teams deploying in on-premise environments.

These are just a few characteristics of deployment in the cloud. We'll discuss this deployment model in more detail in Chapter 7, where we'll go over the details of the cloud mindset, rapid innovation cycles, and how to use an agile approach during your deployment projects. We'll also discuss how the deployment varies between the two landscape options for the cloud (public cloud and private cloud).

1.3.2   On-Premise

Usually, the *on-premise operating model* refers to running and managing software you own on your own hardware. As a result, you're in full control of the hardware and software, mission-critical application data, and software maintenance schedules. Moreover, you have maximum flexibility when it comes to custom enhancements and integration with other systems (in-house solutions or external systems). However, you also are fully responsible for the availability of the software, as well as access, security, and system stability. In addition to the costs for hardware and software, powerful and complex ERP systems incur further costs for the IT experts needed to introduce, manage, and maintain the software.

In some cases, you may decide to subcontract the management of the hardware and software to a managed services provider or deploy the on-premise software on a hardware infrastructure provided in the cloud. In these cases, the operating and deployment model for the software follows the deployment of on-premise software detailed in SAP Activate.

Deployment of SAP S/4HANA in the on-premise model follows the same steps as SAP S/4HANA Cloud deployment, although there are several differences provided by the added flexibility of the solution and typically a larger number of requirements for extensibility of the solution driven by your users. This added flexibility also has one major drawback: heavily tailored solutions are very hard to keep up-to-date and in step with recent software releases and innovations. Customers implementing the on-premise or private cloud solution with the clean core strategy will find more details about the approach in Chapter 2. Additionally, we'll dive into the details of this deployment approach in Chapter 7 and Chapter 8.

The on-premise deployment model is best for those who want to manage their entire IT stack or have requirements for keeping the business application close to other parts of their organization (e.g., manufacturing processes that are sensitive to latency) or for those who have strict rules governing access to their data that don't allow them to operate their systems outside of their premises.

1.3.3   Hybrid

The hybrid operating model enables you to combine the characteristics of the on-premise operating model or private cloud operating model and the public cloud operating model. For example, core areas of your enterprise, where you want a high degree of control and a high level of flexibility, can be operated in private cloud, while other enterprise areas such as subsidiaries can be operated in the public cloud. Many organizations are using this approach to evolve their IT infrastructure while maximizing their existing investment in it. Such companies have adopted public cloud solutions in their landscapes for specific subsidiaries or parts of their business to build cloud knowledge and upskill their resources on this operating model to support their ongoing journey to the cloud.

> **Two-Tier ERP Deployment of SAP S/4HANA Cloud**
>
> If you have complex geographical structures or need distributed systems, you'll benefit from using a hybrid operating model powered by a two-tier ERP system. This model supports solutions in which some parts of the business scenario are operated in the private cloud or on-premise (e.g., central ERP for headquarters, where the corporation consolidates and reports financial results), and some parts are operated in the public cloud (e.g., smaller or dedicated units focusing on sales or exploration). It also caters to situations where some parts of your business are running in the public cloud and others remain on the existing on-premise infrastructure. This deployment model offers maximum flexibility to enterprises transitioning their infrastructure to the cloud.
>
> SAP runs a page called "Two-Tier ERP" in SAP Community where you can find the latest news and updates about this deployment model, including blogs, articles, and resources useful for customers considering this approach for their cloud ERP (*http://s-prs.co/v596601*).

We'll discuss this deployment and operating model in Chapter 9, where we'll go over examples of specific business scenarios of benefit to organizations that run them in this decentralized two-tier deployment approach.

1.3.4   Deployment Considerations for SAP S/4HANA

SAP S/4HANA's simplified data model and modern UX are consistent for cloud, hybrid, and on-premise deployments. Designed for in-memory usage, SAP S/4HANA brings new business capabilities while simplifying the IT landscape.

When deciding which of the previously explained deployment and operating models for SAP S/4HANA is right for your company, you should consider the following:

- Your organization's IT strategy
- Innovation cycles
- Adoption/upgrade efforts
- Total cost of ownership (TCO)
- Commercial models
- Business functionality
- Regulatory, industry, and regional requirements
- Data protection needs
- Localization
- Individualization options

The objective of this section is simply to introduce you to the options. We'll discuss all of these topics in more detail in the appropriate chapters dedicated to each of the deployment models in the second half of this book.

1.4   Deployment Approaches

Now that we've discussed the various ways the SAP S/4HANA application can be deployed, let's go over the options you have for the *transition path*—that is, how the software will be deployed. SAP offers a wide range of deployment options for each SAP S/4HANA variant—both to cater to companies who are new to SAP S/4HANA Cloud and to support existing businesses looking for the most efficient way to move their SAP ERP environments into SAP S/4HANA Cloud.

When determining the optimal path to SAP S/4HANA Cloud for your company, SAP recommends matching your business objectives with the available transition path and destination you're aiming for. Figure 1.6 shows the business objective categories, available transition paths, and destination options.

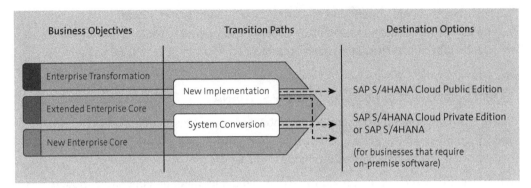

Figure 1.6 Considering Your Deployment Approach Options

Let's now discuss the business objective categories in more detail:

- **Enterprise transformation**
  This category fits companies that are in the middle of a comprehensive business transformation or companies that are implementing new business models in line with their digital transformation goals. Companies in this category typically plan their transition to SAP S/4HANA Cloud Public Edition or SAP S/4HANA Cloud Private Edition via a multistage roadmap aligned with their business transformation goals, and a significant portion of the roadmap activity will be new implementations of new business processes to support their transformation goals. Sponsorship of such transformation typically comes directly from the chief executive officer (CEO). Companies in this category are focused on implementing new business processes that encourage new revenue models or organizations that are implementing intelligent technologies (e.g., internet of things [IoT] or RPA scenarios) or shared services models in their organization.

- **Extended enterprise core**
  Businesses that are looking not only to convert to the new technology but also to immediately benefit from extending their current ERP core solution fit into this category. The focus is on optimization and redesign of selected business processes based on best value or return on investment (ROI). This category also includes companies that are looking for simplification of their IT environment to optimize the cost of operations and enable faster innovation. Companies in this category have a choice of converting their existing environment to SAP S/4HANA Cloud Private Edition or SAP S/4HANA, or implementing the solution from scratch. Selecting the appropriate approach is largely driven by the scope of "outdated" business processes that will need to be redesigned, the age of the existing solution, and its relative ability to support not only current processes but also future business models currently being implemented or anticipated for the future. Typical sponsorship for this category comes from the impacted line of business (LoB) or from the LoB lead co-sponsorship with the chief information officer (CIO).

- **New enterprise core**
  This category fits businesses that are looking to build a foundation for innovation by introducing SAP S/4HANA Cloud Private Edition or SAP S/4HANA as their digital core while minimizing the impact on existing business operations. The focus in this case is on converting the existing landscape and then evolving it along with the business. Typically, companies in this category operate SAP ERP and look for system conversion to SAP S/4HANA Cloud Private Edition or SAP S/4HANA while considering the implementation of innovations such as the Universal Journal, embedded analytics, or the new SAP Fiori UX for selected functions in the organization where this change allows for introducing innovation with minimal disruption. Initiatives in this category typically are sponsored by the CIO.

Now that we've defined the business context for the various transition paths, let's briefly define the characteristics of these paths to set the stage for detailed discussion in each of the chapters dedicated to deployment to the cloud, on-premise, and hybrid environments. Table 1.2 offers an overview of the transition paths.

Type	Reusing via In-Place Conversion	Reengineering with Data Migration	
		Standardized	Customer-Tailored Based on Predefined Content and Scenario
Transition path	System conversion	New implementation	Selective data transition (customer-tailored service based on predefined content and scenario)
Available for	SAP ERP system to SAP S/4HANA Cloud Private Edition or businesses that need to run on-premise SAP S/4HANA	SAP ERP or third-party system(s) to SAP S/4HANA Cloud Public or Private Edition, or businesses that need to run on-premise SAP S/4HANA	SAP ERP or third-party system(s) to SAP S/4HANA Cloud Private Edition, or businesses that need to run on-premise SAP S/4HANA
Purpose	Bringing your business processes to the new platform: ■ A complete technical in-place conversion of an existing ERP software system in SAP Business Suite to SAP S/4HANA Cloud ■ Adoption of new innovations at your speed	New implementation/re-implementation: ■ Reengineering and process simplification based on latest innovations ■ Implementing innovative business processes with preconfigured content on a new platform ■ Performing initial data load	Enabling the right balance between process redesign and reuse with possibility of (selective) history migration

Table 1.2 Overview of Transition Paths to SAP S/4HANA Cloud

Let's take a closer look at each path:

- **New implementation**
  This transition path allows companies to completely reinvent their ERP environment by implementing SAP S/4HANA Cloud Public Edition or SAP S/4HANA Cloud Private Edition as the new solution (or SAP S/4HANA if the business needs to run on-premise) and at the same time migrating data from their existing SAP or legacy environment into this new solution. As we discussed earlier, this strategy is typically used by companies that have determined their existing ERP environment is no longer serving their current and/or future business needs and need to implement a new foundation for innovation that will do the job better.

- **System conversion**
  This transition path is favored by current businesses on SAP ERP 6.0 or newer release that want to minimize the disruption to their existing business operations while updating their existing landscape for future innovations. Companies using this approach have kept their IT environment close to the latest release of SAP software, added custom code selectively, and planned to gradually introduce innovation brought by SAP S/4HANA Cloud Private Edition (or SAP S/4HANA if they require an on-premise software) to their business along a longer innovation path. Although they don't have a need for significant business process innovation at this time, they will benefit from new capabilities, such as the Universal Journal, embedded analytics, SAP Business AI, or SAP Fiori UX.

- **Selective data transition**
  This approach is used by companies that prefer a system conversion but also require sizable work in the standardization of their environment by using the new SAP S/4HANA Cloud Private Edition capabilities (or SAP S/4HANA if they need an on-premise solution). For example, companies might want to innovate their financial processes while reusing their existing logistics functionality and porting it to the new platform. There are other scenarios where this approach is also applicable, such as when a company wants to migrate only a subset of data (e.g., organizational units or specific time slices) into its SAP S/4HANA Cloud Private Edition environment. This approach is delivered as a tailored service based on the specific needs of the company. We'll briefly discuss this approach in Chapter 8, Section 8.4.

1.5   Summary

This chapter introduced the key concepts of SAP S/4HANA Cloud, including an overview of the technologies that companies will have access to in the solution such as SAP Business AI, SAP BTP, SAP HANA, and SAP Fiori. We also discussed, at least on a high level, the functional capabilities of the SAP S/4HANA Cloud system. We spent a bit of time covering the business content for selecting the appropriate deployment model and transition path to help you understand the approach before we get into the discussion of the specific versions of SAP Activate that are appropriate for each transition path. Later, we'll review each of the SAP Activate versions (for new implementation in Chapter 7 and for system conversion and selective data transition in Chapter 8) and discuss how each transition path is supported by the SAP Activate methodology, content, and tools.

In the next chapter, we'll introduce the principles and concepts of SAP Activate for SAP S/4HANA Cloud. We'll introduce the SAP Activate phases, hierarchy, and key preconfiguration assets, such as SAP Best Practices and the enterprise management layer for SAP S/4HANA. We'll briefly discuss the importance of the cloud mindset and clean core strategy for the successful deployment of SAP S/4HANA Cloud. We'll also introduce the SAP Activate community, designed to provide users with a one-stop shop for information and news about SAP Activate.

Chapter 2
Introduction to SAP Activate

This chapter provides a fundamental understanding of the concepts and principles SAP has built into SAP Activate. This is an important chapter to read before you proceed to the later chapters in the book that detail the specific deployment strategies in SAP S/4HANA Cloud projects and SAP S/4HANA projects.

This chapter introduces SAP Activate as the innovation adoption framework that enables your business to deploy new capabilities fast and continue innovating. We'll start by discussing the nature of the SAP S/4HANA Cloud deployment project, where the project team needs to shift their focus to consistently apply the cloud mindset to maximize the value that the new solution creates for the organization. We'll then deep dive into the principles that SAP Activate follows and discuss each in more detail. After that, we'll introduce the SAP Activate phases, outline what happens in each phase, and describe how deliverables created in one phase relate to each other and together support project success. Before closing the chapter, we'll invite you to the SAP Activate community on SAP Community and discuss the available training, enablement, and certification offerings.

2.1   SAP Activate Key Concepts

Organizations that are starting or are in the middle of their SAP S/4HANA transition have questions that SAP Activate aims to answer throughout the entire transition process. SAP Activate's focus is on addressing questions during the actual project, but it also offers guidance for the discovery activities in the discover phase and details how to run and operate the solution after the initial go-live in the run phase. Figure 2.1 shows a few sample questions the project team may have during their transition journey.

SAP introduced SAP Activate at SAPPHIRE in 2015, just as the SAP S/4HANA product was launched, and structured it around a major shift in the mindset that's applied to deployment, as shown in Figure 2.2.

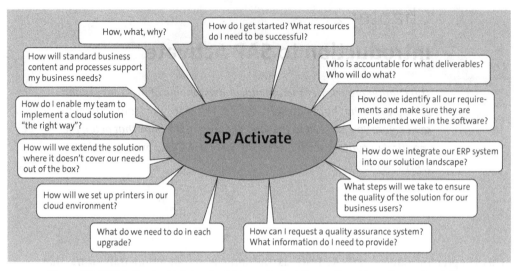

Figure 2.1 SAP Activate: Helping to Address Project Team Questions throughout the Transition to SAP S/4HANA

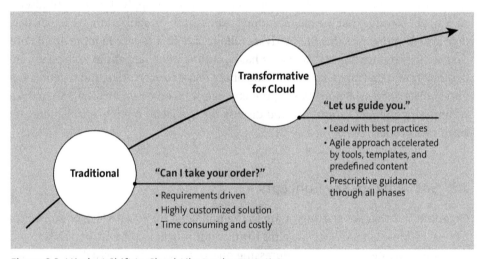

Figure 2.2 Mindset Shift to Cloud-Like Implementation

The shift is represented by the move from the traditional requirements-based approach—heavy on design work in an empty system, resulting in highly customized solutions that take a long time to implement—to an approach that leverages predelivered, ready-to-run, best practice business processes; aims to reuse much of the predelivered functionality and standard functions of the solution; and uses an agile approach to implement the identified delta requirements, extensions, and integrations to meet an organization's needs. SAP Activate also adds prescriptive guidance that expands the traditional methodology with product-specific procedures and accelerators to help not only project managers and project workstream leads but also business key users, IT personnel, and application and technology consultants.

SAP Activate builds on SAP's previous methodologies: ASAP for on-premise projects and SAP Launch for cloud projects. It's designed around the following key principles:

- **Start with ready-to-run business processes**
  The methodology is structured around using a working system that is built on ready-to-run business processes delivered by SAP or an SAP partner. In Chapter 4, we'll discuss two key assets that SAP delivers: SAP Best Practices (available to all customers) and the enterprise management layer for SAP S/4HANA. Both packages offer a starting point for implementing SAP S/4HANA Cloud and SAP S/4HANA, enabling organizations to get started fast with a working system.

- **Confirm solution fit**
  This is done using a working system built on the ready-to-run business processes we discussed in the previous point. Project teams use a fit-to-standard approach to both confirm the fit of the standard predelivered business processes and identify the delta requirements needed to make the solution work for the organization. These delta requirements typically fall into categories of configuration, extensibility, analytics, integration, data, security and access, and so on. The delta requirements are stored in the backlog that the project team uses to capture the work required to deliver the solution to the organization.

Fit-to-Standard or Fit-Gap?

In earlier versions of SAP Activate, on-premise deployments used the fit-gap approach, which was considered better suited to the implementation of on-premise solutions. But in the last few years, as more organizations have embraced the principles of keeping the core clean, project teams have shifted to using the fit-to-standard approach because it's more suitable for keeping close to the standard. There are a few main differences between the fit-to-standard and fit-gap approaches:

- **Fit-to-standard**
  This approach is used in implementations that are applying a cloud mindset—that is, staying close to the standard and keeping the core clean—or where a product has defined boundaries, such as SAP S/4HANA Cloud and SAP SuccessFactors. The approach emphasizes maximizing the use of standard functionality over unnecessary tailoring or extending the solution. This approach still allows for the use of extensibility (key user, developer, and side-by-side) where needed to address critical business requirements that the solution needs to provide to realize the desired business benefit and value the organization requires. At the same time, this approach keeps the core application clean to enable organizations to innovate faster by adopting the innovation SAP releases regularly.

- **Fit-gap**
  This approach was traditionally used in on-premise implementations where the project team has a wider ability or desire to extend the solution with custom code or via the extensibility framework. The focus in this approach is again on the adoption of standard functionality first, but the desire is to allow the project team to use broader options for extending the functionality, including custom code, significant

configuration, and so on. This approach has been used in SAP S/4HANA (on-premise) projects where the project team has decided to use the full development environment inside the application to modify SAP code or develop significant extensions inside the application. This approach isn't recommended as it leads to significant development of custom code, often using technology that makes upgrades more difficult and costly.

In both approaches, the project team must strive to avoid modifying SAP-delivered code; when this is unavoidable, the team must ensure that the changes are properly documented. We'll discuss this in more detail in Section 2.5.

- **Modular, scalable, and agile**

  This principle encompasses three aspects: First, the modularity of the approach allows companies and implementation partners to swap out specific SAP Activate modules as needed. For example, solution adoption activities that include organizational change management (OCM) deliverables and tasks can be swapped with company or partner activities for OCM. Second, scalability is demonstrated by the ability to use the same approach to implement SAP S/4HANA Cloud for growing organizations in a rapid cycle of just a few weeks and to deploy SAP S/4HANA Cloud Private Edition in large multinational companies across a broad number of countries and geographies. SAP Activate can be scaled up or down depending on the needs of the project (influencing factors are project scope, geographical or organizational footprint, number of integrated systems, etc.). Third, the agile approach is used to structure a project into multiple releases built via increments and sprints that allow the team to focus on building the higher-value and higher-priority features first. This approach is embedded in SAP Activate and can be tailored to a company's situation by choosing the desired duration of sprints and structuring the releases according to the company's plans to introduce the solution to the organization. We'll discuss the agile approach in more detail in Chapter 6.

What Is Agile?

The term *agile* is used to describe a unique approach to working in organizations and businesses. It focuses on a change in mindset that individuals and organizations need to apply in the way they approach their work. The key principles are captured in the *Agile Manifesto*, introduced in 2001 as a means to change the approach to software development. You can find the complete text of the Agile Manifesto at *https://agile-manifesto.org*.

The key principles stated in the Agile Manifesto are as follows:

- Individuals and interactions over processes and tools
- Working software over comprehensive documentation
- Customer collaboration over contract negotiation
- Responding to change over following a plan

As the manifesto states, agile practitioners value the items on the left side of the points we've listed more than the items on the right side (e.g., customer collaboration is valued more highly than contract negotiation). This statement doesn't mean that items on the right side are unimportant; instead, it means that agile practitioners prioritize the items on the left. In essence, that approach reflects the change in mindset of increased collaboration, communication, and adaptability.

The agile principles are coded in multiple methods for software development. The most popular among agile practitioners is Scrum, which is also used as the foundation for the agile approach in SAP Activate.

- **Cloud-ready**
  This principle is not only applicable for companies implementing their solution in the cloud but also can be used by project teams implementing SAP S/4HANA in on-premise deployments. In such situations, the cloud technology can be used to access the trial environment or to provide the project team with a working sandbox environment based on the SAP Cloud Appliance Library, which offers a broad selection of predefined systems that companies can use in the early stages of their project. Organizations deploying their solution in the cloud will benefit from the cloud mindset embedded into the methodology and the detailed information about how to request provisioning of the cloud solution and how to access, activate, and use it during implementation. Additionally, a cloud mindset is demonstrated in the way the application is designed, extended, and integrated into customer landscapes.

- **SAP Services and Support, premium engagements-ready**
  We discussed earlier that SAP Activate has been built as a modular methodology that enables companies, partners, and SAP to bring in specific modules. SAP has incorporated links to support and implementation services through SAP Activate where appropriate. This is the most visible for the premium engagement services, such as SAP MaxAttention or SAP ActiveAttention, that are layered onto SAP Activate to provide companies and partners information about how to best leverage SAP Services and Support offerings in their implementation projects. The use of these services is recommended, but customers who don't opt to use them will still benefit from using SAP Activate as it provides instructions for completing the tasks and deliverables regardless of whether SAP Services and Support offerings are used or not.

  As a specific example, inside the **SAP Activate Methodology for Transition to SAP S/4HANA** implementation roadmap in the SAP Activate Roadmap Viewer (see Chapter 3, Section 3.1), you'll find **How SAP Can Support** sections that detail which services from SAP are applicable in the context of a specific deliverable or task. The description text provides more details about the service scope, how to order, and the outcomes the service delivers. See Figure 2.3 for how this text is incorporated into the task description in the methodology.

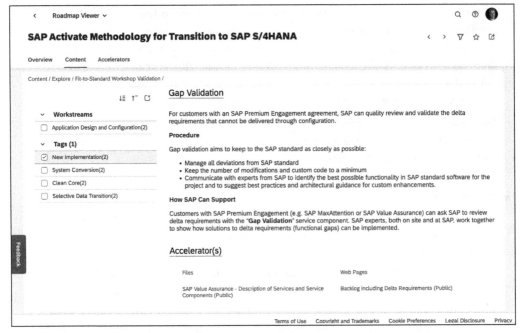

Figure 2.3 SAP Activate for Transition to SAP S/4HANA: How SAP Can Support

Premium Engagement Services from SAP

SAP Services and Support offers a portfolio of services under the umbrella of premium engagement services that are designed to safeguard company implementations, optimize operations, maximize the value of existing investments, and build new capabilities for your organization to become an intelligent enterprise.

The services are structured into a few categories, but these are the primary offerings:

- **SAP MaxAttention**
  This provides a holistic engagement between the company and SAP that aims to cover the company's business and IT needs. The engagement is managed jointly by the company and SAP to plan and execute a portfolio of initiatives, from innovation to optimization of existing solutions and operations, to drive predictable outcomes for the company in a coordinated manner. You can find more details about this service offering at *http://s-prs.co/v596612*.

- **SAP ActiveAttention**
  This service offering focuses on enabling companies to successfully deploy programs and run operations. It's designed to plan and safeguard the portfolio of a company's landscapes, implementation and innovation projects, and operations. SAP offers different levels of services and a portfolio of predefined services that a company can consume to achieve the desired business outcomes. You can find more about these services at *http://s-prs.co/v596613*.

■ **Quality built-in**

Planning and managing quality during the implementation project is one of the critical factors for delivering a successful implementation. SAP Activate provides structured guidance for planning quality in the prepare phase, starting with developing quality management plans for the implementation project, then monitoring and controlling activities throughout the entire project, and finally performing predefined quality gates in each SAP Activate phase. Quality is also targeted in the detailed guidance for planning, execution, and resolution of various testing activities during the course of the project, including unit testing performed early in the realize phase, string testing that ties together multiple unit tests to ensure the data flow through the business process and system, and the ultimate end-to-end integration testing and user acceptance testing (UAT) in later stages of the realize phase. We'll discuss the details of testing in Chapter 5, Section 5.6.

2.2   Components of SAP Activate

The SAP Activate *innovation as a service* is a unique combination of the SAP Best Practices preconfigured business processes, guided and clear methodology, and tools for adoption and extensibility that helps companies and partners implement SAP S/4HANA solutions. Designed for IT and business professionals involved in the implementation, configuration, integration, or extension of SAP S/4HANA solutions, SAP Activate covers new implementations, system conversions, and selective data transition projects.

Figure 2.4 shows the key components of SAP Activate on the left side, which we'll cover in more detail as we progress in this book.

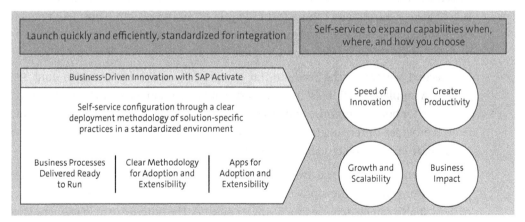

Figure 2.4 SAP Activate: Business Process Preconfiguration, Guided Methodology, and Applications for Adoption and Extensibility

The right side provides a summary of the benefits SAP Activate delivers, including increased speed of innovation, greater productivity for both the project team and the business, and a scalable environment that supports projects from small to large multinational rollouts (growth and scalability), ultimately driving positive business impact for organizations using SAP Activate to implement SAP solutions.

In this section, we'll walk through the key components of SAP Activate: ready-to-run business processes, clear and guided methodology, and applications and tools for adoption and extensibility.

2.2.1   Ready-to-Run Business Processes

Earlier in this chapter, we introduced the foundational principles of SAP Activate, one of which is to *start with ready-to-run business processes*. This principle helps project teams set up the initial system that is then used in the explore phase for fit-to-standard analysis workshops. The current SAP Best Practices packages fall into two categories that are distinguished by branding and the coverage offered. The first is the SAP Best Practices packages that companies and partners can access and download from SAP Signavio Process Navigator (available at *https://me.sap.com/processnavigator/HomePage*).

The SAP Best Practices solution scenarios are structured into logical groups of scope items. Scope items have a wide range of granularity and each represents a business process or end-to-end scenario that is configured inside the SAP Best Practice solution scenario. For example, scope item J78 is Advanced Cash Operations in SAP S/4HANA Cloud Public Edition. The scope item delivers ready-to-run business processes that can be activated with SAP Best Practices in a company's system. These packages include all the necessary configuration, organizational setting (sample), master data (sample), business roles, and—for some scope items—transactional data so that after the scope item is activated, the company can perform the process in the system. Thus, SAP refers to these packages as *ready-to-run business processes* or sometimes as *preconfigured packages*. Figure 2.5 shows the **Solution Scenarios** within SAP Signavio Process Navigator.

The second variant of the ready-to-run business processes for use with your SAP S/4HANA implementation is the enterprise management layer for SAP S/4HANA (available for both on-premise and private cloud deployments). Just like SAP Best Practices, it provides a preconfigured package that can be deployed into a company's environment to start fit-to-standard workshops.

The difference between the two is that the enterprise management layer for SAP S/4HANA provides business processes for multicountry deployment (optionally, upon request, it also can be deployed for a single country). The enterprise management layer covers all major end-to-end business processes by default in both deployment options. Additional scope options can be selected based on each customer's functional requirements. The multicountry deployment option comes preconfigured and localized for up to 49 countries, with a corporate financial template allowing for parallel accounting according to group and local requirements, based on three accounting principles (group/local/tax) and a total of five ledgers. The single-country version comes with one single country and this country's Generally Accepted Accounting Principles (GAAP) as the leading accounting principle (and ledger). A second accounting principle (and ledger) allows for International Financial Reporting Standards (IFRS) reporting. In both versions, the group currency and the fiscal year variant can be adapted to customer requirements.

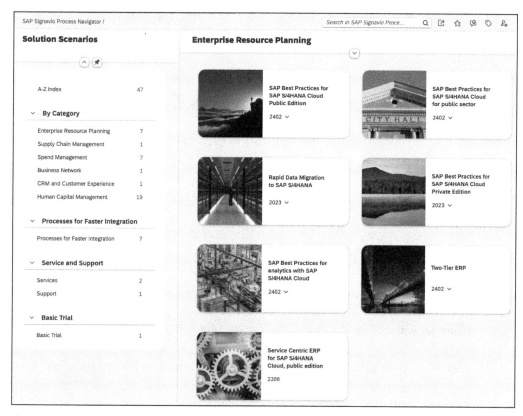

Figure 2.5 SAP Signavio Process Navigator, Providing Access to Ready-to-Run Preconfigured Business Content from SAP

The second difference is the commercial model under which SAP offers these packages. SAP Best Practices are available to all companies and partners with no additional fee. Alternatively, the enterprise management layer for SAP S/4HANA is offered as a service offering for a fee (unless otherwise stated in a company's subscription agreement). You can learn more about the enterprise management layer for SAP S/4HANA via SAP Signavio Process Navigator at *http://s-prs.co/v596602*. The **Enterprise Management Layer for SAP S/4HANA (Version 2023)** overview page from SAP Signavio Process Navigator is shown in Figure 2.6.

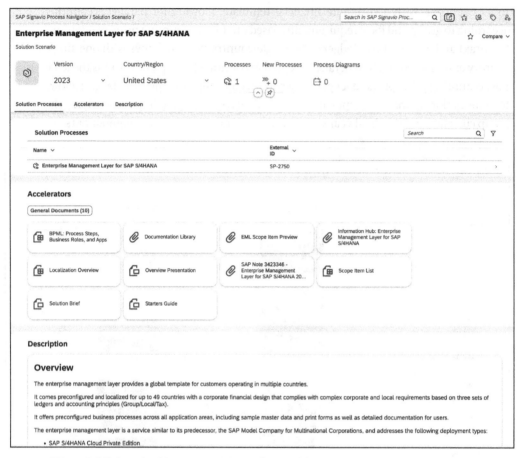

Figure 2.6 Enterprise Management Layer for SAP S/4HANA Overview Page

We'll deep dive into the preconfigured packages and ready-to-run processes in Chapter 4, where we'll discuss their taxonomy, provisioning, and activation processes, as well as show you examples of content that is available in each.

2.2.2   Methodology

As an implementation or migration methodology for SAP S/4HANA Cloud and other SAP solutions, the SAP Activate methodology is a modular and agile framework that builds on its predecessors: the ASAP methodology (for on-premise solutions implementations) and the SAP Launch methodology (for cloud solutions deployments). You can use the SAP Activate methodology on your own, with SAP system integrators, or with SAP Services teams.

With SAP Activate, you'll follow a disciplined project management approach for your SAP S/4HANA Cloud implementation project. The methodology aligns with the industry's best practices for project management documented by the Project Management Institute in *A Guide to the Project Management Body of Knowledge: PMBOK GUIDE*, helping you minimize risk, streamline and accelerate your implementation project, and reduce the total cost of implementation. A standardized work breakdown structure (WBS) helps project managers define and manage project tasks and focus on the deliverables and outcomes that are important for project success.

The traditional project management concepts in SAP Activate are matched with the project team's agile practices based on the Scrum agile framework, which prescribes roles, processes, and ceremonies the team executes during the project. For example, the users of SAP Activate will find a clear explanation of how to create the initial backlog and use it for planning and executing sprints. SAP Activate doesn't stop there: the methodology provides accelerators that explain how to apply agile techniques in the context of an SAP S/4HANA Cloud implementation project. We'll discuss the agile aspects of the methodology in more detail in Chapter 6.

In addition to structured project management techniques and an agile approach, the SAP Activate methodology provides detailed SAP product- and solution-specific guidance aimed for a broad range of project team roles in the SAP project, from application consultants to business users to architects and trainers. SAP Activate significantly expanded the range of users who can benefit by providing prescriptive tasks that detail the procedure for completing work in the project. For example, one task in SAP Activate for SAP S/4HANA Cloud Public Edition details how companies receive the starter environment and how to set up the configuration environment and bring project team users into the system. Consultants will find detailed guides and accelerators explaining how to prepare for, perform, and capture the findings from fit-to-standard workshops. And the team responsible for the implementation of OCM will find documents and guidance in the solution adoption workstream. The solution adoption workstream has been significantly updated, and SAP also offers a standalone OCM roadmap.

All SAP customers and partners can access the SAP Activate methodology in the SAP Activate Roadmap Viewer tool (accessible at *http://s-prs.co/v502705*). We'll explain how to use the tool in Chapter 3, Section 3.1. Companies implementing SAP S/4HANA Cloud (both public and private editions) will get access to the SAP Activate methodology tasks directly in the SAP Cloud ALM application when they use the environment for their implementation project (see Figure 2.7 for an example of a methodology task screen). We'll explain key features of SAP Cloud ALM in Chapter 3, Section 3.3.

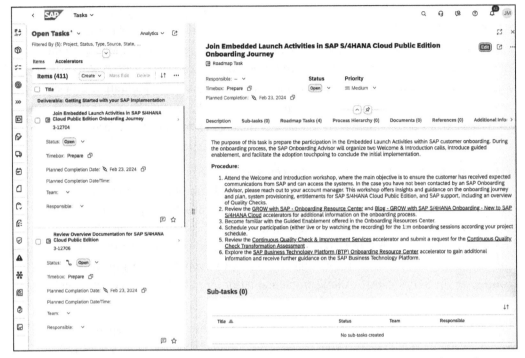

Figure 2.7 SAP Cloud ALM, Showing Implementation Tasks for Deployment of SAP S/4HANA Cloud Public Edition

2.2.3   Tools for Adoption and Extensibility

SAP Activate users will use various tools during the project to implement or convert the solution. SAP Activate recommends the use of specific tools for specific purposes, such as configuration, extensibility, integration, testing, data loads, solution documentation, and so on. We'll introduce some of the tools in this chapter, but the main discussion of the specific tooling required for implementing the different versions of SAP S/4HANA Cloud will be provided in each implementation's chapter because different tools are used when implementing SAP S/4HANA Cloud Public Edition compared to implementing SAP S/4HANA Cloud Private Edition or on-premise.

Now let's outline the key capabilities that the project team needs during the delivery of the project. While the title of this section mentions adoption and extensibility, the scope of these tools is broader and covers at least the following capabilities:

- Configuration
- Documenting the requirements, and solution design, including business process models
- System change management and transport management
- Preparation of data for system loads and productive data migration
- Testing of the solution both during the sprints as well as integration and UAT

- Delivery of end-user training and enablement
- Managing the project work
- Extending the solution
- Integrating the solution with other systems
- Identity and access management (IAM) and security

The topic of tools is so broad that it could fill another book this size, especially if we were to go into the details of how to use each tool. Instead, we'll focus on the key capabilities that project teams need and talk about the tools that provide those capabilities.

Many of these capabilities can be provided by one tool, while other capabilities require different, dedicated tools. Here, we'll use the implementation of an SAP S/4HANA Cloud Public Edition deployment as an example. The key tool for project teams in this situation is SAP Cloud ALM, which provides coverage for capabilities such as solution documentation, business process modeling, transport management, testing, and managing project work, as well as additional capabilities that are necessary for not only implementing but also running the implemented solution productively.

In addition to SAP Cloud ALM, the project team will use specialized tools such as SAP Central Business Configuration to configure the application settings to tailor the solution to a company's requirements. The project team will use in-app extensibility and open application programming interfaces (APIs) along with SAP Business Technology Platform (SAP BTP) to extend the delivered solution capabilities. For migrating data into SAP S/4HANA Cloud Public Edition, the project team will use the SAP S/4HANA migration cockpit. The cockpit provides predefined data load templates the customer team will use for data load, avoiding the need to build the data load templates and routines from scratch. And, finally, for delivery of enablement and training, the project team will use SAP Enable Now to create end-user training and simulations. This is just one example of the tooling that the public cloud project teams can use to get all the work done.

We'll highlight the tools that deliver the SAP Activate content to users in Chapter 5 and discuss the use of tools for specific use cases in the detailed chapters in the later part of this book, starting with Chapter 7.

2.3 SAP Activate Phases and Project Management

The SAP Activate methodology provides guidance over the six phases that support your team throughout the project lifecycle of an SAP S/4HANA Cloud solution. Underlying these phases is a series of deliverables, tasks, and quality checks to ensure that the solution, as implemented, delivers the expected value and can be continuously evolved to match the changing business needs. Figure 2.8 illustrates the phases of the SAP Activate methodology for SAP S/4HANA solutions, which we'll discuss in this chapter.

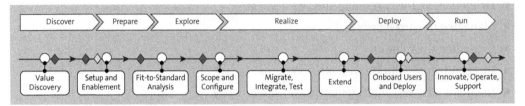

Figure 2.8 SAP Activate Phases and Key Activities in Project Lifecycle

> **SAP Activate Methodology Deliverables**
>
> During each project phase, your project team will produce a prescribed set of deliverables to serve as inputs to subsequent phases. The SAP Activate methodology provides a detailed list of project deliverables, including procedural descriptions explaining how to prepare and complete the deliverable. The methodology also provides accelerators for each phase and workstream, which may include files and assets such as templates, questionnaires, checklists, how-to documents, and guidebooks. Remember, the objective is to facilitate the efficient, consistent, and repeatable delivery of an SAP S/4HANA implementation.

Let's now review the work, deliverables, and activities that the project team performs during each phase of SAP Activate methodology. In this section, we'll provide an example list of deliverables that are created in each phase, talk about the work that is done in each phase, and examine how the work from one phase flows into the next one to progressively build the solution.

2.3.1   Discover

The purpose of the discover phase is to find the solution's capabilities, to understand its business value and its benefits for your business, and to determine an adoption strategy and roadmap in alignment with the solution's capabilities and product roadmap. During this phase, users often access trial environments to get hands-on experience with the application and aid in the selection process.

Example deliverables in the discover phase are as follows:

- Strategic planning
- Application value and scoping
- Trial system access
- Discovery assessment and cloud mindset assessment
- Organizational change overview

2.3.2 Prepare

The prepare phase kicks off the initial planning and preparation for the project. At this time, the project is started, plans are finalized, project governance is established, project team resources are assigned, and work is underway to start the project. In addition, the initial technical and application environment is provisioned or set up during this stage of the project (this is different from previous methodologies that instructed users to set up the initial environment much later in the project as they didn't use the working system during the solution fit confirmation and requirements definition stage).

Example deliverables in the prepare phase are as follows:

- Customer onboarding activities
- Project team (self-)enablement
- Project initiation and governance setup
- Plan project, schedule, and budget
- Project kickoff
- Project standards and infrastructure
- Initial environment provisioning/setup and activation of best practices
- OCM roadmap
- Access to implementation-supporting tools
- Fit-to-standard preparation, including system preparation (functionality/data/authorizations)
- Data migration strategy
- Testing strategy and approach
- End-user learning strategy
- Phase closure and sign-off, including quality gates

2.3.3 Explore

The purpose of the explore phase is to perform a fit-to-standard analysis to confirm the fit of the solution's standard functionality to your company's needs and to determine configuration values, necessary extensions, and analytics requirements. The explore phase also involves identifying required integrations, establishing data requirements, and designing identity and access management. Identified delta requirements and configuration values are added to the backlog to be addressed during the realize phase. During the explore phase, the project team also prepares for the execution of data migration activities, makes plans for testing (including selecting the appropriate testing tools to ensure the quality of the delivered solution), and begins putting together a learning team as part of the adoption workstream that manages the OCM and end-user enablement activities.

Example deliverables in this phase are as follows:

- Performing and monitoring the project activities
- Fit-to-standard analysis
- Company execution of standard processes
- Solution definition
- Integration planning and design
- Extensions planning and design
- Analytics planning and design
- Identity and access management planning and design
- Data load preparation
- Test planning
- Mobilization of the learning team
- Phase closure and sign-off, including quality gates

2.3.4   Realize

During the realize phase, you'll use a series of agile iterations to incrementally build, test, and validate an integrated business and system environment based on the business scenarios and process requirements identified during the fit-to-standard analysis workshops in the explore phase. This phase includes loading company data, performing adoption activities, and planning operations in the new environment. It also includes comprehensive testing of the integrated solution before it's released to the next phase for deployment to productive use by the business.

Example deliverables in this phase are as follows:

- Performing and monitoring the project activities
- OCM alignment activities
- Initial access and setup of the development environment
- Initial access and setup of the test environment
- Configuration and solution documentation
- Setup of integrations
- Development and setup of solution extensibility
- Setup of output management and printing
- Data migration activities (iterative)
- Execution of unit and string testing in sprints
- Solution walkthrough in each sprint
- Technical operations and handover plan
- Planning of Center of Expertise (COE) for operational support

■ Development of key user enablement materials

■ Development of end-user training and documentation

■ Preparation and execution of integration testing

■ Preparation and execution of UAT

■ Cutover planning

■ Phase closure and sign-off, including quality gates

■ Optional activation of additional scope items (optional and relevant especially for planning for cloud solution deployment)

■ System upgrade (optional and relevant, especially for planning cloud solution deployment)

Upgrade during the Implementation Project

The upgrade of your current release could occur during the implementation project, especially when deploying SAP S/4HANA Cloud Public Edition (or other public cloud solutions), where you'll receive regular upgrades per a published schedule. These upgrades can't be delayed or skipped. Project teams need to plan sufficient time and capacity to perform pre-upgrade preparation activities, regression testing, and other post-upgrade actions.

An SAP S/4HANA Cloud Public Edition upgrade takes place in a three-week window where first the test environment is upgraded, and then the development environment and production environment are upgraded simultaneously three weeks later. This time allows for a customer project team to perform regression testing.

During the time between the test environment upgrade and the end of the upgrade window, some activities in the system may be restricted, especially during the physical system upgrade activities—for example, downtime of the data loads or configuration activities during specific stages of the upgrade process. Thus, project teams need to exercise extreme caution when planning critical project activities during the upgrade window. It's strongly recommended not to plan cutover activities during the upgrade window.

2.3.5   Deploy

The purpose of the deploy phase is to set up the production environment, to confirm organizational readiness, and to switch business operations to run in the new environment.

Example deliverables in this phase are as follows:

■ Execution and monitoring of the project

■ Execution of OCM activities

■ End-user learning delivery

■ Dress rehearsal

- Production cutover
- Operation readiness
- Hypercare support
- Stabilization of the production environment after cutover
- Handover to support organization

2.3.6   Run

The run phase is the open-ended phase after going live. Its purpose is to ensure that the solution is running at peak performance and to take advantage of the regular innovations that SAP releases for the SAP S/4HANA Cloud environment. This phase also focuses on the continuous adoption of the solution by new users per your organization's needs.

Example deliverables in this phase are as follows:

- Ongoing system operations
- Continuous OCM activities
- Continuous learning
- Continuous business process and system improvements
- New scope activation
- New country/countries activation
- Setup and onboarding of new users
- System upgrade
- Ongoing execution of quality gates for clean core (especially for customers operating the SAP S/4HANA Cloud Private Edition)

2.3.7   Project Management

The project management deliverables and tasks are comprehensively covered in the SAP Activate methodology. The process follows the standard defined in the Project Management Institute's *PMBOK Guide*, mentioned earlier. The general flow of the project management activities starts in the prepare phase of the methodology with activities for the initiation and planning of the project. Figure 2.9 shows an example of the project management workstream deliverables from SAP Activate for the **SAP Activate Methodology for RISE with SAP S/4HANA Cloud Private Edition** implementation roadmap.

During the prepare phase, the project team completes the following artifacts and events:

- Project charter
- Project WBS
- Project budget

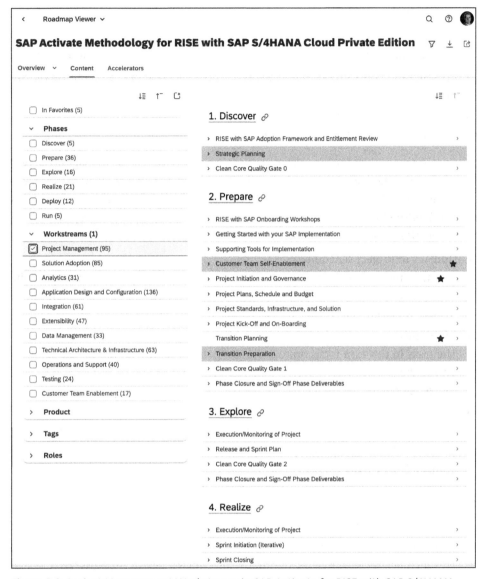

Figure 2.9 Project Management Workstream in SAP Activate for RISE with SAP S/4HANA Cloud Private Edition

- Project management plans to manage the schedule, resources, risk, quality, contracts, and other aspects of project delivery
- Project schedule that will be progressively detailed during the course of the project
- Definition of project team roles and responsibilities
- Establishment of governance for the project, including setting up a Solution Standardization Board (SSB) to control the design of the solution according to standards and best practices established by SAP (discussed in Section 2.4)

- Identification of stakeholders and creation of the stakeholder management plan
- Kickoff of the project in a formal session
- Onboarding of project team members through self-enablement or training sessions
- Provisioning of the environment for application lifecycle management (ALM), SAP Cloud ALM
- Project team infrastructure and workspace, including physical facilities, collaboration space, and the document management environment for project documents

The project team also starts to execute the project activities, such as managing the project, right from the prepare phase. This is indicated in the SAP Activate methodology by the execute and monitor deliverables and tasks that occur in every phase (refer to Figure 2.9). The following is a summary of activities that happen in each phase during the execution, monitoring, and controlling of the project:

- **Updates to project schedule**
  This may include updates to the project timeline, including detailing and refining the high-level timeline for upcoming phases. There is progressive planning of detailed steps in each phase.

- **Directing and managing project execution activities**
  The tasks in this area focus on executing the project activities per the plan defined during the project. This helps the project manager oversee the progress and direct the team to deliver planned results.

- **Monitoring and controlling the project activities**
  This also includes a regular review of progress, assessment of risks and issues, and management of project quality.

- **Manage issues, risks, and changes**
  This area is very important for the project manager to keep under control per defined management plans that the team created in the beginning of the project based on predelivered templates from SAP Activate.

- **Communicate status and progress to project stakeholders**
  This includes regular updates to project stakeholders about progress, risks, issues, and deliverables.

Each phase is also formally closed per the guidance in phase closure and sign-off phase deliverables. The steps in this stage cover the activities of formally closing the phase by conducting a formal quality gate review to assess the completeness of deliverables from the current phase and readiness to start the next phase of the project. In the case of SAP S/4HANA Cloud Private Edition (and some on-premise implementations), it's recommended to perform regular quality checks to confirm adherence to the governance standards for the design of the solution that we'll discuss in the next section about clean core. SAP provides a template for conducting the quality gates in the form of quality gate templates and guides. SAP Activate prescribes one quality gate in each phase to close the phase. Other activities during the phase closure may include collecting lessons learned in a formal knowledge gate, conducting project review activities (e.g., review of project management service), and managing fulfilled contracts.

2.4 Clean Core Strategy

Let's start with the definition of what the clean core strategy means. *Clean core* is a concept to describe a system that is as close to standard as possible. This is achieved by integrating and extending a system in a way that is cloud-compliant, with master data and business process governance and strong operational excellence in running the system.

Often a clean core is thought to be a system without customization. However, being truly "clean" includes adhering to standardized guidelines for all elements of the core, including extensions, integrations, data volumes, and so on. With that, when it comes time to upgrade a system, changes can be put in place without significant manual efforts to test and adapt existing structures, and businesses can adopt the business process innovations or new capabilities with increased agility.

Following the clean core strategy during the design of the business solutions empowers customers' IT to deliver necessary capability while also maintaining organizational agility. The clean core enables organizations to consume innovation delivered in subsequent software upgrades at a faster pace than customers who don't follow this strategy. Organizations adhering to the clean core with their solution design governance and mindset are generally faster to respond to changing business needs, including change in their business processes and business systems. SAP defines the clean core across the core five dimensions, including business processes, data, integration, extensibility, and operational excellence, as shown in Figure 2.10.

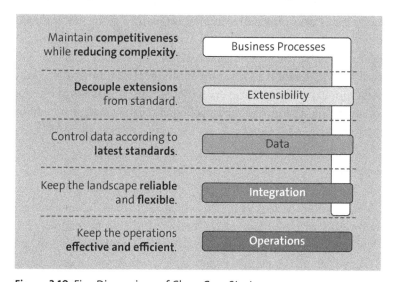

Figure 2.10 Five Dimensions of Clean Core Strategy

To help customers embrace the clean core strategy in their deployment of SAP S/4HANA Cloud, SAP has enhanced SAP Activate with several critical assets and services that help customers ensure they are staying close to the clean core. You can see the key items in Figure 2.11. We'll introduce these elements in this section and deep dive into some of these topics in later chapters.

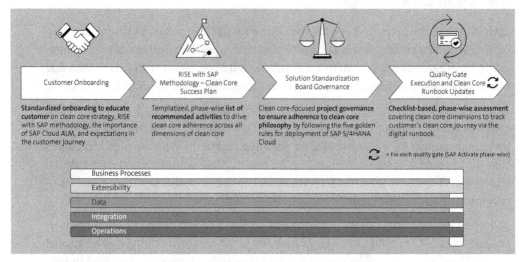

Figure 2.11 Key Elements in SAP Activate Methodology for RISE with SAP S/4HANA Cloud Private Edition Enabling Execution of the Clean Core Strategy

The following elements are part of the SAP Activate for RISE with SAP with SAP S/4HANA Cloud Private Edition roadmap:

- **Structured onboarding activities**
  These activities empower customers during the adoption of their RISE with SAP solution. These activities start immediately after the signature of the RISE with SAP subscription contract when the customer will be invited to attend a series of onboarding sessions to enable the project team regarding clean core principles, SAP Activate methodology, explanation of software entitlements, and more. Basically, this enablement is tailored to ensure that every SAP customer, regardless of whether SAP has direct involvement in the project or not, obtains key information about how to best deploy the solution and take advantage of the software services entitlements included in the RISE with SAP offering.

- **Clean core success plan**
  SAP Activate tasks are selected that directly impact customer's adherence to clean core principles. These tasks are accessible in SAP Activate Roadmap Viewer as a tag in the SAP Activate for RISE with SAP S/4HANA Cloud Private Edition roadmap. SAP also delivers a clean core success plan in SAP Cloud ALM as a predelivered SAP Activate roadmap that you can use to set up a *runbook project* that will be used for the purpose of tracking the adherence to clean core principles during the lifetime of

your system. The runbook will continuously evolve based on the feedback and recommendations SAP provides to customers after running clean core quality gates (explained later in this section) and delivery of the clean core report after each quality gate. The report is based not only on the customer responses to the quality gate checklist but also on telemetry from the system to specifically assess the real situation and adherence to clean core principles.

- **Solution Standardization Board (SSB)**
  This is for strong solution governance based on the clean core dimensions and the five golden rules for implementing SAP S/4HANA Cloud that we'll explain in detail in the next section. We'll first dive into the golden rules for implementing SAP S/4HANA and then expand on how to set up governance in your project to follow this guidance in a structured way with a strong governance body aligned with the overall project governance in your program.

- **Clean core quality gates and clean core report**
  In addition to traditional quality gates that are part of the SAP Activate methodology, SAP added dedicated clean core quality gates into the SAP Activate for RISE with SAP S/4HANA Cloud Private Edition to ensure that customers deploying RISE with SAP regularly review their adherence to the clean core strategy at the end of each phase. SAP will provide the customer with a clean core quality report based on their responses to the quality gate questionnaire at the end of prepare, explore, realize, deploy, and during the operational run in the run phase (recommended repeated every quarter). SAP doesn't produce a clean core report at the end of the discover phase as this clean core quality gate is intended to prepare the customer for running the full-fledged gate at the end of prepare.

You can see how all of these elements come together in Figure 2.12. The flow starts at the bottom right with the customer creating the runbook project based on the SAP Activate roadmap for a clean core success plan in SAP Cloud ALM (steps ❶ and ❷). After that, the project team runs the clean core quality gate 0 at the end of the discover phase (step ❸), and shortly after that, the project team establishes solution governance with the SSB in step ❹. During the execution of clean core quality gate 1 (at the end of the prepare phase, step ❺), the customer completes the quality gate questionnaire, uploads the results to SAP Cloud ALM, and submits them to SAP. SAP reviews the results and provides the customer with a clean core report outlining the positive findings as well as recommendations to implement for close adherence to the clean core strategy (step ❻). The customer then incorporates the key recommendations and follow-up actions as new tasks in their runbook (step ❼).

This process repeats in each phase where the clean core quality gate questionnaire reflects the respective tasks from the clean core success plan and the quality gate checks on adhering to the guidance. In the run phase, it's recommended to continue running quality gate 5, which is partially based on the clean core quality gate questionnaire responses and the actual observations and telemetrics from the customer's system. Like the other quality gates, SAP provides customers with a report containing the positive findings and recommendations to implement to continue the clean core journey.

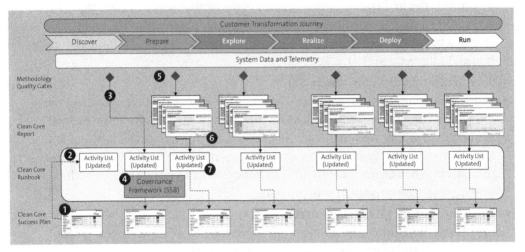

Figure 2.12 Clean Core Strategy in the Context of a Project Delivery

Next, let's deep dive into the golden rules for implementing SAP S/4HANA Cloud and discuss how they reflect the clean core strategy we've defined in this section.

2.5   Golden Rules for Implementing SAP S/4HANA Cloud

Organizations deploying SAP S/4HANA Cloud in their business will benefit from keeping the solution as close to standard as possible, which allows for faster adoption of innovations that SAP delivers both for cloud and on-premise systems. SAP experts often refer to this as a *cloud mindset* or a *clean core strategy*, which we've outlined in the previous section. To help customers adhere to this approach, SAP Activate includes guidance and governance for the application of the golden rules for implementing SAP S/4HANA solutions. In this section, we'll review the approach and rules in more detail to set the foundation for later chapters in this book, including Chapter 7 on deployment of SAP S/4HANA Cloud and SAP S/4HANA (on-premise).

SAP S/4HANA Cloud offers a high level of flexibility and extensibility options that are embedded in the solution and enabled with the full ABAP development environment. Some choices that the implementation team makes during the project could lead to increased total cost of ownership during the regular operations and make upgrades of the environment later challenging. As you implement the solution, SAP recommends project teams stay close to the standard functionality and limit the use of some extensibility and custom coding techniques to absolutely critical cases where the solution needs to be adapted to support the business objectives. This applies to all the dimensions of the clean core strategy we've discussed in the previous section.

SAP has published five golden rules for implementing SAP S/4HANA that provide project teams, architects, technical and functional consultants, and key users with guidelines to implement the solution in a way to make it easier to upgrade and continuously enhance. We'll walk through each of the golden rules in the following sections and explain how to apply that rule in your SAP S/4HANA Cloud project. First, let's look at the rules at a high level and discuss their business benefits.

2.5.1   Golden Rules and Benefits

Let's begin with a high-level overview of the five golden rules and consider their business benefits. The five golden rules are as follows:

1. **Start with preconfigured processes, and foster a cloud mindset by adhering to fit-to-standard and agile deployment detailed in SAP Activate.**
   The following activities fall under this rule:
   - Adopt SAP standard processes via SAP Best Practices, the enterprise management layer for SAP S/4HANA, SAP standard content, or SAP partner templates for fit-to-standard.
   - Where the preconfigured processes don't exist, process configuration and personalization should follow SAP's recommended configuration standards.
   - Use SAP Fiori UX, predefined processes, and data.

2. **Build your solution on quality data (configuration, master, and transactional) to leverage innovations.**
   To keep the data clean and streamlined, follow these guidelines pertaining to this rule:
   - Ensure data quality, including accuracy, completeness, consistency, timeliness, validity, and uniqueness.
   - Manage data volumes to optimize resource utilization and ensure data privacy.

3. **Ensure the use of modern integration technologies.**
   To use modern integration technologies, follow these guidelines:
   - Use public APIs (also known as allow-listed APIs).
   - Provide no native access to APIs that aren't public.
   - Follow SAP Integration Solution Advisory Methodology and SAP Activate guidance for integration.
   - Use SAP BTP functionality for cloud integration.

4. **Ensure the use of modern extensibility technologies.**
   To use modern extensibility technologies, follow these guidelines:
   - Follow guidance to extend SAP S/4HANA in the cloud and on-premise with ABAP-based extensions: (1) extend solution using released remote or local SAP APIs; (2) extend SAP objects only via predefined extension points; and (3) leverage cloud-enabled and released technologies.

- Develop company extensions in a side-by-side approach using SAP BTP.
- Leverage key user extensibility for no-code extensions.
- Use developer extensibility to create custom code where needed.
- Avoid backend enhancements.
- Don't modify SAP source code.

5. **Ensure transparency on deviations.**
   You can ensure transparency via the following methods:

   - Clearly document any deviations as part of the implementation; this will help the company replace these with standard capabilities if they are offered in the future.
   - Use the standard capabilities of ALM tools such as SAP Cloud ALM to document the solution.

Companies that adhere to these rules realize the following benefits:

- **Faster time to value**
  Adopting standard processes and minimization of process variants reduces the number of decisions and effort to configure, tailor, and test the solution, thus resulting in faster time and lower effort for implementation. This approach also allows for tailoring the solution when an organization will gain value from using a customized solution rather than the standard. In many ways, this is a balancing act of implementing the solution close to the standard and maximizing the benefits the organization can extract from the solution.

- **Lower cost of initial deployment and ongoing cost of running the solution**
  Reducing the number of changes in the solution leads to cleaner software that is easier to upgrade and continuously enhance, thus leading to lower overall cost of initial implementation and ongoing upgrades.

- **Ability to absorb innovations delivered by SAP at a faster rate**
  A clean core allows your organization to innovate at a faster rate as you're ready to leverage the regular innovations SAP delivers in your system. Organizations that adhere to the clean core strategy can leverage innovation more quickly and respond to changing business conditions faster.

- **Lower risk during the deployment of the solution**
  Adopting standard software exposes your organization to less risk that could be introduced in custom code during the project, including potential security gaps.

- **Reduction of technical debt and adoption of a high degree of standards, regardless of the transition method**
  By adhering to standard applications, organizations don't introduce potential technical debt in their processes, extensions, integrations, or data as they adhere to SAP-recommended practices, reducing the technical debt of the solution and increasing their ability to embrace innovation regardless of their transition path to SAP S/4HANA Cloud Private Edition or on-premise.

- **Higher flexibility for customers to choose the right, qualified partner**
  Rule 5 stipulates the need to document the key configuration decisions and any deviation from the golden rules. Having clear documentation of the decisions used to design the solution allows organizations to be less dependent on one system integrator and provides them with choices in the market.

- **Transition to future-proof solutions using modern technologies**
  Using modern technologies, such as open APIs for extensibility and integration, sets up the system for the future and allows organizations to benefit from the well-designed system longer as the technologies evolve. Using old technology will lead to them becoming obsolete, and organizations will need to invest in redesigning and rebuilding specific parts of the system that use old technology after they become obsolete or get phased out.

2.5.2   Rule 1

One of the key principles in implementation of the cloud solutions is to stay close to the standard capabilities of the software and to either fully avoid or at least minimize customization of the software. The fit-to-standard approach in your project will help you structure workshops around reviewing the standard functionality delivered in SAP software, whether you're building your solution around SAP Best Practices, the enterprise management layer for SAP S/4HANA, or an SAP-qualified partner package. With all of these packages, the project team starts with a set of predelivered processes that are shown to the business users to secure buy-in and to define delta requirements for capabilities that need to be configured or created during the implementation of the software.

Figure 2.13 shows the application of the fit-to-standard approach in the flow of the project from the prepare phase through the explore phase and into the realize phase.

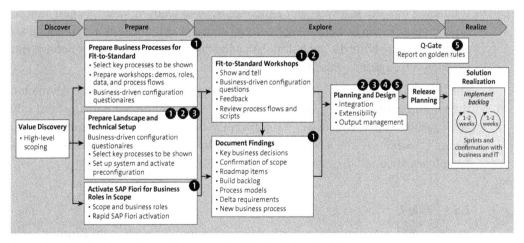

Figure 2.13 Golden Rules 1 and 2 Applied in SAP Activate Methodology

The key steps in each phase that pertain to the rules are referenced with the rule number in the circle. While the focus is on the first two rules in Figure 2.13, all five rules work in conjunction and build on each other. You can see that in cases where the box referencing an activity is linked to multiple rules. For example, the **Prepare Landscape and Technical Setup** activity links to both rule 2 and rule 3 as integrations are a key part of the technical setup.

The preconfigured processes provide a foundation for the fit-to-standard analysis and are critical components of building understanding of the solution capabilities, confirming fit, and identifying delta requirements. We'll provide more details on the structure and components of SAP Best Practices and the enterprise management layer for SAP S/4HANA Cloud in Chapter 4, when we discuss how to get started with a working system. Adopting standard processes often requires driving strong change management to the organization to adopt the new standard instead of tailoring the predelivered processes. This is especially the case with business processes that don't bring differentiation to your business but are necessary to run your organization. In this case, it makes sense to adopt standard processes and rely on SAP for the delivery of innovation. Some examples of these processes are as follows:

- Accounting and financial close
- Asset accounting
- Purchase order accruals
- Preventive maintenance
- Emergency maintenance

Even processes for which you adopt the standard may bring significant innovation into your organization through an ability to use innovation technologies such as machine learning, artificial intelligence (AI), and robotic processing automation (RPA).

It's also important to leverage the SAP Fiori UX to take advantage of the innovation SAP is building into the software with a modern UX that helps process business transactions more efficiently by exposing business information to the user in a new way. SAP Fiori can expose both the analytical data and transactional data on one screen, thus allowing you to analyze the situation and take action.

The last part of the first golden rule is to apply agile techniques in the deployment of the software, which enables your organization to clearly set the focus on the most valuable capabilities first and deliver the software to the business via incremental deployments to maximize the value you're getting from the solution. Refer to the agile techniques discussed in Chapter 6 for more details.

2.5.3   Rule 2

Business software solutions can only deliver business value when they run on top of quality data across all data categories of configuration data, master data (e.g., customer or vendor records), and transactional data of specific business objects created during running the solution (e.g., sales orders, purchase orders, etc.). When you think about data quality, you should consider the following categories of data quality in an ERP system:

- **Accuracy**
  Refers to the correctness of the information stored in the SAP S/4HANA system.

- **Completeness**
  Ensures that all required data fields are populated, and no essential information is missing.

- **Consistency**
  Refers to the uniformity and coherence of data across different processes within the system or across systems.

- **Timeliness**
  Refers to the relevance of data within the ERP system and how current the data is.

- **Validity**
  Ensures that the data conforms to predefined rules and standards.

- **Integrity**
  Ensures the accuracy and reliability of data throughout its lifecycle within the system. This includes internal controls to prevent unauthorized access, unauthorized changes, and data corruption.

- **Relevance**
  Ensures that the data stored in the ERP system is relevant and useful for performing business transactions or analysis.

- **Precision**
  Provides accurate information, enabling analysis and decision-making by the business users.

In the context of the SAP S/4HANA system, managing data volumes is an important topic that falls into the categories of data relevance, validity, timeliness, and accuracy. Customers bringing over data from an existing system that has been operated for decades need to devise a strategy to reduce data volumes before moving to SAP S/4HANA Cloud. Without a reduction of data volumes, the required conversion downtime may become too long to realistically convert the production environment without significant disruption to productive operations.

Other aspects that customers should keep in mind regarding data is how to ensure the data volumes are managed not only during the initial transition but also during the life and ongoing operations of the system. This is done by establishing clear data retention and archiving policies to keep the system data current and relevant. Additionally, customers should consider implementing data quality control processes and deploy solutions that help manage data quality in a productive environment on an ongoing basis.

2.5.4 Rule 3

SAP provides several predefined integrations for SAP-to-SAP integration scenarios as the recommended ways to integrate your SAP S/4HANA Cloud solution with other SAP software in your landscape—for example, SAP SuccessFactors Employee Central or SAP Ariba. For such situations, we recommend using the predelivered integration scenarios you can find in SAP Signavio Process Navigator using search through the available solution scenarios and solution processes (see Chapter 3, Section 3.2). For the integration of homegrown systems or systems from other vendors, SAP recommends using SAP's Cloud Integration capability, available with SAP Integration Suite on SAP BTP. This applies to both cloud-to-cloud and cloud-to-on-premise integration scenarios.

SAP Activate provides specific steps for project teams to follow during the design of integrations that are aligned with the more specific methodology for integrations: SAP Integration Solution Advisory Methodology. The SAP Activate tasks guide project teams to identify the integration needs, define the integration scenario, define the integration styles and use case patterns, and create detailed designs for integrations that aren't delivered out of the box. Then, in the realize phase, you can implement the integration using the available APIs on SAP Business Accelerator Hub (learn more at *http://api.sap.com*).

Figure 2.14 and Figure 2.15 show the flow of these steps in SAP Activate. In Figure 2.14, you can see items from the integration scenario and interface list, which is used to collect a list of integrations. Figure 2.15 shows the flow of activities driving the definition and design of integrations (the numbers correspond to applicable golden rules). The integration scenario and interface list details the functional and technical aspects of the integration, including the API and data the interface uses (such as data type and field length, which are important for technical realization).

Run Simple

Integration Scenario and Interface List

Business Information and Tracking

Role: Technical Consultant

Integration ID	Business Area	Scenario ID	Scope Item (Integration Setup) Title	Process Flow Available?	Details	Business Contact	Technical Contact	Best Practice Setup done by customer? Yes o	Custom Driven
Unique ID to track details and decisions	Name the business area where the integration is used	It is recommended to use scope items for managing the business processes.	Title of the scope item of column H	Is a End to End process flow for the busines sprocess available? See task: *Complete Process models*	Describe hich level the integration containing the business object used. This information is needed to find the right interfaces in the following steps	The business information is handed over to an integration specialist/expert. Name the implementation team member that can be contacted for more details if needed.	Name the implementation team member that can be contacted for more details if needed.	If SAP is providing an integrated solution, then mark this as *No*. *Yes* means that the implementation team has to the necessary steps for the integration.	Is the integration designed by the customer? Yes: a setup guide and a test script needs to be written by the customer. See task *Complete Setup Guides* *No: A setup guide is*
Example									
Example 1	HR	J12	Employee Integration - Employee Central Integration	yes	Person hired in EC, records time in S/4CLD	Jo Miller	Sally Winter	Yes	no
Example 2	Logistics	J45	not available	no	Import POs from 3rd Party system	Anette Bauer	Frank Hoffmann	Yes	yes
Example 3	Finance	J59	Machine learning: Cash Application			Ralph Schultz	Alexander Jones	No	no

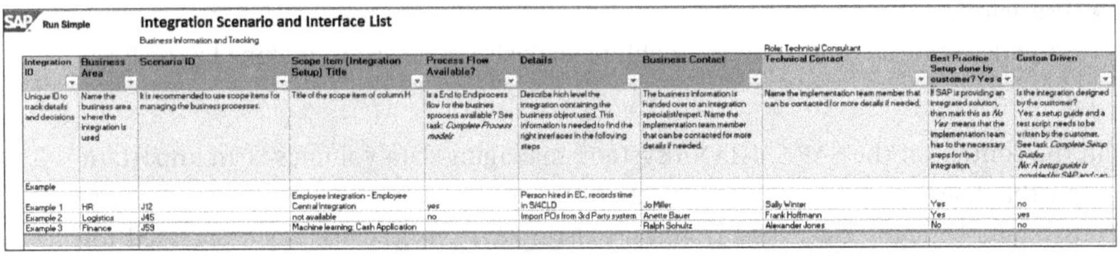

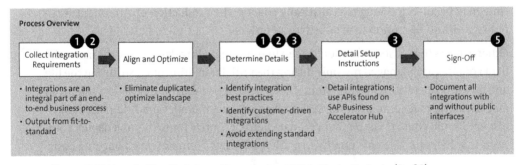

Figure 2.14 How to Handle Integrations during SAP Activate Projects (1 of 2)

Figure 2.15 How to Handle Integrations during SAP Activate Projects (2 of 2)

2.5.5   Rule 4

SAP S/4HANA Cloud supports a wide range of extensibility options that allow businesses to tailor solutions to their needs. The following extensibility options are recommended (introduced in Chapter 5, Section 5.3):

- **Key-user extensibility**
  This allows users to adapt standard functionality to meet their requirements without the need for any external tools, that is, low-code/no-code. It can be used both for applying small changes, such as hiding standard fields for specific user groups, or for including additional business logic. SAP S/4HANA Cloud offers tools that cover diverse extensibility needs. The following is a representative list of key-user extensibility actions:
  - Change and adapt the user interface (UI) layout and context
  - Create a new custom UI
  - Create custom fields
  - Create custom business objects
  - Create and extend forms and email templates
  - Create custom-specific core data services (CDS) views
  - Enhance the current business process by creating custom business logic

- **On-stack developer extensibility**
  This type of extensibility is possible through the integrated development tools in SAP S/4HANA Cloud and SAP S/4HANA, such as the full ABAP development environment in SAP S/4HANA Cloud Private Edition or the ABAP environment for SAP S/4HANA Cloud. This kind of extensibility is usually needed for development projects that involve being near or connected to SAP S/4HANA Cloud data, transactions, or applications.

- **Side-by-side extensibility using SAP BTP**
  This extensibility approach uses SAP BTP (a platform as a service [PaaS]) to extend the application by using the capabilities exposed via services on SAP BTP. The applications built on the platform are then integrated with SAP S/4HANA Cloud and SAP S/4HANA and extend the standard functionality in one of many areas. You can develop applications such as the following:
  - SAP S/4HANA Cloud Product Web Ordering and Reporting (explore more details at *http://s-prs.co/v596603*)
  - Display Created or Changed Sales Orders Using Business Event Handling (see *http://s-prs.co/v596604*)
  - You can find other examples on the SAP Extensibility Explorer site at *http://s-prs.co/v596605* by selecting **Sample Scenarios** at the top of the screen and filtering for side-by-side extensibility

SAP S/4HANA Cloud Extensibility Model

All extensions developed for SAP S/4HANA Cloud should follow the SAP S/4HANA Cloud extensibility model detailed in the "Extend SAP S/4HANA in the Cloud and On Premise with ABAP-Based Extensions" document that you can download from *http://s-prs.co/v596606*. We'll summarize the key extensibility rules that ensure the solution is extended in a cloud-compliant way to allow for smoother upgrades and faster consumption of innovation as well as more flexibility in managing custom code as the solution evolves.

All extensions must adhere to the following rules to ensure cloud-readiness:

- **Released remote or local APIs**
  Extensions can only use released remote or local SAP APIs. SAP keeps these APIs stable.

- **Predefined extension points**
  SAP objects can only be extended via predefined extension points. SAP keeps these extension points stable. Modifications of SAP objects as in on-premise systems are no longer supported.

- **Cloud-enabled and released technologies**
  Extensions can only use cloud-enabled and released technologies.

These rules for extensibility are further expanded in the SAP Application Extension Methodology. SAP Activate tasks in the extensibility workstream follow the same steps. You can access the SAP Application Extension Methodology at *http://s-prs.co/v596607*.

Figure 2.16 shows the flow of the SAP Activate steps for extensibility in the context of a project, where the project team needs to identify the need for extensibility, capture the requirements, detail the design for specific extensibility, and develop and test the extensibility. Figure 2.16 depicts the key sources of information that help you work on extensibility, such as guidance for extensibility and business process flows from standard SAP Best Practices processes used to indicate the extensibility requirements. In the lower portion of Figure 2.16, you can see the process steps that project team extensibility experts follow to define and design extensions in the system. The numbers above the boxes indicate the golden rule(s) applicable to each box.

Further Resources

If you're interested in extensibility, review the details provided via SAP Extensibility Explorer for SAP S/4HANA Cloud at *http://s-prs.co/v502725*, including the example extensibility sample scenarios provided there. You can also explore the extensibility patterns for each type of extensibility we've introduced in this section.

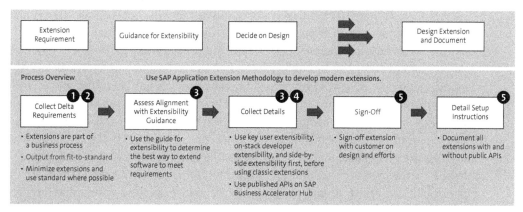

Figure 2.16 How to Handle Extensibility during SAP Activate Projects

2.5.6   Rule 5

The fifth rule is aimed at ensuring that any deviations from rules 1–4 are clearly documented so they can be accessible to the company during future solution upgrades or application of system patches by the service center. This rule has several purposes, the main one being the ability to understand the design decisions that were made during the implementation of the software. This rule ensures that any technical debt is properly documented and that this list of technical debt can be used to further optimize the system after the initial go-live to continue the journey to becoming a clean core enterprise. For example, to remove workarounds and custom code when the functionality is delivered in the standard.

This is especially important during upgrades that may introduce new capabilities requiring reconfiguration of the existing features to work with new software. For example, new functionality introduced in release X+1 may change the way the application runs and may require new configuration. In such cases, access to comprehensive documentation and decision rationales is important. This applies not only to configuration but also to integrations and extensions that have been introduced in the system.

SAP recommends that companies use ALM tools such as SAP Cloud ALM to keep track of key design decisions for configuration, extensions, and integrations as well as the technical debt. The ALM tools provide capabilities to document the process flow decisions, document the design rationale, and capture the key design decisions for the future. It's also important to keep this documentation up to date in the release upgrades as the system gets new release functionality and the design is updated.

2.5.7   Governance to Keep the Core Clean

We've introduced the clean core strategy and the five golden rules in the previous sections. In this section, we'll discuss how to set up project and solution design governance to ensure the clean core strategy is embedded in how the project is run and managed. As we stated at the beginning of this section, the goal of these five golden rules is to help the customer project team keep the core clean and maximize the use of standard functionality wherever possible instead of customizing the system functionality to cater to every single requirement raised by the business users. While this may sound counterintuitive, the experience in many projects has been that many of the requirements raised during the project aren't in use either from the beginning of productive use of the system or shortly after going live. SAP Activate recommends applying the lens of value to the business during the approval process before a requirement is added to the backlog along with the strict adherence to the five golden rules we've detailed in the previous sections. This means following the most current guidance for extensibility, integration, data, process design, and operations to ensure that the solution is built to serve your organization for years to come and that it continues to be flexible with the ability to consume innovations at a fast pace.

To implement such governance, the SAP Activate team has embedded the SSB in the prepare phase. Figure 2.17 shows the **Establish Solution Standardization Board** task as part of the activities in the prepare phase, related to project initiation and governance (see the starred task in the expanded deliverable).

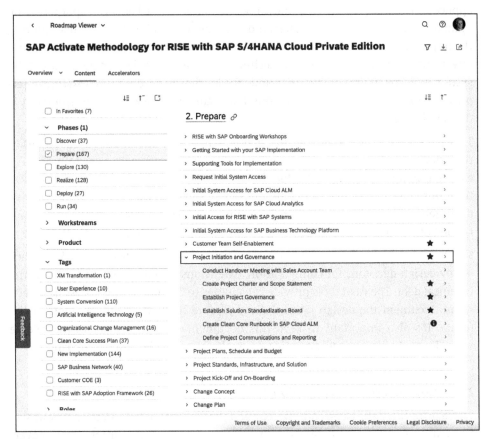

Figure 2.17 Establishing the SSB as Part of Project Initiation and Governance Setup in the Prepare Phase

Along with setting up the project governance and escalation paths, the project team needs to establish the SSB as the body overseeing compliance with the clean core strategy across all five dimensions and in adherence with the five golden rules. Along with this activity, the customer is also instructed to create the clean core runbook project in SAP Cloud ALM.

Let's now talk about the role of the SSB and the scope of its work. The project team establishes this governance function very early in the implementation project, and its role is to ensure that the project standardizes business processes and complies with the five golden rules.

This means that the SSB acts as a body overseeing the standardization of business processes and compliance with five golden rules in line with a clean core strategy. The SSB evaluates, reviews, approves, or rejects delta requirements dispositioned as gaps, in the following categories:

- Process deviations that give rise to impact on program scope and design principles
- Key-user, side-by-side, and developer extensibility, especially when deviating from extensibility guidance for SAP S/4HANA Cloud
- Required integrations with emphasis on the use of allow-listed APIs and compliance with golden rules
- Architectural and cross-team design and data decisions that deviate from clean core principles

Essentially, the SSB functions as the gatekeeper to keep the project team and solution design in line with the five golden rules and clean core strategy. The role of the SSB is to review all the noncompliant requests and decide whether they are going to be implemented. The board meets at least weekly (or more often in large programs with larger numbers of changes) to review all the submitted requests and decide on each. If a request is rejected and the project workstream wants to escalate this decision, they can trigger escalation to the project steering group, as shown in Figure 2.18. Note that Figure 2.18 depicts one page from the SAP Activate SSB template that you can download from the accelerator list in the task shown earlier in Figure 2.17.

The SSB includes representatives from the company and the system integrator; in some cases, when SAP is involved in the implementation, the enterprise architect or other SAP experts may be involved. On specific occasions, the SSB also may include additional participants from project workstreams requesting the change or workstreams that are impacted by the request. The standing participants are as follows:

- SSB chair from the company
- Company and system integration project managers
- Company enterprise architect
- Chief SAP solution architect (system integrator)
- Lead SAP technical architect (system integrator)

- Development leads responsible for SAP development (company and system integrator)
- Data management/harmonization lead

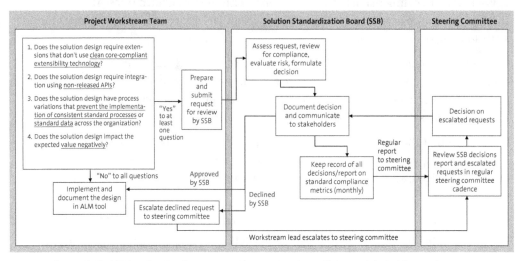

Figure 2.18 SSB Design Review Process to Ensure Compliance with Golden Rules

The role of the SSB is important during the initial implementation project, but it shouldn't cease to exist after the first go-live. It's important to transition the function of the SSB into a permanent role in the IT organization to continue supporting future projects and ongoing enhancements of the implemented system. Figure 2.19 shows the recommended steps for using the SSB during the project and the transition of the function into a permanent role after the initial go-live.

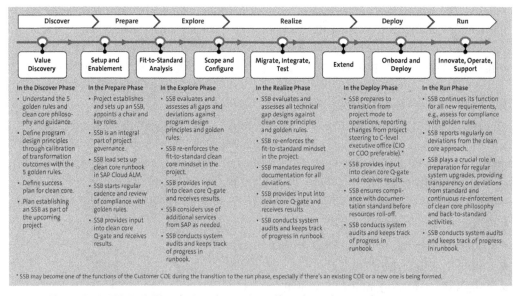

Figure 2.19 SSB Activities during the Project Lifecycle and Beyond

The role and importance of the SSB continues after the initial go-live to ensure continuous focus on implementing the new functionality in a manner compliant with the golden rules and a clean core strategy. Companies with multiple ERP projects should consider establishing an SSB function on the corporate IT level to provide oversight across all projects to monitor compliance with golden rules and ensure adherence to the clean core strategy.

Practical Experience with the SSB

We encourage you to review additional resources about SSB in the SAP Activate community blogs. In particular, the following two blog posts provide (1) more details on the function and role of the governance board and (2) the practical experience of a project manager who established the SSB in their project:

- "Practical Governance to Drive Fit-to-Standard Mindset in Your SAP S/4HANA Implementation": *http://s-prs.co/v546302*
- "The Value of a Solution Standardization Board (SSB) as Part of Implementing SAP S/4HANA Cloud, Extended Edition": *http://s-prs.co/v546303*

2.6 SAP Activate Methodology Taxonomy

In addition to the traditional lifecycle-based hierarchy we've outlined in the previous sections, users can view the content of the SAP Activate methodology by a specific workstream and use tags for filtering and navigation.

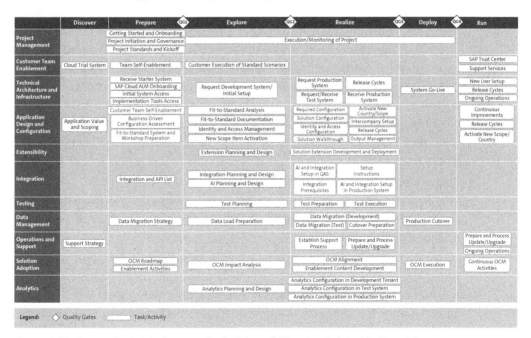

Figure 2.20 SAP Activate Workstream (Left Column) Showing Related Deliverables across Phases (Top Row) in the End-to-End Lifecycle

Figure 2.20 shows the structure of the methodology along the six phases (shown at the top of the image: discover to run), and the rows represent the workstreams of related deliverables and tasks that are shown in the grid. This figure is available for download at *www.sap-press.com/5966*.

In this section, we'll dig deeper into the structure of the SAP Activate methodology and provide additional details about how SAP structured the content and how to best use it in implementation projects.

2.6.1   Workstreams

As shown in Figure 2.20, *workstreams* represent groupings of related deliverables from specific areas, such as project management, application design and configuration, integration, or extensibility. Each deliverable and task in the methodology is assigned to a workstream.

The following is a brief description of workstreams in SAP Activate:

- **Project management workstream**
  This workstream covers planning, scheduling, project governance, controlling, project standards, and monitoring activities for the execution of the project. Project leadership, such as project managers, team leads, or program managers, comprise the audience for this workstream. You'll also find the agile project delivery tasks and deliverables in this workstream.

- **Solution adoption workstream**
  This workstream covers OCM activities such as stakeholder management, change management planning and execution, and value management (VM) in the context of the SAP implementation, where the stream focuses on the realization of the expected value from the implementation of the new system. This workstream closely interacts with the application design and configuration workstream we discuss later in this list. This workstream also includes deliverables and tasks related to planning, preparation, and delivery of end-user training. Organizational change managers, business readiness leads, and trainers comprise the audience for this workstream.

- **Customer team enablement workstream**
  This workstream is related to the enablement activities for the customer project team, which also includes enablement activities for key users that are part of the project team. The critical enablement activities must occur before most of the work starts in the explore phase, especially the fit-to-standard workshops, where customer key users should already be enabled on the application functionality using the initial environment and enablement materials. In addition, key users and administrators (as applicable in specific deployments) must be trained to prepare for the execution of their duties during the project. For example, they must be

enabled on the ALM tool used for capturing requirements, creating solution documentation, and testing. Enablement leads and trainers who are driving the enablement and training activities in the project comprise the audience for this workstream.

- **Application design and configuration workstream**
  This is one of the anchoring workstreams that deals with all aspects of application requirements, design, and configuration activities. The main activities during the project are setting and confirming the solution scope; planning, conducting, and documenting the results of the fit-to-standard analysis workshops; identifying and capturing the delta business process requirements; and creating the solution functional design and technical design documents. This workstream is interconnected with other workstreams for extensibility (including the development of analytics, functional extensions, forms, and workflows) and integration. Functional consultants, key users, and business process experts comprise the target audience for this workstream.

- **Data management workstream**
  This workstream provides the guidance required for the discovery, planning, and execution of moving data from the legacy environment to the new system. It also covers the topics of data archiving and data volume management, data migration activities for cutover planning and execution, and managing the data volumes during the run phase. Data migration experts, system administrators, and system architects comprise the target audience for this workstream.

- **Testing workstream**
  This workstream is related to all the application and technical testing activities that the project team will conduct during the project. The work starts early in the project when the team defines the test strategy that drives the test-planning activities. The testing is conducted repeatedly during the entire project to drive continuous integration of the solution: for example, the project team conducts unit and string testing in the delivery of sprints, and integration testing and UAT are done for each release. To complement the functional testing, SAP Activate guides technical teams to plan and conduct performance, load, and system testing at specific times during the project to mitigate risk to the go-live activities. The work done in this workstream directly contributes to the principle we introduced in Section 2.1: quality built in. Test managers, testing team leads, testing experts, and technical and functional consultants comprise the target audience for this workstream.

- **Technical architecture and infrastructure workstream**
  This workstream covers topics related to architecting and setting up the solution from a technical standpoint. This workstream deals with consultants defining the system architecture; receiving the provisioned environment, whether it's in the public cloud, private cloud, a hybrid deployment, or on-premise; designing the system

landscape; designing and setting up the technical system (primarily for on-premise projects); and handling technical operations standards, governance, and processes. System architects, administrators, and technical users comprise the target audience for this workstream.

- **Extensibility workstream**
  This workstream covers the requirements definition, design, development, and deployment of system functionality that can't be provided by the standard product and needs to be custom developed. Note that this workstream is governed by the SSB that we've introduced earlier in the chapter. SAP offers a wide range of extensibility options that we'll discuss later in this book. For now, we're only going to introduce the types of extensibility that SAP S/4HANA Cloud offers: (1) key user extensibility for low-code/no-code extensibility options such as field extensions; (2) developer extensibility using the ABAP in the cloud or ABAP environment embedded in the application to extend the core functionality; and (3) side-by-side extensibility using SAP BTP to extend the solution outside of the core of the ERP application. Application and technology developers comprise the target audience for this workstream.

- **Integration workstream**
  This workstream covers the activities needed to complete to plan, design, and set up (or develop) integrations between SAP S/4HANA and other applications. The topics included in this workstream are integration requirements identification, integration approach, integration solution design, and integration environment and middleware setup between the solution and external systems. Integration implementation experts and technical users comprise the target audience for this workstream.

- **Analytics workstream**
  This workstream discusses the key activities the project team needs to complete to establish a strong analytical solution for the business. The topics covered in this workstream include design, creation, and testing of the reporting and analytics inside the implemented solution; data modeling; data connections and integration for analytics; creation of stories through analytics; and predictive analysis. Analytics report developers and analytics experts comprise the target audience for this workstream. Note that for some dedicated analytical solutions, such as SAP Analytics Cloud or SAP Datasphere, SAP Activate provides a dedicated implementation roadmap with all the workstreams discussed in this section.

- **Operations and support workstream**
  This workstream is established to guide the project team in defining proper standards and policies for running the solution productively. These standards and policies need to be put in place during the implementation project. The company also needs to create an organization that will be responsible for running the environment.

There is a difference in deliverables for on-premise, private cloud, and public cloud guidance that is given by the scope of cloud services that SAP or other application management service providers cover during the deployment. In general, in on-premise projects, the work in this workstream is much more involved than in public cloud implementations. It's important to set up such an operational organization, even for cloud solutions, to take care of activities such as adding new users, activating new scope, coordinating regular activities during the solution upgrades, or expanding the geographical footprint of the solution after the initial go-live. Sample deliverables in this workstream are the definition and setup of the help desk process and organization; the definition, handling, and management of incidents; the post-go-live change management process; and user-related operations standards and processes. Support agents, power users, and IT organization staff comprise the target audience for this workstream.

2.6.2 Deliverables

A *deliverable* is an entity in the methodology that resides directly underneath the phase. In addition, the deliverable is assigned to a workstream where the work occurs; the two assignments were clearly shown earlier in Figure 2.20 as boxes assigned to a phase and a workstream. Some deliverables may be assigned to multiple workstreams if the related tasks span across workstreams; in such a case, one of the workstreams will be considered leading and will influence the placement of the deliverable, as shown previously in Figure 2.20.

Every deliverable contains a title and textual description in the body, as shown in Figure 2.21. The deliverable represents an outcome from tasks performed in the project. These tasks are assigned to the deliverable and shown as a dynamic list in the SAP Activate Roadmap Viewer. Some deliverables have additional links to accelerators that help project team members complete the work on a specific deliverable.

The following is true for deliverables:

- A deliverable is an outcome of performing one or multiple tasks during a specific phase.
- A deliverable represents a basis for the execution of project quality gates and often represents an element for customer acceptance/sign-off of the project outcomes.
- Each deliverable has at least one task, although often more than one task must be completed to create a deliverable.
- Each deliverable is assigned to a methodology workstream as defined in the previous section.

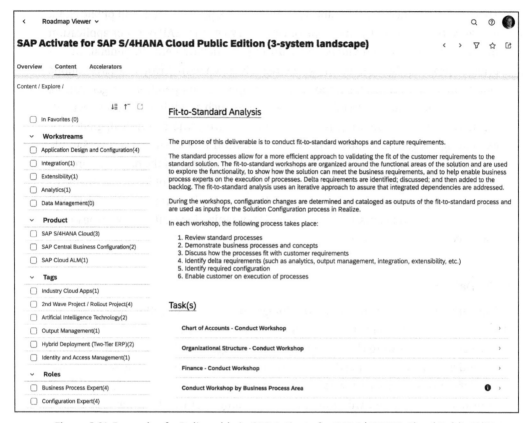

Figure 2.21 Example of a Deliverable in SAP Activate for SAP S/4HANA Cloud Public Edition

2.6.3   Tasks

Tasks in the SAP Activate methodology represent the lowest level of the hierarchy, detailing the work procedure a project team member needs to complete to contribute to creating the deliverable. Tasks generally contain additional links to accelerators that support the owner of the task in completing the task. Accelerators are defined in the next section. The following is true for tasks:

- Tasks describe the work that needs to be done to complete a deliverable; for example, multiple tasks represent the sequence of work on the deliverable.

- The description of the task is more granular than in previous SAP methodologies (e.g., ASAP or SAP Launch) and provides guided details for those assigned to execute the task. For example, a description expands on the how-to guidance outlined in the deliverable and provides detailed procedure steps describing how to execute the task using the assigned accelerators.

- Each task is assigned to one accountable project role that will complete the task. Some tasks may be assigned to supporting roles if other roles need to be involved in the completion of the task.

Figure 2.22 shows an example of a task from SAP Activate for the SAP S/4HANA Cloud Public Edition implementation methodology. Notice the structure of the description, which provides a numbered list detailing the procedure for completing the task and a bulleted list of procedure notes that help the person completing the task understand the additional details and context.

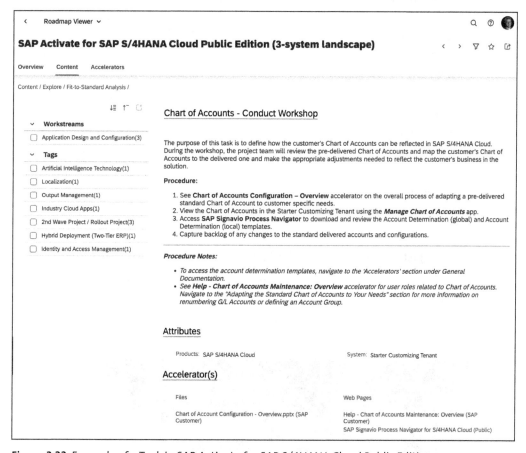

Figure 2.22 Example of a Task in SAP Activate for SAP S/4HANA Cloud Public Edition

2.6.4   Accelerators

SAP Activate provides a rich repository of *accelerators* that are attached to the tasks and deliverables described in the previous sections. The accelerators provide additional documents, templates, links to tools, SAP Help, and descriptions that help project teams complete the tasks and deliverables faster. For example, one accelerator in SAP Activate for SAP S/4HANA Cloud provides project teams with a detailed guide for planning, scheduling, running, and documenting the results of fit-to-standard workshops.

2.7   SAP Activate Community

SAP encourages users of SAP Activate to follow and actively participate in the SAP Activate community space on SAP Community, which is open to all customers, partners, prospects, and SAP internal users. The community provides users access to the latest SAP news, hot topics, and implementation and deployment materials from using SAP Activate methodology in company projects. It's a great place to find answers to your pressing questions. SAP also encourages users of SAP Activate to share their experience with using the approach in customer projects via blog posts, to share examples of how they applied the concepts, and to discuss their project experiences.

The SAP Activate community is the place to stay up to date on new content, learn about the best way to apply SAP implementation and deployment guidance in your next project, and find information about other areas of interest.

In this section, we'll review the key activities that community users can be involved in to maximize the benefit of being part of the community. Note that because SAP continues to evolve the community structure and content, some of the steps outlined here may change over time.

2.7.1   Register and Access the SAP Activate Community

The first step in getting into SAP Community is to register for an SAP Universal ID by clicking on the person icon in the top-right side of your screen at *https://community.sap.com/*. You'll then follow the prompts to complete the registration, as shown in Figure 2.23.

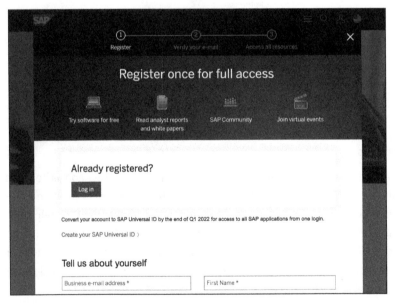

Figure 2.23 Signing Up for SAP Community

Once registered, you can log on directly to the community by clicking the same person icon the next time you access the page. If you already have an SAP Universal ID, you can use it to log in to SAP Community without needing to register. Once you're registered for SAP Community, you can access the SAP Activate community page at *https://community.sap.com/topics/activate* and bookmark it in your preferred web browser of choice.

2.7.2   Find Your Way in the SAP Activate Community

The SAP Activate community offers a simple structure that is represented on the main page shown in Figure 2.24 and gives users easy access to relevant SAP Activate content and resources. At the top of the main page, you'll find a rotating carousel with the most recent updates and blogs. When you scroll a little more down the page, you'll find a streamlined **SAP Activate Minute** videos playlist and more content on the SAP Activate phases with key deliverables, activities, and highlighted accelerators. The page also provides access to additional resources on the right side of the page, where you can find links to topics and areas of the community that help you find relevant information, post blogs or questions, and engage with other users.

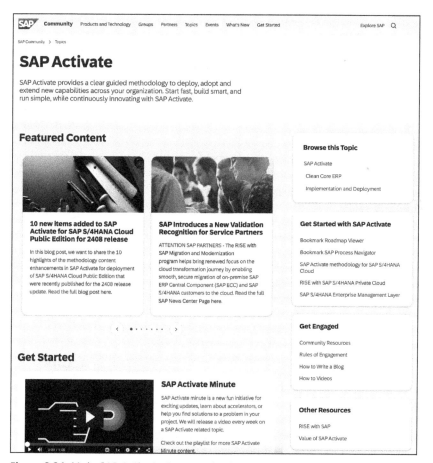

Figure 2.24 Main SAP Activate Community Space

2.7.3   Ask Questions and Find Answers

When accessing SAP Community, you'll likely come with specific questions or topics you need to research. The SAP Activate community provides a search functionality that will help you find answers quickly. You can see the search results screen in Figure 2.25.

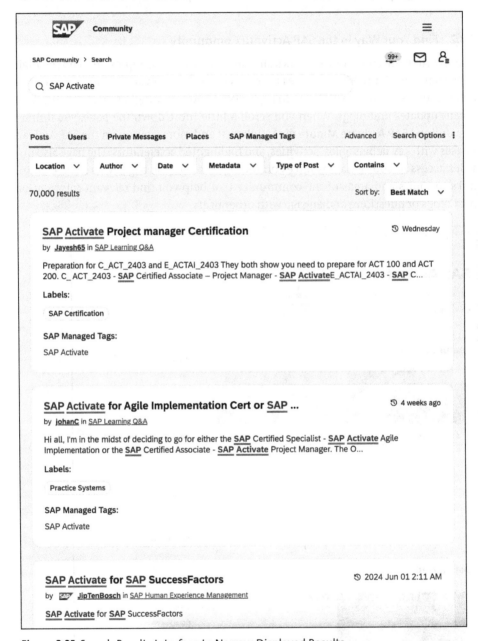

Figure 2.25 Search Results Interface to Narrow Displayed Results

There are multiple ways to search SAP Community. We recommend accessing the **Get Started** link from the SAP Activate community main page, top-level menu navigation. From here, you can find out what SAP Community is about with the following menu choices:

- **Welcome Corner**
  Join the Welcome Corner to search for topics and blogs, introduce yourself, make connections with like-minded community members, enjoy lively discussions, and much more!

- **FAQs**
  You can now access the **Help Pages** by selecting the **FAQs** link. Here, you can find all the answers to your SAP Community navigation questions.

- **All Resources**
  Using this link, you can access a dashboard of how-to videos, SAP Community points of contact, a specific tile for SAP partners, the community rules of engagement, and the SAP privacy statement.

In general, before raising a question, you should first search the community for answers. Over the life of this community, many questions have already been answered, and you may locate an existing answer faster than you could get a response to your own question. If you can't find the answer in the community, you can post your question using the **Ask a Question** link on the SAP community main page; alternatively, you can select **Answers** at the top of the SAP Community navigation and select the **Ask a Question** menu item. Don't forget to assign the SAP-managed SAP Activate tag to your question to make sure it's correctly associated with the SAP Activate community space.

Efficient Questions

Make your question as specific as possible while omitting any details that could identify the project or customer you're working with. Remember that SAP Community is open to diverse types of users and freely searchable by search engines such as Google or Bing.

2.7.4 How to Contribute Blog Posts

If you have examples from your project to share with the community or have experience with SAP Activate you want to discuss, you should post directly to the site as a blog post. The process is like posting the question as just described. You'll need to select **Write a Blog Post** from the SAP Community space.

This will open a new page where you'll input your blog post title, the text of the blog post, and tags that will help users find the content easier. Be sure to use a descriptive title and always assign the SAP Activate managed tag to help users find your blog post in the future. Just like questions, the blog posts are moderated by community moderators before they are posted. If you're contributing your very first blog post, it will be tagged for moderator review before it's approved for publication. A moderator may contact you if the text needs to be adjusted before it's ready to be posted.

You'll receive email notifications from the SAP Activate community when other users post new content (blog posts or questions), comment on your blog post, or provide feedback as a response to your question.

In closing, follow the steps outlined in the "Welcome All SAP Community Members, Start Here!" blog (*http://s-prs.co/v596608*), including taking the **Tour the SAP Community 2024 Tutorial** to familiarize yourself with community guidelines and discover how to get the most out of your membership. You'll also discover how to prepare and manage your blog posts on SAP Community, get tips for better blogging, and learn how to interact with readers.

> **Note**
>
> You must complete the **Tour the SAP Community 2024 Tutorial** to blog in SAP Community.

We believe that community is for everyone, and we welcome you to SAP Community! We're here to help you on your learning journey. To learn even more about SAP Community, read the FAQs in the help section, and watch the how-to videos for detailed guidance on navigating the SAP Community space.

2.8   SAP Activate Training and Certification

If you want to learn more about SAP Activate, SAP offers comprehensive learning journeys consisting of materials to build your implementation skills. You can access the learning journeys on SAP Learning Hub or in an SAP training class. The journeys SAP offers are structured into a logical flow, from overview courses through courses that help attendees become proficient in the SAP Activate approach to courses that help participants stay current. The entire training curriculum is shown in the learning journey for **SAP Activate - Implementation Tools and Methodology** at *http://s-prs.co/v596609*.

You can navigate to specific learning journeys like the one shown in Figure 2.26. This example shows the **Discovering SAP Activate - Implementation Tools and Methodology** learning journey that consists of seven units guiding the learner through the different parts of SAP Activate methodology and tools used during the implementation process.

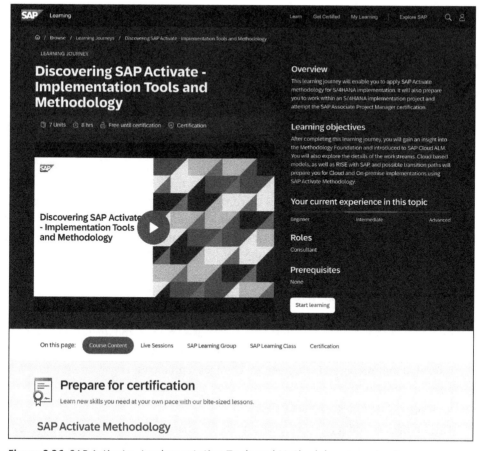

Figure 2.26 SAP Activate - Implementation Tools and Methodology Learning Journey

---

SAP Activate Certification Guide

SAP also offers the SAP Activate certification exam for consultants, project managers, and users of SAP Activate who want to demonstrate their understanding of the approach and obtain certification from SAP. You can take the certification exam on SAP Learning Hub (allow about three hours to complete the exam). We'll share practice certification questions with you in Appendix A to support you in preparation for the exam and provide a review of the materials we cover in this book. We'll provide a more detailed breakdown of the exam topics in Appendix A and offer a series of practice questions for each topic.

We'll conclude this chapter with a detailed list of the enablement channels provided by SAP product management from the SAP cloud ERP engineering team. Those channels are designed to enable and empower SAP customers, SAP partners, and SAP employees with the key product innovations, release after release. You can access the enablement details on the SAP Community page at *http://s-prs.co/v596610*. Now, let's take a look at the available resources:

- **Product expert training**
  These sessions are designed to empower both SAP partners and customers with in-depth product knowledge. Conducted twice a year, these sessions span two weeks and are led by SAP Product Engineering and Product Management teams. Attendees gain comprehensive insights into end-to-end processes and the latest updates, ensuring they are well-prepared to leverage SAP S/4HANA Cloud to its fullest potential.

- **In-depth with SAP S/4HANA Cloud Public Edition**
  This online series, available on SAP Learning Hub, features live product demonstrations and the latest insights from SAP S/4HANA Cloud product experts. Designed for both SAP customers and SAP partners, these sessions aim to extend the reach and impact of SAP S/4HANA Cloud Public Edition by providing deep-dive knowledge transfer independent of release cycles.

- **Early release series: "Show & Tell" sessions**
  These learning sessions keep stakeholders updated on new capabilities with every major SAP S/4HANA Cloud Public Edition release product update. By demoing key innovations before release to customers (RTC), they ensure that all parties are well-informed and prepared for upcoming changes, enhancing engagement and readiness.

- **Podcast: Inside SAP S/4HANA Cloud**
  This dynamic and engaging podcast series shares real-life stories about SAP S/4HANA Cloud implementation projects and successful go-lives. Available on platforms such as SAP Learning, Spotify, and Apple Podcasts, these 15–30 minute episodes feature discussions with customers, partners, and SAP experts, offering valuable insights and best practices to a broad audience. You can sign up for this podcast here in Apple Podcasts: *http://s-prs.co/v596611*.

- **Expert talk videos**
  With the expert talks, the team spreads the word about successful implementation projects and satisfied customers through 15–20 minute biweekly episodes. These sessions share product insights and best practices, featuring SAP S/4HANA Cloud product experts, partners, and customers to highlight success stories and valuable learnings.

- **SAP S/4HANA microlearning**
  Microlearning offers easy-to-consume, short videos (3–12 minutes) that provide product and project insights on demand. Published weekly and driven by customer needs, these videos include demos and product insights, making it easier for everyone to stay informed and proficient in SAP S/4HANA Cloud.

- **SAP Community for SAP S/4HANA Cloud**
  SAP Community serves as a hub for sharing product expert knowledge and supporting customers and partners in their SAP S/4HANA Cloud implementations. You can access the SAP S/4HANA Cloud community at *https://pages.community.sap.com/topics/s4hana-cloud*.

These are amazing resources to stay up-to-date with the innovation SAP delivers with SAP S/4HANA Cloud Public Edition. We encourage all customers and partners to explore these assets and leverage them to stay current on the implementation approach and product capabilities.

2.9 Summary

This chapter introduced the SAP Activate approach and its principles, including the use of SAP Best Practices and the application of the agile approach during the project. We also introduced the six phases of the SAP Activate approach and discussed how the process flows through the phases. We've discussed the five golden rules for implementation of SAP S/4HANA that help organizations live the cloud mindset. And we explained the need for strong governance for these golden rules to ensure that the solution is deployed according to the clean core strategy to enable a faster innovation cycle.

Later in the chapter, you learned about the workstreams that group related deliverables and tasks in the methodology. In addition, we looked at the accelerators that provide you with access to easy-to-use templates, examples, and other tools to accomplish the deliverables faster and with less effort. You've also seen that SAP Activate provides a guided journey to SAP S/4HANA Cloud (and other SAP products).

This chapter also introduced you to the SAP Activate community, including the key actions you can take in the community to engage with other SAP Activate experts and the SAP Activate team in SAP. In the last section, we provided an overview of the training and certification offerings from SAP that will help you learn more about SAP Activate and stay current on its continuous improvements.

In the next chapter, we'll introduce tools for accessing the SAP Activate methodology and preconfiguration assets, as well as discuss tools that project teams use to consume SAP Activate during the course of an implementation or upgrade project.

Chapter 3
Accessing SAP Activate

To implement cloud, hybrid, and on-premise projects, project team members need the support of key tools when accessing and using SAP Activate content. We'll provide an overview of these tools for all deployment options in this chapter.

In this chapter, we'll discuss the key tools that you'll use to access the SAP Activate components: the guided methodology, SAP Best Practices, and the tools for application lifecycle management (ALM).

We'll start by introducing the SAP Activate Roadmap Viewer tool that you can use to view and navigate the SAP Activate methodology content, including access to accelerators. Then, we'll discuss the SAP Signavio Process Navigator environment, in which you can access detailed information about the ready-to-use business process content delivered in SAP Best Practices and the enterprise management layer for SAP S/4HANA (we'll cover the content in Chapter 4). In the second half of this chapter, we'll focus on the SAP Cloud ALM environment that supports deploying and running cloud applications, hybrid deployments, and on-premise environments. SAP Cloud ALM provides capabilities for managing requirements, planning and monitoring the project, creating solution documentation, testing the solution, and running and operating the solution.

Project teams use many other tools to leverage SAP Activate as well, and we'll discuss those in the specific chapters about the deployment of SAP S/4HANA Cloud solutions as well as the deployment of SAP S/4HANA. This chapter will focus on dedicated tools that allow the project team to access the methodology, access and download the ready-to-run business processes, and manage ALM from end to end.

3.1 SAP Activate Roadmap Viewer

You can access the full content of the SAP Activate methodology in the SAP Activate Roadmap Viewer via *https://go.support.sap.com/roadmapviewer/*. The SAP Activate Roadmap Viewer provides easy-to-navigate access to SAP Activate methodology guidance for your specific SAP solution—or, if a solution-specific roadmap isn't available, you can use the generic SAP Activate methodology for the cloud or on-premise solution to get guidance aligned with your deployment approach. (Note that we'll refer to SAP Activate Roadmap Viewer in the rest of this section as Roadmap Viewer.)

The **Roadmap Viewer** entry screen presents you with several tiles that help you understand the role and functionality of the tool, as shown in Figure 3.1. The content behind these tiles helps first-time users explore the key functionality of the Roadmap Viewer and learn how to use it most efficiently. The information includes an explanation of the content provided in the Roadmap Viewer in the **1. Overview** tile, navigational instructions with a short video showing how to get around in the tool in the **2. How to Use** tile, and the **3. Learn More** tile offers a list of additional resources and links. The **4. SAP Cloud ALM** tile brings you to the SAP Support Portal pages that provide more information about the tool's capabilities as well as learning resources (we'll cover this tool in Section 3.3).

On the bottom of the screen in the **Highlights** section, you can quickly access highlighted methodology content for topics such as GROW with SAP, RISE with SAP, and SAP Business Technology Platform (SAP BTP). Next, you can click the blue **Explore All Roadmaps** button to navigate to a list of available SAP Activate methodology roadmaps.

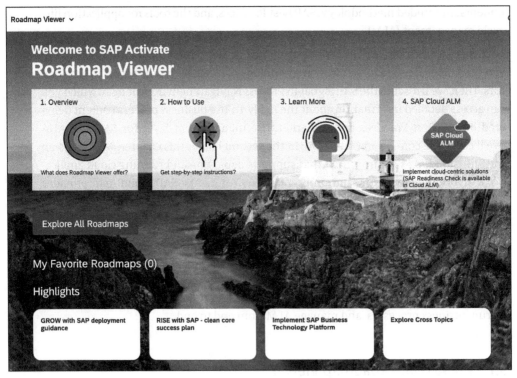

Figure 3.1 Roadmap Viewer Entry Screen

The list of all methodology roadmaps is grouped into the following categories, as shown in Figure 3.2:

- Cloud Specific Methodology
- On-Premise Specific Methodology
- Upgrade Methodology
- General/Cross Topics

Each grouping provides access to individual methodology roadmaps for specific solutions or products. The number in brackets next to the title indicates the number of methodology roadmaps in each category. SAP continues to deliver new content, and in between publishing the previous edition of this book and writing the current edition, there are 10 new methodology roadmaps available to users of the Roadmap Viewer.

You can click on the star symbol in front of one or more methodology roadmaps to make them as favorite specific instances of SAP Activate. Once they are favorited, the tool will show them automatically on the home page when you enter the Roadmap Viewer tool. You can arrange the favorited tiles on the home page in any sequence by simply dragging the tiles to the desired spots. You can open a methodology roadmap either directly from the categorized list or from the home page if you select a favorite roadmap; simply click on the tile on the home page or click on the name of the roadmap.

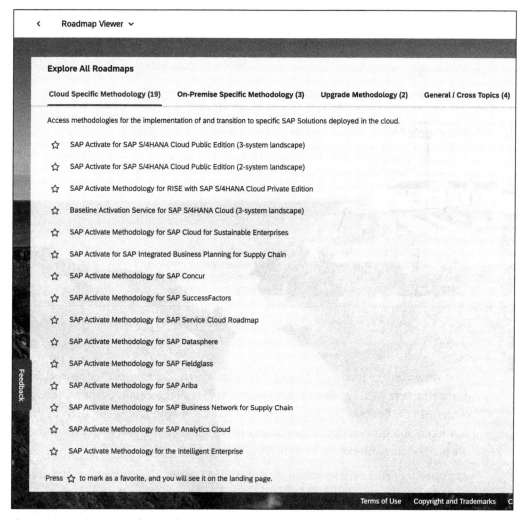

Figure 3.2 Navigation in the Roadmap Viewer: Explore All Roadmaps

After you pick a specific roadmap and open it, the screen will show the roadmap overview information that provides the description of the roadmap's purpose, the solution supported by the roadmap, and an overview of the approach and key deliverables in each phase, as shown in Figure 3.3. This page offers additional details as well, including the following:

- A link to the release notes that provide information about the latest updates to the methodology content
- A link to the overview presentation that helps you understand the overall flow of the methodology for your selected implementation roadmap
- A release date and time stamp, so you know when the content was last published
- Additional links to additional important assets that are available to the users of this roadmap

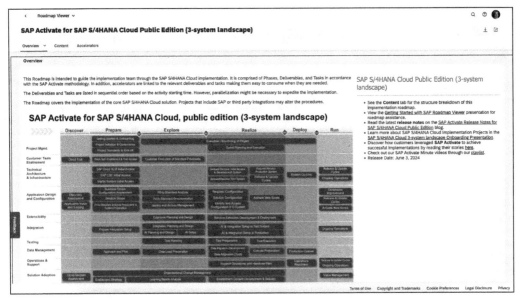

Figure 3.3 Overview Page for the SAP Activate Methodology for SAP S/4HANA Cloud Public Edition

After reviewing the roadmap **Overview** section, you should navigate to the work breakdown structure (WBS) of the methodology to access all the details of the methodology content. In the **Content** tab, you can then browse the methodology hierarchy by phases and access specific descriptions and accelerators attached to the deliverables or tasks in the methodology hierarchy, as shown in Figure 3.4.

You can either click on a specific deliverable to see its description and associated accelerators or expand the deliverable to show the tasks that are contributing to the completion of that deliverable. Use the **>** sign on the left side of the deliverable to expand it and see the tasks, as shown in Figure 3.5. You can also use the up- and down-pointing arrows on the top right of the screen to expand all or collapse all items in the list. This way, you can quickly expand or collapse the entire methodology hierarchy with just one click.

In addition, you can filter the hierarchy by selecting specific (or multiple) **Phases**, **Workstreams**, assigned **Product**, roadmap-specific **Tags**, or project **Roles**. You'll find these selection filters on the left side of the screen. By default, only the Phases list is shown, you'll need to expand the other lists by selecting the **>** symbol to the left of each section. In general, we recommend using the filters when searching for content as in our experience, selecting two filters or, say, **Phases** and **Workstreams**, significantly reduces the number of shown tasks and makes the navigation a lot easier, even for experienced users.

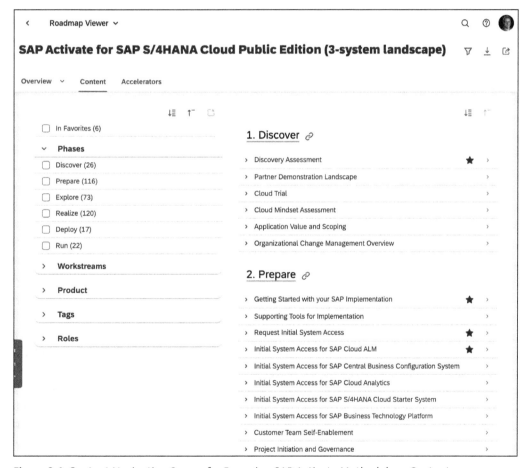

Figure 3.4 Content Navigation Screen for Browsing SAP Activate Methodology Content

Figure 3.5 Expanded Task List under a Roadmap Viewer Deliverable

After you navigate to the deliverable or task description, you'll learn about its purpose and procedure to follow for the successful completion of the task. The Roadmap Viewer will provide access to accelerators and additional web links that support you in completing the task or deliverable. Figure 3.6 provides an example of one task from the SAP Activate methodology for SAP S/4HANA Cloud Public Edition and shows the structure of the task description and additional **Accelerator(s)** and **Web Pages** at the bottom of the description.

You can also make favorites of your frequently used tasks and deliverables by clicking the star icon in the top-right corner of the screen both on the task or in the deliverable (see Figure 3.6). This information can later be used for filtering the content in the WBS. When you want to navigate between tasks under the same deliverable, you can use the < > arrows at the top right of the screen to navigate back and forth in the list of tasks without needing to exit the task. In addition, you can use the breadcrumb links at the top-left side of the screen to navigate back up to the deliverable, the phase, or the list of all deliverables and tasks (note that the filters you select on the complete task list are persistent throughout the navigation).

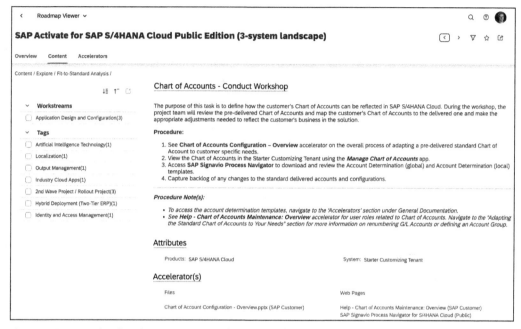

Figure 3.6 Example of Task Description in the Roadmap Viewer

If you're looking for a specific accelerator and don't remember on which task it's assigned, you can navigate directly to the complete list of accelerators assigned to the roadmap by clicking on the **Accelerators** tab at the top of the screen. This will bring you to a page with all accelerators sorted by phase. This page provides similar navigation and filtering capabilities as those for the WBS navigation, shown previously. You can use these filters to narrow the search for an accelerator by phase and workstream to locate the specific accelerator or template you need. Figure 3.7 shows the result of filtering the accelerators screen for the **Explore** phase, **Application Design and Configuration** workstream, and **Business Process Expert** role. This way you can narrow down the list as we discussed earlier in this chapter.

In addition, on the **Overview** page, **Content** page, or **Accelerators** page, you can download the project WBS using the down arrow icon at the top right. The WBS can be imported into your preferred project scheduling tool, or you can leverage the provided formats.

The Roadmap Viewer offers additional capabilities that help you locate specific assets, such as accelerators, tasks, or deliverables, very quickly. You can use the **Search** function (magnifying glass icon) at the top right of every screen to either search all roadmaps in the Roadmap Viewer or search for a specific roadmap or group of roadmaps. Additionally, you can narrow down the results by the content type as shown in Figure 3.8.

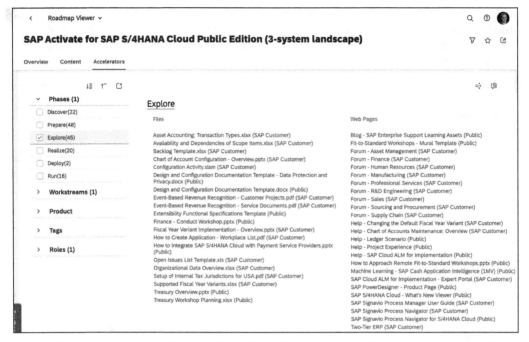

Figure 3.7 Accelerators Screen with Multiple Filters Applied for Phase, Workstream, and Roles

Figure 3.8 Narrow the Search Results by Content Type

We recommend that you, as an SAP Activate user, experiment with the features in the Roadmap Viewer tool as they continue to evolve based on user feedback. You can always send feedback to SAP using the blue **Feedback** button on the left side of the screen.

In the remainder of this book, we'll refer to the Roadmap Viewer when we point out specific accelerators, tasks, or deliverables as we discuss the deployment of SAP S/4HANA Cloud solutions in your environment. Please note that all the SAP Activate content discussed in this section is also accessible in SAP Cloud ALM, as we'll discuss in Section 3.3.

3.2 SAP Signavio Process Navigator

SAP Signavio Process Navigator is a service that provides visibility into significant portions of SAP's process portfolio. It serves as an ideal extension for implementation projects using the SAP Activate methodology. Accessible through the SAP for Me portal, you can directly reach SAP Signavio Process Navigator via *https://me.sap.com/processnavigator*.

SAP Signavio Process Navigator uses the SAP Enterprise Architecture Methodology (SAP EA Methodology) data model, which distinguishes between business and solution architecture entities, as depicted in Figure 3.9.

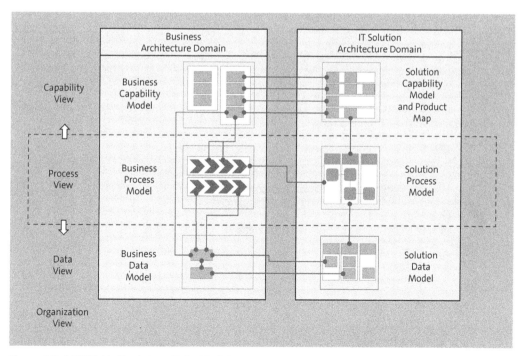

Figure 3.9 SAP EA Methodology Data Model

SAP EA Methodology facilitates the segmentation of business functions, describing typical industry activities through the business capability model. In contrast, the solution map offers an overview of SAP solutions that support and implement these business capabilities.

The process view outlines how the business operates to achieve its objectives, while the solution process model explains how solution components interact to enable business processes. These aspects are accessible via SAP Signavio Process Navigator (see Figure 3.10), which is structured around end-to-end solution scenarios. Within these scenarios, customers can explore individual solution processes, review implemented business value flows, identify necessary solution components, and understand the applications and application roles involved in executing specific activities.

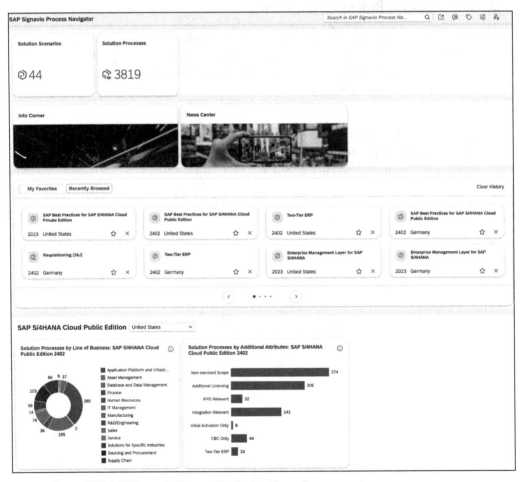

Figure 3.10 SAP Signavio Process Navigator Home Page

SAP Signavio Process Navigator encompasses end-to-end scenarios across various lines of business (LoBs), industries, and technologies, incorporating SAP Best Practices and integration scenarios for efficient deployment. It provides process models, graphical process diagrams (including value flow and solution process flow diagrams), scenarios, and process documentation. These materials are often tailored to specific country or regional localizations. Additionally, SAP Signavio Process Navigator offers a wide range of value accelerators to support all aspects of solution implementations. These value accelerators are available at both the end-to-end scenario level and within dedicated solution processes.

Full access, including the possibility to download value accelerators, is enabled for SAP S-users, but SAP P-users will have restricted access only. You can see the home page of SAP Signavio Process Navigator in Figure 3.10.

You have the flexibility to tailor the home screen according to your preferences. To start, if you frequently use specific solution processes or scenarios, you can bookmark them from the list of recently viewed entities, as shown in Figure 3.11.

Figure 3.11 User Favorites on the Home Screen

Additionally, you can customize the arrangement of tiles on the home screen by hiding or showing them, and even rearrange sections using the drag-and-drop tool via the **Configure Your Page** button on the home screen, as shown in Figure 3.12.

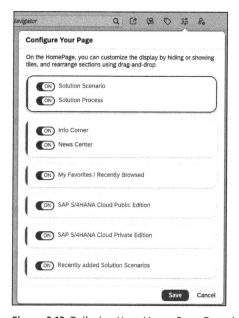

Figure 3.12 Tailoring Your Home Page Experience via Configure Your Page

From the **Solution Scenarios** or **Solution Processes** tiles, you can navigate to dedicated end-to-end solution scenarios or solution processes. The **Solution Scenarios** selection is sorted as follows:

- By product:
  - Enterprise resource planning
  - Business network
  - Supply chain management
  - Spend management
  - Customer relationship management and customer experience
  - Human capital management
- By integration processes
- By industry processes
- By the special category for trial, tools, and demo processes

The A-Z index alternatively provides a sorted list view of all available solution scenarios and their available versions.

The **Solution Processes** tile navigates you to the global search function, as shown in Figure 3.13. This provides multiple options for a detailed search, for example, by solution scenario, solution process, solution capability, application, or application role.

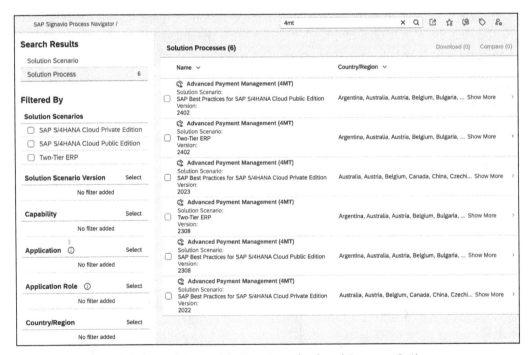

Figure 3.13 Global Search Page with Filter, Download, and Compare Options

Search results can be further refined by applying additional filter criteria. A **Compare** feature allows you to select different release or country versions of the same solution process to get an indication about potential differences, as shown in Figure 3.14.

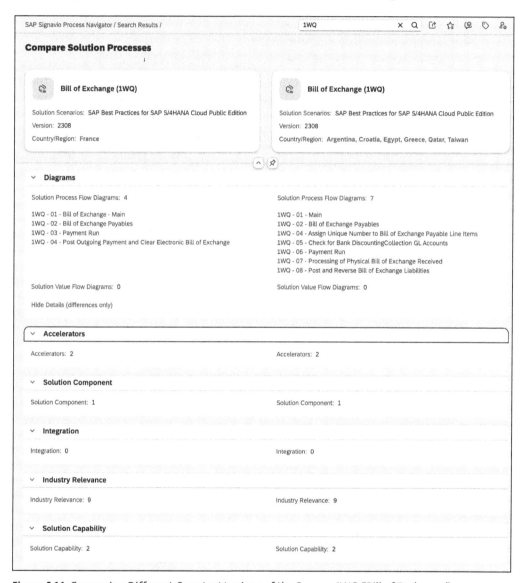

Figure 3.14 Comparing Different Country Versions of the Process 1WQ "Bill of Exchange"

The home screen also provides the most relevant indicators for SAP S/4HANA Cloud Public Edition and SAP S/4HANA Cloud Private Edition, such as the distribution of solution processes by LoB, preselected for a dedicated country/region or specific attributes that need to be considered before or during an implementation project.

3.2.1   Solution Scenario Information

In SAP Signavio Process Navigator, a solution scenario represents a collection of solution processes tailored to specific implementation and deployment requirements. These scenarios serve various purposes:

- **Preconfigured solution processes**
  Solution scenarios may include preconfigured processes that define the scope of an SAP cloud solution, such as those found in SAP Best Practices for SAP S/4HANA Cloud Public Edition. See Chapter 4, Section 4.1.1, for more information.

- **Integrated end-to-end scopes**
  Additionally, solution scenarios describe integrated end-to-end business and technology scopes relevant to customers. Examples include scenarios such as **Lead to Cash for Cloud Deployments**, where integration needs across solution components are well-documented.

- **Dedicated solution areas or industries**
  Some solution scenarios focus on specific areas or industries, such as **Human Capital Management**.

Despite their varying levels of detail, solution scenarios adhere to a common structure for presenting related information.

The first section contains the general scenario data, including its name, version, selected country/region, and specifics regarding the number of delivered processes and process flow diagrams, as you can see in Figure 3.15.

Figure 3.15 Summary of the Solution Scenario Displayed at the Top of the Screen

Following this overview is the list of solution processes included in the scenario version. Note that each individual solution process also has its own version (can be reused in other scenarios). The layout might differ between different scenarios. It can range from a list of alphabetically ordered processes to a sorted layout by LoBs.

The second section starts with a list of relevant value accelerators. Value accelerators are implementation assets that help accelerate the time to value of your implementation project. Value accelerators naturally complement implementation accelerators of SAP Activate; in SAP Signavio Process Navigator, they are sorted according to the following categories:

- Configuration
- Delivery and Positioning
- End-User Information
- Getting Started
- Implementation
- Training and Education
- Reference
- What's New

The final section of the **Solution Scenario** entry page offers a concise description of the scenario. It explains the overall purpose and scope, outlines the associated business benefits, and provides a brief description of the key process flows. You can see both the **Accelerators** section and **Description** section in Figure 3.16.

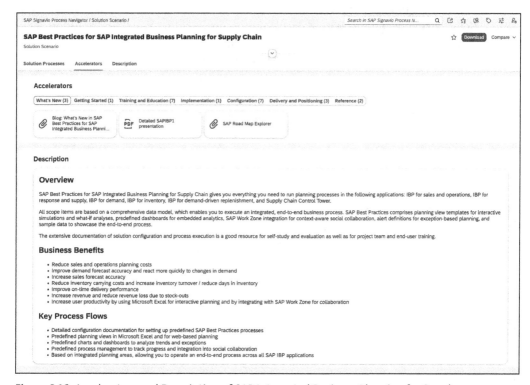

Figure 3.16 Accelerators and Description of SAP Integrated Business Planning for Supply Chain Solution Scenario

3.2.2   Solution Process Information

Now, we'll take a look at the information provided for the solution processes and discuss the screen and information layout in the tool.

At SAP, a solution process is defined as the realization of a business process or parts of a business process in an IT environment. It leverages a defined set of solution components to realize and meet the needs of the business process. A solution process is described using architecture views (that build the "architecture description") and additional meta information (that build the "implementation and optionally the commercial description"). Architecture views provide a detailed visual description for the solution process using solution component, solution value flow, solution data flow, and solution process flow diagrams. (Solution process flow diagrams are typically delivered in Business Process Model and Notation [BPMN].)

Additional meta information associated with the solution process includes, for example, country/region relevance, industry relevance, solution capabilities, integration relevance, deployment-specific information, and license dependencies (optional).

Each solution process is organized into one or more solution process flows. These flows are typically represented using solution process flow diagrams in the BPMN language. BPMN is a standard for process modeling that provides a graphical notation based on a flowcharting technique. Within each solution process flow, you'll find solution activities that outline the specific steps involved. Clicking on a dedicated solution activity in the process flow diagram provides additional information about which application to use for fulfilling the described tasks, along with the associated application role. Both **Application** and **Application Role** are described in more detail in the context window of the solution activity. You can see an example of such solution activity in Figure 3.17.

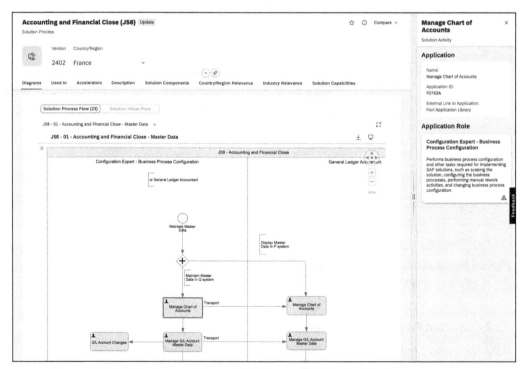

Figure 3.17 Solution Process Flow and Solution Activity in the Solution Process Accounting and Financial Close

SAP Signavio Process Navigator allows you to manipulate the display of the diagrams by adjusting their position (up, down, left, or right), zooming in or out, downloading them in various formats, switching to full-screen mode for detailed viewing, and re-centering the diagram.

The **Used In** section outlines the solution scenario(s) or version(s) in which a specific solution process is used, emphasizing the reusability aspect of solution processes. For solution scenarios, individual solution processes and/or solution process flows can be documented in the **Description** section, following a consistent pattern. This documentation provides a general overview, highlights key process flows, and outlines business benefits. Additionally, the solution process description may include implementation-specific details, as shown in Figure 3.18 (see the highlighted text).

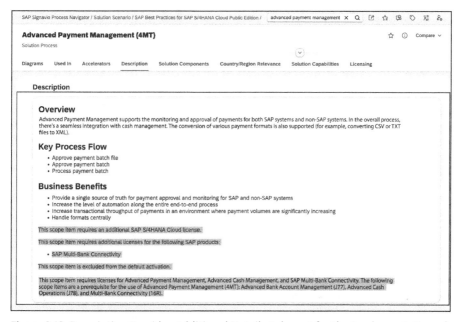

Figure 3.18 Description Provides Additional Details Relevant for the Implementation of Advanced Payment Management (4MT)

The **Accelerators** section contains value accelerators tailored for implementing the solution process. These typical assets include the following:

- **Test scripts**
  Detailed scripts are provided for executing the solution processes with business roles, sample data, and step-by-step execution details. These are very useful especially for new users that need to be guided in the system.

- **Setup instructions**
  Additional setup of integration settings and other setup instructions are provided here for solution processes that require these instructions. Not all solution processes will have setup instructions.

- **Task tutorials**

  These guided enablement materials for business users demonstrate the functionality in easy-to-follow tutorials. The task tutorials are available for many solution processes, and the coverage continues to grow.

In the **Solution Components** section, you'll find a list of software components, packages, or services necessary to technically enable the solution process. In cases when an additional license is required for the solution component, the information is displayed on the component that requires additional licensing, as shown in Figure 3.19, which also shows the **Country/Region Relevance** section.

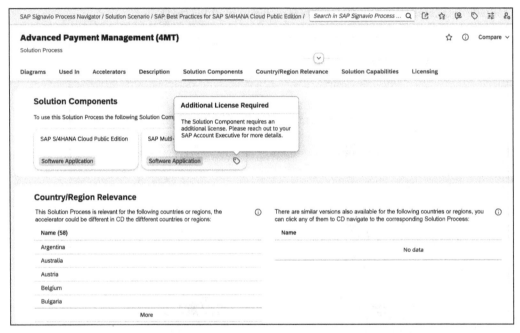

Figure 3.19 Solution Components Section for Solution Process Advanced Payment Management (4MT)

Solution Capabilities refers to the functional ability of one or more software components that address and support specific business objectives. In the context of SAP Signavio Process Navigator, each solution process lists the solution capabilities it supports, organized by higher-level LoBs, as shown in Figure 3.20.

At their core, solution processes typically enhance key solution capabilities within specific industries. Exceptions where solution processes aren't assigned specific industries include solution processes relevant for integrating with generic external cloud solutions, ledger-specific processes, or country-specific processes. In SAP Signavio Process Navigator, we ensure exposure to industries that are specifically relevant, without limitations. You can see the **Industry Relevance** section shown in Figure 3.21.

Figure 3.20 Solution Capability Overview for Solution Process Lot Size of One with Advanced Variant Configuration

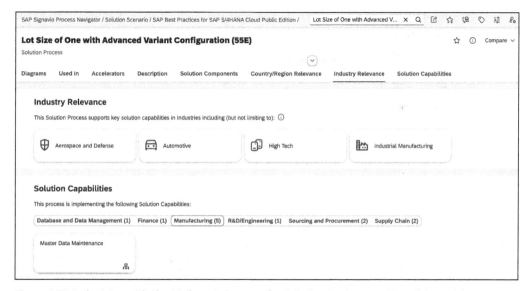

Figure 3.21 Industries with the Highest Relevance for Solution Process Lot Size of One with Advanced Variant Configuration

3.3   SAP Cloud ALM

SAP Cloud ALM is an advanced application lifecycle management (ALM) solution tailored to support customers in implementing and operating their cloud or hybrid solutions. This solution is an integral part of the SAP Activate methodology, providing a comprehensive, guided approach to manage your SAP landscape.

SAP Cloud ALM offers comprehensive lifecycle support, managing the entire application lifecycle from design to operations with built-in, preconfigured, and ready-to-use capabilities that are automatically updated. It supports both cloud-native and hybrid solutions, allowing seamless integration of on-premise and cloud elements. In addition,

SAP Cloud ALM can be provisioned immediately, providing efficient access. Furthermore, it's optimized for SAP technology, running on SAP BTP, and designed for cost efficiency and high performance on SAP HANA.

SAP Cloud ALM is split into two main solutions: SAP Cloud ALM for implementation and SAP Cloud ALM for operations. We'll discuss both in the following sections.

3.3.1   SAP Cloud ALM for Implementation

SAP Cloud ALM for implementation is a comprehensive, cloud-based solution designed to streamline and optimize the management of SAP projects. It centralizes project control, providing real-time visibility into tasks, resources, and timelines. Leveraging the SAP Activate methodology, as shown in Figure 3.22, it guides teams through each project phase, from initiation to go-live, ensuring adherence to best practices. With integrated process management, test management, and change and deployment management, SAP Cloud ALM supports end-to-end capabilities to implement and deploy SAP solutions. Real-time monitoring and analytics enable informed decision-making, ensuring efficient execution and continuous improvement throughout the project lifecycle.

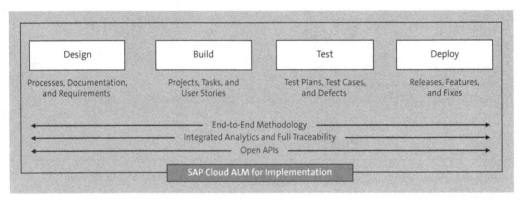

Figure 3.22 SAP Cloud ALM for Implementation

SAP Cloud ALM provides a wide range of features to streamline the project team's workflow. Let's explore them in the following sections.

Benefits

SAP Cloud ALM is a user-friendly and efficient platform for managing implementation projects. Its robust features streamline project management, ensuring reliability from start to finish. For organizations with unique requirements, SAP Cloud ALM's open API strategy offers flexibility in extending functionality. It allows for custom integrations, enhanced reporting, automated workflows, and more, making it adaptable to various business needs. SAP Cloud ALM provides a solid foundation for successful project implementations, with the flexibility to grow and adapt alongside your organization's evolving demands.

Table 3.1 shows the benefits of SAP Cloud ALM for implementation based on user group.

Project Leads	Project Teams	Customers
▪ Instantly available project management platform with no deployment or configuration activities needed ▪ Fast onboarding of and task distribution to your project team ▪ Agile configuration with clear timelines and scope ▪ Faster test planning based on predefined solution processes ▪ Minimized risk by built-in transparency with predefined reporting and traceability dashboards	▪ Clear worklists based on named project tasks, stories, and requirements ▪ Transparency by one central access point to all relevant project data ▪ Accelerated time to value by predefined SAP Activate content and SAP Best Practices solution processes ▪ Predefined user stories and other content assigned to solution processes ▪ Efficient test execution and defect creation	▪ Reduced time to value ▪ Transparency and early results ▪ Stabilized data deployment ▪ Smooth transition to operation ▪ Increased customer satisfaction

Table 3.1 Benefits of SAP Cloud ALM for Implementation

Onboarding and Project Setup

Customers can quickly provision SAP Cloud ALM via SAP for Me, with the system setup taking just a few minutes. SAP Cloud ALM comes preloaded with SAP Activate, SAP Best Practices content, and knowledge of your landscape. The project lead creates a project in SAP Cloud ALM, selecting an SAP Activate roadmap as a task template. All roadmap tasks, including phases, are loaded, and other time information such as project timelines, sprints, milestones, and due dates are manually specified. Team members onboard, receive email invitations, and are assigned tasks based on their roles. The system landscape and deployment plan, including releases, are defined at this stage or later, which is essential for automated testing and change/release management.

Process Management

SAP Cloud ALM offers multiple capabilities for process management as consumption of SAP Best Practices content, scoping, fit-to-standard workshops, and process hierarchies. It gives a comprehensive view of your processes, allowing you to assign custom tags and designate process owners to solution processes. During the fit-to-standard workshop, you can access multilevel SAP Best Practices content, use value flows and solution process flow diagrams, and efficiently capture requirements. In addition, you can attach documents for thorough and detailed documentation.

Figure 3.23 shows the **Open Solution Processes** view in SAP Cloud ALM for implementation in the Processes app, containing a list of solution processes that are within the defined scope.

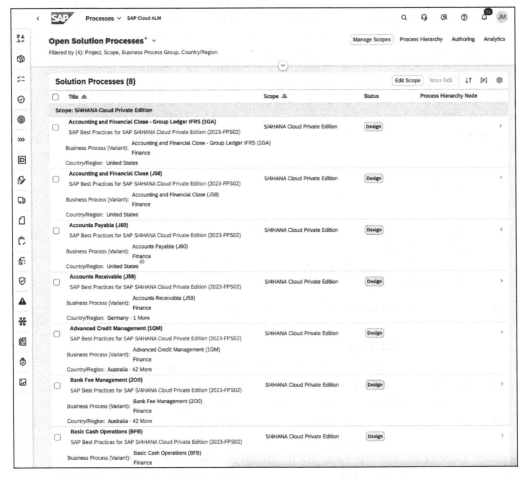

Figure 3.23 Open Solution Process

Figure 3.24 shows how SAP Cloud ALM displays the solution process flow associated with the solution process. In our example, the solution process is **Group Ledger IFRS (1GA)**. The predelivered business processes we discussed in Chapter 4 are available in SAP Cloud ALM to be added to the scope of the project and come with the solution process flow predefined.

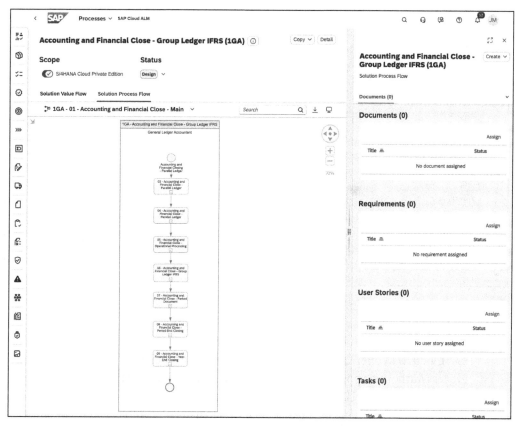

Figure 3.24 Solution Process Flow Diagram

Scoping

After defining the project, the next step in SAP Cloud ALM is to set the scope of the project. The Manage Scopes app allows you to define several scopes and a selection of solution scenarios from the SAP Best Practices relevant for your project. You can even create processes from scratch using the process authoring functionality and then scope them as a part of the project. Following are the main activities:

- **Process scoping**
  After selecting the required solution scenarios, you receive a list of all available solution processes within this solution scenario. You scope each solution process you want to use in your fit-to-standard workshop; an example is shown in Figure 3.25.

- **Process hierarchy**
  Create a central hierarchical structure to organize processes and documentation effectively. Multiple hierarchies can be set up (e.g., by end-to-end process, modular processes, or system architecture). Link elements to these hierarchies and use the Cross-Project Analytics app for an overview.

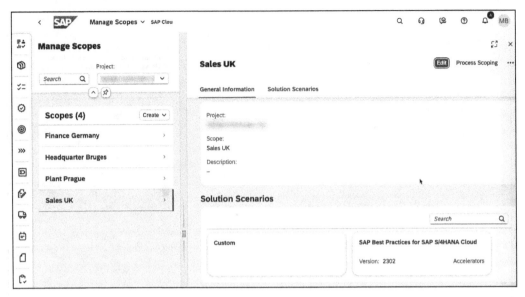

Figure 3.25 Manage Scope

Process Authoring

SAP Cloud ALM offers robust capabilities for managing custom processes through the Process Authoring app. Business process experts can create and maintain custom solution processes, model BPMN diagrams, adapt SAP Best Practices, or import process content from external sources. You can use these custom processes alongside SAP Best Practices content in projects and assign them to your process hierarchy.

Solution processes adhere to the SAP EA Methodology, including solution value flow, process flow, and process flow diagrams. In the **General Information** tab, as shown in Figure 3.26, you can define critical details such as **Title**, **Business Process**, **Country/ Region**, **Solution Component**, and more. These custom processes can be in either a **Draft** or **Published** state. You can scope published processes into projects under the **Custom** solution scenario in the Manage Scope app.

Diving deeper into the **General Information** tab, Figure 3.27 shows the authoring interface for adjusting the solution value flow, and Figure 3.28 shows the interface for adjusting the solution process flow.

These diagrams can be adjusted to reflect the extension of the predelivered business processes as the project team tailors the business process to fit customer needs. These capabilities are typically used as part of the fit-to-standard workshops we'll discuss a little later in this section.

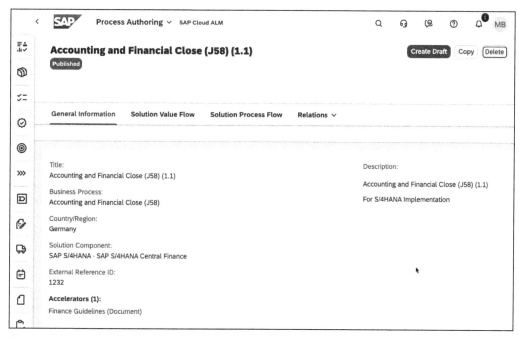

Figure 3.26 Process Authoring: General Information

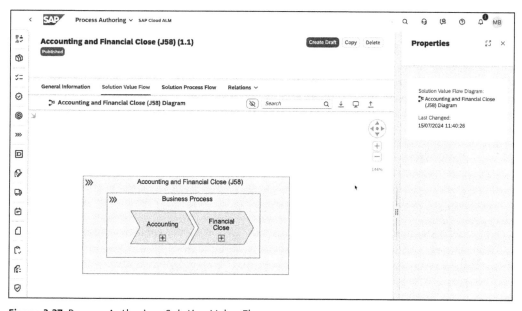

Figure 3.27 Process Authoring: Solution Value Flow

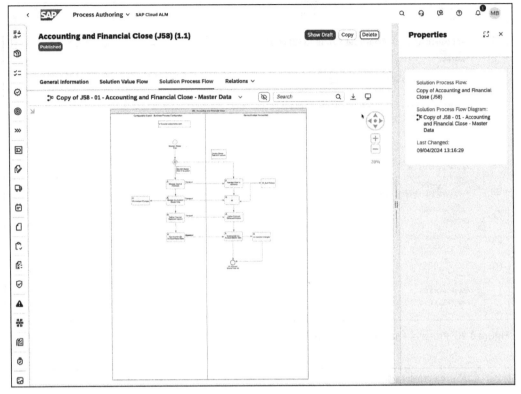

Figure 3.28 Process Authoring: Solution Process Flow

Custom processes can be imported into SAP Cloud ALM using the Custom Process API or directly in the Process Authoring app. The API supports a range of actions, including creating, updating, and deleting process artifacts. You can directly import BPMN files or Scalable Vector Graphics (SVG) process diagrams through the user interface (UI). For detailed information on API options, refer to the API reference available on SAP Business Accelerator Hub at *http://s-prs.co/v596614*.

Fit-to-Standard Workshops

Fit-to-standard workshops in SAP Cloud ALM provide a valuable opportunity for customers to validate SAP Best Practices and pinpoint any additional requirements or necessary adjustments. During these workshops, customers review standard SAP processes to determine whether they should be implemented as is or tailored to better fit their needs. This visualization of business processes facilitates productive discussion and helps organize and prepare the fit-to-standard workshops. Participants can identify gaps or additional needs that require development beyond the standard processes. Any required changes or new requirements can be directly addressed and assigned to the solution processes during the workshop.

You can capture new requirements from scratch in the requirements app, from processes during workshops, or even mass upload using the Microsoft Excel import.

Requirements can be broken down into several user stories for defining the specific tasks the development and configuration experts need to execute. All user stories can be assigned to teams or project members in SAP Cloud ALM as follow-up activities.

Documentation

SAP Cloud ALM centralizes and streamlines documentation management across the project lifecycle, making it easier to access and reuse. It allows the creation, linking, and management of various types of documentation, ensuring consistency and efficiency.

The central Documents app, as shown in Figure 3.29, consolidates all your documentation in one place, including interface specifications, technical designs, and training manuals. You can create new documents, filter and search existing ones, and manage imports and exports. For bulk imports, a template is available to streamline the process using Microsoft Excel.

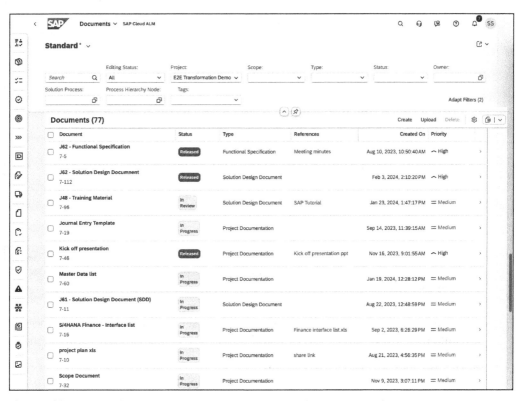

Figure 3.29 Documents App

The **Create** button opens a text editor for crafting documents, categorizing them, and linking them to local or external repositories. Each document entry includes a status, priority, ID, assigned owner, and details about who created or modified it and when, as shown in Figure 3.30. Tags allow you to add customer-specific attributes. For external documents such as Microsoft Word files, Microsoft Excel spreadsheets, or Microsoft PowerPoint presentations, you can store them in local repositories such as Microsoft SharePoint and link them via URL references.

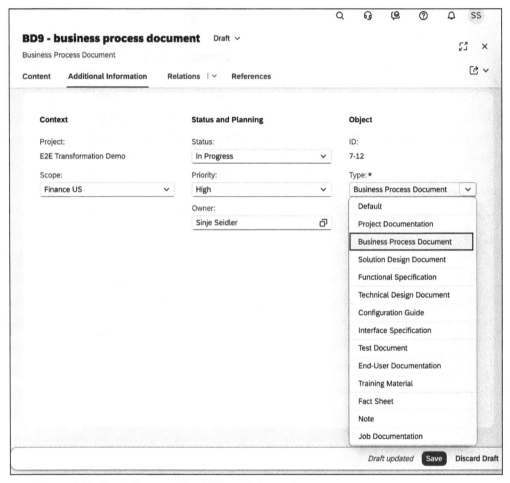

Figure 3.30 Create Document: Additional Information

The **Relations** tab, as shown in Figure 3.31, enables users to link documents to processes, requirements, tasks, and defects, organizing them in a hierarchical structure for better management.

SAP Cloud ALM users can use the analytical view **Solution Process Traceability** to track completeness of solution documentation. It provides the user with a comprehensive overview of the process implementation status from various angles, including requirements, solution documentation, and testing. This is facilitated through dashboards and traceability features, offering clear insights into document status and assignments, as shown in Figure 3.32.

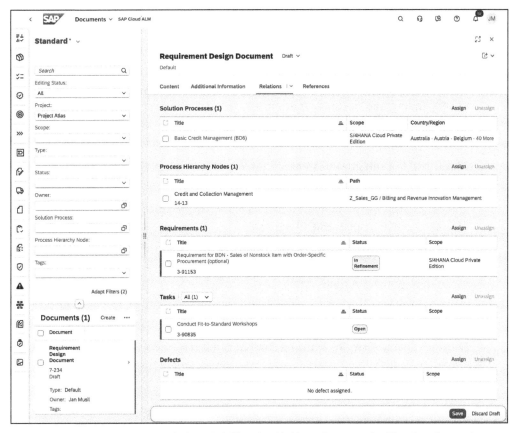

Figure 3.31 Create Document: Relations Tab Showing Linking a Document with a Requirement

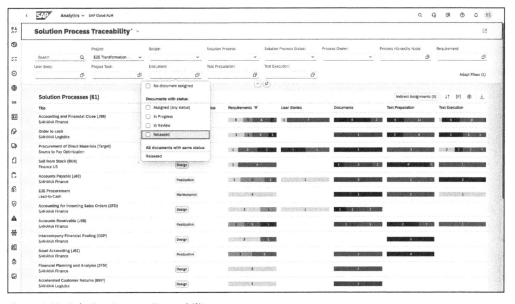

Figure 3.32 Solution Process Traceability

The open API for **Documents** can be used to exchange training material with SAP Enable Now. SAP Cloud ALM supports the inclusion of business process descriptions directly within the tool or through supplementary documents, which is essential for defining custom processes. Integrating with SAP Enable Now enhances training purposes by offering visual representations and system demos of processes, improving understanding and boosting training efficiency. Some best practice processes come with SAP Enable Now recordings, allowing customers to see how processes are executed in the software and providing a comprehensive, hands-on learning experience.

There are a few integration steps to connect SAP Enable Now and SAP Cloud ALM, as shown in Figure 3.33:

❶ As a first step, the tool integration must be set up by connecting the SAP Enable Now work area to a scope in SAP Cloud ALM.

❷ The project scope process content can then be transferred to SAP Enable Now. This simplifies the work of the learning content owner and gives a common structure for the content in both tools.

❸ Now the project documentation created and managed in SAP Cloud ALM can be transferred to SAP Enable Now.

❹ In SAP Enable Now, the learning content can be created using the provided feature to create e-learnings, tutorials, and end-user documentation.

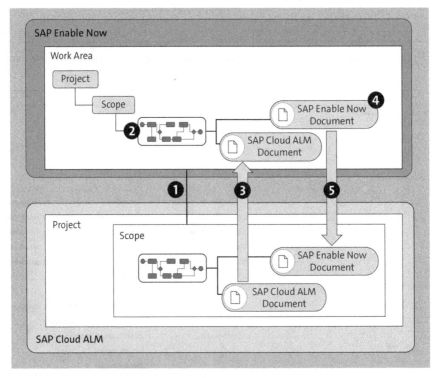

Figure 3.33 Documentation: SAP Enable Now Steps

❺ In the last step, this learning content can be transferred back to SAP Cloud ALM. Here, it can now be tracked as part of the solution process traceability and accessed from the Processes or Documents apps.

During future software changes, the integration can be used to update material to provide the latest documentation to the end user.

Project and Task Management

SAP Cloud ALM significantly accelerates project setup and task management with its integration of SAP Activate, offering a robust starting point for implementation projects. The platform includes several predefined tasks that can be efficiently distributed and managed beyond simple Microsoft Excel lists. Project leads can assign tasks to roles before the project begins, organizing the complete project plan and task distribution in advance. This feature ensures that when onboarding team members, you immediately assign their tasks for the entire project duration. This approach is especially beneficial in the early stages of a project, where time pressure is often high. Project managers quickly set up comprehensive project plans by leveraging these predefined roadmaps, including accelerators such as templates for meeting minutes and kickoff meetings, guaranteeing a streamlined and efficient project start. Users filter, group, and search tasks; view task history; and track project progress through built-in dashboards. This approach ensures seamless project execution, enhanced visibility, and effective resource management. For example, the RISE with SAP roadmap includes accelerators, predefined quality gates, and checklists that provide clear guidelines and structured task management to support project success.

SAP Cloud ALM initially allowed for the use of SAP Activate roadmaps as templates for project guidance, but this was limited to a single product roadmap per project. Recognizing that most implementation projects now involve integrating multiple products, SAP Activate has expanded its capabilities to include combinable roadmaps for various products. Now, SAP Cloud ALM supports the use of these multiple roadmaps within a single implementation project.

Depending on your project's scope and the integration scenarios between the products involved, you can use **Combinable Roadmaps** in the Projects and Setup app when you're creating a new project. In the app, you'll pick relevant SAP Activate roadmaps from the list to create a tailored combined implementation roadmap for your project, as shown in Figure 3.34. You'll find tasks related to different products from the selected roadmaps in the task list, as shown in Figure 3.35.

This enhanced functionality allows for efficient management of cross-product activities within a single implementation project, streamlining your project planning and execution process. This new capability enables you to manage cross-product activities within a single implementation project efficiently.

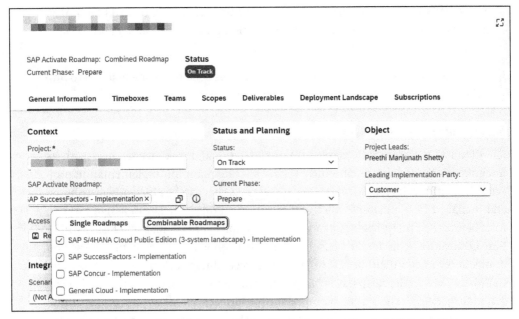

Figure 3.34 Combinable Roadmaps: During the Project Creation in SAP Cloud ALM

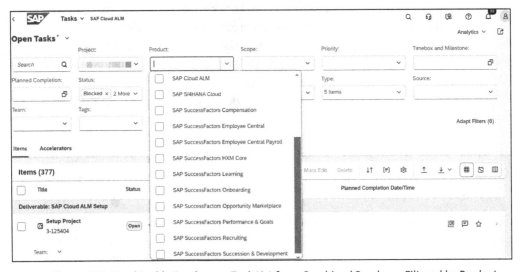

Figure 3.35 Combinable Roadmaps: Task List from Combined Roadmap Filtered by Product

RISE with SAP Methodology: Clean Core Success Plan and Quality Gates

SAP Activate has enhanced the RISE with SAP methodology roadmap by introducing a clean core-focused success plan (refer to Chapter 2, Section 2.4), which includes essential clean core-specific tasks, milestones, and key performance indicators (KPIs) that are crucial for achieving a clean core. This roadmap can be leveraged in your projects to kick-start your clean core journey.

SAP Activate has enhanced the SAP S/4HANA Cloud Private Edition implementation, system conversion, and selective data transition methodology roadmaps with critical assets to support customers embracing the clean core strategy. In SAP Cloud ALM, the content delivered for clean core is available as a dedicated roadmap called **RISE with SAP Methodology - clean core success plan**, as shown in Figure 3.36, and also as part of the new implementation, system conversions, and selective data transition methodology roadmaps.

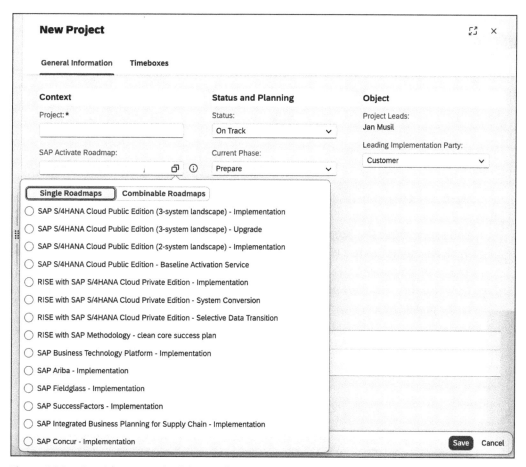

Figure 3.36 RISE with SAP Methodology - Clean Core Success Plan

When you assign this roadmap to your project, you gain access to detailed guidance on task execution and quality gates for each phase—critical milestones tracked in the RISE with SAP methodology. These quality gates come pre-populated with questionnaires that should be completed during the quality gate review at the end of each phase.

As we discussed in Chapter 2, SAP Activate provides customers following the clean core strategy with dedicated clean core quality gates. They are reflected in SAP Cloud ALM in the form of clean core quality gate checklists. You can see example of a clean core quality gate checklist for new implementations in Figure 3.37.

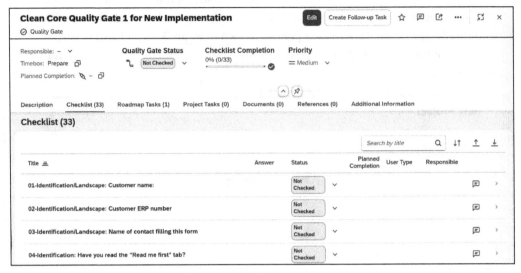

Figure 3.37 Clean Core Quality Gate Checklist

You can monitor the progress of the clean core success plan and the associated runbook directly from the Overview app, as shown in Figure 3.38, ensuring a streamlined and focused approach to achieving not only clean core but also overall project success. Note that the Overview app can be tailored to show progress across various dimensions of the project by leveraging the predefined cards and adjusting the filter options.

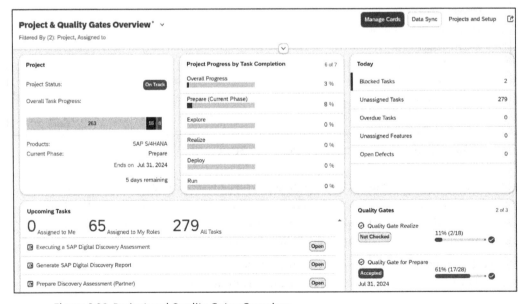

Figure 3.38 Project and Quality Gates Overview

Test Management

SAP Cloud ALM simplifies the testing process by supporting manual and automated test case preparation and execution. Developers and architects conduct initial tests, followed by acceptance testing by end users or key users to confirm that the requirements have been met. This process can be organized through detailed test plans, as shown in Figure 3.39, allowing for coordinated and efficient testing within multiple test cycles using the Test Plans app.

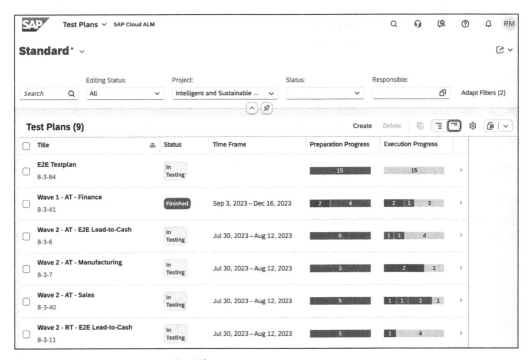

Figure 3.39 Test Management: Test Plans

One of the significant benefits of SAP Cloud ALM is the process-oriented import of test cases. Available information such as process flows can be reused to create new test cases or even whole test assets for SAP S/4HANA can be imported from SAP Best Practices content to save substantial effort and time when creating manual test cases. For public cloud environments, predefined automated test cases are available within the test automation tool for SAP S/4HANA Cloud Public Edition, which is seamlessly integrated in SAP Cloud ALM.

You can create, categorize, and link test cases to requirements and user stories for enhanced traceability. Testers can perform manual tests by following the detailed scripts developed during the preparation phase. SAP Cloud ALM supports manual test cases and integration of automation engines for testing such as test automation tool for SAP S/4HANA Cloud Public Edition and Tricentis Test Automation. It also supports documenting the execution results, capturing screenshots, and recording any discrepancies observed during testing. SAP Cloud ALM also allows users to log, track, and manage defects identified during testing. It supports seamless collaboration between testers and developers to ensure timely resolution of issues. Comprehensive dashboards and analytics provide insights into testing progress, helping your team prioritize and resolve issues effectively, which ensures high-quality and reliable deployment.

Defects can be recorded and tracked through detailed defect views, which include descriptions, related test cases, references, and status updates. This ensures that all issues are addressed promptly and don't hinder the implementation process.

Change and Release Management

SAP Cloud ALM boosts change enablement by integrating various deployment tools, orchestrating transport requests, and ensuring smooth software and configuration changes. This centralized approach simplifies the management of software updates and configuration adjustments, keeping all stakeholders informed about upcoming changes and go-live activities.

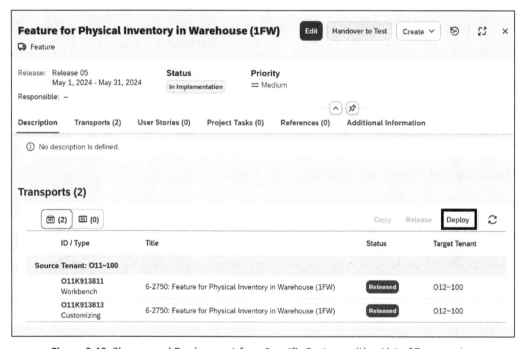

Figure 3.40 Change and Deployment for a Specific Feature with a List of Transports

Features act as containers for the transports required for solution customization. They can be used to deploy customization and development objects across your system landscape, whether for private cloud or on-premise environments. For the public cloud, SAP Cloud ALM supports the central tracking of transports and multiple transport management tools: ABAP-based Change and Transport System used in SAP S/4HANA Cloud Private Edition and on-premise, transport management system (TMS) in SAP S/4HANA Cloud Public Edition, and SAP Cloud Transport Management for all transports and extension built on SAP BTP. SAP Cloud ALM is the orchestration engine that makes sure everything goes consistently to production. The UI of the transport deployment related to one feature is shown in Figure 3.40.

The **Feature Traceability** view in the Analytics app provides a clear view of the current deployment status, as shown in Figure 3.41, ensuring a smooth transition from business requirements to technical execution. Features can encompass multiple transports or a combination of transports and configurations across different systems, which is crucial for integrated software solutions. Once the work on a feature is complete, its status is updated, and the development moves to the quality system for testing. This thorough testing process ensures reliability and success before final deployment.

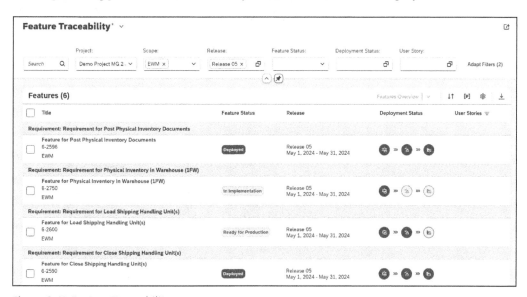

Figure 3.41 Feature Traceability

Analytics

SAP Cloud ALM for implementation provides powerful reports and analytical tools to manage, track, and optimize your implementation projects. It offers a comprehensive suite of options to meet diverse monitoring and reporting needs by transforming change events from various project management applications into meaningful insights. It enables timely, data-driven decision-making through intuitive dashboards and detailed reports.

The **Overview** page serves as a high-level indicator of project progress across various areas and functions as a health check monitor for each card shown. Each card corresponds to a specific topic and presents relevant information related to that topic's projects and also offers drilldown functionality for applications within SAP Cloud ALM. You also can personalize the overview page to suit your role's needs.

The **Analytics Overview** page, as shown in Figure 3.42, acts as a container for detailed standalone analytical pages and includes reports, historical charts, and traceability matrix charts specific to a project. The page enables deeper insights and extensive drilldown capabilities. You can filter and refine your reports for more detailed insight.

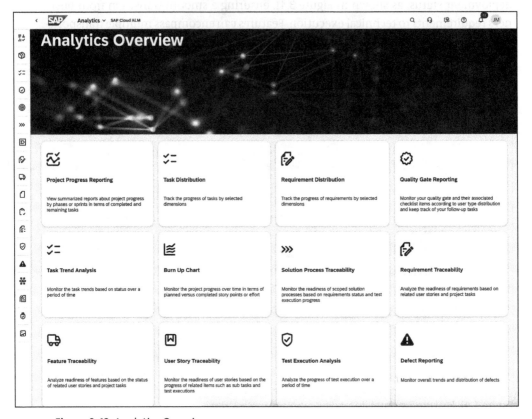

Figure 3.42 Analytics Overview

Table 3.2 provides a list of analytical applications that are currently being offered in the **Analytics Overview** page.

Feature	Purpose
Project Progress Reporting	Provides summarized reports on project progress in terms of completed, remaining and overdue tasks for phases, sprints, milestones, or deliverables. For sprints, it offers tracking based on tasks, effort, or story points.
Task Distribution	Allows granular level of tracking task progresses across various dimensions such as scope, teams, tags, responsible person, or workstreams.
Requirement Distribution	Allows granular level of tracking requirements distributed across various dimensions such as scope, teams, tags, responsible person, or workstreams.
Task Trend Analysis	Monitors task trends over time, using the timebox filter to analyze status changes.
Burn Up Chart	Tracks project progress by comparing completed work to total work using story points and effort metrics.
Solution Process Traceability	Analyzes the readiness of your scoped solution processes based on the progress of related requirements and test executions.
Requirement Traceability	Analyzes readiness of requirements based on the progress of related tasks, features, and test cases. With this tool, you can drill down from the highest level to the lowest level of the entities.
Feature Traceability	Analyzes the readiness of your features based on the progress of its related objects such as user stories, project tasks, and assigned transports.
User Story Traceability	Analyzes the readiness of user stories based on the progress of related items such as subtasks and test executions.
Test Execution Analysis	Shows the test execution progress history grouped by status, test actions, scope, and test plan.
Defects Reporting	Analyzes the overall trends and day-to-day status of defects resolution.

Table 3.2 Analytical Pages Available in the Analytics App

The **Cross-Project Analysis** page in the Cross-Project Overview app is designed for a higher-level view of progress across multiple projects. This page offers standalone cross-project analytical pages to display assignments with their status across multiple projects. It also aggregates data to provide a combined overview at a program level or for specific releases. You can access this analytical page directly from the **Cross-Project Overview** home screen, as shown in Figure 3.43.

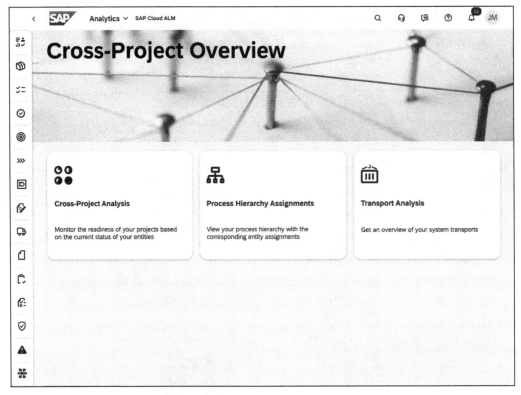

Figure 3.43 Cross-Project Overview App

Table 3.3 provides a list of cross-project analytical applications that are currently being offered in the **Cross-Project Overview**.

Feature	Purpose
Cross-Project Analysis	Provides summarized reports on project progress in terms of completed, remaining, and overdue tasks for phases, sprints, milestones, or deliverables. For sprints, it offers tracking based on tasks, effort, or story points.
Process Hierarchy Assignments	Provides an overview granular structure of process hierarchy nodes, along with the status of its assigned elements allowing for deeper insights into relationships.
Transport Analysis	Provides an overview of your system transports across projects.

Table 3.3 Available Cross-Project Analytical Pages

Application Programming Interfaces

SAP Cloud ALM APIs make it simple to extend SAP Cloud ALM functionalities to provide new features, services, and applications for your SAP application lifecycle. It helps to integrate all ALM tools to ensure that organizations are well-equipped with a platform that can easily integrate with any IT or ALM tools. It ensures accelerated implementation and smooth operations of your end-to-end business solution throughout the entire lifecycle.

With the SAP Cloud ALM API management capabilities, you have three options to integrate all ALM tools:

- Use the direct built-in integration provided by SAP Cloud ALM for selected products such as Tricentis, ServiceNow, Grafana, and SAP Analytics Cloud, to name a few.
- Implement the open APIs available in SAP Cloud ALM with a scope that covers all SAP Cloud ALM processes for implementation and operations.
- Build integration applications and services to combine the SAP Cloud ALM APIs and the SAP platform's functionalities for extensions.

SAP Cloud ALM defines a set of areas called *extension spaces* where partners can innovate and expand standard functionalities. There are areas not covered by the standard set of functionalities to provide opportunities for partners to develop new products and services. SAP Cloud ALM provides APIs to support such extensions in the following areas: incident/problem management, reverse process engineering/process mining, and advanced project management.

Further Resources

The following links contain more information about APIs in this context:
- "Motivation and Concept": *http://s-prs.co/v596615*
- "What's New for SAP Cloud ALM APIs": *http://s-prs.co/v596616*

3.3.2   SAP Cloud ALM for Operations

After implementing the customer solution, it's usually handed over to operations. Today, many challenges are found in solution landscapes, and a company's solution landscape is subject to transformation, including transformation from a monolithic to a hybrid and cloud-centric landscape. The complexity of end-to-end monitoring is also increasing. Therefore, transparency in the communication between the different services and the execution of end-to-end business processes of the intelligent suite is required. SAP Cloud ALM for operations is the latest cloud-based ALM solution and therefore the ideal central solution to address these challenges for cloud-centric companies. SAP Cloud ALM for operations ensures business continuity in the entire landscape via monitoring and alerting, and it increases efficiency by automating operations tasks. It empowers customers to understand the health, availability, and performance of their business solutions, independent of whether they are operated by themselves, other service providers, or by SAP.

Figure 3.44 provides the functional overview of SAP Cloud ALM for operations. SAP Cloud ALM for operations supports the whole problem management process starting from problem detection, over to problem routing, and finally problem resolution. Starting from the inbound integration, SAP Cloud ALM for operations can collect metrics, configuration items, log entries, events, and alerts from the solution landscape for different use cases, such as business process monitoring, integration and exception monitoring, synthetic and real user monitoring, job and automation monitoring, configuration and security analysis, and health monitoring. These use cases can create events, which are distributed by the intelligent event processing to the different problem resolution channels. To manage the problem resolution channels, SAP Cloud ALM for operations includes alert management, notification management, possibilities for operations automation, and management of external APIs. Depending on the process on the outbound side, the events can therefore result in tickets, tasks, emails, chats, operation flows, and external tools to show analytics and raw data. Furthermore, SAP Cloud ALM for operations includes several embedded functionalities for analytics and intelligence. SAP Cloud ALM for operations also features an overarching business service management, including functionalities such as service level management and a detailed event calendar to provide an overview on the status of the solution landscapes at any time.

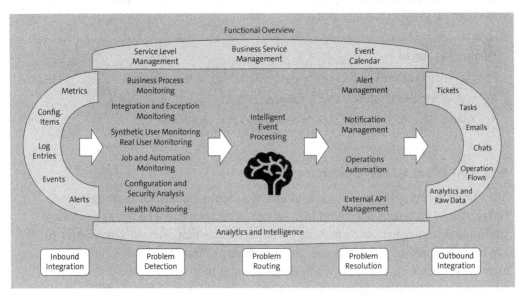

Figure 3.44 SAP Cloud ALM for Operations: Available and Planned Scope

SAP Cloud ALM for operations covers the following use cases:

- **Business service management**
  Business service management includes a business event calendar and business service availability management. In this application, SAP Cloud ALM consolidates the information derived from single technical services to business services. The target group of business service management is business and IT, so the relevant information

is maintained and visualized at the business service level as a kind of common language between business and IT.

- **Business process monitoring**
  By focusing on business process KPIs and documents, business process monitoring provides transparency into the end-to-end processes of the entire intelligent suite. Business process monitoring monitors process health, detects anomalies during process execution, and enables LoB users—but also IT users—to directly identify process disruptions and react to them.

- **Integration and exception monitoring**
  Integration and exception monitoring ensures reliable data exchange processes at the application level in cloud-only and hybrid scenarios. It provides end-to-end monitoring across different SAP cloud services and applications based on the SAP passport mechanism. Integration and exception monitoring closes the gap between business and IT during the issue-resolution process (technical issue versus business issue).

- **User and performance monitoring**
  User and performance monitoring allows you to monitor end-user requests across components and technologies. This type of monitoring is based on synthetic probes (synthetic user monitoring) or real user load (real user monitoring). With real user monitoring, you'll get visibility into the frontends and into the involved cloud services and systems. Synthetic user monitoring provides a simulation of end-user behavior based on scenarios that are scripted and deployed as robots. Figure 3.45 shows the SAP Cloud ALM UI for **Real User Monitoring**.

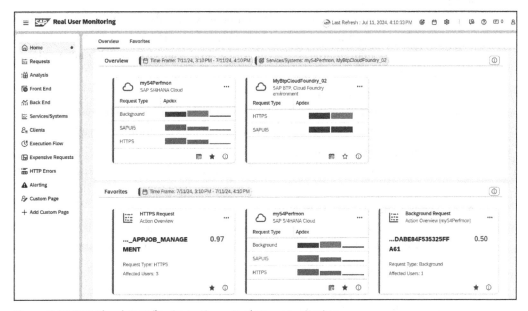

Figure 3.45 SAP Cloud ALM for Operations: Real User Monitoring

- **Job and automation monitoring**
  Besides monitoring of classical jobs, as used in ABAP-based components, the monitoring of automation environments such as SAP Intelligent Robotic Process Automation (SAP Intelligent RPA) and SAP Workflow Management also becomes more and more relevant. Job and automation monitoring addresses mainly IT users, but business users also may be interested in information for business-critical jobs.

- **Configuration and security analysis**
  In the configuration and security analysis application, you can display the items of the technical configuration using the store browser. For selected time frames, changes in these configuration items can be displayed. Thus, configuration and security analysis can be used to supervise in particular security-relevant settings in the landscape.

- **Health monitoring**
  In contrast to system monitoring, SAP Cloud ALM for operations offers health monitoring to monitor components without a dedicated landscape model and auto-discovery. Attributes describing the managed cloud service or system are sent together with the monitoring information. Heath monitoring is offered for on-premise components and for cloud services.

- **External monitoring of metrics and events**
  SAP Cloud ALM for operations will be able to retrieve metrics and events from external monitoring and alerting tools (third-party or open source). This can be relevant to get the complete picture for a solution landscape to cover IT infrastructure aspects or non-SAP components.

- **Intelligent event processing**
  With intelligent event processing, SAP Cloud ALM introduced dedicated event management that can handle events independently on alerts. This is the foundation for correlating manually generated events (e.g., end-user tickets) with automatically generated events (e.g., alerts).

- **Embedded alert management**
  Alerts are calculated per monitoring use case and are visualized in the use case-specific alert inboxes, which are directly embedded into the monitoring applications.

- **Embedded analytics and intelligence**
  Embedded analytics enables use case-specific root-cause analyses and works with raw data as it's collected, as well as with historical data that is aggregated.

- **Embedded operation automation**
  SAP Cloud ALM for operations provides a built-in integration to SAP Build Process Automation, SAP Automation Pilot, SAP Workflow Management, and SAP Intelligent RPA. The goal is to use the content already provided by these platforms for cloud-centric landscapes.

SAP has decided to adopt OpenTelemetry as the standard for observability in SAP Cloud ALM for operations. This decision will simplify the integration of external tools, allowing for the exchange of raw data with third-party tools. OpenTelemetry will also facilitate the onboarding of existing services into SAP Cloud ALM for operations, including SAP software as a service (SaaS) and platform as a service (PaaS) offerings. Regardless of whether the code is managed by SAP or custom-built, OpenTelemetry will be the standard for data retrieval, making it easier to collect data for the different SAP Cloud ALM for operations use cases.

In conclusion, SAP Cloud ALM for operations is the recommended central observability platform for all applications in the solution landscape, with context-sensitive navigation into service-specific local observability tools. While SAP Cloud ALM is the primary tool for problem detection, the local tools are used for deeper root-cause analysis. This central approach allows for unification across various products and custom applications.

3.3.3   Transition from SAP Solution Manager to SAP Cloud ALM

While the previous edition of this book discussed the role and use of SAP Solution Manager, we decided not to cover SAP Solution Manager in this edition. The main reason is the upcoming end of mainstream maintenance at the end of 2027. We recommend all new customers to adopt SAP Cloud ALM and customers currently on SAP Solution Manager are advised to start planning their transition to SAP Cloud ALM. Customers should utilize the **SAP Activate for Transition to SAP Cloud ALM** roadmap for planning and performing the transition to SAP Cloud ALM. You can access the roadmap in SAP Activate Roadmap Viewer (see Figure 3.46) and in SAP Cloud ALM.

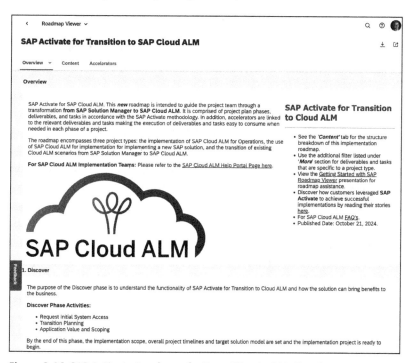

Figure 3.46 SAP Activate Roadmap for Transition to SAP Cloud ALM

SAP recommends customers to transition from SAP Solution Manager to SAP Cloud ALM in the following stages:

1. **Perform switch to SAP Cloud ALM for service and operations**
   This first step enables you to monitor your landscape without additional agents, provides access to additional monitoring use cases, and provides integrated capabilities for services delivery.

2. **Adopt SAP Cloud ALM for implementation**
   Plan and perform the transition of implementation capabilities to SAP Cloud ALM at your own pace.

   Optionally, this step will enable you to leverage implementation functionality we've introduced earlier in this chapter, including requirements management, process management, testing, and more. Table 3.4 outlines some of the data transfer aspects for the process management and testing capabilities.

SAP Solution Manager Capability	SAP Cloud ALM Capability	Data Transfer Aspects
Process management	Process management, documentation, and authoring	Selective data transfer planned for the following: ■ Business process hierarchy ■ Documents ■ Diagrams ■ Libraries ■ Custom Processes
Test suite	Test management	Selective data transfer planned for test cases and test steps

Table 3.4 Transition of Implementation Capabilities

Selective data transfer facilitates migrating relevant data from SAP Solution Manager to SAP Cloud ALM. This approach allows you to tailor the scope and modify data in a single step. It also allows you to combine the redesign of ALM processes with retaining important data aligned to secure your investments.

The readiness check and selective data transfer features streamline the transition to SAP Cloud ALM for customers already using SAP Solution Manager or Focused Build. The readiness check evaluates the current functionalities and identifies their counterparts in SAP Cloud ALM, ensuring that critical features support the new environment.

SAP provides support through the SAP Readiness Check for SAP Cloud ALM, transition methodologies, a roadmap, implementation services, tools for data transfer, APIs, and guidance for typical customer scenarios.

3. **If required, add Focused Run for SAP Solution Manager**
   This is an optional step for customers that require system management capabilities, for instance, customers that have advanced needs to operate hybrid landscapes or have landscapes of significant size and variety of on-premise systems, and/or service provider businesses. We recommend running one scenario exclusively on a single ALM platform for example running system monitoring in Focused Run and integration monitoring in SAP Cloud ALM.

SAP Cloud ALM Product Roadmap

SAP Cloud ALM will continue to evolve in the future. You can review the current state of planning for SAP Cloud ALM in the product roadmap, which provides an overview of planned capabilities for the next few rolling quarters. You can find it at *http://s-prs.co/ v546304*.

Further Resources

For more information about SAP Cloud ALM, check out *Introducing SAP Cloud ALM for Implementations* by Jagmohan Singh Chawla, Wulff-Heinrich Knapp, and Nicolas Alech (SAP PRESS, 2022, *www.sap-press.com/5477*).

3.4 Summary

This chapter introduced the key tools for accessing SAP Activate content: the Roadmap Viewer, which you can use to access the SAP Activate methodology, its descriptions, and accelerators, and the SAP Signavio Process Navigator, which provides you with easy access to the documentation of the ready-to-run business processes delivered in SAP Best Practices and the enterprise management layer for SAP S/4HANA Cloud Private Edition documentation.

We also introduced the concept of ALM and explained how project teams can use tools such as SAP Cloud ALM to control and manage implementation projects and their system environments. We'll use this information in later chapters when we dive into the details of the deployment strategies for SAP S/4HANA Cloud.

In the next chapter, we'll talk about how project teams gain speed when they start with a working system based on SAP Best Practices or the enterprise management layer for SAP S/4HANA.

Chapter 4
Starting with a Working System

SAP Activate uses the principle of "showing and telling" over just telling to help business users understand the capabilities of the solution that's being implemented. Teams should prepare a working system for their show-and-tell sessions in the fit-to-standard workshops. Now, let's discuss the business process content project teams can use to set up the running environment.

One of the foundations of SAP Activate is to start with a working system based on ready-to-use business processes in SAP S/4HANA Cloud. While we often emphasize the use of SAP Best Practices for setting up the working system in some sections of the book, there are other packages that can be used to set up the working environment in SAP S/4HANA Cloud as well. This chapter focuses on introducing the two main sets of packages that SAP delivers for your use: SAP Best Practices and the enterprise management layer for SAP S/4HANA. We introduced the tools that you can use to access this content in the previous chapter, so here we'll drill down into the structure of the content and ways to activate it in your environment.

4.1   SAP Best Practices for SAP S/4HANA

SAP delivers regular updates for SAP Best Practices for SAP S/4HANA Cloud and SAP Best Practices for SAP S/4HANA. In this section, we'll discuss the content available in both packages and provide examples of assets that you can access in SAP Signavio Process Navigator and in SAP Cloud ALM.

4.1.1   SAP S/4HANA Cloud Public Edition

SAP Best Practices for SAP S/4HANA Cloud Public Edition provides ready-to-use business process content for core business processes in finance, human resources, sourcing and procurement, manufacturing, professional services, R&D/engineering, sales, service, and supply chain. Figure 4.1 shows the scope information for SAP Best Practices for SAP S/4HANA Cloud Public Edition 2402, which you can find on the main page in the SAP Signavio Process Navigator.

These predelivered processes are supported by SAP Fiori for a role-specific, intuitive, and simple user experience (UX). In the following sections, we'll outline all the assets that you can access in SAP Best Practices in SAP Signavio Process Navigator, including the What's New Viewer and the release assessment and scope dependency tool.

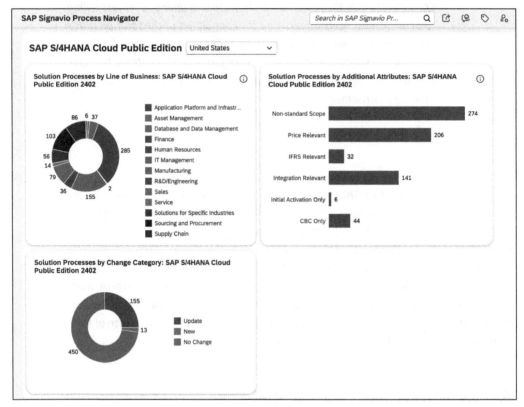

Figure 4.1 Scope of SAP Best Practices for SAP S/4HANA Cloud Public Edition in SAP Signavio Process Navigator

> **SAP Best Practices Scope**
>
> We won't list the current scope of the SAP Best Practices content in this book; by the time it reaches you, the content will have been updated a few times by SAP as the SAP S/4HANA Cloud Public Edition content gets updated several times a year. We recommend that you access the content in SAP Signavio Process Navigator at *https:// me.sap.com/processnavigator/HomePage.*

Structure of the Content

The hierarchical structure of the SAP Best Practices content starts with the *solution scenario,* which serves as the entity that groups together all relevant solution processes items into the line of business (LoB) groups, such as finance, sourcing and procurement, supply chain, manufacturing, and so on. Each of these groups is then split into sub-groups that correspond to business functions; for example, the finance group contains subgroups for accounting and financial close, advanced financial operations, enterprise risk and compliance, and so on.

You can navigate the content in SAP Signavio Process Navigator by expanding the selected group and subgroups in the **Line of Business** section to access specific **Solution Processes**, as shown in Figure 4.2. Note that the updated solution processes are highlighted with the **Update** label in the listing.

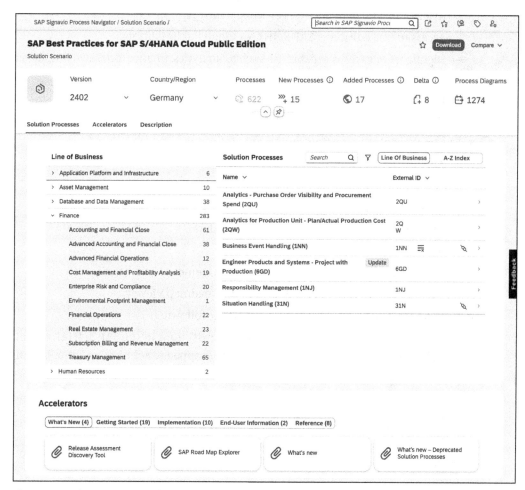

Figure 4.2 Solution Scenario for SAP Best Practices for SAP S/4HANA Cloud Public Edition 2402

In addition, the solution scenario contains the description of the content in the **Description** section and additional accelerators that you can see at the bottom of Figure 4.2. This information is provided to help you understand the solution scope, organizational structure, chart of accounts, key master data that is delivered in the preconfigured solution, and additional details about the preconfigured solution. You can find these assets in the **Accelerators** tab in SAP Signavio Process Navigator.

The key assets and resources on the **Accelerators** tab are as follows:

- The **What's New** section contains the following:
  - Release assessment discovery tool
  - SAP Road Map Explorer
  - What's new
  - What's new—specifically for deprecated solution processes
- The **Getting Started** section contains the following:
  - Availability and dependencies of scope items
  - Access to trial edition of SAP S/4HANA Cloud Public Edition
  - Highlights of various capabilities such as analytics, finance, product compliance, and so on
  - Link to SAP Cloud ALM
  - Note on language availability
- The **Implementation** section contains the following:
  - Application programming interfaces (APIs) on SAP Help
  - Link to business-driven configuration questionnaires
  - List of configuration apps
  - Guidance for creation of your own master data
  - Accelerator with fiscal year variants
  - Preparation steps to test public sector management in the starter system
  - Links to SAP Activate methodology in the Roadmap Viewer
- The **End-User Information** section contains the following:
  - Accelerator with an overview of apps or transactions in the SAP S/4HANA Cloud Public Edition system and how they can be mapped to solution activities that are described by solution processes
  - Task tutorials
- The **Reference** section contains the following:
  - Chart of accounts
  - Financial statement items
  - Forms
  - Master data overview
  - Organizational data overview
  - Preconfigured general ledger account master data for YCOA (global)
  - Preconfigured general ledger account master data for YCOA (local)
  - Preconfigured tax codes

Note

This list is based on the information delivered with release 2402 of SAP S/4HANA Cloud Public Edition; assets may change in future releases.

Now let's look at the individual solution process and the information and assets that are available to you in SAP Signavio Process Navigator. Each *solution process* (also referred to as a scope item) comes with a diagram showing the solution process flow; accelerators providing assets such as setup instructions, task tutorial, and test script that we'll discuss later; and a description of the functionality the scope item delivers, including the business benefits. Additionally, the solution process details provide additional information such as assignment to a solution component(s), country/regional relevance, industry relevance, and list of solution capabilities. For more information, refer to Chapter 3, Section 3.2. Figure 4.3 and Figure 4.4 show examples of one solution process (also referred to as a scope item), **Requisitioning (18J)**, with the previously described content and assets. Figure 4.3 also shows the solution process flow, and Figure 4.4 also displays the assigned accelerators, solution process description, a list of key process flows, and the key business benefits.

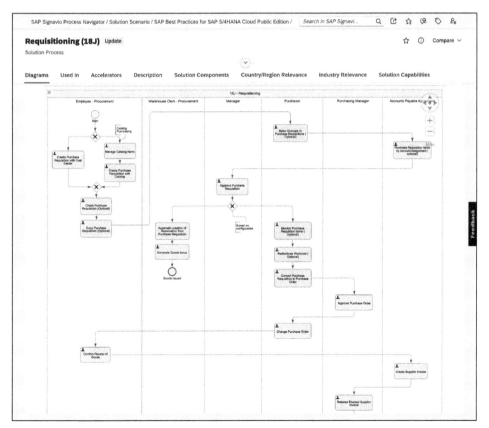

Figure 4.3 Solution Process Requisitioning (18J) Showing Solution Process Flow and Tabs with Additional Details

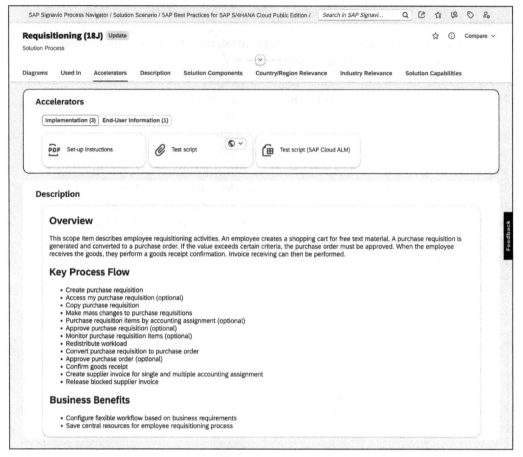

Figure 4.4 Solution Process Requisitioning (18J) Showing Solution Process Description and Business Benefits

SAP Best Practices for SAP S/4HANA Cloud Public Edition is available in multiple languages for many markets. You can find the latest information about country/region and language availability in SAP Note 3369272 at *https://me.sap.com/notes/3369272/E*.

SAP Best Practices for Hybrid Deployment

In addition to SAP Best Practices for deployment of SAP S/4HANA Cloud Public Edition, you can also access content for hybrid (or two-tier) deployment in SAP Signavio Process Navigator. You can find these solution scenarios by accessing the main page and using the search box to search for "Two-tier", as shown in Figure 4.5. Then, select the latest release, and access the content by clicking on the blue text. In our case, we'll access the **2402** version.

Once you access the solution scenario for **Two-Tier ERP**, you can review all the supported solution processes for deploying a hybrid ERP solution, as shown in Figure 4.6.

You can see that the structure of the content follows the same model we've discussed for the SAP Best Practices SAP S/4HANA Cloud Public Edition solution scenario.

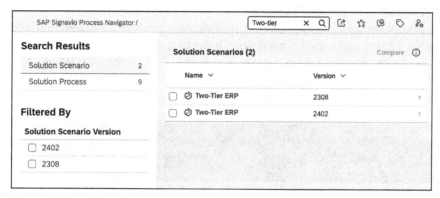

Figure 4.5 Searching for Two-Tier ERP Solution Scenario in SAP Signavio Process Navigator

Figure 4.6 Solution Scenario Two-Tier ERP for Hybrid Deployment

We'll discuss the hybrid deployment/two-tier ERP topic in more detail in Chapter 9.

What's New Viewer

You should also frequently review the information about new, updated, and deprecated scope items in SAP S/4HANA Cloud Public Edition in the What's New Viewer that you can find in the SAP Help Portal at *http://help.sap.com*. Select the **SAP S/4HANA Cloud Public Edition** entry on the main page in the **Enterprise Resource Planning** section, select the **What's New** tab on the next screen, and then click on the **What's New Viewer** link. You can then use the search capabilities or filters to identify changed and updated scope items in the viewer (see Figure 4.7).

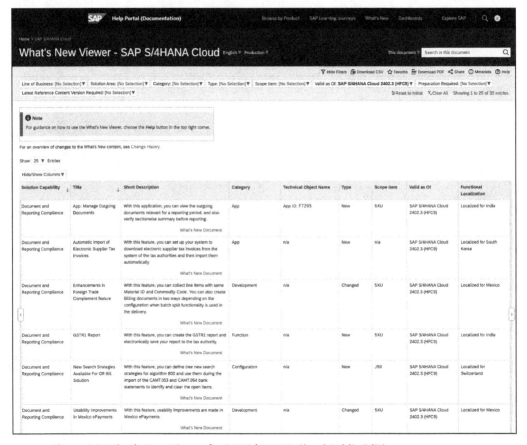

Figure 4.7 What's New Viewer for SAP S/4HANA Cloud Public Edition

Release Assessment and Scope Dependency Tool for SAP S/4HANA Cloud

The release assessment and scope dependency tool for SAP S/4HANA Cloud Public Edition is a simple, self-learning tool for SAP S/4HANA Cloud Public Edition customers. This tool enables the ease of consumption and adoption of impacts, improvements, and innovations rolled out with each release and upgrade.

The tool presents to customers a tailor-made list of deleted, deprecated, new, and changed objects such as apps, APIs, core data services (CDS) views, scope items, and so on for each SAP S/4HANA Cloud Public Edition release, and continuous delivery. This list is filtered based on the customer's used and activated scope, which means that the customers only see the changes relevant to them and not the entire list.

Figure 4.8 shows the **Release Assessment and Scope Dependency for SAP S/4HANA Cloud Public Edition** landing page, which helps you to better understand the impact of the new release or feature delivery of SAP S/4HANA Cloud Public Edition and assess the potential new capabilities that can be activated in your solution. You can access the tool at *www.sap.com/rasd*.

SAP customers can access the tool via their customer S-user IDs. This tool is free for all customers who have implemented SAP S/4HANA Cloud Public Edition. The release assessment and scope dependency tool is also available in six other languages besides English (German, Japanese, Chinese, French, Spanish, and Portuguese). See Figure 4.8 for the view of the landing page of the application providing an overview of the changed, updated, and deleted objects in specific releases of SAP S/4HANA Cloud Public Edition.

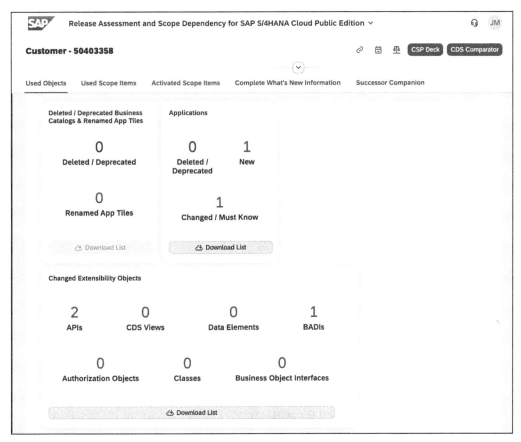

Figure 4.8 Landing Page of the Release Assessment and Scope Dependency Tool for SAP S/4HANA Cloud Public Edition

The release assessment and scope dependency tool is divided into five tabs, each consisting of several tiles. Let's walk through the tabs and tiles:

- **Used Objects**

  This tab provides an overview of the changes introduced in the release for the objects used in the customer system. The following information is available on the tab:

  - **Deleted/deprecated extensibility objects**

    Displays all extensibility objects that are deleted/deprecated based on the customer's usage.

  - **Where-used list for deletions and deprecations**

    Shows custom CDS views and apps impacted by deleted business catalogs and CDS views.

  - **Deleted/deprecated business catalogs and renamed app titles**

    Contains information related to deleted/deprecated business catalogs along with their successors based on the customer's usage. This tile also contains information on renamed app titles along with their current name and changed name.

  - **Applications**

    Contains information on deleted/deprecated applications, along with new/changed/must-know information related to applications.

  - **Changed extensibility objects**

    Displays all extensibility objects that are changed based on the customer's usage.

- **Used Scope Items**

  This tab displays data filtered based on used scope items by the customer. You can find the following information on this tab:

  - **Scope item impact**

    Displays scope items by their impact sorted in descending order.

  - **Personalized What's New Viewer**

    Displays the What's New Viewer filtered by the usage of solution processes by the logged-in customer.

  - **New features**

    Filters features based on category.

  - **Changes**

    Filters based on LoBs.

- **Activated Scope Items**

  This tab displays data filtered based on the customer's activated scope items. You can see an example of the tab information in Figure 4.9. The tab contains the information listed in the **Used Scope Items** tab. In addition to that information, this tab also displays the localization updates, which list all the entries that are linked to the regions localized for the customer.

- **Complete What's New Information**
  This tab displays the entire data set of the What's New Viewer that we've discussed in the previous section. In addition to the information displayed under the **Activated Scope Items** tab, this tab also displays **UI/UX Updates** information, which lists all the changes related to the SAP Fiori UX technology.

- **Successor Companion**
  This tab provides additional information for the customer, including the following data points:

  - **Scope item impact**
    Provides you with a bird's-eye view of a customer's scope item implementation statistics. This compares the used scope item to the activated scope item and gives the customer information on what percentage of scope items are used compared to the scope items that are activated in the system.

  - **Deprecation coverage**
    Identifies the deprecated attributes/objects from previous releases based on their usage metrics from the past three months and recommends their respective successors, facilitating a smooth transition for customers.

Figure 4.9 Activated Scope Items Tab

Additional features that customers can access in the application are as follows:

- **CDS Comparator**
  Compares a deprecated CDS view with its successor and provides a side-by-side comparison.

- **SAP Cloud ALM Integration**
  Allows you to download deletions and deprecations as a spreadsheet and then upload them to SAP Cloud ALM to create project tasks.

- **Downloads**
  Allows you to download all cards in the release assessment and scope dependency tool as spreadsheets. These spreadsheets then can be uploaded to SAP S/4HANA Cloud Public Edition to view the list in the news feed.

- **Release Calendar**
  Shows important release- and upgrade-related dates for SAP S/4HANA Cloud Public Edition.

Further Resources

You can visit *http://s-prs.co/v596630* to learn more about the release assessment and scope dependency tool.

Activating SAP Best Practices for SAP S/4HANA Cloud Public Edition

SAP Best Practices for SAP S/4HANA Cloud Public Edition are delivered ready to be activated in the SAP S/4HANA Cloud Public Edition solution. Customers will use SAP Central Business Configuration to set up a project and activate the best practices content in the starter system. After the fit-to-standard workshops, as the project team enters the realize phase, the SAP Best Practices content will be activated in the development system, and transports will be used to move the activated processes into the test and production systems. We'll discuss these processes in detail in Chapter 7.

4.1.2 SAP S/4HANA Cloud Private Edition

Now that you have a good understanding of the content in SAP Best Practices for SAP S/4HANA Cloud Public Edition, let's look at the content in SAP Best Practices for SAP S/4HANA Cloud Private Edition. The content structure of this package mirrors the structure of what you've seen in Section 4.1.1. The SAP Best Practices content is delivered in the SAP Best Practices for SAP S/4HANA Cloud Private Edition solution scenario with a similar structure and process scope. The scope and coverage of SAP Best Practices differ, though. At the time of writing, the latest SAP S/4HANA Cloud Private Edition release is 2023. The SAP Best Practices for this release provide the scope of functionality shown in Figure 4.10.

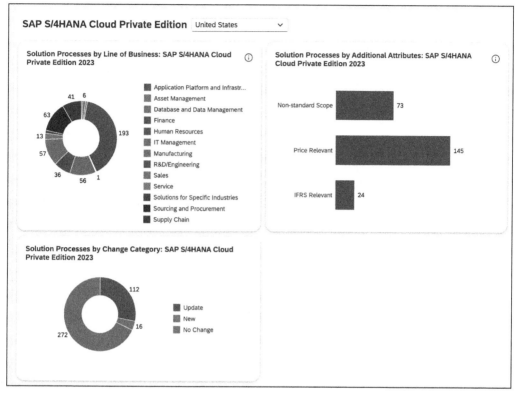

Figure 4.10 Scope of the SAP Best Practices for SAP S/4HANA Cloud Private Edition Solution
Scenario

SAP Best Practices Scope

The process scope of SAP Best Practices for SAP S/4HANA Cloud Private Edition doesn't
provide full coverage of all configuration and industry capabilities available in the SAP
S/4HANA Cloud Private Edition solution. The preconfiguration is used to prepare for fit-
to-standard workshops and serves as a foundation for the show-and-tell workshops.
We'll discuss another option, the enterprise management layer for SAP S/4HANA Cloud
Private Edition, in more detail in Section 4.2.

The scope of the SAP Best Practices for SAP S/4HANA Cloud Private Edition is compara-
ble to the scope of the SAP Best Practices for SAP S/4HANA (on-premise); therefore, this
book won't cover the on-premise solution scenario in detail.

The assets on the solution scenario level provide the same information that we've discussed for SAP S/4HANA Cloud Public Edition. For example, the solution scenario contains a description and key assets such as what's new information, availability and
dependencies matrix, software and delivery requirements document, overview organizational data, master data, task tutorials, and a chart of accounts. On the solution process (also referred to as a scope item) level, the information is structured in a similar

way as for the public cloud solution scenario; for example, the scope item provides a description of the functionality contained in the business process and access to the test script and business process flow.

We'll now look at where the two SAP Best Practices for SAP S/4HANA Cloud Public Edition and SAP S/4HANA Cloud Private Edition differ, which is in the way they are activated.

Activation of SAP Best Practices for SAP S/4HANA Cloud Private Edition

If you're using the SAP Best Practices for SAP S/4HANA Cloud Private Edition in your solution, you'll need to import the package into your system and then use the SAP solution builder tool to activate it. The detailed instructions are provided in the **Administration guide for the implementation of SAP S/4HANA** that you can access from SAP Signavio Process Navigator in the **Accelerators** section and **Implementation** tab, as shown in Figure 4.11.

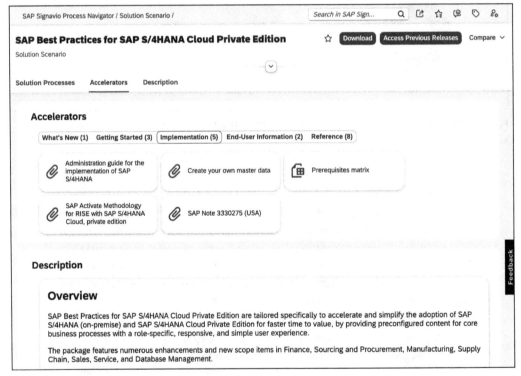

Figure 4.11 Access the Administration Guide for the Implementation of SAP S/4HANA Cloud Private Edition

Now we'll step through the key activities to import, prepare, and activate SAP Best Practices for SAP S/4HANA Cloud Private Edition in your landscape:

1. **Activate the required business functions.**

   During this step, you'll activate the required business functions in your SAP S/4HANA Cloud Private Edition system using the Switch Framework (Transaction SWF5) that allows selective activation of business functions using switches to keep the core solution lean.

> **Further Resources**
>
> For more details on the Switch Framework capabilities and functionality, refer to the SAP Help Portal at *http://s-prs.co/v502717*. These business functions are required for the successful activation of the SAP Best Practices content. You'll find a complete list of required business functions in the **Administration guide for the implementation of SAP S/4HANA Cloud Private Edition**.

2. **Set up a new target client for SAP Best Practices.**

   There are different variants for setting up the target client. The recommended approach for most users is to use the client copy of allowed settings from client 000. In addition, make sure to complete the import of required languages before copying the client.

3. **Perform language import and edit currency settings.**

   In this step, you'll optionally load additional languages into your landscape and confirm that the currency settings haven't been saved as this step is done during the activation process.

4. **Carry out the technical setup steps.**

   During this step, you'll download the SAP Best Practices content, apply the required SAP Notes, execute the SAP Fiori configuration, switch off the creation of activation links for business configuration (BC) sets, create settings in the SAP S/4HANA Cloud Private Edition backend, create basic settings in the SAP Fiori launchpad, set up SAP S/4HANA attachment services (backend and frontend), and set up the email exchange between the SAP system and Simple Mail Transfer Protocol (SMTP) mail server.

5. **Carry out the settings for implementation.**

   In this step, you'll ensure that activation can be executed. You'll provide (or create) users for content activation with the appropriate authorizations, create a dialog user for activation, and adjust system settings to prevent memory dumps or timeouts.

> **Further Resources**
>
> The detailed steps are provided in the **Administration guide for the implementation of SAP S/4HANA Cloud Private Edition**, which you can find in the SAP Signavio Process Navigator at *http://s-prs.co/v502718* inside the solution scenario **SAP Best Practices for SAP S/4HANA Cloud Private Edition** under **Accelerators** in the **Implementation** subsection.

Next, to activate SAP Best Practices, you can follow these high-level implementation steps:

1. Download the SAP Best Practices content.
2. Import the content to your system.
3. Define the scope of the solution by selecting the desired scope items from the package. (Note that some scope items may require additional licenses, so review the list of specially priced scope items in the **Administration guide for the implementation of SAP S/4HANA.**)
4. Generate configuration information.
5. Activate your solution.
6. Execute manual rework activities.
7. Delete the metadata cache.
8. Check and release transports with configuration settings.
9. Perform data migration activities.

Further Resources

Note that the preceding procedure explains how to activate SAP Best Practices for SAP S/4HANA Cloud Private Edition 2023, and the steps can change in future releases. Always refer to the detailed guidance in the **Administration guide for the implementation of SAP S/4HANA** that you can access from the solution scenario in SAP Signavio Process Navigator.

Fully Activated Appliance in SAP Cloud Appliance Library

Additional preconfiguration that you can use in the fit-to-standard workshops is the fully activated appliance with preactivated SAP Best Practices content that is available in SAP Cloud Appliance Library as a 30-day trial environment that can be deployed on Microsoft Azure, Amazon Web Services (AWS), or Google Cloud Platform. This package can be used for demos, proofs of concept, or sandbox environments for fit-to-standard workshops. The preactivated appliance can be started up in a cloud hyperscaler environment in a matter of about 60–90 minutes, compared to a much longer process for the manual activation of SAP Best Practices as outlined earlier in this chapter. At the time of writing, the fully activated appliance is available for SAP S/4HANA release 2023 FPS01.

The appliance is built on top of the SAP S/4HANA solution. Users of the appliance don't have to worry about the technical details as SAP Cloud Appliance Library provides predefined appliance sizing and guides for deployment to the desired cloud infrastructure. The appliance can also be deployed in your own data center.

Figure 4.12 shows the structure of the fully activated SAP S/4HANA appliance for release 2023 that you can access on SAP Cloud Appliance Library and deploy to the desired environment, such as AWS, Microsoft Azure, or Google Cloud Platform (or alternatively in your data center).

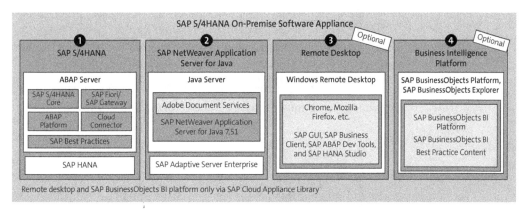

Figure 4.12 Fully Activated Appliance with SAP Best Practices for SAP S/4HANA 2023

Note

The business intelligence platform and remote desktop are only available when using SAP Cloud Appliance Library and aren't for download or Blu-ray shipment.

The business intelligence platform and remote desktop are optional in SAP Cloud Appliance Library (the hosting fee will decrease if you opt out). Both are included by default, but you can opt out in the advanced mode of instance creation. This can't be undone unless you create a new instance that includes these options.

4.2   Enterprise Management Layer for SAP S/4HANA

The enterprise management layer for SAP S/4HANA is a prepackaged, ready-to-use, end-to-end solution template that is tailored to multinational corporations. It isn't specific to an industry and covers most LoBs for up to 49 countries (43 countries based on SAP Best Practices content for SAP S/4HANA Cloud Private Edition and an additional 6 countries with a more limited scope, focusing mainly on finance and basic sales and procurement processes). It provides an extra layer of configuration and content on top of SAP Best Practices and captures the experience from successful, real-life projects. Sold and delivered as a service, a template-driven approach enables any suitable project to increase quality, accelerate adoption, reduce cost, and decrease risk.

The enterprise management layer for SAP S/4HANA can be used during new implementations or to drive innovation of existing SAP implementations. It can be used in SAP-led or individual company/partner-led projects. It can be deployed in SAP S/4HANA Cloud Private Edition (e.g., RISE with SAP), on-premise, or with a cloud provider. Once deployed, the system can be used, configured, enhanced, extended, and connected to other SAP solutions just like any other system. The enterprise management layer for SAP S/4HANA is used to jump-start a project and is ideally suited to drive a fit-to-standard analysis during the explore phase. In addition, the enterprise management layer for SAP S/4HANA can also be deployed in the customer's productive landscape and provide SAP Best Practices for the implementation. This leads to faster deployment, quicker decision-making, and a higher adoption of standard SAP functionality.

In this section, we'll discuss the structure of the enterprise management layer for SAP S/4HANA by explaining the content structure and discussing updates and deployment options.

4.2.1   Structure of Content

The content in the enterprise management layer has been enhanced and adapted for multinational corporations with their complex business and reporting requirements across a multitude of countries. It includes a preconfigured solution, test scripts, process diagrams, and sample organization structures and master data. Whereas SAP Best Practices content for SAP S/4HANA is free of charge but must be activated, the enterprise management layer for SAP S/4HANA is sold and delivered by SAP. The service includes the appliance (in technical terms, a database backup) containing the enterprise management layer for SAP S/4HANA, documentation, and a handover session to the customer's project team.

The enterprise management layer for SAP S/4HANA provides SAP Best Practices for multiple countries in one SAP instance. Simply select which countries you need out of the 49 countries currently available, and you'll get multiple company codes with a harmonized SAP Best Practices chart of accounts and harmonized business processes for multiple LoBs across all countries. Each country is preconfigured with localized business processes to comply with local tax and statutory requirements, hence ensuring document and reporting compliance for the individual countries. Parallel accounting and reporting capabilities according to your group accounting principles, as well as local and tax accounting principles, are the cornerstone of the enterprise management layer for SAP S/4HANA: in technical terms, three accounting principles linked to five ledgers are preconfigured.

The enterprise management layer for SAP S/4HANA is configured with 25 languages. End users can work in any of these languages, and all data and print forms are translated to ensure that correspondence with business partners abroad is possible in their local languages.

The content of the enterprise management layer for SAP S/4HANA is structured into three layers:

- A *standard scope* consists of close to 220+ business processes (or scope items) that are always included and only require the SAP S/4HANA Enterprise Management license.

- *Scope options* allow you to select the additional scope (110+ scope items) that you want and to exclude scope options for which you don't have the required software licenses—for example, scope options for group reporting, cash management, advanced available-to-promise (ATP), or advanced variant configuration, just to name a few.

- *Service options* can be added on customer request and provide additional business processes (22 scope items) that aren't offered by SAP Best Practices: intercompany processes for sales and returns as well as for projects and services between two countries, the Project System module for accounting or for engineering projects, and more.

> **Further Resources**
>
> The latest information can be found in the SAP Signavio Process Navigator at *http://s-prs.co/v596631* (select your country, if not Germany), as well as in the Enterprise Resource Planning Blogs by SAP blog series at *http://s-prs.co/v546306*.

Among other documents, a one-page service summary is available, as shown in Table 4.1. This lists the applications required, the scope options available, and the business processes and capabilities.

Standard Scope	Scope Options	Service Options
<ul><li>Accounting and financial close</li><li>Cost management and profitability analysis</li><li>Financial operations</li><li>Cash management (basic)</li><li>Enterprise risk and compliance</li><li>Production operations</li><li>Production planning</li><li>Maintenance management</li><li>Quality management</li><li>Product engineering</li><li>Sourcing and contract management</li><li>Supplier management</li><li>Operational procurement</li><li>Inventory</li><li>Order and contract management</li><li>Service operations</li><li>Basic transportation management</li></ul>	<ul><li>Document and reporting compliance</li><li>Advanced receivables management</li><li>Advanced cash management</li><li>Lease accounting</li><li>Group reporting</li><li>Treasury and risk management</li><li>Extended warehouse management (EWM)</li><li>Advanced ATP</li><li>Maintenance resource scheduling</li><li>Advanced variant configuration</li><li>Enterprise contract management</li><li>Product compliance</li><li>Product lifecycle management</li></ul>	<ul><li>Intercompany processes</li><li>Cross-plant stock transfer</li><li>Project System for accounting</li><li>Engineering projects</li><li>Billing of projects</li><li>Intercompany billing of projects</li><li>Intercompany billing of services</li></ul>

Table 4.1 Enterprise Management Layer for SAP S/4HANA Summary

4.2.2   Updates

A new version of the enterprise management layer for SAP S/4HANA content is provided for each software release and becomes available roughly one quarter after the new SAP S/4HANA software is released. Regular updates of the functional and localization content, as well as additional content such as new business processes, become available throughout the year and can be downloaded from SAP Signavio Process Navigator. This distinguishes the enterprise management layer for SAP S/4HANA from other template solutions, such as those offered by partners.

Once deployed in the customer landscape, there is no process to upgrade the enterprise management layer content when a new version is released. A software upgrade can be performed in the normal way. Required changes, such as those due to changing legal requirements in some countries, need to be performed by the project team.

4.2.3   Deployment Options

SAP can set up the enterprise management layer for SAP S/4HANA quickly. This means that your organization doesn't need to activate SAP Best Practices and upskill people on how to do this.

There are two main ways to consume the enterprise management layer for SAP S/4HANA:

- **Trial edition with a fixed scope**
  A 30-day trial edition is available for the enterprise management layer for SAP S/4HANA. This is typically used during the discover phase and requires no licenses. The solution is made available through SAP Cloud Appliance Library. In this case, the enterprise management layer for SAP S/4HANA isn't tailored to individual customer requirements and doesn't exclude business processes that require additional software licenses.

- **Custom edition**
  The enterprise management layer for SAP S/4HANA can be adapted to each customer's requirements. Based on a questionnaire, you can choose which countries are needed (countries where you have legal entities), which scope options are needed, and also your group currency and your fiscal year variant. In addition, the local currency and the usual fiscal year variant are preconfigured for each country.

The custom edition requires a signed order form for the enterprise management layer service. The enterprise management layer custom edition can be deployed in the following ways:

- **SAP S/4HANA Cloud Private Edition**
  SAP sets up the enterprise management layer for SAP S/4HANA and hosts and manages the solution.

- **On-premise**
  You get a custom edition built by SAP, and you deploy the database backup that SAP provides in your on-premise landscape.

- **Cloud provider (e.g., Microsoft Azure, AWS, or Google Cloud Platform)**
  As with the on-premise deployment, you can download the enterprise management layer database backup files and use the cloud provider of your choice.

The enterprise management layer for SAP S/4HANA is most frequently used to set up the full productive landscape—the development, quality, and production systems. Having the preconfigured content already deployed helps to accelerate the explore phase and the realize phase. Sometimes the enterprise management layer for SAP S/4HANA will also be deployed in a dedicated sandbox system. The sandbox system is typically used for the explore workshops but can also be used as a reference system for copying configuration into a development system where the enterprise management layer for SAP S/4HANA can't be deployed—for example, in a customer's legacy system.

The system landscape may require multiple servers: an SAP S/4HANA server and an Adobe Document Services (ADS) server. SAP Fiori apps are embedded in SAP S/4HANA and don't require a separate server. You may also require connecting your system where the enterprise management layer for SAP S/4HANA has been deployed to a Cloud Integration tenant to enable end-to-end processes under document reporting and compliance, for example, to exchange electronic documents (eDocuments) with various tax authorities and/or business partners.

To deploy on-premise or with a cloud provider, the installation of the server hardware and operating systems is the customer's responsibility. The solution is deployed via a database backup that needs to be downloaded and restored. The accelerators (documentation) can be downloaded in SAP Signavio Process Navigator at *http://s-prs.co/v596632* (select your country if not Germany).

4.3   Summary

This chapter provided an in-depth understanding of the ready-to-use preconfiguration SAP provides in SAP Best Practices and the enterprise management layer for SAP S/4HANA. These packages and related documentation are major accelerators for any implementation project deploying SAP S/4HANA software in an organization and should be used to accelerate time to value and leverage the investment SAP makes in building and delivering these packages. They provide significant acceleration not only through the preconfiguration but also in the business user's understanding of the solution capabilities by being able to execute business processes in a running system.

In the next chapter, we'll review the key capabilities and processes that are critical in all implementation projects, such as collecting requirements, configuring the solution, extending and integrating systems, and testing.

Chapter 5
Implementation Activities

Now that we've established the importance of working with running systems for the solution requirements and design, we'll cover the configuration, migration, integration, extensibility, business AI, and testing, which are all critical for planning and executing a successful solution implementation.

In this chapter, we'll walk through several key processes related to planning and executing an SAP S/4HANA Cloud or SAP S/4HANA implementation. For the configuration of these solutions, a fit-to-standard analysis is performed to validate the solution functionality included in the project scope and to confirm that the business requirements can be satisfied. Identified delta requirements and configuration values are added to the backlog for use in the next phase. Industry and solution experts from SAP or SAP partners lead a series of structured solution demos and solution design workshops to surface the requirements that will support your business users.

Next, the project team incrementally builds and tests an integrated business and system environment that is based on the business processes and process requirements identified previously and captured in the backlog. The project team loads customer data into the system, plans adoption activities, and prepares cutover plans and plans for operationally running the solution. The configuration and setup activities now also include the steps to activate and set up SAP Business AI capabilities leveraging Joule and generative AI capabilities to improve the end-user experience, productivity, and efficiency. During this process, the project team actively works with business representatives to ensure a good fit of the built solution and its adoption in the business. Note that we'll cover the solution adoption topics, such as organizational change management (OCM) and Customer Center of Expertise (Customer COE), in Chapter 10.

Now, let's dive into these core processes, starting with business-driven configuration.

5.1 Business-Driven Configuration

In this section, we'll discuss how the configuration process—from planning and designing to realizing the planned value—is supported by SAP Activate for the various SAP S/4HANA solutions: SAP S/4HANA Cloud Public Edition, SAP S/4HANA Cloud Private Edition, and others.

SAP S/4HANA Cloud Public Edition in a Three-System Landscape

When we discuss SAP S/4HANA Cloud Public Edition, we're specifically discussing the three-system landscape roadmap. This innovation provides companies with three systems to deploy the solution into—starting with a development system that is used for configuration, extensibility, and integration; followed by a test system predominantly used as a preproduction test and validation environment; and ending with a production system that the company uses for productive operation of its business. We'll discuss the details of this deployment option in Chapter 7.

The configuration process, in all solutions, is supported by the application design and configuration workstream. The purpose of the application design and configuration workstream is to help you plan, prepare, and adapt SAP solutions for your business. This workstream covers the end-to-end configuration process by taking project teams through the following:

- Confirmation of business process scope for the project
- Preparation of configuration with the business-driven configuration assessment
- Fit-to-standard analysis by demoing business processes in the system
- Confirmation of functional design and adaptation of customer-specific configuration
- Identification of business process requirements requiring additional planning and design workshops
- Execution of configurations for production landscape

The configuration process during an implementation project is often compared to the building of a house. If the correct preparation and planning is done up front, and the correct amount of time is spent performing these activities, the configuring or building of the house is more efficient as all major decisions, and the risk of rework is mitigated at the beginning. The goal is to ensure that the actual configuration of the system is as efficient as possible to help the business realize the planned value-add sooner. Deliberate time spent up front enabling, preparing, and planning helps ensure an effective and efficient project with a lower cost of implementation.

We'll walk through the overall configuration process in the following sections. Topics such as integration, extensibility, and testing, which are covered in more detail in other workstreams and later in this chapter, are supported by the application design and configuration workstream.

5.1.1   Preparation for Configuration

The configuration process starts in the prepare phase with the business-driven configuration assessment. The purpose of this assessment is to gain a foundational understanding of the company's current business processes for the discussion and analysis during the fit-to-standard workshops. The business-driven configuration question-naires can be leveraged by the configuration expert as a tool to help drive and docu-ment these discussions. When leveraging these assessments, the configuration expert will download the project-relevant line of business (LoB) configuration questionnaires and refine each so that only the relevant scope for the project is shown. Once com-pleted, the refined questionnaires are provided to the company's business process experts to answer the questions.

In these questionnaires, there are two levels of questions: level 2 and level 3 (level 1 questions have already been asked during the presales and sales discussions in the dis-cover phase). Level 2 questions should be answered during the prepare phase and are geared toward collecting information prior to the execution of the fit-to-standard workshops. The goal is to prevent stop/go execution of the fit-to-standard workshops due to missing information. These questions also help the configuration expert deter-mine the topics that will need to be further discussed and captured during the fit-to-standard workshops. The goal of level 3 questions is to provide more detailed informa-tion on what is needed to make a business decision and to define specific configuration values that will be captured in the backlog. These questions should be further discussed and documented in the fit-to-standard workshop during the explore phase.

Self-enablement is a key component for executing an effective and efficient fit-to-standard workshop that fosters rich discussions. To have a successful fit-to-standard workshop, business process owners and experts should review the necessary SAP Best Practices material (i.e., key assets such as test scripts and process flows) for the related scope items that will be demonstrated during the fit-to-standard workshops. This material can be found in the Processes app within SAP Cloud ALM or in SAP Signavio Process Navigator (see Chapter 4, Section 4.1). There are also other self-enablement accelerators for analytics, data protection, and chart of accounts.

Further Resources

It's important for business process experts to start and continue their self-enablement in parallel with the configuration process. Further details on self-enablement activities for project members can be found in the customer team enablement workstream in the Roadmap Viewer (see Chapter 3, Section 3.1).

While the business process experts are pursuing self-enablement with the solution, the various technical experts begin to create initial requirements lists that will later be used as capturing requirements for specific topics during the fit-to-standard work-shops, such as analytics, identity and access management, extensibility, and integra-tion. These initial lists are created from the results of the digital discovery assessment from the discover phase, or from executive decisions from meetings that took place after the contract was signed.

In addition, business process experts should also make themselves familiar with the golden rules for implementing SAP S/4HANA (discussed previously in Chapter 2, Section 2.5):

1. Start with preconfigured processes, and foster a cloud mindset by adhering to fit-to-standard and agile deployment detailed in SAP Activate.
2. Build your solution on quality data (configuration, master, and transactional) to leverage innovations.
3. Ensure use of modern integration technologies. Use public application programming interfaces (APIs), and provide no native access to APIs that aren't public.
4. Ensure the use of modern extensibility technologies. Develop company extensions in a side-by-side approach using SAP Business Technology Platform (SAP BTP).
5. Ensure transparency on deviations. Any deviation has to be clearly documented.

These rules help to foster a cloud mindset and are referenced throughout the application design and configuration workstream. We discussed the golden rules and Solution Standardization Board (SSB; for governance of the golden rules) in Chapter 2, Section 2.5.7.

An important step for preparing for the fit-to-standard workshops is to set up a system that will be used to demonstrate the functionality of the solution during the fit-to-standard workshops. Configuration experts will prepare the system by enhancing it with additional configuration based on feedback collected from business-driven configuration questionnaires. It's very likely that customer adaptations are required in configuration settings. Demonstrating these options during workshops is important for fostering the discussions and confirming required adjustments needed for execution during the realize phase. Although SAP Best Practices has sample master data, you can create more customer project–specific data (refer to Chapter 3). During the fit-to-standard workshops, the system will be used as a focal point for facilitating discussion; thus, any additional customer project-specific data that can aid this discussion is encouraged.

All business process experts participating in the fit-to-standard workshops should verify access to this system. Then, after access to the system is confirmed, business process experts should continue with self-enablement by executing some of the test scripts for the project scope. The purpose of this activity is for the business process expert to gain hands-on experience in the system, which will help drive fit-to-standard discussions with the configuration experts on the business's processes. This hands-on experience allows the business process experts to become familiar with the tools that will be used during the fit-to-standard workshops and to help guide and contribute to the configuration discussions more effectively. It's recommended to execute transactions in the system to populate data in the analytical reports because it will allow the reporting functionality to be demonstrated during the fit-to-standard workshops.

After the system to be used for demonstration purposes is prepared, the fit-to-standard workshops with the business process experts can take place. The purpose of the fit-to-standard workshops is to validate the predefined scenarios and enhancements in scope for the implementation and to identify potential gaps.

The fit-to-standard workshops and documentation, once completed, are then followed by a series of design workshops. During these workshops, the solutions for the prioritized deltas identified are documented and detailed. These delta design documents are in a format that is suitable for communication and that allows for a formal sign-off by the company, after being reviewed by an independent instance. The signed-off designs are then added to the configuration backlog for execution in the realize phase.

Additional workshops, for topics such as user experience/user interface (UX/UI), security, and data volume, will be executed even after the review and sign off on the delta design documents but prior to the end of the explore phase.

5.1.2 Planning of Configuration

When the preparation is complete, the project team will move into the explore phase. This phase, for the application design and configuration workstream, includes the fit-to-standard workshops, the documentation of the requirements and backlog items, and the planning and designing workshops for technical topics.

Each of the fit-to-standard workshops are organized around the functional areas of the solution and follow an iterative approach, as shown in Figure 5.1. The focus of these workshops is on the business and its requirements. They don't deep-dive into technical topics; rather, the technical discussions are handled during the planning and design workshops. Let's explore the fit-to-standard steps in a bit more detail:

❶ **Review the SAP Best Practices process flow.**
The configuration expert explains a scope item using the SAP Best Practices process flow and responses from the business-driven configuration questionnaires.

❷ **Demonstrate the business process and concept.**
The configuration expert demonstrates the business process using the starter system and delivered master data and then highlights the areas that require configuration decisions. The process flow is used as a point of reference when transitioning in the system.

❸ **Discuss how the processes fit with the company's requirements.**
The team fosters discussion to better understand the company's business requirements, referencing the business-driven configuration questionnaire, and explains how the solution meets these requirements.

❹ **Identify delta requirements.**
The team identifies and catalogs the delta requirements in the backlog for further analysis and closure. Delta requirements are business requirements that can't be satisfied with the standard scenarios.

❺ Identify the required configuration.
The team leverages the business-driven configuration questionnaires to arrive at critical configuration decisions. All configuration values required and any needed in-app extensions are determined and documented in the backlog. The company is responsible for providing value lists (i.e., product group definition).

❻ Enable company execution of standard scenarios.
The configuration expert enables the business process expert to execute the process on his own in the starter system.

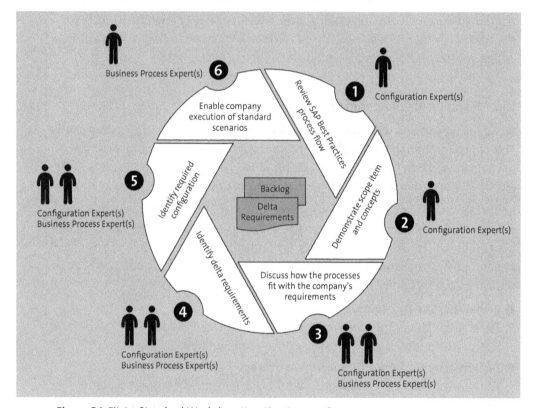

Figure 5.1 Fit-to-Standard Workshop Iterative Approach

During the fit-to-standard workshops, the configuration expert demonstrates the solution in a system and facilitates discussions of some of the key areas identified in the initial business assessment, or the answers for the level 2 and 3 questions in the business-driven configuration questionnaires from the prepare phase.

The goal of these workshops, overall, is to validate the predefined processes of the standard solution with the company requirements, identify customer-specific adaption of configuration settings, and note any delta requirements that need further refinement by technical experts during the planning and design workshops. Any delta requirements identified (for analytics, integration, output management, identity and access management, etc.) are then captured in the initial lists that were created in the prepare phase by the technical experts. Prior to the handover of all these backlog items and delta requirements for the planning and design workshops, the configuration experts validate that all the configuration values and requirements have been captured, and they document any additional outcomes that were discussed after the fit-to-standard workshops.

Keeping in line with the fit-to-standard approach, each of the workshops should be executed in an iterative manner: the solution is demonstrated, how the business process matches the predelivered solution is discussed, and any of the configuration values and delta requirements are documented. The first golden rule, foster a cloud mindset, and the second golden rule, use SAP Best Practices, should act as guidance for fostering discussions during the workshops.

After the business has completed and documented the backlog items and delta requirements from the fit-to-standard workshops in SAP Cloud ALM, any further refinement of requirements for technical configuration then go through a planning and designing process. For this round of workshops, the requirements documented are refined further by technical experts. Some examples of requirements that go through this secondary refinement process are analytics, output management, extensibility, integration, and UI design. These requirements are refined during the workshops and converted to backlog items that will be planned into sprints during the release planning prior to the end of the explore phase.

5.1.3 Execution of Configuration

After all the design workshops are completed and the design documents have been confirmed and signed off on by the company, the execution of the designs that were discussed and determined in the explore phase takes place during the realize phase.

The execution of configuration follows a series of iterations that incrementally build and test the integrated business and system environment. Typically, configuration takes place in sprints that are time-boxed into two-week cycles. During each of these sprints, the configuration expert considers the system configuration, documentation, and unit testing based on the backlog that was planned during the explore phase. This configuration activity is executed per LoB or end-to-end solution.

Each of the configuration sprints follows this iterative configuration approach:

1. Configure
2. Track changes in configuration
3. Execute test
4. Transport configuration
5. Verify with the business

Some required configuration must take place before system use, so the first sprints should focus on this configuration prior to the configuration of the functional areas.

Some of the required configuration before system use includes tax solution, profit center, cost center master data, house bank, and customer-specific fiscal year variant. In addition, during the configuration sprints, additional countries may be added; this additional country activation must be taken into consideration during the planning and the execution of the sprints.

Following the completion of unit testing, a string test is run within the sprint to test initial solution integration with the business priorities or end-to-end solutions in scope. Note, however, this isn't a fully loaded integration test and doesn't replace the text execution that takes place in the testing workstream later in the phase.

What Is a String Test?

A string test is performed when more than one related unit test, which is a test intended to isolate and test a single piece of functionality, is performed one after another to form a string. Rather than test the functionality of a single application, for example, a string test may check the flow of data from one application to another. Further information on testing and different testing types will be discussed later in this chapter (see also Chapter 7, Section 7.3.5).

After the configuration sprints are completed, the configured solution is demonstrated to the business for solution acceptance prior to company testing.

Documentation is important throughout the configuration process as it's used as a reference later in the implementation for key user enablement. Therefore, any changes to configuration that take place after the solution walkthrough and for bug fixing should be captured in the original configuration documentation.

As we've discussed, the efficiency of configuring the solution is directly correlated to the quality and time spent by the business process experts for self-enablement; that is, quality inputs help create quality outputs. With all the planning completed during the explore phase, the actual configuration of the solution takes place during the realize phase. Ideally, this portion of the configuration process should be one of the shortest, as all the heavy work has been completed up front with only the execution step remaining.

Even after the solution has been fully configured and deployed to the business, to realize the planned value, improvements to the solution may be made as the business periodically updates the system and imitates an innovation cycle in the run phase. In addition, new functionality may be released that might cause the creation of a strategic roadmap for continuous improvement.

5.1.4   SAP Central Business Configuration

When doing a deep dive into the configuration process within the application design and configuration workstream, it's also important to understand the configuration tool available to configure specific SAP products.

SAP Central Business Configuration is a new tool used when configuring the end-to-end business processes that span various SAP products from one central place. The vision for SAP Central Business Configuration is to allow the configuration of end-to-end processes across the intelligent enterprise. Although SAP S/4HANA Cloud Public Edition is one of the first solutions to be integrated with SAP Central Business Configuration, additional cloud solutions are planned for the future.

As a configuration tool, SAP Central Business Configuration includes all the configuration activities that take place during an implementation project while not containing any duplicate content from SAP Activate. Instead, the SAP Activate implementation methodology provides the guidance on the right points in time when the configuration tool is needed and allows the tool to take over and guide users through the configuration process.

Much like the configuration process can be broken down into major sections, SAP Central Business Configuration is structured around two parts within the configuration process, as shown in Figure 5.2:

- **Scope and Organizational Structure**
- **Product-Specific Configuration**

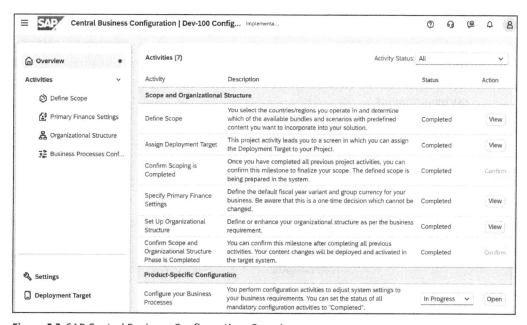

Figure 5.2 SAP Central Business Configuration: Overview

As part of the scope and organizational structure phase, users will select the scope and countries and regions; settings that are required before solution configuration, such as the standard fiscal variant or group currency, as shown in Figure 5.3; and the definition of the organization structure of your company. Note that future activities follow the selection of the scope chosen during the scope and organization structure phase. This functionality means that what you select during the scope and organization structure phase is automatically considered by SAP Central Business Configuration later within the implementation project and matches the decisions needed with the scope chosen. Once these settings are chosen, the initial deployment takes place.

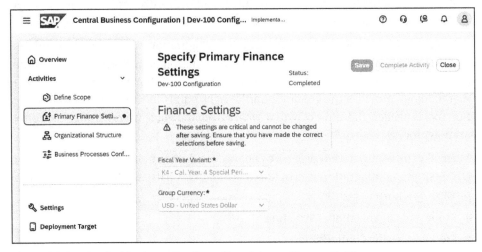

Figure 5.3 SAP Central Business Configuration: Primary Finance Settings

For the product-specific configuration phase, the preconfigured settings are adjusted to better fit the needs of the business. The Business Processes Configuration app, as shown in Figure 5.4, is there for customers to adapt settings per their own business process requirements.

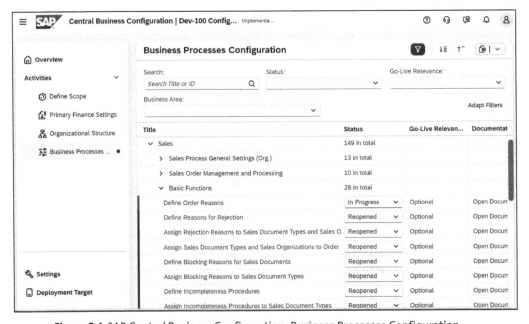

Figure 5.4 SAP Central Business Configuration: Business Processes Configuration

It's organized by LoB and can be accessed via search and filter options. Changes made in these self-service configuration UIs are saved in the SAP S/4HANA system as transport requests, which can then be moved across the landscape to the test and production environments, respectively.

5.2   Data Migration

All SAP ERP systems require customer-specific master data objects to run the business processes configured in the system. To facilitate the entering of potentially very large volumes during the initial implementation, SAP has developed the SAP S/4HANA migration cockpit, along with processes to support the tool; it's available for both SAP S/4HANA Cloud and SAP S/4HANA (on-premise) implementations.

The SAP S/4HANA migration cockpit assists in transferring business data from a source legacy system to a new implementation of SAP S/4HANA Cloud or SAP S/4HANA either through direct transfer from another SAP ERP solution or through staging tables. Migration objects within the migration cockpit are used to identify and transfer the relevant business object data. The migration objects contain information about the source and target structures, as well as the relationships between these structures. Object mapping information for the relevant fields is also stored, as well as any mappings that are required to convert values from the source value to the target value. SAP provides predefined migration templates that are used to structure and load your data. The SAP S/4HANA migration cockpit can be accessed via the Migrate Your Data app.

The migration cockpit supports two different methods of transfer:

- **Migrate data using staging tables**
  The system automatically creates a database table for each migration object. These tables can be populated from an XML or CSV file or from other tools.
- **Migrate data directly from SAP system**
  SAP S/4HANA or SAP S/4HANA Cloud is connected directly to a supported SAP ERP system and the table system within that system.

The process of data migration can be broken down into the planning and execution of data migration. In planning, the following tasks are performed:

- Selecting the required master and transactional data objects
- Determining the migration cockpit field structures (staging tables only)
- Extracting and transforming legacy data (staging tables only)
- Performing data cleansing activities in the source system

For execution, the following tasks are performed, as shown in Figure 5.5:

- Creating the migration project and selecting migration objects
- Populating data into the migration template (staging tables only)

- Loading the data into staging tables (staging tables only)
- Validating data and performing value mapping
- Simulating the data migration
- Executing the data migration

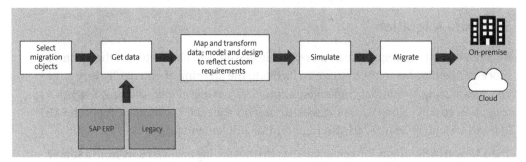

Figure 5.5 Data Migration Process

The process of preparing and executing data migration is detailed in the following sections.

5.2.1   Data Migration Preparation

Data migration is a process that can take longer than expected. It's important to begin preparation shortly after the project start and in parallel with the fit-to-standard workshop. Let's walk through the key tasks.

Selecting Master Data Objects

The purpose of the first task is to determine the master data objects, data sources, migration methods, and extraction plan required for the scope of your implementation. Start by determining all master data objects needed to support the processes detailed in the fit-to-standard workshops. After the list of required objects is determined, the data sources can be mapped to them. In some cases, a legacy equivalent won't be available, and the field data will need to be created or derived. Historical transaction objects (i.e., completed sales orders, completed purchase order, etc.) aren't migrated to the new system. They are typically available via reporting or other archival retrieval tools.

> **Migration Objects**
>
> Note that the coverage and functionality for data migration objects expands with each biannual release of SAP S/4HANA Cloud. A complete list of objects is available via the SAP Help Portal in the **Data Migration** topic area and in the SAP S/4HANA migration cockpit app. Templates should always be checked after an upgrade as they may have changed. SAP also provides the SAP S/4HANA migration object modeler, which allows for modeling custom objects.

Determining the SAP S/4HANA Migration Cockpit Field Structures

If you're using staging tables, the next task is to view the SAP S/4HANA data structures by downloading the template files and associating the structures with the data from the legacy system(s). The templates can be downloaded from your project in the Migrate Your Data app and contains the metadata (fields, data type, mandatory fields, etc.) to help with the data mapping (see Figure 5.6). Downloading the files at this early stage helps you understand the available migration objects and fields, prepare the data, and determine how to fill the templates with the data from the legacy system. It's recommended to open the downloaded files with Microsoft Excel.

The downloaded templates contain an introduction with instructions, a field list, and data sheets per structure. The data sheet contains at least one mandatory structure and additional optional structures depending on the complexity of the migration object. Only mandatory sheets need to be filled; however, after an optional sheet is populated, all the mandatory fields for that structure must be filled.

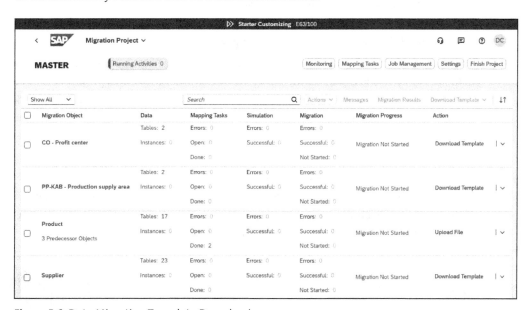

Figure 5.6 Data Migration Template Download

Extract and Transform Legacy Data

The next step isn't relevant if direct transfer from another SAP ERP system is used. Extracting data from the legacy systems to populate into the new system simplifies the manual effort required for starting productive use of a new system. In this task, the specifications for extraction of data from the legacy system are created, and any related legacy system extraction development is initiated. Because master data can change frequently, the process must be created so that it can be efficiently executed during the cutover to production. Data that will be manually entered also requires a specification so that it can also be efficiently executed during the cutover.

Performing Data Cleansing Activities

Prior to converting data from the legacy system to SAP S/4HANA, you have a good opportunity to remove or update records that are obsolete or don't meet current standards. By doing this, the data load volume will be less and the UX better in the new system. This process can be time consuming, and can be started before the implementation projects begins. Data that will be integrated into the new solutions should also be included in the scope.

5.2.2   Data Migration Execution with Staging Tables

Data migration execution takes place during the realize phase. Solution configuration usually uses manually created sample data, but for user acceptance testing (UAT), the final data should be loaded via the processes that will be used during the production cutover. This will allow both business processes and data to be tested together. Let's walk through the key tasks related to the staging tables migration approach.

Creating the Migration Project and Selecting Migration Objects

The migration project is the framework used to manage the data migration process and is the first step in the transfer process. In the development tenant, a project is created, and objects are assigned to begin the process. The scope of the objects and data should be limited at first and then expanded after each successful load. The migration project can be copied once a successful test has been executed.

Populating Data into the Migration Template

In this task, the project team will populate the data extracted from your legacy system into the migration templates that can be downloaded from within the migration project. Figure 5.7 shows the structure of the load template, including descriptions of all fields.

Field List for Migration Object: CO - Profit center

Version SAP S/4HANA CLOUD 2402 - Standard Scope - 06.14.2024 © Copyright SAP SE. All rights reserved.

Sheet Name	Group Name	Field Description	Importance	Type	Length	Decimal
Master Record (mandatory)						
	Key	Profit Center	mandatory for sheet	Text	80	
		Valid From	mandatory for sheet	Date		
		Valid To	mandatory for sheet	Date		
	General Information	Language in Which Texts Are Saved		Text	80	
		Profit Center Name	mandatory for sheet	Text	20	
		Description		Text	40	
		Person Responsible	mandatory for sheet	Text	20	
		User Responsible		Text	80	
	Organizational Unit	Standard Hierarchy Node/Profit Cntr	mandatory for sheet	Text	12	
		Department		Text	12	
		Segment	mandatory for sheet	Text	10	

Introduction   **Field List**   Master Record   Company Code Assignment   ⊕

Figure 5.7 Data Migration Template: Field List

Always use the latest templates provided by the SAP S/4HANA migration cockpit for your release and version. Note that the default size limit for each XML or CSV upload file is 100 MB. Multiple files can be added to a ZIP file, but the combined size can't exceed 160 MB.

Uploading Data into SAP S/4HANA

In the realize phase, iterations of data loads are performed to perfect the data and process. One or more filled-out template files for each migration object are loaded via the project and stored in the staging area of the SAP S/4HANA migration cockpit. The uploaded files can be viewed, deleted, and uploaded again if you encounter errors. For every object in the project, you can find online documentation on how to test and validate the migrated data.

Validating Data and Performing Value Mapping

After the data is loaded into the system, the system validates the data and outputs the errors warnings. After processing the output, value mapping is performed. Value mapping allows for data transformation to occur based on mappings that are proposed, manually entered, or uploaded. The system will, by default, propose mapping values for required objects, but each must be confirmed before proceeding.

Simulating the Data Migration

We recommend that the project team execute a simulation of the data load using the SAP S/4HANA migration cockpit. This activity will simulate the migration of your data through the relevant application interfaces without committing the data to your actual database tables. The team should resolve any issues resulting from the simulation process, which may require adjusting configuration or data.

Executing the Data Migration

After all the steps have been performed, and the project team is confident in the data quality, you can proceed with loading the legacy data into the system. See Figure 5.8 for an example data migration project in the SAP S/4HANA migration cockpit.

This migration can be performed directly or via background processing. By completing this step, the project team delivers the master required by SAP S/4HANA Cloud to run transactions and complete the testing cycles to determine production readiness.

The cutover sequence, estimated runtimes, and person responsible are maintained in the cutover plan so that the process can be repeated in the test and production environments.

When executing data migration in the test and production system, plan around system maintenance times and upgrade downtime periods. Review SAP Note 3024158 for more detailed information.

Figure 5.8 Data Migration Project

5.2.3   Data Migration Execution Using Direct Transfer

As an alternative to data migration using staging tables, the SAP S/4HANA migration cockpit can be connected directly to a supported SAP ERP system. By connecting directly to another SAP ERP system, the staging tables are eliminated, simplifying the process and reducing the overall throughput time. Unlike the staging table process, the migration process can be transported from development to test and production by using the Export Customizing Transport app and the Import Collection app.

5.2.4   Enhancing the Migration Objects Using the Migration Object Modeler

The SAP S/4HANA migration object modeler is an application for enhancing the migration objects that are used in the SAP S/4HANA migration cockpit to support migration objects that are available in the API but not standard to the object. The application supports both migration approaches—data migration execution with staging tables and data migration execution using direct transfer—however, only certain migration objects are supported. A list of objects is available via SAP Note 2999428, and additional objects can be requested via the process listed in SAP Note 2676589. Once the additional source structure is added, mapped, and synchronized, the *.xml* and *.csv* templates will be updated. Additional information is available in the online help and via SAP Note 3216716.

5.3   Extensibility

Most SAP S/4HANA and SAP S/4HANA Cloud systems can be extended to fulfill the company's needs. Therefore, extensibility includes changes to software behavior that go beyond the capabilities of business configuration, data model extensions, data exposure and integration, layout changes to UIs or forms and reports, and creation of new UIs and a business's own applications. Figure 5.9 shows the big picture of SAP S/4HANA Cloud extensibility options, and Figure 5.10 shows their placement and relationships within or outside of the SAP S/4HANA stack.

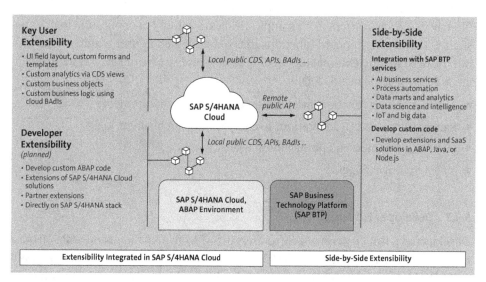

Figure 5.9 SAP S/4HANA Cloud Extensibility: Big Picture

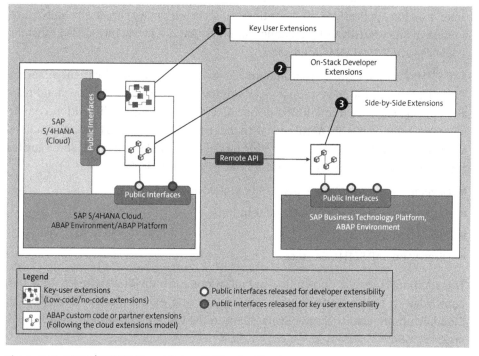

Figure 5.10 SAP S/4HANA Cloud Extensibility: Architecture

As you can see, there are three approaches to extensibility, which we'll discuss in the following sections.

5.3.1 Key User Extensibility

This approach is taken directly within the software stack and allows for extensibility directly in the application—for example, field extensibility or application logic extensibility. This allows standard functionalities to be adapted to user requirements without the need for any external tools. Some important features of key user extensibility are as follows (see Figure 5.10 ❶):

- Adapts standard functionalities to user and business requirements
- Ranges from small UI adaptations to complex custom business logic
- Suited for technical and nontechnical users
- Update-proof changes

5.3.2 Developer Extensibility

Developer extensibility is available to users in SAP S/4HANA Cloud and SAP S/4HANA. Users of SAP S/4HANA Cloud Public Edition in a three-system landscape have access to SAP S/4HANA Cloud, ABAP environment inside the application stack, as shown previously in Figure 5.10. Users of SAP S/4HANA Cloud Private Edition and SAP S/4HANA have access to the full ABAP environment inside their solution, which can be used for extending the application. We'll continue to focus on developer extensibility in the context of SAP S/4HANA Cloud Public Edition as that is a newly introduced capability available to SAP S/4HANA Cloud users.

SAP S/4HANA Cloud, ABAP environment allows you to create development projects in the SAP S/4HANA Cloud system. It gives you the opportunity to develop cloud-ready and upgrade-stable custom ABAP code on SAP S/4HANA Cloud Public Edition, combining the benefits of custom ABAP code with the required restrictions for cloud readiness and with the SAP S/4HANA programming model to build SAP Fiori apps. Some key features of developer extensibility are as follows (see Figure 5.10 ❷):

- Develop custom ABAP code inside SAP S/4HANA Cloud
- Extensions of SAP S/4HANA Cloud solutions
- Partner extensions
- Directly on SAP S/4HANA stack

This additional capability now allows organizations and individuals with existing ABAP knowledge to continue developing applications and extensions for SAP S/4HANA Cloud. For more details about development in the ABAP environment, visit *http://s-prs.co/v596617*.

5.3.3 Side-by-Side Extensibility

In addition to key user extensibility and developer extensibility, you can use side-by-side extensibility to create large extensions and standalone applications that integrate with your SAP S/4HANA solution. This approach uses all the capabilities of SAP BTP as a platform as a service (PaaS) environment to create the required capabilities in a dedicated application running on SAP BTP. This application is then integrated with the SAP S/4HANA Cloud or SAP S/4HANA solution using published APIs that you can access on SAP Business Accelerator Hub at *http://api.sap.com.*

This approach is used for extensions of application capabilities that can't be achieved with key user extensibility or developer extensibility and that are better stored in separate applications for purposes of upgradability or maintenance. This includes the following and can integrate with both cloud and on-premise versions (see Figure 5.10 ❸):

- Developing dependent extensions
- Developing your own custom application
- Consuming existing apps
- Partner-delivered applications extending SAP solution capabilities.

5.3.4 Tools and Implementation

The following resources are used for learning about extending the SAP S/4HANA Cloud and SAP S/4HANA applications:

- **SAP Extensibility Explorer**
  SAP Extensibility Explorer provides a comprehensive overview of extension options for SAP S/4HANA Cloud. You can explore a range of extensibility patterns using different sample scenarios.

> **Further Resources**
>
> For more information about SAP Extensibility Explorer, see http://s-prs.co/v502719.

- **SAP Business Accelerator Hub**
  SAP Business Accelerator Hub is a central, publicly available overview of APIs and other business content on SAP BTP, including API design and API documentation for each API or service. You can access it at *https://api.sap.com.* You can also connect your SAP S/4HANA Cloud application to this service to test the APIs live.

The extensibility tools are designed for the cloud but are also made available in the on-premise solution. Both cloud and on-premise have some differences with respect to transport setup and gateway setup. In the on-premise version, the key user extensibility and classical ABAP development tools can be used in parallel.

The various phases of implementation related to extensibility in cloud and on-premise solutions are shown in Figure 5.11:

1. **Prepare phase**
   During the prepare phase of the implementation, the project team will prepare a list of all the extensions required for smooth running of the company's business. The result of these discussions will be a Microsoft Excel file with a consolidated list of extensions. Alternatively, the initial list of extensions can be captured in SAP Cloud ALM as the basis for the detailed design activities during the fit-to-standard workshop in the explore phase.

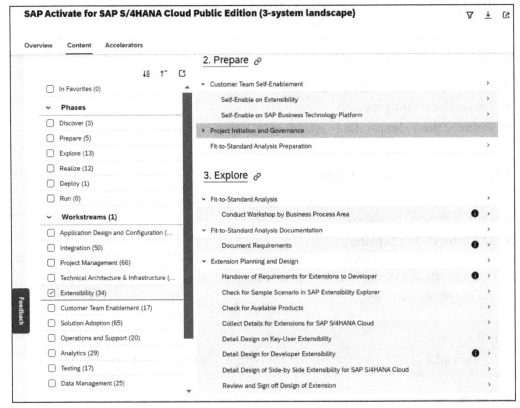

Figure 5.11 Extensibility in SAP Activate Methodology for SAP S/4HANA Cloud Public Edition Three-System Landscape

2. **Explore phase**
   During this phase, the project team should check for available products and review the details for the extensions collected in the prepare phase. After dividing the extensions among key user extensibility, developer extensibility, and side-by-side extensibility, the company does a thorough review and signs off on each extension. The various workshops are conducted by each LoB to identify the list of extensions after reviewing the existing processes in SAP Signavio Process Navigator flows. The

extensions should be reviewed and validated against the golden rules we introduced in Chapter 2, Section 2.5.

The extensibility tools are designed for the cloud but are also made available in the on-premise solution. Both cloud and on-premise have some differences with respect to transport setup and gateway setup. In the on-premise version, key-user extensibility and classical ABAP Development Tools can be used in parallel.

5.4   Integration

An intelligent enterprise is an integrated enterprise. All enterprises are looking to achieve three main scenarios using integration platforms: real-time digital interactions, simplified connected experiences, and process excellence. To do so, the organizations aim to integrate the various systems in their business and IT environments. SAP provides a means to do that in SAP Integration Suite on SAP BTP, which helps you do the following:

- Integrate anything (people, things, processes, data, and applications), anywhere (on-premise, in the cloud, using edge computing), with versatile cloud integration.
- Share real-time data with your supply chain, business networks, and customers with well-managed APIs.
- Orchestrate people, processes, events, and things with process and data integration.
- Automate decision-making with dynamic business rules.
- Enable omnichannel experiences across devices and channels with well-managed APIs.
- Streamline workflows.

The various integration options for SAP S/4HANA are as follows:

- **SAP APIs**
  SAP releases APIs to enable companies digitizing their business to securely connect apps to other systems. The published SAP APIs can be found at *http://s-prs.co/v502720* (cloud) and *http://s-prs.co/v502721* (on-premise).
- **Core data services (CDS) views**
  SAP releases CDS views to read data from the SAP S/4HANA system as OData services.
- **Traditional APIs**
  Business Application Programming Interfaces (BAPIs)/IDocs can be used to connect SAP S/4HANA Cloud with SAP on-premise applications.

The SAP Activate methodology implementation roadmaps help by providing a recommendation of list of deliverables in each phase and a process description in the form of tasks and accelerators (templates, examples, guides, and web links) in a user-friendly format to the project team. Whatever SAP S/4HANA solution you're implementing—SAP S/4HANA Cloud Public Edition, SAP S/4HANA Cloud Private Edition, or SAP S/4HANA—SAP Activate offers a wide range of accelerators and step-by-step processes for implementing any solution.

Figure 5.12 shows the integration-relevant deliverables and tasks in the SAP Activate methodology for an SAP S/4HANA Cloud implementation.

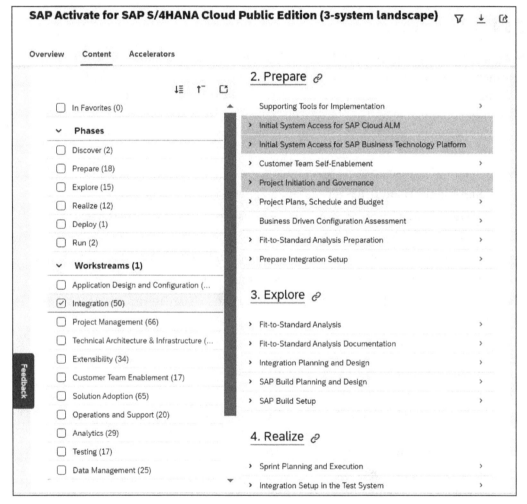

Figure 5.12 Integration Workstream in the SAP Activate Methodology for SAP S/4HANA Cloud Public Edition

The various phases of the SAP Activate methodology for any SAP S/4HANA solution for integration are discussed in the following sections.

5.4.1 Prepare

In the prepare phase, the project team is formed, the scope is refined, and the project gets underway. From the integration standpoint, there are several key decisions and steps that the team needs to walk through that we'll explain in this section.

Let's examine the key deliverables:

- **SAP supporting implementation tools access**
  To begin, we start with accessing the supporting implementation tools. In this deliverable, the company gets access to various tools available in SAP S/4HANA Cloud, such as the following:
  - Set up the SAP BTP global account.
  - Activate SAP Build entitlements, and set up SAP Start and SAP Mobile Start.
  - Subscribe to the Cloud Integration Automation service within SAP BTP.
- **Company team self-enablement**
  Next, the company moves on to team self-enablement. The company team will read all the help related to various tools, which will be useful in the implementation process. Some of these tools are as follows:
  - **SAP BTP, including the Cloud Integration Automation service**
    This is a cloud service that allows users to create their own guided, partially automated procedures for the integration of scenarios. After a procedure is defined and is available, the service can help companies do the following:
    - Role-based execution: Tasks are assigned to the right person based on role assignments.
    - Integrated parameter management: Data can be entered once and reused throughout the workflow.
    - System landscape information: This information is available as a dropdown list from known company SAP systems.
    - Traceability of activity: Information is provided on who did which steps in the integration.
  - **Open connectors**
    The various accelerators provided in the SAP Activate methodology will help users familiarize themselves with open connectors on SAP BTP for customer-driven integration and side-by-side extensions.
  - **Business-to-business (B2B) integrations using electronic data interchange (EDI)**
    This provides information about integration between SAP S/4HANA and third-party systems (e.g., suppliers and buyers) leveraging API-enabled EDI integration. There are various scope items available under EDI integration.
  - **Project plans, schedule, and budget**
    All the planning activities related to the early stages of a project and its schedule

and budget are completed in the next deliverable. The alignment of project schedules and key milestones as follows are considered:

- Different system landscape provisioning
- System landscape configuration start date
- System landscape configuration completion date
- Testing in the quality system landscape and the production system landscape
- System operations related to the software update schedule

- **Business-driven configuration assessment**
  In the business-driven configuration assessment deliverable, various accelerators are provided in the SAP Activate methodology related to questionnaires for each LoB and including questions related to integration considerations.

- **Fit-to-standard analysis preparation**
  Finally, for fit-to-standard analysis preparation, the company will download the SAP Best Practices content and select the various scope items corresponding to their business needs. A list of initial integrations and APIs is provided as an accelerator for preparing the list of the company's current integrations.

5.4.2   Explore

In this phase, the project scope is validated, and it's confirmed that the business requirements can be satisfied by selecting the SAP Best Practices scope items. Any gaps and configuration values are added to the backlog for use in the next phase.

Let's walk through the key deliverables:

- **Fit-to-standard analysis**
  The various LoB-specific workshops are conducted, and SAP Best Practices flows are reviewed. The various accelerators are provided in each roadmap. During the fit-to-standard workshops, the project team identifies the required integration requirements and captures them in SAP Cloud ALM.

- **Solution definition**
  All the documentation captured in each workshop is complete. This includes the detailing of the integration requirements into a formalized set of documented requirements.

- **Integration planning and design**
  The optimized list of integrations is planned and designed, which will be tested in the realize phase of the implementation. The various integrations listed are delegated to the integration expert team that will plan, map, and draft the step-by-step process for each integration. The various tasks involved in this deliverable are as follows:

  - Scenario options for integration
  - Customer-driven integrations
  - Customer-driven integrations using open connectors

- – B2B integrations using EDI
- – Customer-driven integrations with SAP Integration Suite integration flows

5.4.3   Realize

During this phase, both functional and technical implementation takes place. All required interfaces are implemented as designed in the explore phase. All integrations are set up and tested in the test system.

In all the various solutions, the setup instructions for customer-driven integrations are written up and reviewed. An accelerator is already available in the explore phase to consolidate all the integration scenarios in the scope of the company's project.

After all the integrations are set up and approved in the quality system landscape, the setup is completed in the production system landscape.

5.5   SAP Business AI

This section will cover the foundational elements and key considerations your organization should focus on to maximize the benefits of SAP Business AI capabilities, including Joule. We'll address both the consultants responsible for implementing AI-powered business processes and the business users adopting applications with SAP Business AI capabilities. In Chapter 1, we introduced SAP Business AI as one of the core technologies for SAP S/4HANA Cloud and briefly touched on the harmonized UX with SAP Fiori, which will also be discussed here.

As mentioned in Chapter 1, SAP Business AI represents a paradigm shift in how users engage with business applications, enabling them to make data-driven and informed decisions. In this section, we'll dive deeper into the foundational aspects of SAP Business AI within SAP S/4HANA Cloud Public Edition, while highlighting lessons learned, best practices, and key areas to focus on to maximize its business value.

It's important to reiterate that SAP Business AI isn't a standalone feature, but a strategic capability integrated across a wide range of SAP business processes and applications. In this book, we focus on SAP Business AI within SAP S/4HANA Cloud Public Edition, which provides an ideal platform for AI capabilities due to its stable, extensible core; comprehensive data structures; best practices; and intelligent features that enable business process transformation.

For SAP consultants and business users, the objective is to understand that while AI is powerful, its full potential is unlocked when integrated with the intelligent technologies already available within SAP S/4HANA Cloud Public Edition and SAP BTP. The combination of AI and these technologies drives true business transformation by optimizing processes, enhancing the UX, and boosting productivity.

5.5.1   Foundational Elements for Leveraging SAP Business AI

To successfully implement and scale AI capabilities in SAP S/4HANA Cloud Public Edition, organizations must focus on four core elements:

- **Digital core**
  A well-structured and clean data foundation is essential for any AI initiative. SAP S/4HANA Cloud Public Edition ensures "a clean digital core" in all dimensions of the solution. This supports seamless integration of SAP Business AI capabilities and establishes well-defined data structures in the application. As a result, business users can quickly activate and adopt new capabilities, enhancing their efficiency and productivity. The regular updates of SAP S/4HANA Cloud enable their system to stay current, including the AI enhancements that SAP will continue delivering in future releases.

- **User experience (UX)**
  SAP Fiori provides a seamless, intuitive interface, significantly enhancing user productivity. As AI capabilities such as Joule, SAP's AI-powered digital assistant, become more prevalent, it's crucial for users to be familiar with and use the latest UX features. Consultants and IT experts should encourage business users to personalize their experience using tools such as the *My Home dashboard* and *spaces and pages* to maximize efficiency and enjoyment.

  Customers with multiple SAP cloud solutions such as SAP S/4HANA Cloud, SAP Ariba, and SAP SuccessFactors should use SAP Start, which integrates key information from various systems into a unified, easy-to-access interface (see an example of SAP Start in Figure 5.13). Future AI-enabled applications in the system will build on these UX improvements, making seamless, AI-driven business processes a reality for all users.

Further Resources for UX

Learn more about the My Home dashboard and spaces and pages in the following SAP Community blog articles:

- My Home: *http://s-prs.co/v596618*
- Pages and spaces: *http://s-prs.co/v596619*

- **Intelligent technologies**
  Analytics, machine learning, and predictive capabilities are now embedded into SAP S/4HANA Cloud Public Edition. These technologies empower businesses to manage operations by exception, freeing up valuable time for strategic decision-making, and AI adoption. Features such as intelligent scenarios, situation handling, and predictive analytics bring added intelligence to traditional business processes.

Figure 5.13 SAP Start Bringing Together the Most Important Information in an Easy-to-Use UX

Additional Resources for Intelligent Technologies

You can find more information about each of these technologies using the following links:

- Embedded analytics: *http://s-prs.co/v596620*
- Situation handling: *http://s-prs.co/v596621*
- Intelligent business scenarios: *http://s-prs.co/v596622*

- **Business process automation**

  Automation is crucial for modernizing business operations and enhancing user efficiency. By streamlining the business processes and eliminating repetitive manual steps, businesses can achieve greater productivity. SAP BTP capabilities such as SAP

Build Process Automation, SAP Business AI services, and SAP AI Core enable businesses to streamline repetitive tasks, focus on high-value activities, and integrate AI innovations to improve business processes. Automating business processes such as sales order management or predictive accounting not only saves time and reduces human error but also leads to better business outcomes.

Additional Resources for SAP Build Process Automation

We recommend regularly reviewing the latest content for process automation available in the following repositories:

- SAP Business Accelerator Hub: *http://s-prs.co/v596623*
- SAP Signavio Process Navigator: *http://s-prs.co/v596624*

5.5.2   Lessons Learned from Integrating SAP Business AI

Organizations often face challenges when integrating AI into their SAP systems, especially when they lack a well-structured approach. Based on our experiences, here are some key lessons learned in adopting SAP Business AI:

- **Focus beyond generative AI**
  Many organizations mistakenly believe that implementing generative AI alone will revolutionize their business processes. However, it's critical to integrate AI technologies with the existing intelligent technologies available in SAP S/4HANA Cloud Public Edition. The greatest value comes when AI complements existing machine learning models, predictive analytics, and business process automation.

- **Leverage intelligent scenarios**
  SAP S/4HANA Cloud Public Edition offers preconfigured intelligent scenarios that can drive business improvements. For instance, machine learning can monitor goods receipts or automate invoice verification. It's crucial to explore and implement these scenarios based on your specific business needs. You can enable intelligent scenarios through the Intelligent Scenario Management app, allowing users to trust and rely on predictive suggestions for more informed decision-making.

Additional Resources

Review details about the Intelligent Scenario Lifecycle Management app on the SAP Help Portal at *http://s-prs.co/v596625*.

- **Continuous user empowerment**
  Successfully implementing SAP Business AI is not only about improving processes but also about empowering users. Regular updates to the SAP UX and continuous training on new AI capabilities, such as Joule, are essential for ensuring users feel confident in using these tools. Encourage business users to fully leverage the latest

UX improvements we introduced earlier, such as My Home, as well as the SAP Horizon theme, which enable users to tailor their interface and improve productivity by focusing on critical tasks. Additionally, transitioning from older applications such as Web GUI to the most up-to-date AI-embedded SAP Fiori apps (e.g., Manage Sales Orders – Version 2) is key to maximizing efficiency.

- **Automation as a driver of innovation**
  Process automation, enabled by SAP Build Process Automation, should be a top priority for organizations looking to optimize efficiency. SAP consultants should regularly review the latest automation process packages available in SAP Business Accelerator Hub to keep clients informed of new opportunities for automating business processes.

- **Leveraging Joule to assist business users**
  Joule, an intelligent digital assistant, simplifies users' daily tasks through natural language conversations. As AI adoption increases, integrating Joule into workflows will simplify processes and drive more intuitive interactions with the system. From recommending applications to summarizing business data, Joule is set to transform how users engage with SAP systems. You can see an example of Joule in Figure 5.14.

Figure 5.14 Joule Seamlessly Integrated into the UX

- **Adopt the modernized SAP Best Practices**
  SAP's intelligent business processes are constantly evolving, with new capabilities regularly being introduced to support SAP Business AI. Organizations using SAP S/4HANA Cloud Public Edition should consider adopting these AI-embedded business processes to stay ahead of the curve:

– Predictive Accounting for Sales Orders (solution process 2FD): *http://s-prs.co/ v596626*

– Demand-Driven Buffer Level Management (solution process 1Y2): *http://s-prs.co/ v596627*

– Machine Learning for Monitoring of Goods and Invoice Receipts (solution process 2ZS): *http://s-prs.co/v596628*

For each of these solution processes, you'll find additional information such as the business process diagram, setup instructions, and other implementation accelerators. You can see an example of the accelerators, including **Set-up instructions** and **Test script**, for the solution process **Machine Learning for Monitoring of Goods and Invoice Receipts (2ZS)** in Figure 5.15.

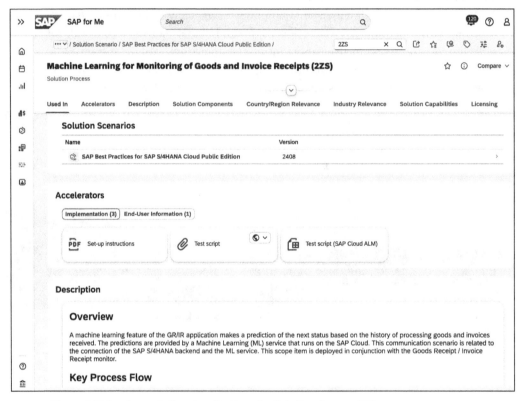

Figure 5.15 Implementation Accelerators for Solution Process 2ZS

5.5.3   The Future of SAP Business AI

SAP Business AI will continue to advance, with capabilities evolving rapidly. SAP will introduce new capabilities with each release, and to fully capitalize on these new advancements, organizations should proactively monitor the SAP product roadmap. Using tools such as the release assessment and scope dependency for SAP S/4HANA

Cloud Public Edition tool (discussed in Chapter 4) is essential for understanding upcoming innovations and adjusting adoption plans to make the most of these new business capabilities. You can see an example of the SAP product roadmap for GROW with SAP and specifically the planned capabilities leveraging generative AI in Figure 5.16.

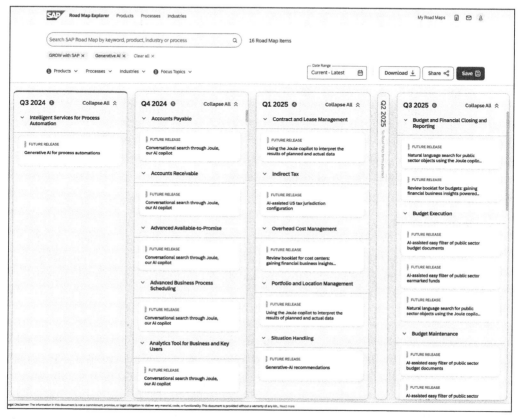

Figure 5.16 GROW with SAP Generative AI Product Roadmap

Organizations should actively track future innovations, such as enhanced human-to-AI collaboration and deeper integrations with other SAP cloud applications such as SAP SuccessFactors. Staying updated on these advancements will help organizations take full advantage of emerging AI capabilities as they become available.

> **Additional Resources**
>
> Review this blog post for more details about considerations for adopting SAP Business AI in your organization: *http://s-prs.co/v596629*.

Unlocking the full potential of SAP Business AI requires more than just implementing generative AI solutions. It requires a holistic approach that integrates SAP Business AI with the robust capabilities of SAP S/4HANA Cloud Public Edition. This approach should focus on enhancing the UX, automating processes, and aligning AI-driven insights with practical business needs. By embracing these key elements and committing to continuous improvement, consultants and business users can drive meaningful transformation within their organizations.

5.6   Testing

SAP Activate covers a range of testing processes and activities across the many SAP solutions, including SAP S/4HANA Cloud Public Edition and SAP S/4HANA Cloud Private Edition. This section will guide you through executing the testing workstream activities and running the upgrade testing activities.

5.6.1   SAP S/4HANA Cloud Public Edition

The SAP Activate for SAP S/4HANA Cloud Public Edition (3-System Landscape) roadmap starts project teams with self-enablement on test management and tools to enable the team on the chosen test management and tools for the project. During this time, the project team should review the test management tool and application lifecycle management (ALM) tool to understand the foundational concepts and tutorials for self-enablement. Enablement of the testing processes should be understood and learned by all testing members.

As with other solutions, test planning activities are performed in the explore phase to set the stage for the remainder of the testing workstream for the project deployment. Paying extra attention to details in the beginning stages of planning will minimize the risk of gaps, rework, setbacks, and additional changes. Test planning for your project starts with creating the test strategy. This strategy can cover the entire project duration and is often owned jointly by the customer and the implementation partner. The test strategy covers the testing objectives and assumptions, scope, testing cycles, approach, tools, defect management, and roles and responsibilities. Before testing starts, all project members and stakeholders must agree to the coordinated approach defined in the test strategy document. Following the test strategy, the next step is to create and schedule a test plan and determine the test scope. A test plan is a group of test cases and processes that reflect the business process sequence and dependencies. It should include the timing of execution from a project timeline standpoint and specify the type of testers that should be made available. In addition, regardless of whether the project is triggered independently or as part of a release, the scope of testing for a project needs to be determined to ensure the testing environments and testing artifacts are available for execution with such a variety of testing cycles (e.g., integration, regression, business process, post-upgrade test (PUT), UAT, etc.).

After the explore phase testing activities have concluded, the realize phase begins. In this phase, test preparation and execution are the main activities the team triggers. Test preparation includes completing the prerequisites, such as knowledge transfer with the testing team and test phase kick-off. Then, complete the test automation tool set-up, including integration with SAP Cloud ALM and user setup. Once the test automation tool is ready, the test cases are defined for end-to-end business processes (SAP Signavio Process Navigator provides predelivered process flows and test scripts), and the team defines the test data for the test case, which is a combination of a test process with test data. Reusing test cases as much as possible or copying and adapting them by adding/removing steps or changing steps is recommended. In addition, your test cases can be created using the test automation tool. You can create custom test processes by copying standard test processes and by creating a new custom test process. The same goes for editing custom test processes: you can adjust test process steps and edit the action data in the test process steps.

After defining the test case, the project team prepares the automated test scripts in the test automation tool for SAP S/4HANA Cloud, which covers individual business scenarios and test data.

As mentioned, standard test automation scripts are delivered with the SAP Signavio Process Navigator content. The team should trigger automated testing via automated test scripts. However, some business processes, such as integration processes, analytics, or output documents, can't be automated via the test automation tool for SAP S/4HANA Cloud. A manual test must be considered for such processes or process steps.

Test Automation Tool

SAP S/4HANA Cloud offers an excellent suite for testing deliverables for project teams and companies. The built-in testing platform in the test automation tool allows you to create manual and customized test cases for more unique business processes. You can also leverage delivered test scripts that are more streamlined and ready immediately for testing activities.

Per industry standards, we strongly recommend that project teams use the test automation tool for SAP S/4HANA Cloud within the solution due to its many advantages.

After every major upgrade, the SAP S/4HANA Cloud testing environment offers the benefit of having (with the consent of the company/project team to allow SAP to run this in the backend) the SAP team run the predelivered test scripts, also known as PUT to ensure the upgrade updates run smoothly. This adds an extra benefit layer of confirming that the test scripts don't have any bugs, defects, or failures so that the company can have peace of mind. Letting SAP take on this action versus the company executing these processes saves time.

The project team can add manual and customized test cases within the PUT scope if the standard scope is insufficient. SAP encourages the company/project team to minimize the use of custom and manual test scripts because as each upgrade release occurs, the test scripts need to be evaluated to ensure they are still running smoothly and accurately. This is required because the automated test tool doesn't test these types of custom scripts, adding additional time and effort to confirm that the steps in these cases were run successfully.

To create and schedule the test plan in the test automation tool for SAP S/4HANA Cloud or within SAP Cloud ALM, you include standard and custom test processes in the sequence that defines the end-to-end business flow. Data should be reviewed and modified using data variants. In addition, the team will modify action data in customer-specific automated test scripts and change the visibility of the test process in the Manage Your Test Processes app.

Next, the test plan is triggered. With the SAP Cloud ALM and test automation tool for SAP S/4HANA Cloud, test scripts can be efficiently run in the solution and give you status updates during the test execution process, including screenshots, status progress (i.e., **Pass**, **Failed**, **In Progress**), and the ability to test scripts with execution schedules that can be run in the background. Figure 5.17 shows an example of one test plan that can be scheduled to trigger and one failed test plan.

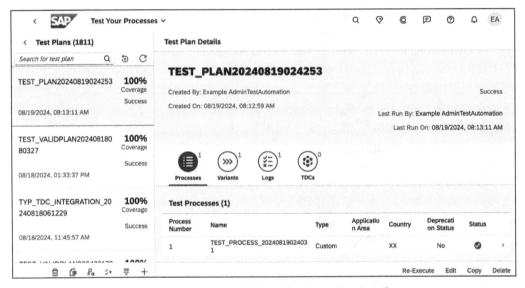

Figure 5.17 Test Your Processes App with Test Plan Execution Details

After the test plan has been triggered, identified errors must be resolved and rerun to ensure accuracy. After all errors have been resolved, the team generates, views, and analyzes the report of the test results shown under **Test Processes** for either **Post-Upgrade Tests** or **Customer Tests** in the **Test Plan Details** dashboard available in SAP S/4HANA Cloud.

The last set of activities of the realize phase are performed under the automated test execution for SAP S/4HANA Cloud deliverables: Execute the Test Cases within SAP S/4HANA Cloud, Defect Management and Retesting for SAP S/4HANA Cloud, and Test Execution Analysis and Reporting for SAP S/4HANA Cloud.

After the test planning, the test execution is performed to trigger the testing cycles. The chosen test suite (e.g., SAP Cloud ALM and the test automation tool) is used, and the outcomes of the analysis and reporting are documented.

The test case and incident message(s) within the test tool(s) are linked and can be called directly from status reporting for further analysis. After every major product upgrade for SAP S/4HANA Cloud is released, the next set of testing activities needs to be considered; these are available in the SAP Activate for Upgrade of SAP S/4HANA Cloud 3-System Landscape implementation roadmap.

Project teams will use the direction for the testing workstream in this implementation roadmap for regression tests and execution. This upgrade roadmap will bring us to regression testing first. Within the regression test deliverable, we'll ensure we're prepared for the PUT by SAP for live customers (this is done for a limited set of SAP S/4HANA Cloud applications and only for productive customers). The test plans are generated by SAP with an option to add a custom scope and decide which variant will be used. Once the test plan is prepared, it will be triggered in the customer's test system. Remember that the customer team must consent for this activity to occur; this consent can be given directly in the test automation tool. If consent is absent, the PUT execution activities won't be performed (consent needs to be presented at least two weeks before the start of the upgrade).

In addition to the SAP-managed PUT, the customer team can trigger the PUT at any time in the Manage Upgrade Tests app.

Reviewing the PUT accelerators is strongly recommended to ensure a smooth upgrade process. The team will analyze the PUT results via the test automation tool to review the statuses and successful execution of the test results. In addition, under the regression test deliverable, the preparation of test cases that need to be triggered by the customer is performed.

Regression test execution is done to close out the final set of testing activities. This is where the regression tests are triggered in the solution to validate previously tested functionalities to ensure they still work as designed after changes are made (e.g., an upgrade, ongoing enhancements, and additional improvements). Re-execution of failed test plans will need to be done after correcting errors.

5.6.2   SAP S/4HANA Cloud Private Edition

The testing workstream in the SAP S/4HANA Cloud Private Edition implementation roadmap guides project teams through the test planning, preparation, execution, and release activities for a successful testing outcome. The SAP Activate Roadmap Viewer includes the entire SAP Activate workstream suite and can be filtered on workstreams, such as testing, for a more focused view of the upcoming testing activities and milestones.

The first step in the testing workstream starts in the prepare phase to enable the team in the testing tools being used for the project as they relate to testing to maximize enablement and learning, create efficiencies in later deliverables (i.e., SAP Cloud ALM and SAP Solution Manager), and set foundational knowledge for the project.

In the explore phase, we focus on test planning activities, including test strategy creation, determining the test scope, and creating and scheduling an overall test plan. When making the test strategy, the elements of the test strategy and documentation are agreed upon before starting testing and signed off on by the team (typically the customer and implementation partner) to define how testing will be performed and completed in the project. Next, the test scope is determined, and the overall test plan is created and scheduled. The test scope needs to be determined early for a project, regardless of whether the project is triggered independently or as part of a release, to ensure the testing environments and materials are available for execution. With such a variety of testing cycles available (e.g., integration, regression, performance, cutover, and UAT), it's essential to define the cycles required to support the planned conversion event. Detailed test planning will cover the dependencies, tasks, criteria, resources, and duration of testing time frames to outline the end-to-end testing activities during the project implementation. To close out the explore phase, the team performs the creation and scheduling of a detailed test plan. This will allow for all scenarios to optimally have the schedule documented to cover tasks, dependencies, and durations, mitigating risk.

At the start of the realize phase, the project team starts the testing preparation activities, which include prerequisites such as preparing for the continuous releases that occur mid-project, identifying the availability of the testers, using a test management system, or ensuring the availability and accessibility of selected test automation tools and chosen test management tools (e.g., SAP Solution Manager and SAP Cloud ALM).

Tricentis Quality Assurance Platform

Tricentis's proven Continuous Testing Framework complements the SAP Activate methodology, specifying the quality engineering steps to take at each phase so you can keep SAP transformation on track—whether you're just getting started or already running on SAP S/4HANA.

Per industry standards, we recommend that project teams use the Tricentis test automation tool or other certified test automation tools for SAP S/4HANA Cloud Private Edition.

The project team must understand the changes that have occurred at the mid-implementation point (where an upgrade has occurred) to ensure that the project's impact has been addressed, understood, and adapted. The project kickoff meeting occurs, and the team is onboarded with the necessary tool setup, knowledge transfers, and user IDs for the systems needed for the project implementation.

Next, manual test cases are created to define the manual test cases and supporting test data to be used for customer solution testing. It's strongly recommended that the number of manual test cases be limited where possible. For automated test cases, the team will use the selected test automation tools to create them directly in the tool.

Project teams can edit the action data and change the visibility of the test processes to modify actions in company-specific automated test scripts and manage the visibility of test cases.

The final set of testing activities in the realize phase is test execution, which includes executing the test plan, correcting and rerunning the test plan to remove any errors or messages, and then analyzing and reporting the testing outcomes. These tasks are based on the project team's previous planning in subsequent phases to ensure the most successful execution of testing activities.

5.6.3   SAP S/4HANA

SAP S/4HANA testing is based on on-premise activities and testing tools different from the two cloud solutions. With the Transition to SAP S/4HANA implementation roadmap, three scenarios can occur for a project deployment: new implementation, system conversion, and selective data transition (see Chapter 8). We'll focus on the on-premise guidance in this section and walk you through the testing workstream in the explore and realize phases.

The testing workstream begins with the test planning activities in the explore phase. The main activities include the following:

- Familiarizing yourself with the tools in test management
- Setting up test management in SAP Solution Manager
- Determining the test scope
- Performing detailed test planning

It's strongly encouraged to finalize the testing planning as early as possible and outline and identify the project scope, testing objectives and assumptions, types of testing, approach, tools, defect management, and roles and responsibilities of the testing team to minimize the number of risks and issues going forward. A solid ground for these key elements sets the road for smoother testing activities and milestones for the project deployment.

Teams must understand the test tools in test management and the setup of SAP Solution Manager, as these will be used heavily during multiple vital events. Various resources are available to the project team so that they can fully familiarize themselves with the testing learning journey (see Figure 5.18).

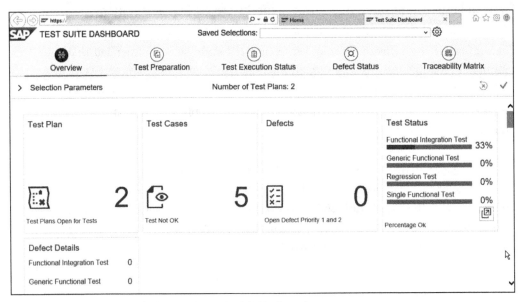

Figure 5.18 SAP Solution Manager Test Suite Overview

Next, the scope of testing for a project, regardless of whether the project is triggered independently or as part of a release, must be determined early to ensure the testing environments and materials are available. With such a variety of testing cycles available (e.g., integration, regression, performance, cutover, and UAT), it's essential to define the cycles required to support the planned conversion event.

The last activity, which closes out the explore phase, is detailed test planning. This is where the scoping and planning of the test is required for the transition project to determine which testing cycles are needed to meet the quality gate conditions for entering the realize phase. This includes evaluating and enabling test management and the test automation tools to support the testing activities across milestones, executing tasks using ALM best practices for test management and tailoring the templates for the test strategy and functional test plan to meet the project team needs. In addition, the detailed testing plan should support the need to mitigate risks that may arise for the end-state solution and during cutover activities.

The last phase in the testing workstream for the Transition to SAP S/4HANA implementation roadmap encompasses the following:

1. Execution plan for the realize phase
2. Test preparation
3. Test execution

Let's dive into these last three critical components of the testing workstream.

The purpose of the execution plan for the realize phase is to trigger the work defined, manage the sprints/testing as described previously, log all issues, and document them in the system for traceability. Furthermore, the project team manages the integration, security, and UAT.

Next, the test preparation task and objective is to prepare all business process-related tests according to customer-specific configurations. Preparing the tests is based on evaluating the existing test materials, which were identified in the explore phase (i.e., testing plan), and other assets for execution of the testing cycles. Any missed test materials and test scripts that are realized must be developed by the detailed test plan to capture all testing-critical materials and documentation. Testing teams can leverage the fully ready and detailed test scripts, process flows, and other documentation via SAP Signavio Process Navigator. SAP Signavio Process Navigator provides scope item content and documentation for project teams to leverage and use ready-to-access content and assets efficiently and quickly with the ease of the tool navigation and its added benefits.

Finally, test execution occurs by performing integration, regression, and UAT testing activities. The testing team prepares a test environment with the required test data defined previously in the testing workstream. After all criteria have been collected and described, test execution can begin.

Typical testing processes for the realize phase are as follows:

1. Software developers perform unit tests in the development systems. Various functional tests are performed depending on the type and scope of the test cycle.

2. Manual testers are provided with the tester handout document and receive details regarding their test package by email.

3. Automated tests are scheduled or started directly.

4. Every triggered test is logged and documented with test notes, and a test status is set manually or automatically.

5. If the system responds unexpectedly during manual testing—for example, if an error message appears—the tester records the incident in the corresponding SAP IT Service Management (SAP ITSM) system, attaching screenshots, log messages, and so on. Usually, this also must be done manually, even for automated tests.

6. The incident is sent to the persons responsible for analyzing and categorizing defects, who then correct the defect in the development system.

7. The correction is transported to the test system according to the existing arrangements and timelines, then retested.

Further Resources

For additional details, see the test execution deliverable in the realize phase in the Transition to SAP S/4HANA implementation roadmap in the SAP Activate Roadmap Viewer.

The objective of integration testing is to perform the end-to-end process integration between all SAP and non-SAP components of the solution landscape and validate that all application systems are functioning correctly as intended. Integration testing and regression testing ensures that all business scenarios have been tested before UAT. UAT is then performed by the users who will be using the solution after the project team finishes the implementation to ensure the solution works as it should with the company's various end-to-end business processes. During the test execution in the various testing cycles, defects and bugs should be logged in SAP Solution Manager for defect resolution and tracking. In addition, all testing details are tracked in SAP Solution Manager, as well as in a central tool location. After these two phases are triggered and completed, the testing workstream concludes.

5.7 Summary

This chapter introduced the key topic areas of fit-to-standard, configuration, data migration, extensibility, integration, business AI, and testing across solutions. It's important to recall that these activities require added attention to ensure that the delivered solution satisfies the business requirements and to any unforeseen setbacks during the project implementation.

We outlined the key activities and focus areas to pay attention to in each of these subjects whether it's the way to surface requirements, design the extensions, or set up SAP Business AI capabilities and testing. In the next chapter, we'll discuss how to apply agile techniques and processes in the context of an SAP S/4HANA Cloud project. We'll describe the agile project team roles, governance, and key agile processes, from release planning through the execution of the sprints that form the foundation for the agile approach.

Chapter 6
Agile Project Delivery

In today's rapidly changing business environment, it's critical for IT organizations to embrace new ways of working to allow for quicker response to the changing needs of their business users. An agile way of working empowers project teams to adjust priorities quickly, allowing them to focus on the highest importance items and thus respond to evolving business needs with urgency and speed.

We introduced the SAP Activate approach and key tools in the previous chapters. Now, let's dive into the details of using the agile mindset during the deployment of your SAP S/4HANA-based solution.

Agile has gained traction over the past years and has become an accepted way of working for IT organizations. While the concepts started with software development, they have been adopted also in other areas of IT and business. SAP Activate was designed as a hybrid approach that leverages the accelerators we talked about in the previous chapters—for example, SAP Best Practices preconfiguration content—to set up the ready-to-use system the project team needs for the fit-to-standard workshops and ultimately to surface the delta requirements and gaps to address throughout the realize phase. SAP has incorporated agile project delivery into the SAP Activate flow to take advantage of the initial backlog coming from fit-to-standard workshops as a basis for agile planning and execution. It allows the team to set a focus for each short time box, called a *sprint*, and deliver value in the form of realized requirements. Sprints are used in the realize phase to work on the highest priority items from the backlog to progressively configure, extend, integrate, and test the system.

In this chapter, we'll go over the details of governance in agile projects, which sets the way team the works in each release and sprint. In addition, we'll discuss the more advanced topic of scaling agile to larger complexity projects with scaling frameworks.

6.1 Roles, Responsibilities, and Governance

SAP Activate builds on the Scrum agile framework for team-level and project-level implementation of agile values, roles, events, and artifacts. The Scrum approach is built around a defined set of values, predefined roles, prescribed processes, and artifacts we'll outline here.

The Scrum framework values are as follows:

- **Courage**
  The teams using the Scrum framework must have the courage to do the right thing and work on challenging problems. The team members who follow the Scrum approach will champion the user's point of view in their work and strive to deliver the best solution for the user and business.

- **Focus**
  All people working in the Scrum framework focus on delivering the stated objectives of the sprint and a release. This is one of the aligning principles to set the focus for every sprint by committing to the delivery of a specified subset of high-priority items from the backlog.

- **Commitment**
  All team members are personally committed to delivering value and agreed-upon deliverables and capabilities.

- **Respect**
  Scrum members have respect for each other and for the users they are working to deliver the solution to.

- **Openness**
  One of the key principles is openness and transparency, which is critical for the agile way of working to function. All Scrum members agree to be open about their challenges and the work they are doing to deliver the goals of the Scrum.

SAP Activate builds on these values and formulates them into principles that are tailored to the context of an SAP project. We reviewed these principles in Chapter 2. In the following sections, we'll take a closer look at the roles, events, and artifacts involved in the Scrum agile framework.

6.1.1   Roles

The Scrum framework defines several key roles, which we'll discuss in the following sections. SAP Activate uses them in addition to the core SAP project roles, which provide a more detailed profile of the role in the context of the SAP project.

Product Owner

The *product owner* is the person responsible for maximizing the value that the Scrum team delivers. The product owner must clearly define the product vision and objectives, translate them into a product backlog as backlog items (e.g., capabilities, key functionality, attributes of the solution), and prioritize the items to give the team clear direction regarding what is more important to deliver the maximum value.

In SAP projects, the product owner's role is played by representatives of the business users, typically a global business process owner or group of process owners. This way, the person(s) in this role can best represent the business user needs and identify the backlog items that help maximize the business value of the solution for the specific group of business users.

Scrum Master

The *Scrum master* role helps the team and product owner follow the Scrum processes and helps with the delivery of Scrum artifacts throughout the project. Their responsibility is to educate all team members on principles, procedures, rules, and values. They also often are responsible for scheduling the Scrum events, such as planning meetings, daily standups, or retrospectives.

The Scrum master is typically a team member who takes on the responsibility of educating the team and directing the Scrum events during the project. We've also seen situations where the Scrum master is a dedicated role in the project; such Scrum masters typically serve multiple Scrum teams. In our experience, the dedicated Scrum master can serve up to three Scrum teams, but not more, as the project teams work on a synchronized Scrum heartbeat; this means that the Scrum events are occurring in the same time frame, limiting the Scrum master's ability to serve more teams.

Team

The Scrum *team* consists of cross-functional experts and professionals brought together to deliver the capabilities stated in the backlog to realize value for the users or business. The team works in an iterative mode, following the sprint model, to deliver increments of work defined in the backlog. Their responsibility is to understand the backlog items and deliver them during the duration of the sprint to reach the definition of done so that the items can be deployed.

Teams in SAP projects consist of cross-functional experts who work on a specific functional or line of business (LoB) area. Each team has a product owner and a Scrum master, as well as a group of expert resources, such as business process experts and functional experts. Figure 6.1 shows an example of the team composition in the SAP Activate methodology. However, this isn't the only way the team can be composed.

There are many ways to set up teams to support the objectives of your project. Some roles and skills may not be available to each Scrum team via a dedicated resource (e.g., user experience [UX] expert or operational support), and multiple Scrum teams will share the capacity of the expert in each sprint. In such cases, it's important that each Scrum team plans for the required capacity of such shared resources in the sprint planning session to ensure they have all the resources needed to deliver the backlog items the team is committing to complete in a particular sprint.

The second consideration for Scrum team composition is the use of configuration or development factories, centralized data management teams, or central organizational change management (OCM)/training teams (centralized function teams). In such cases, the Scrum team also needs to create respective backlog items for such dedicated teams to ensure the centralized function teams deliver what the Scrum team needs in the agreed-upon time frame. Think, for example, about the delivery of test data for the sprint testing activities that are supported by a centralized data migration team. A similar situation may apply to specific data that Scrum teams need for running a sprint review session to demonstrate the delivered functionality on real customer data to gain buy-in from business users and product owners.

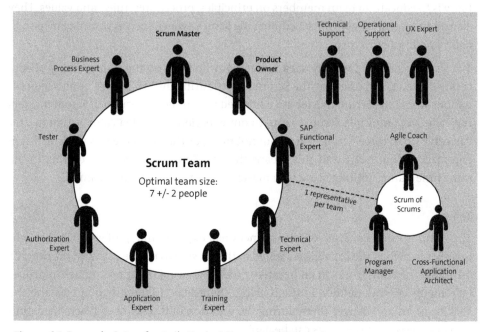

Figure 6.1 Example Setup for Agile Project Team in SAP Project

In addition, note the circle on the right side of Figure 6.1, which shows the regular (typically weekly) meeting between all Scrum team representatives (finance, procurement, sales and distribution, manufacturing, etc.) to work on cross-Scrum team topics. This is extremely important for highly integrated solutions such as SAP where many configuration and setup decisions in one area have an impact on other areas, such as the definition of an organizational structure, setup of the chart of accounts, or definition of number ranges.

In the context of SAP S/4HANA Cloud projects, the project team typically consists of multiple Scrum teams with dedicated product owners responsible for specific functional or business areas and an assigned Scrum master, as shown in Figure 6.2.

For example, the project may consist of the following Scrum teams structured around the key functional areas of the company's solution:

- Finance
- Sales and distribution
- Procurement
- Manufacturing

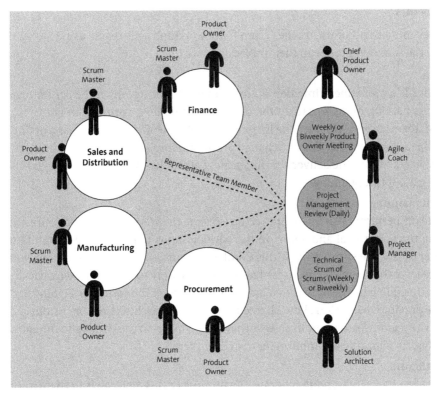

Figure 6.2 Team Composition in SAP S/4HANA Cloud Project: Agile Roles in Scrum Teams

It's important to coordinate among these Scrum teams, and the Scrum approach is extended by having the following coordination meetings:

- Weekly (or biweekly) meetings of all product owners to ensure a consistent definition of the product in the backlog, including the key integrations

- Daily standups to review progress, as well as identify and address any challenges or issues that the individual Scrum team can't address on its own and that need support from the project manager or project leadership

- Weekly (or biweekly) Scrum of Scrums meetings with participation from all Scrum teams to coordinate work on cross-team topics related to configuration and setup that impacts multiple Scrum teams

The composition of the Scrum teams often needs to reflect specific situations. For example, organizations using remote custom code development factories or centralized data management functions will impact the composition of your Scrum teams. In such cases, the project team may have two layers of Scrum team dependencies; for example, the development objects (requiring coding and testing) defined in the finance Scrum team are fulfilled by the dedicated development factory Scrum team. This is like the data preparation example we discussed earlier.

6.1.2   Events

Several events also occur within the Scrum framework, and agile teams using SAP Activate use the same events to run their project:

- **Sprint**
  A sprint is a predefined time box of up to a month during which the Scrum team delivers backlog items to satisfy the definition of done. A sprint is an entity that Scrum teams use to structure the incremental delivery of value and it has a defined and fixed duration that doesn't change during the project. During the sprint, the team works toward the delivery of the sprint goal that has been set in the beginning during the sprint planning.

- **Sprint planning**
  The team performs this collaborative exercise at the beginning of each sprint to define the sprint goal and agree on the backlog items that the team commits to deliver during the sprint. During this event, the team also details the required work to the level that helps them assess feasibility and effort to deliver specific backlog items, including the resources that are required to reach the sprint goal (going back to the previous discussion about shared teams for data, architecture, or custom coding). The team effectively pulls selected backlog items from the backlog to the sprint backlog, thus making a commitment to deliver them.

- **Daily Scrum**
  Also called the daily standup meeting, the purpose of this meeting is to share information among the Scrum team members about the work they are doing, what they plan to do next, and whether they are facing any challenges or blockers. The meeting is set up by the Scrum master, but it isn't a status report to the Scrum master; instead, the team communicates with each other in short sessions every day (about 15 minutes long). The goal is to identify points of synergy where team members can help each other and surface challenges and blockers that the team members need help with (it's the role of the Scrum master to support the resolution of these challenges if team members are unable to resolve them on their own).

- **Sprint review**
  During this event, which is scheduled at the end of the sprint, the team demonstrates the delivered backlog items to the product owner and interested stakeholders in the system. The backlog items are either accepted as delivered and then marked appropriately in the backlog, or they remain in the backlog if there are gaps between what was delivered and the acceptance criteria according to the definition of done. During this event, the product owner and team work jointly to realign the backlog items to ensure that the backlog still reflects the priorities and maximizes value delivery.

- **Sprint retrospective**
  The team holds a retrospective session at the end of each sprint to identify what to keep, what to drop, and what to change or add to their execution of the Scrum process. This event is one of the most critical ones for adapting the approach to the team

and to mature the agile practices. Teams often identify sources of waste and can optimize them very quickly by agreeing to work on that topic and improve it in the next sprint. It's usual to carry a small number of improvement topics into the next sprint to help the team become better.

We'll review the use and sequence of Scrum events while delivering SAP projects in Section 6.3.2.

The SAP Activate methodology provides additional details about how to implement these events in the context of the SAP project. They are embedded in the specific deliverables and tasks in the methodology. You'll find them in the project management workstream as defined tasks with additional guides attached as accelerators. Figure 6.3 shows an example of the **Plan the Sprint for SAP S/4HANA Cloud** task in the **SAP Activate for SAP S/4HANA Cloud Public Edition (3-system landscape)** implementation roadmap in the SAP Activate Roadmap Viewer. There are separate tasks for the sprint execution and closing that detail the use of the events we outlined earlier in the course of the project delivery.

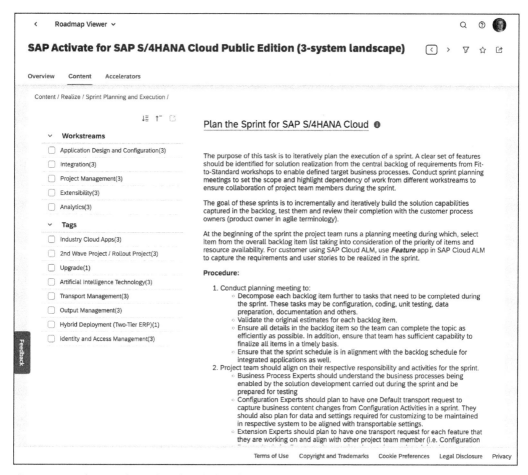

Figure 6.3 Agile-Specific Task Embedded in the SAP Activate Methodology

6.1.3 Artifacts

During the execution of agile processes, the team will produce several artifacts. Scrum defines three key artifacts for the team to manage:

- **Product backlog (or backlog, in short)**
  The backlog is a place that contains an ordered (prioritized) list of backlog items reflecting everything that needs to be delivered in the product or solution. As we mentioned in Section 6.1.1, the product owner is responsible for maintaining the backlog, including the contents, prioritization, and sequencing.

Product Backlog versus ASAP Blueprint

The product backlog is a living document that continues to evolve during the project, unlike an ASAP Business Blueprint document, which used to be created in the ASAP methodology business blueprint phase as a detailed design to address identified requirements and gaps. The blueprint was defined very early in the project timeline and frozen by a formal sign-off.

In SAP Activate, the project team will continue to adjust the product backlog during the sprint review. In addition, the product owners will continue to groom the backlog during the project execution as preparation for the next sprint to provide the Scrum team with detailed backlog items that can be planned into the sprint. In some projects, the backlog items that aren't delivered are used to formulate the scope and timeline of the next wave of deployments or rollouts.

- **Sprint backlog**
  The Scrum team commits to delivering this subset of backlog items during the sprint time box. This sets the focus for the team for the duration of the sprint. Typically, the teams detail the work required during the sprint planning discussed in Section 6.1.2.

- **Increment**
  Increments represent all the backlog items that are delivered during the sprint and meet the definition of done. The team and product owner jointly decide whether to deploy the increment into productive use by users or hold it in the quality environment for larger wave deployment.

We'll discuss the use of these artifacts throughout the rest of this chapter.

6.2 Creating and Managing the Backlog

Fit-to-standard workshops are the mechanism that the project team uses to create the initial backlog to reflect all the capabilities that the solution needs to deliver to maximize its value to the business. During the solution demo and delta design workshops, the team defines and agrees on the required product capabilities and whether they require additional configuration, extension, or integration. These workshops run in parallel, and the process owners define the initial backlog.

The situation may look something like what is shown in Figure 6.4, where you can see the initial product backlogs defined by product owners in individual workshops (first box at the top-left side). Then, the backlog gets consolidated and aligned on the program level. During this exercise, the centralized product backlog reflects the requirements of all teams for feature A in one large backlog item (Scrum teams refer to it as an *epic*) that has subitems from all the teams harmonized so that they can be delivered to the dedicated team during the project. After the central product backlog has been created and the team proceeds to the realize phase, the individual teams will pull backlog items from the central backlog to their team sprint backlogs to drive execution of the requirements.

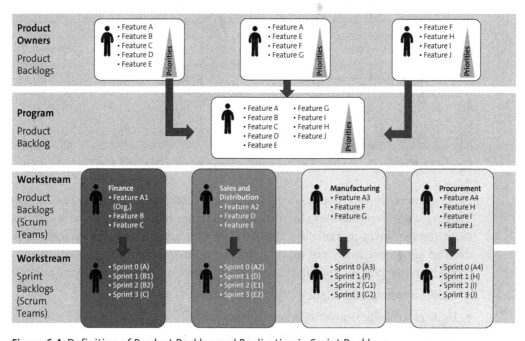

Figure 6.4 Definition of Product Backlog and Realization in Sprint Backlogs

We talked about product ownership in Scrum in Section 6.1.1. In most organizations, the business process ownership is too complex for one central product owner to be defined. This is the case in global organizations that have a multilayered process ownership model that establishes the chief product owner at the top of the hierarchy, with dedicated product owners for each area of the solution that is being implemented. This model allows for the product owners to work directly with their dedicated Scrum team while ensuring a consistent definition of the product along the aligned vision and objectives. Figure 6.5 shows an example of such a setup. Product ownership can be complex in large organizations, and it's important to establish a product ownership hierarchy to involve all key stakeholders in the right stages of the project. Be sure to align the Scrum teams with the product owners for maximum impact.

Another concept for backlog definition is that not all the backlog items are fully detailed right from the beginning. The product owners work through the backlog to help the team understand the backlog items and detail them prior to key activities such as release planning or sprint planning, during which the team needs to have enough information about the backlog item to estimate the effort to complete it and to identify the skills and resources needed for its completion.

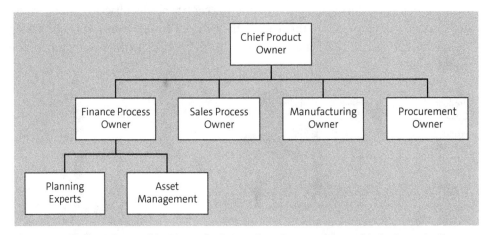

Figure 6.5 Product Ownership Hierarchy Setup along Process Ownership in Organizations

Backlog items are typically created initially in the format of user stories and then detailed to the level that the team members can understand and decide how to implement the required functionality. This detailing process consists of producing more detailed design documents or mock-ups of the desired capabilities. In SAP S/4HANA Cloud projects, these additional details could be one or more of the following artifacts:

- Business scenario description or process description document
- Updates to business process flow/process model
- Functional specifications for extensions or custom objects
- Technical integration design document
- Data requirements document
- Authorization concept or requirement document

Teams also will create more technical realization-specific documents in the realize phase during the sprints to detail technical implementation aspects of the capability being implemented. Typically, more documentation is created in projects that use dedicated development factories where the functional and technical teams aren't collocated. Additional documentation is required to ensure that the development factory understands the requirements in detail and can implement them to meet the user's needs.

Backlog Management Tools

While SAP Activate comes with a template for backlog that is based on Microsoft Excel, this solution will only work for very small teams with a small number of requirements. Larger project teams should consider using SAP Cloud ALM requirement management capabilities that provide more advanced features to plan, sequence, and track the progress of backlog items and tasks. Organizations that already have access to a dedicated backlog management tool such as Jira, VersionOne, or any of the many backlog management tools on the market can use these dedicated tools to manage their backlogs.

SAP Cloud ALM allows for linking the requirements and tasks with external tools via application programming interface (APIs) to keep a connection between the requirement, task, solution documentation, and operational processes. You can find more details about integrating Jira backlog with SAP Cloud ALM using APIs in SAP Community blog post "Integrate SAP Cloud ALM with JIRA" (*http://s-prs.co/v596633*).

We'll now talk about what the team does with the backlog during the realize phase and how they work on the backlog items in the sprint cadence to build up a release.

6.3   Agile Realization

As we outlined in the previous section, the project team and business users jointly define the backlog and prioritize it by business value to establish an agreement between the product owner and the team on what are the highest value (and thus highest priority) capabilities that the system should provide. This prioritization and list of features in the backlog isn't fixed and can change during the project. The backlog serves as input into the team's release and sprint planning activities.

In this section, we'll dive deeper into the concepts of releases and sprints. We'll start with the definitions of release and sprint before going into the details of how sprints are planned, executed, and formally closed.

6.3.1   Defining Release and Sprint

Typically, agile projects define the number of releases and at which times these releases will occur; that is, the team defines how they will deliver the product to the business for productive use in the form of a product roadmap. The term *release* typically indicates a shipment of working software to the business for its productive use. Each release is then structured into multiple sprints that allow the team to set a focus for a time-boxed amount of time to deliver the backlog items the team commits to work on. There is no single number of releases and sprints for a typical SAP project, and the duration of releases is a function of the scope, complexity, and team ability to deliver the capabilities in the solution being deployed. The duration of the sprint should be fixed for the project and should be between one week and a maximum of four weeks. Longer sprints lead to issues in maintaining the team's focus and cadence for the delivery of the selected features. Figure 6.6 shows a schematic of how the backlog initially defined, prioritized, and estimated in the explore phase is used to drive the realization of the requirements during the course of the realize phase. One agile release of working software is shown here, but note that there may be multiple releases of working software to the business in some projects. In such cases, the project team may go through an abbreviated set of activities from the explore phase to reconfirm the backlog, including prioritization, before starting the next release cycle.

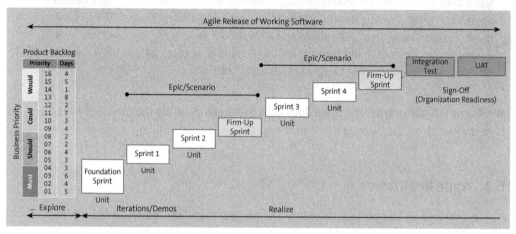

Figure 6.6 Structure of an Agile Release in the SAP Activate Methodology

The second item shown in Figure 6.6 is the series of sprints in a typical SAP project. The design of the sprints is based on experience from SAP projects using agile and consists of the following types of sprints:

- **Foundation sprint**
  During this very first sprint, the project team focuses on setting up the foundational configuration and organizational structure in the SAP system that will allow the project team to proceed into more complex configuration settings. Typical activities in this sprint in the SAP S/4HANA Cloud project include setting up charts of accounts, organizational structures, units of measure, and other general settings for the application that are necessary to proceed with more specific configuration steps.

- **Sprint (also called build sprint)**
  In this traditional sprint, the project team delivers committed features from the backlog and plays them back to the product owners (and business users) at the end of the sprint. We'll cover this further in Section 6.3.2, where we'll explain the activities the project team follows during the time-boxed sprint. During this sprint, the project team conducts unit testing of the features delivered in the sprint. In later sprints, the project team also does string testing, during which they "string together" multiple unit tests to continuously test integration between the components of the system.

- **Firm-up sprint**

  Sometimes these sprints are referred to as *hardening sprints*, and their purpose is to ensure the team continuously integrates the solution and doesn't leave any technical debt in the solution until later stages of the project. Traditionally in the SAP S/4HANA Cloud environment during this sprint, the finished features are moved from the development system to the quality assurance system using the transport management functionality and are then tested in the quality assurance system on real customer data. The teams will also finish the solution documentation during this sprint to capture the rationale for configuration or extensibility decisions. In some cases, the project team may also create end-user documentation for the features delivered in the previous sprint to ensure readiness for key-user and end-user training.

In the next section, we'll go deeper into the concept of the sprint and deconstruct the activities that the project team does in each of the agile sprint cycles.

6.3.2 Anatomy of a Sprint

The sprint is a time-boxed segment of a project during which the project team follows a set of activities to plan, execute, and deliver the committed functionality; confirm that the features meet the customer needs; and conduct activities to continuously improve execution of the agile process. The objective of the sprint is to deliver working software that is ready to be deployed into production. This doesn't mean that the result of the sprint must be deployed to production, however. As SAP environments are usually highly controlled systems in a company's environment, it's typical to only deploy into the production environment at the end of each agile release, when the features committed for release are ready for deployment for productive use.

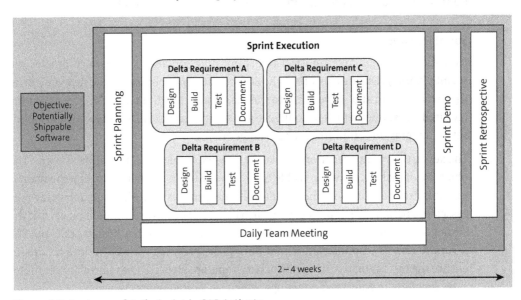

Figure 6.7 Anatomy of Agile Sprint in SAP Activate

All the sprint activities are detailed in the following sections, and they follow the structure of the sprint as it's defined in the agile Scrum framework. We'll go over each of the steps in a little more detail and follow the structure shown in Figure 6.7.

Sprint Planning

During the sprint planning, the project team reviews the backlog for stories that are ready to be worked on in the sprint (some teams refer to these as *sprintable stories*). The project team then takes the highest-value stories from the backlog into the planning meeting. During this meeting, the project team assesses if they understand the story and its acceptance criteria. The project team also discusses what tasks or steps they need to do to complete the story; for example, the story may require configuration, test data, or a special skill set that the team needs to procure from other teams or shared resources. If there is architectural work that needs to be done, for instance, the team will need to secure the capacity of the enterprise architect from the shared resources pool for the sprint to make sure they can deliver the capability at the end of the sprint.

During this process, the team also refines the story estimates to make sure the story hasn't been underestimated in the first pass of estimations that happened before the story was decomposed into individual tasks and activities the team will perform. The team then decides whether the story becomes part of the next sprint (and will be included in the sprint backlog for the team).

Typically, sprint planning is conducted as a workshop, with all Scrum team members participating in the process. The workshop duration should be kept to a maximum of one day, but experienced agile project teams may need much less time—from a few hours to half a day—for the sprint planning activities to be completed.

Sprint Execution

Execution activities cover most of the sprint duration after the team completes the sprint planning. During execution, the Scrum team members select the tasks or stories they will work on and move them to their lane on the Scrum board. They perform the required work, whether it's to configure and test the solution, develop custom code, or set up integration communications arrangements.

The key to the sprint execution is to keep the work visible by using Kanban boards. The objective of making the work visible to everybody in the team and outside the team is to minimize the typical overhead for traditional projects with elaborate reporting processes and meetings. The project team also keeps track of the work spent on each of the stories and estimates the work remaining on each story that has been worked on. The Scrum master is responsible for monitoring the progress with burn-down charts to ensure the team is on track and no backlog items are blocked. The team also communicates regularly in daily team meetings, which we'll discuss next.

Daily Team Meetings

These daily meetings are also called standup meetings and are very short compared to what many consider a meeting. A typical daily standup meeting is between 15 and 20 minutes long, with the objective of exchanging information about what the team needs to work on and whether they have encountered any blockers they need help resolving. Standup meetings are usually structured as a team standing up in a circle, facing each other. Each team member then answers the following questions:

- What have I accomplished since the last meeting?
- What will I work on next?
- Is there anything blocking my progress?

Some teams also include a fourth question in their daily standup: What is my level of confidence that we'll deliver the sprint as planned? This question is helpful in gauging the confidence level of each team member in the delivery of the sprint and assessing if there are hidden challenges that could potentially derail the delivery.

Sprint Demo

Toward the end of the time box, the team schedules a sprint demo session with the product owners (and business key users). The goal of this session is to demonstrate the completed functionality to the business users to gain acceptance and confirm that they meet the user requirements.

The demo is set up as a walkthrough of the backlog items with a live demo of the functionality in the system. It's recommended to minimize the use of tools such as Microsoft PowerPoint in favor of showing the actual capabilities directly in the system. We also recommend that business users are given the opportunity to try the functionality firsthand after the demo. This will help drive the adoption of the new capabilities into the organization. Capabilities that aren't considered complete will remain in the backlog, and the respective backlog items will be updated to indicate the required functional changes and adjustments to the acceptance criteria (for minor fine-tuning of the backlog item).

If the requirement is significantly changed, the product owner needs to create a new backlog item that is then estimated, prioritized, and—in some projects—taken through an additional change request process (for fixed price projects, fixed scope projects, or projects that specify this process in the project governance documents).

Sprint Retrospective

The last activity that the team conducts is the retrospective session to identify potential improvements to the agile process, tools, and interaction for the team. Because this session is internally focused on the team, only the team and Scrum master attend this session (product owners and business users aren't invited). The session is structured into three steps:

1. **Brainstorm and capture**
   During this stage, the project team discusses how the sprint went, including the high points, what should be kept unchanged, opportunities to improve the process, and the potential for eliminating waste. The team members capture their thoughts and input on sticky notes and place them in the collection space on a whiteboard. After enough input has been collected, the Scrum master stops the activity and proceeds to the next step.

2. **Sort and group**
   During this activity, the team groups related input and structures the input into a smaller number of themes that the team can work on in the next step. In some cases, when the team is large, this step is done by the Scrum master and selected team members while others take a short break.

3. **Prioritize and select improvements**
   The last step is to jointly prioritize the improvements that the team wants to drive into the next sprint and select one or, at most, two improvements they will work on in the next sprint.

Retrospectives are critical for all agile project teams because they help teams continuously improve the agile process and tailor it to optimize the throughput and eliminate wasteful activities. In our experience, this is often an underestimated part of the process, and teams that skip this step aren't fully realizing their agile potential as they get stuck executing their agile sprints with no consideration for how the team is evolving and maturing.

6.4   Definition of Ready and Done

The *agile backlog* is a living document that the project team uses to capture all the work that needs to be done during the project to deliver the desired solution outcome. The backlog typically contains pools of items that are in different states. Agile refers to these as *flow regions* inside the backlog. The typical flow regions in the backlog are items that are in the following states:

- **In sprint**
  These backlog items are currently being worked on in a sprint.

- **Ready to be sprinted**
  These backlog items have yet to be assigned to the sprint; these items are cleared to the team and are then prioritized and estimated.

- **In preparation**
  The team works on clarifying these items with the business users, detailing them, or

breaking larger stories into smaller ones that can be done in a sprint (see the "Backlog Grooming" note box).

- **New**
  These are newly added stories that may not have sufficient detail and need to be clarified with the business users before the team can consider working on them.

In each flow region, the granularity of the backlog items is different; that is, the backlog stories in the new flow region may be much too large to fit into one sprint or may not be detailed enough for the project team to be able to estimate the effort. The project team regularly does backlog grooming to ensure there are enough stories to be added to the upcoming sprint.

Backlog Grooming

Agile teams need to continuously review the backlog and prepare the backlog items for the next sprint. This exercise is either done as an ongoing process in each sprint, or the team dedicates a time block for this activity to ensure the backlog always has stories ready to be brought into the next sprint or the next few sprints.

During the grooming, the project team members may break larger backlog items (i.e., epics) into smaller stories that can be inserted into the sprint. The goal of breaking the larger story into smaller ones is to ensure that the sprintable story can be completed during a sprint. During backlog grooming, the team also works with business users to clarify any story that isn't understood by the team or that may need additional detail.

The project team uses the *ready* and *done* states to identify the status of each of the stories. For each story, the project team applies a set of clearly defined criteria to define whether the backlog item (or story) is ready and whether it's completed or done. Project teams can apply this set of criteria on different levels. Traditionally, the criteria are applied for the sprint, and the definition of ready specifies when the team understands the backlog item so they can include it in the scope of the sprint. These criteria generally focus on the following:

- **Understanding why**
  Why is this capability important, what business value does the capability deliver, and who will benefit from this new capability?

- **Understanding what needs to be delivered**
  Sometimes this is also referred to as *acceptance criteria* for the story. In other words, how will the business users judge that the software does what they expect? For example, for a credit card payment on a website, the user can supply a credit card issued by Visa, Mastercard, or American Express or pay with Apple Pay. In such a definition of acceptance criteria, the user can't issue payment via other providers, such as Discover or the Google Pay service. Being clear on what is required for each story is critical to ensure its acceptance during the sprint demo.

- **Being able to determine how the story needs to be realized**
  These criteria allow the team to determine the specific tasks and skills needed to deliver the story. The team needs to be able to determine if the story requires them to do technical design, import specific data, or create a prototype to deliver the capability to the user in the sprint.

Upon satisfying these items, the team can plan the story into an upcoming sprint. You can think of the definition of ready as the contract the team has with the product owner on the minimal required detail for the story to be ready for the sprint.

You can use the following "definition of ready" for stories in the backlog in your SAP S/4HANA Cloud project:

- The story is recorded in the backlog.
- The team understands the problem.
- The team understands why this is important.
- This story has been estimated by the team.
- The team knows how to demo this story to the product owner.
- The team has insight into the context of the story.
- Acceptance criteria from the product owner are clear and agreed upon.
- Acceptance criteria for operations are clear and agreed upon.

The definition of done is used in the context of sprints to determine if the backlog items are completely done. Sometimes, the agile teams will refer to the story as "done, done." In other words, the story is completely implemented, and the other supporting items (e.g., documentation and training materials) have been completed. You'll hear project teams also refer to the story as being done without any outstanding technical debt.

The typical "definition of done" for the sprint in SAP projects has the following characteristics:

- The functionality is configured or built in the system.
- The functionality is unit-tested.
- The functionality is tested by the product owner.
- The functionality is documented; that is, solution documentation exists.
- All outstanding bugs found in testing are fixed.
- The sprint demo has been completed.
- The functionality has been transported to the quality system and is ready for integration and acceptance testing (this may be delayed until the firm-up sprints).

Project teams also apply the "definition of done" for each release to complete the remaining activities that need to be done to deliver an integrated system supporting the business requirements. Here is an example of the definition of done for release in the context of an SAP project:

- The scope of the release is integration tested.
- The scope of the release is user acceptance tested.
- The end-user documentation is completed.
- The training material is completed.
- No technical debt remains—that is, no unfinished work or compromises ("We'll get to this later").
- The functionality is ready for release to the business.

The definitions of ready and done serve as gates. They help the team assess whether the backlog story is ready to be worked on (definition of ready), whether the backlog item has been completed (definition of done for a sprint), and whether it's ready to be delivered to the business users (definition of done for the release). SAP Activate provides an explanation of the concept in the accelerator assigned to the agile deliverables and tasks in the methodology and shows the typical definitions of ready and done that we encourage teams to adapt to their needs.

6.5   Putting It All Together

In this section, we'll review an example of a project that deploys the solution into productive use in one release wave consisting of four sprints to build up the solution and test it fully (see Figure 6.8).

The release starts with the completion of the functional specifications for the scope of the release—see the wave milestones section of the flow right under the **Release 1** chevron. The project team starts the individual sprints and go through the activities in each to finish the technical design, build the solution, unit test it, and prepare it for the sprint demo at the end of the sprint. In parallel, the data management team works to prepare data both for the sprint demo as well as for the single functional test that is done for each sprint to ensure that the functionality delivered in the sprint works correctly. This sequence is repeated for each sprint and concludes with the functional integration test before handover to release. You can see in Figure 6.8 that the data management team continues with the data preparation and the percentages below the milestones show approximate completeness and readiness for the data migration to the productive system. Note that the data management at the bottom of Figure 6.8 shows the mock cutover simulations. In our example, there are three mock cutover runs, but in some projects, it may be sufficient to do one or two.

After the handover to the release event, the project team conducts the full end-to-end integration test that tests the solution and all the required integration points before proceeding to the user acceptance testing (UAT). Upon successful completion, the team proceeds to the productive cutover and the go-live with the new capabilities and the continues to the run phase.

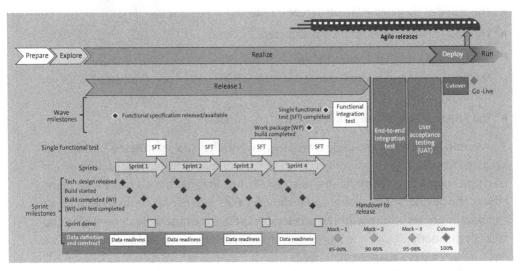

Figure 6.8 Example Project Structure with Four Sprints for the First Release to Productive Use

As you can see from the example, agile project delivery gives project teams a lot of flexibility in how they deploy the functionality to productive use. You can have your project deploy the solution in multiple releases or use a longer release cycle by adding more sprints into the release timeline to effectively stretch it. The goal should be to find the most optimal way to deliver the capabilities to the business without increasing the risk of deployment for the business users.

6.6   SAP Activate in a Scaled Agile Environment

The agile process we've discussed in this chapter is based on the use of Scrum, the agile framework that is most used across various agile teams and industries. In some situations, when the project team size grows, companies use scaling concepts for scaling the execution of agile processes for a large number of project or program team members. One of the best-known scaling frameworks is the Scaled Agile Framework (SAFe) maintained by Scaled Agile, Inc. SAFe is designed to scale agile processes for large teams and organizations. It provides a way for organizations to establish a structure for achieving business agility using lean, agile, and DevOps that is built around integrated principles, practices, and competencies. The framework itself is comprehensive and complex, and it caters especially to the agile management of portfolios, large solutions, and organizations.

In our work with SAP clients that adopted SAFe in their IT organizations, we've designed an approach to benefit from the use of the SAP Activate methodology for the deployment of SAP solutions while retaining the benefits of SAFe for the organization. In this section, we'll discuss how the two work together and outline the key common principles that SAFe and SAP Activate follow. The model described here will be applicable in other scaling frameworks that extend the core Scrum approach for large teams and organizations.

Further Resources

In this chapter, we won't go into the details of SAFe. To explore SAFe further, we recommend reviewing the available documentation and resources at *www.scaledagileframework.com*.

6.6.1   Common Principles in SAFe and SAP Activate

Before we discuss the alignment points and mechanics, let's discuss the common principles that both SAFe practitioners and teams using SAP Activate need to keep in mind.

As we've outlined in this chapter, the SAP Activate agile process is built on the roles, processes, and principles defined in the Scrum agile framework. This includes the execution of agile activities, backlog management, sprint cadence, team structure, and ceremonies during the project. The Scrum framework works well for teams following agile in small or mid-size projects. It has limits, however, in providing guidance for large programs and organizations when it comes to cross-team coordination, management of enterprise backlog, and so on. Scaling frameworks such as SAFe help with the necessary structure, governance, and transparency for large teams. Both SAFe and SAP Activate are built on common principles, which help to show how SAP Activate can be incorporated into the environment that uses SAFe. Let's now review them in more detail:

- **Deliver value incrementally**
  The concept of incremental value delivery is at the heart of agile thinking and is embedded into both approaches, which helps line them up conceptually. SAFe uses terms of *planning interval* and *solution train* to reflect this approach. SAP Activate uses terms of *releases* that represent incremental deliveries of product capabilities to the production environment for use by business users. Both aim to shorten the time to value and deliver value incrementally.

- **Time-boxing and focusing the team in each iteration**
  The SAFe project team plans each planning interval by selecting capabilities and enablers from the appropriate backlog, and then the team works throughout the timeline in iterations to deliver the selected backlog items. Similarly, SAP Activate uses the fit-to-standard workshops to create the initial backlog for the scope of the release and then iterates in time-boxed sprints on selected backlog items that are completed and released to the business via an agile release.

- **Close involvement of business users**

  SAP Activate emphasizes close involvement of business users in the project by making them an integral part of the project team and bringing them to strategic points in the project, such as fit-to-standard or sprint demos. SAFe uses a plan, do, check, adjust cycle common to agile projects, and the team plays back the results of the iteration in the iteration review event.

- **Use of common language and terms**

  SAFe and SAP Activate use common terms such as backlog, sprint/iteration, continuous delivery, built-in quality, product owner, Scrum master, team, product owner, business owners, and many others. These are terms commonly used in agile and have the same meaning in both.

Now we'll dive a little deeper into selected configurations of SAFe and discuss how SAP Activate aligns with each configuration.

6.6.2   Alignment Points for Each Configuration of SAFe

In this section, we'll discuss how SAP Activate lines up with two of the commonly used SAFe configurations. Remember that SAFe is the higher-level framework managing the delivery of a solution or large solution for which we'll outline how SAP Activate fits in each. We won't discuss the alignment with the portfolio-level configuration as most of the alignment points are going to be well explained for the essential configuration and large solution configuration of SAFe.

Essential

In this SAFe configuration, you'll find the most commonality in the deliverables, procedures, processes, and artifacts. The team structure and roles in both SAP Activate and SAFe include Scrum master, product owner, and team members. SAP Activate nicely extends the guidance for how to structure the project team with the relevant experts for SAP solutions, such as solution architects, key users, application consultants, data migration specialists, and so on. The second area for alignment is the actual execution process for running the sprints/iterations within the agile release train of SAFe. Both frameworks use planning activities, execution activities, inspection activities with sprint review, and adjustment activities with retrospective. In terms of artifacts, the alignment is done through the use of the backlog for managing the scope of work and what gets included in each iteration or a release (or as SAFe calls it, *planning interval*). Both approaches build on common agile practices of working as a cross-functional team to deliver value.

The notion of continuous delivery via the release train from SAFe is represented in SAP Activate with the ability to split a larger project into multiple releases, as introduced earlier in this chapter. This concept of grouping deliverables from individual sprints and storing them in the quality system environment until the team is ready to deploy into the production environment is embedded in the SAP Activate methodology. Another key element that ties to the continuous delivery is the execution of the program in increments: SAP Activate refers to them as *releases*, whereas SAFe uses the term *planning interval*. Conceptually these are very similar as both aim to deliver working, tested software that is ready to deploy to productive use.

So, how do you use the SAP Activate approach in SAFe on the essential level? Conceptually, the team will execute the fit-to-standard workshops for the scope of the planning interval in the beginning of each planning interval (during planning and early stages) and then deliver the backlog items that have been included in the planning interval. This occurs regardless of whether the backlog items are configuration, data migration, extensibility, or integration requirements.

Large Solution

In the large solution SAFe configuration, the key additional elements are the solution train backlog and the solution train. They are added to coordinate the execution of multiple agile release trains and involved suppliers.

SAP Activate already includes the notion of delivering large solutions to the business by providing the solution to complex business problems. In the case of SAP solutions, the delivery plans are usually captured in the innovation strategy and high-level roadmap that helps the business plan steps to get from the current as-is solution to the future. These artifacts are detailed in SAP Activate in the discover phase. Equally important is the focus on the business value and adoption of the solution by the business users. To drive the adoption of the solution by the business, SAP delivers the solution adoption workstream that includes the value management (VM) framework, OCM activities, and project team onboarding, as well as business user training. The VM framework in SAP Activate provides the *economic framework* for the solution to deliver business value. In addition, the management of the overall program scope, standards, policies, and governance will be largely represented on this level of SAFe. The program management, including the key program milestones, high-level schedule, and objectives of the program from the SAP Activate project management workstream, will support SAFe deliverables on this level. The solution architecture work represented in SAP Activate in the technical solution management workstream will also support deliverables in this area of SAFe.

SAFe and SAP Activate

The key reason for the use of SAP Activate in organizations that implemented SAFe is that SAP Activate provides an SAP-specific flavor to solution-agnostic frameworks such as SAFe. Thus, companies using SAP Activate inside SAFe will benefit both from the SAP-specific guidance such as the detailed guidance for provisioning, execution of fit-to-standard workshops, configuration approach, solution documentation templates, and so on, and the scaling framework for their organization and team.

You can find additional deep-dive blog posts about the use of SAP Activate in SAFe in the following posts:

- "Innovate Faster: The Power Duo of SAP Activate and Scaled Agile Framework (SAFe)": *http://s-prs.co/v596634*
- "Working with SAFe Epics in the SAP Activate Discover Phase": *http://s-prs.co/v596635*
- "SAP Activate Methodology Prepare and Explore Phases in the Context of SAFe": *http://s-prs.co/v596636*
- "SAP Activate Realize and Deploy Phase Activities in the Context of Scaled Agile Framework": *http://s-prs.co/v596637*

6.7   Summary

In this chapter, we provided details about the agile implementation approach concepts that we introduced in Chapter 2. You learned how the project team roles are defined in an agile project and the responsibilities of each role. We then reviewed the anatomy of the releases and sprints with all their activities, such as release planning, sprint planning, daily standup meetings, and the actual execution of the sprint activities that lead to reviewing and confirming that the delivered work meets the business users' requirements. Finally, we covered the feedback loop and improvement process that the team creates with the use of regular retrospectives to not only capture the lessons learned but also act on the highest-priority improvement to the way the team works in the upcoming sprints. This is one of the most important parts of the agile process that allows teams to evolve and improve the way they work while adhering to simple agile processes.

In the last part of this chapter, we provided guidance for organizations that use scaling frameworks such as SAFe on how to incorporate SAP Activate into their working setup to benefit from the SAP solution-specific guidance in SAP Activate while using the power of the general scaling framework.

In the next chapter, we'll dive into the details of new implementations of SAP S/4HANA Cloud solutions. We'll cover the details of the implementation process in the context of SAP Activate for SAP S/4HANA Cloud and discuss the key content, guidance, and tools that project teams use during the implementation.

Chapter 7
New Implementation of SAP S/4HANA

In this chapter, we'll provide detailed explanations of the new implementation process of three SAP S/4HANA deployment versions: public cloud, private cloud, and on-premise. The new implementation approach is used to introduce SAP S/4HANA in organizations implementing an SAP solution for the first time in their business or for existing SAP customers that want to reimplement their ERP system and adopt the innovation introduced in SAP S/4HANA Cloud or SAP S/4HANA.

This chapter focuses on explaining how to use SAP Activate for new implementations of SAP S/4HANA Cloud Public Edition, SAP S/4HANA Cloud Private Edition, and on-premise SAP S/4HANA. SAP S/4HANA Cloud allows you to benefit from the software as a service (SaaS) consumption model and receive more frequent innovations, among other characteristics, as discussed earlier in Chapter 1.

During the software selection process, before subscribing, the company preferences, geographical footprint, industry, functional requirements, preference for higher level of standardization, or preference for more flexibility help SAP determine which version of SAP S/4HANA software will be deployed to meet your needs.

The SAP Activate roadmaps for different options of SAP S/4HANA follow the same phases and key deliverables, but the technical and functional details differ in specific areas we'll discuss in this chapter. We'll begin with the deployment process for SAP Activate for SAP S/4HANA Cloud Public Edition. Then, we'll discuss the implementation of SAP S/4HANA Cloud Private Edition before we conclude with SAP S/4HANA (on-premise). We'll emphasize the differences between implementing each of these solutions, especially in the solution landscape, and cover capabilities such as configuration, application lifecycle management (ALM), and testing.

7.1 New Implementation of SAP S/4HANA Cloud Public Edition

SAP S/4HANA Cloud Public Edition provides a solid SAP-engineered cloud solution delivered via an SaaS delivery model that includes rapid innovation cycles. The technology behind SAP S/4HANA Cloud Public Edition not only brings a lower cost of ownership but also enables, along with SAP Activate, a more efficient and fast deployment.

In this section, we'll examine the key aspects of the SAP S/4HANA Cloud Public Edition implementation by following the SAP Activate phases as detailed in Chapter 2 and summarized in Figure 7.1.

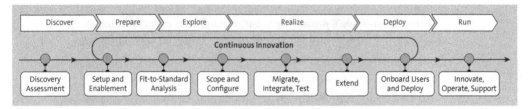

Figure 7.1 SAP Activate Phases and Key Activities

7.1.1 Deployment Approach Overview

Before we start, it's important to note both the landscape of the implementation and the upgrade cycles as these require consideration across the entire project.

SAP S/4HANA Cloud Public Edition leverages a three-system landscape, with an additional starter system to accelerate learning the standard functionality, as shown in Figure 7.2. The starter system is the first system provided at the time the subscription starts and contains preconfiguration and master data based on SAP Best Practices. Test scripts are provided that allow for immediate execution of business processes in the explore phase. The development system will be used in the realize phase to configure the solution based on the output of the fit-to-standard analysis workshops and to conduct unit testing. The business processes are then tested in the test system, verifying that the master data and configuration setup in the development system can meet the business needs. The starter system will be decommissioned approximately a month after the development system is provisioned.

In addition to the SAP S/4HANA systems, three other cloud applications support the implementation:

- **SAP for Me**
  The hub for self-service provisioning of the SAP S/4HANA Cloud Public Edition tenants when they are needed.

- **SAP Central Business Configuration**
  The configuration engine for SAP S/4HANA Cloud and other solutions. We discussed SAP Central Business Configuration in Chapter 5, Section 5.1.1.

- **SAP Cloud ALM**
  The implementation manager loaded with SAP Activate methodology. We discussed SAP Cloud ALM in Chapter 3, Section 3.3.

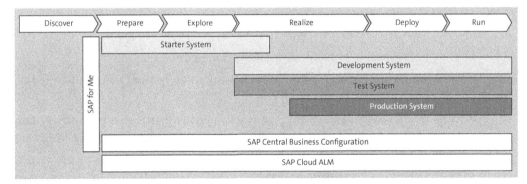

Figure 7.2 SAP Activate Phases and System Landscape

Periodic release updates are applied to SAP S/4HANA Cloud Public Edition to keep the system current and to support continuous innovations. Standard automated tests are executed by SAP, and companies should plan additional custom regression tests. In between releases, corrections are seamlessly applied approximately every other weekend during scheduled maintenance downtime for the productive system. SAP also implements a continuous feature delivery monthly in which companies can adopt needed innovations earlier than the standard upgrade cycle.

Further Resources

See the SAP Activate for Upgrade of SAP S/4HANA Cloud Public Edition (3-System Landscape) roadmap in the Roadmap Viewer for more guidance related to the upgrade.

See the Release and Update Cycles for SAP S/4HANA Cloud Public Edition deliverable in the SAP Activate for Upgrade of SAP S/4HANA Cloud Public Edition (3-System Landscape) roadmap for more information on the release upgrade of SAP S/4HANA Cloud Public Edition.

With that foundation, let's start with the discover phase of SAP Activate.

7.1.2   Discover Your Solution

In this section, we'll discuss how you can test-drive SAP S/4HANA Cloud Public Edition in the trial environment. SAP offers a trial environment for anyone who wants to experience the solution in a real running system that is activated with SAP Best Practices scenarios. The trial system is available for 14 days, but you're able to reregister as often as you need to. While using the trial, you can navigate in a functional system with end-to-end business scenarios for project management, finance, cash management, purchasing, sales, and supply chain.

While the trial system is like the system you'll receive during the implementation project, you'll need to consider the following limitations while using it:

- The trial is available in a limited number of languages.
- As mentioned, the trial is active for 14 days, but it can be reregistered after the expiration.
- Only a subset of predefined scenarios is activated in the trial system; in other words, the complete scope of SAP Best Practices for SAP S/4HANA Cloud Public Edition is much broader than what is available in the trial system.
- Only predefined demo data is available in the system; you can't upload your company data.
- Keep in mind that other trial users have access to the data you input into the trial system.

Let's now go over the steps you can take to discover the capabilities of SAP S/4HANA Cloud Public Edition after signing up for the trial environment.

Sign Up for SAP S/4HANA Cloud Public Edition Trial

To start your own trial, access the SAP S/4HANA trial pages at *http://s-prs.co/v502722*. Select the **Try now** button (see Figure 7.3), and fill out the registration form as prompted.

Figure 7.3 SAP S/4HANA Trial Pages

Access Your SAP S/4HANA Cloud Public Edition Trial Environment

After you've completed the registration process, SAP will send you an email with a link to activate your account. After clicking the link, you'll be directed to a welcome screen that includes your user ID and a link to start the trial. Save the user ID and the link for the SAP S/4HANA Cloud Public Edition trial in a safe place.

The SAP S/4HANA Cloud Public Edition trial environment provides access to detailed guided tours in which you'll assume the role of a specific business user, such as a general ledger accountant, accounts receivable accountant, and others. As shown in Figure 7.4, each business area contains several guided tours. By selecting the tour, you'll be launched into the SAP S/4HANA Cloud Public Edition solution and a guided process that will walk you through the transaction steps in the live system.

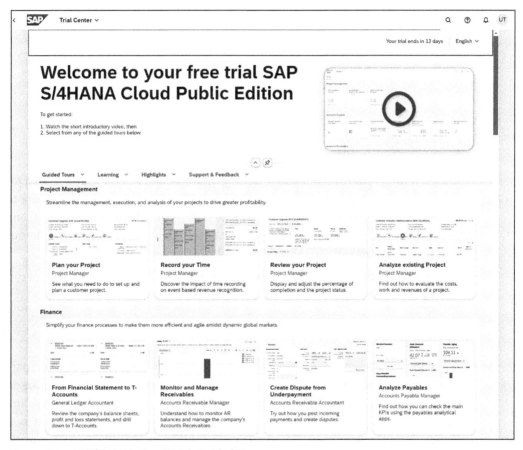

Figure 7.4 SAP S/4HANA Cloud Trial: Guided Tour

The on-screen guidance will tell you which SAP Fiori app tile to select, which buttons to click, and what information you need to input into the application. If you need to get back to the list of guided tours, return to the home screen by clicking **Home** in the dropdown next to the SAP logo and selecting the **Guided Tours** tile.

If you're doing freestyle exploration, you can always activate the help function with the **Open Help** button to learn more about the application. As shown in Figure 7.5, this help function will provide more detailed guidance about the purposes and roles of key screen elements.

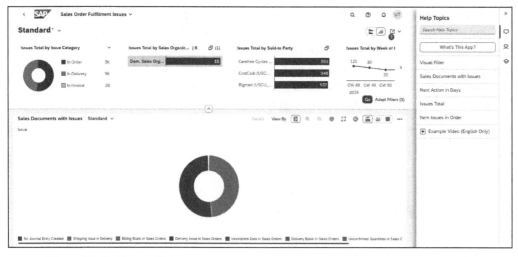

Figure 7.5 On-Screen Help

In addition to the guided tours, select **Getting Started Guides** in the **Learning** area for guides to help you understand how to work with SAP Fiori launchpad, including how to personalize the tiles shown in your launchpad; how to work with SAP Fiori apps; and how to configure your solution. The **Learning Center** link provides access to numerous tutorials on different SAP S/4HANA Cloud Public Edition processes.

Now that you've taken a test-drive with the SAP S/4HANA Cloud Public Edition trial system, let's examine the next SAP Activate project phase: prepare.

7.1.3   Prepare Your Project

This section will cover the activities the project team needs to complete in the prepare phase of an SAP S/4HANA Cloud Public Edition implementation project. We'll focus on activities supporting project initiation and planning, activities related to the provisioning of SAP S/4HANA Cloud Public Edition, and team self-enablement tasks. When used together, these activities prepare business users for the fit-to-standard analysis workshops that the team will later conduct in the explore phase.

After an overview of this phase, the information in this section is structured into several topics that go over the key activities in the prepare phase.

Phase Overview

The purpose of the prepare phase is to provide the initial planning and preparation for the project. In this phase, the project is started, plans are finalized, the project team is assigned, and work gets underway to start the project. The SAP S/4HANA Cloud Public Edition environment is provisioned, and the project team gains access to the starter system and is ready to start planning for the fit-to-standard analysis workshops in the explore phase. Figure 7.6 provides an overview of the deliverables the project team will complete during the prepare phase.

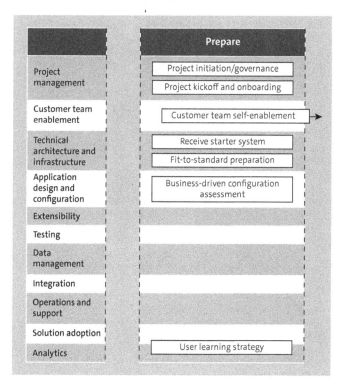

Figure 7.6 SAP Activate Prepare Phase Deliverables for SAP S/4HANA Cloud Public Edition

The prepare phase includes the following activities:

- Defining project goals, a high-level scope, and a project plan
- Securing executive sponsorship
- Establishing project standards, organization, and governance
- Defining roles and responsibilities for the project team
- Validating the project's objectives
- Establishing project management, tracking, and reporting mechanisms for value delivery
- Developing a company project team enablement strategy and starting company project team enablement
- Documenting all initiation activities in the project charter
- Requesting provisioning of SAP Cloud ALM
- Requesting initial access to applicable SAP systems
- Preparing for fit-to-standard workshops, including self-enablement activities
- Closing the phase

Typically, the prepare phase creates the following deliverables:

- Project scope document
- Project organization and governance
- Project schedule, budget, and management plans
- Project standards and policies
- Project risk documentation
- Solution adoption approach, including the organizational change
- Fit-to-standard preparation
- Data migration approach and strategy
- Project quality gate

The prepare phase includes the following typical project milestones and key decisions:

- Project scope validated
- Company project team staffed and enabled
- Project team organization, responsibilities, and location established
- Key stakeholders for communications identified
- Implementation plan defined
- Project environment provisioned

Let's now go over the key activities the project team will perform during the prepare phase of implementing SAP S/4HANA Cloud.

Setting Up the Project

Every SAP S/4HANA Cloud Public Edition implementation project needs to establish a game plan and rules of engagement to keep all project team members moving toward the common goal. The project management workstream in the SAP Activate methodology covers most of the necessary deliverables and tasks that the project manager and project team need to provide as a game plan for everyone involved in the project.

Typical project management deliverables in the prepare phase include the following:

- Project initiation and governance
- Project plans, schedule, and budget
- Project kickoff and project team onboarding materials
- Project standards and project infrastructure

Putting these fundamentals in place will help the project team focus on reaching the project's objectives and enable your business to realize the goals stated in the business case. Let's look at each of these deliverables closely.

Project Initiation and Governance

The purpose of the project initiation and governance deliverable is to formally recognize that a new project exists and to initiate work on the project. During this time, the project sponsor and project manager work to align stakeholders around the project and its scope, provide updated information for planning, and obtain a commitment to proceed.

As part of the initiation activities, the project manager conducts a handover from the discover phase, creates a project charter document and scope statement document, and establishes the project governance to ensure a proper management process for the project. These activities achieve alignment between the SAP system integrator, the company's project team, the company's strategic direction, and the satisfaction of operational requirements for the solution.

Project governance is a critical management framework for the project to ensure that decisions are made in a structured manner. It establishes a policy for the project team, project stakeholders, executives, and system integrators that clearly specifies roles, responsibilities, accountability, and organizational setup. As shown in Figure 7.7, project governance provides a decision-making framework that is robust and logical to ensure that decisions are timely and approved by the authorized personnel.

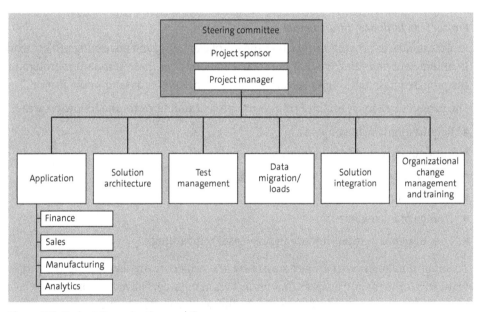

Figure 7.7 Project Organization and Governance

Governance Caution

If you skip this key deliverable, the project isn't formally approved by the company sponsor, and the project manager isn't authorized to apply organizational resources to project activities. You also risk misunderstanding regarding the scope of the project and undefined project governance processes.

Project Plans, Schedule, and Budget

Planning activities during the early stages of the project include developing a project management plan, preparing the project's work breakdown structure (WBS), and defining the project's schedule and budget.

The project management plan is a comprehensive document that details the plans for managing schedules, budgets, issues, risks, project changes, and so on. The SAP Activate methodology provides you with guidance and templates for creating a management plan for your SAP S/4HANA Cloud project. Further, the SAP Activate methodology gives you a detailed WBS in the Roadmap Viewer that your project manager can use to define and sequence required tasks within the scope of the project.

Project Kickoff and Onboarding

To formally start the project, the project manager schedules a project kickoff meeting. This kickoff meeting includes discussion of project objectives, organizational structure, roles and responsibilities, project governance, schedule, scope, communication standards, change request processes, and decision-making processes. The kickoff meeting is attended by the project team, key stakeholders, the project sponsor, and company executives.

Project Standards and Infrastructure

Project standards provide a consistent means of executing and governing project work in an efficient and effective manner. You'll elaborate on these standards throughout the prepare phase, although you can fine-tune some standards later in the project.

The project team must establish minimum project standards for the following areas:

- Requirements management
- Configuration and documentation
- Authorizations and security
- Test planning and execution
- Change management
- Post-implementation support and new user onboarding

To support adherence to project standards, the project team also sets up the project team environment and ensures that project team members have the appropriate level of access to the company facility, project room, and project systems.

This activity also involves IT support to set up project team workstations, including installing and updating the required software, such as internet browsers, communication tools (e.g., Zoom, Microsoft Teams), or collaboration environments (e.g., SAP Community, MURAL).

Provisioning and Setup

The initial admin user can request the provisioning of an SAP S/4HANA Cloud starter system via SAP for Me at *https://me.sap.com* and the **Systems and Provisioning** dashboard. SAP for Me is the central place designed to improve the experience throughout all touchpoints with SAP, including requesting provisioning of cloud systems and tenants. SAP for Me will guide you through the provisioning of the starter system plus trigger the related provisioning of SAP Central Business Configuration and SAP Cloud ALM.

After your starter environment is ready, the initial admin user will receive provisioning emails providing details for access and setup of the systems. The SAP S/4HANA Cloud starter system contains two tenants: the *starter customizing* tenant and *starter development* tenant. One email for each tenant is received along with instructions for accessing the administration console for the Identity Authentication service. Detailed guidance can be found in the Request Initial System Access and Initial System Access for SAP S/4HANA Cloud Starter System deliverables in the Roadmap Viewer.

> **Note**
>
> SAP S/4HANA Cloud Public Edition comes predelivered with initial business role templates that you can use to set up business roles to assign to your users.

Team Self-Enablement

During the prepare phase, the project team learns about different aspects of SAP S/4HANA Cloud Public Edition and the SAP Activate methodology via self-enablement materials such as e-learning, documentation, and self-paced training.

Cloud projects are intended to be implemented over a shorter time, which requires more focus on learning tools. It's important that self-enablement begins prior to project kickoff to maximize the time for learning and to create efficiencies in later deliverables. SAP offers a range of structured training options to learn about the scope and functionality of the solution and to understand the structure and flow of the work in the implementation project. SAP has prepared learning journeys to provide a structured way to enable the various users involved in the project.

Let's discuss an example of the **Grow with SAP S/4HANA Cloud (Public)—Onboarding Fundamentals** learning journey. The learning journey directs learners to enablement and training resources in SAP Learning Hub, at SAP Learning, and with other resources such as blogs or e-learning courses. One of the first steps on this journey is to join the SAP S/4HANA Cloud Public Edition implementation learning room (see Figure 7.8), where you can access a range of materials providing information about implementation approaches, methodologies, and tools. You can find the links to learning journeys in the Roadmap Viewer in tasks under the Customer Team Self-Enablement deliverable.

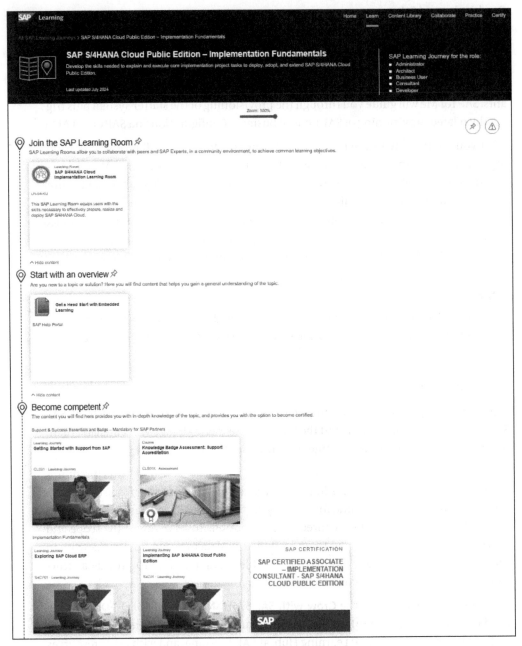

Figure 7.8 Example of Learning Journey for SAP S/4HANA Cloud

Key learning tutorials also are available inside SAP S/4HANA Cloud in the My Learning app.

SAP for Me

SAP recommends that all project team members have access to SAP for Me, where the project team can communicate directly with SAP support and service centers. User details for accessing SAP for Me enable each customer to access SAP Signavio Process Navigator and Roadmap Viewer applications and be recognized as a customer, thus getting access to additional documents and templates needed during the implementation project.

Project team members are encouraged to access the SAP Activate community to find additional resources and to engage directly with SAP Activate experts. You can create a user on SAP Community and access the SAP Activate community at *https://community.sap.com/topics/activate*. We recommend you bookmark this page and frequently visit the space for news and updates.

Organizational Change Management

The purpose of this task is to set up the organizational change management (OCM) team and agree on an OCM concept, which includes the following:

- OCM network concept
- Stakeholder engagement concept
- Communication concept
- Organizational transition concept
- Learning concept
- Change effectiveness concept
- OCM sustainability concept

The change readiness of the organization is assessed by participating in the Cloud Mindset Assessment accelerator and leveraging the results to create awareness for OCM-related topics among the stakeholders. See Chapter 10 for additional details.

Analysis and Planning of End-User Learning Needs

The project team needs to start preparing the end users to use the new application early in the project because, as we discussed previously, cloud implementation projects generally have a compressed schedule compared to on-premise deployments. Therefore, one goal in the prepare phase is to develop a high-level learning plan that provides the recommended approach and activities to prepare end users for using the new system.

The project team executes the following activities to prepare the high-level learning plan:

- **Conduct learning needs identification**
  The project team performs an end-user analysis with a specific focus on determining the current skill levels, knowledge gaps, and training requirements per user group. This activity provides a thorough analysis of required training and helps determine the appropriate learning mechanism for each user group.

- **Develop a detailed end-user learning curriculum**
  Based on the outcome of the learning needs analysis, the project team will develop a working document to formulate an end-user learning curriculum structured by user groups and learning needs identified in the previous step. The team should consider all available options to train users, including formal training, shadowing, and the use of social training such as SAP Learning Hub.

In SAP S/4HANA Cloud Public Edition implementations, the teams prepare learning experiences for key users and end users based primarily on self-enablement using e-learning and easy-to-consume materials online. Additional details are covered in Chapter 10.

Fit-to-Standard Preparation

Preparation for running the fit-to-standard workshop is essential for an effective experience for both the business experts and configuration experts. It includes the following activities:

- Determine the workshop scope based on the project scope statement.
- Review the "How to Approach Fit to Standard Analysis" presentation in the Roadmap Viewer, which provides detailed guidance for running the fit-to-standard analysis workshops.
- Download the scope documentation of the business processes covered in the workshop from SAP Signavio Process Navigator.
- Walk through the SAP Best Practices test scripts in the starter system.
- Adjust the sample data in the system to fit your business. Although the starter system is delivered with master data, some company-specific data can be created to help facilitate understanding by the business experts.
- Review the Expert Configuration and Configuration Activity accelerator in the Roadmap Viewer to help map the configuration required to the scope of the solution. You must understand both the solution abilities and the boundaries of the configuration.
- Anticipate requirements for extensibility and integration that may come up during the workshop.
- Identify the required participants for your workshop and schedule sufficient time to conduct the workshop.

With the prepare phase complete, it's time for the explore phase.

7.1.4   Explore the Solution

This section will provide details about the activities that project team members will execute during the explore phase. The focus will be on planning and running the fit-to-standard analysis workshops that help the project team determine how the SAP Best Practices processes fit your business needs and whether adjustments are needed. We'll also outline how the project team determines configuration values and identifies the necessary extensions and integration points for the solution.

After an overview of this phase, this section is structured into several subsections that cover the key activities of the explore phase.

Phase Overview

In the explore phase, industry and solution experts from SAP or SAP partners lead a series of structured fit-to-standard workshops. The purpose of the fit-to-standard workshops is to validate the solution functionality included in the project scope and to confirm that business requirements will be satisfied. During the workshops, the project team identifies and documents the necessary configuration values, extensions, integration points, and gaps for the end-to-end solution, as shown in Figure 7.9.

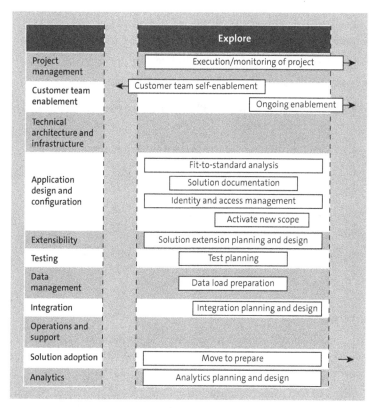

Figure 7.9 SAP Activate Explore Phase Deliverables for SAP S/4HANA Cloud

The following activities are key to the explore phase:

- Managing the project with a strong focus on executing, monitoring, and controlling the results
- Preparing and running company project team enablement activities
- Planning and executing fit-to-standard workshops
- Capturing configuration values to personalize the solution for your business
- Identifying and documenting required integration and solution extensions
- Preparing for data migration
- Designing interfaces, analytics, access management, and enhancements

The following deliverables are typical of the explore phase:

- Fit-to-standard workshops
- Prioritized and documented configuration values in a backlog
- List of required extensions
- Change impact analysis and communication plan
- Integration prerequisites confirmed and resolved
- Data load strategy
- Test strategy
- Inventory of standard and nonstandard interfaces
- Release plan, including confirmation of planned go-live date
- Designs for interfaces, analytics, access management, and enhancements

Finally, the following are typical milestones and key decisions that occur during the explore phase:

- Fit-to-standard workshops for full scope of the implementation completed
- Configuration values captured
- Extensions defined and documented
- Integrations defined and documented
- Project team enabled
- Phase quality assessment conducted

First, let's look at the fit-to-standard analysis workshops.

Fit-to-Standard Workshops

The purpose of fit-to-standard workshops is to validate the predefined SAP Best Practices scenarios delivered in the system with your business requirements. Multiple outcomes can occur from the fit-to-standard workshops, including the confirmation of solution fit; the definition of required configuration values; a list of needed extensions to forms, reports, fields, or business logic; the identification of required integrations; and a list of gaps.

Workshop Tips

At the start of the workshop, we recommend that project teams set rules of engagement during the workshop, as follows:

- Dos
  - Contribute to the discussion.
  - Ask questions if you don't understand something.
  - Be concise in the interest of time.
  - Understand the SAP-delivered best practices.
- Don'ts
  - Use your cell phone, laptop, or tablet.
  - Be afraid to speak up.
  - Forget that you're all on the same team!

Workshops can be conducted remotely. For additional information, see the How to Approach Remote Fit-to-Standard Workshops—Cloud Playbook accelerator in the Roadmap Viewer.

The focused scope of SAP S/4HANA Cloud Public Edition allows for a more efficient approach to validating the fit of the standard solution against your requirements. Fit-to-standard workshops organized around the functional areas of the solution are used to explore the functionality and confirm that the solution can meet your requirements. Gaps are identified and added to the backlog list (gap list). The validation process uses an iterative approach to ensure that integrated dependencies are addressed, including integration requirements and extensibility requirements. In addition, configuration changes are determined and cataloged.

Each fit-to-standard analysis workshop includes the process outlined in Figure 7.10, which is repeated for each business process and process variant. Follow-up workshops may be required if business process requirements are difficult to identify and satisfy.

Let's take a closer look at each step:

❶ Review SAP Best Practices flows
The configuration expert explains the process using the SAP Best Practices process flows, which are available in SAP Cloud ALM.

❷ Demonstrate business scenarios and concepts in the live system
The configuration expert leverages the configured system and delivered data to demonstrate the SAP Best Practices process in the starter system and highlight areas that likely require configuration decisions or may vary for current business processes. The test script documents provided with SAP Best Practices are used to drive the execution of the demonstration in the system.

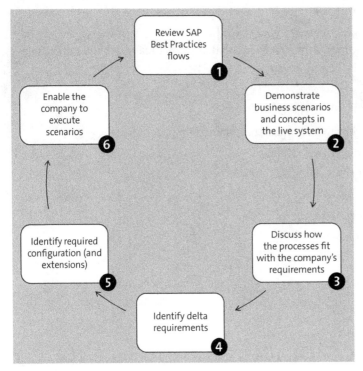

Figure 7.10 Fit-to-Standard Iterative Process

❸ Discuss how the processes fit with the company's requirements

The team engages in discussions to better understand the company's business requirements and to provide understanding of how the solution meets these requirements.

❹ Identify delta requirements

The team identifies and catalogs the delta requirements in SAP Cloud ALM for further analysis and closure. The project team will need to validate identified delta requirements against the product roadmap (*www.sap.com/roadmaps*) to make qualified decisions about whether the gap requires development of extensions or whether the gap can be satisfied with an interim solution until the functionality is delivered in a future update.

❺ Identify required configuration (and extensions)

The team determines and documents the configuration values required. The company is responsible for providing value lists such as product group definitions. The team also captures all required in-app extensions that can be satisfied in the product, items such as adjusting forms, adding business logic, or extending fields. This category also includes standard integrations, where the team can leverage predelivered setup guides for integrating SAP S/4HANA Cloud Public Edition with other systems. Custom integrations are handled as gaps if they require the development of extensions.

❻ Enable the company to execute scenarios
The process flows and test scripts are available in SAP Cloud ALM so that key users can execute the scenarios on their own. If necessary, sample company data can be created to improve learning using more customer-centric examples.

Let's briefly consider the typical workshops conducted when implementing SAP S/4HANA Cloud Public Edition. Note that the list of workshops will vary from company to company, depending on the scope of the solution, and our list is based on selected current capabilities of SAP S/4HANA Cloud Public Edition. Based on the size of the project, many workshops can occur in parallel. First comes the chart of accounts workshop, which is used to define how the company's chart of accounts can be reflected in the solution. During the workshop, the project team reviews the predelivered chart of accounts, maps the company's chart of accounts against the predelivered one, and makes the appropriate adjustments needed to reflect the company's business in the solution.

This is followed by the organizational structure workshop, which defines how the company's organizational structure will be reflected in the solution. During the workshop, the project team reviews the predelivered organizational structure, maps the company's organizational structure against it, and makes the appropriate adjustments to accommodate the company's organizational needs.

From here, the functional workshops begin. Each functional team separately conducts the fit-to-standard analysis for the corresponding functionality. Table 7.1 lists lines of business (LoBs) and topics that are typically covered in each workshop.

Workshop	Typical Topics Discussed
Finance	▪ Accounting and financial close ▪ Advanced accounting and financial close ▪ Financial operations ▪ Advanced financial operations ▪ Cost management and profitability analysis ▪ Enterprise risk and compliance ▪ Real estate management ▪ Subscription billing and revenue management ▪ Treasury management
Human resources	▪ Core human resources
Sourcing and procurement	▪ Central procurement ▪ Invoice management ▪ Operational procurement ▪ Procurement analytics ▪ Sourcing and contract management ▪ Supplier management

Table 7.1 Functional Fit-to-Standard Analysis Workshops

Workshop	Typical Topics Discussed
Supply chain	■ Order promising ■ Advanced order promising ■ Inventory ■ Delivery and transportation ■ Warehousing
Manufacturing	■ Environment, health, and safety ■ Production planning ■ Extended production planning and scheduling ■ Production engineering ■ Production operations ■ Quality management
Sales	■ Sales rebate processing ■ Accelerated company returns ■ Credit and debit memo processing ■ Company consignment ■ Company returns ■ Free delivery ■ Intrastat processing ■ Intercompany sales order processing (domestic/international) ■ Sales inquiry ■ Sales quotation ■ Sell from stock ■ Scheduling agreements ■ Sales contract management ■ Order fulfillment
Asset management	■ Asset operations and maintenance ■ Maintenance management
Professional services	■ Controlling and accounting ■ Projects and engagements ■ Resource management ■ Service-centric billing
Service	■ Service master data and agreement management ■ Service operations and processes
R&D and engineering	■ Enterprise portfolio and project management ■ Product compliance ■ Product lifecycle management

Table 7.1 Functional Fit-to-Standard Analysis Workshops (Cont.)

Determining Configuration Values and Extensions

One of the outputs of the fit-to-standard workshops is documentation of the necessary configuration changes for the team to implement during the realize phase. A blueprint document isn't produced in the SAP Activate approach; however, the project team will record the required configuration and extensions in SAP Cloud ALM that will support the planning and execution of the configuration process in the realize phase.

In each fit-to-standard workshop, the project team determines the following requirements: configuration, master data, forms and reports, identity and access management, extensibility, and integration.

Let's examine these critical decisions in more detail:

- **Defining the organizational structure**
  The team defines the required organizational structure using the Org. Structure Definition Template available in SAP Cloud ALM or the Roadmap Viewer as a starting point or by adopting the standard organizational structure delivered with the starter system. Figure 7.11 shows the default organizational structure delivered with SAP Best Practices for SAP S/4HANA Cloud. The definition will be configured in SAP Central Business Configuration during the initial set up of the development tenant.

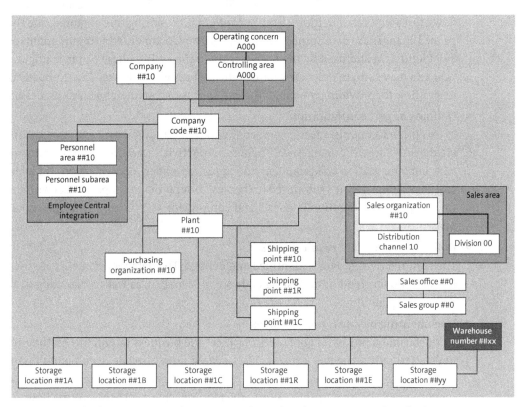

Figure 7.11 Default Organizational Structure Delivered with SAP Best Practices for SAP S/4HANA Cloud

- **Defining the chart of accounts**

  The project team can review the delivered chart of accounts in the starter system using the Manage Chart of Accounts app in SAP S/4HANA Cloud. These accounts can be used as is or as the starting point for a company-specific chart of accounts. In addition, three different chart of accounts type should be considered in the definition:

  - Operating chart of accounts: Mandatory to perform financial postings and used for daily postings to company codes
  - Group chart of accounts: Only necessary if a corporate group exists and financial consolidation is needed
  - Alternative (local) chart of accounts: Required if the customer has any specific local legal requirements

  Unneeded accounts can be marked as **Not Used** and blocked from posting. Don't reuse accounts for purposes other than what is defined in the original description because automatic postings may occur to these accounts.

- **Defining configuration values**

  During the fit-to-standard analysis, the business scenarios are demonstrated and validated using the starter system and SAP Best Practices documentation (process flows, test scripts). In addition, relevant configuration settings are explored, and the needed changes are determined. These changes are documented as requirements in SAP Cloud ALM and used by the project team in the realize phase. Some configuration lists may contain only a few items, while others will be longer. The company is responsible for providing the values that are appropriate to their business processes.

- **Defining expert configuration**

  In exceptional circumstances, expert configuration is required and executed by SAP via the SAP Support Center. The Configuration Activity accelerator in the SAP Activate implementation roadmap lists the approved expert configuration available, and once completed, it's submitted to the service center via a support ticket with the title "Expert Configuration Request" and component XX-S4C-OPR-SRV in the realize phase.

- **Defining master data requirements**

  The required master data is identified and defined. The data requirements are used for master data creation for testing end-to-end scenarios, as well as data migration design and planning.

- **Documenting business process flows**

  As the business processes are tailored to meet the business requirements, they are updated to reflect the new process. The updated flows provide documentation on new processes and are used to support change management and training. Companies can use SAP Cloud ALM to capture the required changes to the process flow.

- **Documenting analytics requirements**
  The standard reports are reviewed during the fit-to-standard analysis workshops. Requirements are added to SAP Cloud ALM or, alternatively, in the Analytics List Template for later review with the analytics experts.

- **Documenting output management requirement**
  Communications channels and the format of output documents are determined. SAP provides form templates that can be used as a starting point to create new templates. The company's current output documents can also be used as documentation of the requirements.

- **Documenting extensibility requirements**
  All extensibility requirements are captured, including business scenarios, user stories, and sources of data. This information will be handed over to the extensibility experts who will develop the detailed designs.

- **Documenting integration requirements**
  All standard and company integrations requirements are documented and cataloged in SAP Cloud ALM as requirements. The Integration Scenario and API List template is available in the Roadmap Viewer and can also be used to track required integration.

- **Documenting identity and access management**
  Special authorization requirements, such as segregation of duties and data visibility, are identified and documented.

The work in fit-to-standard analysis workshops covers the end-to-end solution comprehensively—in other words, both the configuration set directly in the system and also the configuration set via forms, integrations, and extensions. The team needs to determine the scope of the functionality for the initial go-live as a basis for the planning work in the realize phase.

Planning and Design Elements

Areas such as extensibility, integration, analytics, and access management require additional planning and design based on the requirements gathered in the fit-to-standard workshops. The requirements are handed over to the experts in these areas who can develop detailed designs and implementation plans. Because these areas are typically nonstandard items, they often represent bottlenecks in the implementation and should be monitored closely. The output comprises detailed implementation plans and specifications that can be executed in the realize phase.

Data Load Preparation

Data load preparation is the process of taking existing data from a legacy system and preparing it for use in a new SAP system. As of the time of writing, only the staging tables method is supported for SAP S/4HANA Cloud, but direct transfer from another

SAP ERP system is being planned. The staging tables method allows a company to load data from load templates into the staging tables in the SAP S/4HANA Cloud application nondestructively. After the load, the data sits in the staging tables, where it's reviewed for quality. Only after the review is it approved for load into the actual application. This allows the project team to repeat the loads multiple times to ensure the data load templates are accurate without impacting data in the application. This way, the data migration team can resolve any data load issues before the final load to the system and prepare a smooth cutover.

The preparation consists of four tasks:

1. Determining the required master data and transactional data
2. Determining SAP S/4HANA migration cockpit field structures
3. Defining the specification for data extraction from your legacy systems
4. Performing data cleansing activities

It's important that this process begins early in the project because the data extraction and data cleansing activities are typically on the critical path for a successful go-live.

We'll take a closer look at each activity in the following sections.

Determining the Required Master Data and Transactional Data

The purpose of this task is to determine the master data and transactional data required for the scope of your SAP S/4HANA Cloud implementation project and to determine the data sources for these objects. A list of the available migration objects for your SAP S/4HANA Cloud system is available in the solution or in the SAP Help Portal for SAP S/4HANA Cloud Public Edition under **Migration Objects for SAP S/4HANA Cloud.**

Start by determining all master and transactional data objects needed to support the processes detailed in the fit-to-standard workshops. After the list of required objects is determined, the data sources can be mapped to them. In some cases, a legacy equivalent won't be available, and the field data will need to be created or derived.

Historical transaction objects such as completed sales orders and completed purchase orders aren't migrated to the new system. They are typically available via reporting or other archival retrieval tools.

Migration Objects

Note that the coverage and functionality for data migration objects expands with each biannual release of SAP S/4HANA Cloud Public Edition. A complete list of objects is available via the SAP Help Portal under **Data Migration** and in the SAP S/4HANA migration cockpit itself. Templates should always be checked after an upgrade as they may have changed.

Determining SAP S/4HANA Migration Cockpit Field Structures

The purpose of this task is to view the SAP S/4HANA Cloud Public Edition data structures by downloading the template files and associating the structures with the data from the legacy system(s). The specific templates can be downloaded in a Microsoft Excel 2003 XML spreadsheet file or Microsoft Excel format using the **Download Template** button in the Migrate Your Data app (see Figure 7.12). These files contain the metadata (fields, data type, mandatory fields, etc.) and can help with the data mapping. Downloading the files at this early stage helps you understand the available migration objects and fields, prepare the data, and determine how to fill the templates with the data from the legacy system. Additional information about migration templates can be found under **Data Migration** in the SAP Help Portal.

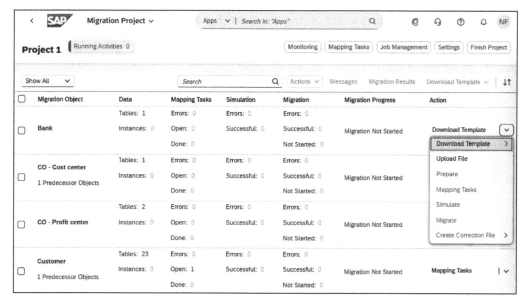

Figure 7.12 Data Migration Download Template

The downloaded templates contain an introduction with instructions, a field list, and data sheets per structure. The data sheet contains at least one mandatory structure and additional optional structures depending on the complexity of the migration object. Only mandatory sheets need to be filled in; however, after an optional sheet is populated, all the mandatory fields for that structure must be filled.

Defining Specifications for Data Extraction from Legacy System

The purpose of this task is to develop the specifications for extraction of data from the legacy system, where necessary, and to initiate the development of the extraction processes. Master and transactional data can change frequently, so a process must be created to assure efficient execution during the cutover to production. Data that will be manually entered also requires a specification so that it can also be created for the cutover.

Performing Data Cleansing Activities

The purpose of this activity is to cleanse the data and eliminate unnecessary legacy data. In addition, the data should be verified to be complete. Unnecessary data should be removed from the legacy data source to reduce the volume of data to load and keep the new system free from extraneous data.

Test Planning

During the explore phase, the project team will start preparing for testing. While most test activities don't start until the realize phase, it's important to prepare not only the testing activities performed during the project but also the regression tests that will be required with each upgrade.

Scoping and planning the tests for the implementation project are required to ensure that the right tests are planned and executed before bringing the system into productive use. Not only is it important to define what types of tests are to be done, but you should also determine who will be accountable for preparing the test plans, executing the tests, and signing off on the results of the testing.

In SAP S/4HANA Cloud Public Edition implementation projects, the project team will need to capture the following testing approach elements in the test strategy document:

- Statement of the project testing objectives and assumptions
- High-level testing schedule to frame what is needed to be completed and when
- Scope of the test to clarify what is to be tested and not to be tested
- Types of testing, including unit testing, business process (string) testing, integration testing, data load testing, and user acceptance testing (UAT)
- Testing approach, including design, construction, and execution of the tests, along with the environments
- Defects management to track and resolve issues encountered
- Governance, roles, and responsibilities to outline the operating model

Along with preparing the testing strategy, the team members responsible for testing should enable and evaluate the test management capabilities in SAP Cloud ALM and the test automation tool in SAP S/4HANA Cloud Public Edition, both of which can support the testing cycles.

7.1.5 Realize Your Requirements

In the previous section, you learned about the steps the project team takes to determine the configuration values and required extensions to the predelivered SAP Best

Practices solution. Let's now shift our attention to how the project team can tailor the predelivered system with company-specific configuration and how the solution can be extended to cover your unique requirements beyond configuration.

After an overview of this phase, this section is structured into several subsections that go over the key activities in the realize phase.

Phase Overview

The purpose of the realize phase is to receive the SAP S/4HANA Cloud systems (development, test, and production) and to incrementally configure, extend, and test the preconfigured solution to reflect your integrated business based on requirements you defined in the explore phase and captured in the backlog. During this phase, the project team also loads company data into the system, tests the business processes, plans adoption activities, and prepares cutover plans and plans for operationally running the solution, as shown in Figure 7.13.

The following activities are key to the realize phase:

- Requesting and initial setup of SAP S/4HANA systems (development, test, production)
- Configuring the company solution in the development environment using agile iterations and the backlog
- Testing the solution in the development environment (unit tests) and test system (string, integration, and UAT)
- Walking through solution processes with stakeholders to confirm that the solution has been configured and meets business needs
- Integrating with other SAP systems and company legacy systems as required
- Executing data migration loads into the development and test environments
- Developing side-by-side extensions and using developer extensibility (on stack) to extend the capabilities of the solution if necessary
- Conducting overall testing of the required business processes in the solution
- Continuing with project team enablement on key concepts and system operations
- Preparing the cutover plan, planning and running change management activities, and preparing to deliver end-user training

During the realize phase, the project team uses a series of agile sprints to incrementally configure, test, and confirm the entire end-to-end solution and to perform legacy data uploads. The project team should actively work with business representatives to ensure a good fit between the built solution and the business requirements. The project team releases the results of multiple agile sprints to business users in a release to production to accelerate time to value and provide early access to the finalized functionality.

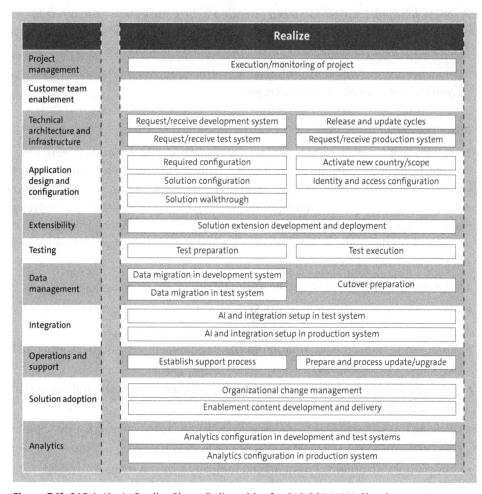

Figure 7.13 SAP Activate Realize Phase Deliverables for SAP S/4HANA Cloud

Typically, the realize phase creates the following deliverables:

- Request and set up the development, test, and production systems
- Initial configuration and system activation using SAP Central Business Configuration
- Organization alignment and user enablement approach
- Solution configuration and solution extensions
- Evaluation and enhancement of security and access controls
- Analytics configuration and artificial intelligence (AI) setup
- Validation of integration points
- Change impact analysis
- Data loaded
- UAT

- Enablement delivery
- Support operations and handover plan
- Cutover and transition plan

The realize phase includes the following typical project milestones and key decisions:

- System activation
- Solution configuration and extensibility completed in each sprint
- Moving configuration and extensions from the development environment to the test environment
- Functionality reviewed and accepted by business users
- Integration testing complete
- Data migration testing conducted
- UAT completed
- Phase quality assessment conducted
- End-user training
- Readiness for production release confirmed
- Defined support and operation processes

Let's begin with provisioning of the infrastructure, starting with the provisioning of and access to the development, test, and production systems.

Development System Provisioning

At the beginning of the realize phase, the company requests provisioning of a development system from the SAP for Me application. You can find detailed steps in the Request the SAP S/4HANA Cloud Development System task. This action will trigger provisioning of two tenants: one will be used by the project team for configuration activities (customizing tenant) and the second will be used for developer extensibility (development tenant). The previously provisioned SAP Central Business Configuration tenant will manage configuration in the development system as well as the starter system.

When the provisioning process is finalized, the company will receive instructions for access to and setup of these tenants, including the steps to set up workspaces for activation and configuration activities through SAP Central Business Configuration. We'll briefly outline these steps next.

Development System Access and Initial Setup

In this section, we'll discuss the first steps that the project team takes after receiving the instructions for access to and setup of the development system. As we mentioned earlier, the development system consists of a customizing tenant and development tenant. A company needs to perform activities to set up and activate each tenant.

The project team will perform the following key activities:

- **Set up the customizing tenant in SAP Central Business Configuration**
  As the project team will be using SAP Central Business Configuration to perform the initial confirmation, the system must be properly activated. The first step is to log into SAP Central Business Configuration and create a new project for a customizing tenant (look ahead to Figure 7.15). The details of these steps are covered in the Set Up Customizing Tenant in SAP Central Business Configuration task in SAP Activate. Then, the configuration experts perform the following activities in SAP Central Business Configuration as they are guided through the implementation project for the customizing tenant:
  - Scoping
  - Assign a deployment target
  - Milestone confirming scoping is completed
  - Primary finance settings
  - Set up organization structure
  - Milestone completing the scope and organizational structure phase

- **Set up the development tenant in SAP Central Business Configuration**
  Next, the configuration expert follows the same steps as in the previous section to set up the development tenant. This way the customizing tenant and development tenant have the same scope and setup to ensure that the developer extensibility, once tested in development tenant, will also work when transported into the test system. You'll find details of this step in SAP Activate in the Set Up Development Tenant in SAP Central Business Configuration task.

- **Initial system access for the SAP S/4HANA Cloud development system**
  During the process, the company will also need to initially access the development system, prepare it for the project team access, and adapt the chart of accounts prior to requesting provisioning of a test system. The detailed steps are provided in the Initial System Access to the Development System task in SAP Activate. The following tasks are performed during this process (once for each tenant in the development system):
  - Gaining initial access to the system (first admin user)
  - Scoping
  - Assigning a deployment target
  - Setting up the organizational structure
  - Entering the primary finance settings
  - Creating users for project team
  - Self-activating of project team members in the Identity Authentication service

After the development system is set up, the test and production systems can be requested from SAP for Me as detailed in the Request the SAP S/4HANA Cloud Test System and Request the SAP S/4HANA Cloud Production System deliverables in SAP Activate. Next, we'll briefly cover the steps to follow when receiving these systems.

Initial Access and Setup of Test System

After the test system access email has been received, the test system is set up using an initial transport from the development system. This transport content is released via the Export Customizing Transports app in the development system. On the receiving side in the test system, use the Import Collection app to import the transport into the test system. Note that the detailed description of the steps is covered in the Initial Access to the Test System task in SAP Activate. Like in the development system, you'll create users and perform self-activation of the project team members in the Identity Authentication service.

Initial Access and Setup of the Production System

After the production system access email has been received and the test system has been set up as outlined in the previous sections, the production system is set up using an initial transport from the development system (the same transport used to set up the test system). This transport content is forwarded to the production system from the test system via the Import Collection app shown in Figure 7.14.

Figure 7.14 Import Collection App in SAP S/4HANA Cloud

Here are the steps to follow:

1. In the test system, identify the transport request, and make sure it shows the **Imported** status.

2. Click on **Forward** to initiate transport to the production system. You can choose to instantly forward all collections. To do this, select **Automation Settings**, and mark the **Instant Forward** checkbox.

3. Switch to the production system and select and import the transport in the Import Collection app once it shows **Ready for Import**.

The detailed process is available in SAP Activate in the Initial System Access for SAP S/4HANA Cloud Production System deliverable and Forward Configuration from Test System to Production System task. Like in the development and test systems, you'll create users and perform self-activation of the productive environment for team members through the dedicated Identity Authentication service for production.

Note that the starter system will remain available to the project as a sandbox environment until 30 calendar days after the production system handover email is sent. If needed, an additional sandbox system subscription is available for longer term needs.

Solution Configuration and Walkthrough

The main purpose of the realize phase is to tailor the system to fit your business needs and confirm that the business process will meet the needs of the company.

The configuration in SAP S/4HANA Cloud is supported by the following processes:

- Guided configuration through SAP Central Business Configuration using easy-to-use configuration activities available to consultants and key users
- Configuration sprints where processes are configured, tested, and moved to the test system
- Configuration in the parallel process line as an alternative for major configuration changes without impacting the main line
- Solution walkthrough where the processes are demonstrated to the stakeholders for approval

Let's take a closer look at each one.

Guided Configuration with SAP Central Business Configuration

For most configuration tasks, such as setting up blocking reasons for billing or adjusting approval limits for purchase orders in your organizational unit, the project team will access the configuration activities in the SAP Central Business Configuration implementation project that is set up during the initial setup of the system after it has been received.

Figure 7.15 shows **Business Processes Configuration**, where configuration experts will find relevant configuration activities for their scope. This application provides a step-by-step view of the required configuration activities and is responsive to the scope selected for the implementation project defined in SAP Central Business Configuration. Consultants and configuration experts use this environment to access the configuration activities and realize the delta requirements and configuration values identified during the fit-to-standard in the explore phase and captured in the backlog.

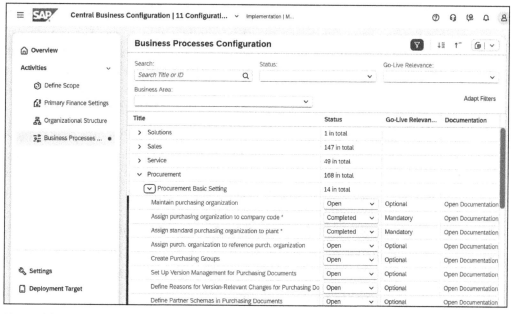

Figure 7.15 SAP Central Business Configuration: Project Experience

Configuration activities are structured into a hierarchy where each hierarchy item provides access to specific configuration activities relevant for the selected scope. The configuration is performed and unit-tested in the SAP S/4HANA Cloud development system, and then transported to the test system for further testing (string and integration tests). The transports to the test system happen at least once every one or two weeks as part of the sprinting process. We'll cover this topic in the next section.

The SAP Activate methodology recommends completing the following configuration activities before opening the system to general configuration and executing of the business processes (even for testing):

- Configuring the tax solution (as applicable)
- Adapting chart of accounts
- Maintaining profit center configuration
- Maintaining cost center master data
- Maintaining takeover date information for asset accounting

- Configuring customer-specific fiscal year variants (as applicable)
- Maintaining data and setting for treasury management (as applicable)

We recommend always referring to the latest information in the SAP Activate methodology in the Required Configuration Before System Use – SAP S/4HANA Cloud deliverable. After these topics are configured, multiple teams can start parallel configuration of finance, sales, sourcing and procurement, supply chain, manufacturing, asset management, and professional services as needed per the scope of the project.

The project team will also need to create sample master data for the purpose of unit-testing the configuration during the short configuration cycles. The sample data should be jointly determined by both consultants and business users so that the data can also be used for business process testing scenarios later. The data should be indicative of your typical data so that it can be used in the solution walkthrough sessions.

Configuration Sprints

Project teams execute configuration in short, one- to two-week agile sprints. In each sprint, the project team performs the required configuration and unit tests the business scenario in the development system. Then, the completed configuration is transported into the test system, where business process testing is conducted, and the completed functionality is reviewed with business users. The configuration experts and business users follow this sequence of steps during the configuration sprints:

- Short configuration cycles, including testing, reviewing, and transporting
- Configuration based on the configuration backlog created during fit-to-standard
- Complete testing of each sprint outcome
- Sprint reviews of what has been configured in the system to verify that business needs are satisfied
- Weekly transports from the development system to the test system via transport management
- Management of solution configuration tasks and user stories maintained in the SAP Cloud ALM system

In this way, the development system and test system are kept synchronized throughout the implementation project. The vehicle to move the configuration between the systems is called a *transport request*, and it enables the project team to move configuration (and extensibility) from the development system through the test system and all the way into the production system. A project team typically doesn't forward the transports from test to production immediately after testing, but rather prior to the cutover to productive use of the features.

Let's now discuss the flow of the configuration shown in Figure 7.16. The process starts with the definition of scope and setup activities in an SAP Central Business Configuration implementation project ❶. Next, the activation of the business content ❷ creates an initial transport that is then used in the setup of the test and production systems, as we discussed earlier in this chapter. In addition, the configuration experts extend and fine-tune the configuration ❸ in the development system to reflect the delta requirements and configuration settings captured in the fit-to-standard workshop. The completed configuration is exported from the development system and imported into the test system, where it's further tested ❹. After successful testing, the transport can be forwarded from the test system to production and later imported into the production system ❺.

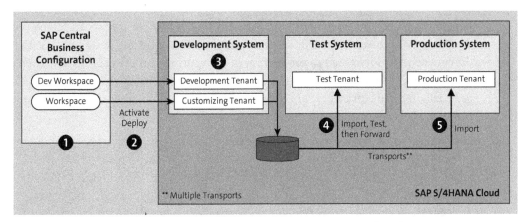

Figure 7.16 Transporting Configuration between Development, Test, and Production Systems

The strategy of employing configuration sprints that each last one or two weeks ensures that the team stays focused on completing the configuration of the business processes and testing and that the size and scope of the configuration stays manageable. In addition to the configuration, there are forms, extensions, and other related nonconfiguration items that are moved via the Export Software Collection app and imported to production using the Import Collection app.

The following is an outline of the steps executed in each configuration sprint:

1. Plan the functionality that will be implemented in the sprint through configuration, key user extensions, developer extensions, output management, master data, and so on.

2. Configure in the workspace for the development system and perform unit and string testing. All configuration is automatically recorded for transport. Any dependent master data (e.g., general ledger accounts) must be manually recreated in the test and production systems before the changes are transported.

3. Using the Export Software Collection app in the development system, export the forms, extensions, or other objects associated with the current transport. A complete list of the objects moved via the Export Software Collection app is available in the application.

4. Use the Export Customizing Transports app in the development system to release the customizing transport with all the configuration changes.

5. In the test system, use the Import Collection app to import the queued changes.

6. After an end-to-end test, system integration test, and UAT in the test system, click on the **Forward** button in the Import Collection app to send all the changes (configuration and extensibility) to the production system.

7. In the production system, use the Import Collection app to import the queued changes.

Repeat the process for each configuration sprint. Note that the transports to the production environment can be done independently from the sprinting process (they don't need to be forwarded to production in each sprint) and instead can be buffered until the complete functionality is ready for release to the production system. This is especially relevant for customers executing subsequent implementation waves after the initial go-live.

Different Transport Modes

SAP S/4HANA Cloud Public Edition supports two different transport modes: simple and flexible. With simple mode, only one business configuration transport is created to collect all changes and has the benefit that the change dependencies are easily managed. With flexible mode, multiple transports can be created in parallel and can have different dependencies. Individual transports can be discarded during the pre-import.

Configuration with the Parallel Project Line

A parallel project line allows significant business configuration changes without disrupting your main transport path. Basically, a copy is created of your mainline project in a separate tenant, the parallel project line, which allows changes, including large and complex ones. Business-critical changes can still flow through the mainline to the production system without impacting the configuration and testing in the parallel project line.

After completing and testing the changes in the parallel project line, you can use the **Merge** function to copy these updates into the mainline development system. From there, the revised configuration is transported to the test system for final validation before being deployed to production.

The prerequisites for creation of a parallel project are as follows:

- In the main line project, all activities and milestones of the scope and organizational structure phase are completed.
- Your main line project is in the product-specific configuration phase.
- All mandatory activities in the main line are completed.
- There are no running lifecycle processes.
- Projects are unlocked.

The parallel project is created with the help of the branching function, as shown in Figure 7.17. Via branching, a full copy of the current project in the main line is created in the parallel project line, including its scope, organizational structure, and configuration. Note that a main line can only have one parallel project line, and changes to the mainline can be sent to the parallel project via the **Rebase** function.

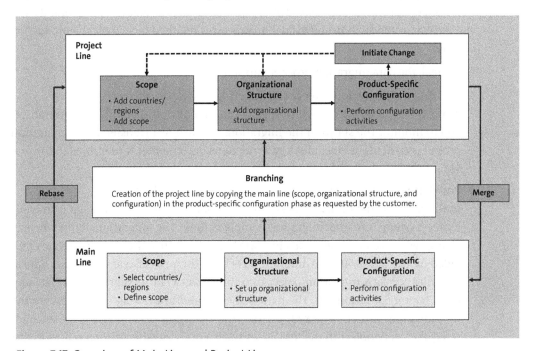

Figure 7.17 Overview of Main Line and Project Line

Solution Walkthrough

The purpose of a solution walkthrough is to demonstrate to the stakeholders that the configured solution meets the organization's business needs. The first step of any solution walkthrough is to prepare the key business scenarios and data needed to demonstrate the functionality to the company's project team. Typically, the company representative presents the functionality to the stakeholders to demonstrate an understanding of the solution and how it will be used to run the business.

The second step is to demonstrate the configured solution to project stakeholders and gain initial approval and confirmation that the solution satisfies the business needs. The initial approval also triggers the beginning of a more comprehensive testing stream.

Data Migration

The purpose of data migration activities is to develop, test, and execute the data migration processes for all the data objects identified in the explore phase. SAP S/4HANA Cloud supports both direct transfer from another SAP ERP system or migration through staging tables. Both processes use the SAP S/4HANA migration cockpit, however, with direct transfer, there is no need for staging the data.

This activity consists of iterative cycles to analyze data quality, refine business rules, and run the migration processes that move, transform, and enrich the company data required to support project test cycles and, ultimately, production. The test cycles enable the migration team to improve data quality, develop a detailed cutover sequencing plan, and exercise the data reconciliation and validation processes required to support the production cutover.

Let's break the data migration process into steps:

1. **Creating the migration project and selecting migration objects**
   A migration project is created to specify the data objects that you want to transfer and to monitor the status of the migration. For each test transfer, a new migration project is created that includes any corrections or refinements identified in the previous test.

2. **Populating the staging tables with the files or preferred tool**
   In this step, the data migration experts will populate the data extracted from your legacy system into the migration template files. The migration template may change with each release, so it's important to always use the latest templates provided by the SAP S/4HANA migration cockpit. The project team will then upload data files for each migration object into the tenant via the Migrate Your Data app (see Chapter 5, Section 5.2). The data is then stored in the staging area, where the uploaded files can be reviewed, deleted, and uploaded again if errors are encountered. For every object in the tool, you can also find documentation on how to test and validate the migrated data from within the migration cockpit itself. Note that this step isn't necessary if transferring data via the direct transfer method.

3. **Performing value mapping**
   After the data is loaded into the staging tables, the migration experts map the required field values of the staging table to fields in the tenant. Once all mapping tasks have been confirmed, the mapping process is complete.

4. **Simulating the data migration**
   This activity will simulate the migration of your data through the relevant application interfaces without committing the data to your actual database tables. The team should resolve any issues resulting from the simulation process, which may require adjusting configuration or business logic.

5. **Executing the data migration**
   After all the steps have been performed and the project team is confident in the source data quality, the data migration experts can proceed with loading the legacy data into the system (see Figure 7.18 for an example data migration project). This migration can be performed online or via background processing. By completing this step, the project team delivers the master data and transactional data required

by the SAP S/4HANA Cloud application. Populating master and transactional data enables the project team to complete the testing cycles and determine production readiness. Parallel project line functionality with data replication can provide a clean environment for validating data migration results, sequencing, and cutover timing.

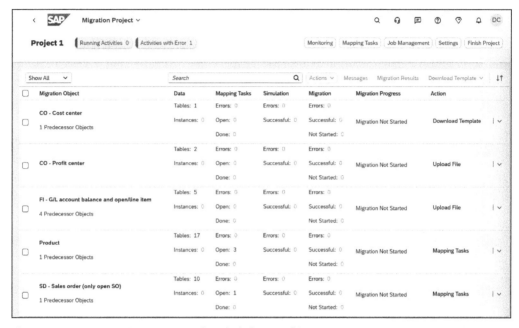

Figure 7.18 Data Migration Project with Included Data Objects

Testing

Progressive testing of the functionality as the system is configured during the realize phase is critical for any project, and this is no different when implementing SAP S/4HANA Cloud. As we mentioned earlier, SAP provides strong built-in testing automation capabilities in SAP S/4HANA Cloud and additional capabilities for test planning and orchestration powered by SAP Cloud ALM. (We introduced SAP Cloud ALM in Chapter 4 and discussed the testing topics in Chapter 5, Section 5.6.1.)

As shown in Figure 7.19, during the implementation, the project team will conduct several types of tests to ensure that the solution is configured properly and performs to the required specification level:

- **Unit test**
  This testing is performed by the configuration expert to ensure that specific units of a solution's functionality (configuration, output, etc.) work as required. This testing is done in each of the one- to two-week-long configuration sprints.

- **String test**
  Think of a string test as a string of unit tests, in which several units of functionality are combined to confirm that the collective functionality works as desired (e.g.,

creating an order and checking the approval levels for both the order item values and the value of the entire order). This type of testing is done during the one- to two-week-long configuration sprints, though in early sprints, the project team may be limited in its scope of testing.

- **Business process test**
  A business process test covers an end-to-end flow with multiple units or strings within a single system. It focuses on testing the ability of the configured, extended, and integrated solution to meet the business requirements using migrated data and real business processes. It may be executed in additional cycles of testing based on the size of the project.

- **Systems integration test**
  A system integration test extends beyond a business process test by including interfaced data from or to other systems in the end-to-end test. A system integration test ensures that data can be imported, exported, or reported as needed in the SAP S/4HANA Cloud or the interfaced system.

- **Data migration test**
  Migrating into the production system is a critical process, so it's essential to thoroughly verify and document data, sequencing, and timing. Data is validated to ensure it meets requirements for completeness and accuracy. Additionally, business process tests are conducted based on the migrated data to confirm data consistency across all business areas.

- **UAT**
  The final testing is performed by the user or a subset of users to ensure that all job functions can be executed successfully in the new system. Using test scripts, training materials, and real experiences, day-to-day operations are simulated by job role to verify that the business can successfully operate after go-live. Successful completion indicates that the system is ready for productive use.

- **Regression test**
  The company validates that the business processes work as expected after changes are made that may impact the system, such as upgrades, extensions, and configuration changes. A company can leverage existing standard automated tests that are applicable to their processes with customer-specific test data and/or create their own processes.

  Within the regression test deliverable, SAP will help ensure live customers are prepared for the major upgrades by triggering post-upgrade tests (PUTs) for customers that have opted into the program. All PUT plans are triggered by SAP after a major upgrade to the test system, and the results are available in the solution in the Analyze Automated Test Results app, along with all applicable screenshots and statuses. Custom automated tests can be added to the scope and triggered with the standard tests.

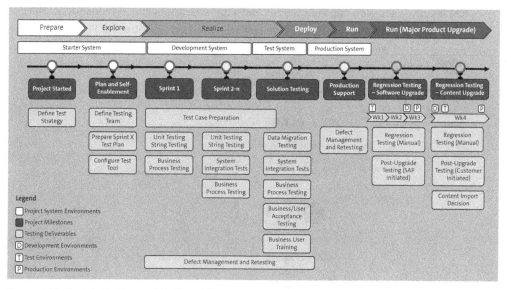

Figure 7.19 Test Activities and Deliverables

SAP S/4HANA Cloud automated testing can be accessed via SAP Cloud ALM or the Manage Your Test Processes app in SAP S/4HANA Cloud. Custom test cases will be done within the test automation tool for SAP S/4HANA Cloud directly. If you're using a third-party testing tool, SAP Cloud ALM can be connected to supported tools to provide a central access point. We recommend that all the project team members involved in testing review the in-application help, user guides, and video recordings demonstrating how to use the tool. The SAP_BR_ADMIN_TEST_AUTOMATION SAP S/4HANA business role is required for access.

Before the tool can be used, the testing team creates the testing users that will be used during the automated test execution.

Further Resources

Step-by-step instructions are included in the Test Management Guide accelerator in the SAP Activate for SAP S/4HANA Cloud Public Edition (3-System Landscape) roadmap in the SAP Activate Roadmap Viewer.

The testing tool comes with predelivered test scripts for coverage of the SAP Best Practices functionality delivered in the system that can be modified or copied to create a new custom test process. SAP recommends using standard test process steps because these processes are updated automatically during the system upgrade. Custom-created process steps require manual updates by the company after a release upgrade, which can cause a delay in executing the tests. The testing will be run in the background, and the system will notify you about the results of the test that has been executed. After the test is completed, you can view details and a log with applicable screenshots of the execution and review the results of every test step in detail, as shown in Figure 7.20.

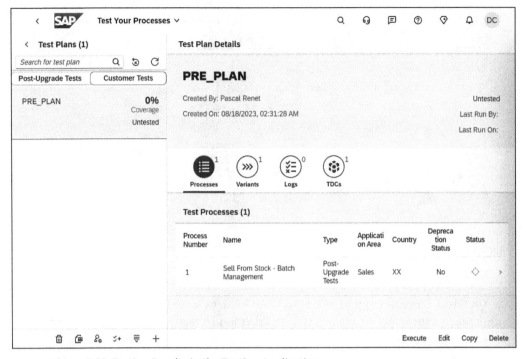

Figure 7.20 Testing Results in the Testing Application

Adapting Forms and Configuring Output Management

Output management is an important part of getting the system ready for company use in the realize phase. During this stage, the project team will configure the output management in their SAP S/4HANA Cloud system and adjust the predelivered forms to meet company requirements. The output channels possible are print, email, and electronic data interchange (EDI).

> **Printing and Form Adjustment Prerequisites**
>
> The project team will need to install both SAP Cloud Print Manager for Pull Integration and Adobe LiveCycle Designer. Both tools are available for download via the Install Additional Software app.
>
> Additional documentation is available in the Output Management Set-Up Instructions (1LQ) SAP Best Practices solution process.

Let's take a closer look at these key activities for adaptation of forms and output management.

Adapting Forms in the Application

SAP S/4HANA Cloud contains SAP-delivered form templates. Simple changes can be completed using the Manage Logos app or the Manage Texts app. More significant changes can be made by downloading the templates from the Maintain Form Templates app and using Adobe LiveCycle Designer.

Print forms use a two-tier concept, as shown in Figure 7.21: the *master* ❶ contains the header information, such as logo ❷ and address ❸, and the *content* ❹ contains the body details. Also note the footer block(s) at the bottom of the template form ❺. The email templates are edited directly in the solution via the Maintain Email Templates app.

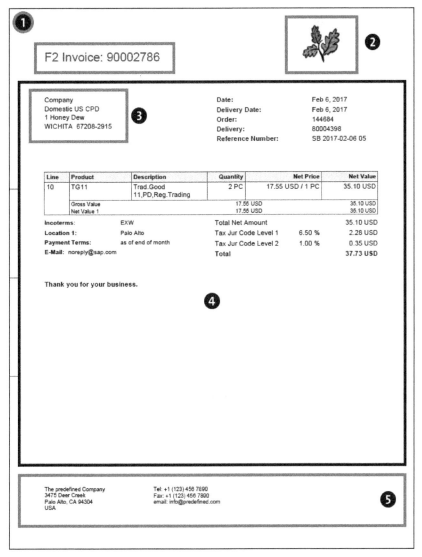

Figure 7.21 Master and Content Form Templates

Enabling Output Management

The purpose of enabling output management is to ensure that forms can be printed, emailed, or sent through an EDI channel. During this step, the project team configures the system through both SAP Central Business Configuration and SAP S/4HANA Cloud apps to support the required output destination.

Figure 7.22 shows the relevant tiles on your home screen for accessing these apps. Follow these steps to set up output management to a printer or set of printers:

1. Set up output channels via the Maintain Print Queues app.
2. Install the SAP Cloud Print Manager for Pull Integration on a local server or PC.
3. Connect print queues and printers via SAP Cloud Print Manager for Pull Integration.
4. Maintain the default print queue in the Output Parameter Determination app, and define the rules that determine which form will be used for each business scenario.

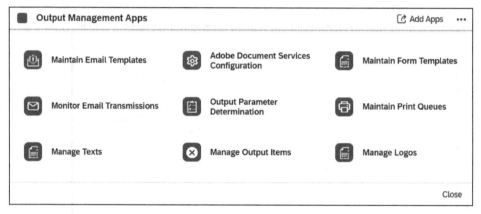

Figure 7.22 Output Management and Output Control Tiles

Application documents in PDF format can be automatically sent to business partners via email. In addition, the output can be configured to send transaction data via EDI.

> **Further Resources**
>
> For complete step-by-step documentation on setting up output management, see the documentation related to the Setting Up Output Management (1LQ) SAP Best Practices solution process.

Extensibility

SAP S/4HANA Cloud provides a range of options to extend the standard capabilities of the application. You can use key user extensibility, developer extensibility, and side-by-side extensibility. We discussed these in more detail in Chapter 5, Section 5.3. Now, we'll go over the key types of extensibility work performed in this phase.

Key User Extensions

Key user extensibility is one part of SAP S/4HANA Cloud's in-app extensibility capabilities that enable your key users to extend the standard functionality without modifying the code. These extensions are only applicable within a restricted organizational context, meaning that key users in this scenario can perform simple extensions of the application. SAP S/4HANA Cloud supports key user extensions to the user interface (UI), including the ability to add new custom fields to the UI and associated logic.

These extensions are created with a web-based key user tool, which provides easy-to-use access to customize the software without making code changes. A key user can make the following modifications on the fly:

- Adapt the UI to your company's naming terminologies by changing the field labels.
- Adapt and simplify the UI by hiding fields that aren't required.
- Organize the layout of fields in the UI to make it more accessible to your organization's needs.

To make changes to key user extensions, the key user must be assigned an appropriate business role that includes the SAP_CORE_BC_EXT business catalog. This assignment will make the key user tools accessible to the user and must be done through the Maintain Business User app in the SAP S/4HANA Cloud launchpad.

The key users will then be able to make the following changes in their SAP S/4HANA Cloud system:

- Make general UI adaptions for forms, tables, or filters, including hiding fields, removing fields, moving fields or UI blocks, creating a new group, adding a new field from the field repository, renaming labels, and so on.
- Add new custom fields to standard existing UIs.
- Add new custom business logic for standard existing UIs.
- Create new custom business objects, allowing data analysis of the underlying database tables.
- Create custom core data services (CDS) views.

The built-in key user extensibility in SAP S/4HANA Cloud provides a wide range of extensibility options for your key users, as we've just outlined. The goal of this stage of the project is to implement the most critical extensions in the system and properly test them before they are transported to the production system.

Further Resources

Refer to the SAP Activate methodology and consult the relevant accelerators in the Roadmap Viewer for the latest guidance on key user extensibility.

Developer (On-Stack) Extensibility

SAP offers an extensibility option as part of SAP S/4HANA and SAP S/4HANA Cloud to complement current key user (in-app) extensibility capabilities. The developer (on-stack) extensibility option empowers ABAP developers to extend standard SAP processes with custom extensions that require tighter integration with the SAP S/4HANA backend while keeping the digital core isolated from the custom code (clean core). This will help minimize the efforts of regression testing during SAP S/4HANA upgrades. We introduced the developer extensibility topic in Chapter 5, Section 5.3.2.

Further Resources

Refer to the "Developer Extensibility" document in the SAP Help Portal at *http://s-prs.co/v546312*.

Side-by-Side Extensibility

You also have option to use side-by-side extensibility, which uses SAP Business Technology Platform (SAP BTP) to build larger extensions or dedicated applications that are then integrated with SAP S/4HANA Cloud using the application programming interfaces (APIs) published on SAP Business Accelerator Hub. We discussed this type of extensibility in Chapter 5, Section 5.3.3.

Integration

For integrations included in the scope of the project, the team sets up the various integrations during the realize phase, following the guidance provided in the SAP Activate framework. SAP provides standard integrations for solutions such as SAP Success-Factors Employee Central, SAP Fieldglass, SAP Ariba, SAP Concur, or SAP Customer Experience, to list a few examples. Always refer to the latest information about available standard interfaces for SAP S/4HANA Cloud Public Edition published in SAP Signavio Process Navigator under the relevant area in the **Line of Business** solution processes and the filter **Integration Relevant**, as shown in Figure 7.23. SAP Signavio Process Navigator provides details about the integration, including setup instructions, process flows, task tutorials, test scripts, and links to the Cloud Integration Automation service.

The Cloud Integration Automation service is available to provide workflow guidance to set up the standard integration in both systems. The steps in the service are from the Solution Process setup guides and are presented in an interactive and guided way to allow quicker execution. The Cloud Integration Automation service subaccount must be created in SAP BTP to access the workflows.

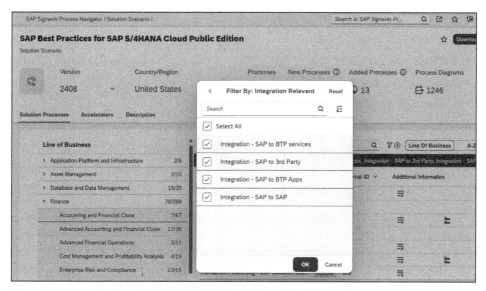

Figure 7.23 How to Access SAP S/4HANA Cloud Integration Scope Items

In addition to standard integrations, you can integrate your custom applications with SAP S/4HANA Cloud using published APIs. SAP Business Accelerator Hub provides comprehensive documentation of all the available APIs for SAP S/4HANA Cloud. The SAP Activate methodology in the Roadmap Viewer provides a framework of tasks for project teams building custom interfaces.

Planning Cutover, End-User Enablement, and User Support

During the realize phase, the project team starts detailed planning for the steps they will take to bring the solution into the production environment and transition to the SAP S/4HANA Cloud system. These activities are documented in a *cutover plan* that captures the strategy, scope, and timelines for moving from the existing solution to the new solution and into the period immediately after go-live.

We'll walk through each activity in the following sections.

Cutover Planning Workshop and Documentation

The purpose of the planning workshop is to document the strategy, scope, and timelines for moving from the "as-is" solution to the "to-be" solution and the post-go-live support period immediately following go-live. This includes a workshop to document activities such as the following:

- Setting up and initializing the production system
- Setting up and verifying interface connections
- Migrating or creating master data manually via a data migration tool and/or via an interfaced system

285

- Testing the complete data migration
- Validating the migrated data
- Creating users
- Notifying impacted third parties
- Determining go/no-go decision points
- Closing the legacy systems
- Completing all required documentation for regulatory purposes (if required)
- Planning timeline and meeting schedule for completing, sequencing, and simulating the cutover schedule

It's important that each team begin the development of the cutover list when starting the configuration and maintain the list throughout the implementation to avoid missing critical details. Estimated durations should also be kept and refined so that the final schedule can be calculated down to the minute. When planning the downtime, always consider planned downtime and restricted uptime related to system patching. Transport movement and data migration can't occur during restricted uptime.

Remote Cutover Playbook

The SAP Activate team has introduced new remote playbooks for activities and tasks that were traditionally done on-site. These playbooks support project teams in a shift to fully remote or hybrid execution of these project tasks. One such playbook is the Remote Cutover Playbook, which has been added to SAP Activate. You can find it in the SAP Activate Roadmap Viewer under the relevant cutover planning and execution tasks. For example, in the task at *http://s-prs.co/v546313*, click on the **How to Approach Remote Cutover** accelerator to access the playbook.

End-User Enablement

During the realize phase, the project team will prepare for user enablement to get new business users started in the system. One key aspect is the development of the learning and training materials for bringing new users into the system. In SAP S/4HANA Cloud implementations, project teams can leverage self-enablement materials such as videos, easy-to-access documentation, and recordings that users can consume at their own pace.

End-user learning content must be designed to encourage effective user adoption and must complement the built-in functionalities of SAP S/4HANA Cloud, including the self-enablement content inside the product. The newly developed learning content must be employee-centric and business process–relevant. Learning experience design considers the type of material needed to target specific groups of end users. Learning content should also reflect the business's priorities in terms of process areas and subjects covered, while focusing on the user experience (UX; i.e., how and when employees will consume learning content). Learning experience design and development work will be undertaken within a clearly defined project plan and quality assurance process.

User Support

Before taking the system live, you'll need to establish a process for supporting your employees in using the new solution. It's critical for end users to know whom they can contact if issues arise and how they can escalate their support requests. Most organizations have existing IT policies and processes in place, and the goal of this activity in the realize phase is to ensure that user support for SAP S/4HANA Cloud is included in support handling and that the IT team can provide such support.

Your support organization must be able to communicate problems internally, troubleshoot data issues or improper system setup (configuration, printing, etc.), research issues, and escalate to SAP support when needed.

7.1.6   Deploy Your Solution

This section will explain how your project team can conduct the final validation of the solution prior to running the cutover activities that will bring the solution into live use by your end users. We'll also discuss end-user enablement capabilities that simplify new user onboarding to SAP S/4HANA Cloud and discuss the salient differences in production support between a cloud environment and the on-premise systems that you're probably more familiar with.

After an overview of this phase, the information in this section is broken into two halves: the cutover to the production process and solution adoption and support.

Phase Overview

The purpose of this phase is to set up the production system, confirm organizational readiness, and switch business operations to the new system. Initiating the deploy phase means that the project team has already completed integration testing in the realize phase and has confirmed that all processes are meeting the business needs, and no issues remain that would hold back the transition to production. Thus, the team transitions to live business operations in the new environment and conducts solution adoption and post-go-live support activities.

The following activities are key to the deploy phase:

- Monitoring operational readiness and tracking goals
- Executing cutover plans
- Monitoring business process results in the production environment
- Establishing solution adoption support processes (e.g., onboarding new users, answering end-user questions, and resolving user issues)

As shown in Figure 7.24, the deploy phase typically creates the following deliverables:

- Organizational and production environment readiness confirmation
- Completion of user enablement
- Verification of integration and output management in production
- Setup processes for adoption of the new live solution
- Cutover to production
- Post-go-live end-user support
- Project closing

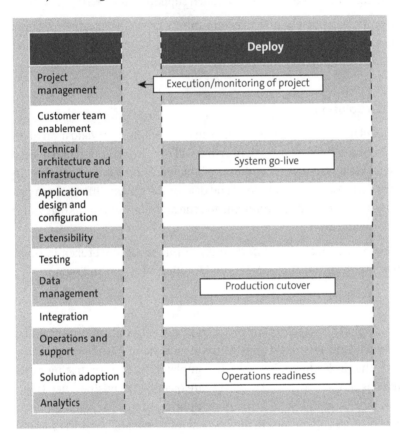

Figure 7.24 SAP Activate Deploy Phase Deliverables for SAP S/4HANA Cloud

The deploy phase includes the following typical project milestones and key decisions:

- Data loads into production completed
- Production environment fully set up and verified
- Organization readiness for transition to production confirmed
- Go-live activities conducted
- Project formally closed

Cutover to Production

The main activity during the deploy phase is to perform the cutover of the business to the new production software and to go live. At this point, the organizational, business, functional, technical, and system aspects of the project are ready to be used in productive manor. We'll walk through two key deliverables in the following sections.

Confirming Operational Readiness for Cutover

Before you can proceed with the cutover activities outlined in the cutover plan, your project team needs to reconfirm that the business is ready to receive the new solution. This step includes confirmation of the following:

- Key users have been identified and trained and are ready to support the solution.
- End users have been enabled on the new solution.
- The production environment has been provisioned and is ready for cutover activities.
- Any business transactions in the legacy system have been stopped per the cutover plan, and contingency plans have been put in place (e.g., manual processing for the duration of cutover).

Now, it's time to perform the cutover.

Performing Cutover per the Cutover Plan

During the realize phase, the project team prepared a cutover plan that details the sequence, duration, and responsibilities for performing the cutover activities. The cutover plan includes but isn't limited to the following:

- Closing the legacy system
- Setting up required integrations in the production environment
- Performing master data and transactional data loads to production per the cutover plan
- Setting up user accounts, including assignment of authorization profiles
- Setting up extensibility in production

After these cutover activities are completed, the project team confirms with the stakeholders the successful conclusion of the cutover before the system goes live for business users and before the company runs business activities in the new environment.

Solution Adoption and Support

The support processes for cloud solutions differ from the traditional on-premise model in several critical ways. You don't need a dedicated IT support organization to support the solution because the environment is managed by SAP; this support includes applying the biannual releases of updates, applying hot fixes and patches, and resolving support tickets.

However, you'll need to establish an organization or appoint a responsible person to ensure the effective onboarding of new users, to drive the use of the solution, and to provide end-user assistance not handled by the SAP support processes. In other words, support must be provided to answer procedural questions that users can't resolve on their own using in-application help functions or questions about company-specific processes and policies.

We'll discuss the key deliverables for solution adoption and support next.

Handover Support to the Operations Team

The purpose of this activity is to transition from project-supported processes and organizational structures to production-supported processes and organizational structures. You'll need to set up sufficient support for end users to ensure that new users can be efficiently onboarded into the system (including creating users, assigning authorizations, and enablement to make end users proficient in using the environment). Such a support organization can also raise support tickets with SAP to resolve any production issues or can create service requests with the service center or other SAP support teams.

The project team will schedule a dedicated handover meeting to formally transition from the project support environment to the company onboarding and adoption environment. Because the new system is a cloud system, the responsible personnel must know how SAP will support the system and the proper methods of engaging with SAP when concerns, questions, or problems arise. The support organization will schedule and conduct the meeting prior to the go-live.

SAP Support Offerings for SAP S/4HANA Cloud Solutions

SAP Enterprise Support, cloud edition is the standard support maintenance agreement embedded in your SAP S/4HANA Cloud Public Edition contract. SAP Enterprise Support provides different levels of proactive support, built on four pillars:

- **Collaboration**
  Receive expert guidance through various collaboration resources such as the value maps, the Customer Interaction Center (CIC), and the Customer Insights Dashboard in SAP for Me.

- **Empowerment**
  Use the SAP Enterprise Support Academy program to acquire knowledge and skills. SAP provides foundational learning assets hosted in the SAP Learning Hub, edition for Enterprise Support powered by SAP Enterprise Support Academy, starting on the first day of your subscription contract. For details on accessing the SAP Enterprise Support Academy learning assets and requesting proactive services, refer to the relevant SAP Activate tasks in the prepare phase.

- **Innovation and value realization**
  Use a wide range of continuous quality checks and assessment services to be proactive during implementation and after go-live.

- **Mission-critical support**
  Cover incident handling for both mission-critical and nonmission-critical applications through real-time support, such as schedule an expert product sessions and expert chat. It also includes service level agreements (SLAs).

SAP Enterprise Support

SAP Enterprise Support is the digital support experience covering all deployment scenarios and included with every cloud subscription. The latest information is available on the SAP Enterprise Support pages at *www.sap.com/services-support/essential-support.html*.

SAP Preferred Success

SAP Preferred Success includes additional features to SAP Enterprise Support designed to provide an advanced success experience. The latest information is available on the SAP Preferred Success page at *www.sap.com/services-support/service-offerings/preferred-success.html*.

The end is in sight! Let's look at the final stage of SAP S/4HANA Cloud implementation with SAP Activate.

7.1.7   Run Your Solution

The final phase of the SAP Activate methodology is the run phase, as shown in Figure 7.25. During this open-ended phase, companies and project teams further optimize the operability of SAP S/4HANA Cloud to maintain the IT systems in operating condition and guarantee system availability to execute business operations. In principle, productive use starts at the company's request right after the deployment of SAP S/4HANA Cloud to production and includes operational maintenance and support. In this phase, the operations team must ensure that the system is running as intended and be able to onboard new users. This phase also addresses the process of updates and upgrades that support the continuous adoption of new innovations.

We'll break up the important topics in the run phase into those that operate and support the implemented solution, and those that continuously improve and innovate.

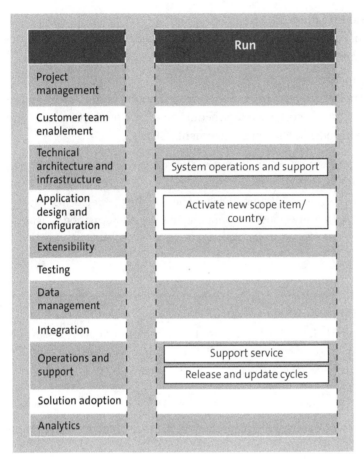

Figure 7.25 SAP Activate Run Phase Deliverable for SAP S/4HANA Cloud

Systems Operations and Support

Like previous SAP Activate implementation phases, the run phase breaks down into workstreams, deliverables, and tasks for end users as they begin to use their new cloud system.

System operations and support is essential to sustain business operations, continue solution adoption, and make incremental value realization. It includes all activities involved in supporting and managing the lifecycle of providing service by SAP, customers' IT support organization, and/or partner to end users. The following functions are included in this framework:

- Support business users.
- Search for solutions within the SAP knowledge database, SAP Community, and SAP Help Portal.
- Track incident resolution progress.

- Escalate incidents if necessary, as required per documented procedures and recommended criteria.

- Communicate provided solutions and time frames to business users.

- Sign off on solutions and confirm incidents (together with business users, if necessary).

We'll walk through key activities for solution operation and support in the following sections.

Onboarding New Users

The purpose of the onboarding and setup task is to determine the appropriate access, security, and authorizations for end users. Authorizations are broken down into simple user categories and are assigned to end users based on their job functions. After the appropriate and applicable roles and authorizations have been assigned, all business users must be authenticated through the Identity Authentication service. Users must then be uploaded into the system and given the necessary access and security authorizations.

> **Application Administrators**
>
> One key role is the company administrator, who serves as the main contact for any provisioning and system access topics. At least one primary and one backup contact should be application administrators.

Resolving Questions

Starting on the effective date of your subscription agreement for SAP S/4HANA Cloud, you may contact the SAP support organization for support services using one of the following methods.

You can contact SAP support through the CIC or SAP for Me. The CIC will respond to your phone inquiries, create incidents on your behalf, and dispatch the incident to match the priority level.

You can also gain direct access to the entire portfolio of SAP Activate implementation roadmaps through the SAP Activate community, available at *https://pages.community.sap.com/topics/activate*. You can get answers in real time directly from SAP Activate experts who can guide you through the SAP Activate methodology phase by phase. We covered the SAP Activate community in more detail in Chapter 2.

On-Demand Support Requests

Recall from Section 7.1.6 that companies need to set up sufficient support for end users to ensure that the new users can be efficiently onboarded into the system. This support organization can raise support tickets with SAP to resolve any production issues or service requests to the service center or support teams.

SAP Trust Center

SAP provides transparent information about the cloud infrastructure and services in the SAP Trust Center. You can access the SAP Trust Center at *http://s-prs.co/v502724*.

Security and trust form the core of any project, especially for cloud projects. SAP offers transparency by releasing current and past reports for companies running live, companies experiencing interruptions, and companies in a maintenance window. The **Cloud Status** area shows details from the past four weeks and can be filtered using SAP S/4HANA Cloud. SAP S/4HANA Cloud companies logged into the SAP Trust Center with their user IDs also will see information about the data center that hosts their solution. In addition to the status of the infrastructure, the SAP Trust Center provides detailed information about cloud services, security, privacy, and available support services.

Continuously Improve and Innovate

With a cloud solution, you'll benefit from frequent updates and periodic upgrades that SAP deploys to the system, which give you the latest improvements and innovations. The upgrade and maintenance release schedule can be found in the Roadmap Viewer.

We'll walk through the key activities in the following sections.

Fast and Continuous Access to Innovation

SAP starts implementing continuous feature delivery via monthly shipments and upgrades two times per year. The continuous feature delivery makes new functionality available to target customers in the time frame between the upgrades, which means faster access to adopt innovation and new capabilities in a nondisruptive manner.

The upgrade process occurs over three weeks, but preparations should be made prior to the start. In addition, it's recommended that no new configuration is added until after the production system is upgraded. Software upgrades are executed by SAP and will start with the test system. The starter (if still available), development, and production systems will be completed afterward. Business content upgrades are deployed and executed at a company's discretion. The upgraded system is tested manually and with the automated testing tool to ensure that business processes can be executed as before. If a defect is found, an incident is entered immediately so that the issue can be resolved prior to the production upgrade.

An upgrade doesn't automatically activate new scope functionality and shouldn't impact existing processes. The enhancements to existing functions can be viewed by scope item using the release assessment and scope dependency tool in SAP S/4HANA Cloud. After the production system is upgraded, additional scopes can be activated.

Product Roadmap

SAP S/4HANA Cloud users receive regular innovations in their environments. SAP provides visibility into planned innovations in the SAP S/4HANA Cloud product roadmap, which is available in the SAP Road Map Explorer at *https://roadmaps.sap.com*. The

SAP S/4HANA Cloud product roadmap for various business areas can be accessed via **Enterprise Resource Planning** and the **Grow with SAP** topic and offers lists of planned innovations, as well as interrelated topics and planned localizations. SAP product roadmaps are updated regularly, and you're encouraged to check this site frequently to determine how you can benefit from innovations to be introduced in the upcoming releases for SAP S/4HANA Cloud. To view innovations available in the current release, the What's New Viewer from the SAP Help Portal gives you a complete overview of new, changed, and deleted features and functions.

Biweekly Patches and Hot Fixes
The blue-green deployment model for the biweekly hotfix collection maintenance procedure means that new corrections are seamlessly deployed in the "green" version, while business users are working in the source release "blue" version. With this model, downtime for the productive system of SAP S/4HANA Cloud is minimized and can be further optimized.

7.2   New Implementation of SAP S/4HANA Cloud Private Edition

We've detailed the deployment of SAP S/4HANA Cloud Public Edition in Section 7.1. The SAP S/4HANA Cloud Private Edition deployment follows the same flow and uses the same fit-to-standard techniques we detailed previously (and discussed in more detail in Chapter 4 and Chapter 5). In this section, we'll focus on explaining the key differences in the preconfiguration content, implementation process, and tools that the project team will use to deploy the solution. We'll also discuss the differences in the system landscape, configuration capabilities, extensibility, and integration that are available in SAP S/4HANA Cloud Private Edition. We won't be discussing the clean core, its importance for the implementation of SAP S/4HANA Cloud Private Edition, and the detailed enhancements to the methodology we already covered in Chapter 2.

This section will follow a similar outline to Section 7.1, where we provided an overview of the deployment before going into specific details for each SAP Activate phase. Let's start with the overview of SAP S/4HANA Cloud Private Edition deployment.

7.2.1   Deployment Approach Overview

SAP S/4HANA Cloud Private Edition provides companies with a highly flexible environment that follows the standardized deployment approach guided by the five golden rules we discussed in Chapter 2, Section 2.5, along with the discussion of the clean core approach and dimensions in Chapter 2, Section 2.4. The golden rules have been established to help companies running SAP S/4HANA Cloud Private Edition systems to deploy the solution in such a way that it allows for frequent upgrades with lower effort than is typically needed for on-premise deployments. They also aim to help companies increase the frequency of consuming innovations SAP delivers with the SaaS model with SAP S/4HANA Cloud Private Edition. The deployment follows the standard six phases of SAP Activate you learned about in Chapter 2 and, on a high level, mirrors the key activities we introduced earlier in this chapter. Figure 7.26 shows a detailed list of deliverables in each phase of SAP Activate for RISE with SAP S/4HANA Cloud Private Edition. This figure is available for download at *www.sap-press.com/5966*.

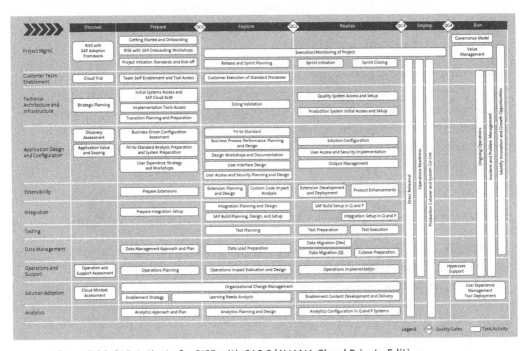

Figure 7.26 SAP Activate for RISE with SAP S/4HANA Cloud Private Edition

In the following sections, we'll discuss the key activities that the project teams complete in each of the phases. Before we do that, we also need to discuss the solution landscape that is typical for deploying SAP S/4HANA Cloud Private Edition.

In general, the solution is provisioned with three systems: development, quality assurance, and production. The solution provides a full transport management system (TMS) for transporting configuration and custom code between the three systems in the landscape. Companies can also elect to add an optional sandbox system to the landscape for additional safety and for evaluation of functionality before they activate the business functions or bring the configuration into their productive landscape (e.g., bring the configuration into the development system and transport it up the transport path to quality and production systems). Note that there is no transport path set up between the sandbox system and any of the systems in the production landscape.

The high-level depiction of the SAP S/4HANA Cloud Private Edition system landscape is shown in Figure 7.27. The figure also shows the key activities and depicts when the different systems in the landscape get used.

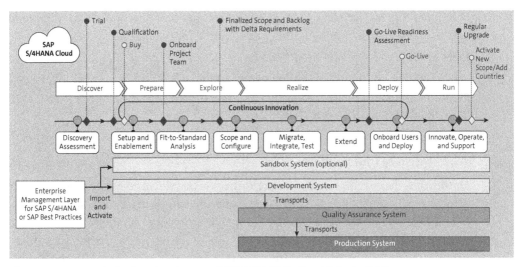

Figure 7.27 Example System Landscape of SAP S/4HANA Cloud Private Edition

In this setup, the development system is used for exploration of the solution, after the preconfiguration content has been deployed into the system. The fit-to-standard approach, which we introduced in Chapter 2 and have seen throughout the book, is used for this solution to confirm the fit of the preconfigured solution, to determine the configuration values for using standard functionality and requirements for extensibility and integration, to define system authentication and security, and to determine data migration requirements.

The Role of the Technical Team in an SAP S/4HANA Cloud Private Edition Project

When implementing SAP S/4HANA Cloud Private Edition, the role of the technical resources is slightly different from that of the technical expert supporting an SAP ERP on-premise solution implementation. Many of the traditional tasks, such as infrastructure management and technical execution of maintenance activities (e.g., upgrades), are handled by the SAP Enterprise Cloud Services team, either as a part of the standard subscription or as an additional on-demand services.

Nevertheless, customer/partner technical resources still play a fundamental role because they manage the system configuration, performance, user/roles, and integration with other solutions. Moreover, they handle new tasks such as SAP Fiori and SAP BTP administration. Additionally, the customer/partner technical resource acts as an advisor and is responsible for interacting with SAP when dealing with service requests, incidents, or other technical requirements.

Note that companies can also opt for a smaller footprint with a two-system landscape that combines the functions of the development and quality systems into one combined system along with the production system in the landscape. In such a setup, the solution is run in a two-tier system environment that uses the combined development and quality system for configuration and testing before changes are transported to the production system for productive use.

When we cover the details of the deployment approach, we'll discuss additional details about the landscape in the relevant subsections. Let's now look at the key project team activities during the discover phase.

7.2.2   Discover Your Solution

During this phase, the project team performs several critical activities that help determine the value and define the high-level scope and approach for the transition to SAP S/4HANA Cloud Private Edition. The key activities include value discovery activities during which the team defines the business case for the transition to the SAP S/4HANA solution, along one of the transition journeys discussed in Chapter 1. In this section, we'll focus on the new implementation (aka greenfield) transition journey. The discovery activities across the application, value, capabilities, transition path, and so on are detailed in the deliverables and tasks in the discover phase of the SAP Activate methodology for RISE with SAP S/4HANA Cloud Private Edition. (Figure 7.28 shows the SAP Activate Roadmap Viewer and corresponding discover phase activities.) Let's now outline the key topics that the project team needs to address during this phase:

- **Strategic planning**
  The aim of strategic planning is to define an innovation strategy and high-level deployment roadmap for all areas of the business that will be transformed. This could span across multiple SAP solutions, including SAP cloud ERP, SAP Success-Factors, SAP BTP, and more. To do so, start with an identification of strategic business and IT objectives, including current pain points. Cluster the objectives into benefit areas, and identify and prioritize the SAP solution enablers for each benefit area. These solutions provide the target enterprise architecture. During this work, the team will also address the topics of clean core and success plan that we introduced in Chapter 2.

- **Discover the value of the new functionality in SAP S/4HANA Cloud for your company**
  During this activity, the project team reviews the new capabilities of SAP S/4HANA Cloud Private Edition for their business. The objective is to thoroughly evaluate the new standard functionality and capabilities that the solution delivers and that the business users can benefit from adopting. The key for this evaluation is access to the SAP S/4HANA Cloud Private Edition trial, which we'll discuss later in this section. Additionally, the digital discovery assessment may be used during this stage to start the definition of the implementation scope and capabilities required for the business.

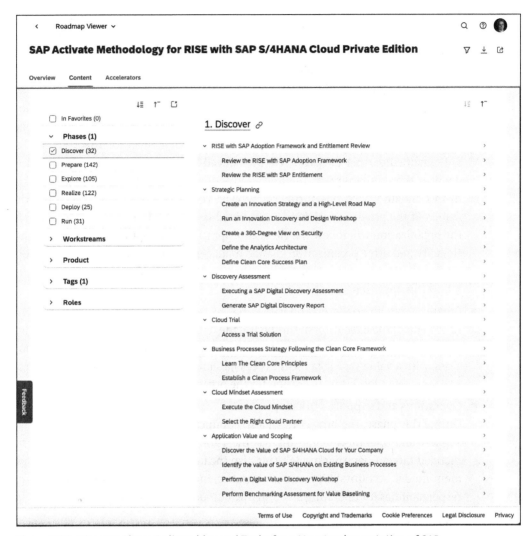

Figure 7.28 Discover Phase Deliverables and Tasks for a New Implementation of SAP S/4HANA Cloud Private Edition

- **Perform application value and scoping activities**
  Along with the evaluation of the new functionality and capabilities, the project team needs to determine the impact of adopting the new standard functionality on the business processes currently in place in the company. This is very important information for understanding the scope and breath of the change management activities that will be required during the implementation project and to adopt the new functionality in the business by the end users. This represents a key touchpoint with the OCM and solution adoption activities we'll detail later in Chapter 10.

  Additionally, SAP Activate provides guidance for teams working through the process to identify the value of the new processes for their existing processes. This can be accomplished with SAP Signavio Process Insights, which enables you to identify issues and blockers for improving your business processes, create an understanding of where those issues are coming from, receive tailor-made recommendations for correcting and improving the processes, and help you find the most suitable innovations for your business transformation.

- **Define the implementation strategy**
  During this activity, the project team will determine the overall implementation strategy, including the selection of the most appropriate preconfiguration package, whether SAP Best Practices, the enterprise management layer for SAP S/4HANA, or SAP-qualified partner packages. We introduced SAP Best Practices in Chapter 4 in detail as the standard preconfigured, ready-to-use set of processes that are used in fit-to-standard workshops during the project. The project team will also look at the results of the previous activities we outlined in this section and determine where the organization will follow the clean core approach of adopting the standard functionality and drive organization change management activities with a much stronger focus. We recommend customers choose the new implementation journey to follow this approach.

- **Create a strategic roadmap and value case**
  At the end of the execution of this phase, the team compiles the results of all activities into a formal strategic roadmap that shows the planned adoption of the solution along with a value case (aka business case) to present the value of the transition to SAP S/4HANA Cloud Private Edition for the organization.

- **Operations and support workshop**
  During this phase, the project team also conducts a workshop to assess customers support and operation needs, discuss the various options and define the recommended target operating model. This also includes the agreement on the engagement model, accountability, and governance, including the definition of roles and responsibilities for operating SAP S/4HANA Cloud Private Edition.

During the execution of these steps, the project team will need access to a trial environment to evaluate the functionality and determine where to stay with the standard functionality delivered through SAP Best Practices processes and where it's warranted to deploy their own practices to preserve the business value of the differentiating processes and practices for the organization. We'll now discuss how project teams can create the trial environment for SAP S/4HANA Cloud Private Edition.

SAP provides companies with access to an SAP S/4HANA fully activated appliance that can be used for trying out the software capabilities before obtaining a subscription. We briefly covered this option in Chapter 4. You can access the SAP S/4HANA fully activated appliance at *www.sap.com/products/erp/s4hana-private-edition/trial.html*. The trial provides access to a system with preactivated SAP Best Practices configuration, ready-to-use business processes, and sample data. You'll find detailed documentation for the step-by-step process to start your 30-day trial on that website. You can also explore additional resources on SAP Community.

You'll find the detailed documentation of the business process content of the trial environment in SAP Signavio Process Navigator, which we discussed earlier in Chapter 3 and Chapter 4. Existing customers with a subscription to SAP Cloud Appliance Library can access the trial environment-ready appliance directly in the SAP Cloud Appliance Library (*https://cal.sap.com/*) and deploy it to their preferred cloud provider environment, whether Amazon Web Services (AWS), Google Cloud Platform, or Microsoft Azure. The appliance comes with a detailed Getting Started Guide, an Architecture and Design document, and predefined sizing for each cloud environment, shown in the **Recommended VM Sizes** section of the website. Figure 7.29 shows the SAP Cloud Appliance Library page for SAP S/4HANA as a fully activated appliance.

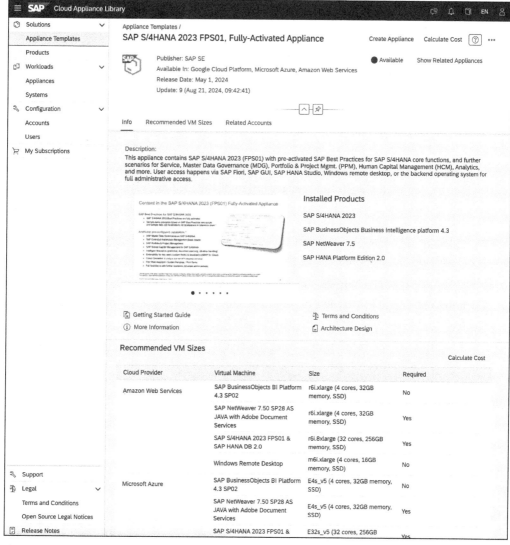

Figure 7.29 SAP S/4HANA 2023 FPS01 Fully Activated Appliance in SAP Cloud Appliance Library

> **Further Resources**
>
> To understand how to deploy SAP S/4HANA as a fully activated appliance and what functionality is delivered, review the following blog post on the SAP website, which was updated for the current release of the software in May 2024 (and continues to be updated for each new release of the appliance): *http://s-prs.co/v596638*.
>
> Note that the SAP S/4HANA fully activated appliance is continually updated to keep pace with the latest software releases. You can check the list of other available appliances when you access SAP Cloud Appliance Library and use the latest release relevant to your project.

7.2.3   Prepare Your Project

Now we'll briefly review the activities the project team executes in the prepare phase. Note that we'll focus on the activities that significantly differ for the deployment of SAP S/4HANA Cloud Private Edition; we won't repeat all the activities from workstreams such as project management, project team onboarding, and so on that are common for deployment of SAP S/4HANA Cloud Public Edition and were covered earlier in Section 7.1.

Phase Overview

The key deliverables in the prepare phase of the SAP Activate methodology for SAP S/4HANA Cloud Private Edition are shown in Figure 7.30. They help the project team set up, plan, and get the project underway. They also support the project team in self-enablement activities, setup of the system landscape, and preparation for fit-to-standard workshops.

We'll only focus on activities that are different because of the landscape setup for SAP S/4HANA Cloud Private Edition. We recommend reviewing the following activities in Section 7.1 and in Chapter 2 if you'd like a refresher:

- Setting up the project, including the setup of governance; definition of roles and responsibilities; preparation of the budget, project plan, and schedule; project kick-off; definition of project standards; and setup of project team environment (Section 7.1)
- Setting up the solution governance to follow the clean core approach during the deployment of the solution in your organization (Chapter 2)
- Project team self-enablement on the solution capabilities, project approach, and use of standard tools and applications during the project (Section 7.1)
- Execution of OCM activities, such as setup of the OCM team, definition of change plan, identification and analysis of the stakeholders, and definition of the communication plan (Section 7.1)

> **Note**
>
> The OCM topic is covered in detail later in the book in Chapter 10.

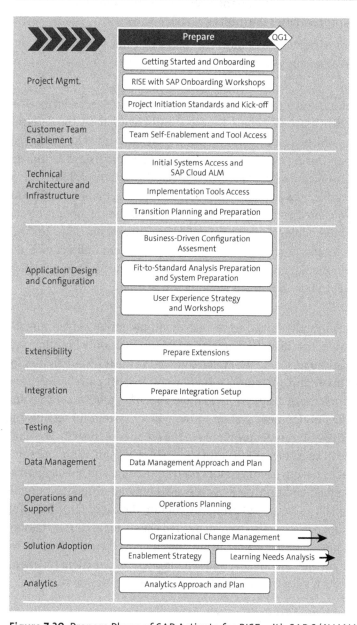

Figure 7.30 Prepare Phase of SAP Activate for RISE with SAP S/4HANA Cloud Private Edition

Next, we'll review the deliverables for which there are differences in SAP S/4HANA Cloud Private Edition.

System Provisioning

We've discussed that the system landscape for SAP S/4HANA Cloud Private Edition consists of three systems that are connected via a TMS. In this section, we'll look deeper into the setup of these systems and explain their role during the implementation and ongoing enhancements process (after the initial go-live).

When the landscape is provisioned, it contains the following three systems (plus one optional system) that are interconnected via a TMS:

- **Development system**
  This system's main purpose is to serve as the environment where the team receives the preconfigured ready-to-use processes. During the discover phase, the determination was made as to which preconfiguration assets were best suited for your organization requirements. During this phase, the landscape is provisioned, and the preconfiguration is installed and activated. The preconfiguration package can be based on the SAP Best Practices package, the enterprise management layer for SAP S/4HANA, or an SAP-qualified partner preconfiguration package. Depending on the package chosen, the methodology provides detailed guidance about steps that are required to be done by the organization to receive the system and activate the appropriate package (note that implementation partner-specific package activation steps will be provided by your chosen implementation partner).

- **Quality system**
  The purpose of the quality system is to serve as an environment for performing the testing for configuration, extensibility, integration of the solution with other systems, and performing the data loads—basically, conducting the testing activities for all these areas of solution implementation. There is a transport path between the development system and the quality system to move the configuration settings and other objects from the development system to the quality system for testing and confirmation before these objects get promoted to the production system. The quality system is also used in later stages of the project for cutover simulation, and some companies may use it as the environment for end-user training and enablement as part of the initial implementation or in subsequent upgrades and continuous enhancements. The quality system will primarily contain the client for integration testing, but some companies may also have dedicated clients for end-user training. In such cases, companies should consider using one client as the golden client for training that will contain the functionality and sample data and one client for execution of training that gets regularly refreshed for repeat training session runs.

- **Production system**
  This environment is dedicated to the productive execution of business processes by the company. This is the environment that the business users access in their daily routine to execute business processes, such as asset management, financial accounting, sales, and logistics. Companies should only import transports to the production system environment after they have been configured in the development system

and thoroughly tested in the quality system. There should be no direct configuration performed in the production system environment at any time. The production environment will contain one productive client where the company performs its daily business activities. There may be additional optional clients set up during the cutover simulation to ensure that the productive client isn't negatively impacted during the cutover simulation weekends in the deploy phase.

- **Sandbox system**
  This is an optional environment. While available to anyone, it's expected that midsize and larger companies are more likely to use this environment than smaller companies. The sandbox environment provides additional safety and a place to prototype functionality that the project team isn't sure they will use in production. For example, some activation of business functions that can't be reverted should be done in the sandbox environment before it's done in the development/quality/production landscape. The sandbox environment will be also important for the execution of release upgrades, as an environment where the new business content for release +1 business content can be evaluated after the release upgrade and considered for use in the productive landscape (through the standard path via the development system to the quality system and then to the production system). This system isn't included in the default subscription at the time of writing this book.

Starter System for SAP S/4HANA Cloud Private Edition

If you've already signed your RISE with SAP deal, depending on your RISE with SAP contract, you may be entitled to receive a starter system for SAP S/4HANA Cloud Private Edition. This 90-day trial system is a fully activated appliance template from SAP Cloud Appliance Library but is provisioned and managed by the SAP Enterprise Cloud Services team. You can leverage this alternative to explore the system capabilities and to run your fit-to-standard workshops.

The entire landscape is provisioned in the prepare phase. Project teams typically use the development system and optional sandbox starting in the prepare phase for purposes of fit-to-standard workshops and solution design. The quality and production systems are used starting in the realize phase when the project team starts to implement the solution through configuration, extensibility, integration, data migration activities, and testing.

Nonreversible Enterprise Extension Activation without Sandbox

For companies that haven't purchased the sandbox environment, the activation of nonreversible enterprise extensions can be done in the development environment with the following considerations:

- A backup needs be made of the development system prior to activation of any nonreversible enterprise extensions that are being evaluated.

- After the evaluation is complete, if the company doesn't want the nonreversible enterprise extensions, then the development environment will need to be restored from the backup.

When this evaluation is taking place, the development environment can't be used to mitigate any production landscape defects because the development environment is technically different from the production environment and quality environment.

SAP recommends all customers use a dedicated environment for application lifecycle management (ALM). Customers of SAP S/4HANA Cloud Private Edition should consider using SAP Cloud ALM for accessing the methodology, capturing and managing the requirements, solution documentation, testing, system change management, proactive monitoring, and operations. We covered these functions in Chapter 3. The use of SAP Cloud ALM is also important for compliance with the clean core strategy and the five golden rules discussed in Chapter 2, Section 2.4 and Section 2.5.

The system landscape is provisioned and given to the companies during the prepare phase to ensure the environment can be set up and prepared for fit-to-standard.

Fit-to-Standard System and Workshop Preparation

Let's now focus on the activities that the project team needs to do to prepare for the fit-to-standard workshops. We've covered the provisioning of the system, including the activation of the preconfigured business processes, in the previous section. We'll now focus on what the team needs to do with the system before the workshops and how to prepare for the execution of the workshops. The following are the key steps that the project team executes during the prepare phase:

1. **Access initial system for fit-to-standard workshops**
   During this stage, the project team will set up users with appropriate authorizations to aid in the execution of fit-to-standard processes. The project team will also perform the activation of the SAP Fiori UX for the business users to show them the new UX during the workshops.

2. **Enhance setup and additional configuration**
   The functional and technical consultants identify the additional configuration that will need to be set up before the workshops are executed. The focus should be on quick wins of functionality that can be configured quickly before the start of the workshops so that the participants can see the functionality in a live system. This is one of the principles discussed in Chapter 2 that helps accelerate learning about the solution with the key business users and is preferred to reviewing documentation or SAP Help.

3. **Activate SAP Fiori in the initial system**
   SAP Activate provides clear guidance about the use of the SAP Fiori rapid content activation functionality in SAP S/4HANA Cloud Private Edition to prepare the SAP

Fiori UX for fit-to-standard for the business roles that are in the project scope. Refer to the SAP Activate task called Activate SAP Fiori in the Initial System (either in SAP Cloud ALM or the SAP Activate Roadmap Viewer) that explains the process and provides references to related blog posts and SAP Help Portal documentation.

4. **Prepare and schedule fit-to-standard workshops**
   This activity includes a review of the fit-to-standard workshop guide accelerator that helps consultants and key users understand the flow of the workshop. They also gain an understanding of the required inputs for the workshops and the output that gets created during the workshop. In addition, the technical consultants together with integration experts prepare an initial list of integrations that will be used during the fit-to-standard process.

Prepare Integration Setup

The project team verifies access to all the systems that will be integrated with the SAP S/4HANA Cloud Private Edition. Next, they will decide which integrations should be working during the fit-to-standard workshops and set these up.

Operations Planning

Plan the transition of the new solution to the operations team early in your project to have enough time to set up the organization, train resources, and transition to the operational setup for productive solution operations. With the introduction of the new solution, your current IT support framework will change. SAP provides guidance on the target IT support process activities, tools, and resources required for you to safely and efficiently operate the new SAP solutions in your environment. We cover aspects of operational excellence in Chapter 10, Section 10.2.

7.2.4   Explore the Solution

Next, we'll review the key deliverables and activities that are done during the explore phase.

Phase Overview

During the explore phase, the project team will engage with the business users to conduct the fit-to-standard workshops with the objective to confirm the fit of the standard solution; determine additional configuration needs, requirements for extensibility, and integration; and determine the data migration plans for loading master data, organizational data, and transactional data such as open balances. The team also focuses on execution of the planned OCM activities, preparing the testing, planning the strategy for delivery of end-user enablement, and training. These are a few highlights of activities that are done during the explore phase. You can see a complete list of deliverables in the explore phase in Figure 7.31.

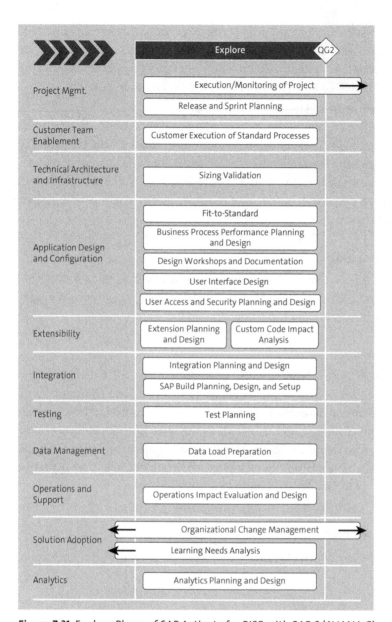

Figure 7.31 Explore Phase of SAP Activate for RISE with SAP S/4HANA Cloud Private Edition

We covered these deliverables in detail in the description of SAP S/4HANA Cloud in Section 7.1. In this section, we'll focus on the deliverables that are approached and completed differently for SAP S/4HANA Cloud Private Edition, as we did for the prepare phase. We'll pay special attention to the following deliverables in the explore phase:

- Additional considerations for fit-to-standard analysis and design
- Analytics planning and design
- Additional capabilities for data load preparation

- Test planning review
- Operations models and capabilities

Let's start with the fit-to-standard analysis and design activities.

Fit-to-Standard Analysis and Design

The general approach and flow of steps in fit-to-standard analysis and design in SAP S/4HANA Cloud Private Edition is the same as in SAP S/4HANA Cloud Public Edition, as discussed in Section 7.1. You'll find the overall flow shown in Figure 7.32, where you can see that the tasks and activities follow the same steps as for SAP S/4HANA Cloud Public Edition:

1. In the discover phase, the strategic planning, solution discovery along with value analysis activities define the value of the solution for the business and help set the initial scope for implementation.

2. In the prepare phase, the project team details out the scope in the project charter and scope statement, and then uses that information to prepare for fit-to-standard workshops (both system and logistics/processes we outlined previously). In parallel, the project team and key users go through self-enablement activities to get familiar with the solution capabilities and implementation approach before the fit-to-standard workshops commence.

3. In the explore phase, the project team conducts the fit-to-standard workshops to confirm the fit of the solution to company needs and to capture any additional configuration values or delta requirements that will be analyzed and designed during the design workshops. The focus is on additional requirements for integration, extensibility, UX, analytics, master data, user access, and security. SAP S/4HANA Cloud Private Edition provides more options for extending the solution, which means that the design phase is typically longer than for SAP S/4HANA Cloud Public Edition. All this information is stored in a requirements backlog and used toward the end of the explore phase for release planning along with planning of the initial few sprints. Note that the sprints are planned progressively and not all planned at the end of the explore phase. Project teams typically plan the next one or two sprints and primarily focus on making sure the desired high-priority backlog items are ready to be inserted into the sprint (we discussed this in detail in Chapter 6 when we reviewed the agile approach).

4. All this work is done as preparation for agile execution during the realize phase, as shown in the solution realization box in Figure 7.32. This figure is available for download at *www.sap-press.com/5966*.

You'll find this schema and all the steps of fit-to-standard analysis and design detailed in the How to Approach the Fit-to-Standard Analysis/Design in the Cloud accelerator in the SAP Activate methodology. You can download it from the SAP Activate Roadmap Viewer (refer to Chapter 3, Section 3.1, for how to access accelerators in the Roadmap Viewer).

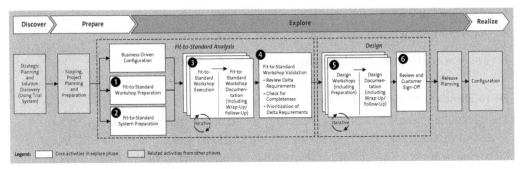

Figure 7.32 Fit-to-Standard for SAP S/4HANA Cloud Private Edition

Use of SAP Cloud ALM for Requirements Capture

As we mentioned, SAP recommends that companies implementing SAP S/4HANA Cloud Private Edition use SAP Cloud ALM for capturing the requirements and solution documentation, which typically includes following:

- Key business decisions impacting the scope or design of the solution
- Confirmation of fit
- Scope information
- Business process models/process flows
- Configuration values
- Design documents (scenario and, optionally, process level)
- Requirements for items covered by the design (e.g., integration, extensibility, analytics, master data, user access, and security)

This documentation should continue to be managed and updated even after the initial go-live to allow the company to manage the upgrade activities. The solution documentation will be critical for any work that will be done after the release upgrade to adjust the system for the new release (e.g., adjust the code in extensions or integrations for the new release level of the software).

Analytics Planning and Design

The project should evaluate the analytics solutions available for SAP S/4HANA Cloud Private Edition. The explore phase should build on the work already done during the discover and prepare phases to document an analytics architecture, landscape, and design.

The detailed task called Review My Fiori Apps Reference Library for Embedded Analytics in SAP Activate guides users through the steps to review the SAP Fiori apps reference library for relevant embedded analytics apps. Later in the deliverables, the project team will perform initial analytics settings and determine details for customer-driven analytics and extension of reports.

Further Resources

SAP Analytics Cloud has its own separate SAP Activate roadmap in the Roadmap Viewer that follows the SAP Activate project phases. You can access this roadmap at *http://s-prs.co/v596639*.

Analytics design covers analytics (e.g., reports, tables, charts, graphs, and geographic analysis), predictive analytics, and planning requirements. Analytics workshops are conducted for LoB-specific processes and requirements. The standard analytics apps and standard business content are reviewed, and a fit-to-standard analysis and design are performed.

Data Load Preparation

We discussed the data load process and capabilities in Chapter 5 and then covered the steps project teams follow in Section 7.1. The same process is used for data loads into SAP S/4HANA Cloud Private Edition with the following key steps:

1. **Determine the required master data**
   The project team will identify the master data objects, data sources, migration methods, and extraction/load plan required for the implementation's scope as determined during the fit-to-standard workshops.

2. **Determine the migration cockpit field structures (only when migrating using staging tables)**
   The project team will create the migration project in the migration cockpit and select migration objects relevant for the scope of the implementation project.

3. **Extract and transform legacy data**
   The project team will extract data from existing legacy systems and use data transformation tools to augment the data for any missing information of fields.

4. **Perform data cleansing activities**
   Before the data can be loaded to the target system, the project team needs to complete activities to review data quality, delete outdated data, harmonize data by removing duplicate entries, identify and resolve inaccuracies, and develop plans to correct critical data issue prior to the planned go-live.

Best Practices for Rapid Data Migration

All of these capabilities are detailed in SAP Signavio Process Navigator in solution scenario Rapid Data Migration to SAP S/4HANA, which you can find at *https://me.sap.com/processnavigator/HomePage*. Once you're logged in with your customer or partner user ID, search for the solution scenario by its name. If you need help with navigation in SAP Signavio Process Navigator, refer to Chapter 3.

The actual data load into the system follows the same process we outlined in Section 7.1 and will be done progressively in the realize phase to prepare data for unit, string, integration, and UAT.

> **Further Resources**
>
> You can find more details about migrating data in *Migrating to SAP S/4HANA* (SAP PRESS, 2024, *https://sap-press.com/5816*).

Test Planning

Test planning is another critical activity that is completed during the explore phase. For SAP S/4HANA Cloud Private Edition, it's recommended to use the SAP Cloud ALM test management capabilities to prepare and run testing of the functionality. We covered these capabilities in Chapter 3.

During the explore phase, the project team needs to ensure that SAP Cloud ALM is available and that it's set up to support the testing requirements. The project team also starts planning the structure of the tests that will be done during the realize phase, whether these are unit tests, string tests bringing together multiple units of testing, or preparations of larger tests for the release—that is, integration tests and UAT.

Operations Models and Capabilities

The aim is to build on the work done in the prepare phase. All the relevant support areas need to be analyzed and defined in detail: roles and skills, processes/procedures, operations documentation, and enabling support tools.

Then, a target operating model is defined that covers the key activities for a Center of Expertise (COE) and the potential use of an external service provider. This will include establishing resources; setting up tools; documenting procedures, knowledge transfer, and operations cutover; and retiring parts of the old operational framework. Information is available on the typical roles and responsibilities for SAP S/4HANA Cloud Private Edition, with details of what aspects of operations and support are covered by SAP.

Later, during the realization phase, the target model is implemented, with knowledge transferred from the project team to the COE and any external service provider.

7.2.5   Realize Your Requirements

Now that we've covered the key aspects in the explore phase, we'll focus on the key differences in the realize phase that companies implementing SAP S/4HANA Cloud Private Edition should be aware of.

Phase Overview

The overall picture of the deliverables completed during the realize phase is shown in Figure 7.33. The execution of these steps follows the same flow as explained for SAP S/4HANA Cloud Public Edition earlier in this chapter. We'll focus on specific considerations that companies implementing SAP S/4HANA Cloud Private Edition should be aware of as the solution offers a broader set of capabilities for configuration and extensibility, which increases the flexibility available to companies in this solution. We'll specifically discuss the considerations for system access and setup, solution configuration, analytics configuration, extensibility, integration, and testing execution.

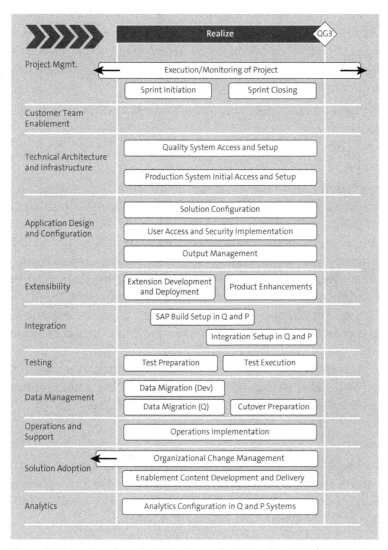

Figure 7.33 Realize Phase in SAP Activate for RISE with SAP S/4HANA Cloud Private Edition

Let's start with considerations for system access.

System Access and Setup

The system access and setup approach are different for SAP S/4HANA Cloud Private Edition. Depending on the company's contract, all system access and provisioning emails are typically shared with the company IT contact/administrator during the prepare phase. It's important for the company's IT contact/administrator to check all communication emails to get access to all the systems by following the instructions in the individual provisioning emails. If it hasn't been done already, the administrator will access the quality system, reset the password and create users for the entire project team to aid in testing and data loads. SAP delivers the system with the same SAP Best Practices or enterprise management layer for SAP S/4HANA as the development system.

The SAP Fiori rapid activation is transported from the development system to the quality system. Existing configuration and development transports are imported into the quality system, and manual rework activities (e.g., nontransportable configuration object activities) are done manually in the quality system.

The production system is accessed later in the realize phase and follows a similar process as the quality system.

Solution Configuration

Organizations implementing SAP S/4HANA Cloud Private Edition have access to a broad set of configuration settings in the Implementation Guide (IMG; Transaction SPRO) in their SAP S/4HANA Cloud Private Edition environment. This environment provides organizations with thousands of possible configuration options, significantly extending the configuration flexibility to reflect an organization's needs with configuration using standard software. The environment for configuring the solution is very similar in scope and functionality to the one used for configuring the SAP S/4HANA solution in an on-premise or hosted setup. Refer to Section 7.3.5 for more details on how configuration is done. The configuration decisions made to extend the scope of preconfigured content that the company or system integrator performs in this environment should be captured as part of the solution documentation, as discussed in Section 7.2.4, using SAP Cloud ALM. In addition, refer to Chapter 2, Section 2.5.6, where we discussed the need for documentation in rule 5.

Analytics Configuration

The analytics solutions are configured based on the design and guidelines documented in the explore phase. The scope may cover analytics, predictive analytics, and planning requirements. The design will typically be based on embedded analytics in SAP S/4HANA Cloud Private Edition or SAP Analytics Cloud to define the UX for analytics and planning.

Examples of the activities to be undertaken in SAP S/4HANA Cloud Private Edition to set up, enable, and use embedded analytics functionality include the following steps (for details, refer to SAP Signavio Process Navigator, solution process Embedded Analytics with SAP S/4HANA [BGH]):

- Configure SAP Fiori Foundation, including the SAP Web Dispatcher, setup of the SAP Fiori launchpad and the Launchpad Designer, and additional configuration following SAP Note 2289865.
- Perform SAP Fiori basic network and security configuration and activation of SAP Fiori apps.

Next, you can either access the View Browser to create analytical reports from available analytical queries or create custom CDS views. We recommend you refer to the detailed documentation of this solution process (BGE) in SAP Signavio Process Navigator for examples of how to create a custom CDS view and how to use the View Browser to find relevant analytical queries.

Integration and Extensibility

In Chapter 2, Section 2.5, we highlighted the need to use modern technologies for integration (rule 3) and extensibility (rule 4). One of the key principles for extensibility and integration in SAP S/4HANA Cloud Private Edition is that SAP code must remain intact. This is to prevent modification of SAP-standard code that would impact the effort and duration of subsequent system release upgrades as well as application of feature packs. We'll now review the options companies should consider for integration and extensibility while implementing SAP S/4HANA Cloud Private Edition.

Integration

When it comes to defining and designing for integration, there is a set of principles to apply:

1. Companies should use the standard predelivered integration scenarios for integrating cloud and on-premise products that SAP delivers.
2. Companies should prioritize the use of open APIs published on SAP Business Accelerator Hub at *http://api.sap.com* before considering other options. The use of open APIs and SAP BTP for integration allows you to build a future-proof solution that uses modern technology. You'll find both the open APIs and the standard predefined integration scenario on SAP Business Accelerator Hub at *https://api.sap.com/package/S4HANAOPAPI/odata*.
3. The use of SAP Integration Suite is the preferred way to integrate with other cloud or on-premise applications. SAP Integration Suite offers a set of predelivered integration content, published as OData and Simple Object Access Protocol (SOAP) service APIs.

Further Resources

You can learn more about the capabilities of SAP Integration Suite at *http://s-prs.co/v502731*.

The SAP Activate methodology provides guidance on how to approach the integration topics throughout the flow of the SAP Activate phases. When it comes to the specific steps for the definition and design of integration, technical experts will follow the steps outlined in Figure 7.34.

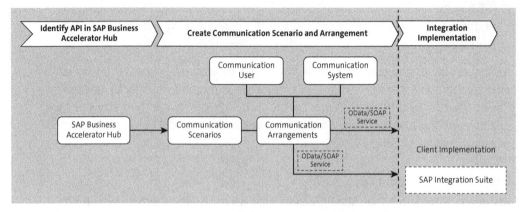

Figure 7.34 Steps to Consume APIs on SAP Business Accelerator Hub

The first steps are to identify the appropriate API on SAP Business Accelerator Hub, set up the communication scenario and communication arrangement with the predetermined user and between the integrated systems, and then implement the integration using SAP Integration Suite. For companies integrating hybrid environments (e.g., on-premise and cloud applications), additional integration options are available. We'll cover the two-tier hybrid integration scenarios in detail in Chapter 9. But before we do that, consider the high-level overview of the integration options available in such situations, as shown in Figure 7.35.

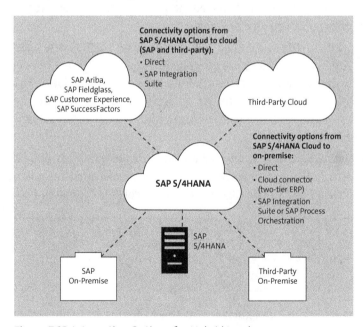

Figure 7.35 Integration Options for Hybrid Landscapes

You can see the options for connecting the cloud-to-cloud applications with SAP Integration Suite, as discussed in this section, and the options for integration of cloud and on-premise products with the cloud connector for two-tier ERP setup and with SAP Integration Suite (preferred) or SAP Process Orchestration.

SAP recommends the Integration Design Support service from SAP Value Assurance services offerings to mitigate risk for the integration planning, design, and setup. The aim is to ensure the technical readiness of the entire solution for go-live, including integrations.

> **Further Resources**
>
> A detailed discussion of integration technologies goes beyond the scope of this book, but if you're interested in these topics, review SAP documentation, or one of the SAP PRESS books on integration technologies available at *http://s-prs.co/v502732*.

Extensibility

Companies that need to extend the standard functionality of the SAP S/4HANA Cloud Private Edition application should use the in-app extensibility, developer extensibility, and side-by-side extensibility options available for the SAP S/4HANA stack (refer to Chapter 5, Section 5.3, for details). We recommend reviewing the clean core strategy topic in Chapter 2, Section 2.4, along with the discussion of the golden rules for implementation of SAP S/4HANA Cloud in Chapter 2, Section 2.5.

In-app extensibility allows companies to accomplish actions such as the following:

- Adapting a new UI using the capabilities in SAP Fiori UX and applications
- Creating their own analytics reports and stories
- Creating email templates and print forms
- Adding application logic
- Adding custom fields to existing database structures

Through developer extensibility, new objects may be created by implementing the ABAP RESTful application programming model in an ABAP Cloud development package offering options to consume these new objects via in-app extensibility options in an upgrade stable manner.

The ABAP RESTful application programming model also provides options to extend existing objects such as SAP Fiori apps using extensibility approaches provided by the framework in the ABAP RESTful application programming model. Note that this approach relates to the approved development concepts of SAP's clean core strategy and development through SAP's ABAP RESTful programming model forbids development of Web Dynpro-based objects, prioritizing usage of SAP Fiori UIs for end-user interaction with the system.

Further Resources

A compilation of the ABAP RESTful application programming model and ABAP Cloud resources is provided here: *http://s-prs.co/v596640*.

In addition to in-app extensibility and developer extensibility, SAP S/4HANA Cloud Private Edition also provides organizations access to classic extensibility, which allows companies to create custom code. SAP strongly recommends using classic extensibility only when the other options aren't possible, and always using it with a stable enhancement point, such as the following:

- ABAP business add-in (BAdIs)
- ABAP-Managed Database Procedures (AMDP) BAdIs to enhance standard SQL script procedures
- User exit enhancements created and managed in Transactions SMOD and CMOD
- Business transaction events (BTEs) for finance

Companies using classic extensibility must avoid the following situations, as detailed in golden rule 4 discussed in Chapter 2, Section 2.5, and also available as a standalone accelerator document in the implementation roadmap for SAP S/4HANA Cloud Private Edition in the Roadmap Viewer:

- **Implicit enhancements, or enhancement spots**
  These don't require a modification key but otherwise are much like modifications. They enable companies to change any SAP code at the start or end of any coding block. In an upgrade, these would need to be processed in Transaction SPAU_ENH. The risk is that the enhancement point may no longer exist or may no longer have access to the same data.

- **Modifications of standard code**
  While technically possible, this should be avoided as a practice in all SAP S/4HANA Cloud Private Edition systems. A company has the ability to modify standard SAP code, but this should be completely avoided. If your company makes these changes, in an upgrade, these modifications will need to be processed in Transaction SPAU. The risk is that the enhancement point may no longer exist or may no longer have access to the same data.

Testing

We discussed in Section 7.2.4 the preparation activities for testing, and we highlighted the need to provision and set up SAP Cloud ALM for testing. In the realize phase, the project team will use the SAP Cloud ALM test management capabilities to plan, structure, execute, and evaluate the various tests that will be done during implementation.

These tests include the unit testing that is usually done during each sprint and the string tests that are done in later sprints to progressively test the integration of various process steps.

String Testing

String testing doesn't replace end-to-end integration testing; instead, the purpose of the string test is to continuously test "strings" of configured and extended processes to avoid finding all the integration issues too late during the integration test, for example, shifting the error-finding and correction process to the left in the timeline, thus reducing the cost of fixing such errors and reducing the risk of missing the production cutover timeline.

The team will also run a full end-to-end integration test and UAT before planning a go-live release to the production system.

7.2.6   Deploy Your Solution

Now that we've completed configuration, extensibility, integration, and testing in the realize phase, we'll proceed to bring the solution to live use and deploy it to production. The goal is to ensure a smooth transition to using the new solution and successfully going live with the new system. We'll now discuss the key activities that are done in this phase. Let's start with the phase overview.

Phase Overview

We covered the deliverables and activities the project team performs in the deploy phase for SAP S/4HANA Cloud Public Edition in Section 7.1. The flow of activities for SAP S/4HANA Cloud Private Edition is the same as covered previously (see Figure 7.36 for an overview of the deliverables).

In this section, we'll only focus on specific considerations companies implementing SAP S/4HANA Cloud Private Edition should keep in mind in their project due to the different system landscape of this solution and the additional ability to create dedicated clients for specific purposes such as cutover simulation and end-user learning. We'll focus on two areas:

- Production cutover considerations
- End-user learning considerations

Let's now discuss cutover activities, focusing specifically on how the flexibility of SAP S/4HANA Cloud Private Edition can be used to structure them.

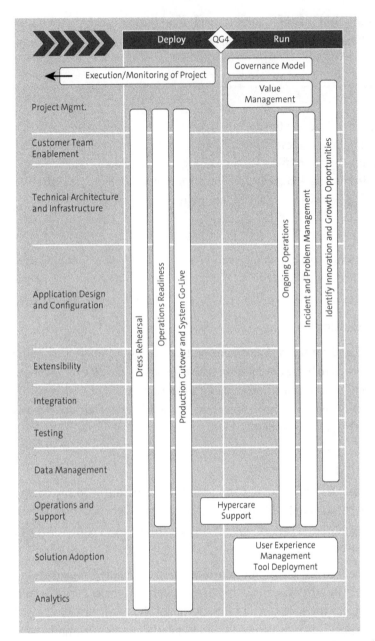

Figure 7.36 Deploy and Run Phases of SAP Activate for RISE with SAP S/4HANA Cloud Private Edition

Production Cutover

We discussed earlier in this chapter the typical landscape for SAP S/4HANA Cloud Private Edition with development, quality, and production systems interconnected with a TMS. During the production cutover, it's common to plan one or multiple cutover rehearsals during which the mock cutover activities are performed to make sure all the steps for the final cutover have been performed at least once. It's also done to ensure that the project team understands and has optimized the effort and duration of each step to make the cutover process optimal.

During these mock cutover runs, the project team will release transports, set up the solution, and load data into the system. After the cutover, the production system should be brought back to its original state. With SAP S/4HANA Cloud Private Edition, companies can request the setup of additional clients dedicated for mock cutovers that will be available temporarily to support the mock cutover process, after which these clients can be removed as they are no longer used.

End-User Learning

During the end-user enablement and learning activities, it's common to set up dedicated clients for delivery of the end-user learning and practice in the system. Typically, these clients are created temporarily in the quality system, and it's a good practice to have two clients:

- **Golden master client**
  This client is for the delivery of training that is accessible for trainers and is kept in its original state as a source for creating the training delivery client. The trainers and project team may make changes to the golden master client when the training exercises and practice are enhanced, but this client isn't accessible to end users.

- **Training delivery client**
  This is the environment where the end users practice using the system functionality. This client is regularly refreshed with fresh copies of the golden master client for training delivery.

7.2.7 Run Your Solution

We've now successfully launched the productive use of the new solution in the business. The run phase provides guidance on key activities that continue to be done to bring new capabilities to the environment during the upgrades and implementation of continuous improvements/enhancements as the system is in use. Let's now look at this area of running the solution.

Phase Overview

We covered the deliverables and activities the project team performs in the run phase for SAP S/4HANA Cloud Public Edition in Section 7.1. The flow of activities for SAP S/4HANA Cloud Private Edition is the same as covered previously (refer to Figure 7.36 for an overview of the deliverables).

In this section, we'll only focus on specific considerations for companies implementing SAP S/4HANA Cloud Private Edition.

Release Upgrade and Continuous Enhancements

Companies using SAP S/4HANA Cloud Private Edition expect frequent releases of new capabilities and the ability to upgrade their software to take advantage of these innovations. SAP delivers one major release every other year starting with release 2023 of the SAP S/4HANA software coupled with delivery of the feature packs every six months in the two years period. These feature packs are much easier to adopt. This two-year release cycle alongside additional feature packs can enhance co-innovation opportunities for customers, minimizing the necessity for product upgrades and thereby easing the adoption while lowering overall implementation cost.

> **New SAP S/4HANA Release and Maintenance Strategy**
>
> We recommend that you review the updated release and maintenance strategy SAP announced in 2022 and that is currently in effect with the SAP S/4HANA release 2023: *http://s-prs.co/v596641*.

The release upgrade for SAP S/4HANA Cloud Private Edition is run as a project during which the development, quality, and production systems are upgraded gradually. After the development system upgrade, the project team works on the resolution of all integration, extensibility, and configuration topics introduced by the new release. We've mentioned often in this book the need to stay close to the standard and to follow the clean core strategy encoded in the five golden rules. This aims to simplify and optimize the execution of upgrades by limiting the deviation from standard software and thus minimizing the number of topics that need to be addressed after each release upgrade. This portion of the project activities focuses on the technical aspect of the software update, with minimum mandatory updates in configuration and custom code.

After the release upgrade of SAP S/4HANA Cloud Private Edition, organizations can request the optional sandbox environment to install the upgraded version of the preconfiguration to evaluate additional functionality that they want to bring into their use in production. SAP S/4HANA Cloud Private Edition doesn't have the content lifecycle management capabilities we've discussed for the SAP S/4HANA Cloud Public Edition and doesn't allow direct load of the release +1 preconfiguration directly into the development system. The selected functionality either needs to be configured manually, following documentation such as the configuration guides in SAP Best Practices, or the configuration experts can package up the selected configuration and data into business configuration (BC) sets to bring them into the development environment. After the configuration is finished and tested in the development environment, the standard TMS will be used to promote it to quality and production systems, just like any other configuration.

With the understanding of the SAP S/4HANA Cloud Private Edition implementation process that this section provided, we'll now take a look at the new implementation of on-premise SAP S/4HANA software.

7.3 New Implementation of SAP S/4HANA

In this section, we'll cover the new implementation of SAP S/4HANA, the on-premise version of the software. The phases and deliverables flow will be the same as in the other new implementations for public and private cloud options, but there will be some differences that customers implementing in an on-premise environment need to consider. Most of these differences will be around installation and setup, as well as in the operations and support activities that are customer-managed (as compared to cloud delivery, where they are covered in full or to a large degree as a service).

We'll discuss the new implementation of an on-premise SAP S/4HANA solution with perpetual licenses in a company or third-party data center, including hyperscalers. In the new implementation approach, a new instance of SAP S/4HANA is implemented to replace a non-SAP legacy system or reimplement and replace an existing SAP solution. There are two business contexts in which companies prefer new implementations. The first is a change in the business model that implies a reevaluation of the way an organization operates. This will mean new demands on the capabilities and agility of an ERP solution. The second context is full business process reengineering, such as consolidating numerous order-to-cash process variants. Regardless of the case, a new implementation enables you to do the following:

- Leverage modern ERP system capabilities.
- Start with a preconfigured new system that you can build with SAP Best Practices.
- Build a new system with a clean core.
- Roll out the solution on a country-by-country basis to worldwide locations rather than use a big bang approach.
- Adopt innovations rapidly.

> **SAP S/4HANA Releases**
>
> SAP plans to release a new updated version of SAP S/4HANA once every two years. Feature packs include enhancement updates shipped between the core version updates. You'll need to decide on the correct release level of your SAP S/4HANA solution-to-be and select the appropriate release-dependent information accordingly.

Figure 7.37 provides an overview of the new implementation approach. This section is organized by SAP Activate phase: discover, prepare, explore, realize, deploy, and run. Some of the activities documented in the prepare phase are often executed earlier in the project in the discover phase.

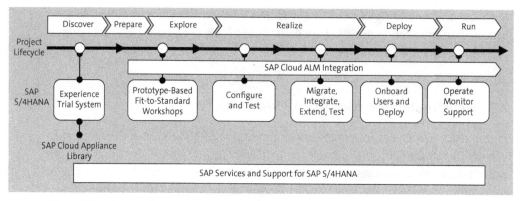

Figure 7.37 New Implementation Approach

7.3.1   Deployment Approach Overview

Your transition to SAP S/4HANA involves many activities throughout the key SAP Activate phases introduced in Chapter 2. Figure 7.38 illustrates the activities within the workstreams and phases. This figure is available for download at *www.sap-press.com/ 5966*.

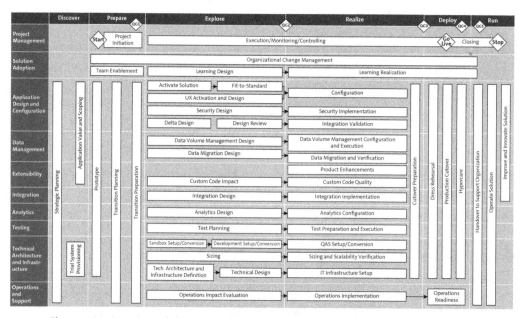

Figure 7.38 Overview of the Transition to SAP S/4HANA Roadmap

There are three implementation approaches for SAP S/4HANA, which we introduced in Chapter 1:

- **New implementation**
  Implement a new instance of SAP S/4HANA by moving either from a non-SAP legacy system or from an old SAP solution.

- **System conversion**
  Convert an existing SAP ERP solution to SAP S/4HANA, including business data and configuration. We'll discuss this further in Chapter 8, Section 8.3.

- **Selective data transition**
  Consolidate an existing SAP software landscape or carve out selected entities or processes as part of a move to SAP S/4HANA. We'll discuss this further in Chapter 8, Section 8.4.

For existing SAP customers, the choice of approach is driven by the following business and IT objectives:

- **New implementation**
  You want to maximize innovation, overhaul business processes, and perhaps adopt new cloud solutions. You may only want essential master data and transactional data from the existing solution.

- **System conversion**
  You don't want to merge or split ERP instances, and you want to keep your existing data and go live with a big bang. You may want to minimize change initially and then innovate selectively afterward.

- **Selective data transition**
  You want to merge or split existing ERP instances or have phased go-lives. You want to reuse only certain parts of the existing configuration, master data, and transaction data.

If you have multiple SAP ERP instances and other connected SAP solutions, you may want to use a combination of the approaches in a phased program. For example, you could do a system conversion of one lead SAP ERP development system, use selective data transition to merge in another SAP ERP system, and do a new implementation for certain parts of the solution.

Let's walk through the SAP Activate phases, in terms of these on-premise deployment options:

- **Discover phase**
  You should create an overall strategy for digital transformation by recognizing the benefits and value of SAP S/4HANA. This is then turned into a roadmap or implementation plan that includes a choice of implementation approach. Finally, you should evaluate the impact on the technical architecture and IT infrastructure, which, together with the implementation strategy, serve as the foundation of the business case.

- **Prepare phase**
  After the business case has been approved, the project is officially initiated in the prepare phase. A first version of an implementation plan includes the findings from the discover phase and sets the stage for the entire project.

- **Explore phase**
  The design-to-be of the SAP S/4HANA solution is defined and documented in the explore phase. In a new implementation, fit-to-standard workshops are performed with the help of a preconfigured sandbox system that represents SAP Best Practices solutions. For a system conversion, a converted version of the existing system is used, and existing custom code is analyzed. By the end of the explore phase, all technical and functional aspects of the implementation project are fully planned, documented in detail, and ready to be executed.

- **Realize phase**
  In a new implementation, you prepare the new technical architecture and infrastructure. In system conversion, the landscape is sequentially converted to SAP S/4HANA. Some of the existing custom code is adjusted. Application and analytics functions are implemented, configured, integrated, and tested. In parallel, IT can adjust operational tools and procedures to prepare for SAP S/4HANA. Finally, end-user training, including project-specific training materials and team setup, is prepared.

- **Deploy phase**
  Finalize the business processes and solution for production go-live. This includes final testing, rehearsing the cutover, and finalizing the IT infrastructure and operations. End-user training sessions are delivered. Finally, the productive instance of SAP S/4HANA is set up or converted on the go-live date. IT operations are further optimized with the help of the project team and SAP. This phase is referred to as *hypercare* and occurs before operational responsibility is fully transferred to the production support team.

- **Run phase**
  Operations are further stabilized and optimized in the run phase. The new SAP system is continuously updated, making the latest innovations from SAP available to the business. Then, the innovation cycle starts again.

To support companies in executing the SAP S/4HANA transition successfully, SAP has several service offerings that provide different levels of engagement and advice:

- **SAP Enterprise Support**
  Provides proactive support during implementation and operation of your SAP S/4HANA system. Remote support enables accelerated problem resolution, fewer business disruptions, and less unforeseen downtime. Access is provided to tools, reports, and services to accelerate innovation.

- **SAP Value Assurance**

  Supports customers on their own or partner-led projects with dedicated planning, design support, and functional and technical safeguarding services throughout the project. It doesn't provide any implementation or delivery services.

- **SAP Advanced Deployment**

  SAP Services and Support provides end-to-end implementation and delivery services, collaborating with partners as required. Relevant SAP Value Assurance services are integrated into the delivery.

- **Premium engagements**

  Provides on-site, premium access to trusted SAP experts and tools that include and go beyond the SAP Value Assurance service portfolio. For example, SAP ActiveAttention and SAP MaxAttention build a long-term relationship with SAP through the project and beyond.

Throughout this chapter, there are notes that highlight the specific SAP service components that can be consumed to reduce risk, provide the best advice, and check the decisions being made. Most of these service components are common to SAP Value Assurance, SAP Advanced Deployment, and premium engagements.

Further Resources

Always refer to the online Roadmap Viewer for more complete descriptions of the service components and the latest links.

7.3.2   Discover Your Solution

The SAP Activate discover phase covers everything done leading up to the decision to proceed with an SAP S/4HANA project. Upon completing the discover phase, an organization will have defined its digital transformation strategy and have an SAP S/4HANA roadmap or plan backed up by a business case. The company will have selected its delivery partners and delivery approach: new implementation, system conversion, or selective data transition. The activities in the discover phase are independent of the delivery approach. Some organizations may push some of the activities described in this section into the prepare phase.

This section begins with strategic planning, where you develop an innovation strategy and high-level roadmap based on SAP S/4HANA and intelligent technology innovations, and you also make early decisions on security and analytics. Then, we'll move on to trial system provisioning and application value and scoping, where you'll assess the value and impact of SAP S/4HANA and check your readiness.

Strategic Planning

The aim of strategic planning is to define an innovation strategy and high-level multi-year roadmap for all areas of the business that will undergo transformation. The roadmap should include, but isn't limited to, SAP S/4HANA.

Start with an identification of strategic business and IT objectives, including current pain points. Cluster the objectives into benefit areas, and for each benefit area, identify and prioritize the SAP solution enablers. These solutions provide the target enterprise architecture. During this planning, the team will also address the topics of clean core we introduced in Chapter 2.

The introduction of SAP S/4HANA into the solution landscape is an ideal opportunity to review and adjust the organization's analytics architecture. It's worth doing this early in the discover phase because there are many changes, new products, and capabilities relevant to SAP S/4HANA. Refer to our discussion of analytics design in the explore phase in Section 7.3.4 for more details.

Another area worth visiting early is your security strategy, including data protection regulations. SAP offers a security strategy advisory service to help determine where security issues exist and how SAP can assist.

Further Resources

SAP offers a North Star service architecture component in which SAP provides the development roadmap, industry practices, and implementation experience.

Innovation services for intelligent technologies are available through SAP MaxAttention and SAP Advanced Deployment.

Trial System Provisioning

To support the value identification and the impact evaluation in the discover phase, it may be beneficial to have access to an SAP S/4HANA system. You can deploy a system within hours or days using an SAP cloud appliance via SAP Cloud Appliance Library (*http://cal.sap.com*). The system is hosted on Microsoft Azure, AWS, or Google Cloud Platform. The provider will charge for hosting, and a user account at the cloud provider is required. SAP Cloud Appliance Library provides a detailed step-by-step guide for setup of the appliance that you'll follow during the installation and setup. Companies with an existing license can deploy an unrestricted SAP S/4HANA sandbox solution directly from SAP Cloud Appliance Library.

A cloud trial system is the fastest option for companies without a license and will provide up to 30 days of access. The trial solution can't be configured and is restricted to a certain number of users (*www.sap.com/products/erp/s4hana-private-edition/trial.html*).

In addition, the SAP Best Practices processes are ready to run immediately as documented in SAP Signavio Process Navigator (refer to Chapter 4, Section 4.1). This allows the team to get hands-on access to the solution and investigate the new features in detail.

Application Value and Scoping

Once you've set your innovation strategy and high-level roadmap, it's time to become familiar with SAP S/4HANA and the value it brings to your company's business. Understand and analyze its impact on your processes, which could influence the implementation method. Along with the evaluation of the new functionality and capabilities, the project team needs to determine the impact of adopting the new standard functionality on the existing business processes. This information is crucial for understanding the scope and breadth of the change management activities necessary during the implementation project, as well as for ensuring end users adopt to the new functionality in the business. It also serves as a key connection to the OCM and solution adoption activities that will be discussed in detail later in Chapter 10.

Application value and scoping contains the following tasks, some of which we'll walk through in this section in more detail:

- Discovering the value of SAP S/4HANA for your company
- Understanding how to design business processes following the clean core paradigm
- Understanding how to achieve clean processes and a clean process framework in SAP S/4HANA (both new implementation and system conversion projects)
- Running a usage and data profiling analysis
- Performing a business scenario and solution mapping
- Establishing the business value of a UX workshop
- Creating a solution architecture
- Performing SAP Readiness Check for SAP S/4HANA for an existing SAP ERP solution
- Defining the implementation strategy
- Creating a strategic roadmap and value case

> **Service Components**
>
> SAP offers various services to support the Application Value and Scoping task, including the Value and Implementation Strategy service, the Discovery Workshop, and SAP Customer Evolution Kit for SAP S/4HANA through SAP Value Assurance, which provides a comprehensive migration analysis, including business scenario and value mapping, a proposed implementation strategy and supporting roadmap, and a value case.

Discover the Value of SAP S/4HANA

Value and benefits drive all projects and must be understood early. The following resources can be used:

- Public web pages such as the SAP Help Portal, What's New Viewer, and SAP Fiori apps reference library
- SAP S/4HANA training, including SAP Learning training on integrations and extensions with SAP BTP
- Learning rooms in SAP Learning Hub
- SAP S/4HANA trial system (refer to our earlier discussion of trial system provisioning)
- SAP Signavio Process Insights, discovery edition, for SAP S/4HANA transformation for existing SAP ERP solutions
- Discovery Workshop for SAP S/4HANA, available from SAP Services and Support
- SAP Customer Evolution Kit for SAP S/4HANA

For organizations new to SAP, the impact of SAP S/4HANA on existing business processes will be evaluated in the explore phase. For organizations moving from an existing SAP ERP solution, the impact is evaluated in SAP Readiness Check for SAP S/4HANA, as described in the next section.

Perform a Business Scenario and Solution Mapping

Strategic planning provides a set of SAP solutions and a target architecture. Business process experts from each LoB should now produce a more detailed solution mapping at a business scenario level. Business scenarios are a level above scope items. To effectively assess business priorities for innovation, organize a workshop with process experts from various LoBs. Analyze each priority by determining its relevance using resources such as SAP Signavio Process Navigator or a simplification item list. If relevant, quantify and describe its value. Ensure all documents are stored centrally for easy access and collaboration across the project team.

For a new implementation, refer to the structure of SAP Best Practices content in SAP Signavio Process Navigator (refer to Chapter 3, Section 3.2, and Chapter 4, Section 4.1).

Define the Implementation Strategy

The next step is to define your implementation strategy. Your strategy should cover the following aspects:

- What is the productive system strategy—that is, one single global instance or regional instances?
- Will the business go live in one big bang or with a multistage transition by country or business unit?
- What are the dependencies and the best sequence for the release plan?
- When will integration between SAP S/4HANA and other SAP and non-SAP solutions go live?
- What are the intermediate architectures in a staged approach?
- Which will be used: SAP S/4HANA Cloud Private Edition, an on-premise data center, or a cloud hyperscaler?

- Will a global template solution be adopted, and how will deviations from the template be managed?

- Will SAP Best Practices content be used, and how?

- What is the strategy for custom development? What development will occur in SAP S/4HANA, and what will SAP BTP be used for?

Organizations moving to SAP S/4HANA from an existing SAP solution need to choose between the three transition approaches described in Section 7.3.1 (new implementation, system conversion, or selective data transition). The team must come to a decision to either reuse existing configuration or reengineer business processes with a reimplementation.

The main aspects to consider are as follows, and their impact is shown in Figure 7.39:

- How much process reengineering is required?

- Is implementing SAP S/4HANA a good opportunity to go back to the SAP standard? And should this be done based on a new implementation or incrementally after a technical conversion to SAP S/4HANA?

- How much of the historical transaction data needs to be retained?

- Will SAP ERP instances be consolidated or split?

- Will SAP S/4HANA or SAP S/4HANA Cloud Private Edition be implemented?

- Does the roll-out have to be phased to reduce risk, or can each instance go live with a big bang approach?

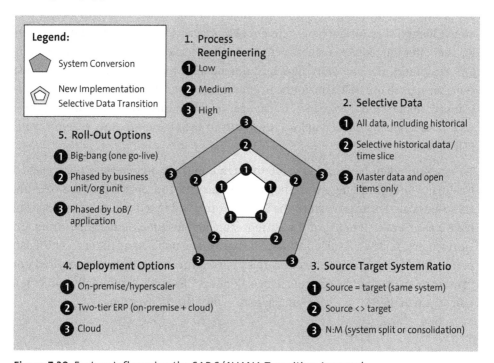

Figure 7.39 Factors Influencing the SAP S/4HANA Transition Approach

Create a Strategic Roadmap and Value Case

A value (or business) case for the project is built based on quantified costs and benefits. The following approach may be used:

1. Define discrete scope blocks required to reach the defined target architecture. Each block will have an organizational, functional, and technical element—for example, the SAP S/4HANA Finance scope for Malaysia.

2. Agree on business transformation objectives, and map value drivers to the scope blocks.

3. Define and link key performance indicators (KPIs) to the value drivers. Use KPIs and value drivers to quantify benefits.

4. Identify cost drivers, and quantify costs.

5. Compose a roadmap or timeline of scope blocks to implement the target solution landscape.

6. Assess the ability to execute the roadmap, considering organizational change, budget, technical capabilities, and previous project experience.

7. Determine the risks of transformation.

8. Summarize the alternative approaches and drive decision-making.

Business Value of the User Experience

SAP S/4HANA comes with a new UI/UX called SAP Fiori. The project team should learn about SAP Fiori, including the technical architecture, role model, and SAP Fiori apps reference library. The SAP Fiori apps reference library provides a set of lighthouse scenarios that offer immediate business benefits to the users of SAP S/4HANA. For existing SAP customers, the SAP Fiori apps recommendation report provides recommendations on apps to use based on your current system usage. This can be used by the LoB teams to understand the scope of UI change. To obtain this, you must run a report in your production system and upload the results to an SAP website. SAP will email you a PDF report.

To establish potential business value through a new UX and create a high-level UX roadmap, start by running a workshop to introduce the concepts of business roles and UX value goals. Ensure you know the SAP solutions and functional areas in scope and have a clear understanding of the current state architecture. Gather input from SAP Fiori scoping, review UX value goals and scenarios, and understand the current UX pain points. Select and prioritize business roles for improvement, discussing desired outcomes and managing the pace of change. Conduct this workshop initially and potentially again in the SAP Activate Run phase to evolve the UX over time.

7.3.3   Prepare Your Project

The prepare phase provides initial planning and preparation for the implementation project. We'll walk through the prepare phase for a new implementation deployment project in this section.

Phase Overview

The purpose of the prepare phase is to kick off the initial planning and preparation for the project. The project officially starts, the team resources are assigned, and the preliminary system setup is done. Although each project has its unique objectives, scope, and priorities, the primary output documents of the prepare phase include the following:

- **Scope document**
  Defines the starting point, goals, target solution, and transition approach.
- **Project charter**
  Includes goals, scope, organization structure, roles and responsibilities, and governance.
- **Project plan**
  Includes a WBS, schedule, and budget.
- **UX/UI strategy**
  Defines how SAP Fiori apps will be adopted and used.
- **Technical architecture**
  Defines the technical components, architecture, and infrastructure for the solution.
- **Interface register**
  Identifies the external systems, applications, and required interfaces.
- **Project standards**
  Defines the approach for requirements management, configuration, and custom code.
- **Operational standards**
  Includes test management and change control.

The rest of this section is organized into topics that appear in the roadmap. SAP Cloud ALM is the recommended solution to support your new implementation of SAP S/4HANA.

Transition Planning

Transition planning defines the scope and execution plan for the upcoming SAP S/4HANA implementation project. The first step is to create a scope document that defines the following:

- **IT and business objectives**
  Success criteria for the implementation project.

- **Starting point**
  SAP and/or non-SAP solutions to be replaced or remain the same.
- **Target solution**
  Target releases, scope, and related SAP systems.

The project plan will be continuously refined throughout the project as part of the project management workstream. SAP can assist with all transition planning topics through SAP Value Assurance or SAP MaxAttention. During the transition planning, start by defining the scope and objectives, and create the initial action plan. Analyze business processes, and outline the technical and data migration architecture.

Check the conversion readiness of the current SAP ERP (system conversion scenarios only), or run a usage and data profiling analysis (system conversions excluded) and decide on the conversion plan. Refer to Chapter 8 for details about system conversion.

Consider the following steps during your transition planning:

- Run a usage and data profiling analysis.
- Define the scope and the objectives of the transition.
- Determine the business process performance baseline.
- Model as-is business processes.
- Define the cutover approach (high-level).
- Clarify the adaption of existing custom code and the development of new custom code (if required).
- Clarify the usage of SAP BTP.
- Create your UX plan.
- Clarify operational readiness.
- Define the technical architecture (if not already done in the discover phase).
- Define the data migration architecture (important for new implementations and selective data transition).
- Plan your data volume management (important for system conversions and selective data transition).
- Clarify the impact on your authorization concept.
- Prepare the interface register to preliminarily identify the external systems, applications, and business objects or transactions that must be integrated with the SAP S/4HANA system.
- Run a legacy impact analysis on interface inventory and data integration to assess the impact on interfaces when moving to SAP S/4HANA.
- Run a first assessment on output management.
- Run a first assessment on training requirements.
- Run a technical security self-check.

Service Components

Refer to the Transition Planning for New Implementation service component within the Roadmap Viewer.

Customer Center of Expertise

Companies that are new to SAP should look at SAP's general recommendations to set up a Customer COE. At least one primary Customer COE certification should be gained. The Customer COE acts as a collaboration hub across IT and LoBs in an organization. Its mission is to provide transparency and efficiency of implementation, innovation, operation, and quality of business processes and systems related to the SAP software solutions and services. See Chapter 10, Section 10.2, for more details.

Transition Preparation

This activity covers the preparation work, which starts before the SAP S/4HANA explore phase. Preparation mainly concerns the tools that will support the implementation project, which you must prepare and set up, such as SAP Cloud ALM or SAP Signavio.

SAP Cloud ALM for implementation is a cloud solution with features, functions, and processes that are provided for running the fit-to-standard workshops and management of some implementation activities. They follow the SAP Activate methodology, content, and tools. It offers specific functionality for project management activities and supports the project start, team setup, solution documentation, and go-live.

The following components may be used:

- Project management
- Process management
- Requirements management
- Documentation management
- Task management
- Test management
- Change and deployment management
- Analytics

Refer to Chapter 3, Section 3.3, for more information.

Project Initiation, Governance, and Plan

The project is formally initiated and set up, including the setup of governance for all involved parties (e.g., the company, the system integrator, and any subcontractors). Key activities include the following:

- Hand over meetings from the previous discover phase.
- Review the commercial contract and resolve any issues.
- Identify stakeholders, and confirm their requirements, expectations, and acceptance criteria.
- Create a project charter based on the scope document.
- Establish baselines for scope, schedule, cost, and quality.
- Create a project management plan.

The project management plan defines the timeline and structure of tasks. It includes the following:

- WBS
- Schedule
- Budget
- Quality standards
- Communications
- Risks and procurement

Prototype

Prototypes enable companies to evaluate specific innovations in a short period using real business scenarios and company data to validate the value of a new solution quickly.

Prototyping is an optional small project on its own. It requires dedicated planning, execution, and evaluation, and it's always driven by business or IT requirements. The main steps of a prototype are shown in Figure 7.40.

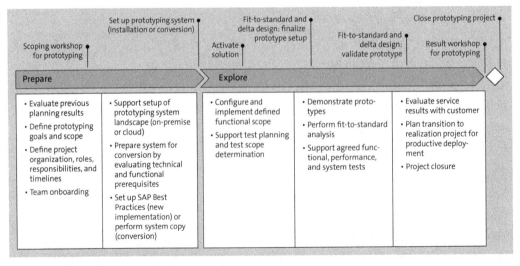

Figure 7.40 Prototyping Framework

SAP Value Assurance

SAP supports this activity with an SAP Value Assurance service that delivers a scoping workshop for prototyping.

Project Team Enablement

This activity ensures that the project team has the necessary knowledge to execute the work during the SAP S/4HANA implementation. Enablement may include different elements of the SAP system, SAP Activate methodology, agile principles and techniques, access to SAP Signavio Process Navigator, and other supporting tools. Self-enablement must begin before the project kickoff to maximize the time for learning and create efficiencies in later deliverables.

Project Standards and Infrastructure

SAP S/4HANA implementation projects need a robust means of executing and governing project work and deliverables. Project standards include requirements management, process modeling, configuration and documentation, custom code, authorizations, agile processes, and use of SAP Cloud ALM if available. Operational standards include test management, change control, incident management, and technical operations.

Project Kickoff and Onboarding

The goal of the project kickoff meeting is to ensure that everybody involved in the project understands its setup. Your project kickoff meeting should cover goals, objectives, scope, organization structure, decision-making process, roles and responsibilities, governance, regular meetings, project standards, infrastructure, schedule, and milestones.

Organizational Change Management Plan

OCM planning prepares an overview of all planned change management activities and ensures that all activities are related to each other. It also ensures consistency in the overall project plan and provides traceability of OCM activities. In the prepare phase, it's crucial for the success of the project to set up the OCM team and agree on its concept. See Chapter 10 for more information.

7.3.4   Explore the Solution

In the explore phase, a backlog of requirements and a design is created based on a fit-to-standard analysis of the solution. A sandbox environment based on the standard functionality of SAP Best Practices is used to drive the explore phase workshops. We'll walk through the explore phase for a new implementation deployment project in this section.

Phase Overview

As described in Chapter 2, Section 2.3.3, the purpose of the explore phase is to perform a fit-to-standard analysis to validate the solution functionality included in the project scope and to confirm that the business requirements can be satisfied. This phase includes designing identified gaps and making configuration decisions. These are added to the backlog for use in the realize phase. In addition, decisions are made on the approach to analytics, integration, security, testing, architecture, infrastructure and data volume design, and data migration. During the explore phase, an end-user training strategy is defined, and change impact analysis is performed.

The main output documents of the explore phase include the following:

- **Design document**
  Overall design documents for business scenarios and end-to-end processes include the scope, objectives, benefits, requirements, KPIs, data requirements, and design.

- **Backlog of requirements**
  Detailed catalog of requirements by business process.

- **Workflows, Reports, Interfaces, Data Conversions, Enhancements, and Forms (WRICEF) list**
  Tracked status, complexity, and progress of WRICEFs.

- **Functional specifications**
  Detailed functional designs for the approved WRICEFs.

- **Data migration approach and strategy**
  Agreed-upon data migration scope and approach to quality, cleansing, ETL, and reconciliation.

- **Technical design document**
  Definition of architecture and infrastructure for productive and nonproductive systems.

- **Test strategy document**
  Definition of the testing scope, approach, deliverables, and tools.

Further Resources

The SAP Activate Roadmap Viewer (see Chapter 3, Section 3.1) contains templates for these project documents.

The rest of this section on the explore phase is organized into topics that appear in the roadmap.

Learning Needs Analysis for Users

The learning need analysis identifies learning and enablement requirements and assesses digital learning opportunities to provide a thorough evaluation of formal and informal learning mechanisms using a "push and pull" methodology. The goal is to ensure that the appropriate learning resources are available when needed, with a focus on intuitive, consumer-focused content, activities, and deployment methods that are directly relevant to the learner's daily tasks.

Activate Solution

As the start of the explore phase, it's essential that a working functional SAP S/4HANA system is used to drive the fit-to-standard workshops. This is done by activating SAP Best Practices and SAP Fiori apps in a sandbox system. There are four approaches:

- **Enterprise management layer for SAP S/4HANA**
  Set up a fresh SAP S/4HANA sandbox system. Engage SAP to activate the enterprise management layer for SAP S/4HANA to maximize speed of deployment of SAP Best Practices. SAP also activates the SAP Fiori apps.

- **SAP S/4HANA fully activated appliance**
  Use this accelerator to speed up the provision of a hosted cloud or on-premise sandbox system with SAP Best Practices.

- **Manual setup and activation of SAP Best Practices**
  Set up a fresh SAP S/4HANA sandbox system. Create a new client by selectively copying Customizing content from client 000. Import and activate selected SAP Best Practices using the SAP solution builder tool. Activate the required SAP Fiori apps.

- **Manual setup without SAP Best Practices**
  If the functional fit of the enterprise management layer for SAP S/4HANA and SAP Best Practices is low, set up and configure the sandbox system from scratch. Then, activate the required SAP Fiori apps. This should be done in the prepare phase because it may delay the start of the workshops.

The enterprise management layer for SAP S/4HANA approach is generally the best choice (refer to Chapter 4, Section 4.2) as it has several advantages. It's the fastest approach and, once done, can be reused to set up the development system. Companies with multiple countries in scope will get a baseline solution for all the countries, including business processes localized for statutory requirements. It includes a financial chart of accounts for each country that is aligned at the group level.

The scope to activate is selected from the SAP Best Practices scope options and/or items. SAP Signavio Process Navigator can be used to examine the scope as described in Chapter 3.

Finally, you can integrate the sandbox system with other SAP systems as identified in the prepare phase. This must be done to support workshops and design cross-system business processes. In many cases, SAP Best Practices scope items are available to accelerate the integration between SAP S/4HANA and SAP cloud solutions such as SAP SuccessFactors and SAP Business Network.

Fit-to-Standard Analysis and Design

The purpose of the fit-to-standard analysis and design process is to approve a scope baseline and design to move into the realize phase. The company validates the activated SAP Best Practices processes and identifies potential gaps between the standard product and business requirements. These delta requirements are prioritized, and a design is verified and accepted by the business owners. Prior to acceptance, SAP can check that there is no standard way of delivering the delta requirements and can review the overall design. A successful explore phase will provide a comprehensive design, minimizing customizations and preventing the need for rework in the realize phase.

The fit-to-standard analysis and design process consists of the following activities (refer to Figure 7.32):

- **Fit-to-standard workshop preparation**
  Plan workshops, and check that the project team has done training and workshop participants have done self-enablement.

- **Fit-to-standard system preparation**
  Check that the SAP S/4HANA sandbox system is ready to demonstrate the processes during the workshops.

- **Fit-to-standard workshops and documentation**
  Present and validate the business processes in workshops, and identify potential delta requirements.

- **Fit-to-standard workshop validation**
  Classify, define, check, document, and prioritize the backlog of delta requirements, and decide which need to be discussed in a design workshop.

- **Design workshops and documentation**
  Define the design during a workshop, and document this afterward.

- **Review and customer sign-off**
  Project architects review and adjust the design. SAP offers services that will make recommendations on potential design improvements and check whether the design is appropriate. Business and IT stakeholders give formal approval.

In the following sections, we'll take a closer look at the sequential activities in fit-to-standard analysis and design.

Fit-to-Standard Workshop Preparation

The workshops are organized by LoB areas (e.g., finance) and end-to-end solutions (e.g., accounting and financial close). This structure matches the hierarchy of content in SAP Signavio Process Navigator. There are typically five or six LoB teams running in parallel. Each team has a series of end-to-end solution workshops, and each workshop covers a set of scope items (or processes).

The project manager will organize the workshop schedule and check that the boundaries and integration points between the workshops are clear. A standard set of workshop input and output template documents are defined. Before LoB-specific workshops start, the team will establish a working model of the SAP enterprise/organization structure and financial chart of accounts.

Fit-to-Standard System Preparation

Key business users will run through the business processes in the sandbox system using SAP Best Practices test scripts. The team will prepare sample master data so that the processes seem familiar during the workshops. Some additional configuration may be done for important requirements that aren't in the processes—for example, a specific type of commonly used sales order discount.

Fit-to-Standard Workshops and Documentation

Each workshop is jointly owned and delivered by an experienced SAP consultant and a business process owner from the business. They should work together closely to prepare a detailed agenda, agree on attendees, distribute prereading, prepare slides, practice the demonstrations, and develop a checklist of questions and required decisions. The SAP consultant needs to understand the as-is business, processes and systems. The business process owner needs to be able to execute the standard SAP processes and use the transaction apps. Both need to review all the content produced before the project started. This may include a business case, value drivers, and an initial fit-to-standard analysis.

The SAP Best Practices test scripts, process diagrams, and master data scripts are key inputs to the workshops. The workshop uses a show-and-tell demonstration to validate the solution, process, organization units, and business roles. The stakeholders are challenged to see if the business can adapt to the standard SAP processes, and any business change impacts are recorded.

The workshop then validates detailed process steps and functionality and defines delta requirements. These are immediately recorded in the backlog. This Microsoft Excel spreadsheet is shown in Figure 7.41. This figure is available for download at *www.sap-press.com/5966*.

Requirements that are met by the standard SAP Best Practices solution don't need to be documented. This saves time compared to the traditional blueprint approach that was used in early SAP ERP implementations.

The following are the different types of delta requirements:

- **Configuration requirements (and values)**
  Specify the requirements for business processes, UIs, and SAP-to-SAP integration scenarios.
- **Authorizations**
  Specify how the standard authorizations are used, and identify delta requirements.
- **Master data**
  Specify how the solution is to be used, and identify delta requirements.

- **WRICEF**
  Identify WRICEF requirements. Enhancements include changes to the UIs and missing functionality.

- **Organization structure requirements**
  Create revisions to the centrally managed enterprise/organization structure, which is revised as each workshop delivers results.

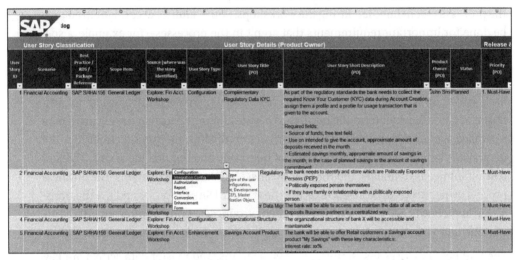

Figure 7.41 Backlog of Requirements

Fit-to-Standard Workshop Validation

The teams research, document, and classify potential delta requirements. This may require discussion between the LoB teams. Some delta requirements may be met using configuration. Each WRICEF item is cataloged in a WRICEF list (Microsoft Excel) and assigned a scope item, initial priority, complexity, owner, and type. Large delta requirements may be treated as custom developments rather than enhancements. These will typically include new custom data objects with new business functionality. Custom development is managed as a mini project.

Before moving ahead with specifying the solution within design documents, it's important to sort out which delta requirements are relevant to fulfill the project objectives. The backlog of requirements is reviewed by the solution architects and project managers. Every item is challenged: Is it vital to meet the business requirement? If so, can it be delivered through standard configuration? A complexity rating can be used to provide a rough-cut estimate. Delta requirements are assigned to sprints considering dependencies, effort, and priorities. This will simplify any future rescoping. Some decisions may need to be escalated to the project steering committee.

Companies with SAP Value Assurance or premium engagement can get a second opinion from SAP when it comes to validating delta requirements. SAP experts, both on-site and at SAP, work together to select the best solutions for functional gaps identified in the project. They look to minimize enhancements and avoid modifications (changes to the standard code outside designated APIs and exits).

Design Workshops and Documentation

The purpose is to design and document functional solutions for the delta requirements. The outputs are as follows:

- Design document
- Configuration requirements updated with outline configuration values
- Functional specifications for each WRICEF item
- Master data design documents
- Business user role documents

The design document summarizes the design for a set of scope items. Each one relates to a business scenario or end-to-end solution. The detailed requirements and WRICEFs relate to the scope items in these documents. Each document includes the following information:

- Process description
- Business objectives and benefits
- Pain points
- Key business requirements
- KPIs
- Organizational change impacts (see Chapter 10 on how these are used)
- Organization structure in SAP
- Process scope by scope item
- Process flow diagrams for scope items (referencing SAP Best Practices process diagrams that are adjusted to reflect the company processes)
- Systems (to be replaced or interfaced with)
- Master data used
- Summary of main delta requirements

Up to this point, the configuration requirements are high level. During design, the team drills down into the detail and, in some cases, defines specific configuration activities and values. This additional information is recorded in the configuration requirements. Configuration in the development system should be able to start at the beginning of the realize phase.

Functional specifications are written to define what is required for each WRICEF item. In some cases, depending on partner contracts and when estimates are required, functional specifications are prepared in the realize phase. How the WRICEF item will be technically delivered is defined in the technical specification written in the realize phase. Data conversions and interface specifications are produced as part of the data management workstream and the integration workstream. For forms, SAP Best Practices contains an accelerator that lists the predefined forms provided.

A master data design document is often created for each master data object. It defines the proposed design and controls. These documents will help drive the data volume design and data migration design later in the explore phase. SAP Best Practices contains master data scripts that show how to create the master data.

A business user role document is created for each role in the organization and defines how the role will operate. A matrix is often used to relate the user role to specific SAP authorization roles. SAP Best Practices contains an accelerator that lists the standard SAP Best Practices roles and their scope items and transaction apps.

User Experience Activation and Design

The project team needs to maximize the value of the SAP Fiori apps that provide an enhanced UX in SAP S/4HANA. SAP recommends that a UX lead work across the LoB teams. UX-specific working sessions are required after the fit-to-standard workshops. The lead can define, estimate, and prioritize UI configuration and delta requirements.

A process to look at UX requirements is shown in Figure 7.42. The UX lead will decide how to use the following:

- Theming, branding, and personalization
- UI enhancements (with key user tools) and UI extensibility (with SAP Web IDE)
- SAP Screen Personas for "classic" non-SAP Fiori apps: SAP GUI for HTML and Web Dynpro for ABAP
- New SAP Fiori apps

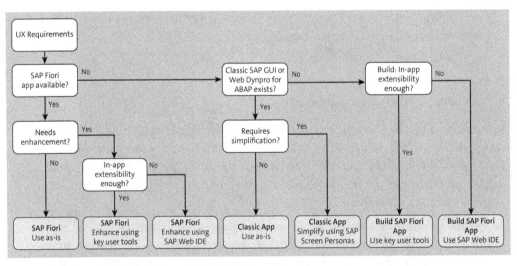

Figure 7.42 Design Options for UX Requirements

The UX lead will assist in the definition of business user roles and design the SAP Fiori launchpad experience and SAP Fiori tile setup. In some cases, low-fidelity UX mock-ups may be produced.

Further Resources

Refer to the Roadmap Viewer for details about how SAP can support UX work in the project.

Review and Customer Sign-Off

The project architects review and adjust the end-to-end design. SAP offers services that will make recommendations on potential design improvements and check whether the design is appropriate. Companies with SAP Value Assurance can use the Design Evaluation service. If there is uncertainty on the design of complex processes or concerns about robustness, operability, and sustainability of a process and solution design, premium engagements offer the Application Architecture Evaluation service.

The project obtains formal approval of the fit-to-standard analysis and design by business and IT stakeholders. This is done toward the end of the explore phase and incorporates all the design documents produced. It's important that the stakeholders genuinely understand the documents. They should be written in clear business language with SAP terminology clearly explained. Successful demonstrations and workshops are the key to truly informed approval.

With the sign-off, all stakeholders agree that the design is complete and the solution proposals for requirements are understood and accepted. Issues identified during acceptance need to be documented and classified.

The backlog is updated and now represents the backlog for the realize phase. If an agile approach is adopted (see Chapter 6), the updated backlog is the baseline for sprint planning in the realize phase.

Data Volume Design

After the fit-to-standard analysis and design is complete, it's time to move on to data volume design. The purpose of data volume design is to document and agree on a data volume management strategy. It will define what data is stored where and for how long (i.e., defining the residence and retention time). This considers and includes aspects such as the following:

- External reporting requirements (tax audits, product liability)
- Internal reporting requirements (i.e., fraud detection)
- Business process requirements
- Data privacy
- Dependencies between data archiving and document management

It defines the infrastructure (e.g., content servers), use of data aging and operation, sequencing and monitoring of data archiving, and data deletion jobs.

The following techniques are used to manage data volume:

- **Data aging**
  An SAP HANA database allows data to be divided into current/hot data (stored in main memory) and historical/cold data (primarily stored on disk).

- **Data archiving**
  Data with a long retention period (legal compliance, product liability data, etc.) is transferred from the online database to an alternative storage medium, which provides display access to the transferred data.

- **Data deletion**
  Out-of-date records that are no longer used by the business nor required for legal compliance are deleted from the online database.

> **Service Components**
>
> In SAP Value Assurance, you can use the Data Volume Design service to assist in this task.

Data Migration Design

Effective data migration from legacy systems to the new SAP S/4HANA solution is a critical success factor for new implementations. This will include automated processes and manual data migration through keying. It covers master data (e.g., customers, banks, and cost centers) and open transaction data (e.g., open sales or service orders). In many cases, legacy data may include sensitive or classified information that requires special handling procedures.

The steps in the explore phase are as follows:

1. **Prepare and conduct the data migration assessment**
   Finalize the list of data objects to be migrated based on the design. Consider the alternative data migration approaches and tools that can be used and learn how to use them.

2. **Perform the data audit**
   Identify the legacy systems that will supply data, and use data profiling to assess the quality of the legacy data.

3. **Prepare the data migration scope and requirements document**
   Use SAP's questionnaire to drive the requirements document that covers each data object in detail. This includes data volumes and the criteria for selecting the data records to be migrated. It also covers any special security requirements for classified information.

4. **Create the data migration approach and strategy document**
   Define the approach and tools to be used in the realize phase. This includes production of a data dictionary/catalog, data cleansing, ETL, testing, and reconciliation. It also defines the infrastructure requirements, use of data migration pilots and rehearsals, and the ultimate sign-off process.

5. **Manage test data**
   The realize phase will require many sets of data to execute testing. This includes system, integration, performance, and regression testing. This activity defines the data to be migrated or created in the development and systems.

6. **Define specifications for data migration**
   Define the functional specifications required for data migration requirements not delivered through the toolset. These include extract (e.g., legacy data extraction programs), transform, validate, load (e.g., APIs for custom objects), and reconcile (e.g., reports to compare source and loaded data).

The most commonly used tools are the following:

- **SAP S/4HANA migration cockpit**
  Provides predefined Microsoft Excel XML file upload templates that are mapped to standard load APIs in SAP S/4HANA. It provides tools to validate, convert, and load data, including reworking and loading incorrect data that fails. For larger data volumes, it can work with SAP HANA staging tables instead of Microsoft Excel templates. The staging table approaches are covered in SAP Best Practices scope item Data Migration to SAP S/4HANA from Staging (2Q2).

- **SAP S/4HANA migration object modeler**
  Used in on-premise projects to adjust or create migration objects and mappings for the SAP S/4HANA migration cockpit.

- **SAP Data Services**
  ETL software that can be used as an alternative to the SAP S/4HANA migration cockpit or alongside through the filling of SAP HANA staging tables. It's used to cleanse, standardize, de-duplicate, enrich, and load legacy data. It can also connect directly to legacy systems to extract data. Rapid data migration to SAP S/4HANA in SAP Best Practices offers out-of-the-box SAP Data Services content for 40-plus data objects.

Data migration is often on the critical path of the overall project timeline. For this reason, some of the realize phase activities may be started before the explore phase is complete. This may include data cleansing and pilot data migrations for the high-volume or complex data objects.

See Chapter 5, Section 5.2, for more about the SAP S/4HANA tools for data migration.

Further Resources

See the Roadmap Viewer for online resources and the range of services that SAP offers to assist companies with data migration.

Technical Architecture and Infrastructure Definition

A target technical architecture and infrastructure is defined in a technical design document. The technical architects need to create a detailed infrastructure design that includes the selection of hardware vendors for servers and storage, mapping of technical components, network design, and definition of cloud integration options.

The approach in the explore phase is as follows:

1. **Discover technical boundary conditions**
   These include technical solutions required, size and purpose of nonproduction systems, data center strategy, system availability requirements, SLAs for planned and unplanned downtime, high availability (HA), and disaster recovery (DR).

2. **Create a technical solution map**
   Collect detailed information on each technical component, for example, deployment model, nonfunctional requirements, integration requirements, minimum releases, and release dependencies.

3. **Decide on integration with cloud applications**
   Define integration by considering available bandwidth, peak times, availability requirements, and recovery procedures.

4. **Select hardware and perform hardware sizing**
   Work with the hardware supplier to undertake hardware sizing.

5. **Develop the virtualization strategy**
   Determine how a virtualization platform will fit into the design to use virtual servers rather than dedicated hardware per server.

6. **Design the network**
   Consider data center interconnectivity, network zones, and local area network (LAN)/wide area network (WAN) bandwidth and latency.

7. **Prepare testing**
   Prepare meaningful test cases for flexibility, workload management, HA, DR, backup, and restore.

8. **Document the technical design**
   Technical design is developed and documented in a series of workshops. This includes technical components, scalability, load balancing, backup, HA, DR, architecture, infrastructure, deployment plan, and data center and third-party integration.

SAP Activate Roadmap Viewer provides accelerators such as white papers, checklists, and a Technical Solution Map template and Technical Design Document template.

Service Components

SAP can assist through the Technical Platform Definition service component and the Advanced Sizing service component.

Integration Design

The purpose of this activity is to define the architecture and design required for interfaces between all systems. This activity is executed in close cooperation with the work on interfaces in the WRICEF list and design. The integration requirements between SAP systems are documented in the configuration requirements.

The interface architecture identifies all the systems-to-be and interfaces. An interface register lists the middleware technology, protocol type, frequency, and directions of communication of each interface.

After the architecture and scope are agreed upon, an integration design document is produced. The following aspects should be described for each integration aspect or interface:

- Short description of the integration aspect
- General business requirements (e.g., frequency and required fields)
- IT systems interfaced to SAP S/4HANA
- Identification of integration requirements (referencing the backlog)
- Solution for requirements (middleware, field mapping, or configuration)
- Important customizing
- Developments
- Organizational aspects
- Process quantification (i.e., expected data volume)

Functional specifications for interfaces between SAP and non-SAP systems are produced during the explore or realize phase depending on the milestone definitions of the project.

The SAP middleware solution to manage the operation of end-to-end integration processes is either SAP Process Integration (on-premise) or SAP Integration Suite. You can find APIs and predefined integrations scenarios online on SAP Business Accelerator Hub.

Service Components

SAP offers the Integration Validation service component to companies using SAP Value Assurance and premium engagements.

Analytics Design

The project should evaluate the strategic and business value of all the analytics solutions available for SAP S/4HANA. The explore phase should build on the work already done during the discover and prepare phases to document an analytics architecture, landscape, and design. The following SAP solutions may be considered:

- **SAP S/4HANA embedded analytics**
  Includes LoB-specific prebuilt solutions. New real-time reports can also be produced based on the SAP HANA CDS views.

- **SAP BW/4HANA**
  SAP's second-generation data warehousing solution for SAP and non-SAP data.

- **SAP Analytics Cloud**
  Cloud-based analytics solution that can operate across all SAP on-premise and SAP cloud solutions, SAP BW/4HANA, and non-SAP solutions.

- **SAP Digital Boardroom**
  An add-on to SAP Analytics Cloud to provide real-time analysis and decision support for C-level leadership.

- **SAP BusinessObjects Business Intelligence**
  On-premise alternative to SAP Analytics Cloud.

Further Resources

SAP Analytics Cloud and SAP BW/4HANA have their own separate SAP Activate roadmaps in the Roadmap Viewer that follow the SAP Activate project phases.

Analytics design covers analytics (e.g., reports, tables, charts, graphs, and geographic analysis), predictive analytics, and planning requirements. Analytics workshops are conducted for LoB-specific processes and requirements. The standard analytics apps and standard business content are reviewed, and a fit-to-standard analysis and design are performed. Note that the SAP Best Practices for analytics are currently for SAP S/4HANA Cloud and aren't yet available for SAP S/4HANA.

Analytics design guidelines are produced that define the following:

- When and how to use the different analytics solutions
- When to use the different connection types between the solutions
- Data modeling guidelines
- User access and security concepts

Service Components

SAP can assist through SAP Value Assurance with the Analytics Design service component.

Security Design

The purpose of the security design deliverable is to scope security and design user management. The security topics include infrastructure, network, operating system, database, and frontend access. User management topics cover roles, authorizations, user maintenance, and segregation of duties.

Security activities are prioritized (mandatory/recommended/optional) to create a detailed security roadmap for implementation in the realize phase and beyond. The required security topics are as follows:

- Planning SAP HANA security following the SAP HANA Security Guide
- Defining communication security
- Defining authentication mechanisms

There are also topics that are recommended but may not be required or prioritized by all companies:

- Planning the implementation of single sign-on (SSO)
- Defining processes for SAP auditing, logging, and monitoring
- Planning the security of the IT infrastructure
- Planning remote function call (RFC) connections and gateway security
- Patching SAP Notes for security
- Creating custom code security

The business roles and authorization requirements determined during the design drive the user management design.

Segregation of duties is the assignment of steps in a process to different people to avoid fraud resulting from individuals having excessive control. The management of access risks is supported by SAP Access Control, which is part of SAP governance, risk, and compliance (GRC) solutions.

Service Components

SAP can assist through SAP Value Assurance with the Security Design service component.

Test Planning

The purpose of this critical deliverable is to manage the quality of the solution and to minimize issues during and after go-live. A risk-based approach should be used to define test planning. This means that the testing effort is high for high-risk topics and low for low-risk topics.

The test strategy document covers the following topics:

- **Project testing**
  Determine project testing objectives and assumptions.
- **Test scope**
  Results from the design drive the scope. Compile a list of test cases and test scripts focusing on the business-critical and frequently used business processes.

- **Types of testing**
  Select test cycles, including unit testing, business process (string) testing, integration testing, data conversion testing, performance testing, UAT, and regression testing.

- **Testing approach**
  Determine how different test types relate to each other; for example, a successful unit test is a prerequisite for doing a string test.

- **Testing deliverables**
  Define test processes per project phase, test environments, and test data (aligned with the data migration design).

- **Testing tools**
  Determine which tools will be used to perform different tests.

- **Test automation**
  Decide whether automation will be used, and evaluate and select the appropriate tools.

- **Defect management**
  Describe how defects will be documented.

- **Roles and responsibilities**
  Describe the test lead and the responsibilities of individual project team members.

Detailed test planning should be done to plan the timing, duration, criteria, dependencies, and resources for each of the test cycles.

> **Service Components**
> SAP can assist through SAP Value Assurance with the Test Planning service component.

Set Up Development Environment

Before configuration and development work starts in the realize phase, the development environment needs to be set up. There are three main approaches:

- **Enterprise management layer for SAP S/4HANA**
  Set up a fresh development system by reusing the enterprise management layer for SAP S/4HANA originally created for the sandbox.

- **Manual setup and activation of SAP Best Practices**
  Set up a fresh SAP S/4HANA development system. Create a new client, and then import and activate selected SAP Best Practices using the SAP solution builder tool. The SAP S/4HANA fully activated appliance can't be used to create a development system.

- **Empty development system**
  This approach provides complete flexibility and control. After the new client is available, configuration is entered from scratch manually using the SAP Best Practices in the sandbox system as a reference.

> **Service Components**
> SAP can provision the development environment through the Platform Execution Enablement service component.

Technical Design

Detailed technical specifications are produced for all WRICEFs based on the functional specifications prepared earlier. The technical specifications will include details such as entry point in the system, enhancement logic, process flow diagram, data model, and required authorizations. Template documents are available in the Roadmap Viewer. Unit test case documents are prepared and reviewed by the application design team to check that they fit with the evolving design.

Sizing

Run a capacity estimation on the required hardware for application server and databases (CPU, RAM, storage, network). There are several levels for sizing:

- Budget sizing for smaller companies using very simple algorithms
- Advanced sizing for medium to large companies using throughput estimates, questionnaires, formulas
- Advanced sizing using standard tools (e.g., Quick Sizer) and focusing on core business processes
- Expert sizing based on a custom capacity model, which may also include custom coding

The outcome of this activity is to document the estimated hardware requirements, which can be discussed with the hardware vendor.

Custom Code Impact

As part of the transition to SAP S/4HANA, you need to identify custom code that must be adjusted. This activity is relevant if custom code needs to be taken over from an old SAP ERP system. In the prepare phase, a first analysis of the custom code has been done. Analyze all custom objects from the list and prioritize with respect to business clarity and urgency. Unused custom objects can be stored in transport requests and excluded from migration by the Software Update Manager (SUM) tool during conversion.

Operations Impact Evaluation

An operations impact evaluation is undertaken. With the introduction of a new solution such as SAP S/4HANA, the current IT support framework will change.

The deliverables from the explore phase, such as the technical design document and other design documents, are important sources of information on what needs to be supported and how by IT after the new solution is live.

The aim is to identify new operational activities, modifications to existing activities, and activities that can be retired. All the relevant support areas need to be analyzed: roles and skills, processes/procedures, operations documentation, and enabling support tools. Then, a roadmap is defined that includes the key activities for IT to fill the gaps and prepare the future IT support framework. This will include establishing resources; setting up tools; documenting procedures, knowledge transfer, and operations cutover; and retiring parts of the old framework.

Service Components

SAP can support this task with the Operations Impact Evaluation service component document management. Project documents, such as design documents and WRICEF specifications, are stored with document versioning.

Operations impact evaluation involves the following:

- **Requirements**
  The backlog of business requirements is transferred from a Microsoft Excel spreadsheet into SAP Cloud ALM. This allows configuration and developments done in the realize phase to be linked back to specific requirements.

- **Task management**
  The project deliverables and tasks can be managed and tracked in SAP Cloud ALM via task management, which contains the SAP Activate roadmap content.

- **Change and deployment management**
  Change and deployment management describes a multistep process that involves planning, executing releases, monitoring progress, and managing deployment tasks. It allows deployment and release planning features to help users stay updated on go-live activities and ensure seamless software and configuration changes.

Additional details on SAP Cloud ALM can be found in Chapter 3.

Communication Plan Execution

To enhance the information level of all stakeholders involved in the SAP S/4HANA implementation project, a proper communication plan must be available to foster understanding and commitment and facilitate fast and sustainable user adoption. This involves tailoring communication strategies to meet the unique needs of different target audience while maintaining a consistent message. As a result, it's strongly recommended to develop a change story that clearly explains the rationale and benefits of the SAP S/4HANA implementation, which will serve as the narrative for all your communication efforts throughout the project. Refer to the OCM concept in Chapter 10 for more details about managing OCM in the explore phase.

7.3.5   Realize Your Requirements

In the realize phase, business process requirements are implemented based on the design. Testing is done in the quality assurance system before deploying the SAP S/4HANA production system in the deploy phase. We'll walk through the realize phase for a new implementation project in this section.

Phase Overview

During the realize phase, a series of cycles are used to incrementally build, test, and validate an integrated business and system environment based on the business scenarios and process requirements identified during the explore phase. Configuration, extensions, integration, security, and analytics are implemented. The technical infrastructure is commissioned, including the quality assurance and production environments. Company legacy data is migrated or ready to migrate, and data volume management is set up. Adoption activities occur, and the operations support framework is prepared. The phase ends with preparation for the cutover.

The main outputs of the realize phase in a new implementation include the following:

- The system is configured, and configuration documentation is created.
- Technical specifications, test cases, and custom code for WRICEFs are completed.
- Infrastructure, integration, security, and operational procedures are in place and tested.
- Quality assurance and production environments are set up with transports from the development system.
- Data migration processes are tested, and a data quality assessment report is delivered.
- Data aging, data archiving, and data deletion are ready.
- Tests, including UAT, are complete based on a test plan, test cases, and test scripts.
- The support operations framework and procedures are ready.
- Cutover from legacy systems to SAP S/4HANA has been planned and rehearsed.

The realize phase must be planned in detail with dependencies coming together in the plan for testing. Carefully defined entry and exit criteria must be transparent to the whole team to ensure that the workstreams remain coordinated. The plan must be frequently updated to reflect progress and changes in scope and timescales.

The LoB teams (e.g., finance or manufacturing) from the explore phase continue to operate through the realize phase. The project will have iterative build cycles with a specific set of user stories and scope assigned to each cycle. If an agile delivery approach is being used, the build cycles are called sprints, as mentioned earlier, and have a much shorter duration than in a traditional waterfall approach. Refer to Chapter 6 for more details about agile delivery and planning and managing sprints.

The following sections on the realize phase are organized into topics that appear in the roadmap.

Enablement Content Development

During the enablement plan, develop readily accessible, easily digestible, and end user–specific enablement content. This helps to facilitate and ensure an easy and effective adoption of solution knowledge and skills needed by the organization's end users for higher system adoption and productivity. The first step is to create a content development plan with defined roles and responsibilities for the developers creating the content. Next, undertake the learning enablement content design and development work with the clearly defined content development plan, a clear quality assurance process. The content development should be monitored against the project deadline.

Configuration

The purpose of this activity is to configure the solution settings according to the design defined and agreed upon during the explore phase. Configuration is done in the development environment, and steps are executed in cycles (or agile sprints). SAP Best Practices provide the baseline configuration in the development system, or configuration is done from scratch referring to the SAP Best Practices in the sandbox. A configuration guideline is produced to document the approach and define the standards to be used.

The configuration sequence depends on the business scope but typically follows this order:

1. Organizational unit settings
2. General settings for each LoB
3. Master data settings
4. Processes within each LoB for high-volume process variants (e.g., procurement of direct materials)
5. Processes that span LoB teams, which are done in one company code for high-volume process variants (e.g., sales orders to payment receipt or goods receipt with warehouse management)
6. Functions that cross processes and have a high impact (e.g., available-to-promise [ATP], pricing, or credit management)
7. Medium-volume process variants (e.g., production subcontracting or customer returns)
8. Replication and process testing in different company codes and countries
9. Complex cross-LoB functions (e.g., intercompany transfers and batch management)
10. Low-volume process variants (e.g., purchasing rebate processing or dangerous goods)
11. Country-specific localizations for statutory requirements or process variants

Each configuration cycle consists of the following stages:

1. **Handover session**
   Handover occurs from the design team to the configuration team.

2. **Perform configuration**
   Configure settings in the development system by LoB and end-to-end process.

3. **Unit test**
   Test the newly configured functions.

4. **String test**
   Test the end-to-end process or solution impacted by the configuration change.

5. **Solution walkthrough**
   Present the new capability to the project team.

6. **Bug fixing**
   Resolve issues identified in the unit test, string test, and solution walkthrough.

7. **Documentation**
   Document the configuration settings and any impacts on the design.

Much of the configuration is done using the IMG in Transaction SPRO. SAP Fiori apps are configured using adaptation at runtime. Configuration of integration between SAP products and configuration of analytics are covered later.

The following sections cover the sequential stages of configuration in detail.

Handover Session

The handover is done from the design team (in charge of the design documents) to the configuration team. The handover session is typically done via a workshop to hand over all important design documents for a business priority/business area from the design team to the configuration team. The configuration team may be offshore or split across multiple physical locations. This is a good time to check the completeness and detail of the documentation.

Documents to hand over may include the following:

- Delta design documents from the explore phase
- Organizational structure design
- Master data design
- Roles and security
- Configuration requirements
- Functional specifications for WRICEF objects
- UX design documentation
- SAP Best Practices configuration and documentation
- Configuration guidelines

Perform Configuration

Configuration settings are made in the development system. Some are manually entered, some may be copied and pasted from the sandbox system, and some might be activated using the SAP solution builder tool. As this is a development system, all changes are recorded in transport requests. These will be used later to transfer configuration from the development system to the quality assurance and production systems.

Most of the configuration is done using the IMG in Transaction SPRO. This consists of a hierarchy of individual IMG activities, as shown in Figure 7.43. Help documentation is available within the IMG and under **Product Assistance** in SAP Help Portal. The team should follow the configuration guidelines that govern the naming and numbering of new configuration records.

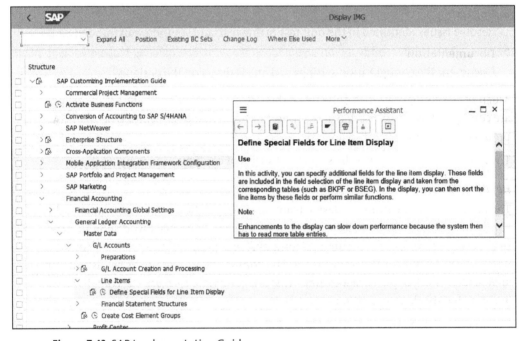

Figure 7.43 SAP Implementation Guide

Examples of IMG configuration settings include the following:

- **Organization structure**
  Company codes and plants
- **General settings**
  Chart of accounts and value-added tax (VAT) numbers
- **Master data**
  Settings for cost centers and business partners
- **LoB**
  Document types and correspondence

To understand what configuration is delivered for each SAP Best Practices scope item, use the Prerequisite Matrix accelerator in SAP Signavio Process Navigator, as highlighted in Figure 7.44. The SAP Best Practices IMG configuration is organized into building blocks. Each SAP Best Practices scope item is shown as a row (e.g., **US_16R**) and has several prerequisite building blocks shown in columns (e.g., **3Y5**, **J90**). Each building block contains configuration for several IMG activities.

If you want to activate this Scope item/ Process		You have to activate first					
Scope item/ Process	Scope item/ Process Description	1	2	3	4	5	6
US_16R_OP	Bank Integration with SAP Multi-Bank Connectivity	3Y5 (XX)	J90 (XX)	4M6 (XX)	4C7 (XX)	2MZ (XX)	J19 (XX)
US_18J_OP	Requisitioning	3Y5 (XX)	J90 (XX)	4M6 (XX)	4C7 (XX)	2MZ (XX)	J19 (XX)
XX_1BS_OP	SAP Fiori Analytical Apps for Sales	HB1 (XX)					
US_1E1_OP	Quality Management in Discrete Manufacturing	3Y5 (XX)	J90 (XX)	4M6 (XX)	4C7 (XX)	2MZ (XX)	J19 (XX)
US_1EZ_OP	Credit Memo Processing	3Y5 (XX)	J90 (XX)	4M6 (XX)	4C7 (XX)	2MZ (XX)	J19 (XX)
US_1F1_OP	Debit Memo Processing	3Y5 (XX)	J90 (XX)	4M6 (XX)	4C7 (XX)	2MZ (XX)	J19 (XX)
US_BKP_OP	Customer Returns	3Y5 (XX)	J90 (XX)	4M6 (XX)	4C7 (XX)	2MZ (XX)	J19 (XX)
US_19I_OP	Sales Contract Management	3Y5 (XX)	J90 (XX)	4M6 (XX)	4C7 (XX)	2MZ (XX)	J19 (XX)
US_1EG_OP	Bank Integration with File Interface	3Y5 (XX)	J90 (XX)	4M6 (XX)	4C7 (XX)	2MZ (XX)	J19 (XX)
US_1GA_OP	Accounting and Financial Close - Group Ledger IFRS	3Y5 (XX)	J90 (XX)	4M6 (XX)	4C7 (XX)	2MZ (XX)	J19 (XX)
US_1GB_OP	Asset Accounting - Group Ledger IFRS	3Y5 (XX)	J90 (XX)	4M6 (XX)	4C7 (XX)	2MZ (XX)	J19 (XX)
US_1GF_OP	Asset Under Construction - Group Ledger IFRS	3Y5 (XX)	J90 (XX)	4M6 (XX)	4C7 (XX)	2MZ (XX)	J19 (XX)
US_19C_OP	Activity Management in Procurement	3Y5 (XX)	J90 (XX)	4M6 (XX)	4C7 (XX)	2MZ (XX)	J19 (XX)
US_19E_OP	Supplier Classification and Segmentation	3Y5 (XX)	J90 (XX)	4M6 (XX)	4C7 (XX)	2MZ (XX)	J19 (XX)
US_1HB_OP	Financial Plan Data Upload from File	3Y5 (XX)	J90 (XX)	4M6 (XX)	4C7 (XX)	2MZ (XX)	J19 (XX)
US_1FD_OP	Employee Integration - SAP S/4HANA Enablement	3Y5 (XX)	J90 (XX)	4M6 (XX)	4C7 (XX)	2MZ (XX)	J19 (XX)
XX_1JI_OP	Real-Time Reporting and Monitoring for Procurement	HB1 (XX)					
US_1J2_OP	Compliance Formats - Support Preparation	3Y5 (XX)	J90 (XX)	4M6 (XX)	4C7 (XX)	2MZ (XX)	J19 (XX)
US_1FM_OP	Quality Management in Procurement	3Y5 (XX)	J90 (XX)	4M6 (XX)	4C7 (XX)	2MZ (XX)	J19 (XX)
US_1JW_OP	Advanced Available-to-Promise Processing	3Y5 (XX)	J90 (XX)	4M6 (XX)	4C7 (XX)	2MZ (XX)	J19 (XX)
US_1GI_OP	General Ledger Allocation Cycle	3Y5 (XX)	J90 (XX)	4M6 (XX)	4C7 (XX)	2MZ (XX)	J19 (XX)
XX_1MN_OP	SAP Fiori Analytical Apps for Treasury and Risk Management	HB1 (XX)					
XX_1O0_OP	Planning Apps for Sales	HB1 (XX)	3SK (XX)	2C9 (XX)			
US_1IQ_OP	Sales Inquiry	3Y5 (XX)	J90 (XX)	4M6 (XX)	4C7 (XX)	2MZ (XX)	J19 (XX)
US_1IU_OP	Customer Consignment	3Y5 (XX)	J90 (XX)	4M6 (XX)	4C7 (XX)	2MZ (XX)	J19 (XX)
US_1MI_OP	Delivery Processing Without Order Reference	3Y5 (XX)	J90 (XX)	4M6 (XX)	4C7 (XX)	2MZ (XX)	J19 (XX)
US_1B6_OP	Sales Rebate Processing	3Y5 (XX)	J90 (XX)	4M6 (XX)	4C7 (XX)	2MZ (XX)	J19 (XX)
US_1K2_OP	Event-Based Revenue Recognition - Sell from Stock	3Y5 (XX)	J90 (XX)	4M6 (XX)	4C7 (XX)	2MZ (XX)	J19 (XX)
US_1MP_OP	Quality Management in Sales	3Y5 (XX)	J90 (XX)	4M6 (XX)	4C7 (XX)	2MZ (XX)	J19 (XX)
US_1MR_OP	Quality Management in Stock Handling	3Y5 (XX)	J90 (XX)	4M6 (XX)	4C7 (XX)	2MZ (XX)	J19 (XX)
US_SL4_OP	Supplier Evaluation and Performance Monitoring	3Y5 (XX)	J90 (XX)	4M6 (XX)	4C7 (XX)	2MZ (XX)	J19 (XX)
US_1NR_OP	Engineering Bill of Material - Versions Management	3Y5 (XX)	J90 (XX)	4M6 (XX)	4C7 (XX)	2MZ (XX)	J19 (XX)
XX_1QR_OP	Predictive Analytics for Purchase Contract Quantity Consumption	HB1 (XX)	1VT (XX)				
US_1QA_OP	Specification Management for Recipes	3Y5 (XX)	J90 (XX)	4M6 (XX)	4C7 (XX)	2MZ (XX)	J19 (XX)
US_1QC_OP	Formulation - Recipe Development	3Y5 (XX)	J90 (XX)	4M6 (XX)	4C7 (XX)	2MZ (XX)	J19 (XX)
Prerequisite Building Blocks	+						

Figure 7.44 SAP Best Practices Accelerator: Prerequisite Matrix

SAP Best Practices content is also made available in SAP Cloud ALM. Choose the **Solution Documentation** tile, select a solution, and then browse in the **Business Processes** section. The SAP Best Practices content for SAP S/4HANA Cloud Private Edition can also be used for on-premise scenarios.

Further Resources

Detailed instructions are provided in "Administration Guide to Implementation of SAP S/4HANA with SAP Best Practices" on SAP Help Portal.

Configuration of the SAP Fiori UI is done with UI adaptation at runtime. It's possible to move, rename, and remove sections, groups, and fields. You can also combine fields or add standard fields or custom fields. Classic non-SAP Fiori apps (SAP GUI for HTML and Web Dynpro for ABAP) can be configured using SAP Screen Personas.

Unit Test

The objective of this task is to properly unit test the newly implemented functions in the development system and to log and fix issues. Each of the LoB teams create and manage a list of unit tests to cover all their processes. Each unit test has a test script that documents the precise steps to be followed in the system, the data to use, and the expected results. The SAP Best Practices test scripts can be extended to reflect the solution-specific scope.

String Test

A test is done for an end-to-end process by stringing together unit tests. The string test will often cross multiple LoB teams. Tests may be done in the development or quality assurance systems.

Because a full integration test is executed later in the realize phase, the recommendation is to test with manually created test data rather than migrated data. The focus should be on SAP processes and functionality. This can include standard integration between SAP products, such as SAP S/4HANA and SAP Business Network. Testing of company-specific WRICEF objects and interfaces with non-SAP systems is done during integration testing.

Test execution and results should be documented and stored in a central location. Issues should be logged and fixed. See SAP Signavio Process Navigator for test script examples.

Solution Walkthrough

The aim of this task is to present the solution capability and business process to business process owners in the LoB teams via live demonstration. Their early feedback is incorporated into the solution. If open questions can't be resolved within the project, the business process owner takes the queries to the business for resolution. Changes to the scope or design must be managed through the change request process.

Bug Fixing

Issues and bugs identified during tests and the solution walkthrough should be resolved directly within the current build cycle or logged in the project issue list. The string test should be repeated to check that changes haven't produced any unwanted side effects.

Documentation

The LoB teams document the configuration settings and impacts on the design. Solution documentation can be stored in SAP Cloud ALM. Refer to Chapter 3.

Custom Code Quality

During the SAP S/4HANA implementation project, a custom code quality check should be conducted based on the SAP S/4HANA development guidelines and following a clean core concept. Before the development work can starts (see the following section on product enhancements), SAP recommends establishing the required quality as part of the software development process.

The following aspects should be considered during the quality check:

- Create, enrich, and update your development guidelines for SAP S/4HANA, SAP HANA, and SAP S/4HANA Cloud, considering the clean core concept.
- Empower and train your development teams according to your development guidelines.
- Ensure the new and changed rules and regulations are checked in your development process (e.g., via peer quality reviews, periodic use of the ABAP test cockpit).
- Enable custom development quality measures in your software development process (e.g., to limit the number of SAP modifications) and code reviews.
- Support the future readiness of your code, for example, by using cloud extensions.
- Constantly rethink and question your custom code concept to enable a modern and innovative custom development environment.

Product Enhancements

In a new implementation, product enhancement covers the development of custom code to close the delta identified during the fit-to-standard workshops defined in the explore phase. It also covers the adjustment of already-existing custom code identified in the Custom Code Impact Analysis activity. Product enhancement may also include larger custom developments that may be executed by the company, a partner, or SAP Innovation Services. If a new implementation is being done in SAP S/4HANA to replace an old SAP ERP solution, the team may decide to reuse some of the old custom code. Refer to Chapter 8, Section 8.3.3, on system conversion guidance.

The following sections cover the product enhancement activities during the realize phase.

Select Development Technologies

Before developing new code in SAP S/4HANA, developers should be aware of the latest technical options available—for example, using in-app or side-by-side extensibility options via SAP BTP, which helps you keep the SAP S/4HANA system clean as your digital core.

Extensibility apps provide a more readily maintainable alternative to classic extensibility for a growing list of objects and enhancements. This includes adapting SAP Fiori UIs, adding custom fields, adding application logic, and creating reports, email templates, and forms.

Extensions via SAP BTP allow development to be done in parallel with the SAP S/4HANA implementation to keep the core clean and make software upgrades faster. It also allows the team to consume the latest technology platform for innovation use cases such as mobile, machine learning, big data, and internet of things (IoT).

Developers should also be aware of the latest SAP Best Practices associated with the newest techniques. Where possible, these approaches should be considered before classic extensibility. As always, modifications outside stable enhancement points should always be avoided. The golden rule for modern extensibility technologies in the cloud can also be applied on-premise. Decisions on the approach should be documented in a project-specific development guideline and reviews put in place to check that approaches are adopted.

Adjust Affected Existing Custom Code

This task focuses on adjusting affected custom code to make it ready for SAP S/4HANA. This activity is relevant in case the custom code needs to be adjusted. To adjust custom code affected by the conversion to SAP S/4HANA, first ensure your developers have the necessary skills for the task. Then, prioritize the list of custom objects that need adjustment, and wait for the development system to be converted. Once it has been converted, make the necessary adjustments to the custom code objects, and log all changes in transport requests. After this, transport your changes to the quality system once it has been converted to SAP S/4HANA, and test your changes. If corrections are needed, make them in the development system, and transport them to the quality system again. Finally, populate all transport requests in the production system buffer in preparation for import during the go-live. It's essential to properly retrofit changes made in the production support landscape to the new development system to ensure the latest business requirements are accounted for within the project landscape.

Adjust Custom Code with Redesign and Replatforming

Rather than fixing custom code, and for significant code extensions (e.g., complex code that requires high maintenance effort or processes that are critical to the business or that differentiate from the competition), you might want to consider recoding or redesigning within SAP S/4HANA (e.g., using in-app extensibility), or alternatively, you can move the extension to SAP BTP as a side-by-side extension.

Develop Extensions Following the Clean Core Strategy

The developers build, unit test, and document all the code enhancements. After development is complete, the application design team tests and retests them until all issues are resolved. To follow a clean core approach, we recommend reviewing Chapter 2, Section 2.4 and Section 2.5, where we discuss the clean core strategy and the golden rules for implementation of SAP S/4HANA in great detail.

> **Service Components**
>
> SAP Value Assurance offers the Technical Performance Optimization service component to support customers in configuring the solution in an optimal way.

Custom Developments

It's recommended to manage development requirements that are critical or exceed a certain threshold as custom developments. These are typically managed as small standalone agile projects. The functional specification, technical specification, development, and testing are managed through agile sprints (refer to Chapter 6, Section 6.3.2). It's recommended to manage those as custom developments with the help of SAP Services and Support.

User Experience Implementation

The UX implementation covers the new implementation of SAP UIs, or adjustment of existing ones as defined in the UX Activation and Design activity in the explore phase. The focus is on the implementation of SAP Fiori. The process includes configuring and developing customer-specific UIs (e.g., SAP Fiori UX and SAP Screen Personas), creating custom business roles with tailored launchpad content, developing enhancements based on functional requirements, and performing unit testing to ensure readiness for deployment.

Data Volume Management and Configuration

Data volume management is configured based on the design from the explore phase. This includes cleaning up or archiving business data, configuring data archiving, and testing execution of data archiving. Ensure that data volume management has been configured and tested successfully. The settings can be taken over into the productive system once transferred to the new SAP S/4HANA system.

> **Further Resources**
>
> Refer to SAP Help Portal for documentation on how to do the configuration (design time) and test the solution (runtime).

Data Migration

For a new implementation, this activity develops, implements, and tests the data migration processes defined in the explore phase. This activity consists of iterative development and testing cycles focused on the analysis of data, refinement of business rules, and deployment of migration processes and programs. The test cycles enable the migration team to improve data quality to an acceptable production level, develop a detailed cutover sequencing plan, and exercise data reconciliation and validation processes required to support the cutover.

The project team develops the specific architecture, processes, and programs that support the extraction, validation, harmonization, enrichment, and cleansing of the legacy data. This is done based on the data migration approach and strategy document and the data migration functional specifications developed in the explore phase. The processes depend directly on the tools and utilities selected in the explore phase (refer to Section 7.3.4). These deliverables can range from fully automated programs based on an ETL software platform to a series of manual processes based on tools such as Microsoft Excel and Microsoft SQL Server. SAP supports data migration with the SAP S/4HANA migration cockpit and/or SAP Data Services.

The data migration approach for each data object may vary. Whatever the approach, multiple test rounds are executed. The results are recorded, and the defects are eliminated. The data migration test results are statistics that provide a detailed account of data load issues and successfully loaded data.

If data volumes are very large, the initial test cycles may need to use samples of representative data. Data profiling should be done to ensure representative variations are used; otherwise, defects and unique mappings and requirements may remain hidden. Runtimes for the production cutover process may need to be optimized. Master data that is likely to be static may be migrated early with delta updates run during the cutover.

A final data quality assessment report is produced at the end of the realize phase. This summarizes the results and assesses the overall data migration quality. This is reviewed with the project stakeholders. At the end of this task, the data migration team can move into the deploy phase with the confidence that a majority of data quality issues and migration issues have been resolved and mitigated.

> **Note**
>
> For more information on the data migration process, refer to Chapter 5, Section 5.2.

Sizing and Scalability Verification

The sizing estimation performed in the explore phase (see the "Sizing" subsection under Section 7.3.4) is further detailed out and verified. At this step of the project, the initial assumptions are now being reevaluated based on real-world KPIs.

The scalability verification tests and validates whether the new system can handle increased workloads, users, or data volume efficiently as it scales up. To guarantee the success of the smooth processing of core business processes, these processes need to be measured, tested, and compared between the source and target systems. As a goal, the converted SAP system will deliver the same or better performance indicators as compared to before the conversion. Therefore, the results must be compared against the predefined performance baseline.

Service Components

SAP can assist through SAP Value Assurance with the Size to Scale service component. SAP can provide support for the test and optimization of the volume test, and/or provide specific business case optimization where required.

Set Up Infrastructure and Security

In the realize phase, the technical infrastructure must be installed and configured as defined in the technical design document created in the explore phase.

The IT infrastructure setup work includes the following:

- Server hardware, operating system, and virtualization platform
- Storage solution—that is, the physical setup of the storage infrastructure usually done by the storage supplier
- Integration of the new components into the existing IT environment—for example, integration into the existing network and backup solution
- HA, DR, and backup

The company-specific results from the security design phase are also implemented, including the following:

- User management, including roles, authorizations, and user maintenance
- Infrastructure and network security
- Operating system and database security
- Frontend access and authentication

The team must execute infrastructure tests based on the test cases and test plan. This will measure the performance against the defined KPIs to ensure the infrastructure operates within the boundary conditions of the business. The team resolves, documents, and retests issues and defects. Tests should include the following scenarios:

- Performance, as issues may require changes to the functional design in addition to infrastructure changes
- Flexibility procedures (e.g., by moving the system load to other hosts, adding instances, or changing instances)
- HA
- DR
- Backup and restore
- Infrastructure security

If already available, the productive hardware is tested to validate the configuration. Otherwise, the productive hardware is tested in the deploy phase (Section 7.3.6).

> **Service Components**
>
> SAP can assist through SAP Value Assurance with the Technical Feasibility Check, Business Process Performance Optimization, Technical Performance Optimization, and Volume Test Optimization service components. These may lead to changes in the functional design, configuration, and tuning for optimum performance; elimination of bottlenecks; and SAP Fiori-specific performance improvements.

Integration Implementation and Validation

During integration implementation, the customer-specific design from the explore phase is implemented. This activity should be executed in close cooperation with the configuration and product enhancement activities. The project team should do the following:

- Implement standard SAP Best Practices scope items for specific integration scenarios, such as Automated Purchase-to-Pay with SAP Ariba Commerce Automation (J82).
- Configure and customize SAP-to-SAP integration scenarios not covered by SAP Best Practices.
- Implement interfaces between SAP and non-SAP solutions based on interfaces built and unit tested in the product enhancement activities.

When implementing and running landscapes that drive mission-critical business processes, the integration of solutions can be complex and challenging. The implementation work is typically distributed across many teams and many stakeholders, including custom-built and third-party software.

SAP recommends the Integration Validation service to mitigate risk based on the use of SAP Value Assurance services. The aim is to ensure technical readiness of the entire solution for go-live. It includes analysis of critical business processes and interfaces to validate scalability, performance, data consistency, and exception management. A comprehensive monthly status of technical go-live readiness for core business processes is recommended and includes these aspects:

- **Data consistency**
  In distributed solution landscapes, the consistency of the data across software systems must be subject to checks and validations. This requires transactional security, and all integration queues and interfaces must be monitored.
- **Business process monitoring and exception management**
  There must be 100% transparency into the status and completion of business processes. The flow of documents must be monitored.

- **Performance and scalability**
  Response time for critical transactions and runtime for batch jobs should meet business requirements. Adequate load balancing must be in place.

Service Components

SAP recommends the use of the following service components through SAP Value Assurance: Integration Validation, Interface Management, and Technical Integration Check. These tried-and-tested processes, provided by SAP Services and Support, give you access to lessons learned from hundreds of other live SAP implementations. See the Roadmap Viewer for more details.

Analytics Configuration

The analytics solutions are configured based on the design and guidelines documented in the explore phase. The scope may cover analytics, predictive analytics, and planning requirements. The design will typically be based on embedded analytics in SAP S/4HANA, SAP Datasphere, and SAP Analytics Cloud to define the UX for analytics and planning. SAP BW/4HANA provides a data warehouse for structured and unstructured data from SAP on-premise, SAP cloud, and third-party solutions.

Further Resources

Refer to the SAP Analytics Cloud and SAP BW/4HANA roadmaps in the SAP Activate Roadmap Viewer for more details.

Examples of the activities to be undertaken in SAP S/4HANA include the following:

- Configure the SAP Fiori launchpad.
- Perform the technical setup of SAP S/4HANA CDS views and SAP S/4HANA embedded analytical apps based on CDS views.
- Customize prebuilt SAP S/4HANA embedded analytics.
- Create custom CDS views for custom SAP S/4HANA embedded analytics.

Examples of the activities to be undertaken in SAP BW/4HANA include the following:

- Install the SAP BW/4HANA content add-ons, and activate the required content areas.
- Establish the system connection between SAP S/4HANA and SAP BW/4HANA.
- Set up a live data connection between SAP S/4HANA and SAP BW/4HANA to enable analytics without persistent data in SAP BW/4HANA.
- Build SAP BW/4HANA models, extract SAP S/4HANA data, and configure queries.
- Work with third-party data in SAP BW/4HANA.

Examples of the activities to be undertaken in SAP Analytics Cloud include the following:

- Configure general settings such as the import functionality, database connector, and cloud connector.
- Import and enable prebuilt content for SAP Analytics Cloud.
- Configure the underlying SAP Analytics Cloud data models, planning models, and predictive models.
- Set up a live data connection between SAP Analytics Cloud and the SAP S/4HANA and SAP BW/4HANA systems to enable analytics without persistent data in the cloud.
- Import data into the data models and perform data preparation for analytics with persistent data in the cloud.
- Configure SAP Analytics Cloud stories for reports, tables, charts, graphs, and geographic analysis.

Service Components

SAP recommends the use of the Analytics Design Support service components through SAP Value Assurance. This service delivers guidance on how to leverage new analytics capabilities such as SAP S/4HANA embedded analytics, implement strategic SAP products for analytics and enterprise data warehousing (SAP Analytics Cloud, SAP Digital Boardroom, SAP Datasphere, SAP BW/4HANA, or SQL-based SAP HANA data warehousing), and integrate them into existing infrastructures.

Testing

In this deliverable, the test strategy and test plan produced in the explore phase is put into action. Figure 7.45 provides an overview of the testing approach, which illustrates what systems are used and the sequence of test cycles. You can also refer to Chapter 5, Section 5.6, for more information on testing.

Test cases and test scripts with expected results are produced for all the test cycles. Process flow diagrams and test scripts from SAP Best Practices scope items serve as accelerators. Testing tools are set up, and the testing teams are trained. A combination of manual testing and automated testing is used. The scope and source of the required test data is agreed upon. The details of the approval procedure for UAT are finalized, and the test plan is turned into a detailed schedule of activity.

During all test execution, defects are formally logged for traceability, fixes are applied and transported, and the process is retested until the issue is resolved. Errors can hide in the variants of processes, so ensure that test scripts mix these up well—for example, a foreign currency order with batch management.

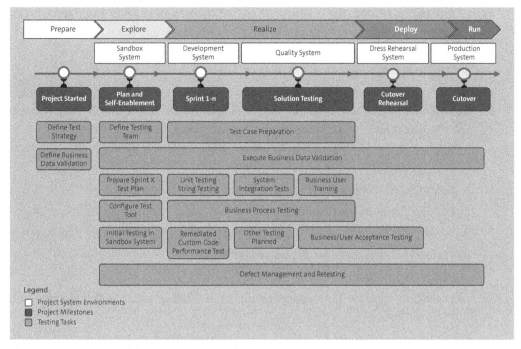

Figure 7.45 Overview of the Testing Approach

All the different workstreams come together in the test process. As we've seen throughout our discussion of the realize phase, unit tests and string tests are part of configuration, for example.

The following tests are available:

- **Integration tests**
  Integration testing is performed to verify proper execution of the entire application, including all WRICEFs, integration between SAP solutions, and interfaces to external applications. Integration testing is conducted in the quality assurance system using migrated data. Integration testing is approved after all tests have passed.

- **Regression tests**
  During integration tests, many fixes are transported into the quality assurance system. Later fixes may break processes that had already passed their tests. To mitigate risk, regression tests are executed alongside the cutover rehearsals. The scope and approach are similar to integration testing. The quality assurance system is monitored as if it were the production system, as this will provide an indication of end state operations. For example, errors in the system log, which may not be noticed by testers, could cause instability in the production system.

- **UAT**
  UAT provides formal approval from actual users that the solution works as specified and meets the business requirements. The scope and approach are similar to

integration testing. The UAT team is guided by the project team and starts with the integration test cases and scripts and then adds real-world scenarios.

Set Up Quality Assurance and Production

A quality assurance environment is made available to test configuration and development in an environment sized like the production system to be as similar as possible to the existing solution. This must be done early enough in the realize phase to enable data migration and integration tests. Refer to the technical design document produced in the explore phase. Steps include the following:

1. Execute the technical installation of the required SAP products.
2. Run the technical system setup.
3. Set up the transports from the development system to the quality assurance system.
4. Transport development and configuration.
5. Perform manual rework activities for configuration that isn't transported.
6. Execute integration set up between the SAP S/4HANA solution and SAP and non-SAP solutions.
7. Document the detailed procedure to streamline the process for production.

> **Further Resources**
>
> For detailed information, refer to the Administration Guide for the Implementation of SAP S/4HANA on the SAP Help Portal.

Before the cutover activities start, a production environment is made available to execute final go-live simulations and cutover. This environment will be used as the future production system on go-live.

Operations Implementation

Changes to the support operations are implemented following the operations roadmap defined in the explore phase. The following areas are covered:

- **Detailed operations**
  The changes to the support framework are implemented. This is often managed through detailed IT change requests.

- **Roles and responsibilities**
  Changes to resources and their roles and responsibilities are implemented.

- **Support processes and procedures**
  Changed IT support processes are documented and tested. This includes incident management, problem management, access management, change management, test management, job management, and system recovery.

- **Operations support tools**
  Tools are adjusted or newly set up. Old operational tools are turned off.

- **Operations documentation**
  An operations handbook is produced, and all documentation is updated and stored in a central repository.

- **Knowledge transfer**
  The IT support resources prepare to run the new solution. Knowledge transfer is done through a combination of activities, including formal training, self-study, shadowing, and on-the-job training.

Cutover Preparation

Now, it's time to prepare for cutover with the following tasks:

- Create a detailed hour-by-hour cutover plan to mitigate risk.
- Plan the rehearsal and simulation of cutover activities in legacy and SAP systems.
- Define contingency processes for problem scenarios.
- Get approval from informed stakeholders.

During simulation, the tasks, sequence, and duration are optimized, and the responsibilities in the project team and business are finalized. Rehearsals are repeated until the go-live risk is mitigated to an acceptable degree.

The scope of rehearsals will include work in the legacy systems—for example, parking of logistics and warehouse processes, financial closing, blocking access to users, and stopping operational jobs. The cutover rehearsal will include backups, transports, manual configuration steps, data migration, data reconciliation, testing, business acceptance of the cutover, and contingency processes. The overall communication approach may include coordination with the company, suppliers, and other third parties.

A new implementation may require the following three or more simulations:

- **Technical**
  Definition and validation of the steps with the project team.

- **Dry run**
  Full execution of the cutover schedule with the entire team to validate steps, sequence, and data.

- **Final**
  Full execution of the entire cutover schedule to streamline execution and obtain exact timings.

Detailed Change Impact Analysis

This activity aims to understand how implementing the new SAP S/4HANA system will impact different stakeholder groups. It emphasizes that the implementation project affects the entire organization not just IT. To achieve this, a change impact analysis is needed and can be conducted in workshop settings with experts from various areas to uncover insights and prepare for the transition. After the assessment, it's important to address the identified challenges with specific actions. It includes the following tasks.

- Prepare change impact workshops
- Conduct change impact assessment
- Manage impacts

Organizational change impacts were identified in the explore phase and help drive OCM activities. During the realize phase, these are reassessed with a focus on changes in the project scope, design, and assumptions. In particular, the alignment of OCM with the test, data migration, and cutover processes is checked. See Chapter 10 for more information.

Enablement Delivery

It's important to cover all the different methods of enablement delivery available to an organization. Some examples include on-site classroom learning, virtual classroom learning, e-learning self-enablement, blended learning, short micro videos, webinars, social collaboration, blogs, and on-the-job coaching. Each enablement delivery should cover the following aspects:

- **Train the trainer**
  Soft skills for trainers to learn all the tips and tricks for effective training delivery, both in person and virtually.
- **Pilot delivery**
  Dry run of the course, either virtually or in person.
- **UAT training**
  Usually solution overview, basics and navigation, high-level introduction to how testing works before UAT starts.
- **Knowledge transfer**
  An SAP trainer delivering content and knowledge transfer to the trainer.
- **Coaching**
  One-on-one with users, answering general queries or covering specific areas; can also include floorwalking—trainers are made available postimplementation to walk around the customer's office to respond to individual queries, problems and tasks.

The steps include the following:

1. **Plan learning logistics**
   Consider all the training, planning, and logistics required to deliver enablement content and courses.

2. **Set up system landscape and data**
   Establish a system landscape and data for training purposes. Provide learners with a hands-on practice system to use during training.

3. **Deliver enablement**
   Equip the designated trainers and end-user with the knowledge and expertise needed to perform their roles effectively.

7.3.6 Deploy Your Solution

During the deploy phase, the solution, supporting tools, and processes are made ready for the SAP S/4HANA production system go-live. We'll walk through the tasks in the deploy phase for a new implementation project in this section.

Phase Overview

At this point in the project, a production environment is already available. All configuration, enhancements, and UAT are complete. Final go-live simulations and cutover are executed. This phase includes a go or no-go decision and ensures that the organization is ready to run in the new environment.

The primary activities of the deploy phase in a new implementation include the following:

- End-user learning and organizational change readiness
- Finalize testing
- Final production data load
- Operation and infrastructure readiness
- Cutover rehearsal
- Production cutover
- System go-live and hypercare support
- Handover to support organization

Integration Validation

The integration validation activities initiated in the realize phase are finalized. SAP recommends the Integration Validation service to mitigate risk based on the use of SAP Value Assurance services. The aim is to ensure technical readiness of the entire solution for go-live. It includes analysis of critical business processes and interfaces to validate scalability, performance, data consistency, and exception management. A comprehensive monthly status of technical go-live readiness for core business processes is recommended.

Operation and Infrastructure Readiness

The technical infrastructure and SAP S/4HANA production environment must be ready. Ensure the operations and support organization is prepared to run the new solution. The activity provides a defined support approach for monitoring and measuring the day-to-day support operations. The following topics need to be covered:

- Roles and responsibilities
- Support processes, governance, and procedures
- Operations support tools and documentation
- Knowledge transfer

Service Components

SAP can support this activity with the Operations Readiness service component. It includes a status review of the IT operation changes defined during the operations impact evaluation. Ideally, the check is performed a couple of weeks before go-live.

Dress Rehearsal

Before performing the cutover to production, it's important to rehearse the cutover plan entirely in a test system that reflects the future state of the production system. The rehearsal is intended to confirm the ownership, sequence, and duration of the cutover activities to production. There may be a need to postpone the go-live date if significant changes and critical items are raised as a result of this rehearsal. The cutover schedule is likely to be complex, with many dependencies and owners from the business and IT. Therefore, communication plays a crucial role in ensuring a successful production cutover.

Final Production Data Load

After all preparations and configuration on both the technical and application levels are complete, data can be loaded from the legacy systems into the production environment of SAP S/4HANA. Static master data may be migrated before the cutover and more dynamic data during the cutover. This approach can be used to reduce the work and duration of data migration in the cutover.

Production Cutover

The purpose of the cutover is to execute the cutover plan and get the solution ready for productive use and operation. The main activities in the cutover are the following:

- Execute the cutover, following the tasks defined in the cutover plan.
- Complete the final production data load if needed (e.g., open items).

- Document the actual duration of each step to support future projects.
- Capture any variances to the plan, along with decision-makers who approved the change.
- Cutover managers should proactively notify task owners of upcoming tasks to ensure their availability.
- Regularly communicate the status to stakeholders.
- After the data is loaded, complete testing and data reconciliation.
- Complete all required documentation for regulatory purposes.
- Obtain system sign-off.

Service Components

SAP offers the production installation as part of the Platform Execution service component. The service provides a variety of predefined packages that are highly standardized, cost-effective, and scalable.

System Go-Live and Hypercare Support

The system go-live is the final milestone of a successful SAP S/4HANA implementation project. The solution is now running live in the production environment, and the hypercare period follows to ensure seamless adoption of the new system.

Hypercare is the period that comes directly after the go-live. Its purpose is to support questions and issues that might arise. During this period, predefined checks will be executed daily to closely monitor adoption of the new solution. It's essential to verify how the new system behaves and improve system performance if needed.

The main activities in the hypercare period should include the following:

- Monitor resource consumption.
- Analyze workload.
- Check system scalability.
- Follow-up on going-live check.
- Perform security monitoring.
- Delete obsolete data.

Service Components

The following SAP Value Assurance services are provided during the hypercare period: going live support, technical performance optimization, and business process improvement.

Handover to Support Organization

After the hypercare phase ends, it's crucial to fully enable the regular support organization to operate the new SAP system safely and securely. The following activities are covered:

- Finalize system documentation.
- Complete operational procedures as part of the operations handbook.
- Check the customer support organization.
- Resolve and close open issues.
- Perform the handover from the project team to operations.

7.3.7   Run Your Solution

The final phase of the SAP Activate methodology is the run phase. After the successful completion of the implementation project, companies and project teams further optimize the operability of the new SAP S/4HANA solution. In this open-ended phase, the operations team must ensure that the system is running as intended. This phase also supports the continuous adoption of the solution by new users.

The main topics in the run phase include the following:

- Operate the solution
- Improve and innovate the solution

We'll walk through each in the following sections.

Operate the Solution

With the implementation project completion, the customer support organization will have to take responsibility for operating the new SAP S/4HANA solution. The goal of this step is to ensure efficient day-to-day operations, impacting IT support personnel, processes, and tools.

Additionally, it's essential to perform routine actions to ensure that the system is running as expected. For example, this is necessary to maintain the systems in a functioning and operating condition, guaranteeing systems availability and required performance levels.

The customer support organization should continuously improve and optimize the IT operations. This may include implementing automation and shifting from reactive to proactive approaches.

SAP MaxAttention

SAP has a large set of offerings for SAP MaxAttention customers for safe and efficient operations. For example, SAP can configure application operations in your environment and train your IT support experts in using the tools. If you want to get the full potential of your SAP solutions and understand cloud opportunities, the Hybrid Operations services that are part of premium engagement services might be the right selection for you. If you want SAP to execute IT operation tasks, then SAP Cloud Application Services can help you.

Improve and Innovate the Solution

To support the business and end users, IT maintenance processes must be set in place to continuously improve the solution. It requires periodic updates by implementing feature and support packs to bring the latest software updates from SAP into the solution. A planning cycle involving business and IT should identify innovations to be deployed.

SAP S/4HANA provides visibility into planned innovations in the SAP S/4HANA product roadmap, which is available at *https://roadmaps.sap.com/*. SAP Road Map Explorer displays innovations and describes how the product capabilities are planned to progress over time to help detail the transformation journey.

Improving and innovating the solution contains the following tasks:

- Access the value of the SAP S/4HANA transformation.
- Run the User Experience Business Benefit Workshop.
- Periodically update your SAP system and initiate a new innovation cycle.

Access the Value of the SAP S/4HANA Transformation

This task helps customers evaluate the value of the SAP S/4HANA new solution by using SAP Signavio. SAP Signavio Process Insights allows the generation of standardized process performance indicator (PPI) analysis in SAP ERP and SAP S/4HANA, comparing the performance of business processes before and after the migration. This approach ensures that the expected value of the transformation is achieved while supporting ongoing process improvement within the SAP S/4HANA new environment.

> **Note**
>
> This task is only possible if SAP Signavio Process Insights and SAP Signavio were used throughout the implementation project.

Run the User Experience Business Benefits Workshop

It can be valuable to run a workshop to review the UX business benefits achieved with the implementation of the new solution. It's during this workshop that the UX/UI strategy and UX adoption roadmap can be adjusted based on the decisions made in the workshop. You can also review and discuss feedback provided, lessons learned, areas of improvement, and statistics on app usage and user behaviors. At the end of the workshop, you should review and adjust the UX adoption roadmap for future business roles as required.

Periodically Update Your SAP System and Initiate a New Innovation Cycle

Companies that want to implement significant business change should revisit the overall strategy developed at the start of the project. This may drive an upgrade focused on business change. Upgrades focused on technical goals should be planned in parallel because technical upgrades keep the SAP system current by implementing corrections and selected innovations.

An upgrade is managed as a project. The upgrade project, including tools, phases, and activities, is covered as a separate roadmap in the Roadmap Viewer. You can access it at *http://s-prs.co/v546315*. A first check of the upgrade readiness of SAP S/4HANA is usually performed before the new upgrade project starts. This will reveal what administration activities must be done before the upgrade can start. The maintenance planner can be used to plan the change event.

> **Service Components**
>
> SAP offers various service components to support the improvement and innovation cycle, including business transformation services, business process improvement for SAP solutions, and planning and execution of SAP maintenance.

7.4 Summary

This chapter comprehensively covered the new implementation of SAP S/4HANA Cloud Public Edition, SAP S/4HANA Cloud Private Edition, and SAP S/4HANA in your environment. We recommend all teams deploying SAP S/4HANA solutions to always check for the latest and most up-to-date guidance and content for their implementation in the SAP Activate Roadmap Viewer (implementation guidance) and SAP Signavio Process Navigator (preconfigured, ready-to-use business processes). While we made every effort to represent the current state of the solution as of the time of writing, the software continues to evolve, as do some processes for provisioning, configuration, extensibility, and testing. We've covered three versions of the SAP S/4HANA solution deployment to highlight some of the differences in capabilities that provide a higher level of standardization, in the case of SAP S/4HANA Cloud Public Edition, and some of the extended flexibility options offered by SAP S/4HANA Cloud Private Edition.

In the next chapter, we'll review how existing SAP ERP customers can transition to SAP S/4HANA Cloud Private Edition or SAP S/4HANA (on-premise). We'll discuss the system conversion and selective data transition journeys in detail.

Chapter 8

System Conversion and Selective Data Transition to SAP S/4HANA

This chapter covers the transition to SAP S/4HANA Cloud Private Edition (or on-premise) for organizations that want to move from an existing SAP ERP solution to an SAP S/4HANA-based solution.

This chapter covers the transition project to move to an SAP S/4HANA solution. It's relevant for organizations that want to move their old SAP ERP solution to SAP S/4HANA Cloud Private Edition. The content applies if you have your own data center or use a cloud hyperscaler with an infrastructure as a service (IaaS) contract. Note that the transition scenario for new implementations of SAP S/4HANA is covered in Chapter 7.

In this chapter, we'll provide an overview of the transition project, discover the new solution, and plan your journey. We'll then walk through the SAP Activate phases step-by-step for a system conversion. We'll conclude by looking at another deployment option: selective data transition. This chapter is focused on SAP S/4HANA Cloud Private Edition, but it can also apply to on-premise SAP S/4HANA.

Roadmap Viewer

For additional information, refer to the SAP Activate Methodology for RISE with SAP S/4HANA Cloud Private Edition for System Conversion roadmap. The purpose of the roadmap is to support transition projects and to help you with the following:

- Creating a foundation through transparency of all activities and tasks
- Making implementation and transition projects predictable
- Managing risk proactively

This chapter's content is structured to mirror the roadmap in the Roadmap Viewer. For more details, accelerators, and the latest links, refer to the Roadmap Viewer at *http://s-prs.co/v502733*.

8.1 Deployment Project Overview

Your transition to SAP S/4HANA involves many activities throughout the key SAP Activate phases introduced in Chapter 2. Figure 8.1 illustrates the activities within the workstreams and phases (figure is available for download at *www.sap-press.com/5966*).

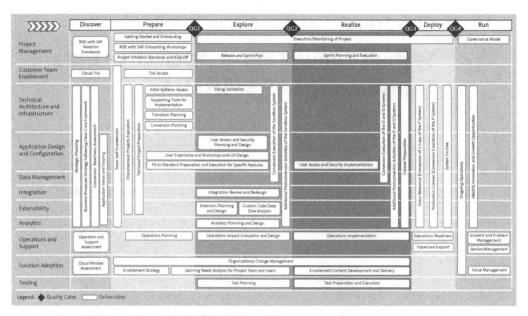

Figure 8.1 Transition to SAP S/4HANA Roadmap

> **Note**
>
> The deployment project overview in this section and the discover phase discussion in Section 8.2 will be very similar to our coverage in Chapter 7, Sections 7.3.1 and 7.3.2. For completeness, we've included this discussion for both new implementations and system conversions of SAP S/4HANA. If you've already read Chapter 7, Section 7.3, please skip to Section 8.3.

There are three implementation approaches for SAP S/4HANA, which we introduced in Chapter 1:

- **New implementation**
  Implement a new instance of SAP S/4HANA by moving from a non-SAP legacy system or an old SAP solution. Chapter 7 covers this in detail.

- **System conversion**
  Convert an existing SAP ERP solution to SAP S/4HANA, including business data, custom code, and configuration.

- **Selective data transition**
  Consolidate an existing SAP software landscape, or carve out selected entities or processes as part of a move to SAP S/4HANA.

For existing SAP customers, the choice of approach is driven by the following business and IT objectives:

- **New implementation**
  You want to maximize innovation, overhaul business processes, and adopt new cloud solutions. You may only want essential master and transactional data from the existing solution.

- **System conversion**
  You don't want to merge or split ERP instances, but you do want to keep your existing data and go live with a big bang. You may want to minimize change initially and then innovate selectively afterward.

- **Selective data transition**
  You want to merge or split existing ERP instances or have phased go-lives. You want to reuse only certain parts of the existing configuration, master data, and transaction data.

You may want to use a combination of the approaches in a phased program if you have multiple SAP ERP instances and other connected SAP solutions. For example, you could do a system conversion of one lead SAP ERP development system, use selective data transition to merge in another SAP ERP system, and do a new implementation for certain parts of the solution.

Let's walk through the SAP Activate phases in terms of these deployment options:

- **Discover phase**
  You should create an overall strategy for digital transformation by recognizing the benefits and value of SAP S/4HANA. This strategy should then be turned into a roadmap or implementation plan that includes a choice of transition approach. Finally, you should evaluate the impact on the technical architecture and IT infrastructure, which, together with the implementation strategy, serve as the foundation of the business case.

- **Prepare phase**
  After the business case has been approved, the project is officially initiated in the prepare phase. The first version of an implementation plan includes the findings from the discover phase and sets the stage for the entire project. In system conversion, the pre-projects defined are executed, and the conversion strategy is confirmed.

- **Explore phase**
  The explore phase defines and documents the design of the SAP S/4HANA solution. For a brownfield project, the first sandbox system is converted, and the custom code is analyzed in depth. By the end of the explore phase, all technical and functional aspects of the implementation project are fully planned, documented in detail, and ready to be executed.

- **Realize phase**
  In a system conversion, the landscape is sequentially converted to SAP S/4HANA, and the remaining custom code is adjusted. Application and analytics functions are

implemented, configured, integrated, and tested. In parallel, IT can adjust operational tools and procedures to prepare for SAP S/4HANA. Finally, end-user training, including project-specific training materials and team setup, is executed.

- **Deploy phase**
  Finalize the business processes and solution for production go-live. This includes final testing, rehearsing the cutover, and finalizing the IT infrastructure and operations. Continue delivering the end-user training sessions. Finally, the productive instance of SAP S/4HANA is set up or converted on the go-live weekend. IT operations are further optimized with the help of the project team and SAP. This phase is referred to as *hypercare* and occurs before operational responsibility is fully transferred to the production support team.

- **Run phase**
  Operations are further stabilized and optimized in the run phase. The new SAP system is continuously updated, making the latest innovations from SAP available to the business. Then, the innovation cycle starts again.

8.2   Discover Your Solution

The discover phase covers everything done leading up to the decision to proceed with an SAP S/4HANA project. On leaving the discover phase, an organization will have defined its digital transformation strategy and have an SAP S/4HANA roadmap or plan backed up by a business case. The company will have selected its delivery partners and delivery approach: new implementation, system conversion, or selective data transition. The activities in the discover phase are independent of the delivery approach. Some organizations may push some of the activities described in this section into the prepare phase.

This section begins with strategic planning, where you develop an innovation strategy and high-level roadmap based on SAP S/4HANA and intelligent technology innovations. You also make early decisions on security and analytics. Then, we'll move on to trial system provisioning and application value and scoping, where you assess the value and impact of SAP S/4HANA and check your readiness.

8.2.1   Strategic Planning

SAP's intelligent enterprise features the following key components:

- **Intelligent suite**
  This integrated suite retains the modularity and flexibility of independent solutions, such as SAP S/4HANA, SAP Customer Experience, SAP Ariba, and SAP SuccessFactors.

- **Digital platform**
  With SAP Business Technology Platform (SAP BTP), SAP can facilitate the collection, connection, and orchestration of data, as well as the integration and extension of processes within the intelligent suite.

- **Intelligent technologies**
  SAP BTP enables companies to leverage their data to detect patterns, predict outcomes, and suggest actions using advanced technologies such as machine learning, artificial intelligence (AI), and robotic process automation (RPA).

Strategic planning aims to define an innovation strategy and a high-level multiyear roadmap for these three key components. The roadmap should include SAP S/4HANA and analytics, but it isn't limited to them.

Start with an identification of strategic business and IT objectives, including current pain points. Cluster the objectives into benefit areas, and for each benefit area, identify and prioritize the SAP solution enablers. These solutions provide the target enterprise architecture.

SAP provides some tools that can assist in the strategy definition:

- **SAP Value Lifecycle Manager**
  This tool helps customers measure expected value, monitor actual value, identify critical gaps, and understand where to optimize value throughout their transformation journey.

- **Digital Discovery Assessment**
  This tool helps customers assess their requirements and determine the SAP S/4HANA Cloud solution to better suit their business needs.

- **SAP Signavio Process Insights, discovery edition**
  This tool provides tailored insights into the operational business process based on the current SAP ERP source system. For each line of business (LoB), it includes a list of correction recommendations to be carried out, ideally before the project, and innovation recommendations to be considered along with the project, such as intelligent technologies, SAP Fiori apps, and other SAP cloud solutions.

Introducing SAP S/4HANA into the solution landscape is an ideal opportunity to review and adjust the organization's analytics architecture. It's worth doing this early in the discover phase because there are many changes, new products, and new capabilities relevant to SAP S/4HANA. Refer to our discussion of analytics design in the explore phase in Chapter 7, Section 7.3.4 (new implementation), and Section 8.3.2 (system conversion) for more details.

Another area worth visiting early is your security strategy, which includes topics such as data protection regulations.

8.2.2   Trial System Provisioning

To support the value identification and the impact evaluation in the discover phase, it may be beneficial to have access to an SAP S/4HANA system. You can deploy a 30-day trial system within hours using an SAP cloud appliance via SAP Cloud Appliance Library (*http://cal.sap.com*). The system is hosted on Microsoft Azure, Amazon Web Services (AWS), or Google Cloud Platform. The provider will charge for hosting, and a user account at the cloud provider is required. SAP Cloud Appliance Library provides a detailed step-by-step guide for the appliance setup you'll follow during the installation and configuration. The SAP S/4HANA Fully-Activated Appliance template provides the SAP Best Practices processes ready to run as documented in SAP Signavio Process Navigator (refer to Chapter 4, Section 4.1). This allows the team to get hands-on access to the solution and investigate the new features in detail.

Starter System for SAP S/4HANA Cloud Private Edition

If you've already signed your RISE with SAP deal, depending on your contract, you may be entitled to receive a starter system for SAP S/4HANA Cloud Private Edition. This 90-day trial system is an SAP S/4HANA Fully-Activated Appliance template from SAP Cloud Appliance Library but is provisioned and managed by the SAP Enterprise Cloud Services team. You can leverage this alternative to explore the system and run your fit-to-standard workshops.

8.2.3   Application Value and Scoping

Application value and scoping contains the following tasks, which we'll walk through in this section:

- Discovering the value of SAP S/4HANA
- Identifying the value of SAP S/4HANA on existing business processes
- Defining the implementation strategy
- Creating a strategic roadmap and value case

Discover the Value of SAP S/4HANA

Value and benefits drive all projects and must be understood early. For that, the following resources can be used:

- Public web pages such as the SAP Help Portal, What's New Viewer, and SAP Fiori apps reference library
- SAP S/4HANA training, including SAP Learning Site training on integration and extensions with SAP BTP
- Learning rooms in SAP Learning Hub
- SAP S/4HANA trial system (refer to Section 8.2.2)

Identify the Value of SAP S/4HANA on Existing Business Processes

Strategic planning provides a set of SAP solutions and a target architecture. Business process experts from each LoB should now produce a more detailed solution mapping at a business scenario level. Business scenarios are a level above scope items.

Existing customers can request the SAP Signavio Process Insights, discovery edition report to identify issues and blockers as the first step in improving their business processes, understand where those issues are coming from, get tailor-made recommendations for correcting and improving the processes, and find out the most suitable innovations for their process transformation.

You must run a report in your production system and upload the files to an SAP website. Then, you can access the results from a dashboard. Figure 8.2 shows an example of SAP Signavio Process Insights, discovery edition.

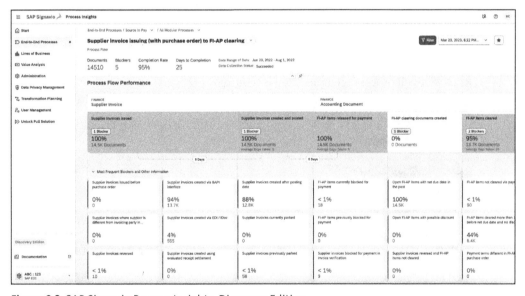

Figure 8.2 SAP Signavio Process Insights, Discovery Edition

Define the Implementation Strategy

The next step is to define your implementation strategy. Your strategy should address the following questions:

- What is the productive system strategy, that is, one single global instance or regional instances?
- Will the business go live in one big bang or with a multistage transition by country or business unit?
- What are the dependencies and the best sequence for the release plan?
- When will integration between SAP S/4HANA and other SAP and non-SAP solutions go live?

- What are the intermediate architectures in a staged approach?
- Will SAP S/4HANA Cloud Private Edition, an on-premise data center, or a cloud hyperscaler be used?
- Will a global template solution be adopted? And how will deviations from the template be managed?
- Will SAP Best Practices or enterprise management layer for SAP S/4HANA content be used, and how?
- What is the strategy for custom development? What development will occur in SAP S/4HANA and what will SAP BTP be used for?

Organizations moving to SAP S/4HANA from an existing SAP solution need to choose from among the three transition approaches described in Section 8.1 (new implementation, system conversion, or selective data transition). The team must decide whether to reuse the existing configuration or reengineer business processes with a new implementation.

The main aspects to consider are as follows, and their impact is shown in Figure 8.3:

- How much process reengineering is required?
- Is SAP S/4HANA a good opportunity to go back to the SAP standard, and should this be done based on a new implementation or incrementally after a technical conversion to SAP S/4HANA?

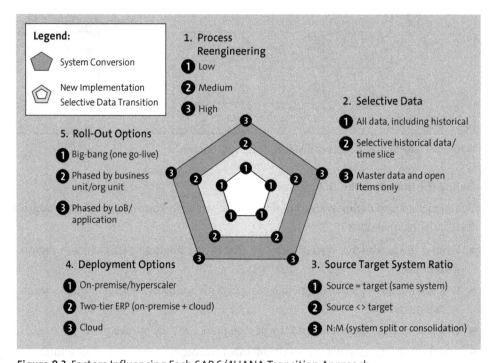

Figure 8.3 Factors Influencing Each SAP S/4HANA Transition Approach

- How much of the historical transaction data needs to be retained?
- Will SAP ERP instances be consolidated or split?
- Will SAP S/4HANA Cloud Private Edition or SAP S/4HANA be implemented?
- Must the roll-out be phased to reduce risk, or can each instance go live with a big-bang approach?

Create a Strategic Roadmap and Value Case

A value (or business) case for the project is built based on quantified costs and benefits. The following approach may be used:

1. Define discrete scope blocks required to reach the defined target architecture. Each block will have an organizational, functional, and technical element—for example, the SAP S/4HANA scope for Malaysia.
2. Agree on business transformation objectives, and map value drivers to the scope blocks.
3. Define and link key performance indicators (KPIs) to the value drivers. Use KPIs and value drivers to quantify benefits.
4. Identify cost drivers and quantify costs.
5. Compose a roadmap or timeline of scope blocks to implement the target solution landscape.
6. Assess the ability to execute the roadmap, considering organizational change, budget, technical capabilities, and previous project experience.
7. Determine the risks of transformation.
8. Summarize the alternative approaches and drive decision-making.

8.2.4   Conversion Readiness Assessment

For organizations moving from an existing SAP ERP solution, the impact of SAP S/4HANA is evaluated in SAP Readiness Check for SAP S/4HANA, as described in the next section.

SAP S/4HANA is the result of SAP rearchitecting the SAP ERP suite for modern business processes and the world's ever-increasing digitization. This means that parts of SAP ERP have been improved, simplified, replaced, removed, or categorized as nonstrategic. All of these changes are documented in the simplification list for SAP S/4HANA, which you can find on SAP Help Portal.

If you have an existing SAP ERP solution, understanding the simplification items that impact the system is a key activity in the discover phase. SAP Readiness Check for SAP S/4HANA is an automated self-service toolset used to evaluate the current state of your SAP ERP system in preparation for a transformation project. It identifies not only the relevant simplification items but also analyzes many other aspects, including custom code, add-ons, active business functions, recommended SAP Fiori apps, sizing, and so on. Some of them could be showstoppers or requirements that must be addressed before the project starts.

This tool also lists currently used features that are part of the compatibility scope. This means functionalities that were originally created for SAP ERP and usage rights in SAP S/4HANA expire at the end of 2025, with a few exceptions that will be available until 2030. Therefore, these features must be replaced as part of the system conversion.

SAP Readiness Check for SAP S/4HANA provides a dashboard (see Figure 8.4) that addresses these questions:

- Is functionality used that will need to be replaced or changed? Are the simplification items mandatory, conditional, or optional? Should the work be done in the current SAP ERP system or in the new SAP S/4HANA system?
- What features currently used are in the compatibility scope?

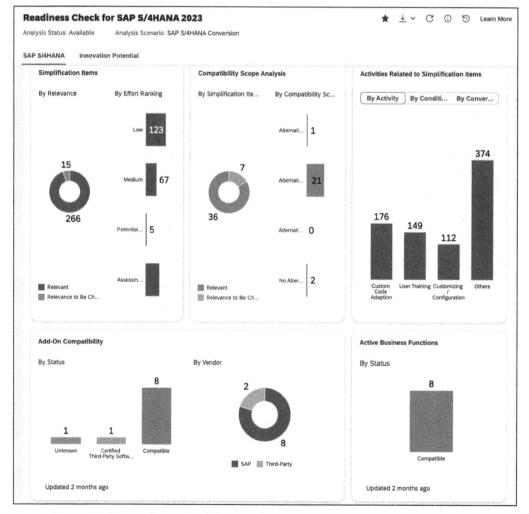

Figure 8.4 SAP Readiness Check for SAP S/4HANA Dashboard

- Are there incompatible add-ons (e.g., third-party add-ons) or incompatible business functions?
- Are there custom solutions or add-ons delivered by SAP Innovation Services that must be investigated by SAP before a project starts?
- Are all technical system requirements fulfilled (e.g., software levels, single stack system, Unicode)?
- How many custom objects are impacted by the data model and software changes?
- Which business-critical reports and transactions will be replaced or removed?
- What SAP Fiori apps are relevant for your current scope?
- What configuration needs to be adjusted?
- What is the estimated SAP S/4HANA system size? Are there options to reduce the size before the conversion?
- Are there live SAP Business Warehouse (SAP BW) extractors that will be impacted?
- What interfaces/integrations will be impacted?
- What issues must be solved before running customer-vendor integration?
- What inconsistencies does the financial data have, and how do we fix the errors?

Further Resources

If you need SAP support to learn how to interpret the results of SAP tools such as SAP Signavio Process Insights, discovery edition, and SAP Readiness Check for SAP S/4HANA, as well as to identify the value of SAP S/4HANA for your business, you can enroll in the SAP Customer Evolution Kit program (*https://events.sap.com/customer-evolution-kit/*). This program will help you understand how to leverage SAP solutions to transform your business into an intelligent, sustainable enterprise. The engagement provides you with a streamlined methodology to clearly define the incremental value potential of SAP S/4HANA and other cloud solutions to explore new capabilities, identify the preferable transition path, build a journey map, and create a benefit case.

8.3 System Conversion

In the system conversion approach, an existing SAP ERP solution is converted to SAP S/4HANA Cloud Private Edition or SAP S/4HANA (on-premise) and taken live. System conversion may be combined with a new implementation or selective data transition in a hybrid approach (Section 8.4). This might be relevant where multiple SAP ERP instances are to be merged. For example, one development instance might be converted to SAP S/4HANA to form a baseline, parts of another instance are added with selective data transition, and a third is added with a new implementation.

Figure 8.5 illustrates the sequence of some of the main activities in the system conversion approach.

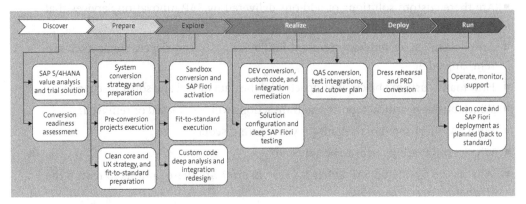

Figure 8.5 Overview of the System Conversion Approach

The SAP Readiness Check for SAP S/4HANA and identification of SAP S/4HANA simplification items are normally undertaken in the discover phase (refer to Section 8.2.3).

Some simplification item activities are best undertaken in the current SAP ERP system before the main project starts. Then, in the explore phase, the production system is copied to a sandbox system, and a complete conversion is performed. This is used to identify unknown issues and create the first version of the runbook to be used in the upcoming conversions. In the realize phase, new scope and simplification items are implemented, custom code is adjusted, and SAP Fiori is activated. Testing is done in a converted quality assurance system before a dress rehearsal and deploying to a conversion of the production system.

This section is organized by the SAP Activate phases: prepare, explore, realize, and deploy. In each of the following sections, we'll walk through the key deliverables for a system conversion. Note that some of the activities documented in the prepare phase may be executed earlier in the discover phase before the project starts.

8.3.1   Prepare Your Project

The prepare phase provides initial planning and preparation for the implementation project. In this section, we'll walk through the prepare phase for a system conversion project.

The purpose of the explore phase is to execute a full end-to-end conversion of the old SAP ERP system to SAP S/4HANA in a sandbox system. Much of the existing configuration will work unchanged. However, other tasks must be considered after the conversion, such as enabling SAP Fiori or resolving inconsistencies in the productive landscape before moving to the next conversion cycle.

After that, the project team performs initial testing to confirm that the conversion hasn't affected processes that weren't supposed to be impacted. This environment is also used to identify opportunities to improve the processes leveraging SAP Fiori.

As this first conversion cycle may reveal unknown issues/activities, the project plan must be evaluated and adjusted accordingly. Depending on the issues, additional sandbox iterations may be needed.

Other important activities during this phase include an initial analysis of the current custom code and impacted integrations.

Phase Overview

The purpose of the prepare phase is to kick off the initial planning and preparation for the project. The project starts, and the scope, approach, and plans are finalized. The project team resources are also assigned.

The key technical aspects of this phase include deciding the system conversion strategy, which means defining the system conversion approach, conversion cycles, and dual maintenance. Moreover, complete the technical project preparation, finish all preconversion projects defined during the discover phase, and prepare the fit-to-standard workshops for specific processes.

The main output documents of the prepare phase include the following:

- **Scope document**
  Defines the starting point, objectives, target solution, and transition approach
- **Project charter**
  Includes goals, scope, organization structure, roles and responsibilities, and governance
- **Project plan**
  Includes a work breakdown structure (WBS), schedule, and budget
- **System transition roadmap**
  Defines how systems will be used and the sequence of conversion
- **User experience (UX)/user interface (UI) strategy**
  Defines how SAP Fiori apps will be adopted and used
- **Technical architecture**
  Revised to show the impact of the move to SAP S/4HANA
- **Project standards**
  Includes requirements management, configuration, and custom code
- **Operational standards**
  Includes test management and change control

The rest of this section on the prepare phase is organized into topics that appear in the roadmaps.

Customer Team Self-Enablement

You must train the project team on the project scope, system conversion approach, simplification items, and related SAP topics such as SAP Cloud ALM, SAP Fiori, or SAP BTP. Enablement may include different elements of the SAP system, SAP Activate methodology, agile principles and techniques, and other supporting tools. It's important that self-enablement begins prior to the project kickoff to maximize the time for learning and to create efficiencies in later deliverables.

The SAP Learning site is a good resource for this. For instance, for system conversion, your team can take the "System Conversion to SAP S/4HANA" course and the "Gain Experience with a System Conversion to SAP S/4HANA" course (*https://learning.sap.com/*).

Project Initiation, Governance, and Plan

The project is formally initiated. Refer to Chapter 6 for project management topics, including project governance. Activities include the following:

- Hold handover meetings from the previous discover phase.
- Review the commercial contract and resolve any issues.
- Identify stakeholders, and confirm their requirements, expectations, and acceptance criteria.
- Create a project charter based on the scope document.
- Establish baselines for scope, schedule, cost, and quality.
- Create a project management plan.

The project management plan includes the following:

- WBS
- Schedule
- Budget
- Quality standards
- Communications
- Risks
- Procurement

Project Standards and Infrastructure

SAP S/4HANA projects need a robust means of executing and governing project work and deliverables. You should revise, approve, and communicate project and operational standards. The infrastructure, including computers, software and licenses, security, phones, meeting rooms, email, and remote access, should be ready for the project team.

Project standards include requirements management, process modeling, configuration and documentation, custom code, authorizations, agile processes, and tools used. Operational standards include test management, change control, incident management, and technical operations.

Project Kickoff and Onboarding

The kickoff provides the project team, key stakeholders, and anybody else involved in the project with the information they need. Everybody involved in the project should understand the project charter, which includes goals, objectives, scope, organization structure, decision-making process, roles and responsibilities, governance, regular meetings, project standards, infrastructure, schedule, and milestones.

Organizational Change Management Plan

All change management activities are planned in a roadmap, which ensures that all activities align with each other and the project plan. In the prepare phase, it's important for the project's success to set up the organizational change management (OCM) team to agree on its concept. See Chapter 10 for more information.

Technical Project Preparation

This refers to the preparation tasks that must occur in the source SAP ERP solution before the main SAP S/4HANA project starts. The critical tasks are as follows:

- **Check interoperability**
  Before starting your project, you must check the version interoperability among all SAP solutions that will interact with the target SAP S/4HANA system to evaluate whether the conversion to SAP S/4HANA affects any other systems already installed in the landscape. If additional preparatory tasks are identified, they must be considered in the project plan.

- **Define a clean core approach for extensibility**
  During this phase, it's relevant to identify opportunities to transition custom code to clean core options. This will help enhance stability, improve lifecycle management, reduce maintenance costs, and accelerate innovation. You can use the Cloud Readiness Check Variant from the ABAP test cockpit tool to assess whether your custom code complies with the ABAP for Cloud Development language and receive recommendations for updating to the ABAP Cloud coding language.

  In addition to the analysis, it must be defined when the code modifications will be executed, for instance, as part of a second project phase or along with custom code remediation for system conversion.

- **Define objects and tools for business data validation**
  During an SAP S/4HANA conversion, you must ensure that the source business data was migrated consistently and accurately as expected. Thus, you must evaluate and

identify the tools and objects that will be considered to guarantee data integrity. This will be achieved by comparing the defined objects before and after the SAP S/4HANA conversion.

- **Learn about the role of the technical team in an SAP S/4HANA Cloud Private Edition project**
  When moving to SAP S/4HANA Cloud Private Edition, the role of the technical resources is slightly different from that of the technical expert supporting an SAP ERP on-premise solution. Many of the traditional tasks, such as infrastructure management and technical execution of maintenance activities (e.g., upgrades), are handled by the SAP Enterprise Cloud Services team, either as part of the standard subscription or as additional on-demand services.

  Nevertheless, customer/partner technical resources still play a fundamental role because they still manage the system configuration, performance, user/roles, and integration with other solutions. Moreover, they handle new tasks such as SAP Fiori and SAP BTP administration. Additionally, the customer/partner technical resource acts as an advisor and is responsible for interacting with SAP when dealing with service requests, incidents, or other technical requirements.

Preconversion Projects Execution

Before the first conversion cycle, make sure to complete all the pre-conversion projects defined during the conversion readiness assessment as part of the discover phase, or as an outcome of any other task during discovery or prepare. Some examples of these pre-conversion projects are listed here:

- Perform data volume management
- Synchronization of customers/vendors into business partners (customer-vendor integration [CVI])
- Reconciliation of financial data
- Review add-on compatibility
- Clean up unused custom code
- Unicode conversion
- Full sandbox conversion

Transition Planning

In this deliverable, the team defines the scope and high-level execution plan for the SAP S/4HANA transition project. The key tasks are as follows:

- **Define the scope and the objectives of the transition**
  A scope document is produced that defines the following:
  - IT and business objectives: Success criteria for the transition project
  - Starting point: SAP solutions to be converted, replaced, or remain the same

- Target solution: New target releases, new scope, quick wins, and related SAP systems

- Transition approach: Preparation activities, infrastructure changes, landscape changes (e.g., system splits of consolidations), and maintenance windows

- **Define cutover strategy**
  Cutover planning starts with a system transition roadmap that documents the conversion sequence and the creation of temporary systems for production support.

- **Custom code initial analysis**
  As part of your SAP S/4HANA system conversion, a considerable amount of standard SAP-delivered code is expected to be optimized/remediated/replaced due to the multiple simplifications delivered in SAP S/4HANA. Although most of your custom code is expected to continue to work without any (or minimum) changes, SAP recommends running an initial analysis of custom code to correctly understand the "as is" and "to be" status of your custom code, including SAP clean core concepts to ensure future code compatibility.

  Running custom code analysis will help you identify how many custom objects are impacted by the conversion, document the results, and determine the roadmap for custom code objects. For that, you must follow these steps:

  - Learn how custom code adaption is managed and executed.
  - Familiarize yourself with the SAP clean core strategy.
  - Use SAP tools to identify unused code that can be retired.
  - Use SAP tools to identify custom ABAP source code that must and should be adjusted.
  - Based on SAP's clean core strategy, decide which code can be decoupled to cloud solutions, moved to newer development paradigms, or replaced by SAP standard features.
  - Prepare a rough-cut estimate of the work required, assuming the use of semiautomated quick fixes where possible.

- **Revise technical architecture and security**
  The existing technical architecture is revised to reflect the changes defined in the scope document. It may also include the switch to an SAP HANA database and the introduction of SAP Fiori frontend components.

  You also must document the new technical and functional security requirements related to SAP S/4HANA. These will include security role changes documented in simplification items and the introduction of SAP Fiori. Using SAP tools, a technical security self-check can be executed.

- **Perform data volume planning**
  Data volume management should be considered prior to a system conversion to reduce the amount of data to be converted (this impacts the duration and downtime of the cutover) and the amount of data in memory (this impacts the hardware costs).

The team must define the scope of cleanup work in the prepare phase, and the scope of data volume work to be done in the explore and realize phases.

- **Assess interfaces and integration**
  Check existing documentation and identify the external systems, applications, and business objects that must be integrated with SAP S/4HANA. These should be captured in an interface register (e.g., a Microsoft Excel spreadsheet). Then, assess the impact of moving from SAP ERP to SAP S/4HANA on interfaces. SAP has kept most of the official interfaces to and from SAP ERP stable in SAP S/4HANA. This isn't necessarily the case for nonofficial interfaces (e.g., the use of Open Database Connectivity [ODBC] on the database level).

System Conversion Strategy

In this phase, you must define the technical system conversion approach. Based on that, the number of conversion cycles and the dual maintenance strategy. The key tasks are as follows:

- **Define the technical system conversion approach**
  SAP offers different conversion approaches and downtime optimization techniques for different technical requirements (e.g., in-place conversion or system move to a different infrastructure) and technical downtime reduction needs. You must evaluate those options and select the most suitable one in an early project stage because they may directly influence the conversion project plan activities, timelines, effort, and costs.

  Figure 8.6 shows the different approaches that can be considered depending on factors such as the source system, database, and business downtime expected.

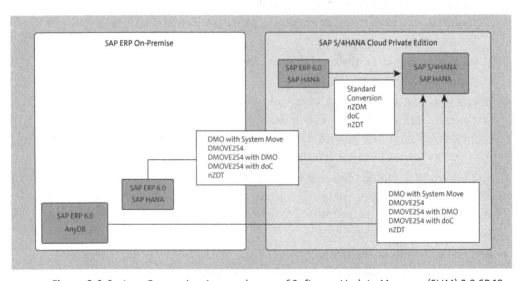

Figure 8.6 System Conversion Approaches as of Software Update Manager (SUM) 2.0 SP 18

- **Define conversion cycles**

  An efficient conversion process tailored to your environment is essential to ensure a smooth transition to SAP S/4HANA. Thus, the number and sequence of the conversion cycles must be defined and considered in the conversion project plan.

  It's recommended to consider a minimum of five conversions, including sandbox, development, quality, dry run, and production. However, additional iterations may be needed depending on the conversion approach and issues encountered.

  Figure 8.7 shows an example of a six-cycle conversion project listing the main tasks by cycle.

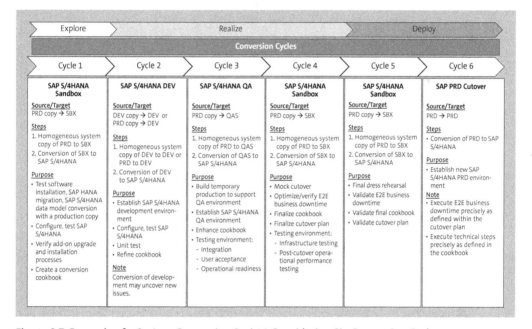

Figure 8.7 Example of a System Conversion Project Considering Six Conversion Cycles

- **Define the need of dual maintenance**

  During the conversion project, the business may require changes to the production environment, prior to the final conversion, to continue their operations. A temporary additional landscape may be necessary to support the production system changes while your landscape is converted to SAP S/4HANA. At the same time, the changes mentioned previously must be synched to the already-converted systems. Therefore, it's imperative to evaluate the need for a dual maintenance process and establish the procedures, tools, roles, and resources to execute it. Figure 8.8 exemplifies how a dual maintenance process can be managed.

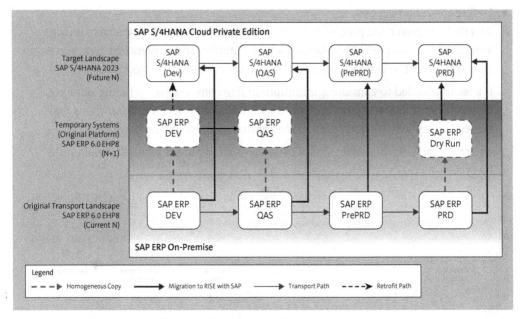

Figure 8.8 Example of the Dual Maintenance Process

User Experience Strategy and Workshops

The UX strategy and workshops will help you manage and grow your UX adoption over time. UX, by nature, spans many functional and technical areas, so the aim is to encourage effective collaboration between business and technical teams. You can use the recommendations provided during and after your move to SAP S/4HANA whenever you want to grow your UX adoption, adding value to the business.

The content covers SAP S/4HANA and related RISE with SAP extensions in SAP BTP. It includes the User Experience Strategy Workshop and Template to agree on guiding principles and governance; workshop templates to establish the business value, scope the future, and envision the future to explore high-value apps and features and update your now/next/later UX adoption roadmap; and guides for how to select apps, evaluate fit, review extension options, design launchpad layouts, and communicate changes to users.

Fit-to-Standard Preparation for Specific Features

You must familiarize yourself with the fit-to-standard framework and prepare for the fit-to-standard workshops. In the context of a system conversion, the fit-to-standard workshops are a direct outcome of the Conversion Readiness Assessment – Conduct Functional Review Workshop in the discover phase. The simplification items analyzed in those workshops are typically categorized into three main groups:

- Group 1: Need functional/technical remediation
- Group 2: Need fit-to-standard workshops
- Group 3: Simplification item nonrelevant

This activity focuses on the list of simplification items in Group 2: Need fit-to-standard workshops. Some examples are as follows:

- SAP ERP features not available in SAP S/4HANA: Settlement management implementation to replace SD rebates processing.
- SAP ERP features available in SAP S/4HANA but not in compatibility scope: Implement EWM to replace WM.

Additionally, the fit-to-standard workshops must include functionalities you don't currently use, which will be implemented along with your system conversion project.

The fit-to-standard analysis and design in the prepare and explore phases consists of the following activities, as listed in Figure 8.9 (available for download at *www.sap-press.com/5966*):

❶ Fit-to-standard workshop preparation
The workshops are organized by LoB areas (e.g., finance) and end-to-end solution (e.g., accounting and financial close). In a system conversion, the workshops focus on where the solution changes. There is an initial fit-to-standard workshop, which is followed by a design workshop where required. The project manager will organize the workshop schedule and check that the boundaries and integration points between the workshops are clear. A standard set of workshop input and output template documents are defined.

❷ Fit-to-standard system preparation
Another important aspect is selecting the system to carry out this activity. Several options must be discussed, such as the starter system for SAP S/4HANA Cloud Private Edition, SAP S/4HANA fully-activated appliance, or a previously converted sandbox system (if available). You must be sure to complete any pending activity, such as enabling SAP Fiori, to leave the environment ready for the workshops.

Steps ❸ through ❻ are relevant to the explore phase and will be covered in the next section.

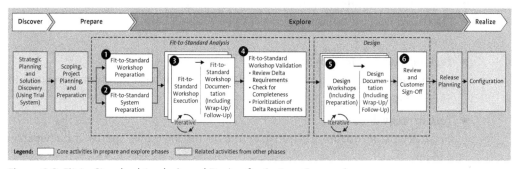

Figure 8.9 Fit-to-Standard Analysis and Design for System Conversion

8.3.2   Explore the Solution

In the explore phase, a sandbox system is created based on a recent copy of the productive system. This system is used to perform the first conversion cycle and initial testing.

In this section, we'll walk through the explore phase for a system conversion project.

Phase Overview

The purpose of the explore phase is to execute a full end-to-end conversion of the old SAP ERP system to SAP S/4HANA in a sandbox system. Much of the existing configuration will work unchanged. However, other tasks must be considered after the conversion, such as enabling SAP Fiori, or resolving inconsistencies in the productive landscape before moving to the next conversion cycle.

After that, the project team performs initial testing to confirm that the conversion hasn't affected processes that weren't supposed to be impacted. This environment is also used to identify opportunities to improve the processes leveraging SAP Fiori.

As this first conversion cycle may reveal unknown issues/activities, the project plan must be evaluated and adjusted accordingly. Depending on the issues, additional sandbox iterations may be needed.

Other important activities during this phase include a deep dive analysis of the current custom code and a review of the integrations. This analysis not only focuses on listing the impacted custom code and interfaces but also on defining how and when to move to the options aligned with the clean core principles.

The main output documents of the explore phase include the following:

- **Detailed conversion cookbook**
  Covers the end-to-end migration and conversion process and is specific to the company environment.
- **List of impacted custom code objects**
  Prioritized list of custom objects and code that need to be adapted because of the system conversion.
- **List of impacted integrations**
  Prioritized list of interfaces that need to be adapted because of the system conversion.
- **Technical design document**
  Updates existing documentation to reflect the architecture and infrastructure for SAP S/4HANA.
- **Test strategy document**
  Updates existing documentation to define the testing scope, approach, deliverables, and tools.
- **Fit-to-standard workshops for specific features signed-off**
  Formal approval of the design documents, configuration requirements, and functional specifications.

This section on the explore phase is organized into topics that appear in the roadmap.

System Conversion Execution of the Sandbox System

In system conversion, an SAP S/4HANA sandbox system is created at the start of this phase by copying the existing SAP ERP production system to a sandbox and doing an end-to-end SAP S/4HANA migration and conversion. This activity's deliverables are a successfully converted sandbox system and a check of whether the process is feasible for the business, including an initial business downtime estimation. The realize phase can't be kicked off until the sandbox conversion is successful.

The sandbox conversion activities in sequence are as follows:

- **Technical preconversion activities**
  After the sandbox system creation as a copy of the production system, guarantee that the source system technical requirements for the selected system conversion approach are met. The technical preparation activities mentioned in the conversion guides and related notes must be executed. This is also the moment to execute the maintenance planner tool to validate the conversion path and other compatibility requirements (e.g., add-ons and business functions) and to prepare the target landscape for the conversion process (e.g., validate access credentials, storage availability, availability of necessary tools and media files). If not done before in the production system, update the SAP Notes relevant for the simplification item checks.

  Document every step from the activities to build an initial version of the runbook that must be refined on the next conversion cycles.

- **Functional preconversion activities**
  Some SAP S/4HANA simplification items must be addressed by implementation work in the existing SAP ERP solution before the technical conversion. If these steps haven't been done as part of the preprojects listed previously, they must be completed in the sandbox as part of the functional preconversion activities. The errors in the simplification item check tool must be solved. Otherwise, the SUM will fail to execute.

  Another important aspect of this activity is to execute and document the results of the reports defined as part of the business data validation strategy.

- **System conversion execution**
  Perform the technical steps for the SAP S/4HANA conversion using the SUM tool according to the selected conversion approach. After the conversion and some technical post-activities are done, fill out the information required by the SAP Enterprise Cloud Services team and hand over the system so they can proceed with their post-processing activities. When those tasks are completed, the system will be delivered back, so you can continue with the required post-conversion and project activities.

- **Functional postconversion activities**
  The "Conversion Guide for SAP S/4HANA" details mandatory postprocessing activities. In the finance area, these consist of updates to configuration, data migration of financial accounting, and additional activities after the data migration.

  When the sandbox is converted, you must execute the reports defined as part of the business data validation strategy one more time. After that, the results should be compared with those obtained in the source system. If you find differences, you must identify the root cause and confirm that it's possible to continue with the system conversion.

Additional Postconversion Activities of the Sandbox System

After the technical conversion has been successfully completed, some additional activities must be performed to guarantee the project's readiness for the next phase.

The additional activities are as follows:

- **Enable SAP Fiori**

  In the converted sandbox system, SAP Fiori won't be active. Consequently, you must run the activation steps of SAP Fiori in this system. It means running the setup activities for activating SAP Fiori prerequisite frameworks (e.g., enterprise search and embedded analytics) and running the SAP Fiori rapid activation procedure to ensure proper activation of SAP Fiori apps along with their dependencies (such dependencies occur at the service, role, or app navigation level).

  It's important for your business that you start exploring additional features, apps, and intelligent experiences during this phase. Doing so will help you get the most out of the SAP S/4HANA system. Additionally, running a proper system exploration via SAP Fiori will help you define the initial versions of your SAP security roles, including the new SAP Fiori security artifacts.

- **Run initial testing**

  In the converted sandbox system, you must validate that the conversion hasn't affected processes that weren't supposed to be impacted. This means running end-to-end processes following the steps you currently follow in SAP ERP.

  Additionally, you must search for opportunities to improve your processes, running the same scenarios but considering SAP Fiori to cover some steps. Testing SAP Fiori with your business data will show you the value of SAP S/4HANA. Thus, this task will help you reevaluate your UX strategy.

- **Resolve inconsistencies in the productive landscape**

  The issues identified before and after the conversion must be remediated in the productive landscape. For master data, this could be directly addressed in the productive system. Corrections that need other remediations, such as the application of SAP Notes or configuration, must be solved in the development system and transported through the productive landscape.

  Completing this task before moving to the next conversion cycle is important because it will reduce the effort required to convert the following systems.

Fit-to-Standard Workshops for Specific Features

The fit-to-standard analysis and design aim to approve changes to scope and design before proceeding to the realize phase. As explained before, these workshops directly result from the discover phase's Conversion Readiness Assessment. The Functional Review Workshop task focused on identifying the critical elements for simplification that should be addressed during the fit-to-standard workshops. It includes SAP ERP features not available in SAP S/4HANA and SAP ERP features available in SAP S/4HANA but in the Compatibility scope that will be replaced along with the system conversion. It may also include functionalities not currently used but chosen for implementation as new features within the same project.

The fit-to-standard analysis and design in the explore phase consists of the following activities, as listed in Figure 8.10 (available for download at *www.sap-press.com/5966*):

❸ Fit-to-standard workshops execution and documentation

Through this workshop, you ensure that the solution aligns with the business requirements and processes outlined in the prepare phase. The workshops enable business process experts to understand how the solution can support their needs by exploring functionality and identifying delta requirements. Any configuration decisions and additional requirements identified during these workshops are carefully documented and added to the backlog or integration and interface list.

After that, you must ensure that all the decisions and requirements from the fit-to-standard workshops are fully documented. By conducting a careful analysis, any missing documentation must be found and added to ensure that the project is completed. Additionally, technical experts will document all change requirements meticulously, providing detailed and refined information.

Following are the different types of delta requirements:

– Configuration requirements: Most of the configuration from the old SAP ERP solution will remain unchanged. Requirements to change the configuration may relate to simplification items, business processes, UIs, and SAP-to-SAP integration scenarios.

– Authorizations: Specify changes to how authorizations are used.

– Master data: Specify changes in how the solution will be used.

– Workflows, reports, interfaces, data conversions, enhancements and forms (WRICEF): Existing WRICEFs may need to be changed, or new WRICEFs may be required. Enhancements include changes to the UI and missing functionality. Data conversions aren't necessary unless the project has a new solution scope.

– Organization structure requirements: Identify any changes to the centrally managed enterprise/organization structure.

❹ Fit-to-standard workshop validation

The solution architects and project managers work closely to ensure that all requirements are accurately captured and classified. This will help determine the best approach for addressing each requirement and ultimately guide the decision-making process for adopting new solutions or retaining older ones. By challenging each requirement and evaluating its necessity and feasibility, the team can better prioritize and plan for the design and implementation of the solution.

❺ **Design workshops and documentation**

Then, you must run a design workshop and document the configuration and WRICEFs. The focus of the documentation should be on the delta requirements that have been identified and prioritized during the fit-to-standard analysis. This information is crucial for creating accurate estimates for the realize phase, as the functional specifications may undergo revision or finalization during this stage.

❻ **Review and customer sign-off**

Finally, the project architects thoroughly review the end-to-end design and make necessary adjustments. These final steps are important to ensure all stakeholders agree that the requirements are complete and that the proposed solutions are understood and accepted. Any issues identified during this stage are documented and classified. The backlog is then updated to represent the backlog for the realize phase. The project can confidently move into the next phase by obtaining formal approval and incorporating all necessary documentation.

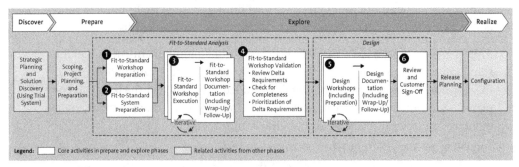

Figure 8.10 Fit-to-Standard Analysis and Design for System Conversion

Figure 8.11 shows an example of a backlog of delta requirement that is an output of the Design Workshops and Documentation activity.

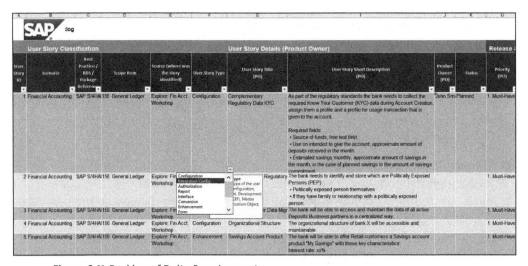

Figure 8.11 Backlog of Delta Requirements

Custom Code Deep-Dive Analysis

When running a system conversion to SAP S/4HANA, you're required to analyze your custom code to determine "must-change," "should-change," or "nice-to-change" code. This process should ideally start during the prepare phase (as discussed in Section 8.3.1, under "Transition Planning").

Custom code deep-dive analysis starts by using SAP tools to assess custom code such as the following:

- Usage Monitor (Transaction SUSG) to collect custom code usage statistics
- Custom Code Migration app to identify unused code and create technical deletion packages
- Transaction SUM, to automatically remove unused code during the conversion process
- ABAP test cockpit (Transaction ATC) to check for SAP S/4HANA simplifications in custom code and identify automated remediation options derived from such simplifications
- Transactions SPDD and SPAU to adjust the dictionary objects and custom code

Based on the results provided by the SAP tools, a prioritized list of custom code objects needs to be defined with a focus on modifications due to upgrades, database changes, new data models and processes, and business criticality or urgency.

Using this list, code design decisions need to be made to determine whether to update the code to fit new SAP features, redesign completely following clean core approaches, or maintain the code as is, considering the technical debt associated with each option and the benefits or impacts of such decisions.

The result of such analysis is then a well-rounded roadmap of how custom code should be managed in your implementation project, a clear picture of the efforts needed for custom code remediation, a good understanding of where you'll leverage new features from the newer SAP S/4HANA stack or features, and a starting point for your business to comprehend where the introduction of cloud-like approaches can optimize business operations and ease custom code maintenance.

> **Further Resources**
>
> The "Custom Code Migration Guide for SAP S/4HANA" on the SAP Help Portal (*https://help.sap.com/docs/*) provides more details. The guide is updated for each release of SAP S/4HANA software.

Integration Review and Redesign

In this phase, you must assess current integrations in your SAP ERP system to identify those affected by the upcoming system conversion. It means developing a strategic plan to mitigate impacts through remediation or replacing outdated integrations with new SAP technologies. The following tasks must be considered:

- **Current integrations impact analysis**
  Analyzing inbound and outbound integrations using SAP Readiness Check 2.0 and ABAP test cockpit to classify interfaces by technology, frequency, and direction. Identify impacted interfaces, and, if needed, adjust business processes for SAP S/4HANA compatibility.

- **Define target integration**
  Develop a strategy to replace outdated technologies with SAP Integration Suite or SAP Process Orchestration, focusing on transitioning from old methods, such as IDocs, to current ones, such as APIs or OData services, for improved functionality and maintenance. Although this initially targets integrations affected by the system conversion, it also represents an opportunity to make a roadmap and define when to move all the integrations to the new technologies.

- **Apply clean core principles for integration**
  The clean core principles for integration focus on implementing standard SAP integration methods (OData, SOAP, events), leveraging orchestration between SAP S/4HANA and external platforms, and ensuring updated security. A key element is prioritizing standard integrations and only considering custom interfaces when there is no other option. These custom interfaces must be appropriately documented and planned to be replaced when a standard feature is released.

In addition, emphasize a clear integration strategy using the SAP Integration Solution Advisory Methodology and maintain "keep clean" practices for any new integration scenario. Moreover, you must revise and renew the architecture and design for all systems' interfaces, including integrations with other SAP cloud solutions.

Analytics Planning and Design

The project should evaluate the strategic and business value of the new analytics solutions available for SAP S/4HANA. The explore phase should build on the work done during the discover and prepare phases to complete an analytics architecture, landscape, and design. The following SAP solutions may be considered:

- **SAP S/4HANA embedded analytics**
  This includes LoB-specific prebuilt solutions and comprehensive real-time reports based on SAP Fiori and virtual data model in SAP S/4HANA.

- **SAP Datasphere**
  Cloud-based SAP's data warehousing solution for SAP and non-SAP data.

- **SAP BW and SAP BW/4HANA**
  SAP's on-premise data warehousing solutions for SAP and non-SAP data.

- **SAP HANA/SAP HANA Cloud**
  SAP's in-memory database which could work as a data warehouse.

- **SAP Analytics Cloud**
  Cloud-based analytics solution that can operate across SAP S/4HANA, SAP cloud solutions, and SAP data warehouse solutions (SAP Datasphere, SAP BW/4HANA, SAP HANA) and non-SAP solutions. Planning and predictive solutions are also included in SAP Analytics Cloud as well as analytics solutions.

- **SAP BusinessObjects Business Intelligence**
  On-premise alternative to SAP Analytics Cloud.

Analytics design covers business intelligence (e.g., reports, tables, charts, graphs, and geographic analysis), predictive analytics, and planning requirements.

If SAP BW or SAP BW/4HANA are part of the old landscape, the business benefits of moving some use cases to SAP S/4HANA embedded analytics should be assessed. Some operational aggregates in SAP BW will no longer be required, and extracts and reports can be decommissioned.

When moving to SAP S/4HANA, the impact on the standard and custom SAP BW data sources and SAP BW extractors used in SAP ERP must be analyzed. Many standard extractors will continue to work with SAP S/4HANA, but some aren't on the allowlist. The design must address how this will be resolved.

Analytics workshops are conducted for LoB-specific processes and requirements. Existing and new business requirements are analyzed and designed according to a fit-to-standard process. The design should document which analytics use cases remain unchanged, updated, or replaced.

Analytics design guidelines are produced that define the following:

- When and how to use the different analytics solutions
- When to use the different connection types between the solutions
- Data modeling guidelines
- User access and security concepts

User Access and Security Planning and Design

The purpose of user access and security planning and design is to consider the impact of the SAP S/4HANA conversion on security and user management. It covers roles, authorizations, user maintenance, and duties segregation.

In general, SAP Fiori apps will replace old transactions for two main reasons: the transaction is deprecated, or new SAP Fiori apps are adopted to improve business processes. Users running those SAP Fiori apps via the SAP Fiori launchpad need access to all launchpad content (apps, UIs, features), related authorizations, and the default layout. This is controlled through business roles. Thus, an update of the authorization concept is required, leading to changes in the backend Transaction PFCG roles and authorizations.

There are also other topics that are recommended but may not be required or prioritized by all companies, such as the following:

- Planning the implementation of single sign-on (SSO)
- Defining processes for SAP auditing, logging, and monitoring
- RFC connections and gateway security
- Custom code security

In SAP S/4HANA Cloud Private Edition, security topics related to infrastructure, network, operating system, and database are managed by the SAP Enterprise Cloud Services team, which is governed by standardized processes. In addition, some services will be provided by SAP or a hyperscaler operating your environment as part of the subscription services. Refer to SAP Trust Center for details on security, cloud operations, data center details, and agreements.

Further Resources

You can access the SAP Trust Center at *www.sap.com/about/trust-center.html*.

Test Planning

The purpose of this critical deliverable is two-fold: (1) to manage the quality of the solution and to minimize issues during and after the go-live, and (2) to streamline the multiple system conversions that will be done during the project. A risk-based approach should be used to define test planning. The test strategy document covers the following topics:

- **Project testing**
  Use project testing objectives and assumptions, focusing on new or changed areas of the solution.

- **Test scope**
  Define the scope using regression tests from the old SAP ERP solution and the new design in SAP S/4HANA. The result is a revised list of test cases and scripts focusing on the business-critical and frequently used business processes.

- **Types of testing**
  Select test cycles, including regression testing, unit testing, business process (string) testing, integration testing, performance testing, and user acceptance testing (UAT).

- **Testing approach**
  Define how the different test types relate to each other (e.g., a successful unit test is a prerequisite for doing a string test).

- **Testing deliverables**
  Describe the test processes per project phase, test environment, and test data.

- **Testing tools**
  Determine which tools will be used to perform different tests.

- **Test automation**
  Decide whether automation will be used, and evaluate and select the appropriate tools.

- **Defect management**
  Describe how defects will be documented.

- **Roles and responsibilities**
  Define the test lead and the responsibilities of individual project team members.

Detailed test planning should be done to define the timing, duration, criteria, dependencies, and resources for each of the test cycles.

For better control and efficiency, you should consider using SAP Cloud ALM as a central platform for test management a test automation tool.

End-User Learning and Change Impact Analysis

During the explore phase, the training requirements for key users and end users are analyzed and documented. A learning needs analysis identifies the skill levels, knowledge gaps, and training requirements. Based on the analysis, a training strategy and plan is designed. See Chapter 10 for more information.

A change impact analysis is done after the fit-to-standard workshops for specific features are complete. An OCM expert will usually join the project team. They will gather the organizational and technical changes identified in the workshops and refine these by comparing the business processes and solutions as is and to be. See Chapter 10 for more information.

Operations Impact Evaluation

An operations impact evaluation is undertaken. The current IT support framework will change with the introduction of a new solution such as SAP S/4HANA. This task is especially important if you're moving from SAP ERP on-premise to SAP S/4HANA Cloud Private Edition because some activities currently handled by your IT team will now be performed by SAP.

The deliverables from the explore phase, such as the technical design document and design documents, are important sources of information on what and how IT should support the new solution after it goes live.

The aim is to identify new operational activities, modifications to existing activities, and activities that can be retired. All the relevant support areas need to be analyzed: roles and skills, processes/procedures, operations documentation, and enabling support tools. Then, a roadmap is defined that includes the key activities for IT to fill the gaps and prepare the future IT support framework. This will consist of establishing resources, setting up tools, documenting procedures, knowledge transfer, operations cutover, and retiring parts of the old framework.

8.3.3 Realize Your Requirements

In the realize phase, simplification item changes and new requirements are implemented based on the design. The existing custom code is adjusted, and the integrations are set up. A conversion of the development and quality systems are completed and used for testing. We'll walk through the realize phase for a system conversion project in this section.

Phase Overview

During the realize phase, a series of cycles are used to incrementally test, extend, and validate the system environment based on the business scenarios and process requirements defined during the explore phase. The existing custom code and interfaces impacted are adjusted. A new or changed scope is implemented using configuration, extensions, integration, and analytics.

The main outputs of the realize phase in a system conversion include the following:

- The custom code is adjusted and tested.
- Updates are made to configuration and configuration documentation.
- Technical specifications, test cases, and custom code are created for new WRICEFs.
- Infrastructure, integration, security, and operational procedures are updated and tested.
- Development and quality assurance environments are migrated and converted to SAP S/4HANA.
- Data aging, data archiving, and data deletion are ready.
- Tests, including unit, integration and UAT, are complete based on a test plan, test cases, and test scripts.
- Support operations framework and procedures are ready.
- The cutover process is planned.

The realize phase must be planned in detail, with dependencies coming together in the testing plan. Carefully defined entry and exit criteria must be transparent to the whole team to ensure that the workstreams remain coordinated. The plan must be frequently updated to reflect progress and changes in scope and timescales.

The LoB teams (e.g., finance or manufacturing) from the explore phase continue to operate through the realize phase.

System Conversion of the Development System

The development system needs to be set up at the start of the realize phase. After that, you must execute all the functional and technical activities required to complete the development system's conversion following the defined technical system conversion approach. The system conversion execution of the sandbox system includes the same tasks listed in Section 8.3.2:

- Technical preconversion activities
- Functional preconversion activities
- System conversion execution
- Functional postconversion activities

Furthermore, this is the moment to consider the previously defined dual maintenance strategy (if any) to support the business changes needed to be transported through the productive landscape during the system conversion project.

Ideally, there will be a soft freeze to minimize production support changes during the project. Take care to properly retrofit changes performed in the production support landscape to the new development system to ensure the latest business requirements are accounted for.

Additional Post-Conversion Activities of the Development System

Once the technical conversion of the development system is completed, several functional and technical tasks must be performed to prepare the system for testing. The additional activities are as follows:

- **Enable SAP Fiori in the development system**
  In this task, your team will set up SAP Fiori apps for your project. The starting point of this activity is completing the fit-to-standard workshops and ensuring you have a list of the SAP Fiori apps you pretend to use in your production system.

  Based on these inputs, you can run system activation as described in the Enable SAP Fiori task as part of the explore phase. With the foundation setting in place, custom business roles and SAP Fiori launchpad spaces and pages need to be created to ensure users validate and test the app navigation experience in the SAP Fiori launchpad. Depending on the validation/test results, refinement of SAP Fiori spaces, pages, and roles might be needed.

- **Custom code remediation**
  In this phase, you must execute the remediation of custom code based on a prioritized list of impacted objects, considering those that might be candidates to move to clean core and predefining approaches for remediation or redesign (with a clean core perspective) of impacted custom code objects.

  The procedure includes performing functional adaptations and optimizations (e.g., performance tuning, code pushdown, simplification, and renewing UX) and potentially implementing a clean core approach.

  When needed, consider retrofitting changes in your production landscape to the "new" development system.

- **Implementation of adjustments and redesign of integrations**

  The task involves implementing necessary adjustments to impacted interfaces and introducing new integrations to replace obsolete ones identified in the Integration Review and Redesign tasks as part of the explore phase.

  This includes modifying existing custom code, implementing new standard integrations, and creating wrappers for custom scenarios where standard solutions are unavailable. Extensive testing is conducted to ensure all integrations function correctly before deployment to the quality and productive systems. Training and documentation updates are also carried out to familiarize users with the changes and ensure the smooth operation of business processes linked to the integrations.

- **Solution configuration of additional features**

  The configuration activities aim to systematically build and test a unified business and system environment through a series of iterative cycles, using the defined and agreed-upon business scenarios and process requirements specified in the explore phase. The configuration process will be split into two-week sprints, with each sprint concentrating on system setup, documentation, and unit testing based on the backlog previously agreed. All configuration settings and modifications will be documented, and any customizing transports will be collected.

- **Product enhancements of additional features**

  In this task, you'll review the options to enhance the solution with new features and fix identified gaps. SAP recommends solving those gaps or innovation opportunities through extensibility capabilities in SAP BTP.

  All extensions/enhancements/innovations should follow the three-tier extensibility model:

  - **Tier 1: For cloud development**

    Using ABAP Cloud coding language and the RESTful ABAP application programming model.

  - **Tier 2: For custom API wrappers**

    Leveraging preexisting legacy coding and enabling such objects for temporary consumption in ABAP Cloud coding language until a proper tier 1 replacement is available.

  - **Tier 3: For legacy development**

    In cases where the ABAP Cloud model can't fulfill business requirements, keeping in mind the possibility of moving these objects to tier 1 or tier 2 in future opportunities.

  For all generated objects, the development process must consider the following tasks before moving to the next phase:

  - Design of technical/functional specifications

  - Creation of development objects

  - Documentation and unit testing

- **Testing and performance review of the remediated custom code**
  You must ensure your custom code was properly fixed by testing all the code adjustments run in the Custom Code Remediation task. To successfully execute this task, your developer team must be familiar with tools such as ABAP test cockpit for iterative code quality assessment, ABAP SQL Monitor for performance quality assessment, and advanced coding techniques for additional improvements not easily identified by automated tools. Keep in mind that the steps in this task should be run in the customer client, avoiding the need for client 000 access.

  Before testing, it's recommended to enable runtime checks via the Runtime Check Monitor (Transaction SRTCM) to catch issues such as empty tables or missing "ORDER BY" clauses and fix any detected problems. Additionally, enabling the ABAP SQL Monitor to gather performance data and resolve any issues after testing is a good practice. Preferably, this should be executed in the system used for the UAT, but a productive system may also need to be considered for final tuning.

Analytics Configuration

The analytics solutions are changed and implemented based on the design and guidelines documented in the explore phase. The scope may cover analytics, predictive analytics, and planning requirements. The design will typically be based on embedded analytics in SAP S/4HANA and SAP Analytics Cloud to define the UX for analytics and planning. SAP Datasphere, SAP HANA Cloud, or SAP BW/4HANA provide a data warehouse for structured and unstructured data from SAP on-premise, SAP cloud, and third-party solutions. Parts of the existing solution (e.g., SAP BW, SAP BW/4HANA, and SAP BusinessObjects Business Intelligence) may need to be changed or superseded altogether.

Examples of the activities to be undertaken in SAP S/4HANA include the following:

- Perform the technical setup of SAP S/4HANA core data services (CDS) views and SAP S/4HANA embedded analytical apps based on CDS views.
- Customize prebuilt SAP S/4HANA embedded analytics.
- Create custom CDS views and SAP Fiori apps with key user tools for custom SAP S/4HANA embedded analytics.

Examples of the activities to be undertaken in SAP Analytics Cloud include the following:

- Configure general settings such as the import functionality, database connector, and cloud connector.
- Import and enable prebuilt content for SAP Analytics Cloud.
- Configure the underlying SAP Analytics Cloud data models, planning models, and predictive models.

- Set up live data connections between SAP Analytics Cloud and SAP S/4HANA, SAP Datasphere, HANA Cloud, and SAP BW/4HANA to enable analytics without persistent data in the cloud.

- Import data into the data models, and perform data preparation for analytics with persistent data in the cloud.

- Configure SAP Analytics Cloud stories for reports, tables, charts, graphs, and geographic analysis.

Further Resources

Refer to the SAP Analytics Cloud, SAP Datasphere, and SAP BW/4HANA SAP Activate roadmaps in the Roadmap Viewer for more details.

Testing

The test strategy and plan produced in the explore phase are implemented during testing. Figure 8.12 provides an overview of the testing approach, illustrating the systems used and the sequence of test cycles. For more information on testing, refer to Chapter 5, Section 5.6.

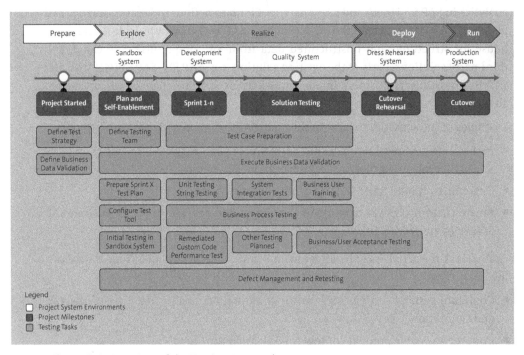

Figure 8.12 Overview of the Testing Approach

Test cases and scripts are created and updated. Testing tools are checked, and the testing teams are trained. A combination of manual and automated testing is used. The scope and source of the required test data are agreed upon. The details of the approval procedure for UAT are finalized, and the test plan is turned into a detailed activity schedule.

During all test executions, defects are formally logged for traceability, fixes are applied and transported, and the process is retested until the issue is resolved. Errors can hide in process variants, so ensure that test scripts mix these well (e.g., a foreign currency order with batch management). All the different workstreams come together in the test process.

During realize, you must consider at least the following tests:

- **Unit tests**
  Unit testing is executed in the development system to stress out each process that potentially was impacted during the conversion. This will avoid finding errors such as dumps, missing configuration, or losing crucial business information only in a later project stage.

- **Integration tests**
  Integration testing is performed in the quality system to verify the proper execution of the entire application, including all WRICEFs, integration between SAP solutions, and interfaces to external applications. It's conducted in the quality assurance system and approved after all tests have passed.

- **Regression tests**
  During integration tests, many fixes are transported into the quality assurance system. Later fixes may break processes that had already passed their tests. To mitigate risk, regression tests are executed alongside the cutover rehearsals. The scope and approach are similar to integration testing. The quality assurance system is monitored as if it were production, as this will indicate end-state operations. For example, errors in the system log, which testers may not notice, could cause instability in the production system.

- **User acceptance tests (UATs)**
  UAT provides formal approval from actual users that the solution works as specified and meets the business requirements. The scope and approach are similar to integration testing.

System Conversion Execution of the Quality System

Before integration starts, the quality assurance system needs to be set up. Then, you must execute all the functional and technical activities required to complete the quality system conversion following the defined technical system conversion approach.

The outcomes from the previous conversion cycle(s) should be considered to optimize the conversion procedure and update the runbook document.

Operations Implementation

Changes to the support operations are implemented following the operations road-map defined in the explore phase. The following areas are covered:

- **Detailed operations**
  The changes to the support framework are implemented. This is often managed through detailed IT change requests.

- **Roles and responsibilities**
  Changes to resources and their roles and responsibilities are implemented.

- **Support processes and procedures**
  Changed IT support processes are documented and tested. This includes incident management, problem management, access management, change management, test management, job management, and system recovery.

- **Operations support tools**
  Tools are adjusted or newly set up.

- **Operations documentation**
  An operations handbook is produced, and all documentation is updated and stored in a central repository.

- **Knowledge transfer**
  The IT support resources prepare to run the new solution. Knowledge transfer is done through a combination of activities, including formal training, self-study, shadowing, and on-the-job training.

Cutover Preparation

The conversion of the production system requires a clearly defined cutover plan and will typically be controlled by a cutover manager. The cutover plan documents the end-to-end activities of the cutover, from the steps leading up to the event through to the end of the conversion. Tasks commonly found in a cutover plan include the following:

- Prerequisite steps for the production conversion
- Ramp-down activities (e.g., batch jobs and interfaces)
- Pre-conversion validation reports
- End user lockout
- Technical migration and business data conversion
- Post-conversion changes (e.g., transports and parameter changes)
- Technical post-conversion validation reports that check for business data consistency
- Business-driven system validation and comparison of the pre- and post-conversion reports
- Go/no-go decision

- Ramp-up activities
- Users unlock

The cutover plan doesn't detail the technical conversion to the level that is captured in the runbook. However, it's common to highlight specific tasks from the runbook within the cutover plan to ensure the process is on schedule. The cutover plan should also include a contingency plan to revert the changes in the event there is a no-go decision.

Enablement: Content Development and Delivery

Training material is created for end users. SAP recommends the SAP Enable Now tool (see Chapter 10, Section 10.1.4) for creating the training material, supporting translations, and developing e-learning. It can be used for SAP and non-SAP applications. Possible training documents include the following:

- **Course concept**
  Goal and structure of each training event
- **Training manual**
  Instructions for the trainers
- **Work instructions**
  Step-by-step explanations of each process and transaction
- **Exercises**
  Instructions and data for hands-on use of the solution
- **Simulations**
  Recorded walkthroughs of processes and transactions with guidance
- **E-learning**
  Self-learning for less complex topics
- **Web-based training**
  Alternative to classroom training that provides communication with the trainer via video, chat, and phone

Finally, the trainings are delivered according to the schedule and material previously created. This activity will help ensure that end users are prepared for the new solution.

Organizational Change Management Alignment

Organizational change impacts were identified in the explore phase and helped drive OCM activities. During the realize phase, these are reassessed with a focus on changes in the project scope, design, and assumptions. In particular, the alignment of OCM with the test and cutover processes is checked. See Chapter 10 for more information.

8.3.4   Deploy Your Solution

During the deploy phase, the solution, supporting tools, and processes are prepared for the SAP S/4HANA production go-live. In this section, we'll walk through the tasks in the deploy phase for a system conversion deployment project.

Phase Overview

Final go-live rehearsals are executed. This phase includes a go or no-go decision and ensures that the organization is ready to run in the converted environment.

The primary activities of the deploy phase in a system conversion project include the following:

- Organizational change readiness
- Finalize testing
- Operation and infrastructure readiness
- System conversion execution of the dress rehearsal system
- System conversion execution of the production system (cutover)
- System go-live and hypercare support
- Handover to support organization

Organizational Change Readiness

In the deploy phase, the OCM activities ensure that all relevant stakeholders are ready to go live. Monitoring OCM activities, including the communication plan, is crucial to ensure end-user adoption. See Chapter 10 for more information.

Finalize Testing

The testing activities initiated in the realize phase are finalized. The following testing activities must be closed and confirmed before cutover to production:

- Integration validation
- Infrastructure and security tests
- Performance tests

Operation and Infrastructure Readiness

The technical infrastructure must be ready. Ensure the operations and support organization is prepared to run the converted solution. The activity provides a defined support approach for monitoring and measuring the day-to-day support operations. The following topics need to be covered:

- Roles and responsibilities
- Support processes, governance, and procedures

- Operations support tools and documentation
- Knowledge transfer

System Conversion Execution of the Dress Rehearsal System

Before the actual production cutover, a dress rehearsal system needs to be set up. It must be created from the most up-to-date copy of the production system. After that, execute all the functional and technical activities following the cutover plan. If needed, update the runbook document and/or the cutover plan accordingly.

The rehearsal is intended to confirm the ownership, sequence, and duration of the conversion activities. Considering the cutover schedule is likely to be complex with many dependencies and owners from IT and business, communication plays a crucial role in ensuring a successful conversion.

The result of this conversion cycle is a key input for the go/no-go decision. If everything goes as expected, the production system should continue in a freeze period, so no changes are expected until the conversion go-live date.

System Conversion Execution of the Production System (Cutover)

At this point, the organizational, business, functional, technical, and system aspects of the project are ready for production. To complete the conversion of the production system, you must execute all the functional and technical activities needed per the cutover plan tasks refined and validated in previous conversion cycles. The detailed conversion procedure must be precisely executed as documented in the runbook document.

The main activities in production conversion are as follows:

- Request a restore point of the production system prior to the final conversion process.
- Execute the conversion of the production system following the runbook updated during the rehearsal.
- Capture any variances to the plan along with the decision-makers who approved the change.
- The cutover managers should proactively notify task owners of upcoming tasks to ensure their availability.
- Regularly communicate the project status to stakeholders.
- Test and validate the system.
- Complete all required documentation for regulatory purposes.
- Obtain system sign-off.

System Go-Live and Hypercare Support

The system go-live is the final milestone of a successful SAP S/4HANA conversion project. The solution is now running live in the production environment, and the hypercare period follows to ensure seamless adoption of the new system.

Hypercare is the period that comes directly after the go-live. Its purpose is to support questions and issues that might arise. During this period, predefined checks will be executed daily to closely monitor the adoption of the solution. It's essential to verify how the system behaves and improve system performance if needed.

The main activities in the hypercare period should include the following:

- Monitor resource consumption
- Analyze workload
- Perform system health check
- Perform sizing verification
- Monitor security

Handover to Support Organization

After the hypercare phase ends, it's crucial to fully enable the regular support organization to safely and securely operate the new SAP system. The following topics are covered:

- Finalizing system documentation
- Completing operational procedures as part of the operations handbook
- Checking the customer support organization
- Resolving and closing open issues
- Performing the handover from the project team to operations

8.3.5 Run Your Solution

The final phase of the SAP Activate methodology is the run phase. After the successful completion of the system conversion project, companies and project teams further optimize the operability of the new SAP S/4HANA solution. In this open-ended phase, the operations team must ensure that the system is running as intended. This phase also supports the continuous adoption of the solution by new users.

The main topics in the run phase include the following:

- Ongoing system operations
- Continuous OCM
- Continuous end-user learning activities
- Continuous improvement and innovation
- System upgrade

> **System Conversion versus New Implementation**
>
> With the conversion project completed, the run phase is the same for both a new implementation and a system conversion. The key deliverables that we'll discuss in this section don't differ from Chapter 7, Section 7.2.7 and Section 7.3.7.

Ongoing System Operations

It's essential to perform routine actions to ensure that the system is running as expected, for example, to maintain the systems in a functioning and operating condition, guaranteeing systems availability and required performance levels.

In SAP S/4HANA Cloud Private Edition, SAP executes standard, optional and additional monitoring services related to the technical platform per the roles and responsibilities service catalogue. For example, monitoring the database for technical issues and backup scheduling. SAP also triggers event notifications to customers/partners in case of any events related to the technical platform (e.g., infrastructure, database) and offers additional technical services that could be requested on demand. However, you're still responsible for operating the new solution, business processes, users, data, and configuration tailored to your needs to ensure effective and efficient operations.

Continuous Organizational Change Management

The purpose of this activity is to continue the OCM tasks after your go-live to ensure continuous solution adoption by relevant stakeholder groups. The change management team regularly measures end-user adoption and plans and implements OCM activities by leveraging lessons learned. See Chapter 10 for more information.

Continuous End-User Learning Activities

In the run phase, it's good practice to monitor the users after the training has been completed and regularly update the training materials to ensure they stay relevant. Processes must be in place to enable new users and upskill current users. Based on many years of experience with global software deployments, the SAP Training and Adoption organization has developed a continuous learning framework with clearly defined steps and training activities.

> **Further Resources**
>
> For more information on implementing the continuous learning framework from SAP, visit *https://learning.sap.com*.

Continuous Improvement and Innovation

To support the business and end users, IT maintenance processes must be set in place to improve the solution continuously. This requires periodic updates by implementing feature packs and support packs to bring the latest software updates from SAP into the solution. A planning cycle involving business and IT should identify innovations to be deployed.

SAP S/4HANA provides visibility into planned innovations in the SAP S/4HANA product roadmap, available at *www.sap.com/roadmaps*. The roadmap describes how the product capabilities are intended to progress over time. It provides information on recent innovations, planned innovations, and a summary of the product's future direction.

System Upgrade

Technical upgrades keep the SAP system current by implementing corrections and improvements. Companies that want to implement significant business change should revisit the overall strategy developed when moving to SAP S/4HANA. This may also drive an upgrade focused on business change.

An upgrade is managed as a project. A first check of the upgrade readiness of SAP S/4HANA is usually performed before the new upgrade project starts. SAP tools, such as SAP Readiness Check for SAP S/4HANA and the maintenance planner, play an important role here. These checks will reveal what administration activities must be done before the upgrade can start.

The upgrade process, including tools, phases, and activities, is covered as a separate roadmap in the SAP Activate Roadmap Viewer.

8.4   Selective Data Transition

Selective data transition is an alternative to the new implementation or system conversion approach and is relevant for companies moving from an existing SAP ERP solution to SAP S/4HANA. We recommend reading Chapter 7 on new implementations and Section 8.3 in this chapter on system conversions first because this section only describes the differences between those approaches and this one. As its name implies, this approach involves transferring data from one or more existing SAP ERP solutions to a new SAP S/4HANA solution.

Complex scenarios, such as consolidating multiple systems into a single SAP S/4HANA, require the involvement of SAP Services and Support and its specialized tools and services. Less complex business requirements indicate the use of SAP Business Transformation Center, which comes without additional subscriptions. In addition, some partners have their own tools and services. Note that this section focuses on selective data transition using SAP tools.

The data selectively transferred can include the following:

- ABAP repository of objects and developments
- Configuration (Customizing) data
- Master data
- Transaction data (historical closed items and open items)

There are two common approaches for the target system creation within selective data transition: shell conversion and mix and match. In *shell conversion*, a shell copy of a production system is made without master data and transaction data and is converted to SAP S/4HANA. In *mix and match*, a new SAP S/4HANA install is created, and then elements of the configuration and ABAP repository are transported or manually transferred. Both scenarios require data migration to follow, including master data, balances, and open items. A comparison of the approaches is shown in Table 8.1.

Criteria	System Conversion	Selective Data Transition		New Implementation
		Shell Conversion	Mix and Match	
Process reengineering	Simplification items adopted during project; innovations usually done after conversion	Organization structure changes; possible process changes in some areas	Extensive changes in several areas, including organization structure changes	Fundamental process redesign, including organizational restructuring
Data cleansing	Optional archiving prior to the project; data inconsistencies to be fixed	Selection of active data; cleansing on the fly possible	Selection of active data; cleansing on the fly possible	New data construction—fully clean for new processes
Data transformation	Only mandatory changes adopted	Structural and field mappings possible	Structural and field mappings possible	New data construction—fully clean for new processes
Phased go-live	Full system conversion, no phased approach possible	Fully supported (per company code, ideally)	Fully supported (per company code, ideally)	Fully supported (per company code, ideally)

Table 8.1 Comparison of Implementation Approaches

Criteria	System Conversion	Selective Data Transition		New Implementation
		Shell Conversion	Mix and Match	
Historical data	● Full transactional history converted	● For example, per time slice, functional area, or organizational unit	● For example, per time slice, functional area, or organizational unit	○ Only master data and open items
System split or consolidation	○	● For either split or consolidation scenarios	● For either split or consolidation scenarios	● For either split or consolidation scenarios

Table 8.1 Comparison of Implementation Approaches (Cont.)

The data is moved using Data Management and Landscape Transformation (DMLT) software and related services. For more than 10 years, DMLT tools and services have provided well-established solutions for organizational changes, acquisitions, divestitures, or harmonization of SAP landscapes. The software provides highly automated processes that move large amounts of data between SAP instances quickly. Similar software and services are provided by third-party vendors but fall outside of SAP's support arrangements.

Next to DMLT and third-party vendors, the SAP Business Transformation Center offers standard SAP tooling for selective data transition approaches.

Selective data transition should be considered when organizations need to do the following:

- Go live in phases (e.g., by country or business unit)
- Reduce the risk of a big-bang go-live
- Split or merge existing SAP ERP instances
- Leave behind large amounts of old data—for example, to reduce the duration of system conversions and cutovers
- Reduce reimplementation effort by reusing elements of the solution while redesigning others

The split and consolidation of SAP ERP instances is a large topic and won't be covered in detail in this book. Instead, this section focuses on how selective data transition can be used to phase go-lives and accelerate projects. This may be required in SAP ERP solutions with large data volumes or with many users in multiple countries.

The starting point is to create a parallel SAP S/4HANA sandbox or development system. A new clean install of SAP S/4HANA can be used (mix-and-match approach). Alternatively, you can use DMLT tools to create a shell copy of an existing SAP ERP system (shell conversion). The shell contains the ABAP repository and configuration data without master data or transactional data. A system conversion is done to turn this into an SAP S/4HANA instance. The conversion process is simpler and faster without the master data and transactional data, and certain simplification items can be more easily implemented without business data.

DMLT or SAP Business Transformation Center are used for selective data migration of master and transactional data. If no historical transactions are required and only open transaction items are needed, the SAP S/4HANA migration cockpit (direct transfer scenario) may be the best option. DMLT allows a time slice of historical transactional data to be migrated.

Let's consider an example project scenario using shell conversion. This assumes a two-stage project. The first stage is a technical transition followed by a second stage to implement business transformation innovations.

Let's walk through the phases of the first (technical) stage, which is led by a technical team:

- **Prepare phase**
  In the prepare phase of a selective data transition using shell conversion, you perform the following activities:
  - Engage the DMLT team or a partner to advise you on the approach. This may lead to preparation work in the existing SAP ERP system.
  - Analyze DMLT source system functionality.
  - Analyze the existing landscape using SAP Readiness Check for SAP S/4HANA, SAP Business Transformation Center, and SAP Signavio Process Insights for SAP S/4HANA transformation.
  - Execute the SAP S/4HANA preparation activities in the existing SAP ERP solution; for example, archive data to reduce the data footprint and remove unwanted custom code and configuration. In addition, perform CVI to make the business partner the lead object.

- **Explore phase**
  In the explore phase of selective data transition using shell conversion, you perform the following activities:
  - Create a new SAP S/4HANA sandbox system. Create a shell copy using a recent copy of a production SAP ERP instance.
  - Perform an SAP S/4HANA system conversion of the shell system.
  - Make configuration changes required to execute the planned workshops.
  - Conduct fit-to-standard analysis and design, focusing on mandatory SAP S/4HANA simplification items.

- **Realize phase**
  In the realize phase of selective data transition using shell conversion, you perform the following activities:
  - Set up data migration tools and environment.
  - Create a new SAP S/4HANA development system using a shell copy of the sandbox system.
  - Set up a production support track for ongoing maintenance of the live solution.
  - Make configuration changes required for simplification items.
  - Adapt ABAP code for SAP S/4HANA.
  - Implement any changes required for integration and analytics solutions.
  - Execute multiple data migration test cycles using the selected tools.
  - Set up a quality assurance system and production system with a copy of the SAP S/4HANA development shell without master data and transaction data.
  - Test selective migration of master data and transaction data in the quality assurance system.
  - Set up SAP Information Lifecycle Management (SAP ILM) and a retention warehouse to move old data into a low-cost infrastructure.
  - Run testing previously planned, such as integration and UAT.

- **Deploy phase**
  In the deploy phase of selective data transition using shell conversion, you perform the following activities:
  - Rehearse the cutover.
  - Migrate master data and, if required, historical transactional data into the production system.
  - Cut over to the production system.
  - Migrate open transaction item data and master data that have changed since the last migration cycle.

After the technical transition stage is complete, a second project stage can be kicked off to implement business transformation innovations (e.g., adoption of SAP Fiori apps). The second stage is led by the business.

This approach is flexible and can be adjusted depending on your organization's requirements, for example:

- The first go-live could include the business transformation scope in addition to the technical conversion.
- The SAP S/4HANA preparation activities could be done in the sandbox rather than the existing SAP ERP solution.
- In the explore phase, you might jump straight to a development system instead of using a sandbox. (sandbox is still required later to do the test cycles of data migration).

- During the technical transition, configuration and ABAP code adaption could be done in the sandbox system and then could be moved to the development system. This can reduce the duration of the production support track.

- Multiple sequential go-lives could occur, with master and transaction data migrated as required (e.g., by country and company code).

- You can selectively transfer business data and master data from multiple source SAP ERP systems. Compatibility of the ABAP repository and configuration is a prerequisite for working with multiple source systems. Harmonization work is required in the prepare phase.

- You can use the SAP S/4HANA migration cockpit only for selective data migration (excluding historic transactions), which can provide a more application-focused approach when compared to the technical migration involved in DMLT services. Less harmonization work may be required.

- The old production system may be decommissioned to a dormant status to access historic data and archived data.

The following DMLT scenarios may be relevant in selective data transition. Scenarios 1 and 2 are used in our previous example.

- **Create shell system**
  Create a copy of a system without master and transaction data, which includes configuration (Customizing) and the ABAP repository.

- **Company code transfer**
  Transfer data related to one company code from a source SAP ERP 6.0 system to a single client in the target SAP S/4HANA system. The scope can include master data and transaction data only or configuration (Customizing) with or without master data. This can include custom tables. Because data is merged at a client level, organization structure mapping may be required.

- **Client transfer**
  Transfer configuration (Customizing), master data, and transaction data from a source system and client to a target SAP S/4HANA system. Where there is more than one source system, a client merge is possible.

- **System merge**
  Combine master data and transaction data from two or more clients from different SAP ERP source systems into a target SAP ERP system. Configuration data isn't included. This is suitable for single and multiclient production systems.

In scenarios 2 to 4 with multiple source SAP ERP systems, the ABAP repository and configuration of the source systems must be compatible. These approaches require manual harmonization work in the source systems and target development system. Analysis tools that compare the source systems can identify the harmonization work required. The transformation can include data model conversion, Unicode conversion, and database changes to SAP HANA in one step. The project can take several months. Multiple test cycles are required in a dedicated sandbox system. SAP uses the test cycles to finalize configuration and generate programs to do the transfer.

Service Components

SAP offers the Data Migration Execution service to deliver DMLT solutions for SAP S/4HANA.

8.5   Summary

This chapter described how to transition from an existing SAP ERP solution to a new SAP S/4HANA Cloud Private Edition solution following the SAP Activate methodology through the discover, prepare, explore, realize, and deploy phases. We've seen that three approaches can be used:

- New implementation, for existing SAP customers that want to start again and reimplement (covered in Chapter 7)
- System conversion, for existing SAP customers that want to convert to SAP S/4HANA with a big-bang go-live
- Selective data transition, for existing SAP customers that want to convert to SAP S/4HANA in phases or split or merge their existing SAP ERP instances

Now that we've covered both cloud and on-premise deployment, we're left with a final option: hybrid. We'll discuss hybrid deployments in the next chapter, including the available business scenarios that organizations can use to maximize their existing technology investment while transitioning their business processes to the cloud.

Chapter 9
Deploying Hybrid System Landscapes

In this chapter, we'll look into how SAP S/4HANA Cloud can be used to run two-tier deployment landscapes, examine various recommended deployment types, and deep dive into a few important end-to-end business processes available with such two-tier deployments of SAP S/4HANA Cloud.

Organizations across the globe are in the midst of a major transformation. Digital technologies are forcing them to reimagine their business models, business processes, and how they can create more value for their customers. As a result, many are opening sales offices in new regions and growing existing sales and distribution operations, acquiring new companies to either consolidate their position in existing market segments or expand into new areas, and setting up new joint ventures and centralized shared services for certain back-office functions (e.g., HR, procurement, and travel management) to obtain efficiencies of scale and synergies from acquisitions.

From an IT perspective, the best approach for these subsidiaries is to standardize via an integrated business solution that meets their functional requirements and is less expensive to deploy, easier to change, and simpler to manage. Yet these systems should also satisfy corporate requirements, which typically include regulatory transparency, visibility into operational metrics, use of centralized business processes, and key data roll-up.

To ensure efficiency, simplify processes, and drive innovations, organizations are moving away from complex processes and integrations and from the practice of maintaining disparate IT landscapes from different IT vendors. As shown in Figure 9.1, a complex IT landscape with complex integration doesn't help organizations standardize. In general, companies expect predelivered integrations from a software provider not only to accelerate the adoption journey but also to make it easier to maintain a system throughout its lifecycle.

In this setup, data and processes are streaming through many different applications, vendors, and locations. Such high IT complexity results in misaligned business processes, inconsistent data models, and uncommon user experiences, which increases operational costs and reduces operational efficiency. Another result is limited governance and compliance across subsidiaries, which increases the risk for organizations.

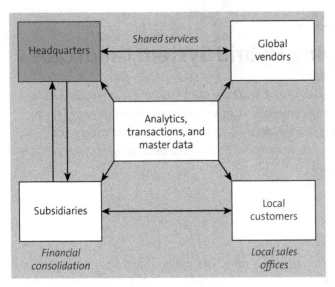

Figure 9.1 Complex IT Landscape

The answer to all these issues is a two-tier ERP setup. In this chapter, we'll explain this two-tier ERP setup and master data, walk through key deployment scenarios, explore integration accelerators, and discuss analytics options.

9.1 What Is a Two-Tier ERP Setup?

The hybrid ERP setup is shown in Figure 9.2; in the SAP world, this is known as a *two-tier ERP setup*. In this scenario, the complex processes continue to run in their proven on-premise applications, shown in the top half of Figure 9.2; meanwhile, simplified and standard processes shift into a cloud-based ERP system, shown in the bottom half of Figure 9.2, for business functions or subsidiaries.

Customers who choose the two-tier ERP journey might also choose to integrate with the existing systems subjected to their business needs. Organizational readiness for integration and an end-to-end process view play critical roles in deciding the level of integration, as shown in Figure 9.3. SAP's tools and resources are designed to support varying levels of integrations from loosely coupled to tightly coupled. For example, as demonstrated, a loosely connected scenario could be achieving a financial consolidation by integrating data from various entities into a centralized system for accurate reporting and analysis. Tightly integration often involves two ERP systems working together to complete a business process, such as when a regional sales office needs to acquire goods and services from headquarters. It makes sense in cases where the second-tier operations share data, such as customer records or product master records. As a prerequisite, it's required to align the master data and foundational data such as organizational structures to simplify the process of aggregating the data as mid-path.

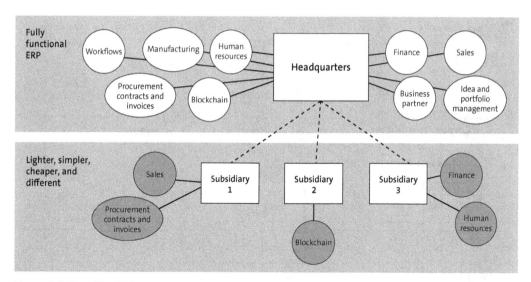

Figure 9.2 Two-Tier ERP

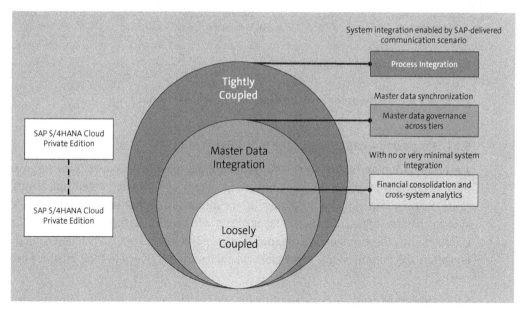

Figure 9.3 Two-Tier ERP with Varying Levels of Integration

A two-tier ERP setup can be deployed in the following ways, as shown in Figure 9.4:

- Headquarters and subsidiaries
- Central services
- Ecosystem

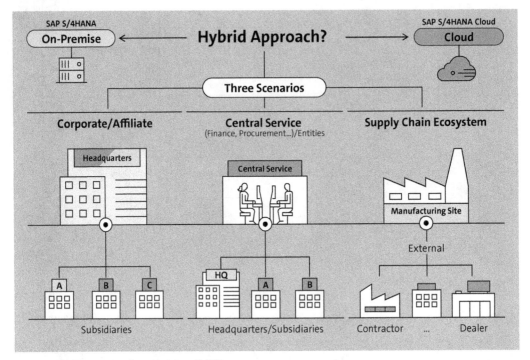

Figure 9.4 Deployment Possibilities

We'll look into these options in detail in subsequent sections.

9.1.1   Corporate Headquarters and Subsidiary Setup

The headquarters and subsidiaries setup is most applicable when organizations are growing inorganically by expanding into different geographies through mergers and acquisitions; in this scenario, if subsidiaries aren't integrated with the headquarters' ERP system, then the organization can't reap true growth benefits in this competitive world. Consequently, these expanding organizations need to integrate all subsidiaries rapidly and affordably to achieve real-time global visibility and efficiency in their business processes.

SAP's software as a service (SaaS) solution for two-tier ERP deployment provides standard integration scenarios between headquarters and subsidiaries through SAP S/4HANA Cloud for the subsidiaries and on-premise SAP S/4HANA, SAP S/4HANA Cloud Private Edition, or a non-SAP system for headquarters. This hybrid ERP model between a headquarters and its subsidiaries helps organizations safeguard their investments while equipping global subsidiaries with more agile and flexible cloud-based software.

Subsidiaries require a degree of agility to meet their markets' needs quickly and innovate at their own pace; consequently, they need their own ERP systems to control their own destinies. Having a cloud ERP system means subsidiaries don't have to worry about infrastructure, hardware, and IT management.

9.1.2   Central Services Setup

To remain competitive in the current market, organizations need to start reimagining and reexamining their business processes. Part of this procedure is to identify which business processes are complex and which can run on a shared setup. Organizations can think of different business models in which certain business functions can be seen as profit centers or shared services, which brings us to the topic of line of business (LoB) functions in the cloud.

Imagine that a global organization has multiple ERP systems in different geographical locations, or even a single instance of an ERP system in which multicounty operations are carried out. For example, a global organization in the automobile industry might have operations in multiple countries with different business models and different business strategies to meet the customer requirements. If you take procurement as a central service, the local entity will follow its own terms and conditions, but headquarters will have standard guidelines that might not be followed at local subsidiaries. Such an organization would have a complex architecture and complex business processes.

The example of moving the finance functions to the cloud for a global organization applies to nonglobal/local organizations as well. For example, IT services are normally central business functions that serve the entire organization and its LoBs. Organizations can reimagine their business functions to see IT as a profit center as well or outsource IT by taking it to the cloud without losing control.

9.1.3   Supply Chain Ecosystem

An *ecosystem* is a closed environment in which entities are both interdependent and connected. A classic example is the case of the automotive dealers for an automobile company.

Some organizations don't require a headquarters and subsidiaries setup but still want to adopt cloud systems and have a two-tier ERP setup.

Let's again take the example of an organization in the automobile industry, in which the organization deals with multiple small vendors or dealers; each vendor and dealer operates its own disconnected systems. In this situation, the organization doesn't currently have visibility across its entire supply chain. Some companies aspire to build networks of their small vendors or dealers by encouraging everyone to implement a cloud solution that can be easily connected to the organization's ERP system. Here, the dealers that sell the organization's finished goods will place orders with the organization, and the organization will issue the finished goods to the dealers.

Similarly, an organization could connect its ERP system to vendors running a cloud solution, which would result in collaborative manufacturing with its suppliers. An organization can also track the stages of manufacturing, as well as the inventory of raw materials available from its suppliers. Such visibility at the suppliers' end gives organizations the power to have accurate materials planning, thus reducing the cost of carrying inventory; now they can know how much raw materials to order for the day's production.

Further Resources

For more on this topic, refer to the white paper titled "Two-Tier ERP Deployment for SAP S/4HANA Cloud: A Practical Guide for Senior Leadership," available at *http://s-prs.co/v546319.*

9.2   Move Options

In this section, we look at move options that will help customers transition from an existing landscape to a two-tier ERP landscape. Essentially, this boils down to two ways to transition for existing SAP ERP customers:

- **Monolith-to-federated landscape**
  Many customers want to embrace the SaaS world by using two-tier ERP as the vehicle to get into the cloud world. For example, large organizations have chosen to implement SAP S/4HANA Cloud in one of their standard subsidiaries. That means existing on-premise SAP ERP systems can still be connected to cloud solutions so that customers have a phased approach to transition into the SaaS world. A two-tier ERP setup gives companies a way to leverage the best of both the on-premise and cloud worlds while planning to embrace the SaaS world in the future, as shown in Figure 9.5.

- **Federated-to-federated landscape**
  We see in many large enterprises the existence of multiple ERP instances to take care of various entities worldwide; for them, it's a matter of mapping systems to the cloud and then planning the move.

  A federated-to-federated landscape is applicable when organizations plan to transition to a public cloud solution by deploying multiple cloud ERP instances in a distributed manner.

  To better illustrate, let's take the headquarters-subsidiaries setup as an example deployment option for this move option. However, this will work too for other variants of deployment: corporate subsidiary, central services, and supply chain ecosystem setup. Figure 9.6 shows the move option from a highly federated landscape leaning toward on-premise to a federated landscape, which is a more hybrid option with a mix of cloud and on-premise.

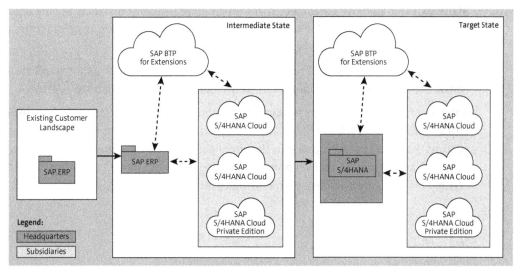

Figure 9.5 Monolith-to-Federated Landscape

Data Residency-Related Guidance for Residency Norms

Many countries have mandated organizations to have their ERP systems hosted in the same data center as their business operations. Many more have asked organizations to have their data back kept within the same data as their business operations. However, considering all the regulations, customers are advised to segregate multiple geographies, divisions, subsidiaries, and ledgers with global and country-specific content. In other words, many cloud instances that are connected to various business reasons will be considered as a federated-to-federated landscape.

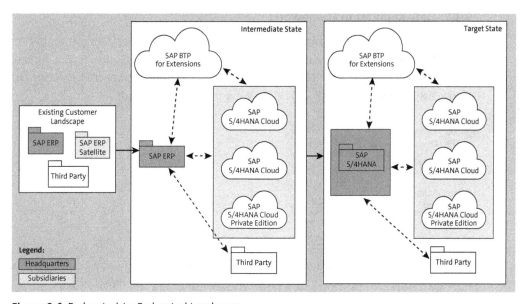

Figure 9.6 Federated-to-Federated Landscape

Many existing SAP ERP customers run a single monolith ERP instance. Such a landscape inhibits the freedom for smaller, more nimble entities in their conglomerate to innovate at a pace faster than headquarters/corporate entities.

For such landscapes, it's ideal to move subsidiaries to the cloud as a first step before considering moving their headquarters to the cloud or to on-premise SAP S/4HANA.

A two-tier ERP setup provides standard end-to-end business processes between subsidiaries running SAP S/4HANA Cloud and headquarters running an on-premise ERP. This ensures that subsidiaries moving to the cloud get to consume innovation faster, stay standard, and be nimble, and yet don't lose the flexibility demanded by corporate leadership or headquarters to have better visibility into and control of subsidiaries.

9.3   Master Data

In any two-tier ERP deployment, master data plays an important role. The need to create and manage master data centrally is vital. Business partners, product masters, and some financial master data elements can be managed centrally in a two-tier ERP deployment with SAP S/4HANA Cloud. In this section, we'll discuss the recommended replication options for managing master data in a two-tier ERP deployment.

Additionally, we'll discuss how the SAP Master Data Integration multitenant cloud service for master data integration can be leveraged. Large enterprises with specific business needs can also use API capabilities to replicate master data from SAP S/4HANA Cloud Public Edition to SAP S/4HANA Cloud Private Edition using the middleware of their choice.

9.3.1   Data Replication Framework

The Data Replication Framework (DRF) is used to replicate master data elements from the SAP Master Data Governance (SAP MDG) hub system (see Figure 9.7) or directly from SAP S/4HANA or SAP ERP without SAP MDG to target connected systems (see Figure 9.8). In both cases, SAP S/4HANA Cloud is the target system.

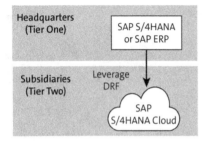

Figure 9.7 Data Replication Framework without SAP MDG

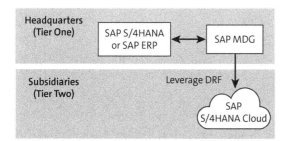

Figure 9.8 Data Replication Framework with SAP MDG

Further Resources

For more information on data replication, visit *http://s-prs.co/v546318*.

9.3.2   API-Based Replication

SAP S/4HANA Cloud also provides allowlisted APIs to propagate master data changes to a subsidiary running SAP S/4HANA Cloud. For example, let's consider the Profit Center: Create, Update, Delete API. This inbound service enables you to create, update, and delete profit center master data through Simple Object Access Protocol (SOAP) messages. The allowlisted API can be used to propagate changes from a source system into the target SAP S/4HANA Cloud system.

Compared to the DRF approach, the API-based approach can be used to handle many more master data elements centrally; all we need is an allowlisted API on SAP S/4HANA Cloud. Handling master data changes via allowlisted APIs also provides the added advantage of enriching data before propagating it into target subsidiary systems.

Further Resources

For a complete listing of all available allowlisted APIs, refer to SAP Business Accelerator Hub for SAP S/4HANA Cloud at *https://api.sap.com*.

9.4   Finance

Finance is a core function for every company because every organization's success and sustainability largely depend on efficient management of its finances.

In this section, you'll see key finance scenario highlights in a two-tier ERP system with SAP S/4HANA Cloud running at subsidiary companies.

9.4.1   Financial Planning

Financial planning involves determining the capital required across a business to meet its strategic goals and objectives for a given period. Financial plan data is created for different dimensions: cost centers, market segments, functional areas, and much more.

For companies working in a two-tier ERP deployment model, consolidated financial planning for the entire corporate group is performed in one of two ways. In a *top-down approach*, financial planning is done at headquarters for the entire business and then cascaded to the subsidiaries. On the other hand, in a *bottom-up approach*, the subsidiaries provide a financial plan proposal to headquarters, and headquarters then consolidates the same for all the subsidiaries for group-level financial planning.

SAP provides the following options for financial planning in a two-tier ERP setup:

- Integrated financial planning using SAP Analytics Cloud
- Group reporting planning using SAP Analytics Cloud
- Financial planning and analysis with SAP Analytics Cloud

Let's look at all these options now.

Integrated Financial Planning Using SAP Analytics Cloud

Headquarters and subsidiary companies in both on-premise SAP S/4HANA and SAP S/4HANA Cloud can use integrated financial planning for profit and loss (P&L) and balance sheet planning in SAP Analytics Cloud, as shown in Figure 9.9. SAP Analytics Cloud is fully integrated and allows the import of actual data from SAP S/4HANA Cloud, SAP S/4HANA, SAP SuccessFactors, and SAP Integrated Business Planning (SAP IBP). It comes with predefined business content with demo data and supports planning on actual data from different connected systems with integrations in financial planning processes, including the cost center, product cost, sales and profitability, investments, P&L, balance sheets, and cash flow planning. The different planning areas seamlessly integrate; for example, the consensus demand plan quantity from SAP IBP flows into sales quantity planning, workforce planning from SAP SuccessFactors flows into cost center planning, cost center planning provides the activity cost rates for product cost planning, and product cost planning provides the product cost rates for the cost of goods sold calculation within profitability planning. In the end, a complete plan P&L, balance sheet, and cash flow statement are derived.

The plan values can be transferred back to planning table ACDOCP, and this plan data is available in analytical reports for comparison with the actuals such as Cost Center – Plan/Actuals, Cost Center – Plan/Actuals YTD, Internal Order – Plan/Actuals, and Internal Order – Plan/Actuals YTD. Activity cost rates and planned statistical key figures can also be exported back. The plan data from table ACDOCP can be consolidated into group reporting table ACDOCU.

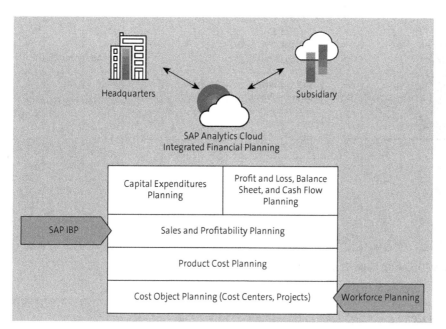

Figure 9.9 Integrated Financial Planning Using SAP Analytics Cloud

Scope Item

The required SAP S/4HANA Cloud scope item for is 4RC for integrated financial planning, and it's 1YB for import connection setup with SAP Analytics Cloud.

The required communication arrangement is SAP_COM_0087 (SAP Analytics Cloud).

Group Reporting Planning Using SAP Analytics Cloud

Subsidiary companies on SAP or non-SAP systems can send actual financial data to headquarters on SAP S/4HANA Cloud or on-premise SAP S/4HANA. Headquarters then can perform the consolidation and group reporting, as shown in Figure 9.10. This actual data can then be sent to SAP Analytics Cloud for group reporting planning. Group reporting planning in SAP Analytics Cloud is based on the SAP S/4HANA data model and is fully integrated with it. Planning administrators can prepopulate planning screens based on past actual data.

Group reporting planning allows headquarters to plan the P&L and balance sheet at the group level based on the group reporting dimensions such as the consolidation unit, functional area, financial statement item, and partner consolidation units in SAP Analytics Cloud.

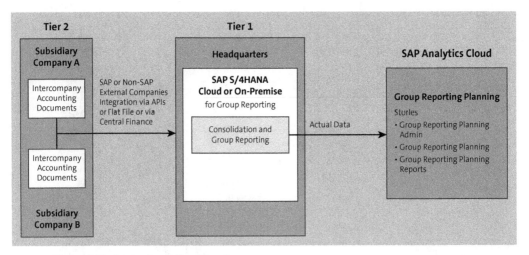

Figure 9.10 Group Reporting Planning

Scope Item

The required SAP S/4HANA Cloud scope item for group reporting planning on SAP Analytics Cloud is 5PU. The required communication arrangement needed is SAP_COM_0087 (SAP Analytics Cloud).

Financial Planning and Analysis with SAP Analytics Cloud

SAP S/4HANA offers financial planning and analysis in SAP Analytics Cloud based on SAP S/4HANA financial structures. Headquarters on SAP S/4HANA (on-premise) and subsidiaries on SAP S/4HANA Cloud can connect to SAP Analytics Cloud as a centralized planning tool. The solution includes a model, reports, dashboards, and a preconfigured integration process. The solution includes financial planning and analysis for P& Ls (including cost center and profit center planning), balance sheets, and cash flow. The multicurrency solution includes a set of financial analysis reports to enable variance analysis, trend analysis, year-over-year reporting, and financial statement analysis.

Scope Item

The required SAP S/4HANA Cloud scope item for SAP Analytics Cloud is 2EB. Refer to SAP Signavio Process Navigator for more details on this scope item.

Plan Data Retraction

Plan data retraction from SAP Analytics Cloud to SAP S/4HANA Cloud is possible via a flat file. In all three approaches for financial planning with SAP Analytics Cloud, financial planning data can be imported into subsidiaries running SAP S/4HANA Cloud via ready-to-use CSV-formatted Microsoft Excel templates that are delivered as part of the SAP Best Practices content.

> **Scope Item**
>
> The required SAP S/4HANA Cloud scope item is 1HB. Refer to SAP Signavio Process Navigator for more details on this scope item.

9.4.2   Advanced Financial Closing

The existing traditional financial closing process has huge potential for optimization. Customers can now streamline and optimize the financial closing process with SAP Advanced Financial Closing. Advanced financial closing in SAP Business Technology Platform (SAP BTP) can be seamlessly integrated with heterogeneous system landscapes. It supports the planning, execution, monitoring, and analysis with workflow-supported processes of period-end closing tasks for all entities (i.e., typically headquarters and all subsidiaries) of a corporation, as shown in Figure 9.11. Customers benefit from the standardized process, faster closing cycle, high-quality compliant results, end-to-end monitoring through embedded analytics, situation handling, automation using SAP Intelligent Robotic Process Automation (SAP Intelligent RPA), and transparency across all subsidiaries and headquarters companies.

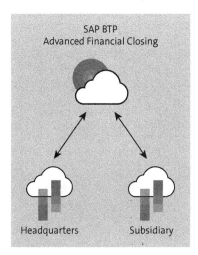

Figure 9.11 Advanced Financial Closing

> **Scope Item**
>
> The required SAP S/4HANA Cloud scope item for advanced financial closing is 4HG, and the relevant communication scenario is SAP_COM_0566. Refer to SAP Signavio Process Navigator for more details of this scope item.

9.4.3   Intercompany Reconciliation Automation

The traditional process of intercompany reconciliation (ICR) is tedious and labor-intensive. Subsidiaries traditionally required a lot of communication to resolve discrepancies, and it was difficult to reconcile at headquarters due to large volumes of data taking a much longer time for group closing.

These drawbacks of the traditional approach are overcome with the advanced intercompany matching and reconciliation (ICMR) solution available with SAP S/4HANA Cloud or on-premise SAP S/4HANA, which offers predefined rules for auto-matching. Users can also get intercompany accounting document auto-matching proposals using the intelligent machine learning ICR service in SAP BTP. These innovations provide automation and modernization and increase matching accuracy and transparency among headquarters for subsidiary companies, streamlining the local closing to corporate closing and speeding up the entity closing to group closing process.

As shown in Figure 9.12, subsidiary companies on SAP or non-SAP systems can send the intercompany accounting documents to headquarters running on SAP S/4HANA Cloud or on-premise SAP S/4HANA through file upload, APIs, or via the Central Finance solution. Within headquarters, the intercompany documents will be first matched by predefined rules, and the remaining unmatched documents can be sent to the intelligent ICR service in SAP BTP, which will do the line-item matching and reason code assignment and will send the matched documents proposal back to the headquarters system.

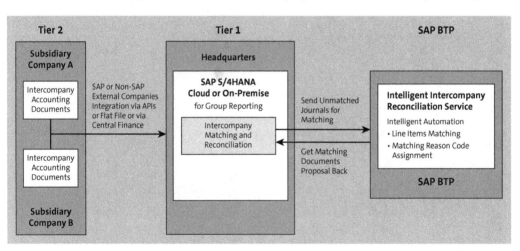

Figure 9.12 Intelligent ICR

Scope Items

The required SAP S/4HANA Cloud scope items for ICR automation are 4LG and 40Y. The relevant communication scenarios for the setup are SAP_COM_0553 and SAP_COM_0377. Refer to SAP Signavio Process Navigator for more details on these scope items.

9.4.4   Financial Consolidation

Financial consolidation is a process in which the financials of different legal entities—perhaps organizational subsets operating in different sectors and/or countries but belonging to one parent entity—are combined and reported centrally. The central reporting takes care of combining assets, revenues, and expenses of the parent and sublegal entities on the parent's balance sheet, giving shareholders, investors, and customers a complete overview of the company's financial health. This isn't just a pure number aggregation; it needs to be mindful of established principles, accounting standards, and legal and regulatory compliance guidelines.

In a two-tier ERP setup, financial consolidation at headquarters is an absolute need. Depending on the flexibility and complexity of an organization's operations worldwide, ownership pattern, and legal rules, its consolidation requirements can vary.

SAP S/4HANA Cloud provides many options for enabling financial consolidation:

- Statutory consolidation with SAP S/4HANA Cloud
- Central Finance
- Enabling consolidation via a third-party consolidation stack

Let's consider each of these options.

Statutory Consolidation with SAP S/4HANA Cloud

SAP S/4HANA Cloud also comes with built-in consolidation capabilities mainly for legal/statutory purposes. This option is targeted for companies that currently don't have any consolidation layer investments and need quick, template-based functionality for consolidation based on the International Financial Reporting Standards (IFRS).

In the landscape shown in Figure 9.13, the consolidation engine is already part of SAP S/4HANA Cloud; it can also integrate with external subsidiary systems via flexible uploads and a powerful data management tool for validating data and maintaining data integrity.

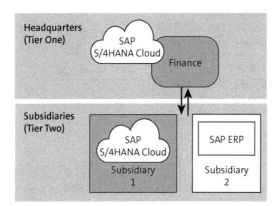

Figure 9.13 Cloud-Based Statutory Consolidation

Scope Items

The required SAP S/4HANA Cloud scope item is 1SG, the data extraction from external system scope item is 2U6, the data from the group reporting data collection scope item is 287, and the multiple group currency scope item is 4VB. Refer to SAP Signavio Process Navigator for more details on these scope items.

The SAP S/4HANA Cloud statutory consolidation functionality is an ideal fit for organizations with the following goals:

- Moving accounting to the cloud
- Accessing consolidation functionalities in addition to local accounting
- Consolidating subsidiaries that are running ERP solutions from multiple vendors

You can easily control which positions of the financial statements should be eliminated against each other. Any elimination rule generates a fully adjustable journal entry. For example, the following typical elimination steps are available out of the box with SAP S/4HANA Cloud: accounts payable/accounts receivable, operational income/expenses, financial income/expenses, dividends, and reporting.

Central Finance

SAP S/4HANA Cloud can connect seamlessly with Central Finance deployed at headquarters. Central Finance is an SAP S/4HANA deployment model in which customers connect multiple ERP systems in their group entities into a central SAP S/4HANA Finance system with real-time replication, resulting in a central, unified financial reporting view. This deployment is preferred if real-time speed and agility are key to an organization's digital transformation. It's considered nondisruptive because the source systems are untouched, and financial postings are replicated in real time via the SAP Landscape Transformation Replication Server, as shown in Figure 9.14.

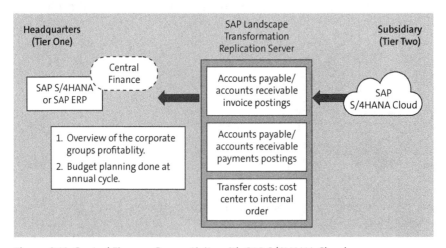

Figure 9.14 Central Finance Connectivity with SAP S/4HANA Cloud

SAP Business Planning and Consolidation (SAP BPC) optimized for SAP S/4HANA is the business planning and consolidation functionality implemented on premise as part of SAP S/4HANA. In a two-tier ERP setup, it's common to see companies run SAP BPC optimized for SAP S/4HANA on the on-premise SAP S/4HANA instance because they seek to leverage real-time planning and consolidation capability at headquarters and want to integrate subsidiary systems directly with their real-time planning and consolidation instance. Therefore, when SAP S/4HANA Cloud connects to on-premise SAP S/4HANA, it eliminates the need for extract, transform, load (ETL) processes and the need for a separate planning and consolidation system. SAP BPC optimized for SAP S/4HANA comes with many predefined planning models for easy and faster adoption of planning templates, such as cost center planning, profit center planning, P&L planning, balance sheet planning, and functional area and work in progress (WIP) planning. Once set up, it provides for replication of financial transaction data from SAP S/4HANA Cloud to SAP S/4HANA Central Finance 1610 FPS 02 or later.

> **Scope Item**
>
> The required SAP S/4HANA Cloud scope item is 1W4. The communication scenarios provided for integration are SAP_COM_0083 and SAP_COM_0200. Refer to SAP Signavio Process Navigator for more details on this scope item. For a detailed setup guide, refer to the setup instructions in scope item 1W4.

Third-Party Consolidation Stack via APIs

SAP S/4HANA Cloud provides a rich and open set of APIs that enable third-party consolidation stacks to read financial data relevant for consolidation from SAP S/4HANA Cloud for further processing.

As shown in Figure 9.15, if headquarters runs a non-SAP ERP solution, then financial measures relevant for consolidation can be retrieved via allowlisted APIs for reading trial balances, journal entries, and accounting documents.

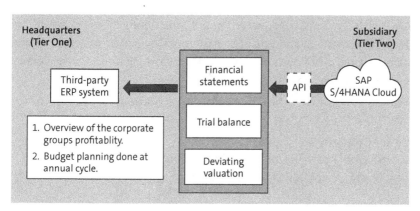

Figure 9.15 Read Financial Measures via Allowlisted APIs

9.4.5   Cash Visibility of Subsidiary at Headquarters

In a typical headquarters-subsidiaries relationship, headquarters needs visibility and control for decision-making and needs visibility specifically into the subsidiary operations and cash position for group-level reporting. Headquarters needs to ensure that subsidiaries have access to liquidity for their day-to-day activities and that there is no impact on subsidiary operations.

With this scenario, the cash manager at headquarters gets cash visibility into subsidiary companies and can provide the reporting of the cash position for the entire enterprise. As shown in Figure 9.16, the cash specialists at subsidiaries perform daily banking duties related to disbursement and receivable accounts, including cash transfers, cash pooling, and approvals. A cash manager can then provide reporting of the cash position to headquarters with comprehensive information, including opening and closing balance. With cash visibility, headquarters can know the cash position at subsidiaries and allocate funds as needed.

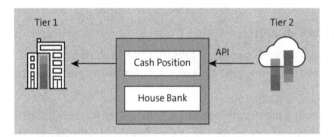

Figure 9.16 Cash Flow Visibility

With advanced cash operations, headquarters gets a consistent view of the actual cash position, as well as the short- and mid-term cash forecasts. A comparison view between the actual and forecasted cash flow is available with drilldown features for the detailed transactions and rich dimensions for the analysis.

Scope Item

The required SAP S/4HANA Cloud scope item for advanced cash operations is J78. The communication scenario provided for integration is SAP_COM_0654. Refer to SAP Signavio Process Navigator for more details on this scope item.

9.5   Sales

A rapidly changing business environment often poses challenges to a business. Many organizations are exploring the issues posed by inorganic growth specifically from mergers and acquisitions for meeting the market demand and gaining competitive advantage. For a business, managing the upstream and downstream stakeholders in an endeavor to gain a competitive advantage has become more complex. Sales activities will become even more important in the scattered environment in which the different entities within a business use different system landscapes. In this section, we'll look at two-tier ERP business processes in sales and how a business can overcome the accompanying challenges with SAP S/4HANA Cloud. We'll start with two-tier ERP sales, examining sales from a local sales office, drop shipments, and returns handling with an eye on both the current challenges and the processes with SAP S/4HANA Cloud.

9.5.1   Subsidiary as a Local Sales Office

In a setup in which a subsidiary is established as a local sales office, managing sales operations independently requires starting the sales activities, independently fulfilling customers' requirements, and handling subsequent processes such as returns.

A business might choose to set up a subsidiary as a local sales office if it has the following business objectives:

- Capturing a strategically important market
- Lowering the financial expenditures by bringing in business model optimization
- Targeting certain geographic regions for its products

Figure 9.17 represents the sales process from an independent subsidiary. This process usually begins when a customer approaches the sales office for quotations. Alternatively, a salesperson may identify an opportunity through the marketing campaign and directly approach a customer in their region to provide insights about the new products the company offers that might be of interest to the customer. As shown in Figure 9.17, headquarters has visibility into the process of converting an opportunity into sales order fulfillment, even if it doesn't manage the sales directly.

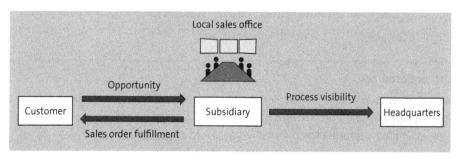

Figure 9.17 Sell from Local Sales Office

Communication between subsidiaries and headquarters is a key challenge for independent sales subsidiaries. Headquarters depends on manual communication channels for visibility of the process and for the overall performance of subsidiary; such access is even more critical if a business has multiple subsidiaries that collectively affect its overall performance.

Let's examine the two-tier ERP deployment model with either SAP ERP or on-premise SAP S/4HANA implemented at headquarters and SAP S/4HANA Cloud implemented at the subsidiary. As highlighted in Figure 9.18, a salesperson converts the predecessor documents from sales activities such as quotations to a sales order. The subsidiary confirms whether it can deliver the product on the date requested by the customer. It then performs follow-up actions such as shipping and billing activities to complete the order-to-cash process.

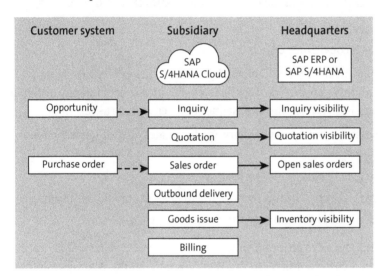

Figure 9.18 Sell from Local Sales Office with SAP S/4HANA Cloud

SAP has published four allowlisted APIs for integrating with SAP S/4HANA Cloud for these points:

- `API_SALES_QUOTATION_SRV` and `API_SALES_INQUIRY_SRV` for leads and opportunities
- `API_SALES_ORDER_SRV` for sales orders and their statuses
- `API_MATERIAL_STOCK_SRV` for inventory position

Further Resources

SAP has envisioned essential APIs for other critical information—specifically, customer credit details and customer account balances—that are under consideration for future releases. For more information on required APIs, visit *https://api.sap.com*.

9.5.2 Drop-Shipping

Drop-shipping is a supply chain management technique in which the retailer doesn't keep goods in its own stock but instead transfers customer orders and shipment details to the manufacturer or wholesaler. In the drop-shipping process, a subsidiary doesn't hold or manage the inventory but instead requests that headquarters replenish the inventory directly to the customer. This is the case for a dependent subsidiary setup in the two-tier ERP system. In principle, two drop-shipping models are possible, depending on a business's deployment model:

- Drop-shipping from headquarters
- Drop-shipping from subsidiary

Let's look at each of these in detail.

Drop-Shipping from Headquarters

This scenario is applicable for a business that has a subsidiary as a sales office that doesn't manage the inventory. In this scenario, the subsidiary depends on headquarters for inventory replenishment.

In this process, a customer approaches the subsidiary for the required product. As highlighted in Figure 9.19, the subsidiary will pass on the requirements to headquarters because the subsidiary doesn't manage the inventory. Headquarters will perform the delivery of the product directly to the end customer and create the billing document for the subsidiary. The subsidiary then creates the final billing document for the end customer.

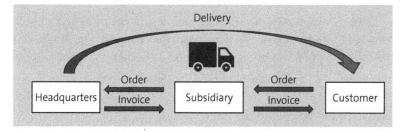

Figure 9.19 Drop-Shipping from Headquarters

From a business perspective, real-time collaboration between headquarters and its subsidiaries is required to realize this drop-shipping process. From an IT perspective, this requires enormous manual effort to integrate the software in such a way to avoid the need for manual intervention. The following are common challenges with this setup:

- A lot of manual interaction due to more data entry points
- Limited or lacking information on the goods movement between headquarters and the subsidiary

- Enormous effort needed to establish the integration between headquarters and the subsidiary

With SAP S/4HANA Cloud, SAP offers prepackaged integration content with SAP Best Practices scope items. These result in seamless integration, reduced implementation time, and end-to-end business coverage.

There are two variants of the drop-shipping process from headquarters that come into play, depending on business requirements:

- Drop-shipping without advanced shipping notification (ASN)
- Drop-shipping with ASN

Figure 9.20 illustrates the end-to-end business process view of drop-shipping from headquarters when SAP S/4HANA Cloud is implemented at a subsidiary. Depending on whether the company is drop-shipping with or without an ASN, several integration points are required in SAP S/4HANA Cloud, which are marked with solid arrow lines:

- **Outbound service for sending purchase order**
  This is one of the critical integration points through which the requirements from a customer are transferred to headquarters. In this process, the third-party sales order is created manually based on the customer's requirements via the customer's purchase order. On saving the sales order, a purchase requisition will be generated; this is converted into a purchase order in SAP S/4HANA Cloud. Once the purchase order is generated, it needs to be communicated to headquarters as a sales order to automatically capture mandatory information such as product details, required quantity, requested delivery date, and ship-to party information.

- **Inbound service for receiving order confirmation**
  Once the sales order is created at headquarters, headquarters performs an inventory availability check for the requested delivery date from the customer. The result needs to be communicated back to the subsidiary so that the subsidiary can communicate it to the end customer. The **Purchase Order Confirmation** tab of SAP S/4HANA Cloud is updated with the details of the confirmed quantity.

- **Outbound service for sending purchase order**
  This is one of the critical integration points through which the requirements from a customer are transferred to headquarters. In this process, the third-party sales order is created manually based on the customer's requirements via the customer's purchase order. On saving the sales order, a purchase requisition will be generated; this is converted into a purchase order in SAP S/4HANA Cloud. Once the purchase order is generated, it needs to be communicated to headquarters as a sales order to automatically capture mandatory information such as product details, required quantity, requested delivery date, and ship-to party information.

- **Inbound service for creating supplier invoice**
  This is the last critical integration point required to capture the account payables information in SAP S/4HANA Cloud. The subsidiary gets the supplier invoice created

automatically through the integration once the billing document is generated at headquarters for the subsidiary. This integration saves massive effort and takes significantly less time than creating the supplier invoice document manually for the end user.

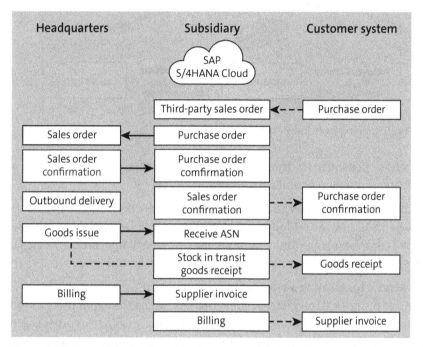

Figure 9.20 Drop-Shipping from Headquarters with SAP S/4HANA Cloud

Drop-Shipping from Subsidiary

This scenario is applicable when the subsidiary acts as a manufacturing unit and/or a warehouse that manages the inventory. In this case, headquarters depends on the subsidiary for inventory replenishment.

Figure 9.21 shows the business process flow between headquarters and the subsidiary. In this process, a customer approaches headquarters for the product required and provides the quantity and the expected delivery date.

Headquarters will pass on the requirements to the subsidiary because headquarters doesn't manage the inventory. The subsidiary performs the delivery of the product directly to the customer and creates the billing document against headquarters. Headquarters then creates the final billing document for the end customer.

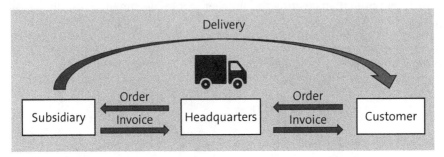

Figure 9.21 Drop-Shipping from Subsidiary

Businesses whose headquarters handle fulfillment encounter similar challenges as businesses whose subsidiaries handle fulfillment.

Figure 9.22 illustrates the end-to-end business process view of drop-shipping from the subsidiary when SAP S/4HANA Cloud is implemented there. Depending on whether the company is drop-shipping with or without an ASN, several integration points are required in SAP S/4HANA Cloud, which are marked with solid arrow lines:

- **Inbound service for creating a sales order**
  This is one of the critical integration points through which the requirements from the customer are transferred from headquarters. In this process, a sales order is generated based on the customer requirements via the purchase order at headquarters.

- **Outbound service for sales order confirmation**
  An availability check is performed during the sales order creation at the subsidiary with SAP S/4HANA Cloud. The availability check helps confirm availability of the quantities of a product needed to send to a customer by the requested delivery date. This information needs to be communicated to headquarters so that headquarters can communicate it to the end customer.

- **Outbound service for delivery request**
  This integration is required if a business is implementing a drop-shipping process with an ASN. In this process, once the outbound delivery is generated and the goods dispatched from the subsidiary, delivery details must be sent to headquarters. The ASN is generated at headquarters and contains the details of the quantities dispatched.

- **Outbound service for billing document**
  This is the last critical integration point, in which the billing document is sent to headquarters to automate the creation of the supplier invoice. Once the billing document is generated at the subsidiary with SAP S/4HANA Cloud, it's communicated to headquarters as a supplier invoice. This integration saves massive effort and takes significantly less time than creating this document manually from the end user.

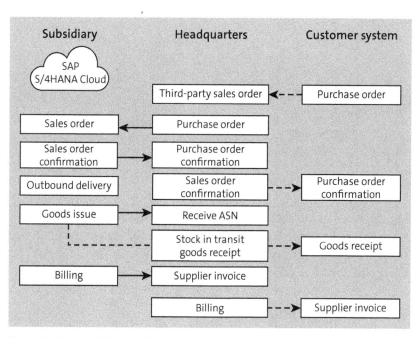

Figure 9.22 Drop-Shipping from the Subsidiary with SAP S/4HANA Cloud

> **Scope Item**
>
> The required SAP S/4HANA Cloud scope item is 2EL. Refer to SAP Signavio Process Navigator for more details on this scope item.
>
> The communication scenario provided for integration is SAP_COM_0223.

9.5.3 Returns Handling

In the previous sections, process details have been provided for sell-from-stock and drop-shipping scenarios. In both scenarios, after the product is sold, the customer may return it for various reasons. Returns processing will become perilous if a business doesn't have a proper channel of communication for capturing the return information and communicating as necessary with headquarters for making certain decisions.

Returns processing is classified based on the scenarios provided in the previous sections: either returns for sales from local sales offices or returns from drop shipments. Returns processing for sales from local sales offices is applicable when a customer returns the product to a subsidiary sales office that manages all of its operations as an independent subsidiary. Figure 9.23 shows the returns process to an *independent* subsidiary; note that system integration gives headquarters visibility into the returns process.

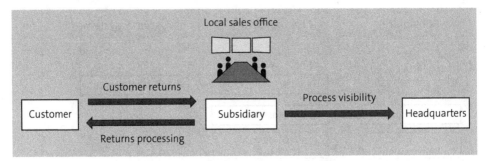

Figure 9.23 Returns Processing for Local Sales Office

This process begins when a customer wants to return the product to the subsidiary. The return can be initiated through a customer return note or through manual information. From here, two options are possible, depending on the company's returns practices: either a returns order is created and processed alone, or a follow-on process occurs in which a credit memo is created or a product is replaced. Let's look at each:

- **Returns sales order without follow-on functions**
  Once the return order is generated, the subsidiary will perform shipping activities such as creation of delivery and goods receipt once the goods have physically arrived. As soon as the goods receipt is performed, the subsidiary can decide whether the product is to be sent back to the supplier or scrapped. As a final step, a billing document is created. To map this business requirement, SAP S/4HANA Cloud offers scope item BDD as a part of its SAP Best Practices content.

- **Returns sales order with follow-on functions**
  In this process, the subsidiary may initiate the quality check once the customer returns the product physically. A quality inspection also may be carried out at the customer premises. Once the return order is generated, the subsidiary will perform shipping activities such as creation of delivery and goods receipt. The subsidiary decides whether the product is to be replaced or refunded based on various factors. Accordingly, a sales order is generated for a free-of-charge product for replacement, or a credit memo is created for a refund. To map this requirement, SAP S/4HANA Cloud offers scope item BKP as a part of its SAP Best Practices content.

In both scenarios with SAP S/4HANA Cloud at the subsidiary, SAP has published two allowlisted APIs for integrating with SAP S/4HANA Cloud for the following points:

- `API_CUSTOMER_RETURN_SRV` for information on customer returns order
- `API_CUSTOMER_RETURNS_DELIVERY_SRV` for information on customer returns delivery

Returns handling for other scenarios, such as drop-shipping, is anticipated in future product releases.

So far, the existing sales scenarios have been largely applicable to all kinds of businesses; however, there is always a chance of variations. Based on customer adaptation and requirements, SAP will release more scenarios or variants in later product releases of SAP S/4HANA Cloud.

9.6 Services

Never before has technological advancement offered more innovation and transformation opportunities for the services industry. Systems integrations allow firms to grow revenue without increasing or modifying their entire business process. There are increased opportunities in manufacturing for companies to streamline the merger activities between their subsidiaries or retail channels for the betterment of services with digital technologies.

A company's revenue will stem from not only sale of products but also customer-specific solutions that transform the business and differentiate it from their peers in the marketplace. These solutions include value-added services, predictive analytics, proactive maintenance, and more.

In this section, we'll look at two-tier ERP business processes in services and how a business can build new processes with the integration of an existing landscape into SAP S/4HANA Cloud. We'll start with two-tier service order management, repair order integration, and sales installation processes, with an eye on both the current challenges and the processes in SAP S/4HANA Cloud.

9.6.1 Service Order Management

Service order management is used to manage the end-to-end lifecycle of service requests. Service requests are generally raised for customer queries in terms of servicing or repairing of products purchased.

As mentioned earlier, drop-shipping is a supply chain management technique in which the retailer doesn't keep goods or service in its own stock but instead transfers customer orders and shipment details to the manufacturer or service provider. This drop-shipping concept applies to both sales and services capabilities, as you'll see in the following sections.

Service or repair of products are generally outsourced by headquarters to a subsidiary. In service order management, similar to drop-shipping (as discussed in Section 9.5.2), a setup exists between headquarters and subsidiary wherein headquarters doesn't manage service operations such as installation, but instead requests that a subsidiary carries out the activities at a customer location directly. This is the case for a dependent subsidiary setup in the two-tier ERP system.

Figure 9.24 shows service order management from an independent subsidiary. The process starts when the customer places an order at headquarters for services. The internal sales representative at headquarters creates the customer's sales order. Headquarters will contact the service provider, depending on the service to be provided. Headquarters has visibility into the process of converting a customer requirement into a service opportunity, even if it doesn't manage the services directly.

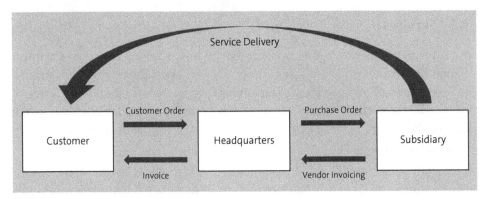

Figure 9.24 Service Order Management

Communications between subsidiaries and headquarters need to be seamless for independent service subsidiaries. A subsidiary depends on manual communication channels for visibility of the process and for the overall performance of headquarters; such access is even more critical if a business has multiple subsidiaries that collectively affect its overall performance.

Let's examine the two-tier ERP deployment model with either SAP ERP or on-premise SAP S/4HANA implemented at headquarters and SAP S/4HANA Cloud implemented at the subsidiary. As highlighted in Figure 9.25, the process begins with a salesperson interaction with the customer and continues as follows:

1. A sales order is created in headquarters with a material that generates the purchase requisition. A purchase order is created against the purchase requisition.

2. The purchase is approved, and an electronic data interchange (EDI)-based approach is used to automatically transfer the purchase order information for the creation of a service order at the subsidiary.

3. A service manager receives the automatically generated service order at the subsidiary with sold-to, ship-to, bill-to, and pay-to information coming from headquarters. The ship-to information contains details of the end customer.

4. The service order is confirmed, and the EDI-based approach is used to confirm the purchase order at headquarters for receipt of details.

5. A service technician in the subsidiary delivers the service required to the customer and confirms the service order.

6. Based on the service delivered and confirmation, the purchaser at headquarters posts the service entry sheet.

7. A vendor invoice or billing document is created at the subsidiary and billed to headquarters; consequently, a corresponding supplier invoice is created automatically at headquarters.

8. Headquarters raises an invoice against the initial sales order.

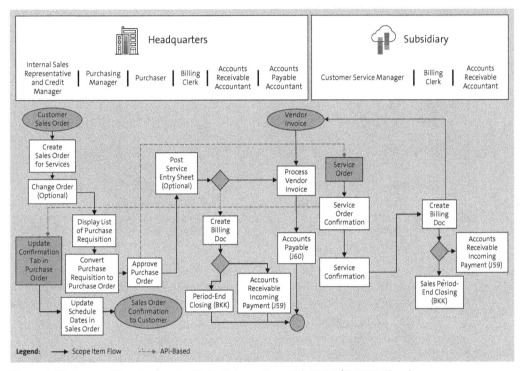

Figure 9.25 Process Flow for Service Order Integration with SAP S/4HANA Cloud

Scope Items

The required SAP S/4HANA Cloud scope items are 3D2 and 2EL. Refer to SAP Signavio Process Navigator for more details on these scope items.

The communication scenario provided for integration is SAP_COM_0224.

9.6.2   Repair Order Integration

A repair order is a sales document for recording all the business processes that are involved in processing faulty goods that a customer sends in for repair. Headquarters employs resellers/retailers/service providers as a channel through which a product can be delivered to the end customer. Customers reach out to the same channels if they need to repair a product they purchased. Subsidiaries help customers access the product warranty coverage and amount of repair through in-house repairs. Quality checks ensure that the repair is needed and determines if spare parts are to be added or replaced. These spare parts are procured from headquarters.

Figure 9.26 represents the repair order integration from an independent subsidiary. The process starts with a customer walking into a retailer store or reaching out to a service provider/reseller with a product complaint. A subsidiary receives the customer material and places it under the customer stock. A customer service representative performs a precheck and assesses the repair. A repair order is created with parts to be procured from headquarters.

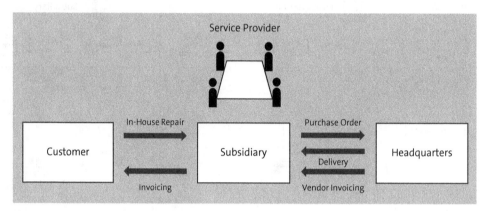

Figure 9.26 Repair Order Integration

Let's examine the two-tier ERP deployment model with either SAP ERP or on-premise SAP S/4HANA implemented at headquarters and SAP S/4HANA Cloud implemented at the subsidiary. As highlighted in Figure 9.27, the process begins with a service representative interaction with the customer and continues as follows:

1. A product is received from the customer through post goods movement and placed under the customer stock.

2. An in-house repair is created for the customer with the product and serial number details.

3. A customer service representative performs a precheck as part of the quality inspection.

4. A repair order is created from the in-house repair with a product that generates the purchase requisition. A purchase order is created with the vendor as headquarters against the purchase requisition.

5. The EDI output type in the purchase order is used to send the details to SAP BTP.

6. In SAP BTP (specifically, the Cloud Integration capability), using standard artifacts, an integration flow is built that creates a sales order in the on-premise SAP S/4HANA system with a purchase order reference document.

7. The sales order triggers an EDI output for confirmation of receipt.

8. Delivery creation (post goods issue) from the on-premise SAP S/4HANA system is done for shipping the procured product to the subsidiary. In the subsidiary system (SAP S/4HANA Cloud), an inbound delivery is created against the purchase order, and receipt of the material for repair is taken.

9. The repair confirmation is done against the repair order and goods issue for delivery of product to the customer.

10. A vendor invoice or billing document is created at the subsidiary and billed to headquarters; consequently, a corresponding supplier invoice is created automatically at headquarters.

11. Headquarters raises an invoice against the initial sales order.

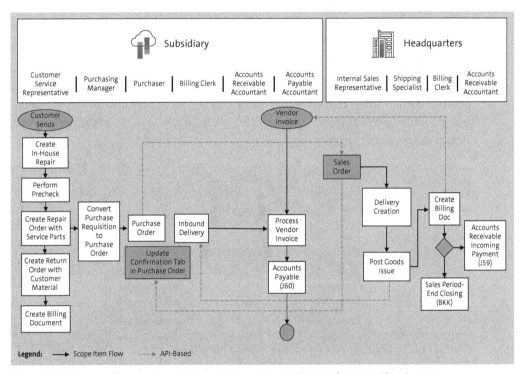

Figure 9.27 Process Flow for Repair Order Integration with SAP S/4HANA Cloud

Scope Items

The required SAP S/4HANA Cloud scope items are 3XK and 2EJ. Refer to SAP Signavio Process Navigator for more details on these scope items.

The communication scenario provided for integration is SAP_COM_0223.

9.6.3   Sales and Installation

When a customer requires a product along with installation, this is known as the sales and installation process. In SAP S/4HANA Cloud, sales and installation is referred to collectively as *solution order management*, which represents an end-to-end process that spans from creating a solution order to delivering products, one-time services, longrunning services, and subscriptions. This includes integration with invoicing and controlling.

Subsidiary core business processes include services and installation activities. With the sales and installation process, a setup exists between headquarters and subsidiaries wherein headquarters doesn't manage service operations such as installation; instead, subsidiaries procure the materials from headquarters and carry out the activities at a customer location directly. This is the case for a dependent subsidiary setup in the two-tier ERP system.

In a setup in which a subsidiary is established as a local sales and service office, it receives a customer's request to manage the service activities at the customer location and gets the materials from headquarters.

Figure 9.28 represents the sales and installation process from an independent subsidiary. The process starts when the customer places an order at the subsidiary for product and service. The internal sales representative at the subsidiary creates the customer's order. Headquarters ships the material to the subsidiary, which takes care of installation at the customer location.

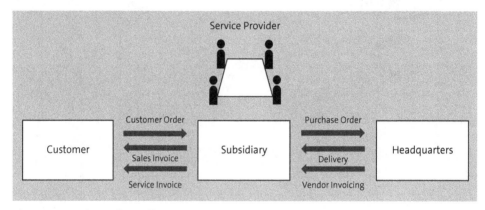

Figure 9.28 Sales and Installation Process

Let's examine the two-tier ERP deployment model with either SAP ERP or on-premise SAP S/4HANA implemented at headquarters and SAP S/4HANA Cloud implemented at the subsidiary. As highlighted in Figure 9.29, the process begins with a salesperson interacting with the customer and continues as follows:

1. A service representative creates a solution order with the product required and service (installation) as additional line items.

2. The sales item in the solution order is released, which creates a sales order containing the product that generates the purchase requisition. The purchase order is created with the vendor as headquarters against the purchase requisition.

3. The EDI output type in the purchase order is used to send the details to SAP BTP.

4. In SAP BTP (specifically, the Cloud Integration capability), using standard artifacts, an integration flow is built that creates a sales order in an on-premise SAP S/4HANA system with a purchase order reference document.

5. The sales order triggers an EDI output for confirmation of receipt.

6. Delivery creation (post goods issue) from the on-premise SAP S/4HANA system is done for shipping the procured product to the subsidiary. In the subsidiary system (SAP S/4HANA Cloud), the inbound delivery is created against the purchase order for receipt of product.

7. The service item in the solution order is released, which creates a service order that is replicated to field service management (FSM).

8. A service technician is assigned to the service request with details of the installation, containing product and customer information.

9. Service order confirmation is done in FSM and replicated to the SAP S/4HANA Cloud system at the subsidiary.

10. A vendor invoice or billing document is created at the subsidiary and billed to headquarters; consequently, a corresponding supplier invoice is created automatically at headquarters.

11. Headquarters raises an invoice against the initial sales order.

12. With a solution order, there is an option to bill the sales and service items together or separately, depending on the customer's requirement or request.

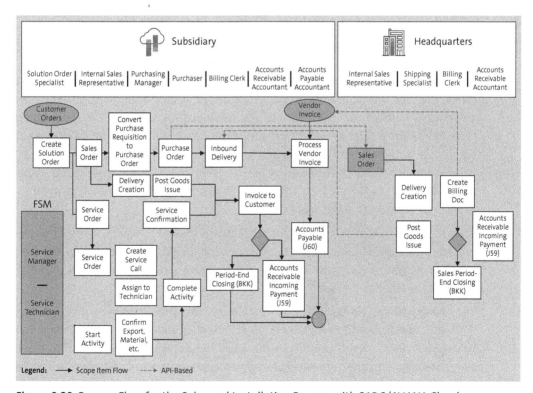

Figure 9.29 Process Flow for the Sales and Installation Process with SAP S/4HANA Cloud

So far, the service scenarios have been largely applicable to service-centric processes that are widely expanding; however, there is always a chance of variations. Based on customer adaptation and requirements, SAP will release more scenarios or variants in later product releases of SAP S/4HANA Cloud.

> **Scope Items**
>
> The required SAP S/4HANA Cloud scope items are 5GT, 49X, and 2EJ. Refer to SAP Signavio Process Navigator for more details on these scope items.
>
> The communication scenario provided for integration is SAP_COM_0223.

9.6.4 Warranty Claim Process

The warranty management process enables users to manage customer warranty and vendor warranty details for an equipment/asset through the predefined process. Typically considering after-sale operations, smaller service divisions running on cloud instances can leverage end-to-end process to manage their warranty budgets against available original equipment manufacturers (OEM) configured as headquarters.

Customers using equipment may reach the nearest service centers for asset servicing. System users at service centers can create a claim on behalf of customers using the Manage Customer Claims app. Based on the type of the claim, the validation is done automatically in the claim. For example, a customer claim is created for an asset, and a customer warranty is maintained, which is applicable at the point of the claim creation range, and then the claim will be validated against the latest valid warranty. Similarly, an external supplier claim created will be validated against the latest warranty maintained for the asset. Claims can also capture important details such as registration date, repair date, and repair end dates, as well as organization-specific details such as plant. It's also possible to add the responsible person, labor involved, and spare part information, if used during the process. If the claim is covered under vendor warranty, those details can be sent to supplier recovery.

After the initial validation, a corresponding claim is created at headquarters for further processing. Claim validation rules can also be built, or existing rules can be leveraged per the business need. Finally, output can be triggered to share the details manually with responsible stakeholders.

The end-to-end process is designed in such a way that the finance postings action on both the subsidiary and headquarters of the supplier and vendor claim applications respectively clears out the account postings on both sides of the transaction. The responsible subsidiary creating a supplier claim generates the claim creation event, which can be listened to, and then an API call from headquarters to the public cloud fetches the details of the supplier claim. Based on the available details, a corresponding customer claim is created in headquarters using the IDoc. Further, when a claim is validated, the output management configured in the system helps to generate different types of output, including PDF files and auto-generating emails.

Users can manually maintain the Maintain Supplier Response action in the Manage Supplier Claims app corresponding to the response from headquarters.

Scope Items

The required SAP S/4HANA Cloud scope items are 63Y and 5HR. Refer to SAP Signavio Process Navigator for more details on these scope items. The communication scenario provided for integration is SAP_COM_0766.

9.7 Procurement

Let's now turn our attention to the procurement business processes, their challenges, and how a business can overcome the challenges with SAP S/4HANA Cloud in a two-tier ERP deployment.

In a headquarters and subsidiary model, headquarters often lacks visibility into procurement activities at connected subsidiaries in real time. That means the central headquarters is unable to plan, guide, and control procurement spend at subsidiaries.

Deployed in a two-tier ERP model, SAP S/4HANA Cloud helps businesses streamline procurement processes for both a headquarters and its subsidiaries, thereby improving compliance. To optimize procurement processes in a standard headquarters-subsidiaries setup, let's examine the following four scenarios to streamline procurement operations using SAP S/4HANA Cloud:

- Procurement handled directly by the subsidiary with process visibility provided for headquarters
- Centralized purchasing from headquarters for subsidiaries
- Centralized contracting from headquarters for subsidiaries
- Centralized scheduling agreements from headquarters

We'll consider each one now.

9.7.1 Procurement Handled Directly by Subsidiary

In this deployment scenario, the subsidiary is modeled to run like an independent entity with an efficient purchasing organization that has a strong presence in a geographical location. The subsidiary is equipped to run its own procurement operations and manage local inventory. Supplier management and evaluation, source of supply management, and contract management are handled locally by the subsidiary.

Figure 9.30 shows the end-to-end business process view of independent procurement operations at a subsidiary with necessary procurement visibility available for headquarters. With SAP S/4HANA Cloud implemented at a subsidiary, headquarters also prefers that purchasing operations be independently carried out by the subsidiary for operational ease and cost effectiveness. Predelivered reporting content makes sure that headquarters reporting requirements are managed with ease.

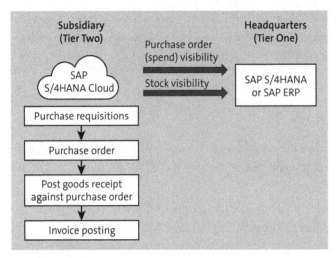

Figure 9.30 Independent Procurement Unit

The process typically starts with the creation of purchase requisitions at the subsidiary. Based on the material requirements planning (MRP) configuration, the SAP S/4HANA Cloud system can trigger purchase requisitions automatically, but these can also be created manually in the system.

As a next step, the purchaser converts purchase requisitions to purchase orders in the system. Based on the business requirements, a purchase order can be sent for required approvals. The vendor is informed about the requirement to supply the goods and services per agreed-upon terms and conditions.

SAP S/4HANA Cloud offers allowlisted APIs and CDS views to meet headquarters' reporting/analytical needs; these can be consumed to make customized reports. SAP has published the following allowlisted APIs to realize this two-tier ERP scenario:

- `API_SALES_ORDER_SRV` to integrate external applications with sales order processing
- `API_MATERIAL_STOCK_SRV` to retrieve material stock information
- `API_PURCHASEORDER_PROCESS_SRV` to create and update purchase orders with the data

9.7.2   Centralized Procurement at Headquarters

In a centralized purchasing setup, all purchasing activities are designed to flow through headquarters. This is attractive for organizations that aim to do the following:

- Leverage purchasing volumes as a means to reduce the cost of their operations
- Improve transparency at subsidiaries previously running decentralized local processes
- Migrate existing procurement systems to an efficient central purchasing setup

Centralized purchasing has become an integral building block of the SAP S/4HANA Cloud two-tier ERP procurement setup. Strategic procurement tasks such as supplier management benefit from both the transparency and the ability to initiate strategic activities from a single digital procurement control center. The central purchasing scenario of SAP S/4HANA Cloud gives a single point of access and visibility to purchasing documents such as purchase requisitions and purchase orders from the connected subsidiary systems.

Figure 9.31 shows the end-to-end business process view of central purchasing with both subsidiaries and headquarters. First, all unsourced purchase requisitions are sent to headquarters for consolidation. Consolidation is handled at the SAP S/4HANA central purchase organization to leverage the benefits of purchasing volumes. Responsibility management gives an organization more flexibility for its approval processes. This feature is provided to display the attributes of purchase requisition items on the list page. It can facilitate centralized approval based on business requirements.

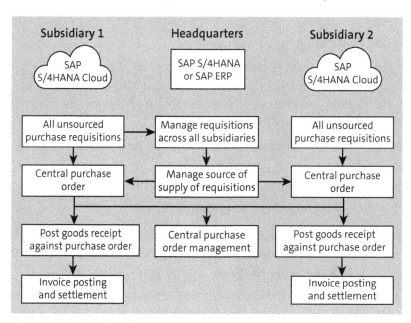

Figure 9.31 Central Purchasing

Managing the source of supply of all requisitions is another key function managed at headquarters. A source of supply defines how or where a product is procured. This includes many other checks that are carried out: the vendor must not be deleted, an info record must exist, and so on.

A purchase order can be triggered from any system. However, central purchase order management is handled at headquarters. An SAP Fiori app (Approve Purchase Orders) for the approval and flexible workflow framework in the headquarters' central SAP S/4HANA system facilitates the approval process for central purchase documents either at subsidiaries or at headquarters, subject to business requirements. Purchasers can use a central processing feature on the list page of the central system to block or unblock the automatic creation of purchase orders in the connected systems. They can edit the purchase requisitions/purchase order items that are created in the central system or those that have been extracted from the connected system.

Follow-on purchasing activities such as goods receipt against the purchase order and invoice posting and settlement are handled at subsidiaries locally.

Scope Item

The required SAP S/4HANA Cloud scope item is 2XT. Refer to SAP Signavio Process Navigator for more details on this scope item.

The communication scenario provided for integration is SAP_COM_0200.

9.7.3 Centralized Contracting from Headquarters

Centralized contract management is used to negotiate a global, long-term agreement between an organization and a supplier for the supply of materials or the performance of services within a certain period per predefined terms and conditions. This is a common practice for organizations with the following goals:

- Streamlined contracting process across headquarters and subsidiaries
- Lowered costs and better conditions based on scaled purchasing activities across multiple subsidiaries
- Compliance with complex regulations across subsidiaries

Figure 9.32 shows the end-to-end business process view of the procurement process at a subsidiary using central contracting from headquarters. In our example, headquarters is running SAP S/4HANA and the subsidiary is running SAP S/4HANA Cloud.

Once negotiated at headquarters, the central contract is created at headquarters and then distributed to the relevant subsidiaries. Operational purchasing activities such as goods receipt against a purchase order and invoice posting and settlement are handled at subsidiaries locally. Users can select the type of central contract from the available options (i.e., quantity contract or value contract). The system also enforces that users add valid values in case of mandatory requirements.

Central contracts are associated to a central purchasing group, central purchasing organization, and company code for reporting purposes. To monitor usage on an ongoing basis, users can add a target value; this is mandatory when the contract is a value contract but optional when the contract is a quantity contract. Creation of an item for lean services is possible for a free-text service.

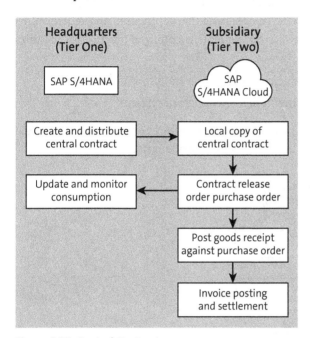

Figure 9.32 Central Contract

Users can access the Job Schedule Import of Catalog Data app to extract the master data from different subsidiary systems into the central system. Modification of distributed contract information is possible before the distributed contract is created in the connected subsidiary system from the central purchase contract. The MM_PUR_S4_CCTR_MOD_DISTR_CTR business add-in (BAdI) can be used to modify this information.

After the central contract has been put into effect, follow-on purchasing activities such as the goods receipt against the purchase order and invoice posting and settlement are handled at the subsidiary locally.

Consumption at each subsidiary is updated back to headquarters. The central on-premise SAP S/4HANA purchase system helps monitor contract consumption and renewal of expiring contracts across all subsidiaries on a real-time basis.

Scope Item

The required SAP S/4HANA Cloud scope item is 2ME. Refer to SAP Signavio Process Navigator for more details on this scope item.

The communication scenario provided for integration is SAP_COM_0200.

9.7.4   Centralized Scheduling Agreements from Headquarters

In a business environment, when there is an established source of supply, creating and managing purchase orders might become a very tedious task. To manage purchase activity over the long run, a scheduling agreement may be required.

A *centralized scheduling agreement* is a long-term agreement between a vendor and an ordering party for a predefined material or service that is procured on predetermined dates over a given time. Creating such agreements is common practice for organizations with the following goals:

- A streamlined business process across headquarters and subsidiaries
- Monitoring of long-term agreements across connected systems

Figure 9.33 illustrates the end-to-end business process view of procurement at a subsidiary using centralized scheduling agreements from headquarters.

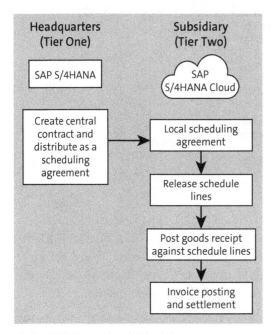

Figure 9.33 Centralized Scheduling Agreements

In the central buyer's SAP S/4HANA system at headquarters, a central contract is created and then distributed across various connected subsidiary systems. The scheduling agreement outline agreement type is distributed to subsidiaries. Scheduling agreements both with and without release information (document types LP and LPA, respectively) are enabled. Scheduling agreements aren't editable in the connected subsidiary systems, but schedule lines can be added manually in such systems.

9.8 Manufacturing

With recent changes in technology and digitization, the world has drastically changed; for manufacturers, the digital world has opened immense possibilities and new markets. Manufacturers want to reach their customers faster and exploit digitization without losing their competitive edge. Acquisitions and mergers have become the fastest modes of reaching out to customers in new and emerging markets. With each acquisition, an organization can extend its LoBs while maintaining the core at its headquarters. To leverage the advantages of such a model, organizations are always on the lookout to simplify the processes at and get complete visibility into subsidiaries.

SAP S/4HANA Cloud's two-tier ERP capabilities target this market need, which not only helps organizations have smoother and faster mergers and acquisitions thanks to simplifying the integration between headquarters and subsidiaries but also helps organizations reduce their costs. With SAP's two-tier ERP approach, organizations can now have integrated processes running between their subsidiaries and headquarters and can have complete visibility into their subsidiaries without affecting the flexibility and freedom of the same.

In this section, we'll cover how integrated manufacturing processes can be executed in a two-tier ERP mode, thus allowing organizations to use the core capabilities of subsidiaries and become competitive in a true sense. We'll discuss the following manufacturing scenarios:

- The subsidiary as a production unit and internal supplier to headquarters
- The subsidiary as the materials manager for headquarters' assembly processes
- How SAP S/4HANA Cloud integrates with manufacturing execution systems (MESs)
- Predictive material and resource planning with scheduling agreements
- MRP visibility scenarios

9.8.1 Production at Subsidiaries

When it comes to two-tier ERP deployment for manufacturing, one of the most common use cases occurs when headquarters has settled and matured the main production line for the final finished goods, but its subsidiaries manufacture the required components or subassemblies. This model is commonly seen in many industry sectors, such as the automobile and pharmaceutical industries, in which the component manufacturing unit will be the subsidiary supplying units to the OEMs—in other words, headquarters.

In this two-tier ERP deployment, headquarters will be running an on-premise ERP system (either SAP ERP or SAP S/4HANA), and the subsidiary runs SAP S/4HANA Cloud. In such deployment models, organizations will expect seamless technical integration between headquarters and the subsidiary to support an integrated business process.

In this manufacturing scenario, master data becomes the critical factor; in this case, the most important master data elements are the material master and the business partners. As a prerequisite, master data should be in sync between the subsidiary and headquarters. In this two-tier ERP scenario, headquarters plays the role of master data guardian and maintains the sanctity of the data; the carefully maintained master data should be replicated from headquarters to subsidiaries. (For SAP S/4HANA Cloud master data replication best practices, see scope item 1RO.) You can leverage several master data replication approaches, such as the DRF- or API-based approaches.

Another school of thought says that subsidiaries can have their own master data that may not be available at headquarters; in such cases, the subsidiaries are still allowed to create their own master data.

In this section, we'll focus on the approach in which master data is replicated from headquarters to subsidiaries. First, IDocs are used to send the master data from headquarters (running on either SAP ERP or on-premise SAP S/4HANA) to the subsidiary (running on SAP S/4HANA Cloud). On the receiving side, the appropriate API needs to be enabled with proper communication arrangements.

Make sure configurations such as RFC connections between the source and target system and the partner profile configuration are in place. For customer masters, use standard DEBMAS and material master MATMAS IDoc message types.

In this scenario, headquarters starts with demand management by creating planned independent requirements, either manually or by generating the forecast for the finished product. Based on this, headquarters runs MRP to create a procurement plan for finished goods, which is procured from the subsidiary location. As a result, purchase requisitions are generated. On approval, the purchase requisition will be converted to a purchase order with the vendor as the subsidiary. (Note that the purchase requisition/purchase order is an optional process.) At headquarters, the planners can analyze and evaluate the capacity load situation in subsidiary location by using two-tier ERP analytics. Planners can also manually create the purchase order directly without using the MRP run.

As shown in Figure 9.34, after issuing the purchase order from headquarters on the subsidiary, the corresponding sales order will be created automatically at the subsidiary. A document reference in the sales order and purchase order will help link the demand and the supply: the sales order will reflect the customer purchase order number, and the purchase order will show the reference document number under the **Confirmation** tab.

If an available-to-promise (ATP) check is activated at a subsidiary, then the SAP S/4HANA Cloud system will perform the availability check and propose the delivery schedule back to headquarters. The delivery date is updated in the purchase order issued from headquarters.

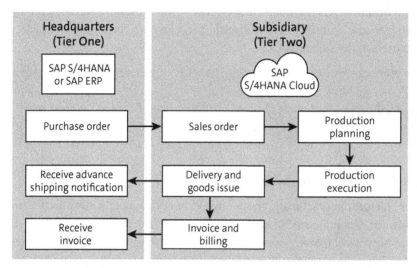

Figure 9.34 Subsidiary as Production Unit and Internal Supplier to Headquarters

At the subsidiary, the sales order becomes the primary demand. Subsequently, the MRP is run to fulfill the demands received from headquarters. This will generate the planned orders and purchase requisitions for produced and procured items (raw materials). These planned orders and purchase requisitions are converted into production orders and purchase orders.

Next, the production order must be released and confirmed. Headquarters can receive the update on the production bookings from the subsidiary through the two-tier ERP analytics report. Headquarters can also get a report on the production performance of the subsidiary location, scrap generated during the production process, raw material inventory levels, and an overview of any deviation from the raw material consumption.

Once the stock is available, the shipping specialist will review the sales order, and an outbound delivery is created against the sales order. This outbound delivery from the subsidiary will automatically create the ASN for the inbound delivery at headquarters against the purchase order. This is the next level of integration provided by the two-tier ERP approach, in which the purchase order at headquarters will be updated with inbound deliveries from the subsidiary.

Subsequently, at headquarters, the goods receipt will be made against the inbound delivery.

Finally, the billing document will be generated at the subsidiary, and a supplier invoice will be created at headquarters. This will create the accounts payable liability to the subsidiary at headquarters.

This is the third level of integration with headquarters provided by SAP's two-tier ERP approach. Now headquarters will make the payment to the subsidiary, in the same way as clearing its vendors' liability. This will settle the accounts receivable transaction from headquarters at the subsidiary.

Scope Item

The required SAP S/4HANA Cloud scope item is 21T. Refer to SAP Signavio Process Navigator for more details on this scope item.

9.8.2   Assembly at Subsidiaries with Components Provided by Headquarters

With two-tier ERP for manufacturing, another use case occurs when a subsidiary manages assembly for headquarters using components provided by headquarters. In today's competitive world, many organizations outsource small assemblies to their subsidiaries, which have expertise in particular areas. (In the previous scenario, the subsidiary only prepared the components and subassemblies, not the entire assemblies.)

In the auto industry, for example, the assembly of a wire harness requires expertise and specialized equipment; many auto manufacturers prefer that their sophisticated subsidiaries handle this rather than their headquarters. In this scenario, headquarters will supply the component to the subsidiary against the subcontracting purchase order.

In a two-tier ERP context, the subsidiary (runs on SAP S/4HANA Cloud) has expertise in particular products and supplies these products to headquarters (runs on either SAP ERP or SAP S/4HANA). Let's see in detail how the subsidiary manages assembly for headquarters with components provided by headquarters.

As a prerequisite, the master data between headquarters and the subsidiary should be in sync. In general, master data will be created in headquarters and shared across subsidiaries.

Figure 9.35 explains how the materials are handled by the subsidiary to make assemblies for headquarters. The process starts when a purchase order is created at headquarters. As part of integration in a two-tier ERP setup, an automatic sales order will be created at the subsidiary system with reference to the purchase order from headquarters. If prices are within the limits, then an automatic order confirmation will be sent back to headquarters, and the information will be updated in the **Confirmation** tab of the purchase order. In a two-tier ERP system, purchase order to sales order automation supports change and delete processes also.

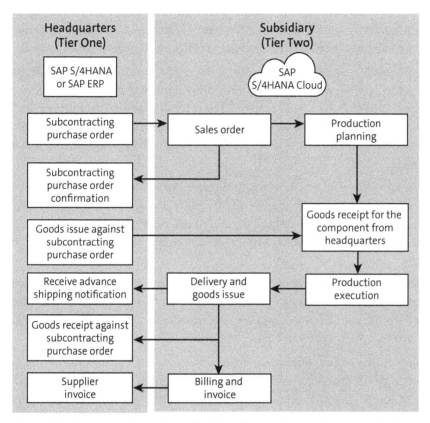

Figure 9.35 Managing Materials at the Subsidiary to Manage the Assembly for Headquarters

At the subsidiary, the demand fulfillment process starts with the MRP run for the demand, which comes in the form of sales orders from headquarters. The planned orders for the assemblies and the purchase requisitions for the components will be generated from the MRP run at the subsidiary. The purchase requisition for the components will be converted to purchase orders with zero value because these components are provided by headquarters for assembly processing. The components, which will be received by the subsidiary from headquarters, will be part of the headquarters' books of account; the subsidiary will be the custodian, and these components' inventory won't hit the subsidiary's books of account. The components requirements information will be communicated to headquarters manually via email or over the phone.

Headquarters will already have the bill of materials (BOM) for the subassembly and the components required for it. Headquarters will then issue the components against the subcontracting purchase order on the subsidiary and communicate the same to the subsidiary manually via email or over the phone.

A goods receipt will be posted for the components at the subsidiary with zero price against the purchase order created at the subsidiary with headquarters as the supplier. Once received, these components will create inventory in the subsidiary system and won't hit the subsidiary's books of account. From the headquarters' point of view, the components inventory will still show in its books of account, and though the components are physically at the subsidiary, headquarters has visibility of the components.

Once components are available at a subsidiary, the production process starts with the conversion of a planned order to production. Components will be staged for the production order; then the order will be released to carry out the real production. Once production is complete, the order will be confirmed against produced quantities, along with scrap if there is any. Finally, a goods receipt will be posted against the production order.

The shipping specialist will start the order fulfillment process by creating an outbound delivery against the sales order once assembly is ready. The warehouse clerk will pick the order and post goods issue against the outbound delivery. Once goods issue is posted, an automatic ASN will be sent to headquarters under the two-tier ERP approach.

At headquarters, an inbound delivery will be created automatically and will be updated in the **Purchase Order Confirmation** tab. This will be helpful for goods receipt planning. Once goods are received from a subsidiary, the warehouse clerk will post the goods receipt against the inbound delivery at headquarters against the purchase order.

At the subsidiary, the billing clerk will create a billing document against the outbound delivery. Once the billing document is posted, an automatic invoice will be sent to headquarters for payment. Headquarters will review the subsidiary's invoice and release payment.

Scope Item

The required SAP S/4HANA Cloud scope item is 2WL. Refer to SAP Signavio Process Navigator for more details on this scope item.

9.8.3   Integration with Manufacturing Execution Systems

The main purpose of a manufacturing execution system (MES) is to monitor, track, and report the manufacturing process from the beginning stages of the process through the finished product level, recording the WIP. An MES also helps enhance production efficiency and increase adoption of Industry 4.0 concepts.

As part of two-tier ERP deployment, a subsidiary using SAP S/4HANA Cloud will leverage the headquarters MES to monitor and control the production process at the subsidiary.

Figure 9.36 shows the end-to-end manufacturing process at the subsidiary location that shares the headquarters MES. As a prerequisite step before MES integration with SAP S/4HANA Cloud, master data and transaction data should be replicated in the MES.

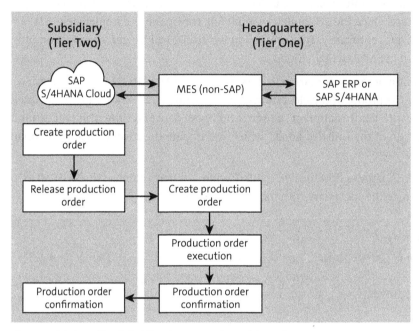

Figure 9.36 Supplier Subsidiary's Integration with MES

The manufacturing cycle starts with demand management. In this process, the production planner will have a forecast from the sales team or a concrete sales order from a customer for the finished goods. Now the sales plan needs to be synced with the production plan.

The next step is to create the production plan. Production planning is the core step of the end-to-end manufacturing process. Based on this production plan, subsequent steps are decided, and the planner will schedule the MRP. MRP will perform the net requirement calculation for the complete BOM structure and check whether the requirements are covered by the existing stock. If not, it will create the procurement proposals. Based on the procurement type, planned orders for produced items and purchase requisitions for procured items will be generated. The production planner will evaluate the MRP results and convert the planned order to a production order. The production supervisor will release the production order. This will release not only the production order header but also the operations.

The MES will get only production orders with the released status; the released production orders are replicated in the MES. Use communication scenario SAP_COM_0156 to integrate a MES through application link enabling (ALE) IDocs, business application programming interfaces (BAPIs), and OData calls.

On receiving the production order in the MES, the shop order is generated in the MES. Once this is released, a unique shop floor control (SFC) number will be generated. This SFC number can have a quantity of 1 or greater than 1 based on the material being built. The production operator will pick the SFC and start the build, using a production operator dashboard. Once the SFC build is completed, the operator completes the SFC and records any nonconformity. The completion of the SFC will trigger a production order confirmation in SAP S/4HANA Cloud.

The production order confirmation in the subsidiary's SAP S/4HANA Cloud system will also include the production yield, raw material consumption, scrap, and rework quantities, along with confirmation of the start and finish date and time. This will result in the production of the finished goods, which will update the inventory and the financials.

This scenario illustrates how the two-tier ERP approach helps connect the SAP S/4HANA Cloud system at the subsidiary with the MES at headquarters.

> **Scope Items**
>
> The required SAP S/4HANA Cloud scope item is 1Y5. To integrate with a third-party MES, use scope item 2JN. Refer to SAP Signavio Process Navigator for more details on these scope items.

9.8.4   Predictive Material and Resource Planning with Scheduling Agreements

This two-tier ERP scenario covers the process of medium-term planning with predictive material and resource planning (pMRP), as shown in Figure 9.37. A business use case example is where headquarters running on SAP S/4HANA manufactures the final assembly, and the subsidiary running on SAP S/4HANA Cloud supplies a key subassembly as part of the final product.

Using this scenario's capabilities, headquarters and the subsidiary can share details of targets and constraints for a quantity per period bucket through collaborative planning. Headquarters initiates the planning process through pMRP. The constraint quantity received from the subsidiary for the subassembly is considered at headquarters to arrive at the final plan to manufacture the final product.

Business benefits include the following:

- Capability to create simulations at both headquarters and the subsidiary, considering types of flexible constraints, enabling you to plan effectively with resource-based simulations

- Joint planning between headquarters and subsidiaries to arrive at a consensus plan for the final product and subassembly

- Operative planning with forecast-based schedules for the subsidiary to initiate MRP

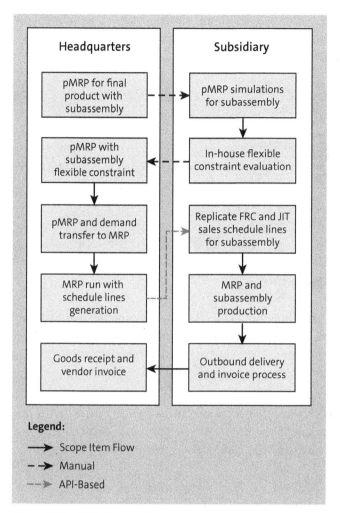

Figure 9.37 pMRP Process Flow

9.8.5 MRP Visibility Scenarios

In a two-tier ERP setup, MRP visibility scenarios involve synchronizing planning and inventory data between a central (tier 1) and subsidiary (tier 2) ERP system. MRP visibility ensures that both tiers have accurate, real-time access to material availability, demand forecasts, and production schedules across locations. This helps avoid stockouts and overproduction, and ensures efficient resource allocation by maintaining clear visibility and coordination of material needs across all levels of the organization. It's possible to enable visibility scenarios either at headquarters or at the subsidiary based on the business needs. We'll discuss both ways in this section:

- **MRP visibility at headquarters**

  In this case, as shown in Figure 9.38, usually the subsidiary receives the demand from the external customer, which then triggers creating customer sales orders manually. The planner can perform the MRP run, which generates procurement proposals. Procurement proposals are shared as demand to headquarters, and the production planning process follows.

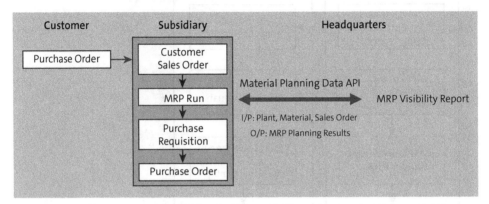

Figure 9.38 MRP Visibility at Headquarters

Headquarters can access the MRP Results view app by entering the material number/MRP element category/plant, and it displays the list of demands with the required stock for the given material. The app helps planners act proactively by planning for the underlying components to produce the assembly on time.

- **MRP visibility at subsidiaries**
  Users at subsidiaries, as shown in Figure 9.39, can have better visibility of MRP results of the production materials at headquarters. It also helps with transparency by providing access to the demand planned for the materials.

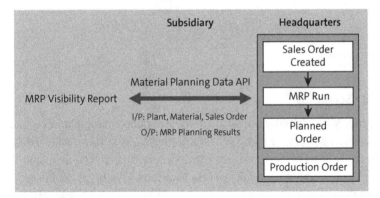

Figure 9.39 MRP Visibility at Subsidiaries

At the subsidiaries, the process starts with the creation of the purchase order, then triggers the automatic creation of the sales order at headquarters, and sends back the purchase order confirmation. Planners can perform the MRP run at headquarters to generate the planned order against the customer sales requirement. The planned order will be converted to a production order to proceed with the production activities. Users at subsidiaries can access the MRP Results View app to check the status of production planning. The list of replenishment elements, along with stock availability for the given material/sales order, is provided for planners at the subsidiary to act proactively to fulfill the customer requirement on time.

Scope Item

The required scope items for SAP S/4HANA Cloud are J44, J45, and 1BM. Refer to SAP Signavio Process Navigator for more details on these scope items.

9.9 Integration

In a two-tier ERP setup with SAP S/4HANA Cloud, integration plays an important role in an organization's digital transformation. On their journey to adopt innovations in the cloud, customers increasingly extend and integrate their existing on-premise applications into the cloud. In this section, we'll cover available integration approaches, monitoring, and accelerators that can be managed in a two-tier ERP deployment with SAP S/4HANA Cloud.

Integration has become a key enabler for the digital transformation of organizations. Therefore, one goal of the future SAP integration strategy is to increase the simplicity of integration between SAP applications by aligning their processes and related data models, including the publication of APIs. The target is to simplify new integration solutions, especially for LoB cloud integration scenarios, and to further deepen integrations between SAP applications over time.

Enterprise architects defining the integration strategy in their company's system landscape usually try to find the best possible way to provide integration guidance across multiple teams, projects, and system integrators. For them, it's important to look for the most suitable integration technologies to approach new integration domains. Integration is a critical component of the two-tier ERP solution. As shown in Figure 9.40, SAP S/4HANA Cloud can be integrated with both on-premise and cloud solutions from SAP and third-party providers.

The connectivity landscapes are illustrated in Figure 9.41. Factors to consider when determining the best connectivity option include the dominant system landscape, the availability of prepackaged content, go-live timelines, and the total cost of ownership. For example, standard content is available for the Cloud Integration capability, which reduces the total cost of implementation; in contrast, a custom interface needs to be built for SAP Process Integration or SAP Process Orchestration, which can extend the implementation process.

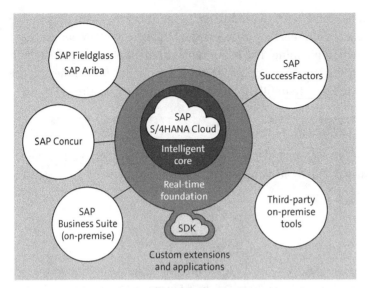

Figure 9.40 SAP S/4HANA Cloud Integrated into SAP Landscape

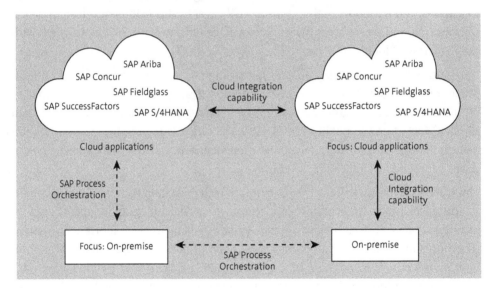

Figure 9.41 Two-Tier ERP Integration Approaches

Together, these integration approaches can support prepackaged integrations, template-based integrations, and allowlisted API-based integrations.

9.10   Analytics and Reporting

Analytics is information resulting from the semantic analysis of data presented in a meaningful pattern. Using analytics, companies can gain fast and accurate insights into their business and implement new processes and applications based on those insights. A growing number of organizations are looking for public cloud analytics solutions that can be implemented quickly without the need for manual upgrades and migrations. Similarly, analytics in a two-tier ERP deployment is an important consideration while deploying subsidiary ERP solutions. If pockets of analytics solutions remain in silos, then a company can't see the complete picture, thereby inhibiting the ability of the group organization to spot opportunities for growth and potential savings that can be obtained either due to overlap in operations or inefficient processes.

It's important that a decision-making chief analytics officer (CAO) or another C-suite executive has ownership of analytics across all groups' concerns and ties it into the groups' visions and corporate priorities. Business benefits of central analytics include streamlined processes between headquarters and subsidiaries for better planning and reporting, ability of headquarters to have visibility into subsidiaries' expenses and revenue, and process centralization.

Let's take analytics via SAP BTP one step further with analytics via SAP Analytics Cloud, a product built on SAP BTP. From planning predictive analytics to creating compelling data visualizations and from exploring data analytics to gaining smart insights along with data transformation, SAP Analytics Cloud has become the recommended solution for end-to-end business analytics in the cloud.

In a two-tier ERP deployment, as shown in Figure 9.42, headquarters and subsidiary systems' data can be combined in SAP Analytics Cloud for planning (planning models for data-driven budgeting and forecasting), collaboration (access-controlled alignment across plants/segments/business entities), and forecasting (machine learning-driven forecasting).

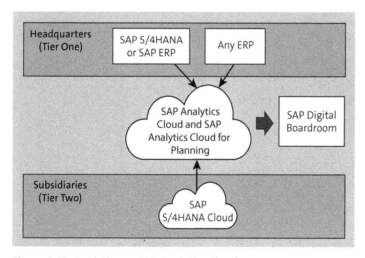

Figure 9.42 Analytics on SAP Analytics Cloud

9.11   Summary

In this chapter, we introduced the concept of two-tier ERP deployment with SAP S/4HANA Cloud and recommended deployment options in such hybrid deployments, and we did a deep dive into various end-to-end business processes, starting with master data and continuing through finance, sales, services, procurement, manufacturing, and sustainability. Toward the end, we touched upon integration approaches and central analytics supported in two-tier landscapes.

The next chapter will introduce the organizational change management (OCM) and enablement topics that are critical for both the project team and for driving the adoption and use of SAP S/4HANA in your organization.

Chapter 10

Organizational Change Management

In the ever-evolving world of business and technology, organizations constantly seek ways to adapt, innovate, and optimize their operations. One of the key factors that play a pivotal role in this process is organizational change management. Managing change effectively can be a game-changer for businesses, ensuring that their people, processes, and technology seamlessly align with evolving goals and strategies.

This chapter introduces SAP's global *organizational change management (OCM)* framework and approach that is fully available as cross-topic in the SAP Activate methodology. We'll also discuss the importance of the Customer Center of Expertise (Customer COE) for ongoing operational excellence in running the SAP solution. We'll discuss a wide range of topics from how to ensure organizational reading for transition from project organization to COE setup, the capabilities framework, and the progression of the transition activities through the phases of SAP Activate.

Now, let's start with the details of the OCM framework.

10.1 Organizational Change Management

Recognizing digital transformations as holistic business transformations, we'll start our discussion by describing the people-related challenges associated with implementing digital technologies. We'll then outline SAP's global OCM framework, providing a brief overview of its six dimensions. Next, we'll focus on the OCM methodology embedded in SAP Activate. After a visualization of the OCM deliverables aligned with the different SAP Activate phases, we'll guide you through an SAP implementation from an OCM perspective. This includes information on the specific people-related challenges and dynamics of each phase and the way OCM activities are orchestrated to address these topics. This supplements the OCM content available in the SAP Activate methodology, where detailed descriptions of the different deliverables and their practical implementation can be accessed.

We'll also highlight learning and enablement as integral part of OCM. It starts with elaborating how SAP implementations can profit from a structured learning and enablement approach, followed by an input on the learning and enablement support throughout an SAP project lifecycle. We'll highlight the specific challenges of cloud implementations and their implications for OCM, and the final section offers guidance on scoping OCM in an SAP implementation, considering both the project's and the company's characteristics as significant influencing factors on the OCM setup.

10.1.1   The People Side of Digital Transformation

We live in a digital age. Digital technologies are key triggers for progress and innovation. Therefore, almost every company currently follows up with digitalization, striving to improving operations, developing new products and business models, and thus reaching a competitive advantage.

The related implementation projects often focus on the technical aspects of digitalization, which of course can be very challenging. However, this is only one aspect of digitalization. Fully leveraging the potential of new digital technologies usually implies the adaptation of business processes, roles and responsibilities, and the development of new skills. In addition, it often requires alternative forms of collaboration across silos, a different mindset, and a new way of working. Overall, digital implementations are holistic business transformations, impacting the entire organization.

People-Related Challenges in Digital Transformations

Along with digitalization, the pace and intensity of change has accelerated dramatically: digital technologies allow a worldwide, quasi real-time handling of information, unprecedentedly speeding up decision-making processes. And the disruptive implications of artificial intelligence (AI) have only started to become visible and tangible. However, in this digital business world, people are still analogue creatures. They don't always behave logically, they need time to adapt to changes, and they have emotions, hopes, fears, and concerns. There is no "reset" button to make employees instantly adopt a new digital solution.

Imagine a company introduces new digital technology, yet users persist with their old routines or invent creative workarounds as if nothing changed. This scenario may be somewhat exaggerated, but it makes clear that digitalization is as much about people as it is about technology. Employees must be willing to adopt all the changes resulting from a digital transformation and be committed to use new digital tools and technologies in the intended way.

Importance of User Adoption

This leads to the concept of user adoption. *User adoption* is defined as the process users go through when they transfer from an old solution to a new solution, and finally adopt the new solution as well as start working with it. Low user adoption can manifest itself in very different ways. For example, users make handling errors, stick to old habits and processes, use workarounds wherever possible, don't enter data in the required quality, or refuse to use additional, value-adding functionalities. All of this can have multiple negative consequences for a company, for example, increased training needs, additional costs, a longer project duration, reduced efficiency—and even a complete failure of the entire transformation. Hence, user adoption is a key success factor and a continuous process that starts with the beginning of the project and goes beyond the go-live date!

Components Determining User Adoption

User adoption is the indicator of how willingly and to which extent users work with the new solution and consume the offered functions and features for their daily work. Whether employees finally use the new system in the intended way depends on three components:

- **Affective component**
  If an employee has positive emotions toward the new system and looks forward to working with it, he will more likely use the new system after go-live.

- **Cognitive component**
  If an employee believes that he'll benefit from working with the new system, this will increase the likelihood of his later system usage.

- **Behavioral component**
  If an employee actively looks for ways to integrate the system into the daily working routines, this will most probably lead to a high user adoption.

To summarize, user adoption is more than just people clicking the right buttons in the system—it's first and foremost an attitude.

Hoping for a kind of "big bang" user adoption on the go-live date without thoroughly preparing the users is a risky endeavor. Companies are well advised to not only manage the technical and functional aspects of their transformations but also address the equally important people-related challenges right from the project start.

Definition of OCM

This is exactly what OCM is about. According to the Project Management Institute, OCM can be defined as "a comprehensive, cyclic, and structured approach for transitioning individuals, groups, and organizations from a current state to a future state with intended business benefits." Having a closer look at the different elements of this definition helps to get a good understanding of the role OCM plays within a digital transformation:

- **OCM is a comprehensive, cyclic, and structured approach.**
  This means that OCM requires repeated activities and ideally provides a framework with tools and templates that give orientation and guidance for the complex dynamics during organizational change.

- **OCM is targeted at transitioning individuals, groups, and organizations.**
  When dealing with the people side, OCM addresses three different layers: individuals, groups, and the entire organization. OCM tries to best support the individual transition of each impacted employee. However, OCM can't just directly address every single individual; it also has to focus activities on different stakeholder groups. And, of course, a change manager will always have an eye on the organizational level.

- **OCM guides the way from a current to a future state.**
  This aspect of the definition points out that OCM supports the *process* from the as-is situation to the desired to-be situation. It's not responsible for the project *content*, for example, analyzing the current state or defining the future state. This is usually done by the functional experts of the transformation project.

- **OCM focuses on the intended business benefits.**
  OCM isn't an end in itself. It's clearly targeted at supporting the project to reach the predefined goals and realize the desired business benefits.

Added Value of OCM

Supporting a digital transformation with OCM is an investment. Planning and executing change management activities requires manpower and financial resources. Some companies ask themselves if these investments pay off in the end. The answer is a clear yes! Although it's challenging to calculate an exact financial benefit, many studies indicate that OCM has a positive impact on the overall project success.

By acting as a bridge between the business and the project team, the change manager fosters constructive dialogue with all relevant stakeholder groups, ensuring that the respective needs are seen, taken seriously, and addressed appropriately. This enhances stakeholder commitment and reduces resistance, making it easier to stick to the project plan and more likely to finish the project on time, in scope and on budget.

Above all, by driving a fast and sustainable user adoption, companies can immediately benefit from the advantages the new digital technology provides. This has positive effects on both the productivity of the impacted workforce and on the project's return on invest.

10.1.2   OCM Framework

SAP's comprehensive OCM framework is the result of more than two decades of practical experience. It has been developed to professionally manage the people side of SAP projects and to foster fast and sustainable user adoption. The framework consists of six dimensions, supporting the entire implementation lifecycle by addressing all relevant OCM action areas (see Figure 10.1).

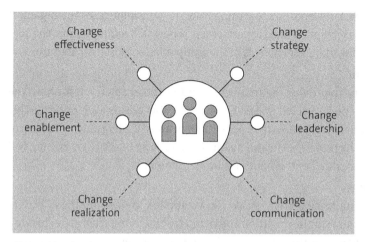

Figure 10.1 SAP's Organizational Change Management Framework

Each of the six OCM framework dimensions has a specific focus aimed at supporting the implementation process of an SAP solution:

- **Change strategy**
  This dimension covers activities that are required to set up OCM properly. This includes both outlining the direction of the OCM support for the SAP project and identifying which specific challenges should be tackled. The definition of corner-stones for the OCM setup and the development of an initial plan that summarizes the upcoming OCM activities also belong to the change strategy dimension.

- **Change leadership**
  This dimension is about managing all relevant stakeholders to create a positive atti-tude toward the SAP project and to reduce resistance. As business leaders are important role models, it's crucial that they actively support the project and spread consistent messages within their teams. Especially useful for larger implementation programs, one change leadership activity is to work with change agents who take over local change management tasks.

- **Change communication**
  This dimension aims to deliver the right message to the right people at the right time. Missing information is an often-neglected reason for resistance during an SAP implementation. The change communication dimension contains the planning, de-velopment, and execution of suitable communication activities for all relevant stakeholders. By creating awareness and commitment for the SAP project, change communication enhances the willingness of the users to embrace upcoming changes.

- **Change realization**
  This dimension encompasses the identification and management of the change impacts associated with the SAP implementation. This emphasizes not only system

10

and process changes, but also shifts regarding roles, responsibilities, or the organizational setup, as well as people-related aspects, such as new skill requirements, changes in the overall way of working, or changes of the companies' mindset and culture.

- **Change enablement**

  This dimension aims to provide the required learning and enablement for both the project team and the impacted users throughout the entire SAP project. This includes the development of an enablement strategy and the identification of learning needs for both the project team and business users. Role-based user training will be developed and provided as the system is implemented.

- **Change effectiveness**

  This dimension contains all activities that can be applied to measure the effectiveness of OCM activities. Monitoring their impact helps find out if they are achieving the desired objectives or if they must be adjusted. Furthermore, change effectiveness contains the tracking of criteria such as business readiness or user adoption, detecting potential issues at an early stage and thus allowing the project team to react accordingly.

10.1.3   OCM in SAP Activate

SAP's OCM methodology is fully aligned with SAP Activate. Figure 10.2 illustrates the alignment of all OCM deliverables with the different SAP Activate phases. A core set of OCM deliverables is located within the solution adoption workstream for all roadmaps. In addition, the full OCM methodology is also accessible as a cross-topic in SAP Activate Roadmap Viewer (see Chapter 3, Section 3.1).

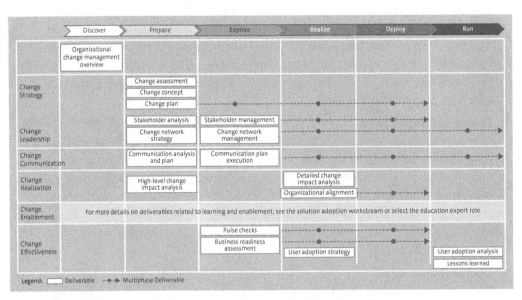

Figure 10.2 SAP's OCM Methodology Aligned with SAP Activate Phases

The OCM methodology supports organizations of all sizes embarking on SAP projects, offering a systematic approach to effectively manage the people side of such transformations. It provides guidance on how to set up and implement OCM throughout the entire project lifecycle. The subsequent sections will help explain how OCM addresses the unique dynamics and challenges of each SAP Activate phase, with a focus on providing a general overview. More detailed information is available in the cross-topic section of the SAP Activate Roadmap Viewer. For each deliverable, this section contains step-by-step descriptions of the required tasks and procedures, supplemented with hands-on tools and templates.

The change enablement dimension focuses on the learning and enablement activities of an SAP project, which are described in a separate chapter. There are practical reasons for this. First, the responsibility for the enablement activities is often assigned to specific project roles and resources, such as a learning and enablement architect. Second, the deliverables, tasks, and accelerators associated with the change enablement dimension are directly integrated into the solution-specific roadmaps of SAP Activate Roadmap Viewer. Lastly, the two important supporting tools—SAP Enable Now and SAP Learning Hub—will also be highlighted in this chapter.

Discover

The overall purpose of the discover phase is to get a good understanding of the solution capabilities and to comprehend the business value of the solution for the organization. The focus of the project team is usually on the functional and technical side of the upcoming project. However, it's highly recommended to also start the discussion on the people side of the transformation. Especially in companies with no or limited practical experience regarding OCM, there is often a broad range of diverse stakeholder opinions on the responsibility, scope, tasks, and added value of OCM. Thus, the perception of whether OCM is needed in an SAP project and which topics should be addressed often varies substantially across the decision-makers. These different views can lead to time-consuming decision-making processes, a delayed start of OCM, and to unrealistic or conflicting expectations, making a later setup and execution of OCM unnecessarily difficult.

Thus, creating a shared understanding of OCM among the key project stakeholders is an important task during the discover phase. SAP's global learning platform (*https://learning.sap.com*) offers comprehensive OCM-related learning journeys to support an effective and fast knowledge transfer to the relevant stakeholders of an upcoming SAP project.

Learning Offers on SAP's Global Learning Platform

In addition to technical, functional, and product-related content, SAP Learning Hub also contains learning journeys (*https://learning.sap.com*) regarding the people side of SAP transformations:

- **Discover Organizational Change Management for SAP Cloud Projects** (*http://s-prs.co/v596642*)
  This learning journey explains how OCM contributes to the success of an SAP implementation and provides an overview about key OCM activities.
- **Getting Started with Learning and Enablement in SAP Projects** (http://s-prs.co/v596643)
  This learning journey provides foundational knowledge about all learning and enablement activities within an SAP project and a clear methodology to follow.

Both learning journeys can be completed with a record of achievement. Further learning assets are added to the platform on an ongoing basis.

Another focus for OCM in this phase is to collect information regarding the potential people-related challenges of the SAP implementation. Based on these insights, the scope for OCM is defined and the required resources are identified and assigned (Section 10.1.6). Finally, in this phase, how OCM will be integrated into the project organization can be determined or at least discussed.

Prepare

During the prepare phase, the SAP project is set up, project team members are assigned, and the initial project plan is finalized. Everything is done to ensure a good project start. The same applies for OCM: based on a systematic as-is analysis, the change plan and the communication plan are developed.

Because the prepare phase is rather short, collecting the required information for the OCM setup can be challenging. The project leaders sometimes don't perceive an added value of the analysis activities and expect OCM to begin with concrete activities right away. However, a thorough *change assessment* is the foundation for all upcoming OCM steps. It's important to understand the special characteristics of the business units impacted by the project, for example, their previous experience with IT-driven transformations, the way change is handled, the key values, and the general dos and don'ts in the cooperation. This knowledge allows for identifying the assets OCM can build upon, avoiding pitfalls, and enabling OCM to design OCM interventions that are compatible with the organization. Furthermore, the change assessment targets collecting information about the project, such as the generic implications for the impacted units, the expected reactions of the users, and the key challenges OCM should address. Overall, the insights gained during the change assessment are a prerequisite for prioritizing action areas, maximizing the impact of OCM interventions, and making the best use of the available resources.

Like the overall OCM setup, initiating the change communication also starts with investigating the current status. In general, the *communication analysis and plan* and the execution of communication activities requires a significant time investment not only from the OCM resources but also from the project team. Functional experts must provide input for creating compelling communication assets, and the project leaders are especially actively involved in the communication delivery, for example as speaker in all-employee meetings or Q&A sessions. To make the best use of this investment, project-related information must be delivered via appropriate communication channels to the appropriate user groups. In this context, the communication channel analysis plays an important role. Creating an overview of the existing channels, such as internet pages, newsletters, meetings, or collaboration platforms, and evaluating their advantages and limitations for the change communication, enables the identification of suitable methods and media for conveying project-related information. Furthermore, additional channels can be implemented, if needed.

Another up-front activity for setting up change communication professionally is the *communication needs analysis*. By clustering the impacted users in distinct target groups, assessing the existing knowledge about the implementation project, and identifying the respective information needs, communication activities can be tailored to best meet the specific requirements of each group.

A valuable source of information for the definition of these groups is the *stakeholder analysis*. Usually conducted both on the individual and group level, the stakeholder analysis provides a systematic overview of the stakeholder landscape for the SAP project. Dividing the impacted users into subgroups with similar characteristics and capturing information such as the number, business unit allocation, and geographic location, is a prerequisite not only for an effective change communication but also for setting up learning and enablement activities. On an individual level, the stakeholder analysis assesses key individuals regarding their attitude toward the project and their power to influence the project success. Being aware of these aspects is the basis for deriving stakeholder engagement activities and setting up a systematic stakeholder management.

As already mentioned, these analysis activities are not an end in themselves. The communication channel analysis and communication needs analysis are the input for creating the initial version of the communication plan. This plan supports the setup, synchronization, and tracking of all project-related communication measures. It helps to identify required resources, assign clear responsibilities, and foster consistent messaging throughout the project.

In a similar way, the *change plan* documents all intended OCM activities to support the SAP implementation. The initial version developed in the prepare phase is still rather generic. As the project proceeds, the plan will be refined and adjusted on an ongoing basis. In addition, the change plan has to be synchronized with the project plan. Thus, if the project plan is adapted, the change plan must be updated accordingly.

If the organization decides to support the SAP implementation with a change network, the development of a *change network strategy* is another task during the prepare phase. Working with decentral change agents helps OCM especially in designing change communication activities to meet the requirements of different location, coordinating on-site communication efforts and in establishing feedback channels into the organization. The change network strategy documents the cornerstones, for example, a role description, including tasks and skill requirements, and the nomination procedure.

Toward the end of the prepare phase, conducting a *high-level change impact analysis* may be necessary. Especially for transformations with a medium to high complexity, this analysis helps to obtain insights regarding the level and type of impact of the SAP project on the different business units. These insights help to create awareness of impending changes, to focus OCM activities and to identify people-related risks, which then can be tackled at an early stage. Once important additional information regarding change impacts is available, the high-level change impact analysis should be updated.

In the following project phases, OCM will be able to build upon the different analysis steps when getting into a more execution mode in the next phases. Nevertheless, despite the undisputable importance and added value of the analyses during the prepare phase, OCM should also invest time in hands-on activities, providing immediate, visible added value for the impacted users. An example of such activities is the creation of generic communication assets addressing all impacted users, such as a project presentation, short explanatory videos, FAQ lists, or a project glossary.

Overall, finding a good balance between conceptual work and delivering first visible, hands-on activities right from the start helps to position OCM well within the project team and fosters good, trusting cooperation between change management and project management.

Explore

After the project has been successfully set up, the project team conducts a detailed examination of the company's current business processes and performs the fit-to-standard analysis. During the fit-to-standard workshops, the implications of the new solutions become clearer. In this context, some resistance is likely to occur, especially in business units that don't yet perceive an added value of the new way of working.

To create a broad commitment to the project, OCM follows up upon the initial stakeholder engagement activities defined during the prepare phase. This includes implementing these activities, reviewing and updating the stakeholder analysis, and establishing *stakeholder management* as an ongoing process throughout the project duration. Especially regarding the management of individual stakeholders, a close collaboration with the project leadership team is required. Winning critical key stakeholders to support the project and thus ensuring a broad leadership commitment is important, as the leaders are important multipliers for the project, conveying messages into the organization and winning employees for the transformation.

Furthermore, implementing the change network is an OCM task during the explore phase. Usually, OCM takes over the preparation and facilitation of the network meetings, starting with a kickoff. Especially in the first meeting, members of the project leadership team also join and provide information on the SAP project. For successful *change network management*, it's important to create an open atmosphere that allows the change agents to raise any issues or concerns that came up in the units they represent. Furthermore, targeted training initiatives, especially regarding soft skills, as well as compelling supporting material (e.g., communication packages) are prerequisites for the change agents to fulfill their tasks.

Following the initial planning of the change communication during the prepare phase, the focus of change communication in all subsequent project phases is on the *communication plan execution*. As the project proceeds and more detailed information is available, the change communication activities in the explore phase start addressing the different stakeholder groups, referring to their respective needs and concerns, and conveying specific information. The activities strive to further foster awareness for the SAP project, to promote the project's benefits both for the company and the respective user groups, and to motivate the users to actively support the project. The communication plan is the central steering tool, providing an overview of both already completed and upcoming activities. Therefore, a constant, thorough update of the plan is indispensable.

As some of the key activities have now been set up, OCM can also start to tackle the first change effectiveness topics. *Pulse checks* are usually conducted repeatedly as short surveys to collect feedback and to track the development regarding a specific topic, for example, the collaboration within the project team, the overall perception of the SAP project, or the evaluation of OCM interventions. Depending on the topic, the survey can address the project team or a subset of the project team members, all impacted users, or specific target groups, such as the employees of a business area or the change agents. Deriving implications and providing feedback to the pulse check participants is key for ensuring a high participation rate in follow-up surveys.

The end of the explore phase is usually the earliest point in time to conduct the first business readiness assessment. It targets assessing the overall readiness of the business areas affected by an SAP implementation as the go-live date approaches, striving to ensure a seamless transition to the new system. Like pulse checks, the *business readiness assessment* can be carried out repeatedly in different project phases. The focus is on identifying people-related project challenges as soon as possible, allowing enough time for their effective resolution. In subsequent surveys, the business readiness assessment can also evaluate the impact of conducted mitigation activities.

All OCM measures derived from the different activities described previously must be integrated in the change plan. This should be done with appropriate granularity, avoiding unnecessary updating and tracking effort, but allowing for a comprehensive overview of the OCM support at any point in time. In general, OCM in the explore phase should succeed in transferring the preparatory activities of the previous phase into routines that will be carried out throughout the project, switching from a planning mode to an executing mode.

Realize

After exploring SAP's best-practice standard and agreeing on the to-be processes and solution, the project team starts configuring the new solution. In addition, the realize phase includes project activities such as data migration, system integration, and extensive testing to ensure the solution meets performance and functionality expectations. As the go-live comes closer, general attention for the project rises. Users are interested in concrete information on how they will be impacted by the new SAP solution.

Therefore, the detailed *change impact analysis* is a key activity for OCM. The task should be performed at the beginning of the realize phase, when the to-be processes and solution are defined. This allows enough time for preparing the organization well for the go-live. The change impact analysis is best conducted in a series of short workshops, each one focusing on a specific part of the overall implementation scope, for example, a process scope area. Experts from various business units and diverse backgrounds, such as subject matter experts, process owners, and key users, discuss the upcoming changes. They not only holistically consider technological and processual aspects but also reflect changes regarding roles and responsibilities, organizational setup, and implications for people, for example, new skill requirements or the need to adapt the mindset and culture. An additional quantitative rating of the change impacts (e.g., high, medium, and low) facilitates the visualization of the results and enables easy detection of topics requiring high OCM support. Already during the workshops, initial ideas for supporting measures should be collected and documented. Following the assessment, these ideas are then further elaborated on, and responsibilities for the implementation are assigned.

The results of the detailed change impact analysis provide important input for the change communication. OCM must aggregate the gained insights for the different user groups and convey easy-to-understand information on the upcoming changes to make the transformation tangible. This reduces uncertainty and rumors, enhances commitment to the transformation and contributes to motivating the users to prepare well for the upcoming go-live.

Preparing the business units for the transition also includes the *organizational alignment*. This step ensures that the organizational setup aligns with the requirements of the new standard processes. The focus of OCM in this context is the facilitation of the role mapping process: using the stakeholder list of affected business users, the new SAP roles are allocated to the employees. Typically, this step takes place in a workshop setting involving the relevant business process owners and the authorization team. Organizational alignment also includes the alignment of organizational policies, procedures, and structures. This requires the active contribution of many different parties, including the project team, leadership team of affected business units, business process owners, and HR department. OCM should ensure a clear assignment of responsibilities throughout this process to avoid misunderstandings or duplication of effort. Overall, OCM plays a supportive role in this process; it's not tasked with providing functional advice, elaborating the new organizational structure, or determining the target operating model.

Another activity of OCM in the realize phase is the development of the *user adoption strategy*. The user adoption strategy aims to systematically identify and manage factors that influence user adoption in the SAP project. By measuring key adoption and experience metrics, issues and potential risks can be proactively identified at an early stage. During the realize phase, it's possible to monitor influencing factors on user adoption; the actual user adoption can only be assessed after go-live. The user adoption strategy defines key performance indicators (KPIs) for both phases and describes the data gathering process. Integrating insights from the detailed change impact analysis provides information for choosing appropriate KPIs and helps prioritize mitigation measures in business areas expected to experience high change impacts. After the conceptual setup is completed, the KPIs defined before go-live are collected, and mitigation activities derived and implemented.

Deploy

During the deploy phase, the project team conducts preparation activities, such as setting up the system and migrating data from the legacy system to the new solution. After go-live, the project team supports the users in working with the new system, helping them to solve technical issues and answering any system-related questions that might come up. At the end of this intensive hypercare period, the project team hands the system to the IT department that then takes care of ongoing system operations, continuous user support, and enablement.

OCM plays a crucial role in supporting the transition. As the deploy phase is rather short and many different topics must be handled in parallel by the project team, OCM ensures that the people side of the transformation isn't neglected. Besides the completion of open organizational alignment tasks, OCM is engaged preparing and delivering the go-live communication. The content includes concrete, user group–specific information on the go-live timeline; system access; contacts for issues and problems; learning and enablement opportunities; and details on additional support offers. This enhances trust among users that the transition is well prepared and reduces concerns and insecurity.

Furthermore, it's recommended to conduct a business readiness assessment close to go-live. Identifying and addressing existing hurdles for a successful start of the new solution provides valuable input for the project team and helps to target the final preparation activities.

Overall, the deploy phase is characterized by high pressure, challenging timelines, and unexpected issues popping up, sometimes requiring immediate actions. Thus, a close collaboration and ongoing, frequent alignment between project management and change management, high flexibility, and a mutual support during this phase are key.

Run

After the go-live has been completed and the new system is running, the project team hands over to the IT department and the business units. The focus of the run phase is to ensure that the solution is running at peak performance and to take advantage of the regular innovations that SAP releases for the solution. This includes ongoing system operations, continuous business process and system improvements, new scope activation, and onboarding of new users.

OCM can now conduct the *user adoption analysis*, collecting the agreed-on KPIs for tracking the actual user behavior. This evaluation of users' interactions with the new system and adherence to new processes helps pinpoint obstacles and issues hindering user acceptance and derives measures to reinforce the use of the new system. As sustainable user adoption is key to realize all benefits of the standards and ongoing updates the SAP solution provides, establishing ongoing monitoring processes for user adoption after project completion is essential. Thus, OCM fosters the implementation of support structures and the delegation of distinct responsibilities within the organization to drive and sustain user adoption.

Before the project is closed and OCM terminates its support, it's recommended to derive *lessons learned* regarding the OCM delivery during the project. This is usually done in a workshop setting. In an open, constructive discussion without blaming or finger-pointing, teams can identify successes, best practices, challenges, and difficulties regarding the OCM project support and then make recommendations for the future handling of derived people-related project matters. These recommendations enhance both the successful management of upcoming SAP projects and also the competency of the organization to professionally address the people side of business transformations in general.

10.1.4   Learning and Enablement

Learning and enablement is critical for any SAP project. While a comprehensive learning offering helps the users to acquire the right knowledge and skills related to SAP systems and processes, enablement focuses on practical application and ongoing support to ensure users can effectively leverage the SAP solution in their daily work. An SAP project benefits from a professional and structured learning and enablement approach in multiple ways:

- **Mitigation of project risks and higher return on investment**
  - Well-trained project team members and users reduce implementation risks.
  - Effective training ensures that organizations get the most value out of their SAP investment by fully leveraging system capabilities.
  - Proper enablement reduces the number of support tickets and issues after go-live.

- **Facilitation of knowledge transfer and development of internal expertise**
  - Enabling key users creates internal SAP experts who can support others.
  - Exhaustive training materials preserve and enhance system knowledge within the organization.
- **Faster adoption and better usage of the new SAP system**
  - Comprehensive learning and enablement offerings help users understand how to effectively use the new SAP solution in their daily work.
  - Well-trained users can work more efficiently in the new system, reducing handling errors and increasing productivity.
- **Continuous improvement and innovation**
  - Ongoing learning allows users to stay up to date with new features and optimizations.
  - A culture of continuous learning makes it easier to adapt to future SAP upgrades and enhancements.

The learning and enablement approach is an integral part of the OCM methodology and fully aligned with the SAP Activate phases. The key deliverables and tasks aligned to each phase are briefly described.

Prepare

In the prepare phase, the project team is onboarded and starts building the foundation for the SAP project and subsequent project phases. From a learning and enablement standpoint, it's crucial to ensure that the project team members have the right competencies to fulfill their project roles. This includes knowledge and skills related to the SAP systems and best-practice processes in scope of the project, as well as the tools, technologies, and methodologies used to implement the SAP solution.

One of the first activities to support knowledge building is the *learning needs analysis for the project team*. Based on the project scope, the learning requirements for each project team member are identified and aligned with key project stakeholders. The results of the learning needs analysis are used to develop a learning curriculum, outlining the SAP standard courses that the different project roles require. A valuable source for available training content is SAP Learning Hub and the global learning platform (*https://learning.sap.com*). After validating and approving the curriculum, the project team members get specific learning courses assigned to them and are asked to complete them.

SAP Learning Hub

As mentioned earlier, SAP Learning Hub (*https://learning.sap.com*) is a digital learning solution that supports learners in building and maintaining SAP software skills. It offers various learning formats. With access to both self-study and guided learning

---

resources, learners can follow learning journeys tailored to specific roles and skill levels, to upskill in SAP solutions and topics. Learners can also access guided learning resources, to deepen their knowledge across the SAP solution portfolio. A subscription to SAP Learning Hub provides access to an extensive number of guided learning resources and management capabilities, such as the following:

- Expert-led live sessions covering deep dives and preparations to stay certified
- Access to hands-on practice systems and sandbox SAP environments, prefilled with data and exercises to experiment with solutions
- Four SAP certification exam attempts per year and access to enablement and assessment to stay certified
- Learning analytics capabilities to support individual and team management

In parallel to the training activities for the project team, the learning and enablement lead builds the *enablement strategy*, which is the foundation for the learning and enablement stream in the subsequent project phases. The enablement strategy provides a clear framework and guidance for all enablement activities within the SAP project. An important step in developing the strategy is an assessment of the current learning culture and the existing learning and enablement capabilities of the company that can be leveraged in the SAP project. This covers existing training and education resources, content development tools, enablement platforms, knowledge sharing channels, or governance processes. Based on the assessment results, all necessary enablement activities to support the SAP implementation are defined and documented in an enablement strategy document and plan.

Overall, it's advisable to assign a dedicated *enablement project manager* to oversee the learning and enablement activities. This role can set up and manage the learning and enablement stream in an SAP project on the basis of best practices, tools, and methods from SAP.

Explore

After the functional project workstream teams have built their knowledge through attending training and completing self-study, they start exploring the business requirements during the fit-to-standard workshops. At this point in time, the learning and enablement team turns their attention to the *learning needs analysis for users*. The team usually conducts workshops per workstream with subject matter experts to identify target user groups and learning needs for the SAP solutions and best practice processes in scope of the project. The results of the stakeholder analysis serve as a useful data source for this activity by providing information about the type and number of user groups impacted by the SAP project. If available, the results of the change impact analysis can be used to detect further learning needs for the different target groups. The results will be shared with the business managers, giving them the opportunity to address potential skill gaps before go-live.

After identifying the learning needs for the different user groups, a learning curriculum must be created. The resulting course catalog contains the preferred content types such as videos, concept slides, e-learning, work instructions, simulations, exercises, and assessments that must be created. It's structured by process area, including key tasks, process overviews, targeted business role, learning duration, method of delivery, and any prerequisites. Based on the course catalog, a high-level content development plan will be created to estimate the resources and time needed for the enablement content development and delivery work. The results of the learning needs analysis will be presented to the business subject matter experts and key project stakeholders for review and final sign-off.

Especially in SAP projects with a huge process scope and many stakeholders, it's advisable to streamline and standardize the learning content. Therefore, using an authoring and performance support tool is highly recommended to make learning content development efficient and the distribution to users as easy as possible. If customers want to use SAP Enable Now as their preferred content development tool, a parallel activity in the explore phase is the *deployment of SAP Enable Now*. This task includes preparing and technically installing the content development tool, creating the necessary templates, and enabling authors and administrators on how to use the tool.

SAP Enable Now

SAP Enable Now is a comprehensive content authoring, curation and delivery platform. It gives each user the role-based information, guidance, and eLearning they need to adopt any new technologies that will be implemented. At the same time, SAP Enable Now helps to create, manage, and deliver enablement content—from videos to virtual training—across all channels and formats. By providing in-application help and eLearning content to users, SAP Enable Now increases their competence and confidence, while fostering adoption, productivity, and performance across the business. You can see SAP Enable Now Info Center in Figure 10.3.

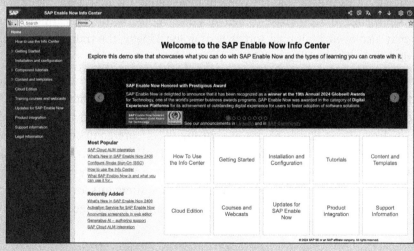

Figure 10.3 SAP Enable Now Info Center

More information about SAP Enable Now is available on the following websites:

- SAP product overview: *www.sap.com/products/hcm/enable-now.html*
- SAP Help Portal: *https://help.sap.com/docs/SAP_ENABLE_NOW*
- SAP Enable Now Info Center: *https://enable-now.sap.com*

Realize

An important outcome of the learning needs analysis is the approved plan for *enablement content development*. This plan contains the defined roles and responsibilities for the content development team members, assigned resources (e.g., subject matter experts, content developer, and trainer), and timelines for development. During the realize phase, the learning and enablement team executes the plan and develops the enablement content for the SAP project.

A variety of learning and enablement content will be created for classroom training, online learning, and self-study. Providing a wide range of engaging learning content enhances the user's overall learning experience, their knowledge retention, and the adoption of the new solution. An important part of this development activity is a continuous review process to ensure the content is developed to the right quality and adheres to customer branding standards and tone of voice. At the end of the review process, the enablement content is approved and ready for delivery.

Deploy

During the deploy phase, *enablement delivery* commences for targeted users of the SAP project. Usually, this process begins with pilot training. The pilot serves as a "dry run" to test that content has been developed correctly and to ensure delivery readiness. For scaling the training delivery to many users, it's often necessary to start with a "train the trainer" activity. This means that the content development team equips the trainers with the knowledge and expertise to deliver effective instructor-led learning. Some trainers may also need additional soft skills training. Finally, the trainer delivers the courses directly to the business users.

Enablement delivery is usually supported by comprehensive communication activities, such as announcements for the upcoming training activities, information about available training courses, and trainer and contact persons for any learning and enablement-related questions. Furthermore, it's an important prerequisite for a smooth delivery to ensure courses are administered correctly. Typically, an enablement administrator will take care of the learning logistics, such as the availability of sufficient on-site learning rooms, booking of classrooms, technical requirements for virtual session, invitation management, attendance tracking processes, and course feedback.

Run

After go-live and during the run phase, the trainers can support further knowledge transfer and coaching with a blend of technical support, refresher training, or ongoing user support. It's important that the trainers capture feedback during enablement delivery to facilitate the continuous improvement of enablement content and activities. In addition, leveraging a performance support tool such as SAP Enable Now can be very helpful to assist users with adopting newly deployed functions and features for their day-to-day business.

Overall, learning and enablement are important elements of the OCM methodology and contribute substantially to the success of an SAP project. A timely start to the learning and enablement activities and sufficient resources allocated to them are crucial prerequisites for developing and delivering high-quality enablement content to the business. Therefore, project stakeholders and decision-makers shouldn't neglect the effort required to manage and deliver effective enablement to the business user.

10.1.5 OCM in the Cloud Context

Cloud-driven transformations have some special characteristics. Probably the most obvious one is a mindset change from the fit-gap approach in the on-premise world to the fit-to-standard approach in the cloud context. In this approach, the company adapts to the solution instead of the solution being adapted to the company's requirements. Overall, there are some important aspects change managers should keep in mind when supporting a cloud project.

Promoting the Cloud Standard

One asset of SAP cloud solutions is that they provide best practice processes. Companies profit the most from implementing cloud software when they stick to the predefined standard. Unfortunately, some decision-makers and project leaders tend to think that moving to the cloud standard with a modern, easy-to-handle interface and best practice processes automatically leads to happy, committed users. They underestimate that even a change for the better is still a change. Users want to know why the change is necessary and what it means for them. They want to be supported in building up new skills and unlearning previous habits. In brief—they want to be taken seriously.

OCM plays an important role in convincing and winning over users. At the same time, change management must take into consideration the special characteristics of cloud projects. Most importantly, OCM in these projects is *not* about broad participation! Other than in transformations with more degrees of freedom, it's not opportune to ask the users how they would like to design the user interface and the new business processes. Change managers should avoid falling into this trap because pseudo-participation causes a lot of disappointment, frustration, and even resistance on the users' end and can cause significant harm to the project.

Keeping Up with Fast Cloud Implementations

SAP cloud solutions can be implemented very fast. The closer a company sticks to the standard, the easier is the technological side: the cloud software is more or less ready to use right from the project start. The new solution and the new "look and feel" can be shown immediately, making the future way of working tangible for the users at an early stage. However, human beings don't adapt to changes in real time! It can take a while to develop new skills and habits and—let's not forget—to unlearn the way things have been done so far. If companies "rush to adapt" and don't invest enough time and energy into the transition process, this might cause stress and frustration as well as lead to unnecessary frictions during the implementation. Thus, OCM activities should be initiated as early as possible because a delayed start can hardly be compensated for. Already in the on-premise world, integrating OCM only after the first people-related issues came up was difficult; in the cloud world, this "firefighting-approach" is now completely outdated. Furthermore, assigned OCM resources should be available throughout the entire project duration because an exchange leads to additional onboarding activities. The required time investment is often not reflected in the tough project timeline. Finally, OCM must be delivered fast, for example, by leveraging digital tools and technologies, whenever possible. This reduces the time for collecting and analyzing data and creating compelling visualizations.

Supporting Continuous Adoption

Preparing the users for go-live is an important task for OCM—and usually one of the last OCM activities. The cloud project normally ends shortly after the go-live with a hypercare phase. But the official project end doesn't mean that the change is over: cloud solutions are refined and further improved on an ongoing basis. With every release cycle, the users receive updates, for example, new functions and features driving innovation. Therefore, companies should prepare the users for the need of constant adaptation throughout the entire software lifecycle and foster a mindset of embracing permanent change beyond the go-live. Change managers should initiate the development of suited support structures and expert networks together with the business, taking care of clear responsibilities for the implementation and maintenance of these structures. This helps users integrate updates into their daily working routines and thus foster a consistently high user adoption.

10.1.6   Scoping OCM for an SAP Project

Companies differ strongly in the way they handle change. For some, ongoing change is part of their DNA, while others stick to old attitudes and habits and often struggle with getting accustomed to something new. Similarly, every SAP implementation has its own characteristics and dynamics, especially when it comes to the people side. Thus, when it comes to setting up OCM for an SAP implementation, there is no "one size fits all." The amount of required OCM support depends on the project characteristics. As a rule of thumb, the higher the complexity of the project and the stakeholder landscape, the more change impacts are expected, and the higher the strategic relevance of the project for the company, the more should be invested in OCM. Other influencing factors are the experience and capabilities of the organization to deal with digital transformations.

Systematically assessing the drivers before the start of an SAP implementation helps to tailor OCM appropriately. Of course, such an assessment is a little time investment, but the follow-up costs for either deciding for too little or too much OCM support are significantly higher.

Scoping OCM to Support an SAP Project

Before getting started with an SAP project, a structured analysis of the as-is situation is highly recommended. Identifying both potential project challenges and the company's assets to manage people-related issues helps to get a clear picture of the required OCM support. In addition, an assessment of individual change management skills identifies suitable resources to take over OCM tasks in the project team.

Each of these three topics is covered in a separate short questionnaire:

- The *project assessment* enables the company to identify the people-related challenges of its cloud project.
- The *organizational capability assessment* evaluates the company's change culture, experience with change, and existing competencies regarding OCM.
- The *individual skill assessment* allows interested individuals to detect both their current skills and areas of development regarding OCM.

All questionnaires, guides for result interpretation, and helpful additional information can be accessed free of charge at *http://s-prs.co/v596644*.

When it comes to the topics OCM should address, the structure of the OCM content in the SAP Activate Roadmap Viewer provides a good orientation: Key OCM activities are integrated in the functional roadmaps. In addition, the entire OCM approach is available as a cross-topic. This provides an overview of the full picture, so the company can decide from there which deliverables are suitable to support the upcoming SAP implementation. Follow are two examples: (1) A change network is only required for medium- to large-size projects, with impacted users distributed across various locations or countries. (2) If an implementation project leads only to minor changes for the business, the high-level change impact analysis will most probably not reveal important insights justifying the effort for its conduction and might as well be skipped.

Overall, accompanying SAP implementations with OCM isn't a "nice to have"; it's an important investment in helping users embrace the changes triggered by the project, fostering user adoption and contributing significantly to the project's success.

10.2   Transition to the Customer Center of Expertise

This section focuses on the Customer COE and addresses how a company should adapt and reconfigure its support model, service offerings, processes, and roles and responsibilities required with hybrid SAP solutions.

As projects transition into the run phase, OCM responsibilities and activities are to be handed over from the implementation project to the practice embedded in the business and IT (see our coverage of the run phase in Section 10.1.3 and of continuous adoption in Section 10.1.5). Organizations that already have a Customer COE in place may benefit from expanding its capabilities to OCM for cloud or hybrid IT landscapes and assume the role of this practice. Where no such Customer COE is in place yet, you may want to consider establishing one. Hence, this section introduces the concept, roles, and benefits of Customer COEs.

A Customer COE is a team of experts drawn from across an organization tasked with maximizing the return on a company's business software investment or the lifetime business value. This is achieved by optimizing business processes, IT applications, and resources, as well as by applying continuous innovation and improvement. A company's investment in SAP may consist of several solutions. With the move to the cloud, a company may have a mix of on-premise and cloud solutions. A Customer COE should be put in place regardless of the company's landscape, system complexity, or integration needs. The Customer COE should focus on increasing the business value of the solutions while meeting the needs of the business. This is accomplished by designing organizational and operational excellence, adopting effective governance, and developing the appropriate skills—all while lowering costs.

10.2.1   Organizational Readiness in the Customer Center of Expertise

OCM plays a vital role in preparing and transitioning the organization to the new ways of working. Transition planning occurs in the prepare phase of the project, as we saw in Section 10.1.3.

Continuous change management supports an organization's ability to continually improve organizational efficiencies through expanded use of the solution and adoption of the new system functionality. Reskilling IT resources and businesspeople is therefore an essential element in ensuring that the Customer COE has the right skills and resources available as part of the transformation. To help drive innovation, IT departments will be required to develop new skills and roles within the organization focused on continuous improvement practices. This change in focus impacts both business and IT employees to support the digital transformation and requires an early transformation of employees. Typically, highly technical and detail-focused IT professionals will gain a deeper understanding of the business goals and vision; similarly, strategic business professionals will understand the more technical intricacies of an

SAP cloud ERP system and know how to use the capabilities of the solution to realize their business value potential.

10.2.2   Capability Framework

SAP has defined a Customer COE capability framework that will drive effectiveness through business value and efficiency by focusing on delivering best-in-class services. The framework consists of the following:

- Strategy
- SAP architecture and innovation
- Organization and governance
- Processes, tools, and standards
- People and skills and digital change

Figure 10.4 shows a holistic approach to safeguarding investments in SAP software and maximizing business value from subscriptions.

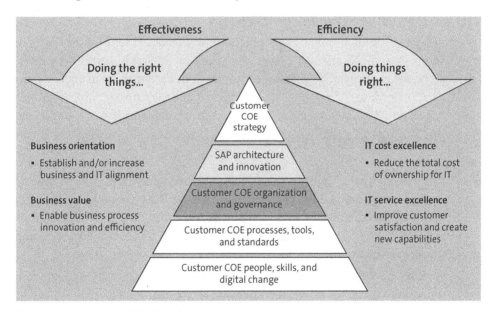

Figure 10.4 Customer COE Capability Framework

The Customer COE forms crucial links among the business, SAP solutions, and the IT department to achieve the company's goals and performance objectives. It requires exceptional end-to-end solution orchestration underpinned with system availability, performance and security goals, and dynamic business innovation.

To achieve the appropriate end-to-end solution orchestration, the Customer COE needs to do the following:

- Implement standardized end-to-end operation processes flexible enough to react to fast-changing business needs.

- Balance the need to implement automated and proactive processes with having manual and reactive processes, according to a risk-based assessment and value to business.

- Define KPIs that will support a continuous improvement mindset, ensuring state-of-the-art IT that is ready for new challenges.

- Maintain knowledge of the latest innovation by maintaining a close connection to experts from the SAP ecosystem (internal and external skills).

For organizations with hybrid SAP solutions that include SAP cloud ERP, the Customer COE capability framework should be reviewed and revised to reflect the business objectives set out with the SAP cloud ERP implementation. Business process standardization and automation introduced with SAP cloud ERP solutions may require adjustment of the strategy, governance model, and IT processes.

10.2.3   Roadmap for Organizational Readiness

A company's transition from the project to the deployment and setup of the Customer COE begins during the discover phase. The speed of transition to the new model depends on the maturity of the existing Customer COE. It's important to understand at the start what needs to change, who will be impacted, and the path to getting to an effective organization that supports governance of the future digitalization of the business.

Let's walk through some key activities for the Customer COE for each phase:

- **Discover**
  During this phase, you identify the business value and benefits, as well as define the adoption strategy and roadmap. You should leverage the Customer COE capability framework to drive initial discussion and ensure a common understanding of the Customer COE organization model to manage all SAP-related topics. For a Customer COE, some key recommendations are as follows:
  - Identify and onboard business process owners and digital business analysts to support the SAP cloud implementation and future operations.
  - Determine the business scope and the number of planned end users to perform an initial identification of Customer COE roles that might be affected with the implementation of SAP cloud solutions.

- **Prepare**
  During the prepare phase, it's recommended that you conduct a workshop to focus on the company-specific scope for the Customer COE, roles, and a high-level definition of innovation services. The workshop helps the organization focus on decisions such as what to deliver with internal versus external resources, nominating Customer COE leadership roles, and creating a project plan for your Customer COE

establishment or transformation based on your current and strategic organizational needs.

- **Explore**
  Key activities that facilitate the setup of the Customer COE include the following:
  - Provide clarity on the future operation of the Customer COE and its capabilities after going live to enable management to identify and plan for internal and external resources.
  - Provide ongoing guidance to employees earmarked for the Customer COE on roles and responsibilities throughout the implementation project and the run phase.
  - Identify tools and standards for IT service and operations management that need to be used or established for future Customer COE support and operations.

- **Realize**
  Key activities to facilitate the setup of the Customer COE include the following:
  - Define what success looks like for an SAP cloud implementation in daily business operations.
  - Define the right business KPIs to drive and guide continuous business improvement.
  - Adapt existing service-level agreements (SLAs), and prepare the internal service desk accordingly. This includes adapting to new categorizations of incidents and service requests, along with the related communication with their SAP counterparts.
  - Train the business on testing and other relevant tasks to support SAP release cycles.

- **Deploy**
  During the deploy phase, it's recommended that you implement the defined processes and tools, prepare key users to train the end user community, and support an efficient business operation after go-live.

- **Run**
  During the run phase, it's recommended that business and IT resources work together under the Customer COE model to establish normal business operations with increased focus on user adoption, business optimization, innovation, and digitalization, while lowering total cost of ownership.

10.2.4   New Roles with SAP S/4HANA Cloud

Digital transformation with SAP cloud solutions might require new skills. Roles and responsibilities within the business and IT teams will be impacted. Use this opportunity for change by reskilling current operations staff to support the new digital strategy. Being able to actively engage in an online community such as SAP Community (*https://community.sap.com*) is an essential skill for all existing roles to stay current, find answers to common questions, and get tips on known or emerging challenges. The following new roles will also need to be introduced to successfully run the organization:

- **Digital business analyst**

  The role of the digital business analyst is the biggest change in business roles. It evolved from a traditional business analyst role to a key player in developing prototypes driving the digitalization of business. The digital business analyst works closely with business architects in IT.

  Companies with a digital transformation office may not be required to differentiate between the roles of digital business analyst and business architect. Both roles leverage business digitalization to create business value.

- **Cloud business architect**

  The cloud business architect may traditionally come from an SAP S/4HANA solution architect role. Reskilling or upskilling may be required to serve in a cross-functional cloud architect capacity to ensure technical feasibility and realization of current and planned business requirements.

- **Prototyper/user experience (UX) developer**

  The prototyper may come from the traditional ABAP development role and is only required for companies with a need for extensions (either using in-app extension capabilities in SAP S/4HANA Cloud or SAP Business Technology Platform [SAP BTP] for side-by-side extensions). Employees in this role should be enabled to guide users toward simple and effective business solutions.

- **Data scientist**

  With the rise of generative AI, large language model-based chat bots, big data, and other technologies, the role of a data scientist is highly desirable in a Customer COE. Traditional developers can be reskilled with mathematical and algorithm knowledge and machine learning tools to perform this role.

- **Change agent**

  A leader focused on change management promotes and enables change to happen and is an essential part of a Customer COE. People in this role should have good understanding of business culture, be experienced in business disciplines that are impacted by the change, and be comfortable in working through uncertainty.

Figure 10.5 provides a comparison of Customer COE roles found in an SAP ERP environment on-premise and the change required with SAP S/4HANA Cloud Public Edition.

The increased granularity of role descriptions provides the visibility required to map and transition each employee role. Note that there is no direct relation between the role description and the full-time equivalent (FTE) required in the target Customer COE: several roles may be combined into a single job position. For example, companies replacing their traditional ERP with SAP S/4HANA Cloud or implementing a hybrid two-tier ERP setup might significantly reduce the need for basis experts or database administrators. In addition, some roles, such as enterprise architect or developer, might not warrant staffing with FTEs in all organizations. One FTE might need to play multiple roles. Outsourcing, ad hoc service acquisition, or subscription to respective services offered by certified SAP partners may also deserve consideration.

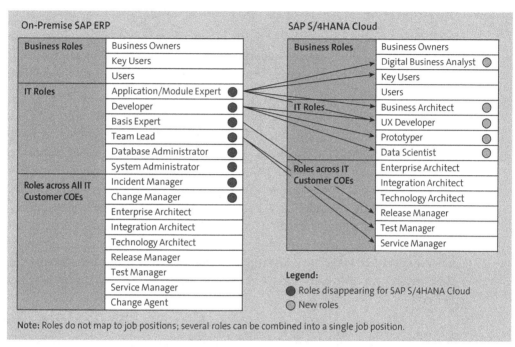

Figure 10.5 ERP Customer COE Roles versus Roles Required with SAP S/4HANA Cloud Public Edition

Companies with a hybrid solution that includes SAP S/4HANA Cloud Public Edition should note that traditional operational roles are supported by SAP under the SAP S/4HANA Cloud subscription model. A good example is that the role of the traditional Basis expert tasks and the application management (for more complex changes) now form a part of the periodic releases. Many maintenance tasks for data—for example, creating a new purchase group or a new cost center—will be performed in the business by authorized personnel. Line of business experts with strong knowledge of discrete business processes may transfer from the IT organization to the business organization, thereby strengthening the business's native IT solution skills.

To define a successful support model, companies are required to define and assign new roles and responsibilities to employees or third parties and adjust existing support practices. A collaboration governance model between business, IT, and other stakeholders of your SAP solution should be considered from the outset in the discover phase.

To realize business value quickly and sustainably define the new governance model at the start of the SAP S/4HANA Cloud journey. Don't wait until the deploy or run phases to prepare your organization!

10.3   Summary

This chapter provided an overview of the OCM activities covered across the six phases of SAP Activate and discussed the importance of Customer COE for operational excellence, continuous improvements of the solution, and adoption of new capabilities (staying current).

Additionally, we stressed that investing in OCM yields significant returns for SAP implementations by mitigating concerns and resistance, bolstering commitment, and thereby promoting swift and enduring user adoption. With the fast-paced technological progress, digital transformations will remain an important constant in the business world and, at the same time, will lead to further changes in the way we're working. This will also influence the evolution of SAP solutions. AI, in particular, has the potential to greatly enhance the value proposition for SAP solutions. Predictive analytics and forecasting can accelerate decision-making processes, an improved customer experience can boost operational efficiency, and the personalization of solutions—reflecting individual preferences and behavior patterns—can support their adoption at critical moments.

In addition, AI-supported solutions will further boost innovation and the creation of new business models and—in the long run—determine which companies will survive in the market. These developments will also impact the way OCM is delivered. Digitalization will speed up the OCM delivery, make OCM activities easily scalable, and allow tailored, personalized support of users both during the implementation and after go-live. We're convinced that successful digital transformation will always involve both technology and people. Therefore, as SAP solutions evolve, OCM will continue to be a crucial element in ensuring smooth and effective transitions to new technologies.

In the next chapter, you'll learn about the SAP Activate methodology for other SAP products, such as SAP SuccessFactors, intelligent enterprise, SAP BTP, conversion from an SAP S/4HANA Cloud two-system to three-system landscape, and the roadmap for SAP S/4HANA upgrade and product integration.

Chapter 11
SAP Activate for Other SAP Products

We've discussed how SAP Activate is used in the context of an SAP S/4HANA Cloud project, but SAP Activate provides coverage of other SAP products as well. We'll introduce those additional versions of SAP Activate for other products in this chapter and show you assets that you can use in implementation of products such as SAP SuccessFactors and SAP Business Technology Platform or while upgrading your SAP S/4HANA solution.

This book has provided detailed information about the use of SAP Activate in the context of deploying the SAP S/4HANA Cloud solution in your organization. This chapter will focus on introducing other "flavors" of SAP Activate for SAP solutions across a wide range of cloud and on-premise products. We'll focus on a few key examples of SAP Activate, and we'll share links for each to the implementation roadmaps currently available and SAP Best Practices packages (where available) that you can use in your next project.

The SAP Activate methodology assets are available in SAP Activate Roadmap Viewer, and the SAP Best Practices assets can be accessed in SAP Signavio Process Navigator (refer to Chapter 4). We'll introduce a few flavors of SAP Activate content for other products in this text in more detail and then provide a list of all currently available SAP Activate methodology packages that companies and partners can access in SAP Activate Roadmap Viewer.

11.1 SAP Activate for SAP SuccessFactors

SAP Activate provides comprehensive coverage of the SAP SuccessFactors solution, with assets for planning and managing the project in the form of a dedicated SAP Activate methodology for SAP SuccessFactors. This methodology is available in the Roadmap Viewer via the main page at *http://s-prs.co/v502741*. Once there, click on the **Explore All Roadmaps** button, and then select the **Cloud Specific Methodology** tab. Finally, click on **SAP Activate Methodology for SAP SuccessFactors** in the list of available roadmaps. The main page of the methodology for SAP SuccessFactors is shown in Figure 11.1.

The methodology follows the same six phases we defined in Chapter 2 of this book, but the content inside the guidance is specific to the deployment of the SAP SuccessFactors solution.

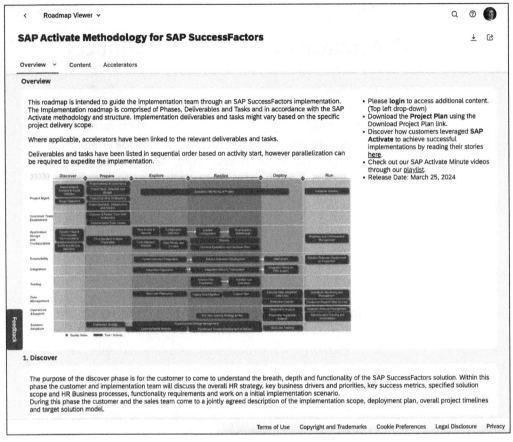

Figure 11.1 SAP Activate Methodology for SAP SuccessFactors

To complement the methodology, SAP has also released several packages of SAP Best Practices content for SAP SuccessFactors. At the time of writing, the following packages are available for SAP SuccessFactors in the SAP Signavio Process Navigator:

- SAP Best Practices for SAP SuccessFactors Employee Central
- SAP Best Practices for SAP SuccessFactors Employee Central integration
- SAP Best Practices for SAP SuccessFactors Workforce Planning
- SAP Best Practices for SAP SuccessFactors Time Tracking
- SAP SuccessFactors MHR-120 Employee Experience
- SAP SuccessFactors MHR-20 HR Administration
- SAP SuccessFactors MHR-40 Benefits
- SAP SuccessFactors MHR-10 Organizational Management
- SAP SuccessFactors MHR-30 Time and Attendance Management
- SAP SuccessFactors MHR-130 Service Center

- SAP SuccessFactors Recruiting
- SAP SuccessFactors Onboarding
- SAP SuccessFactors Performance and Goals
- SAP SuccessFactors Employee Central Payroll
- SAP SuccessFactors Opportunity Marketplace
- SAP SuccessFactors Succession and Development
- SAP SuccessFactors Learning
- SAP SuccessFactors Compensation
- SAP SuccessFactors Dynamic Teams

You can find these packages in the SAP Signavio Process Navigator by following these steps:

1. Open SAP Signavio Process Navigator at *https://me.sap.com/processnavigator/ HomePage*.
2. Select the **Solution Scenarios** tile on the top left of the screen.
3. Select **Human Capital Management** in the left side selection box in the **By Product** section.

The list of available SAP Best Practices for SAP SuccessFactors will be displayed on the right side of the screen. As shown in Figure 11.2, you can navigate to a specific package and its contents from there.

Figure 11.2 SAP Best Practices for SAP SuccessFactors

SAP Best Practices for SAP SuccessFactors provide the same navigation structure we explained in Chapter 2. The key assets that are provided in the package are delivered inside the scope items as the following documents:

- Solution process flow
- Solution value flow
- Task tutorial
- Test scripts
- SAP Help Portal link

SAP Best Practices for SAP SuccessFactors cover a wide range of country-specific configurations that you can select on the main page of each package using the selection box below **Version** on the **Solution Scenarios** overview screen. You can also change the **Country/Region** on the overview page to get a view of the content for a specific country or region.

11.2   SAP Activate for the Intelligent Enterprise

This SAP Activate roadmap has a special role: it has been used to prototype and deliver implementation methodology guidance that spans multiple distinct SAP products to support end-to-end business scenarios that go beyond one product—for example, the hire-to-retire, source-to-pay, external workforce, and total workforce management business scenarios. Companies implementing multiple SAP products need SAP Activate to support the scope of their projects, and that is why this methodology roadmap exists—to provide the right content for such situations. This roadmap, like all other SAP Activate methodology roadmaps, continues to evolve and bring new content to users. SAP has added SAP Concur content to the SAP Activate for the Intelligent Enterprise roadmap to expand the existing coverage that includes SAP SuccessFactors, SAP S/4HANA Cloud, and SAP Fieldglass.

Additionally, this roadmap has been a prototype for *combination roadmaps* that are now starting to be available to users of SAP Cloud ALM, as you can see in Figure 11.3. SAP Cloud ALM users can select one or multiple combinable roadmaps to flexibly scope their project task list based on multiple SAP Activate roadmaps that are enabled for combination to work. As of this writing, SAP Cloud ALM offered users a combination of the following SAP Activate methodology roadmaps:

- **SAP S/4HANA Cloud Public Edition (3-system landscape) - Implementation**
- **SAP SuccessFactors - Implementation**
- **SAP Concur - Implementation**
- **General Cloud - Implementation**

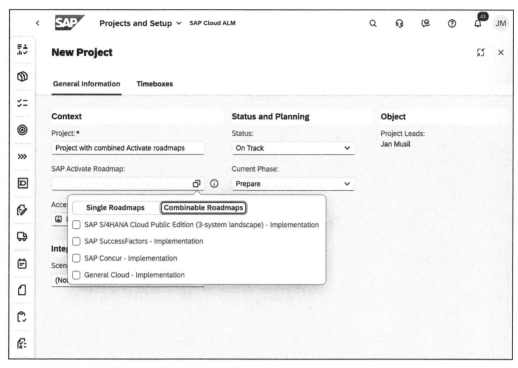

Figure 11.3 Combinable SAP Activate Methodology Roadmaps in SAP Cloud ALM

Now back to the SAP Activate for the Intelligent Enterprise roadmap: you can access this methodology content in SAP Activate Roadmap Viewer via the main page at *http://s-prs.co/v502741*. Once there, click on the **Explore All Roadmaps** button, and then select the **Cloud-Specific Methodology** tab. Finally, click on **SAP Activate Methodology for the Intelligent Enterprise** in the list of available roadmaps. To browse the detailed guidance, you can select the **Content** tab at the top of the page and then select the appropriate filter selection on the left side of the screen in the **Tags** section. You can filter the content by specific business scenarios, by a selection of products, or by a combination of the two, as you can see in Figure 11.4.

The methodology content's navigation is the same as for all the other roadmaps, and the guidance includes details specific to all covered solutions, including solution-specific accelerators. SAP continues to evolve this methodology content and add coverage for additional business scenarios and solutions.

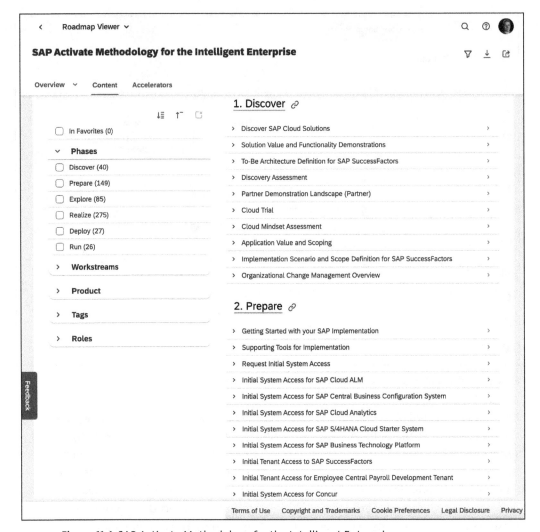

Figure 11.4 SAP Activate Methodology for the Intelligent Enterprise

11.3   SAP Activate for SAP Business Technology Platform

SAP Business Technology Platform (SAP BTP) offers customers a broad range of capabilities to extend and personalize SAP applications, integrate and connect across landscapes, and enable business users to connect processes and user experiences, make confident decisions, and drive continuous business innovation. For customers needing help to get started with SAP BTP, the *SAP Activate Methodology for SAP Business Technology Platform* roadmap is designed to provide implementation guidelines for customers implementing SAP BTP-based solutions.

You can access the SAP Activate Methodology for SAP BTP roadmap in the Roadmap Viewer, which you can access via *http://s-prs.co/v502741*. Once there, click on the

Explore All Roadmaps button, and then select the **Cloud-Specific Methodology** tab. Finally, click on **SAP Activate Methodology for SAP Business Technology Platform** in the list of available roadmaps. See Figure 11.5 for an overview of the content provided in this methodology roadmap. The methodology will guide you through specific steps that help your team access the platform, enable your team using the predelivered self-guided enablement materials, help prepare a proof of concept, set up a solution architecture, develop and test the architecture, and assist with other key activities to adopt the solution.

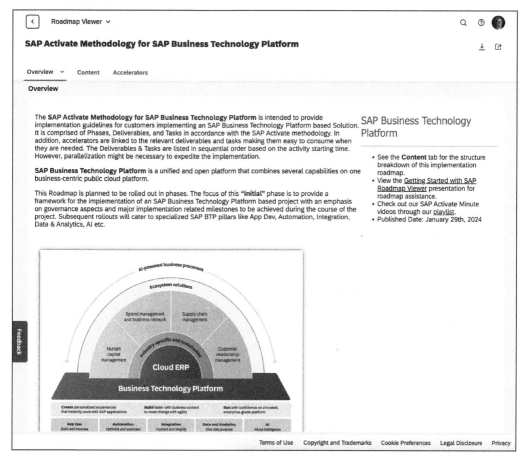

Figure 11.5 SAP Activate Methodology for SAP Business Technology Platform

11.4   SAP Activate for Two- to Three-System Landscape Conversions

Some of the SAP Activate roadmaps that SAP introduced have a narrow focus, like this one that has been designed to help customers on the SAP S/4HANA Cloud Public Edition two-system landscape prepare and execute a conversion to the three-system landscape that offers additional capabilities and flexibility for SAP's public cloud customers.

In this case, the process is specifically tailored to the conversion project with the phases shown in Figure 11.6. We'll now review the key activities that are performed in each phase of this conversion roadmap. Note that in this roadmap, there is no explore phase, and in the run phase, there are activities to finalize the setup of the new test system that the customer receives as part of the conversion along with enabling users on the new capabilities that this three-tier system landscape solution offers. Let's now have a look at each of the phases:

1. **Discover**
   During this phase, the customer is onboarded and educated on the new capabilities that the three-system landscape provides. Additionally, the contractual setup is put in place to enable the customer to consume the three-system landscape functionality.

2. **Prepare**
   In this phase, the project is formally launched, the planning activities are underway, and the customer starts the self-enablement activities for the new capabilities of the three-system landscape. A critical part of this phase is preparing for the post-conversion setup of the new landscape, including planning for data migration to the test system, planning integration setup, and performing the pre-conversion checks and release transports. Toward the end of the phase, the customer formally confirms their readiness for the conversion process to begin.

3. **Realize**
   As opposed to other SAP Activate roadmaps, in the case of conversion, the realize phase is relatively compact and focuses on performing the critical post-conversion steps to access the system, set up the configuration engine, and prepare the full landscape for productive use. Note that the production system isn't touched during the conversion process, and the productive operations are never impacted. The conversion only works on the development and test systems that both need to be accessed and set up for the entire landscape to work for the customer long term. During the realize phase, the team only performs the critical steps to bring the entire landscape to operation to ensure business continuity.

4. **Deploy**
   This is a short phase to formally bring the three-system landscape to productive operations while recognizing some of its limitations. For example, the test system isn't being used for testing purposes until the rest of the setup activities are completed in the run phase.

5. **Run**
   During this phase, the project team finalizes the setup of the new test system, including the setup of output management, integration rewiring, data migration to the test system, and continuous enablement of the users on the new three-system landscape capabilities, such as embedded ABAP Cloud environment for developer extensibility or the new more flexible transport management system.

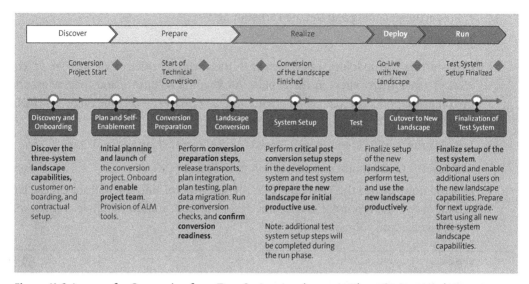

Figure 11.6 Journey for Conversion from Two-System Landscape to Three-System Landscape in SAP S/4HANA Cloud Public Edition

You can access the SAP Activate for Conversion of SAP S/4HANA Cloud Public Edition 2-System to 3-System Landscape roadmap in the Roadmap Viewer, which you can open via *http://s-prs.co/v502741*. Once there, click on the **Explore All Roadmaps** button, and then select the **Cloud-Specific Methodology** tab. Finally, click on **SAP Activate for Conversion of SAP S/4HANA Cloud Public Edition 2-system to 3-system landscape** in the list of available roadmaps.

11.5   SAP Activate Methodology for SAP S/4HANA Upgrades

The last methodology roadmap we want to introduce in this chapter is for planning and conducting an upgrade from one release of SAP S/4HANA to a newer or latest release of the product. This upgrade roadmap also provides information about the implementation of additional capabilities that are embedded in the SAP S/4HANA solution. Customers upgrading to a new release of SAP S/4HANA usually want to add new capabilities to their solution, so this roadmap covers both the functional upgrade and implementation of additional capabilities. The following selections can be made in the roadmap to select a company-specific scenario:

- Technical Upgrade
- Upgrade with Functional Enhancement
- SAP Transportation Management
- SAP Extended Warehouse Management
- SAP S/4HANA Service

- **Production Planning and Detailed Scheduling**
- **Advanced ATP**

Users of this methodology can access it in the Roadmap Viewer via *http://s-prs.co/ v502741*. Once there, click on the **Explore All Roadmaps** button, and then select the **Upgrade Methodology** tab. Finally, click on **SAP Activate Methodology S/4HANA Upgrades** in the list of available roadmaps.

To select the specific scenario, you'll need to continue navigating as follows:

1. Select the **Content** tab on the screen shown in Figure 11.7.

2. Scroll down to see the **Tags** option in the selection of filtering options on the left side, as shown in Figure 11.8. Select the desired option, and the roadmap content will adjust based on your selection.

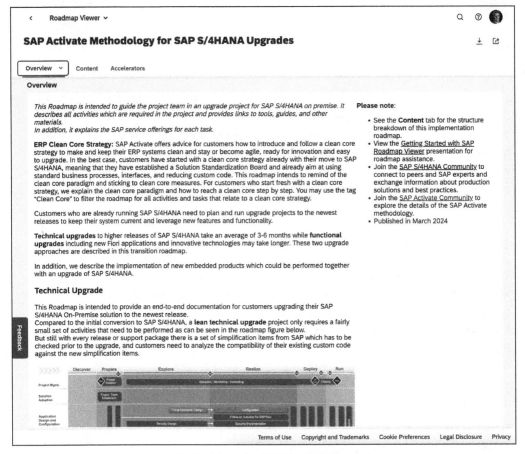

Figure 11.7 SAP Activate Methodology for SAP S/4HANA Upgrades

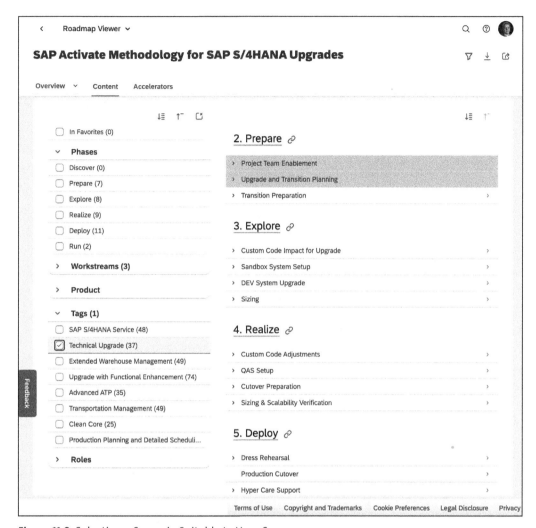

Figure 11.8 Selecting a Scenario Suitable to Your Scope

The filtering process is like the one we explained when discussing the SAP Activate for the Intelligent Enterprise roadmap in Section 11.2.

11.6 Additional SAP Activate Methodology Roadmaps

We've introduced several examples of SAP Activate assets that are available to use in projects that include other SAP solutions, products, specialized projects, and end-to-end business scenarios. You can always find the latest methodology content on SAP Activate Roadmap Viewer. All of these assets are also accessible in SAP Cloud ALM as SAP Activate Roadmap Task Templates in the setup of a new project.

As of the time of writing (fall 2024), the following methodology roadmaps are available to SAP customers and partners:

- **Cloud-specific roadmaps**
  - SAP Activate for SAP S/4HANA Cloud Public Edition (3-System Landscape)
  - SAP Activate for SAP S/4HANA Cloud Public Edition (2-System Landscape)
  - SAP Activate Methodology for RISE with SAP S/4HANA Cloud Private Edition
  - Baseline Activation Service for SAP S/4HANA Cloud (3-System Landscape)
  - SAP Activate Methodology for SAP Cloud for Sustainable Enterprises
  - SAP Activate for SAP Integrated Business Planning for Supply Chain
  - SAP Activate Methodology for SAP Concur
  - SAP Activate Methodology for SAP SuccessFactors
  - SAP Activate Methodology for SAP Service Cloud Roadmap
  - SAP Activate Methodology for SAP Datasphere
  - SAP Activate Methodology for SAP Fieldglass
  - SAP Activate Methodology for SAP Ariba
  - SAP Activate Methodology for SAP Business Network for Supply Chain
  - SAP Activate Methodology for SAP Analytics Cloud
  - SAP Activate Methodology for the Intelligent Enterprise
  - SAP Activate Methodology for SAP Sales Cloud Roadmap
  - SAP Activate for Conversion of SAP S/4HANA Cloud Public Edition 2-System to 3-System Landscape
  - SAP Activate for SAP S/4HANA Cloud Public Edition (3-System Landscape) - Early Adopters
  - SAP Activate Methodology for SAP Business Technology Platform
- **On-premise-specific methodology roadmaps**
  - SAP Activate Methodology for Transition to SAP S/4HANA
  - SAP Activate Methodology for Transition to SAP BW/4HANA
  - SAP Activate Methodology for SAP S/4HANA Central Finance
- **Upgrade methodology**
  - SAP Activate for Upgrade of SAP S/4HANA Cloud Three-System Landscape
  - SAP Activate Methodology for SAP S/4HANA Upgrades
- **General/cross topics methodology roadmaps**
  - SAP Activate Methodology for New Cloud Implementations (Public Cloud – General)
  - SAP Activate Methodology for Business Suite and On-Premise – Agile and Waterfall

- – Experience Management
- – Organizational Change Management

You can find all of these assets in the Roadmap Viewer at *http://s-prs.co/v502741*.

11.7   Summary

This chapter provided an overview of the available SAP Activate methodology and SAP Best Practices assets across all SAP solutions. The examples were selected to show you the various assets that you can use in your next implementation, upgrade, or conversion project. We recommend that you regularly check the SAP Activate Roadmap Viewer and SAP Signavio Process Navigator for new content as SAP continues to add to the portfolio of available assets. You should also consider following the SAP Activate community on SAP Community to keep up to date on any new additions or updates to existing content (*https://community.sap.com/topics/activate*).

Appendix A
SAP Activate Certification Preparation

In this appendix, we offer practice questions and answers to test your understanding of SAP Activate and to prepare for the certification exam. Note that these questions are based on the information presented to you in this book, information available to you in SAP Activate tools we've introduced throughout this book (e.g., SAP Activate Roadmap Viewer and SAP Signavio Process Navigator), and on the SAP Activate community (*https://pages.community.sap.com/topics/activate*).

We recommend that you also consider taking SAP-recommended courses to prepare for the SAP Activate certification exam. Details of the certification exam are available in the **Discovering SAP Activate Implementation Tools and Methodology** learning journey at *https://learning.sap.com/learning-journeys/discovering-sap-activate-implementation-tools-and-methodology*.

In this chapter, we'll present all the questions in Section A.2 and the correct answers with explanations in Section A.3. Both sections use the same hierarchy to allow you to find answers to questions at your convenience. We highly encourage you to follow the SAP Activate community for additional information about strategies shared by users of SAP Activate to prepare for the certification exam. You can also post your questions about preparing for the exam in the community to engage directly with the SAP Activate team at SAP and other SAP Activate experts.

A.1   Exam Structure

The certification exam questions are structured into the following categories (the number in brackets indicates the number of practice questions in each category):

- SAP Activate Overview (6)
- SAP Activate Elements (5)
- Workstreams Overview (5)
- Transition Path "New Implementation SAP S/4HANA Cloud Public Edition" (6)
- Transition Path "New Implementation SAP S/4HANA Cloud Private Edition" (6)
- Agile Project Planning (5)
- Agile Project Delivery (5)
- Transition Path "System Conversion to SAP S/4HANA" (4)
- Transition Path "Selective Data Transition to SAP S/4HANA" (3)

Each category is assigned a relative percentage weight in the exam that provides insight into the number of questions from this category that you can expect in the exam (see the SAP Training website for a detailed breakdown of the certification exam in Figure A.1).

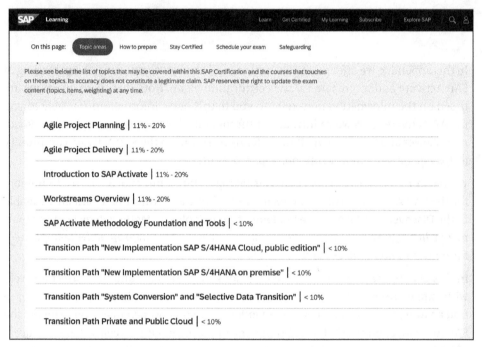

Figure A.1 Structure of SAP Certified Associate – Project Manager – SAP Activate Exam

A.2   Practice Questions

This section will present the practice questions in the same categories that SAP uses for the certification exam. We'll follow the sequence of categories presented in the list in the previous section.

These practice questions will help you evaluate your understanding of the topics covered in this book. The questions shown are similar in nature to those found on the certification examination. Although none of these questions will be found on the exam itself, they will allow you to review your knowledge of the subject. Select the correct answers, and then check the completeness of your answers in Section A.3. Remember that on the certification exam, you must select *all* correct answers and *only* correct answers to receive credit for the question.

A.2.1   SAP Activate Overview

This section focuses on the definition of the SAP Activate approach and examines your knowledge in this area. You can find answers to the questions with explanations in Section A.3.1.

1. Which statement best defines SAP Activate? (Select one correct answer.)

☐ **A.** SAP Activate is a methodology for implementation and upgrades of SAP S/4HANA software.

☐ B. SAP Activate provides users with prescriptive guidance, ready-to-use business processes, and tools for implementation and upgrades.

☐ C. SAP Activate provides tools for SAP customers who are deploying the SAP S/4HANA Cloud solutions in their organizations.

2. When was SAP Activate released to the market? (Select two correct answers.)

☐ **A.** SAPPHIRE 2015

☐ **B.** When SAP shipped SAP ERP 6

☐ **C.** TechEd 2019

☐ **D.** Along with the introduction of SAP S/4HANA

3. What are the components included in SAP Activate? (Select two correct answers.)

☐ **A.** Methodology

☐ **B.** SAP Best Practices

☐ **C.** SAP Fiori

☐ **D.** SAP HANA

4. Which resource can you use to get answers to your questions about SAP Activate from experts? (Select one correct answer.)

☐ **A.** SAP Activate community on *www.sap.com*

☐ **B.** SAP Cloud ALM

☐ **C.** SAP Signavio Process Navigator

☐ **D.** SAP Readiness Check

5. Where can you access the SAP Activate methodology? (Select one correct answer.)

☐ **A.** SAP Signavio Process Navigator

☐ **B.** SAP Activate community

☐ **C.** Roadmap Viewer

☐ **D.** SAP Roadmap Navigator

6. Where can you download SAP Activate accelerators for project management? (Select two correct answers.)

☐   **A.** Roadmap Viewer

☐   **B.** SAP Signavio Process Navigator

☐   **C.** Digital discovery assessment tool

☐   **D.** SAP Cloud ALM

A.2.2   SAP Activate Elements

This section focuses on your understanding of the SAP Activate elements and examines your knowledge in this area. You can find answers to the questions with explanations in Section A.3.2.

1. What other components can be used to set up the initial system/landscape for the SAP S/4HANA Cloud Private Edition implementation? (Select one correct answer.)

☐   **A.** SAP Best Practices

☐   **B.** Enterprise management layer for SAP S/4HANA

☐   **C.** Qualified SAP partner packages

☐   **D.** All of the above

2. What are the hierarchy levels of the SAP Activate methodology? (Select three correct answers.)

☐   **A.** Program

☐   **B.** Project

☐   **C.** Phase

☐   **D.** Task

☐   **E.** Deliverable

3. What do the SAP Best Practices for SAP S/4HANA Cloud Public Edition deliver? (Select three correct answers.)

☐   **A.** Standard operating procedures (SOPs)

☐   **B.** Preconfiguration

☐   **C.** Business process flows

☐   **D.** Building block documentation

☐   **E.** Test scripts

4. What capabilities does SAP Cloud ALM offer for users of SAP Activate? (Select two correct answers.)

☐ **A.** Ability to run robotic process automation

☐ **B.** Ability to display the SAP Activate methodology content into the tool

☐ **C.** Ability to generate test automates based on the requirements and design documents

☐ **D.** Ability to use SAP Best Practices content for business process modeling

☐ **E.** Ability to automatically mark completed activities in a project schedule based on the progress of work

5. What configuration capabilities in the SAP S/4HANA Cloud Private Edition solution can users access to configure the software to the company's needs? (Select one correct answer.)

☐ **A.** Implementation Guide (IMG)

☐ **B.** SAP configuration cockpit (SCCP)

☐ **C.** SAP setup framework (SSF)

☐ **D.** Self-Service Configuration UIs (SSCUIs)

A.2.3 Workstreams Overview

This section focuses on your understanding of the fundamentals of the SAP Activate methodology workstreams, their content, and structure. The questions examine your knowledge in this area. You can find answers to the questions with explanations in Section A.3.3.

1. What options for transition to SAP S/4HANA Cloud Private Edition from SAP ERP are supported by the SAP Activate methodology? (Select three correct answers.)

☐ **A.** New implementation

☐ **B.** System conversion

☐ **C.** Data migration

☐ **D.** Selective data transition

☐ **E.** Upgrade

2. Which of the following statements are included in the SAP Activate principles? (Select two correct answers.)

☐ **A.** Use SAP consulting services

☐ **B.** Start with ready-to-run business processes

☐ **C.** Confirm backlog with sponsor

☐ **D.** Confirm solution fit

3. Which techniques does SAP Activate use to confirm solution fit for the business and define delta requirements? (Select one correct answer.)

☐   **A.** Backlog

☐   **B.** Blueprinting

☐   **C.** Fit-to-standard

☐   **D.** Fit-gap

4. Which key templates/accelerators can the project manager use to explain how the project will be managed from time, quality, and risk perspectives? (Select one correct answer.)

☐   **A.** Project Scope Statement

☐   **B.** Project Schedule Template

☐   **C.** Project Management Plan Template

☐   **D.** Fit-to-Standard Overview Presentation

5. What technologies are delivered with SAP S/4HANA Cloud applications? (Select two correct answers.)

☐   **A.** SAP Concur

☐   **B.** SAP Fiori

☐   **C.** SAP Fieldglass

☐   **D.** SAP HANA

A.2.4   Transition Path "New Implementation SAP S/4HANA Cloud Public Edition"

This section focuses on your understanding of SAP Activate for implementation of SAP S/4HANA Cloud Public Cloud solution and examines your knowledge in this area. You can find answers to the questions with explanations in Section A.3.4.

1. Which system is used for fit-to-standard workshops in SAP S/4HANA Cloud Public Edition? (Select one correct answer.)

☐   **A.** Development

☐   **B.** Starter

☐   **C.** Test

☐   **D.** Production

2. In which workstream will you find organizational change management (OCM) assets? (Select one correct answer.)

☐ **A.** Project management

☐ **B.** Solution adoption

☐ **C.** Project team enablement

☐ **D.** Data management

3. Which working environment can project teams use to structure their work around SAP Activate tasks, access SAP Best Practices documentation (including business process diagrams) in one place, and run their projects? (Select one correct answer.)

☐ **A.** SAP Activate community

☐ **B.** SAP Activate Roadmap Viewer

☐ **C.** SAP Signavio Process Navigator

☐ **D.** SAP Cloud ALM

4. Which asset in the SAP Activate methodology provides project managers with a list of items that must be completed in each phase? (Select one correct answer.)

☐ **A.** List of SSCUIs

☐ **B.** Quality gate checklist

☐ **C.** Project management plan

☐ **D.** Sign-off template

5. In which tool can you access test script documents for SAP S/4HANA Cloud Public Edition? (Select one correct answer.)

☐ **A.** SAP Road Map Explorer

☐ **B.** SAP Business Accelerator Hub

☐ **C.** SAP Signavio Process Navigator

☐ **D.** SAP Activate Roadmap Viewer

6. What configuration environment do you use to configure SAP S/4HANA Cloud Public Edition? (Select one correct answer.)

☐ **A.** SAP Central Business Configuration

☐ **B.** Data migration cockpit

☐ **C.** SAP Cloud ALM

☐ **D.** SAP Implementation Guide (IMG)

A.2.5   Transition Path "New Implementation SAP S/4HANA Cloud Private Edition"

This section focuses on your understanding of SAP Activate for implementations of the SAP S/4HANA Cloud Private Edition solution and examines your knowledge in this area. You can find answers to the questions with explanations in Section A.3.5. Note that many of the questions in this section also apply to the case of the new implementation for on-premise SAP S/4HANA.

1.   Which tools can you use to prepare for the transition to SAP S/4HANA Cloud Private Edition? (Select one correct answer.)

☐   **A.** SAP Activate community

☐   **B.** Implementation Guide (IMG)

☐   **C.** SAP Readiness Check for SAP S/4HANA

☐   **D.** Transport management system (TMS)

2.   Where will the project team access SAP Best Practices documentation and adjust business process models for delivered preconfiguration? (Select one correct answer.)

☐   **A.** Roadmap Viewer

☐   **B.** SAP Activate community

☐   **C.** SAP Cloud ALM

☐   **D.** SAP Signavio Process Navigator

3.   What is the sequence of workshops in the explore phase for SAP S/4HANA Cloud Private Edition implementation? (Select one correct answer.)

☐   **A.** Prepare system, conduct fit-to-standard, and perform delta design

☐   **B.** Perform delta design, prepare the system, and conduct fit-to-standard

☐   **C.** Prepare system, perform delta design, and conduct fit-to-standard

☐   **D.** Conduct fit-to-standard, perform delta design, and prepare system

4.   Which of the following items are outputs of the realize phase of a new SAP S/4HANA Cloud Private Edition implementation project? (Select two correct answers.)

☐   **A.** Configuration and configuration documentation

☐   **B.** Cutover to production

☐   **C.** Landscape sizing

☐   **D.** Support operations framework and procedures

☐   **E.** Project scope statement

5. Which types of testing are recommended by SAP Activate in the realize phase to test configuration and extensibility? (Select two correct answers.)

☐ **A.** Unit testing

☐ **B.** Peer testing

☐ **C.** Integration testing

☐ **D.** Change management testing

6. Which of the following items are part of the five golden rules for implementation of SAP S/4HANA Cloud Private Edition? (Select two correct answers.)

☐ **A.** Start with preconfigured processes

☐ **B.** Inform stakeholders about new functionality

☐ **C.** Review the operations process before going live

☐ **D.** Ensure transparency on deviations

A.2.6   Agile Project Planning

This section focuses on examining your understanding of the agile approach in SAP Activate—specifically, the planning activities in the context of your project. Section A.3.6 provides answers to the questions with additional explanations.

1. Which new roles are introduced in SAP Activate with the use of the agile approach? (Select two correct answers.)

☐ **A.** Scrum master

☐ **B.** Product owner

☐ **C.** Agile train master

☐ **D.** Backlog manager

2. How frequently does the agile project team plan? (Select one correct answer.)

☐ **A.** Only after fit-to-standard

☐ **B.** Every iteration/sprint

☐ **C.** At the beginning of the project

☐ **D.** Once in each phase

3. Who estimates the effort needed for each backlog item? (Select one correct answer.)

☐ **A.** Scrum master

☐ **B.** Product owner

☐ **C.** Team

☐ **D.** Project manager

4. Who sets the priority of the backlog item? (Select one correct answer.)

☐ **A.** Scrum master

☐ **B.** Product owner

☐ **C.** Team

☐ **D.** Project manager

5. What artifacts and data points will be used during the release and sprint planning? (Select three correct answers.)

☐ **A.** Backlog

☐ **B.** Retrospective

☐ **C.** Sprint duration

☐ **D.** Team size and capacity

☐ **E.** Burn-down chart

A.2.7 Agile Project Delivery

This section examines your understanding of the agile approach in SAP Activate—specifically, the executing and closing activities in your project. Section A.3.7 provides answers to the questions with additional explanations.

1. What agile practices do agile teams use to continuously improve? (Select one correct answer.)

☐ **A.** Backlog grooming

☐ **B.** Retrospective

☐ **C.** Sprint planning

☐ **D.** Daily standup

2. How does the project team continuously align and communicate progress? (Select one correct answer.)

☐ **A.** During daily standup

☐ **B.** Making work visible

☐ **C.** Tracking progress in burn-down charts

☐ **D.** All of the above

3. Which key artifact gets updated every sprint? (Select one correct answer.)

☐ **A.** Backlog

☐ **B.** Project schedule

☐ **C.** Management plans

☐ **D.** Scope document

4.   Who signs off on the completion of the backlog items during the sprint demo? (Select one correct answer.)

☐   **A.** Project manager

☐   **B.** Scrum master

☐   **C.** Team

☐   **D.** Product owner

5.   What is the purpose of the daily standup meeting? (Select two correct answers.)

☐   **A.** Debrief project sponsor

☐   **B.** Identify blockers

☐   **C.** Update status report

☐   **D.** Communicate progress

A.2.8   System Conversion to SAP S/4HANA Cloud Private Edition

This section focuses on examining your understanding of using SAP Activate for system conversion to SAP S/4HANA Cloud Private Edition. You can find answers to the questions with explanations in Section A.3.8. Note that many of the questions in this section also apply to the case of the system conversion to SAP S/4HANA (on-premise).

1.   Which of the following steps are part of the planning system conversion? (Select three correct answers.)

☐   **A.** Perform blueprinting workshops

☐   **B.** Clarify custom code adaption

☐   **C.** Perform data volume planning

☐   **D.** Define cutover approach

2.   What pre-conversion projects does SAP recommend customers complete prior to starting the system conversion to SAP S/4HANA Cloud Private Edition? (Select one correct answer.)

☐   **A.** Data volume management

☐   **B.** Reconciliation of financial data

☐   **C.** Cleanup of unused code

☐   **D.** All of the above

3.   Where can you find a list of functions that have changed from SAP ERP to SAP S/4HANA Cloud Private Edition? (Select one correct answer.)

☐   **A.** SAP Business Accelerator Hub

☐   **B.** Simplification list

☐   **C.** SAP Cloud ALM

☐   **D.** Implementation Guide (IMG)

4.   Which solution supports the system conversion approach from SAP ERP? (Select one correct answer.)

☐   **A.** SAP SuccessFactors

☐   **B.** SAP Fieldglass

☐   **C.** SAP S/4HANA Cloud Private Edition

☐   **D.** SAP S/4HANA Cloud Public Edition

A.2.9   Selective Data Transition to SAP S/4HANA Cloud Private Edition

This section examines your understanding of using SAP Activate for selective data transition to SAP S/4HANA Cloud Private Edition. Section A.3.9 provides answers to the questions with additional explanations. Note that many of the questions in this section also apply to the case of the selective data transition to SAP S/4HANA (on-premise).

1.   Which objects can be transitioned to the SAP S/4HANA Cloud Private Edition system during the selective data transition approach? (Select one correct answer.)

☐   **A.** ABAP repository objects (e.g., custom code)

☐   **B.** Transactional data

☐   **C.** Master data

☐   **D.** All of the above

2.   Which tools are used during the selective data transition to move data from the SAP ERP system to the SAP S/4HANA Cloud Private Edition system? (Select one correct answer.)

☐   **A.** SAP Cloud ALM

☐   **B.** SAP Signavio Process Navigator

☐   **C.** Data Management and Landscape Transformation (DMLT)

☐   **D.** SAP Transport Management (SAP TM) system

3. What are the common approaches to selective data transition? (Select two correct answers.)

☐   **A.** Conversion

☐   **B.** Mix and match

☐   **C.** New installation

☐   **D.** Shell conversion

A.3   Practice Question Answers and Explanations

In this section, we'll provide the answers to the practice questions. We'll also provide short explanations for each answer and sometimes refer to more details about the topic earlier in the book.

A.3.1   SAP Activate Overview

This section provides correct answers and explanations (where necessary) to the questions listed in Section A.2.1.

1. Correct answer: **B**
    Answer **B** touches best on all the aspects of SAP Activate (methodology, ready-to-run business processes, and tools/applications for configuration and extensibility). Answer **A** focuses too heavily on just one aspect of implementation—the methodology—and only on the SAP S/4HANA solution, while SAP Activate is available for a range of SAP solutions. Answer **C** only considers the tools and doesn't highlight the availability of preconfigured processes and prescriptive methodology.

2. Correct answers: **A, D**
    Both **A** and **D** are correct as SAP Activate was first introduced at SAPPHIRE 2015 along with the release of the SAP S/4HANA solution.

3. Correct answers: **A, B**
    SAP Activate includes prescriptive guided methodology, preconfigured processes delivered in SAP Best Practices, and tools/applications for configuration, extensibility, data migration, and testing.

4. Correct answer: **A**
    The SAP Activate community provides SAP customers, partners, and interested parties with access to the experts that designed SAP Activate and use it in their implementation projects. You can find blog posts, ask questions, and engage with SAP Activate experts from both SAP and the broader community.

5. Correct answer: **C**
   The full version of the SAP Activate methodology can be accessed in SAP Activate Roadmap Viewer using your computer, tablet, or mobile device. It provides you with access to all available SAP Activate methodology roadmaps, phases, deliverables, tasks, and accelerators. Roadmap Viewer is an environment to review SAP product and solution roadmaps to see what new capabilities are planned to be delivered in the future.

6. Correct answers: **A, D**
   SAP Activate Roadmap Viewer provides users with access to a complete set of accelerators delivered within the SAP Activate methodology. All users can access and download accelerators such as project scope documents, WBSs, and project management plans. Note that access to accelerators is based on access level; users are recommended to log on to the tool using their SAP IDs to get access to all available materials. Customers using SAP Cloud ALM have access to the same set of accelerators once they create a new project and assign the specific SAP Activate methodology roadmap to it. Then you can access the accelerators in the Task Management capability of SAP Cloud ALM.

A.3.2 SAP Activate Elements

This section provides correct answers and explanations (where necessary) to the questions listed in Section A.2.2.

1. Correct answer: **D**
   During the implementation of SAP S/4HANA Cloud Private Edition software, the project team can deploy the initial preconfiguration from either SAP-offered content and services (e.g., SAP Best Practices and the enterprise management layer for SAP S/4HANA Cloud Private Edition), which we outlined in Chapter 4, or preconfigurations delivered in packages from SAP partners that are qualified for use in the SAP S/4HANA Cloud Private Edition system.

2. Correct answers: **C, D, E**
   The SAP Activate methodology hierarchy levels are *phase → deliverable → task*, which is the structure of the SAP Activate methodology roadmap in SAP Activate Roadmap Viewer. Note that in some environments, such as SAP Cloud ALM, the deliverable level may be shown, but not act as the structure level with additional information.

3. Correct answers: **B, C, E**
   The SAP Best Practices package for SAP S/4HANA Cloud Public Edition provides users with access to preconfigured processes, business process documentation, business process flows, and test scripts that provide a detailed, step-by-step description of how to execute the business processes in the system.

4. Correct answers: **B, D**

Of the listed answers, SAP Cloud ALM allows users to leverage both the SAP Activate methodology roadmap template to set up the task list and WBS and the SAP Best Practices content in the tool for the fit-to-standard and process modeling. Users can adjust both the WBS and business process documentation and process flows.

5. Correct answer: **A**

SAP S/4HANA Cloud Private Edition software provides configuration capabilities through the Implementation Guide (IMG) in Transaction SPRO. This same capability is used to configure SAP S/4HANA. Note that the SSCUIs are used to configure SAP S/4HANA Cloud Public Edition only.

A.3.3   Workstreams Overview

This section provides correct answers and explanations (where necessary) to the questions listed in Section A.2.3.

1. Correct answers: **A, B, D**

The three available strategies for transition to SAP S/4HANA Cloud Private Edition from an SAP ERP solution are the new implementation, system conversion, and selective data transition. There is no upgrade option because SAP S/4HANA Cloud Private Edition is a different product from SAP ERP. Data migration, while part of the transition paths mentioned here, is not by itself a valid transition path because it only considers the movement of master and transactional data; it omits the configuration, extensibility, and integrations.

2. Correct answers: **B, D**

SAP Activate principles are discussed in Chapter 2 of this book and are as follows:

   – Start with ready-to-run business processes
   – Confirm solution fit
   – Modular, scalable, and agile
   – Cloud ready
   – SAP Services and Support engagement-ready
   – Quality built-in

3. Correct answer: **C**

SAP Activate uses fit-to-standard to confirm solution fit and identify the delta requirements for the customer solution. We've discussed the approach in Chapter 2. The term *blueprint* is used by the ASAP methodology that was used to implement previous versions of the SAP ERP solution; SAP Activate today offers support for SAP S/4HANA Cloud solutions using the fit-gap approach.

4. Correct answer: **C**

   The Project Management Plan Template provides project managers with a structured way to document the management plans for all knowledge areas of the Project Management Institute's Project Management Body of Knowledge (*PMBOK Guide*), including time management, quality management, and risk management.

5. Correct answers: **B, D**

   The SAP S/4HANA Cloud application is built on top of the SAP HANA in-memory database and provides a modern user experience powered by SAP Fiori. The two other answers, SAP Concur and SAP Fieldglass, are additional SAP products that aren't delivered with SAP S/4HANA Cloud; however, they can be integrated with SAP S/4HANA Cloud using standard integration scenarios.

A.3.4   Transition Path "New Implementation SAP S/4HANA Cloud Public Edition"

This section provides correct answers and explanations (where necessary) to the questions listed in Section A.2.4.

1. Correct answer: **B**

   SAP S/4HANA Cloud Public Edition has four systems in the landscape. The starter system is provisioned first and used to complete the fit-to-standard workshops. The development system, test system, and production system are only provisioned after fit-to-standard workshops are completed and are used to activate the desired scope, configure, extend, integrate, and test the solution before going live.

2. Correct answer: **B**

   The SAP Activate methodology provides the OCM deliverables and tasks in the solution adoption workstream, where users can find adoption activities, including end-user training, OCM, and value management.

3. Correct answer: **D**

   SAP Cloud ALM provides users with access to SAP Activate tasks, via which the project team can keep track of their progress. Users can access the SAP Best Practices documentation in the same environment in SAP Cloud ALM. The other tools mentioned in answers **B** and **C** don't provide combined access and aren't environments for teamwork, only for viewing the content. The SAP Activate community is a community space that doesn't contain SAP Activate tasks and SAP Best Practices process documentation.

4. Correct answer: **B**

   The quality gate checklist provides project managers with the list of key deliverables that need to be completed in each phase of the SAP Activate methodology. The SAP Activate for RISE with SAP S/4HANA Cloud Private Edition roadmap also offers a dedicated clean core quality gate checklist that focuses on listing all the activities and tasks that are related to clean core. You can find more details about clean core in Chapter 2.

The SSCUI list provides a complete list of SSCUIs in SAP S/4HANA Cloud Public Edition. The project management plans detail the management plans for all project management knowledge areas (e.g., risk management, quality management, time management, etc.), and the sign-off template provides a template for formal sign-off that needs to be adjusted for each sign-off event.

5. Correct answer: **C**

SAP provides the test scripts within the SAP Best Practices content that you can access in SAP Signavio Process Navigator (as discussed in Chapter 4). Additionally, you can access the test scripts in SAP Cloud ALM when you scope in the SAP Best Practices content into your project.

6. Correct answer: **A**

Customers can use SAP Central Business Configuration to activate the business scope and configure the solution capabilities using the fine-tuning configuration capabilities. We've discussed these topics in Chapter 5.

A.3.5   Transition Path "New Implementation SAP S/4HANA Cloud Private Edition"

This section provides correct answers and explanations (where necessary) to the questions listed in Section A.2.5.

1. Correct answer: **C**

SAP customers are advised to use the SAP Readiness Check for SAP S/4HANA tool to assess their existing environment to understand the impact of simplification on SAP S/4HANA, custom code scope, add-ons, data volumes, and so on.

2. Correct answer: **C**

Out of the listed tools, only SAP Cloud ALM allows users to access the SAP Best Practices documentation (after it has been imported) and modify the predelivered business process models in the modeling functionality in SAP Cloud ALM.

3. Correct answer: **A**

During the explore phase, the project team will first prepare the system for fit-to-standard analysis workshops by adjusting the master data and organizational structure and implementing the quick-win configuration that can be shown during the workshops. After the system has been prepared, the project team will proceed to fit-to-standard workshops to confirm the fit of the standard processes and to capture delta requirements. After that, the project teams proceed to delta design workshops to design the resolution of design delta requirements and gaps. These workshops can happen on different schedules for each area, such as finance, procurement, logistics, and so on; however, they follow the same pattern of preparing the system, conducting fit-to-standard sessions, and designing for delta requirements and gaps. Note that this sequence of workshops is common across all versions of SAP Activate for implementation of SAP solutions.

4. Correct answers: **A, D**

   During the realize phase, a lot of work is done on configuration, extensibility, data migration, integration, testing, and so on. **A** and **D** reflect the work that is done in the realize phase. The cutover to production (**B**) is done in the deploy phase, and the landscape sizing (**C**) and project scope statement (**E**) are done in earlier phases of the project.

5. Correct answers: **A, C**

   SAP Activate recommends the following types of testing during the realize phase:

   - Unit testing to confirm that configuration or custom code works as required per the requirement definition
   - String testing to start testing data flows between integrated business functions
   - End-to-end integration test to confirm the integrated solution works
   - Data migration testing
   - User acceptance testing to expose selected end users to the new functionality and uncover issues the project team might have missed
   - Performance and load testing to stress test the application for specific use cases, such as a storm test for a utility company or inclement weather test for an airline

6. Correct answers: **A, D**

   The five golden rules are as follows (as discussed along with clean core in Chapter 2):

   - Start with preconfigured processes, and foster a cloud mindset by adhering to fit-to-standard and agile deployment detailed in SAP Activate
   - Build your solution on quality data (configuration, master, and transactional) to leverage innovations
   - Use modern integration technologies
   - Use modern extension technologies
   - Ensure transparency on deviations from these golden rules for operational excellence

A.3.6   Agile Project Planning

This section provides correct answers and explanations (where necessary) to the questions listed in Section A.2.6.

1. Correct answers: **A, B**

   The SAP Activate methodology follows the Scrum agile approach that introduces the following agile roles:

   - Scrum master
   - Team
   - Product owner

2. Correct answer: **B**

   Planning in agile projects occurs on multiple levels. In the SAP implementation project context, the planning activities occur when the project is planned in the prepare phase; then, in each subsequent phase, project plans are detailed, and the agile project team plans each sprint/iteration during the regular agile cycle. Sprint planning is part of every sprint/cycle.

3. Correct answer: **C**

   The effort estimation for each backlog item is up to the experts in the project team. It's not the role of the Scrum master or product owner.

4. Correct answer: **B**

   Prioritization of backlog items is the responsibility of the product owner in the agile project. The product owner should use a value-based prioritization framework to assess the benefits of each backlog item and properly prioritize them in the project.

5. Correct answers: **A, C, D**

   During planning, the project team uses the backlog (**A**) to understand the prioritized backlog items and to make the commitment. This sets the scope of work for the sprint. The second variable in planning each sprint is to know the fixed duration of the sprint (**C**). The last variable is to know the size of the team and, most importantly, the capacity of the team (**D**) to do the work that is being planned.

A.3.7   Agile Project Delivery

This section provides correct answers and explanations (where necessary) to the questions listed in Section A.2.7.

1. Correct answer: **B**

   In each sprint, the agile project team will use a retrospective meeting to identify the improvement opportunities by asking a series of questions, such as the following:

   - What do we want to keep?
   - What do we want to change in the next sprint?
   - What do we want to stop doing?

   Out of each retrospective, the project team decides on one or a few improvement steps that are then implemented for the next sprint to continuously improve the process.

2. Correct answer: **D**

   All the listed practices are used by project teams to align the resources and communicate progress both inside the team and to project stakeholders. The agile approach is based on radical transparency, which helps everybody understand the plans, status, and what needs to be done to achieve the goal set for the sprint or release.

3. Correct answer: **A**

   Of the listed artifacts, only the backlog is typically updated each sprint, even if it's to indicate that some backlog items have been completed. The backlog is a living artifact in every agile project. The other listed artifacts are typically updated less frequently.

4. Correct answer: **D**

   The product owner is responsible for reviewing and approving that the backlog items have been delivered and that they meet the definition of done.

5. Correct answers: **B, D**

   Agile teams perform daily standup meetings to communicate progress to the rest of the team and to identify blockers that may be preventing them from progressing in work on specific backlog items. During the standup, each team member addresses the following questions:

   - What have I done since our last meeting?
   - What do I plan to do until the next meeting?
   - What blockers am I facing?

   Some teams may add additional questions to gauge the confidence of the project team in their ability to deliver committed backlog items.

A.3.8   System Conversion to SAP S/4HANA Cloud Private Edition

This section provides correct answers and explanations (where necessary) to the questions listed in Section A.2.8.

1. Correct answers: **B, C, D**

   SAP Activate doesn't prescribe any blueprinting workshops. The other three steps are part of the planning system conversion, as we described in Chapter 8. Refer to Chapter 8, Section 8.3 for an overview of all the planning and execution steps.

2. Correct answer: **D**

   Customers planning system conversion of their SAP ERP environment to SAP S/4HANA Cloud Private Edition should complete all of the listed projects prior to starting the conversion activities. Managing data volumes prior to transition is a critical step in managing the size and complexity of your future environment as is the reconciliation of financial data and cleanup of unused custom code. Refer to the prepare phase in the SAP Activate for RISE with SAP S/4HANA Cloud Private Edition roadmap for a complete list of projects to complete prior to conversion.

3. Correct answer: **B**

   SAP provides detailed information about new, updated, and changed functions in SAP S/4HANA Cloud Private Edition in the simplification list.

4. Correct answer: **C**

   Of the listed solutions, only SAP S/4HANA Cloud Private Edition software supports the system conversion from previous versions of SAP ERP software. The other solutions listed don't support the system conversion approach.

A.3.9   Selective Data Transition to SAP S/4HANA Cloud Private Edition

This section provides correct answers and explanations (where necessary) to the questions listed in Section A.2.9.

1. Correct answer: **D**

   All of the listed items can be transitioned during the selective data transition approach.

2. Correct answer: **C**

   During the selective data transition, data is moved using the DMLT software and related services. For more than 10 years, DMLT tools have provided well-established solutions for organizational changes, acquisitions, divestitures, or harmonization of SAP landscapes. The software provides highly automated processes that move large amounts of data between SAP instances quickly. Refer to Chapter 8, Section 8.4.

3. Correct answers: **B, D**

   There are two approaches for selective data transition: shell conversion and mix and match. In shell conversion, a shell copy of a production system is made without master and transaction data, and this is converted to SAP S/4HANA Cloud Private Edition. In mix and match, a new SAP S/4HANA Cloud Private Edition install is created, and then elements of the configuration and ABAP repository are transported or manually transferred.

Appendix B
The Authors

Sven Denecken is the senior vice president and chief marketing and solutions officer for industries and customer experience (CX) at SAP SE. He drives product marketing across SAP's industry and CX solutions, enabling customers' digital transformation.

The industries that customers operate in define their core business, and from the outset, SAP has worked together with customers and partners to build business solutions that address industry-specific processes and enable their digital transformation.

Sven Denecken leads product marketing for industries and CX at SAP. In this role, Sven is charged with strengthening the go-to-market approach, driving product marketing across SAP's industry and CX solutions.

Sven has many years of experience working with customers and partners to create success and value within the SAP network. He has held a variety of roles across functional areas, including ERP product management, driving acquisition post-merger integrations, and in product engineering as head of product success and chief operating officer for the flagship solution, SAP S/4HANA Cloud.

As a senior executive, Sven works closely with customers, partners, influencers, and SAP experts to shape and deliver effective outcomes for industry customers to support their digital transformation.

You can connect with Sven at *www.linkedin.com/in/sdenecken/en*.

Jan Musil is the SAP Activate chief product owner at SAP. Jan heads a team of seasoned product managers responsible for SAP Activate, the innovation adoption framework aiding SAP customers and partners in deploying SAP solutions like SAP S/4HANA, SAP SuccessFactors, SAP Ariba, SAP Integrated Business Planning, and SAP BTP. His team keeps SAP Activate content current with product capabilities and deployment best practices, coordinating closely with product engineers, field consultants, customers, and partners.

Throughout his career, Jan has worked in SAP product engineering, quality management, customer support, project management, and services operations across the

United States, Germany, and the Czech Republic. He is dedicated to advancing SAP solution deployment strategies, with a particular focus on agile implementation, cloud deployment, leveraging standard software packages, employing a structured quality methodology, program management, and value management.

Jan often speaks at SAP and industry events, has coauthored books on SAP Activate, and contributed to publications on application lifecycle management, project management, and other industry topics.

You can connect with Jan at *www.linkedin.com/in/musiljan/*.

Srivatsan Santhanam, vice president of spend engineering, has been with SAP Labs India since 2004, and is the head of the SAP Concur engineering product unit in SAP Labs India. He has nearly two decades of industry experience and is one of the early pioneers and thought leaders in the hybrid cloud/two-tier ERP with SAP S/4HANA Cloud product space.

Srivatsan has seven US patents to his credit and many more in a filed state. He is a regular blogger and a coauthor of an SAP PRESS E-Bite, *SAP S/4HANA Cloud for Two-Tier ERP Landscapes*. He is an alumnus of the Indian Institute of Management-Ahmedabad and has a master's degree in data science from IIIT Bangalore. Srivatsan is a regular speaker at many SAP, technology, and innovation events worldwide.

You can connect with Srivatsan at *www.linkedin.com/in/srivatsansanthanam/*.

B.1   Contributors

Vital Anderhub is a member of the product management team for SAP's operations platforms. His tasks involve solution management and knowledge management for SAP Focused Run and SAP Cloud ALM.

Jorge Javier Baltazar is a senior technology and development consultant for the User Experience and Mobility practice in SAP's Adoption Services Center and a member of the SAP S/4HANA Customer Care and Regional Implementation Group, focusing on the adoption of SAP Fiori and clean core developments. Jorge has helped deliver multiple SAP S/4HANA implementation projects, including one of the first ever system conversions in the world, and some of the first SAP Fiori implementations back in 2013. Jorge joined SAP in 2011.

Kiran Bose is a senior product manager for SAP Activate methodology and is the product owner for the SAP Activate for SAP Business Technology Platform roadmap. His primary focus is the extensibility and integration workstreams across all roadmaps. Kiran joined SAP in 2007 and has spent most of his career as an SAP solution architect, helping customers in their implementation and transformation projects.

Janko Budzisch is the chief product owner for SAP's operations platforms, SAP Focused Run and SAP Cloud ALM. His main task is to drive the strategic direction of these product lines with input from customers, partners, and SAP's internal stakeholders. His mission is to provide SAP customers and SAP-centric service providers with the most suitable operations platforms to support their transformation into intelligent enterprises.

Bob Byrne is a senior product manager in the product engineering board area. His focus is on SAP S/4HANA Cloud and the SAP Activate methodology—specifically, the SAP Activate implementation methodology for SAP S/4HANA Cloud. Bob also manages the SAP Activate community space. Bob has been with SAP for 20 years.

Dan Ciecko is a senior product manager for SAP Activate methodology and is the product owner of the SAP S/4HANA Cloud Public Edition roadmap. Dan joined SAP in 1997 and has spent most of his career as a platinum consultant implementing various SAP products for customers. Through this experience, he mastered the mechanics of software implementations of both on-premise and cloud environments and how to efficiently bring quality and value to customers. He was a core contributor to the development of SAP Activate and prior cloud implementation methodologies. In addition to the SAP S/4HANA Cloud Public Edition roadmap, Dan works on the strategic direction of the SAP Activate methodology and supporting tools and processes. He manages several other SAP Activate cloud roadmaps that guide the successful implementation of other SAP products.

Xavier Dejaegher works in the SAP Product Engineering organization, where he's responsible for building product content for SAP S/4HANA to help SAP customers succeed locally and globally. With more than 25 years of experience in the areas of financial accounting and localization, Xavier worked until a few years ago as a consultant for SAP in the United Kingdom, mainly on international projects, before he focused on building content for the enterprise management layer for SAP S/4HANA.

Nicole Fuller has been part of SAP's Cloud ERP Product Success organization since 2019. Currently, she is a product manager for the SAP Activate methodology, focusing on the analytics workstream across all roadmaps. Prior to joining the SAP Activate team, she worked as a product expert for SAP S/4HANA Cloud Public Edition as part of cloud customer care. During her time in this role, she guided several customers to successful go-lives on SAP S/4HANA Cloud Public Edition and supported regional cloud customer care activities to oversee all public cloud implementations in the Americas region.

Christina Galbreath is a product manager within SAP Activate, responsible for the SAP Activate Methodology for New Cloud Implementations roadmap and the project management, customer team enablement, and solution adoption workstreams. She has been with SAP for 20 years.

Chandan Gurav joined SAP in 2017. He is a product manager for SAP Activate in the SAP S/4HANA organization in North America. Chandan focuses on testing and industries content to guide customers. Besides managing testing and industries content, Chandan is a product manager for the tools and applications that the SAP Activate team uses for managing and publishing roadmaps.

Ying Huang is a product expert for SAP S/4HANA. Her journey with SAP solutions started with SAP R/3 3.1H. She has both consulting and industry experience in implementing and running SAP solutions, including SAP's master data, analytics, and reporting solutions. She has extensive business knowledge in the areas of supply chain, sales operation planning, and project portfolio planning and management for IM&C. Her focus for SAP Activate is on the software lifecycle events, design and configuration, and operations and support workstreams, as well as the Customer COE and business process transformation-related topics.

Adnette Kamugisha joined SAP in 2013 and is currently a product manager for SAP Activate methodology. She is the product owner of the SAP Activate methodology for the RISE with SAP S/4HANA Private Cloud Edition roadmap. Adnette played a pivotal role in the creation and successful release of the first version of the RISE with SAP implementation roadmap. Within the SAP Activate methodology team, she also contributes to the technical architecture and infrastructure workstream, providing guidance to customers during system provisioning. Additionally, she collaborates with various stakeholders to enhance the deployment experience of other SAP solutions. Adnette is passionate about improving the SAP Activate methodology content through collaboration with SAP experts and partners, actively incorporating customer feedback.

She is equally dedicated to people development, serving as a people colead within Product Success & Cloud Co-Innovation and as an objectives and key results (OKR) coach with the SAP Activate methodology team. Her commitment stems from a strong desire to help people excel, develop, and contribute to SAP's outstanding products and experiences, recognizing that people are the driving force behind SAP's success.

Oliver Kohnke is global director at SAP Learning services and is responsible for SAP's organizational change management service. For more than 30 years, he has been managing the people side of business transformations for international organizations of all sizes and in many industries. His current role involves standardizing the change management service, developing digital learning formats, and enabling customers and partners. Oliver holds a PhD in industrial and organizational psychology and is an adjunct senior lecturer at the University of Mannheim. The focus of his research and teaching is on digital transformation and technology adoption. He is editor and author of several scientific and practitioner publications. You can connect with Oliver at *https://www.linkedin.com/in/oliver-kohnke-3ba758a0/*.

Jose Marquez Mares Ramos is part of SAP's Cloud ERP organization and heads the SAP S/4HANA Customer Care and Regional Implementation Group for the Americas. In this role, Jose is responsible for supporting the overall customer adoption of SAP S/4HANA Cloud Private Edition.

Prior to this role, Jose was a logistics consultant and integration manager, leading and delivering successful projects related to business transformation and SAP ERP implementation in North and Latin America. He joined SAP Peru in 2012 and was relocated to SAP Canada in 2016.

Prasanth P. Menon is the product owner of the release assessment and scope dependency for SAP S/4HANA Cloud Public Edition tool at SAP Labs India. He has also been working as a subject matter expert who takes care of technology topics for the two-tier ERP product space with SAP S/4HANA Cloud. He helped the two-tier ERP team with integration and all technical setup related to data replication and extensibility.

Fernando Moreira is a principal technology consultant and architect in the Data and Technology Services practice from SAP's Adoption Services Center SAP BTP organization. With a degree in computer engineering, he joined SAP in 2004. Over the past 20 years, he has been involved in numerous SAP implementation projects as a technology team lead and delivered specialized services from the areas of SAP Support and Business Transformation Services. Since 2020, he has also served as a project coach and SAP S/4HANA technology expert from the Regional Implementation Group, aiding customers in their transition to SAP S/4HANA Cloud Private Edition through the SAP S/4HANA Customer Care program. Fernando is also dedicated to knowledge sharing, contributing to SAP Community, and co-authoring and presenting SAP S/4HANA enablement sessions for SAP customers, partners, and internal audiences.

Andreas Muno works in the SAP S/4HANA Cloud expertise services team on solution adoption, organizational change management, cloud mindset, and other cross-topics. A trained economist, patented innovator, and startup cofounder, he has more than 20 years of SAP experience in consulting and developing business software in Europe and as an industry solution and product manager in the US, with a variety of focus areas from public services, supplier relationship management, mobile applications, business process modeling and optimization, records management, and best practices to integrated business scenarios with SAP S/4HANA Cloud and its extension capabilities. More recently, he dialed in on the human factor in cloud software adoption success, enabling SAP's partners to bring about excellent outcomes at their joint customers, strengthening ecosystem relationships, and mentoring and coaching colleagues to become the best they can imagine.

Ritu Patil works in Customer Experience and Solutions within the SAP Cloud ALM product management team. In this role, she supports product owners and the CPO by managing responsibilities that ensure the successful implementation of SAP Cloud ALM solutions. Since joining SAP in 2022, she has contributed to various projects and strategic content initiatives, focusing on optimizing SAP Cloud ALM deployments and improving customer experiences within SAP Cloud ALM offerings.

Yannick Peterschmitt is head of enablement in SAP's Cloud ERP Product Success organization. Yannick and his team focus on holistic SAP customer and partner enablement and success. The enablement team drives global and highly scalable knowledge transfer programs. The team supports key customers and partners with their expertise and best practices. Beside an extensive bill of materials of product assets, the enablement team launched new and innovative channels, including the podcast Inside SAP S/4HANANA Cloud and the Expert Talk Series available on YouTube, in order to offer customers and partners simpler access to product expertise. Yannick graduated from a business school in Paris and started his SAP career the field organization. He was first a consultant for presales with SAP France, then moved to the EMEA region for business development roles, until he went to corporate positions in solution management, product marketing, and product management.

Monica Reyes is a member of Digital Finance NA – Global Customer Engagement and Services and the SAP S/4HANA Customer Care and Regional Implementation Group. She has more than 25 years of diverse experience in procure to pay, order to cash, and tax engines. Prior to joining the America's SAP S/4HANA Customer Care and Regional Implementation Group, Monica worked as a finance consultant, focusing on tax engines and external invoice vendor management solutions. In her current role, she supports customers transitioning to SAP S/4HANA Cloud Private Edition.

Holger Steffens, vice president at SAP SE, leads the Process Content Tooling and Delivery team within the SAP S/4HANA organization. In this capacity, Holger delivers process modeling tools that empower SAP enterprise architects and business process owners to efficiently design, model, and develop business processes across SAP's solution portfolio. Holger oversees the development of SAP Enterprise Architecture Reference Library, an SAP process design and modeling environment that seamlessly integrates with the graphical modeling capabilities of SAP Signavio. Additionally, he spearheads the development of SAP Signavio Process Navigator, a publicly accessible service on the SAP for Me customer portal, which showcases significant portions of SAP's predefined and preconfigured processes. With more than 25 years of experience at SAP, Holger has held various management positions across SAP Services, SAP Solution Adoption and Knowledge Experience, strategic projects, and SAP Product Engineering. He has been a key knowledge holder of the SAP Best Practices concept for more than a decade.

Esteban Stransky is a principal technology consultant and architect in the SAP HANA Latin America and the Caribbean practice within SAP's Adoption Services Center SAP BTP organization. He holds a degree in telecommunications and IT engineering, and joined SAP in 2016. With more than 15 years of experience, Esteban has worked with partners and customers and has been involved in numerous SAP implementation projects as a technology team lead. Since 2021, he has also served as a project coach and SAP S/4HANA technology expert in the Regional Implementation Group, supporting customers in their transition to SAP S/4HANA and SAP S/4HANA Cloud Private Edition. Additionally, Esteban is committed to knowledge sharing, contributing to SAP Community, and delivering SAP S/4HANA enablement sessions for SAP customers, partners, and internal audiences.

Marco Valencia is the vice president for SAP S/4HANA Product Success in the Cloud ERP organization, overseeing cloud customer care. In this role, Marco is responsible for supporting the overall customer adoption of SAP S/4HANA Cloud Public Edition by assessing customer and market requirements and helping to define customer adoption strategies.

With more than 30 years of professional experience, Marco focuses on customer advocacy, product management, implementations, upgrades, value engineering, and cloud transformation of SAP solutions. He has extensive experience in implementing and supporting strategic customers with SAP S/4HANA Cloud Public Edition. Marco joined SAP in 1996.

Doris Wieser is a principal business consultant in the Digital Change and Adoption team of SAP's Business Transformation Services. She has worked in the areas of change management and organizational development with a focus on IT-driven transformations for more than 25 years, as both an internal and external consultant. With her PhD in organizational psychology on the challenging role of middle managers in change processes, she followed her passion to integrate applied research in her practical work.

Index

S

- Learn about the SAP Activate certification test structure and how to prepare

- Review the key topics covered in each portion of your exam

- Certified Associate Exam

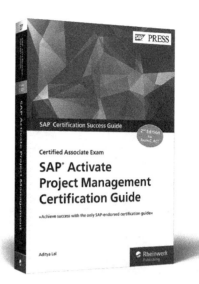

Aditya Lal, Jeyaganesh Viswanathan

SAP Activate Project Management Certification Guide

Certified Associate Exam

Get ready for the SAP Activate project management exam with this certification study guide for C_ACT_2403! Master all the important exam topics, from agile project planning and delivery to new implementations and system conversions. Reinforce your knowledge with a review of key terminology and practice questions and answers for each subject area. Set yourself up for success on test day!

approx. 400 pp., 2nd edition, avail. 03/2025
E-Book: $74.99 | **Print:** $79.95 | **Bundle:** $89.99

www.sap-press.com/6032

Rheinwerk Publishing

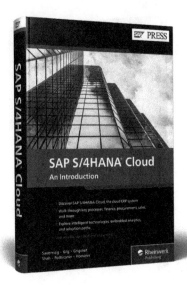

- Discover SAP S/4HANA Cloud, the cloud ERP system

- Walk through key processes: finance, procurement, sales, and more

- Explore intelligent technologies, embedded analytics, and adoption paths

Saueressig, Gilg, Grigoleit, Shah, Podbicanin, Homann

SAP S/4HANA Cloud

An Introduction

SAP S/4HANA Cloud has a lot to offer—see what's possible! Explore core functionality like finance, logistics, and reporting with embedded analytics. Learn how SAP S/4HANA Cloud impacts your users and how it can be extended, integrated, and adopted by your organization. Get information on the latest intelligent technologies and see how SAP S/4HANA Cloud can help unify and streamline your business. A bold new world awaits in the cloud!

538 pages, 2nd edition, pub. 05/2022
E-Book: $74.99 | **Print:** $79.95 | **Bundle:** $89.99
www.sap-press.com/5457

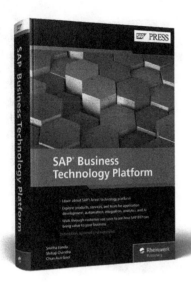

Interested in reading more?

Please visit our website for all new book
and e-book releases from SAP PRESS.

www.sap-press.com